Greenhill Books

THE AMERICAN ARSENAL

GREENHILL MILITARY PAPERBACKS

The American Arsenal
Anatomy of the Zulu Army
The Art of War
Brave Men's Blood
A History of the Art of War in the
Middle Ages (two volumes)
A History of the Art of War in the
Sixteenth Century
The Illustrated Encyclopedia of
Handguns
The Luger Story
The Viking Art of War

Napoleonic
Napoleon's Campaign in Poland,
1806–1807
The Note-Books of Captain Coignet
On the Napoleonic Wars
Wellington at Waterloo
Wellington in the Peninsula

World Wars I and II
Battle of Britain Day
Bomber Offensive
Born of the Desert
Dawn of D-Day
Disaster at D-Day
Guderian
The Hitler Options
I Flew for the Führer
Infantry Attacks
Invasion
Kesselring: German Master
Strategist
The Last Year of the Luftwaffe
Long Range Desert Group
The Memoirs of Field Marshal
Kesselring
The Moscow Option
The Red Air Fighter
SAS: With the Maquis
The Sky My Kingdom
War on the Eastern Front
Why the Germans Lose at War

THE AMERICAN ARSENAL

The World War II Official Standard Ordnance
Catalog of Small Arms, Tanks, Armored Cars,
Artillery, Antiaircraft Guns, Ammunition,
Grenades, Mines, Etcetera

INTRODUCTION BY IAN V. HOGG

Greenhill Books, London
Stackpole Books, Pennsylvania

Greenhill Books

This edition of *The American Arsenal*
first published 2001 by Greenhill Books, Lionel Leventhal Limited,
Park House, 1 Russell Gardens, London NW11 9NN
www.greenhillbooks.com
and
Stackpole Books, 5067 Ritter Road, Mechanicsburg, PA 17055, USA

British Library Cataloguing in Publication Data
A catalogue record for this book is available from the British Library

ISBN 1-85367-470-2

Library of Congress Cataloging-in-Publication Data available

The American Arsenal is based upon the U.S. Army manual *Catalog of
Standard Ordnance Items* produced by the Office of the Chief of Ordnance
Technical Division, Washington D.C., 1944. The first Greenhill edition was
published in 1996, and is now reproduced in paperback complete and
unabridged.

Designed by DAG Publications Limited
Printed and bound in Singapore by Kyodo Printing

CONTENTS

1. TANK AND AUTOMOTIVE

Light Tanks, 10
Medium Tanks, 22
Heavy Tanks, 32
Light Tank Engines, 36
Medium and Heavy Tank
    Engines, 37
Tank Transporters, 39
Gun and Howitzer Motor
    Carriages, 44
Vehicular Gun Mounts, 62
Armored Trailers, 65

Armored Cars, 66
Carriers, 71
Snow Tractors, 74
Scout Cars, 75
Half-Tracked Vehicles, 76
Armored Utility Vehicles,
    Prime Movers, etc., 80
High-Speed Tractors, 83
Tracked Landing Vehicles,
    87
Service Trucks, 89

Trailers, 91
Maintenance and
    Recovery Trucks, 95
Passenger Sedans, 100
Motorcycles, Bicycles and
    Scooters, 102
Trucks (including Jeeps
    and Amphibians), 105
Cargo Trailers, 126
Fording Equipment, 130
Airborne Equipment, 131

2. ARTILLERY

Mobile Artillery, 133
Railway and Seacoast
    Artillery, 169

Tank Armament, 177
Antiaircraft Artillery, 184
Sub Caliber Guns, 199

Harbor Defense Mines,
    208
Aircraft Armament, 213

3. SMALL ARMS

Machine Guns, 221
Submachine Guns, 230
Rifles, 231
Shotguns, 236
Projectors and
    Dischargers, 239

Grenade and Rocket
    Launchers, 242
Machine Gun Mounts,
    245
Small Arms Ammunition,
    251

Helmets, 255
Body Armor, 256
Bayonets, Knives and
    Sabers, 257
Miscellaneous Items,
    258

4. AMMUNITION

20mm Ammunition, 261
37mm Ammunition, 263
40mm Ammunition, 269
57mm Ammunition, 271
60mm Ammunition, 273
75mm Ammunition, 275
3 inch Ammunition, 281
81mm Ammunition, 289
90mm Ammunition, 291

105mm Ammunition, 293
4.5 inch Ammunition, 298
120mm Ammunition, 299
6 inch Ammunition, 300
155mm Ammunition, 302
8 inch Ammunition, 315
240mm Ammunition, 320
12 inch Ammunition, 322
16 inch Ammunition, 324

Hand and Rifle Grenades,
    326
Mines, 330
Sub Caliber and Practice
    Ammunition, 336
Artillery Fuzes. 338
Bomb Fuzes, 354
Rockets, 370
Rocket Launchers, 379

Introduction

One of the things about the American Army of 1941–5 which impressed British soldiers was its profligacy with paper – instructional paper, that is. I have before me the British Army's instructional pamphlet on the Lewis machine gun; it is 22 pages long and illustrated with a handful of amateurish line drawings. I also have before me the U.S. Field Manual 23–15 on the Browning Automatic Rifle, more or less the American equivalent of the Lewis gun; it is of 208 close-printed pages illustrated with line drawings, diagrams and photographs. When I had a Jeep, it came with a driver's manual that must have been 200 pages long and covered every aspect of maintenance and operation; when I had a Morris gun tractor I was given a 'Guide to the Task System', a generalised 15-page pamphlet which detailed the orderly routine by which vehicle maintenance had to be done – any vehicle, from a tank to a motorized lawnmower. The fact that this particular Morris had the accelerator between the clutch and brake pedals was something I had to find out for myself, the hard way.

Soldiers are a curious lot; they always want to know a bit more about what they are doing, and they are always curious about what people with other cap or collar badges are up to. But in European armies such curiosity was frowned upon; why do you, a field gunner, wish to know what weapons arm the coast defences? You must be a spy. In the U.S. Army, on the other hand, such curiosity was welcomed; it showed that the man was taking an interest in the 'big picture' and it indicated a willingness to cooperate with other arms of the services which was not, in the past, readily apparent.

And so, in order to satisfy this thirst for knowledge, and, if the truth be known, to boost morale by revealing as much as could safely be revealed about the nation's armaments, various military agencies began producing compendia or catalogues to fill in the spaces which the official War Department manuals failed to reach. The Ordnance School at Aberdeen Proving Ground appears to have been among the first and most effective of these agencies, producing a six-volume ammunition encyclopedia, a two-volume set on coast artillery equipment, and useful volumes on sights, motor vehicles and similar subjects. And doubtless the Artillery, Armor, Transportation and other schools did likewise.

This was all very well in 1940–2 when the army was expanding faster than the distribution of official pamphlets could cope, but once the initial expansion was over some order had to be laid upon the scene, if only to make sure everybody was singing the same song to the same tune; it was no use TM 9-2005 *'Ordnance Material, General: Vol 4; Railway and Seacoast Artillery'* saying that the 12in Railway Mortar M1890 on Carriage M1 weighed 176,800 pounds when TM 4-210 *'Coast Artillery Weapons and Materiel'* said that it weighed 176,000 pounds. Sooner or later somebody would notice and questions would be asked. Moreover the amount and diversity of equipment being produced for the army needed to be properly catalogued for the benefit of staff officers and planners so that they could see whether there was a particular piece of equipment that would fill a need which had suddenly appeared, or whether they would have to go to some agency and have a new device designed and produced. (A point of view which, it seems, was lost sight of somewhere in the 1960s and led to the parallel development of similar equipment by all three services and the waste of large sums of money – but that's another story.)

As a result of this sort of thinking, the Ordnance Department set about the production of a master catalogue which would cover in detail every piece of equipment, even the most modern – for which reason it was graded 'Confidential'. It was a luxurious production, on expensive, coated paper, supplied in loose-leaf form in a series of ring binders, and kept up to date by frequent amendments and issues of new pages. Blocks of pages were allocated to specific groups of equipment; some groups were filled, others were not, which accounts for gaps in the pagination, and the system stuttered somewhat when equipment for which small provision had been made – such as rockets – began to appear in bulk and had to be fitted in where it could. It was an ambitious programme, and it took time to get going; and before it could be completed, second thoughts were being had. There was, for example, no good reason to fill a 'Confidential' manual with details of things like motor-scooters or binoculars, which were commercial products bought off the shelf. More so when the War Department, now beginning to catch up on its original responsibilities, began producing its own series of catalogues such as TM9-2800 *'Standard Military Motor Vehicles'* of 1 September 1943, catalogues which were perhaps to a lesser standard of erudition but certainly to a lesser standard of production and hence cheaper and hence given far greater distribution. And they were simply 'Restricted' documents, making distribution even more generous.

Faced with these War Department volumes, the Ordnance Department production began to look superfluous. We have now no way of knowing, but long experience of the institutional military system leads me to suspect that the sub-department in charge of the *Catalog* saw the writing on the wall and began to wonder how they could continue to produce this Confidential series in the face of the Restricted competition. Somebody spotted the lifebelt and grabbed it: include the latest information on *Enemy* equipment! This had to be confidential – you didn't want them to know what you knew about their stuff – so it was the very thing to be included in this prestigious publication. And so two new sections appeared, 'German Equipment' and 'Japanese Equipment', and were tacked on to the end of the final volume.

As the war entered its final year, the amount of enemy equipment in Allied hands, and the amount of information acquired about it, had reached such proportions that many other specialised volumes were being published on this subject. Most of them were graded 'Secret' and therefore held much more detailed information than could be included in a 'Confidential' document, and so the provision of enemy material information soon began to shrink. And by the summer of 1945 it seems that the whole project had come to a halt. I have never seen any formal notice of its termination, and it was not until many years later that I ever saw a complete volume of this series and then, eventually, the complete set.

For all its faltering progress, though, the *Ordnance Standard Catalog* is the ultimate compendium of equipment used by the U.S. Army in 1944/45. In no other single source can so much detail on weapons, vehicles, ammunition and ancillary combat equipment be found, together with an authoritative statement of the development and introduction process. Moreover, it is authenticated by reference back to Ordnance Committee Minutes and similar authorities, so that every figure, date, specification or description can be accepted as being correct. And because it was meant to introduce staff officers to unknown elements of the army, only here will you find such things as coast defence mines, anti-aircraft directors and shrapnel shells for the 75mm Gun M1897. But don't just take my word for it: say 'Open Sesame' and take a look into Aladdin's Cave.

There is, however, one small disclaimer. Due to damage, some pages cannot be photographically reproduced, and therefore have had to be carefully reconstructed. The text has followed the original style as closely as possible, but some illustrations have had to be provided from other sources, which accounts for a British soldier standing in front of the 155mm GMC M40 among other things. Nevertheless, the information on these 'reconstructed pages' has been taken from authentic U.S. official documents and is as accurate as the information in the rest of the book

1

TANK AND AUTOMOTIVE

Light Tanks, 10
Medium Tanks, 22
Heavy Tanks, 32
Light Tank Engines, 36
Medium and Heavy Tank Engines, 37
Tank Transporters, 39
Gun and Howitzer Motor Carriages, 44
Vehicular Gun Mounts, 62
Armored Trailers, 65
Armored Cars, 66
Carriers, 71
Snow Tractors, 74
Scout Cars, 75
Half-Tracked Vehicles, 76
Armored Utility Vehicles, Prime Movers, etc., 80
High-Speed Tractors, 83
Tracked Landing Vehicles, 87
Service Trucks, 89
Trailers, 91
Maintenance and Recovery Trucks, 95
Passenger Sedans, 100
Motorcycles, Bicycles and Scooters, 102
Trucks (including Jeeps and Amphibians), 105
Cargo Trailers, 126
Fording Equipment, 130
Airborne Equipment, 131

LIGHT TANK M3 SERIES

LIGHT TANK, M3, standardized in July, 1940, and produced in quantity beginning in March, 1941, was supplied to our Allies, under Lend-Lease, as well as to our own Army through 1941 and 1942. Nicknamed the "General Stuart" by British troops, these tanks won high praise during the Libyan campaign, and are now considered obsolete only because of the great improvements in later vehicles.

Based on Light Tank, M2A4, but using heavier armor and incorporating other improvements, Light Tank, M3, for its day, was heavily armed and armored and provided a high standard of mechanical reliability.

Through the production period, numerous improvements were made, so that the final M3s were vastly different from the first. First models were entirely riveted, with a seven-sided turret. Later a welded, seven-sided turret was used, and still later, a rounded, welded, homogeneous turret. The final models were entirely welded.

The volute spring suspension is used, with the rear idler "trailing" on ground level, rather than "mounted" above the ground as on Light Tank, M2A4. This lengthens the ground contact of the track, thus decreasing the pressure per square inch, and gives additional support to the rear of the tank.

Power is supplied by a 7-cylinder Continental W670–9A gasoline engine. Some models of Light Tanks, M3 and M3A1, were powered by a Guiberson T1020-4 Diesel engine. A synchromesh transmission provides five forward speeds and one reverse.

The driver and assistant driver occupy seats in the hull, with vision ahead through hatches equipped with windshields. In combat areas, the armored hatch cover may be closed, whereupon vision is possible through a protectoscope, a form of periscope.

The gunner and commander-loader occupy seats in the turret, which may be traversed through 360° by a hand-operated mechanism. Entrance to the turret is through the cupola hatch, which also provides an observation post for the commander. In noncombat areas, the commander may operate with his head and

LIGHT TANK, M3, WITH SEVEN-SIDED, WELDED TURRET, RIVETED HULL

PISTOL PORT DOOR AND PROTECTOSCOPE

TOP OF ROUNDED, HOMOGENEOUS TURRET

LIGHT TANK, M3, WITH ROUNDED, HOMOGENEOUS, WELDED TURRET

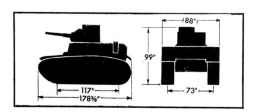

10

LIGHT TANK, M3A1, HAS POWER-TRAVERSED TURRET WITHOUT CUPOLA

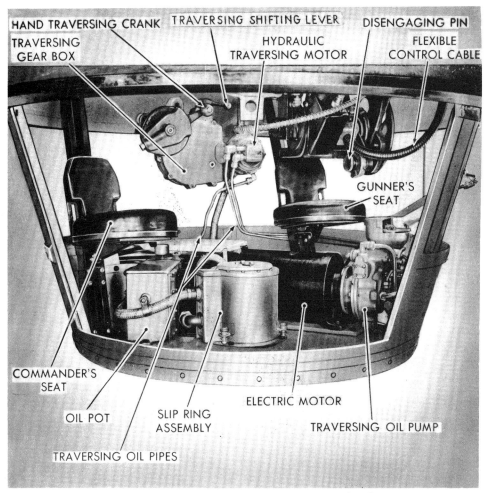

HAND TRAVERSING CRANK — TRAVERSING SHIFTING LEVER — DISENGAGING PIN

TRAVERSING GEAR BOX — HYDRAULIC TRAVERSING MOTOR — FLEXIBLE CONTROL CABLE

GUNNER'S SEAT

COMMANDER'S SEAT

OIL POT — SLIP RING ASSEMBLY — ELECTRIC MOTOR — TRAVERSING OIL PUMP

TRAVERSING OIL PIPES

LIGHT TANK, M3A1, TURRET BASKET SHOWING TRAVERSING MECHANISM

shoulders above the cupola. In danger zones, vision from the cupola is through pistol ports equipped with protectoscopes. (Early models used direct vision "peepholes" instead.)

Principal armament is a 37 mm gun, M5 or M6, mounted with a cal. .30 machine gun in a combination mount in the turret. The turret guns have elevations from −10° to +20°. An A.P.C. projectile, fired from the 37 mm gun, has a muzzle velocity of 2,900 feet per second. It has a maximum range of 12,850 yards, and will penetrate 1.8-inch face-hardened armor plate at 1,000 yards.

Late models are provided with a gyrostabilizer to increase the accuracy of aiming and firing the turret guns when the vehicle is in motion.

Other armament includes a cal. .30 machine gun, in the bow, one on the turret for antiaircraft use, and one in each sponson.

Normal fuel capacity of 56 gallons may be increased when necessary by the use of two 25-gallon jettison fuel tanks. These can be abandoned upon entering a combat zone. The vehicle is equipped with a two-way radio.

Light Tanks, M3 and M3 (Diesel), were declared obsolete by Ordnance Committee action in July, 1943. These and later vehicles of the Light Tank, M3, Series, were built by the American Car and Foundry Co.

References—TM 9–726; OCM 15920, 15932, 16135, 16258, 16370, 16531, 16583, 16603, 16610, 16611, 17200, 17107, 17201, 17235, 17578, 17949, 17984, 20076, 20317, 20852, 21015.

LIGHT TANK, M3A1, was standardized in August, 1941, as a modification of Light Tank, M3. It was declared obsolete in July 1944.

The turret is similar to that used in the final version of Light Tank, M3, but omits the cupola. A fighting compartment is integrated with the turret and is rotated with it, either by a hydraulic mechanism or by hand. This compartment contains seats for the gunner and commander-loader as well as the traversing and gyrostabilizer mechanisms and ammunition.

An improved Combination Gun Mount, M23, for the turret guns has a periscopic sight. An additional periscope, with 360° traverse, is provided in the turret roof. Other armament is the same as on Light Tank, M3, except that the sponson guns are omitted.

The vehicle is equipped with an improved radio and with an interphone

LIGHT TANK, M3A3, HAS IMPROVED TURRET WITH RADIO BULGE. FRONT PLATE IS STRENGTHENED AND SPONSONS ARE EXTENDED FORWARD

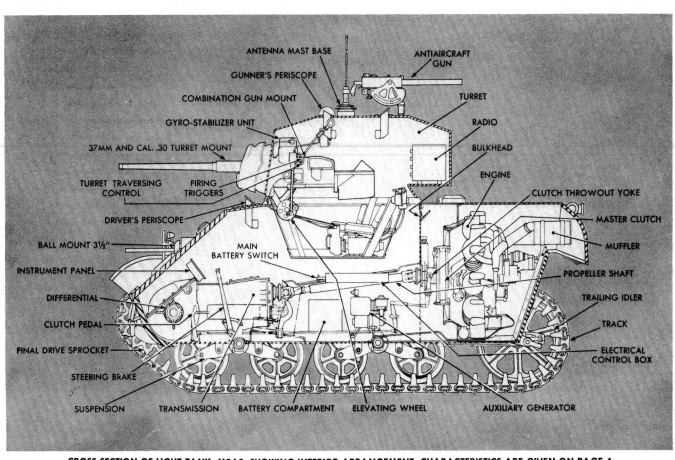

CROSS SECTION OF LIGHT TANK, M3A3, SHOWING INTERIOR ARRANGEMENT. CHARACTERISTICS ARE GIVEN ON PAGE 4

system, with connections for each crew member.

Light Tank, M3A1 (Diesel), was declared obsolete in July, 1943.

REFERENCES—TM 9–727; OCM 17235, 17330, 17578, 17680, 17906, 17952, 17984, 18639, 19396, 20076, 20317, 20852, 21015, 21037, 24120; SNL G–103, Vol. 5.

The nomenclature, Light Tank, M3A2, was authorized in March, 1942, for a tank to be similar to Light Tank, M3A1, but with a welded hull. This model was never put into production.

REFERENCES — OCM 17984, 18639, 20076.

LIGHT TANK, M3A3, was standardized in August, 1942, as a modification of Light Tank, M3A1. It was reclassified as Limited Standard in April, 1943.

An improved turret, with a radio bulge at the rear, provides greater space in the fighting compartment. The hull is welded and streamlined in design. The front plate is extended forward and reinforced, providing more space and greater safety for the driver and assistant. The drivers' hatches, formerly in the front plate, are relocated in the top plate and equipped with periscopes to provide indirect vision in combat zones. Three additional periscopes are provided in the turret.

Sponsons are lengthened to the rear of the vehicle and contain additional gasoline tanks as well as additional ammunition storage. Sand shields are provided over the suspensions. A storage box is located at the rear.

Other improvements include easier steering, improved fire protection and ventilation, relocation of battery, switch and instruments and provision of detachable head lamps and a detachable windshield and weather cover.

The redesigned Combination Gun Mount, M44, includes a telescope which may be used through all degrees of gun elevation.

REFERENCES — TM 9–726C; OCM 18639, 19119, 19182, 19396, 20076, 20153, 20317; SNL G–103, Vol. 7.

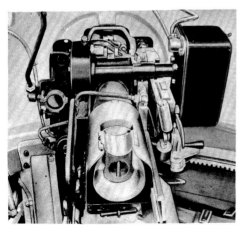

COMBINATION GUN MOUNT, M44

TYPICAL CHARACTERISTICS
LIGHT TANK, M3

Crew..4

Physical Characteristics

Weight (gross)	27,400 lb.
Length (hull)	14 ft., 10⅜ ins.
Width	7 ft., 4 ins.
Height	8 ft., 3 ins.
Turret ring diameter	46¾ ins.
Ground clearance	16½ ins.
Tread (center to center of tracks)	73 ins.
Ground contact length	117 ins.
Ground pressure	10.47 lb./sq. in.

Armor

	Actual	Basis
Hull, Front, Upper	1½ ins.	1¾ ins.
Lower	⅝–1¾ ins.	1¾–3 ins.
Sides and rear	1 in.	1 in.
Top	⅜ in.	
Bottom	⅜–½ in.	
Turret, Front	1½ ins.	1¾ ins.
Sides and rear	1¼ ins.	1¼ ins.
Top	½ in.	

Performance

Maximum speed on level	36 m.p.h.
Maximum grade ability	60%
Trench crossing ability	6 ft.
Vertical obstacle ability	24 ins.
Fording depth (slowest forward speed)	36 ins.
Turning radius	21 ft.
Fuel capacity—without jettison tanks	56 gal.
with jettison tanks	106 gal.
Maximum drawbar pull	14,800 lb.
Cruising range (approx.)	70 miles

Engine,

	Continental	Guiberson
Make		
Model	W670–9A	T1020–4
Type	Radial A.C.	Radial A.C.
Cylinders	7	9
Fuel	Gasoline (80 octane)	Diesel (50 cetane)
Max. governed speed	2,400 r.p.m.	2,200 r.p.m.

Rated hp.	250 at 2,400 r.p.m.
	220 at 2,200 r.p.m.

Max. torque	584 lb.-ft.	580 lb.-ft.
	at 1,800 r.p.m.	at 1,400 r.p.m.

(See additional engine characteristics on page 27)

Vision and Fire Control

Protectoscopes	2
Direct vision slots	2

Communications — Radio ... SCR-245

Battery, Voltage, Total 12

Fire Protection and Decontamination

Fire Extinguisher, CO₂–10 lb. (fixed)	1
CO₂–4 lb. (hand)	1
Decontaminating Apparatus, M2, 1½ qts.	1

Transmission, Type .... Manual shift

Gear ratios

First speed	5.37:1
Second speed	2.82:1
Third speed	1.72:1
Fourth speed	1.09:1
Fifth speed	.738:1
Reverse speed	6.19:1

Differential, Controlled, Gear Ratio .. 2.62:1

Steering Ratio 1.845:1

Final Drive, Type .... Herringbone

Gear Ratio	2.41:1
Sprocket, no. of Teeth	14
Pitch diameter	24.56

Suspension, Type .... Volute spring

Wheel or tire size	20x6
Wheel construction	Welded

Idler, Trailing, Type .... Ind. vol. spring

Wheel or tire size	30x6
Wheel construction	Welded

Track, Type .... Rubber block

Width	11⅝ ins.
Pitch	5½ ins.
No. of shoes per vehicle	132 or 134

LIGHT TANK, M3A1

Characteristics same as for Light Tank, M3, except as noted:

Physical Characteristics

Weight	28,500 lb.
Height	7 ft., 6½ ins.
Ground pressure	10.56 lb./sq. in.

Vision—Protectoscopes 5

Periscopes	2
Direct vision slots	2

Communications—Radio SCR-508

Interphone stations 4

LIGHT TANK, M3A3

Characteristics same as for Light Tank, M3A1, except as noted:

Physical Characteristics

Weight (gross) (with Track, T16)	31,752 lb.
Length (with bustle box)	16 ft., 6 ins.
Width	8 ft., 3 ins.
Height	7 ft., 6½ ins.

Fuel Capacity .... 102 gals.

Vision and Fire Control

Periscopes	5
Protectoscopes	Omitted
Direct vision slots	Omitted
Telescope, M54	1

Armament—Light Tanks, M3, M3A1, M3A3

37 mm Gun, M5 or M6, and	In Combination Mount, M22, M23 or M44, in turret
1 cal. .30 Browning machine gun	
1 cal. .30 Browning machine gun	In ball mount in bow
1 cal. .30 Browning machine gun	On turret, antiaircraft
2 cal. .30 Browning machine guns	Sponsons: on M3 only
1 Tripod Mount, cal. .30, M2	
Provision for 1 cal. .45 submachine gun	

Ammunition Stowage

	M3	M3A1	M3A3
37 mm (A.P.C., M51B1; A.P.C., M51B2; H.E., M63; Can., M2)	103 rds.	116 rds.	174 rds.
Cal. .30	8,270 rds.	6,400 rds.	7,500 rds.
Cal. .45	500 rds.	510 rds.	540 rds.
Grenades, Hand (Fragmentation, Mk. II, 4; Offensive, Mk. IIIA2, w/Fuze, Detonating, M6, 2; Smoke, W.P., M15, 4; Thermite, Incendiary, 2)	12	12	12

LIGHT TANKS M5 LIMITED STANDARD—M5A1 SUBSTITUTE STANDARD

LIGHT TANK, M5, WITH PISTOL PORTS AND HATCHES CLOSED; HULL AND TURRET PERISCOPES UP; GROUSERS ON SIDE OF TURRET

LIGHT TANK, M5, standardized in February, 1942, was designed as a modification of Light Tank, M3A1, to use twin Cadillac engines and Hydra-Matic transmissions, providing automatic gear shifting. It was reclassified as Limited Standard in April, 1943.

The hull is fabricated of welded, homogeneous armor plate with the reinforced front plate, extended sponsons, and streamlined effect subsequently adopted for Light Tank, M3A3. Elimination of bolts and rivets reduced the danger of having these parts driven inside the tank by the impact of projectiles on the exterior.

The welded, power-operated turret and integrated turret basket are similar to those used on Light Tank, M3A1. However, because of the lower driveshaft tunnel required by the use of the Cadillac engines and Hydra-Matic transmissions, it was possible to relocate the turret-traversing mechanism and portions of the gun stabilizer under the turret basket, thus providing more space in the fighting compartment.

The turret, of welded, curved-plate armor plate, is covered on the front by a

LEFT SIDE OF COMBINATION GUN MOUNT, INCLUDING 37 mm GUN, M6

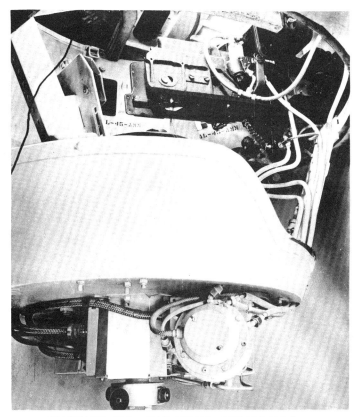

TRAVERSING MECHANISM BENEATH TURRET BASKET

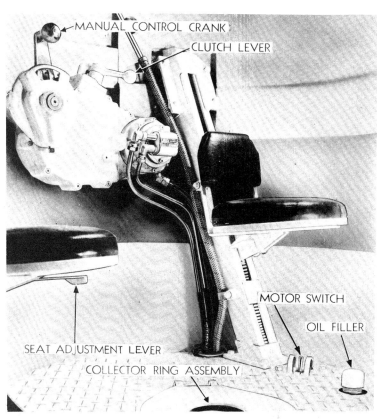

ADJUSTABLE SEATS AND CONTROLS IN TURRET BASKET

heavy armor-plate casting which serves as a base for the combination gun mount. The turret can be rotated through a traverse of 360° either by a hydraulic mechanism or by hand.

Principal armament is a 37 mm Gun, M6, mounted with a cal. .30 Browning machine gun, in the turret. Elevation is from −10° to +20°. An A.P.C. projectile, when fired from the 37 mm gun, has a muzzle velocity of 2,900 feet per second. It has a maximum range of 12,850 yards, and will penetrate 1.8 inches of face-hardened armor plate at 1,000 yards.

A gyrostabilizer is provided to keep the turret gun sufficiently close to a fixed elevation while the tank is in motion over normal terrain so that the gunner can accurately aim and fire the gun.

The two 8-cylinder, 90°, V-type, liquid-cooled Cadillac engines are located in the rear of the hull. The flywheel end of each engine is connected to a Hydra-Matic transmission. These transmissions, plus a two-speed stepdown in the transfer unit, provide six forward speeds and one reverse speed.

An auxiliary power plant consisting of a generating set powered by a single-cylinder gasoline engine supplements the engine generators for charging the battery.

Seats for the driver and assistant driver are adjustable horizontally or vertically. Seats go up under spring pressure and

down under body weight and can be locked in any position.

The vehicle is provided with dual controls and has four escape hatches, one for each member of the crew. It is equipped with 360° periscopes for the driver, assistant driver, and commander and a periscopic gun sight, as well as with three protectoscopes in the turret ports. Two knockout plugs cover ports in the front armor plate. The tank is wired for radio and for an interphone system.

REFERENCES—TM 9–732, 9–1732A; OCM 15959, 16135, 17428, 17451, 17471, 17578, 17680, 17827, 17906, 17952, 17984, 18544, 18639, 19119, 20076, 20317; SNL E-103, Vol. II.

LIGHT TANK, M5A1, was standardized in September, 1942, and replaced Light Tank, M5, in production. It was reclassified as Substitute Standard in July, 1944.

Principal change was in the use of an improved turret with a radio bulge at the rear, similar to the turret of Light Tank, M3A3. The improved turret provides more room for turret crew members and permits desirable rearrangements in stowage. A radio antenna bracket is mounted above the bulge. A removable plate in the rear of the bulge permits removal of the 37 mm gun.

The antiaircraft gun mount is improved

and repositioned to the right side of the turret. Dual traverse is incorporated, permitting the commander to traverse the turret while firing the antiaircraft gun.

Larger escape hatches, with improved positive water-sealing door latches, are provided, and there is an additional escape hatch for emergency use in the floor of the hull.

The improved Combination Gun Mount, M44, for the turret guns, incorporates a direct-sighting 3-power telescope. The breech guard permits hinging upward, facilitating travel from one seat to another by personnel. A new mount for the commander's periscope permits 360° traverse. An additional periscope in the turret facilitates rear vision for the commander.

Pistol port doors are redesigned and relocated, and equipped with locking devices. A direction finder fastened to the turret roof ahead of the commander's periscope indicates the straight ahead position. A spotlight is provided.

Sand shields, which extend down from the sponsons and cover the top portion of the track, are supplied when required.

Pilot models for Light Tanks, M5 and M5A1, were manufactured by the Cadillac Motor Car Division, General Motors Corp.

REFERENCES—TM 9–732; OCM 17471, 17827, 18639, 18925, 19182, 19396, 20153, 24175; SNL G-103, Vol. VIII.

190½" 90"
94½"
117" 73½"
170¾"

LIGHT TANK, M5A1, SHOWING REDESIGNED TURRET WITH SHIELD FOR ANTIAIRCRAFT GUN MOUNT; SAND SHIELDS OVER SUSPENSIONS

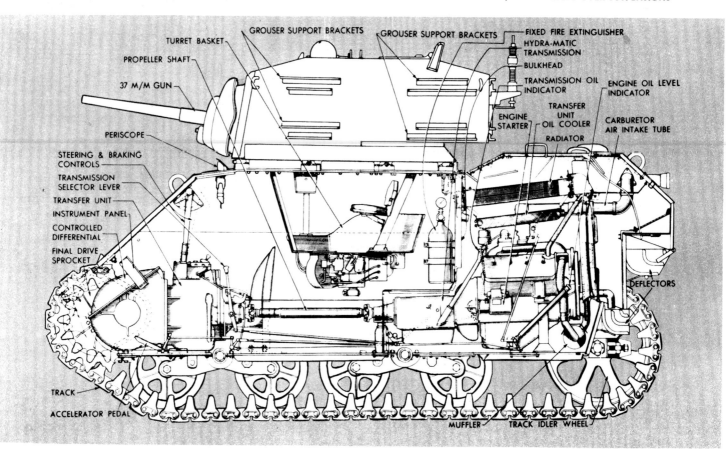

CROSS SECTION DIAGRAM OF LIGHT TANK, M5A1, SHOWING INTERIOR ARRANGEMENT. CHARACTERISTICS ARE GIVEN ON PAGE 8

LIGHT TANK, M5A1, REAR VIEW SHOWING EXTERIOR STOWAGE

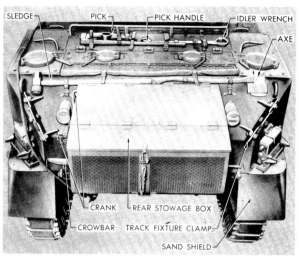

REAR VIEW SHOWING USE OF STOWAGE BOX

TYPICAL CHARACTERISTICS

LIGHT TANK, M5

Crew 4

Physical Characteristics

Weight (gross)	33,000 lb.
Length	14 ft., 2¾ ins.
Width	7 ft., 4¼ ins.
Height	7 ft., 6½ ins.
Height—to center line of bore	6 ft., 5⅜ ins.
Turret ring diameter	46¾ ins.
Ground clearance	13¾ ins.
Center of gravity—above ground	33½ ins.
rear of sprocket	79½ ins.
Tread (center to center of tracks)	73½ ins.
Ground contact length	117 ins.
Ground pressure	12.4 lb./sq. in.

Armor

	Actual	Basis
Hull, Front, Upper	1⅛ ins.	2½ ins.
Lower	2–2½ ins.	2–2½ ins.
Sides and rear	1–1⅛ ins.	1–1⅛ ins.
Top	½ in.	
Bottom	⅜–½ in.	
Turret, Front	1¾ ins.	2 ins.
Sides and rear	1¼ ins.	1¼ ins.
Top	½ in.	

Performance

Maximum speed on level	36 m.p.h.
Maximum grade ability	60%
Trench crossing ability	5 ft., 4 ins.
Vertical obstacle ability	18 ins.
Fording depth (slowest forward speed)	36 ins.
Fuel capacity	89 gals.
Cruising range	100 miles
Turning radius	21 ft.

Vision and Fire Control

Periscopes (M6, 3; M4, 1)	4
Protectoscopes (in pistol ports)	3

Communications

Radio	SCR–508, 528 or 538
Command tank	SCR–506
Interphone stations	4
Flag Set, M238	1

Battery, Voltage 12

Fire Protection and Decontamination

Fire Extinguisher, CO₂–10 lb. (fixed)	1
CO₂–4 lb. (hand)	1
Decontaminating Apparatus, M2, 1½ qts.	1

Engine, Make and Model . . . Cadillac, Series 42

Type	Dual, V–8, L.C.
No. of cylinders	16
Displacement	346 cu. ins.
Fuel (gasoline)	70 and 80 octane
Max. governed speed	4,000 r.p.m.
Net h.p.	220 at 4,000 r.p.m.
Max. torque	488 lb.-ft. at 1,200 r.p.m.*

(Additional engine characteristics on page 27)

Transmission, Type . . . . Hydra-Matic

Gear ratios

First speed	3.26:1
Second speed	2.26:1
Third speed	1.44:1
Fourth speed	1.00:1
Reverse	3.81:1

Transfer Case, Type . . . . Hydraulic

No. of speeds	2
Gear ratios	2.37:1; 1.00:1

Differential, Controlled, Gear Ratio . . 2.62:1

Steering ratio 1.845:1

Final Drive, Type . . . . Herringbone

Sprocket, No. of teeth	13
Pitch diameter	22.8
Gear ratio	2.57:1

Suspension, Type . . . Vertical volute spring

Wheel or tire size . . . . 20x6 ins.

No. of wheels per vehicle	8
Wheel construction Rubber tired, spoked or disk

Idler, Type . . . . Trailing

Wheel or tire size . . . . 30x6 ins.

Track, Type . . . . T16, T55E1, or T36E6

Width	11⅝ ins.
Pitch	5½ ins.
No. of shoes per vehicle	132

*Transmission output in direct drive.

LIGHT TANK, M5A1

Characteristics same as for Light Tank, M5, except as noted.

Physical Characteristics

Weight (gross) (with T16 tracks)	33,907 lb.
Length—over stowage box	15 ft., 10½ ins.
Width—with sand shields	90 ins.
Height—over gun mount	7 ft., 10½ ins.
Ground clearance	13¾ ins.
Ground pressure	12.5 lb./sq. in.

Vision and Fire Control

Periscope, M4, w/Telescope, M40,
or Periscope, M4A1, with Telescope,
M40, and Instrument Light, M30 1

Periscopes, M6	4
Protectoscopes	Omitted

Telescope, M70D, with Instrument Light,
M39C 1

Armament—Light Tanks, M5 and M5A1

1 37 mm Gun, M6, and . . . . {In Combination Mount, M23, in turret
1 cal. .30 Browning Machine Gun, M1919A5 (fixed) . . . . } (Mount, M44, in Light Tank, M5A1)
1 cal. .30 Browning Machine Gun, M1919A4 (flexible) . . . . In bow
1 cal. .30 Browning Machine Gun, M1919A4 (flexible) . . . . On turret, antiaircraft
1 Tripod Mount, cal. .30, M2
Provision for:
1 cal. .45 submachine gun . . . . Equipment of crew

Ammunition, Stowage

	M5	M5A1
37 mm (A.P.C., M51B1; A.P.C., M51B2; H.E., M63; Can., M2)	123 rounds	147 rounds
Cal. .30	6,250 rounds	6,500 rounds
Cal. .45	420 rounds	540 rounds
Grenades, Hand (Fragmentation, Mk. II, 4; Offensive, Mk. III (w/Fuze, M6), 2; Smoke, H.C., M8, 4; Thermite, Incendiary, 2)	12	12

LIGHT TANK M22—LIMITED STANDARD

LIGHT TANK, M22, IS BUILT SMALL AND LIGHT TO PERMIT CARRYING BY AIRPLANE. NOTE BRACKETS AT SIDES

Light Tank, M22, is designed to provide light tank firepower in a vehicle light enough to be carried by airplane. It weighs approximately 16,000 pounds, completely stowed and with a crew of three, or approximately half the weight of Light Tank, M5A1. Size and silhouette also are much less. To achieve the weight saving, armor thickness was reduced and all but the most essential stowage was eliminated.

Four brackets, located above and to the rear of the bogie suspension are provided for attaching the vehicle to an airplane. The fighting compartment and turret are readily removable for transport purposes.

Armament consists of one 37 mm Gun, M6, and one cal. .30 machine gun mounted in a Combination Gun Mount, M53, in the turret. The guns can be elevated from 10° to +30°, and can be traversed 360° in the hand-operated turret. The A.P.C. projectile fired from the 37 mm gun has a muzzle velocity of 2,900 feet per second. It has a range at 30° elevation of 12,000 yards and will penetrate 1.8-in. of 20° obliquity face-hardened armor plate at 1,000 yards.

Provision is made for carrying a cal. .45 submachine gun.

Because of weight limitations, no power traverse or gyrostabilizer are provided. Maximum armor thickness is 1 inch. The crew consists of the commander-loader and gunner, seated in the turret,

LIGHT TANK, M22, WITHOUT TURRET, SUSPENDED BENEATH AIRPLANE

LIGHT TANK, M22, TURRET BASKET WITH TURRET REMOVED

and the driver, seated in the hull. There is no assistant driver.

A volute spring suspension with a trailing idler is used. Tracks are of steel.

Power is supplied by a 6-cylinder, horizontally opposed, air-cooled Lycoming 0-435-T gasoline aircraft engine located at the right rear. The power train, located at the front of the vehicle, consists of a fixed-ratio transfer case, a 4-speed transmission, and controlled differential.

The vehicle has a fuel capacity of 55 gallons and a cruising range of approximately 135 miles.

The driver's hatch in the front plate can be fastened upward for direct vision in non-combat zones. A detachable windshield with weather cover is provided. There are two hatches in the turret and an emergency escape hatch in the floor of the hull.

The tank is equipped with a two-way radio and an interphone system. It has three periscopes for vision and a gunner's periscope.

Development of Light Tank, T9, was approved by Ordnance Committee action in May, 1941. Action in May, 1941, authorized limited procurement of Light Tank, T9E1, which has an improved front hull and improved turret. In September, 1944, the vehicle was redesignated Light Tank, M22, and reclassified as Limited Standard.

REFERENCES — OCM 16747, 17087, 17953, 19545, 19726, 20680, 21002, 23958, 24935, 25333; SNL G-148.

TYPICAL CHARACTERISTICS

Crew 3
Physical Characteristics
 Weight (gross w/o crew) . . . . 16,000 lb.
 Length . . . . 12 ft., 11 in.
 Width . . . . 7 ft., 3¾ in.
 Height . . . . 5 ft., 8½ in.
 Turret ring diameter . . . . 47½ in.
 Ground clearance . . . . 10 in.
 Tread (center to center of tracks) . . . . 70½ in.
 Ground contact length . . . . 104 in.
 Ground pressure at 0 penetration . 7.03 lb./sq. in.

Armament
 1 37 mm Gun, M6, and
 1 cal. .30 Machine Gun, M1919A4 (flexible)
  In Combination Mount, M53, in turret
 Elevation . . . . −10° to +30°
 Traverse . . . . 360°
 1 Tripod Mount, cal. .30, M2
 Provision for:
  3 cal. .45 Submachine Guns, M3, or
  1 cal. .30 Carbine and
  2 Submachine Guns, M3

Ammunition, Stowage
 37 mm (A.P.C., M51B1 or M51B2;
  A.P., M74; H.E., M63;
  and Can., M2) . . . . 50 rounds
 Cal. .30 (in belts and boxes) . . . 2,500 rounds*

*2,250 rounds in command tank.

Cal. .45 . . . . 450 rounds
Grenades, Hand (Fragmentation, Mk. II,
 4; Smoke, M8, 4; Thermite, Incendiary,
 2; Offensive, Mk. III, 2) 12

Armor

	Actual	Basis
Hull, Front, Upper	1 in.	
Lower	1 in.	
Sides, Upper	¾ in.	
Lower	½ in.	
Rear	½ in.	
Top		⅜ in.
Bottom		½ in.
Turret, Front	1 in.	
Sides	1 in.	
Rear	¾ in.	
Top	¾ in.	

Performance
 Maximum speed on level . . . . 35 m.p.h.
 Maximum grade ability 50%
 Trench crossing ability . . . . 5 ft., 5 in.
 Vertical obstacle ability . . . . 16 in.
 Fording depth . . . . 36 in.
 Fuel capacity . . . . 55 gal.
 Cruising range . . . . 110 miles
 Turning radius . . . . 20 ft.

Vision and Fire Control
 Direct vision for driver
 Periscopes, M6 3

Periscope, M8 or M8A1
 (w/Telescope, M46) 1
Communications
 Radio SCR-510
 Interphone stations 3
 Flag Set, M238 1
Battery, Voltage, total 12
Fire Protection and Decontamination
 Fire Extinguisher, CO₂-10 lb. (fixed) 1
  CO₂-4 lb. (hand) 1
 Decontaminating Apparatus, M2, 1½ qts. . . 1
Engine, Make and Model . . Lycoming 0-435-T
 Type . . . . Opposed, A.C.
 Number of cylinders 6
 Fuel (gasoline) . . . . 80 octane
 Maximum governed speed . . . . . 2,800 r.p.m.
 Net hp. . . . . 162 at 2,800 r.p.m.
 Maximum torque . . 332 lb.-ft. at 2,100 r.p.m.
(See additional characteristics on page 27.)

Transmission, Type . . . . Manual shift
 Gear ratios
  First speed 1.857:1
  Second speed 1:1
  Third speed 463:1
  Fourth speed 304:1
  Reverse 1.666:1

Transfer Case, Type . . . . . . 3-gear, Fixed ratio
 Gear ratio 2:1

Differential, Controlled, Gear ratio 3.05:1
 Steering ratio 2:1

Final Drive, Type . . . . Spur gear
 Sprocket, Number of teeth 22
 Pitch diameter 21:08
 Gear ratio 2.23:1

Suspension, Type . . . . . . Vertical volute spring
 Wheel or tire size 15x6

Idler, Trailing, Type . . . . Volute spring
 Wheel or tire size 28x6

Track, Type . . . . T78, Steel
 Width . . . . 11¼ in.
 Pitch . . . . 3 in.
 Number of shoes per vehicle 212

Brakes, Type . . . . Mechanical

OVERHEAD VIEW SHOWING ENTRANCE HATCHES AND COMBINATION GUN MOUNT

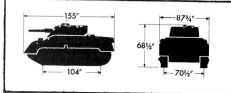

LIGHT TANK M24—STANDARD

LIGHT TANK, M24, HAS LOW SILHOUETTE AND TORSION BAR SUSPENSION. IT MOUNTS 75 MM AIRCRAFT GUN IN TURRET

TYPICAL CHARACTERISTICS

Crew 4

Physical Characteristics
Weight (gross, approx.) . . . . .38,750 lb.
Length—hull . . . . .16 ft., 3 ins.
   overall, with armament . . . . .18 ft.
Width . . . . .9 ft., 4 ins.
Height—top of cupola . . . . .8 ft., 1 in.
   top of A.A. mount . . . . .8 ft., 4 ins.
Turret ring diameter (inside) . . . . . . .60 ins.
Ground clearance . . . . .17 ins.
Tread (center to center of tracks) . . . .96 ins.
Ground contact length . . . . .112 ins.
Ground pressure . . . . .10.7 lb./sq. in.

Armament
1 75 mm Gun, M6, and
   1 cal. .30 Machine Gun, M1919A4 (flexible)
   In Combination Gun Mount, M64, in turret
   Elevation . . . .−10° to +15°
   Traverse . . . . .360°
1 cal. .50 Machine Gun, M2, HB
  (flexible) . . . . .On turret, antiaircraft
1 cal. .30 Machine Gun, M1919A4
  (flexible) . . . . .In bow mount
1 2-Inch Mortar, M3 . . . . .In turret
1 cal. .30 Tripod Mount, M2
Provision for:
4 cal. .45 Submachine Guns, M3, or
3 cal. .45 Submachine Guns, M3, and
  1 cal. .30 Carbine, M1, with Grenade
  Launcher, M8

Ammunition, Stowage
75 mm . . . . .48 rounds
Cal. .50 . . . . .440 rounds
Cal. .30 . . . . .3,750 rounds
Cal. .45 . . . . .720 rounds
2-Inch Smoke Bombs, Mk. I/L (British) 14 rounds
Grenades (Smoke, 2; Fragmentation, 6) 8

Armor

	Actual	Basis
Hull, Front, Upper	1 in.	2½ ins.
Lower	1 in.	1½ ins.
Sides, Forward	1 in.	1 in.
Rear	¾ in.	¾ in.
Rear, Upper	¾ in.	¾ in.
Lower	¾ in.	1¼ in.

Top	½ in.	
Bottom (first 36 ins.) .	½ in.	
(remainder) . . .	⅜ in.	
Turret, Front and sides .	1 in.	1¼ ins.
Rear	1 in.	1 in.
Roof	½ in.	
Gun shield, Upper . . .	1½ ins.	2 ins.
Lower	1½ ins.	2¼ ins.

Performance
Maximum speed on level . . . . .35 m.p.h.
  3% grade . . . . .17 m.p.h.
  10% grade . . . . .11 m.p.h.
Maximum grade ability 60%
Trench crossing ability . . . . .6½ ft.
Vertical obstacle ability . . . . .36 ins.
Fording depth (slowest forward speed) . .40 ins.
Turning radius . . . . .40 ft.
Fuel capacity . . . . .110 gals.
Cruising range (approx.) Highway . .175 miles
   Cross country . . . . .100 miles
Maximum drawbar pull . . . . .22,000 lb.

Vision and Fire Control
Periscope, M6 3
Telescope, M71G, with Instrument Light,
  M33 (or Telescope, M70N, with Instru-
  ment Light, M39C) in Telescope Mount,
  M65, with Headrest 1
Periscope, M10C, in Periscope Mount, M66
  (or Periscope, M4A1) 2
Azimuth Indicator, M21 1
Elevation Quadrant, M9, with Instrument
  Light, M30 1
Gunner's Quadrant, M1 1
Vision Blocks (in cupola) 6

Communications
Radio . . .SCR–508, 528, 538, or British No. 19
   Command tank SCR–506
Interphone stations 5
Flag Set, M238 1

Battery, Voltage, total 24

Fire Protection and Decontamination
Fire Extinguisher, CO₂–10 lb. (fixed) 1
   CO₂–4 lb. (hand) 1
Decontaminating Apparatus, M2, 1½ qts. . . .2

Engine, Make and Model . . .Cadillac, Series 42
Type .Dual, V–8, L.C.
No. of cylinders .16
Fuel (gasoline) . . . . .80 octane
Max. governed speed . . . . .4,000 r.p.m.
Net hp. . . . . .220 at 3,400 r.p.m.
Max. torque . . . . . .488 lb.-ft. at 1,200 r.p.m.
(Additional engine characteristics on page 27.)

Transmission, Type. Hydra-Matic, with transfer
                   unit and synchronizer
Gear ratios (with transfer unit)
  Forward—First speed 9.19:1
    Second speed 5.96:1
    Third speed 3.62:1
    Fourth speed 2.34:1
    Fifth speed 4.05:1
    Sixth speed 2.62:1
    Seventh speed 1.59:1
    Eighth speed 1.03:1
  Reverse—First speed 9.57:1
    Second speed 6.17:1
    Third speed 3.78:1
    Fourth speed 2.44:1

Transfer Case, Type . . . . .Synchromesh
Gear ratios—Forward 2.34:1; 1.03:1
   Reverse 2.44:1

Differential, Controlled, Gear ratio . .2.625:1
Steering ratio 1.55:1

Final Drive, Type . . . . .Herringbone
Gear ratio 2.571:1
Sprocket, No. of teeth 13
Pitch diameter 23.108

Suspension, Type . . . . .Torsion bar
No. of wheels . . . . .10, dual
Wheel or tire size 25½x4½
Wheel construction . . . . .Stamped disk

Idler, Type .Fixed
Wheel or tire size . . . . .22½x4½, dual
Wheel construction . . . . .Stamped disk

Track, Type . . . . .Steel block, single pin,
              rubber bushed, with center guide
Width . . . . .16 ins.
Pitch . . . . .5½ ins.
No. of shoes per vehicle 150

Light Tank, M24, was designed to provide an improved light tank mounting a 75 mm gun, and having increased flotation and mobility and greater accessibility of all components. It was standardized in July, 1944.

The crew consists of four men.

Principal armament consists of a 75 mm Gun, M6, in a concentric recoil mechanism, mounted with a cal. .30 machine gun in Combination Gun Mount, M64. A gyrostabilizer is provided. The combination mount has an elevation from $-10°$ to $+15°$, and can be traversed 360° in the power-operated turret.

A cal. .50 machine gun is pintle mounted at the rear of the turret for antiaircraft protection. A cal. .30 machine gun is in the bow, and a 2-inch mortar in the right front turret. Provision is made for carrying four cal. .45 submachine guns.

There is no turret basket. Seats for the turret crew members are suspended from the base ring. The 75 mm ammunition is stowed on the floor of the vehicle in water-protected containers.

Power is supplied by two 8-cylinder, 90°, V-type, liquid-cooled Cadillac engines, through two Hydra-Matic transmissions. Right and left engines are interchangeable. A manual shift transfer unit with two speeds forward and one reverse is incorporated in the gear train used to couple the two engines together.

A controlled differential for steering and braking is located in the front of the hull.

A synchronizer incorporated in the transfer unit permits a speedy shift from the low to high range or vice versa, and allows a total of eight speeds forward with an overlap of third and fourth speeds in the low range with the first and second speeds in the high range. In addition, four speeds can be obtained in reverse, making possible reverse speeds up to 18 miles per hour.

As compared with Light Tank, M5A1, the vehicle has a 22% increase in overall low gear ratio, with correspondingly increased grade ability and pulling capacity.

An individually sprung, compensated torsion bar suspension, together with a single pin, rubber-bushed, center guide track, 16 inches wide, provides better riding qualities, a more stable gun platform, and reduced ground pressures, allowing better cross-country mobility than could be obtained with Light Tank, M5A1.

Radiators are of larger capacity, and are so placed that they can be readily cleaned from openings in the fighting compartment bulkhead. Fans are directly in the rear of the radiators.

Doors for the driver and assistant driver are larger and can be opened and closed without interference irrespective of turret position. The turret doors are also larger. An escape hatch is provided in the floor of the hull.

Wherever possible, unit assemblies have been made so that they can be easily removed and rapidly replaced in the field. Interchangeability of components and assemblies has been applied throughout the design.

Three periscopes for vision, a commander's vision block cupola, a sighting periscope, and other sighting equipment are provided. The vehicle is equipped with a two-way radio and an interphone system. A quick release pintle of 69,000 pounds capacity is provided.

Development of this vehicle as Light Tank, T24, was authorized by Ordnance Committee action in March, 1943. Limited Procurement of the vehicles was authorized in September, 1943.

The pilot vehicle was manufactured by the Cadillac Motor Car Division, General Motors Corporation.

REFERENCES—TM 9–729; OCM 19674, 20078, 20316, 21038, 21446, 21699, 22642, 22870, 23446, 24175, 24395, 25324.

LIGHT TANK, M24, LEFT REAR VIEW, WITH CAL. .50 GUN ON TURRET

ENTRANCE HATCHES ARE LARGER THAN ON EARLIER LIGHT TANKS

MEDIUM TANK M3 SERIES

These were the first American medium tanks produced in quantity under the defense program prior to the entry of the United States into World War II. Supplied to the British and Russians as Lend-Lease materiel, they compared favorably with other medium tanks at that time.

They were the first of our tanks to employ 75-mm guns, gyrostabilizers, and power-traversed turrets with integral fighting compartments. Their armor was thicker than that of our earlier tanks.

Battle experience in Africa and Russia suggested improvements, some of which were introduced as production continued. Most of the improvements, however, were incorporated in the design of Medium Tank M4. When the latter was standardized in October 1941, tanks of the M3 series were designated Substitute Standard. In April 1943 they were reclassified as Limited Standard, and in April 1944 they were declared obsolete.

MEDIUM TANK M3—This was the original vehicle of the series. It had a riveted hull and was powered by a Continental (Wright) R-975-EC2 or R-975-C1 gasoline engine.

MEDIUM TANK M3A1—This was similar to Medium Tank M3 but had a cast hull.

MEDIUM TANK M3A2—This was similar to Medium Tank M3 but had a welded hull.

MEDIUM TANK M3A3—This was similar to Medium Tank M3A2, with a welded hull, but was powered by twin General Motors 6-71 Diesel engines.

MEDIUM TANK M3A4—This was similar to Medium Tank M3, with a riveted hull, but was powered by a Chrysler multibank engine.

MEDIUM TANK M3A5—This was similar to Medium Tank M3, with a riveted hull, but was powered by twin General Motors 6-71 Diesel engines.

Principal armament was a 75-mm Gun M3, in a rotor mount in the right front of the crew compartment. This gun had an elevation from $-9°$ to $+20°$ and could be traversed $15°$ in each direction. The gun could be fired manually or electrically. The A.P.C. projectile M61, fired from this gun with a muzzle velocity of 1,920 feet per second, has a maximum range of 13,090 yards and will penetrate 2.9 inches of face-hardened armor plate at 1,000 yards.

A 37-mm Gun M6 and a Cal. .30 Machine Gun M1919A4 were mounted in a Combination Gun Mount M24, in the turret, which had a traverse of 360°. The turret guns were fired electrically and had elevations from $-7°$ to $+60°$. The

MEDIUM TANK M3 HAD RIVETED HULL AND CAST TURRET WITH 360° TRAVERSE

MEDIUM TANK M3A1 HAD CAST HULL AND CAST TURRET, GIVING STREAMLINED EFFECT

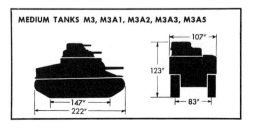
MEDIUM TANKS M3, M3A1, M3A2, M3A3, M3A5

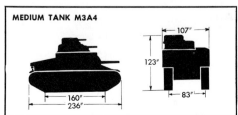
MEDIUM TANK M3A4

A. P. C. projectile, fired from the 37-mm gun with a muzzle velocity of 2,900 feet per second, has a maximum range of 12,850 yards and will penetrate 1.8 inches of face-hardened armor plate at 1,000 yards.

A cal. .30 machine gun for antiaircraft use was mounted on the cupola, and two cal. .30 machine guns were in the bow. Provision was made for carrying one cal. .45 submachine gun.

The turret and integrated fighting compartment could be traversed by a hydraulic mechanism or by hand. The cupola normally rotated with the turret but could be rotated by hand.

The crew consisted of six men. The driver and radio operator occupied seats forward in the hull. The 75-mm gunner sat on the left side of the gun mount. The 37-mm gunner and gun loader and the commander were seated in the turret.

Both the 75-mm gun and the 37-mm gun were provided with gyrostabilizers, which aided in keeping the guns aimed at their targets while the tank was in motion.

Periscopic sights were provided for the 75-mm and 37-mm guns. The driver's door and the pistol port doors were provided with protectoscopes for indirect vision.

The armor of the front upper section,

cupola, and turret sides was 2 inches thick, and that on the sides of the hull and the front lower section was 1½ inches thick.

The tank was wired for radio installation and for an interphone system.

An auxiliary generating set provided additional electric power when required.

The vehicle had five forward speeds and one reverse.

REFERENCES—TM 9–750; OCM 16052, 16111, 16258, 16610, 16728, 16935, 16699, 16911, 16860, 17090, 17159, 17293, 17201, 17301, 17316, 17503, 17440, 17503, 17578, 17591, 17613, 17677, 17722, 17723, 17799, 17800, 17906, 23185, 23495; SNL G–104, Vols. 1, 3, 5, 10, 12.

TYPICAL CHARACTERISTICS

	M3 (riveted)	M3A1 (cast)	M3A2 (welded)	M3A3 (welded)	M3A4 (riveted)	M3A5 (riveted)
Crew	6	6	6	6	6	6
Physical Characteristics						
Weight (gross)	60,000 lb.	60,000 lb.	60,000 lb.	63,000 lb.	64,000 lb.	64,000 lb.
Length	18 ft., 6 in.	18 ft., 6 in.	18 ft., 6 in.	18 ft., 6 in.	19 ft., 8 in.	18 ft., 6 in.
Width	8 ft., 11 in.	8 ft., 11 in.	8 ft., 11 in.	8 ft., 11 in.	8 ft., 11 in.	8 ft., 11 in.
Height	10 ft., 3 in.	10 ft., 3 in.	10 ft., 3 in.	10 ft., 3 in.	10 ft., 3 in.	10 ft., 3 in.
Turret ring diameter (inside)	57 in.	57 in.	57 in.	57 in.	57 in.	57 in.
Ground clearance	17⅛ in.	17⅛ in.	17⅛ in.	17⅛ in.	17⅛ in.	17⅛ in.
Tread (center to center of track)	83 in.	83 in.	83 in.	83 in.	83 in.	83 in.
Ground contact length at 0 penetration	147 in.	147 in.	147 in.	147 in.	160 in.	147 in.
Ground pressure per sq. in.	13.36 lb.	13.36 lb.	13.36 lb.	13.36 lb.	12.9 lb.	13.36 lb.
Performance						
Maximum speed	26 m.p.h.	26 m.p.h.	26 m.p.h.	29 m.p.h.	26 m.p.h.	29 m.p.h.
Maximum grade ability	60%	60%	60%	60%	60%	60%
Trench crossing ability	6.2 ft.	6.2 ft.	6.2 ft.	6.2 ft.	6.2 ft.	6.2 ft.
Vertical obstacle ability	24 in.	24 in.	24 in.	24 in.	24 in.	24 in.
Fording depth (slowest forward speed)	40 in.	40 in.	40 in.	36 in.	40 in.	40 in.
Fuel capacity	175 gal.	175 gal.	175 gal.	150 gal.	160 gal.	175 gal.
Cruising range	120 miles	120 miles	120 miles	160 miles	120 miles	160 miles
Turning radius	37 ft.	37 ft.	37 ft.	37 ft.	39 ft.	37 ft.
Engine, Make	Continental	Continental	Continental	G.M. 6-71	Chrysler	G.M. 6-71
Model	R-975-EC2 or C1	R-975-EC2 or C1	R-975-EC2 or C1	6046	A-57	6046
Type	Radial A.C.	Radial A.C.	Radial A.C.	Twin, In-Line, L.C.	Multibank, L.C.	Twin, In-Line, L.C.
No. of cylinders	9	9	9	12	30	12
Fuel, Octane or cetane	92 or 80	92 or 80	92 or 80	50	80	50
Type	Gasoline	Gasoline	Gasoline	Diesel	Gasoline	Diesel
Max. governed speed	2,400 r.p.m.	2,400 r.p.m.	2,400 r.p.m.	2,100 r.p.m.	2,400 r.p.m.	2,100 r.p.m.
Net hp. at r.p.m.	340 at 2,400	340 at 2,400	340 at 2,400	375 at 2,100	370 at 2,400	375 at 2,100
Max. torque, lb.-ft. at r.p.m.	800 at 1,800	800 at 1,800	800 at 1,800	1,000 at 1,400	1,020 at 1,200	1,000 at 1,400

(See additional engine characteristics on page 28.)

Armament
1 75-mm Gun M2 or M3 . . . . . . In Mount M1
1 37-mm Gun M5 or M6 and ⎫ In Combination
1 Cal. .30 Browning Machine ⎬ Mount M24
  Gun M1919A4 (flexible) ⎭ in turret
1 Cal. .30 Browning Machine Gun
  M1919A4 (flexible) . On cupola, antiaircraft
1 Cal. .30 Browning Machine Gun
  M1919A4 . . . . In bow
Provision for:
1 Cal. .45 submachine gun . Equipment of crew

Ammunition, Stowage
75-mm	46 rounds
37-mm	178 rounds
Cal. .45	1,200 rounds
Cal. .30	9,200 rounds
Hand Grenades	12

Armor	Actual	Basis
Hull, Front, Upper	2 in.	4⅜ in.
Lower	1½ in.	2¾ in.
Sides	1½ in.	1½ in.
Rear	1½ in.	1⅝ in.
Top	½ in.	
Bottom	½ in.–1 in.	
Turret, Front	2¼ in.	6½ in.
Sides and rear	2¼ in.	2 in.
Top	⅞ in.	

Vision and Fire Control
Periscope M1	1
Periscope M3	1
Protectoscopes	7

Communications
Radio (with interphone)	SCR-508
Command tank	SCR-506

DETAIL OF SUSPENSION BOGIE AND TRACKS

Battery, Voltage, total 24
Fire Protection
Fire Extinguisher, CO$_2$–10 lb. (fixed) 2
  CO$_2$–4 lb. (hand) 2
Transmission, Type . . . . Synchromesh
Gear ratios
First speed	7.56:1
Second speed	3.11:1
Third speed	1.78:1
Fourth speed	1.11:1
Fifth speed	0.73:1
Reverse	5.65:1
Differential, Controlled, Gear ratio . . . 3.53:1
Steering ratio 1.515:1
Final Drive, Type . . . . Herringbone
Gear ratio	2.84:1
Sprocket, No. of teeth	13
Pitch diameter	25.038
Suspension, Type . . . . Volute spring
Wheel or tire size 20x9
Idler, Type . . . . Adjustable eccentric
Wheel or tire size 22x9
Track, Type . . . . Rubber block
Width	16⁹⁄₁₆ in.
Pitch	6 in.
No. of shoes per tank	158 (166 on M3A4)

MEDIUM TANK, M3A3, HAS WELDED HULL, CAST TURRET. M3 SERIES MEDIUM TANKS MOUNT 75 mm GUN IN RIGHT ROTOR, 37 mm GUN IN TURRET

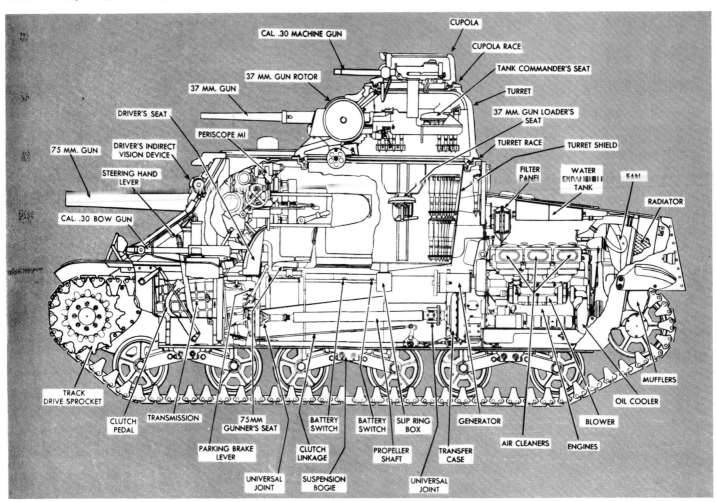

DIAGRAM OF MEDIUM TANK, M3A3, SHOWING INTERIOR ARRANGEMENT. ARRANGEMENT OF OTHER M3 SERIES MEDIUM TANKS IS GENERALLY SIMILAR

MEDIUM TANK M4* SERIES—STANDARD

MEDIUM TANK, M4, WITH WELDED HULL AND SAND SHIELDS. 75 MM AND CAL. .30 GUNS ARE IN COMBINATION GUN MOUNT, M34A1

These medium tanks, nicknamed "General Shermans" by British troops, have played an important part in Allied victories in Africa, Sicily and Russia ever since they first helped rout Marshal Rommel's troops at El Alamein.

Standardized in October, 1941, they introduced a number of improvements over the Medium Tank, M3, Series, which they replaced in production.

The 75 mm gun was relocated in the turret, providing 360° traverse and greater elevation and depression than was possible in Medium Tank, M3. The silhouette was lowered by the elimination of the cupola, thus making the tank a less conspicuous target and also resulting in a lowered center of gravity, making the tank more stable. The 37 mm gun was eliminated. The crew was decreased to five, including an assistant driver.

The 75 mm gun breech was turned 90° from the vertical, allowing for easy right-hand loading. The radio was relocated in a turret "bulge." Greater comfort and safety were provided for all crew members.

Produced simultaneously by different manufacturers, the various models differ from each other principally in their engines. A further difference is that the M4A1 has a cast hull, whereas the others have welded hulls. In addition, the M4A5, produced in Canada, embodies differences requested by the Canadian government. All have cast turrets.

Principal armament (except for the M4A5) is a 75 mm Gun, M3, mounted with a cal. .30 machine gun in a combination gun mount in the turret. The turret guns may be elevated from −10° to +25°. They are fired electrically by means of foot and hand switches. A gyro-stabilizer is provided.

An A.P.C. projectile, fired from the 75 mm gun, has a muzzle velocity of 2,030 feet per second, and will penetrate 3.1 inches of face-hardened armor plate at 1,000 yards.

Other armament includes a cal. .30 machine gun in the bow, operated by the assistant driver; a cal. .50 machine gun, mounted at the top of the turret, operated by the commander for antiaircraft use, and a 2-inch smoke mortar. A clip is

OVERHEAD VIEW OF MEDIUM TANK, M4A1, SHOWING ENTRANCE HATCHES

*See also Medium Tanks, M4 (105 mm), and M4A3 (105 mm), page 21, and Medium Tanks, M4 (76 mm), Series, page 22.

mounted in the turret to carry a cal. .45 submachine gun, which can be used through the pistol port in the side of the turret.

The turret is a one-piece casting of armor which rotates on a ball bearing race recessed and protected against direct hits and lead splash from enemy fire. The turret basket is rigidly fastened to the turret by means of a ring of bolts around its circumference. The turret hatch ring acts as antiaircraft gun mount.

The driver sits at the left bow of the tank. The assistant driver sits at the right bow. The loader sits in the turret, to the left of the 75 mm gun, and the gunner to its right. The tank commander sits in the rear of the turret, behind the gunner. Adjustable seats, allowing 12 inches of movement up and down and 5 inches fore and aft, are provided for the gunner, driver and assistant driver.

Access to the tank is through two hatches in the bow and a revolving hatch in the turret. An emergency escape hatch is located in the tank floor, behind the assistant driver.

Indirect vision is provided for each member of the crew by means of periscopes. The gunner's periscope is synchronized with the gun, contains a telescopic sight, and changes its line of sight only if the gun is elevated or depressed or the turret rotated. All other periscopes are mounted so that they can be tilted up or down and rotated through 360°. Early models had direct vision slots, protected by thick glass plates and hinged covers, for the driver and assistant driver. Because of their vulnerability to bullet splash, these were eliminated in later production, and additional periscopes were provided.

The transmission has five forward speeds and one reverse speed. A parking brake is built into the transmission. The

MEDIUM TANK, M4A1, HAS CAST HULL. PHOTO SHOWS EARLY PRODUCTION GUN MOUNT, M34

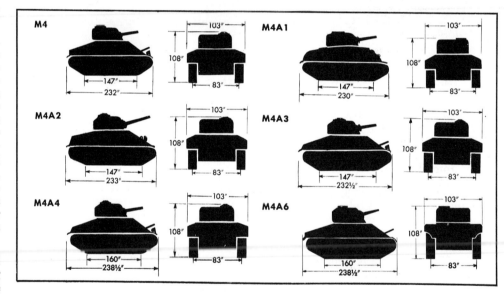

MEDIUM TANK, M4A3, WELDED, WITH CAST LOWER FRONT HULL

MEDIUM TANK, M4A4, WELDED, WITH THREE-PIECE LOWER FRONT HULL

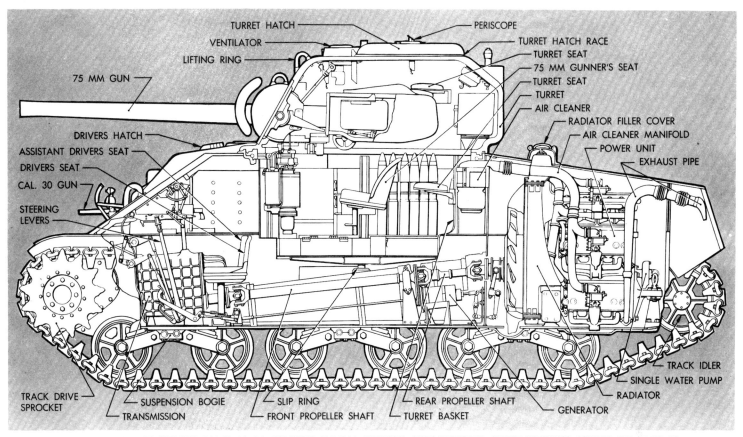

CROSS SECTION OF MEDIUM TANK, M4A4 SHOWING TYPICAL INTERIOR ARRANGEMENT. CHARACTERISTICS APPEAR ON PAGE 20

controlled differential transmits engine power to the final drive unit, and contains a brake system for steering and stopping the vehicle. The final drive units transmit power from the controlled differential to the hub of the driving sprockets through a set of reduction gears. The entire power train can be removed from the vehicle when necessary.

Six 2-wheeled, rubber-tired bogies or suspensions, bolted to the hull, support the vehicle on volute springs. The tracks are driven by sprockets on the front of the vehicle. Two idlers are mounted on eccentric shafts at the rear end of the hull, and provide for adjustment of the track tension. The weight of the upper portion of the track is carried by track-supporting rollers. (Some vehicles have the track-support roller directly over the suspension bracket. A second type has the roller offset to the rear of the bracket and is fitted with a track skid on top of the bracket.)

Two fixed 10-lb. fire extinguishers are provided in the engine compartment, and may be operated from the driver's seat or from outside the tank. Portable 4-lb. fire extinguishers are provided in the driver's compartment and in the turret.

The tank is equipped with a two-way radio and an interphone system. An auxiliary generator provides additional current at times of unusual drain, and

may also be used in preheating the engine compartment in cold weather.

The pilot tank, designated Medium Tank, T6, was built at Aberdeen Proving Ground, and had a cast hull. The vehicle had an entrance hatch at the side and had two additional machine guns in the bow, which were eliminated from the production tanks.

A number of changes were made during production, with the result that newer vehicles differ somewhat from those produced earlier.

The original Combination Gun Mount, M34, had a front shield which protected the 75 mm gun only. Ordnance Committee action in October, 1942, standardized Combination Gun Mount, M34A1, a modification which incorporated a direct sighting telescope. This mount may be recognized by its front shield which protects the Cal. .30 machine gun and the direct sighting telescope, as well as the 75 mm gun. It has two "ears" projecting a few inches over the 75 mm gun.

The lower front plate of the hull on early models consisted of three pieces, bolted together. Later production vehicles used a one-piece plate.

Introduction of sand shields over the suspensions, and of water-protected ammunition chests, were among other changes on later vehicles.

MEDIUM TANK, M4, standardized in October, 1941, is built with a welded hull and a cast turret.

Power is supplied by a Continental R975, 9-cylinder, radial, aircraft-type engine.

The turret may be traversed manually or by a hydraulic mechanism. In the past, some models used an electric power traverse.

These tanks are built by the Baldwin Locomotive Works, American Locomotive Co., Detroit Tank Arsenal (Chrysler); Pressed Steel Car Co., and Pullman Standard Car Mfg. Co.

REFERENCES — TM 9–731A; OCM 16052, 16111, 16556, 16744, 16861, 17202, 17316, 17387, 17570, 17578, 17800, 17906, 17952, 17981, 18391, 18518, 18661, 18843, 18874, 18961, 20155, 20518, 20531, 20680, 20719, 20724, 20798, 20848, 21002, 21111, 21286, 21462.

MEDIUM TANK, M4A1, standardized in December, 1941, is similar to Medium Tank, M4, but has a cast hull which is curved to present less opportunity for a direct hit on a flat surface from any angle. It is powered by a Continental R975 engine. These tanks are built by the Lima Locomotive Works, Inc., Pacific Car and Foundry Co. and Pressed Steel Car Co.

REFERENCES — TM 9–731A; OCM 17578, 19277, 19279, 19983, 19984, 20518, 20984, 21414, 22199.

MEDIUM TANK, M4A2, standardized in December, 1941, has a welded hull and a cast turret and is generally similar to Medium Tank, M4, except that it is powered by twin General Motors 6–71 Diesel engines, which are assembled as a single unit known as the G.M. 6046 power unit. Either engine may be operated independently of the other, if necessary.

These vehicles are manufactured by the Fisher Tank Division, General Motors Corp.; Pullman Standard Car Mfg. Co., and the Federal Machine and Welding Co.

REFERENCES — TM 9–731B; OCM 17578, 19456, 19724, 19725, 19983.

MEDIUM TANK, M4A3, standardized in January, 1942, has a welded hull and a cast turret and is generally similar to Medium Tank, M4, except that it is powered by a 500 hp. Ford tank engine. This is an 8-cylinder, liquid-cooled "V" type engine designed for tanks.

These tanks are built by the Ford Motor Co.

REFERENCES—TM 9 759; OCM 17678, 19982, 19983, 20205, 20518, 21053.

MEDIUM TANK, M4A4, standardized in February, 1942, has a welded hull and a cast turret, and is generally similar to Medium Tank, M4, except that it is powered by a Chrysler tank engine power unit, consisting of five banks of cylinders, each of which is in itself a conventional "L" head, water-cooled engine. The five units are geared together and operate as a single unit.

These tanks were built by the Detroit Tank Arsenal (Chrysler).

MEDIUM TANK, M4A5, THE CANADIAN RAM, MOUNTS 57 MM AND CAL. .30 GUNS

REFERENCES—TM 9–754; OCM 17855, 19280, 19983, 20205.

MEDIUM TANK, M4A5, was given this designation for record purposes by OCM 17856. It is produced in Canada under the designation, RAM II. It is generally similar to the Medium Tank, M4, but has variations requested by the Canadian Government.

Principal armament is a 57 mm gun in a combination mount with a cal. .30 machine gun in the British type cast turret. A small cupola is added on the left front of the hull roof and mounts a cal. .30 machine gun. A smoke projector is mounted on the right side of the turret front plate.

The tank is powered by a Wright R975 engine.

The pilot tank was manufactured by the American Locomotive Co.

REFERENCE—OCM 17856.

MEDIUM TANK, M4A6, is similar to Medium Tank, M4A4, but is powered by an RD–1820 Ordnance engine manufactured by the Caterpillar Tractor Co. This is a radial Diesel-type engine with a displacement of 1,820 cubic inches. This tank is manufactured by the Detroit Tank Arsenal (Chrysler).

REFERENCES — OCM 19200, 19439, 19630, 19631, 20716.

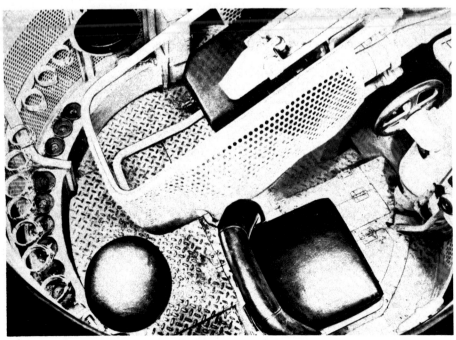

GUN MOUNT AND GUARD AND TURRET SEATS IN MEDIUM TANK, M4A1

STEERING LEVERS AND OTHER DRIVING CONTROLS

TYPICAL CHARACTERISTICS

	M4	M4A1	M4A2	M4A3	M4A4	M4A6
Crew	5	5	5	5	5	5

Physical Characteristics

	M4	M4A1	M4A2	M4A3	M4A4	M4A6
Weight (gross)	66,500 lb.	66,500 lb.	69,000 lb.	68,500 lb.	71,000 lb.	71,000 lb.
Length	19 ft., 4 ins.	19 ft., 2 ins.	19 ft., 5 ins.	19 ft., 4½ ins.	19 ft., 10½ ins.	19 ft., 10½ ins.
Width	8 ft., 7 ins.	8 ft., 7 ins.	8 ft., 7 ins.	8 ft., 7 ins.	8 ft., 7 ins.	8 ft., 7 ins.
Height	9 ft.	9 ft.	9 ft.	9 ft.	9 ft.	9 ft.
Ground clearance	17⅛ ins.	17⅛ ins.	17⅛ ins.	17⅛ ins.	15¾ ins.	15¾ ins.
Tread (center to center of tracks)	83 ins.	83 ins.	83 ins.	83 ins.	83 ins.	83 ins.
Ground pressure, per sq. in.	13.7 lb.	13.7 lb.	14.2 lb.	14.1 lb.	13.4 lb.	13.4 lb.
Ground contact length at 0° penetration	147 ins.	147 ins.	147 ins.	147 ins.	160 ins.	160 ins.

Performance

	M4	M4A1	M4A2	M4A3	M4A4	M4A6
Sustained speed on level	24 m.p.h.	24 m.p.h.	29 m.p.h.	26 m.p.h.	25 m.p.h.	25 m.p.h.
Maximum grade ability	60%	60%	60%	60%	60%	60%
Trench crossing ability	7 ft., 5 ins.	7 ft., 5 ins.	7 ft., 5 ins.	7 ft., 5 ins.	8 ft.	8 ft.
Vertical obstacle ability	24 ins.	24 ins.	24 ins.	24 ins.	24 ins.	24 ins.
Fording depth (slowest forward speed)	36 ins.	36 ins.	40 ins.	36 ins.	42 ins.	42 ins.
Fuel capacity	175 gals.	175 gals.	148 gals.	174 gals.	150 gals.	150 gals.
Cruising range	120 miles	120 miles	150 miles	130 miles	100 miles	100 miles
Maximum drawbar pull	42,350 lb.	42,350 lb.	44,800 lb.	43,050 lb.	47,600 lb.	47,600 lb.
Engine, Make	Continental	Continental	G.M. 6–71	GAA–III	Chrysler	Caterpillar
Model	R975–C1	R975–C1	6046	V–W.C.	5-line W.C.	RD–1820
Fuel (gasoline)	80	80	—	80	80	—
(Diesel)	—	—	50	—	—	45
Max. governed speed	2,400 r.p.m.	2,400 r.p.m.	2,100 r.p.m.	2,600 r.p.m.	2,400 r.p.m.	2,000 r.p.m.
Net hp. at r.p.m.	353 at 2,400	353 at 2,400	375 at 2,100	450 at 2,600	370 at 2,850	450 at 2,000
Max. torque (lb.-ft. at r.p.m.)	800 at 1,800	800 at 1,800	1,000 at 1,400	950 at 2,100	1,025 at 1,200	1,470 at 1,200

(See additional engine characteristics on pages 28 and 29.)

ASSISTANT DRIVER'S STATION IN RIGHT BOW

Armament and Ammunition

75 mm Gun, M3, and
1 cal. .30 Browning Machine Gun, M1919A4 (flexible) . . In Combination Gun Mount, M34A1, in turret
1 cal. .30 Browning Machine Gun, M1919A4 (flexible) . . . . In bow
1 cal. .50 Machine Gun, M2, H.B. (flexible) . . . . On turret (antiaircraft)
1 Mortar, 2-Inch, M3
1 Tripod Mount, M2, Cal. .30
Provision for:
1 cal. .45 Submachine Gun . . . . Equipment of crew

Ammunition, Stowage	M4, M4A2, M4A3, M4A4, M4A5	M4A1
75 mm (H.E., M48, A.P., M72; A.P.C., M61)	97	90
Cal. .30 (A.P. and tracer)	4,750	4,750
Cal. .45	600	600
Cal. .50 (A.P. and tracer)	300	300
Grenades, Hand (Fragmentation, Mk. III, 4; Smoke, H.C., M8, 4; Offensive, Mk. III, w/fuze, Detonating, M2; Thermite, incendiary, 2)	12	12
Smoke Ammunition (minimum)	12	12

Armor

	Actual	Basis
Hull, Front, Upper	2 ins.	2–4 ins.
Lower	1½–2 ins.	2–2½ ins.
Sides	1½–2 ins.	1½–2 ins.
Rear	1½ ins.	
Top	1 in.	
Bottom	½–1 ins.	
Turret, Front	3 ins.	3¾ ins.
Sides	2 ins.	2 ins.
Top	1 in.	

Vision and Fire Control

Periscope, M4 (w/Telescope, M38)	1
Periscope, M6	6
Gunner's quadrant, M1	1
Bore sight	1
Telescope, M70F	1
Azimuth Indicator, M19	1
Elevation quadrant, M9	1

Communications

Radio	SCR-508
Command tank	SCR-506
Interphone stations	5
Flag set, M238	24

Battery, Voltage Total 24

Fire Protection and Decontamination

Fire Extinguisher—CO₂–10 lb. (fixed)	2
CO₂–4 lb. (hand)	2
Decontaminating Apparatus, M2, 1½ qts.	2

Track, Type . . . . Rubber block

Width	16½ ins.
Pitch	6 ins.

No. of shoes per vehicle
158 (Medium Tank, M4A4, uses 166 shoes)

Suspension, Type . . . . Volute spring

Wheel or tire size	20x9

Idler, Type . . . . Fixed

Wheel or tire size	28⅛x9

Final Drive, Type . . . . Herringbone

Gear ratio	2.84:1
Sprocket, no. of teeth	13
Pitch diameter	25.038

Differential, Controlled, Gear ratio 3.53:1

Ring gear, no. of teeth	60
Pinion, no. of teeth	17
Steering ratio	1.515:1

Transmission, Type . . . . Mechanical syncromesh

Gear ratios, First speed	7.56:1
Second speed	3.11:1
Third speed	1.78:1
Fourth speed	1.11:1
Fifth speed	.73:1
Reverse	5.65:1

MEDIUM TANKS M4 (105 MM HOW.), M4A3 (105 MM HOW.)—STANDARD

These modifications of Medium Tanks, M4 and M4A3, were designed to combine the firepower of a 105 mm howitzer with the performance characteristics of a medium tank. They are supplied in addition to the medium tanks with 75 mm guns authorized by Tables of Basic Allowances, and to replace the 75 mm Howitzer Motor Carriages, M8, in Battalion Headquarters Companies, Medium Tank Battalions.

The 105 mm Howitzer, M4, is mounted in a Combination Gun Mount, M52, with one cal. .30 Machine Gun, M1919A4, flexible, in a 360° hand-traversed turret. No gyrostabilizer is provided. The howitzer is a redesign of 105 mm Howitzer, M2A1.

Other armament is the same as for Medium Tanks, M4, and M4A3.

The cast turret has a partial turret basket. A fighting seat for the gunner, a convoy seat for the tank commander and a riding seat for the loader are provided. All seats traverse with the turret.

A commander's vision cupola is provided above the turret. Equipped with six prismatic vision blocks, of 3 inch, laminated, bullet-resisting glass, it affords a wide field of view.

There is a suitable floor over the stowage space on either side of the power tunnel. Pistol ports and lifting hooks are the same as for Medium Tanks, M4, and padding and safety belts are furnished wherever required. A pintle for towing an ammunition trailer is provided.

Construction of two pilot Medium Tanks, M4A4, mounting the 105 mm howitzer, was authorized by Ordnance Committee action in December, 1942. Designated Medium Tank, M4A4E1, the vehicle was tested at Aberdeen Proving Ground and at Fort Knox, Ky. Modifications deemed necessary were incorporated in new pilot models designated Medium Tank, M4E5. Standardization of the vehicles was approved in August, 1943.

MEDIUM TANK, M4 (105 mm HOW.), is based on Medium Tank, M4, using a Continental R975–C1 engine.

MEDIUM TANK, M4A3 (105 mm HOW.), is based on Medium Tank, M4A3, using a Ford GAA engine.

REFERENCES — OCM 17202, 17316, 19394, 21113, 21347.

MEDIUM TANK, M4 (105 MM HOWITZER), SHOWING DETAILS OF TOP OF HULL AND TURRET

TYPICAL CHARACTERISTICS

Crew 5

Physical Characteristics

Weight (gross, approx.) { M4—66,500 lb.
{ M4A3—68,500 lb.
Length { M4—19 ft., 4 ins.
{ M4A3—19 ft., 4½ ins.
Width .... 8 ft., 7 ins.
Height .... 9 ft., 2¹¹⁄₁₆ ins.
Ground clearance .... 17⅛ ins.
Tread (center to center of tracks) ...... 83 ins.
Ground contact length .... 147 ins.
Ground pressure { M4—13.7 lb./sq. in.
{ M4A3—14.1 lb./sq. in.

Armament

105 mm Howitzer, M4, and { In Combination
1 cal. .30 Machine Gun, { Gun Mount,
M1919A4 (flexible) { M52
Elevation .... −10° to +35°
Traverse .... 360°
1 cal. .30 Machine Gun,
M1919A4 (flexible) .... In bow mount
1 cal. .50 Machine Gun, M2, HB
(flexible) .... On turret
1 Mortar, 2 inch, M3
1 Tripod Mount, cal. .30, M2
Provision for:
1 cal. .45 Submachine Gun

Ammunition, Stowage

105 mm Howitzer .... 66 rounds
Cal. .30 .... 4,000 rounds
Cal. .50 .... 300 rounds
Cal. .45 .... 600 rounds
Grenades, Hand (Fragmentation, MK. II, 6;
Smoke, W.P., M 15,6) 12
Smoke Bombs, 2 Inch, MK. I 18

Armor

Armor	Actual	Basis
Hull, Front, Upper	2 ins.	2–4 ins.
Lower	1½–2 ins.	2–2½ ins.
Sides	1½–2 ins.	1½–2 ins.
Rear	1½ ins.	
Top	1 in.	
Bottom	½–1 in.	
Turret, Front	3 ins.	3¾ ins.
Sides	2 ins.	2 ins.
Top	1 in.	

Performance

Maximum speed on level—M4 .... 24 m.p.h.
M4A3 .... 26 m.p.h.
Maximum grade ability 60%
Trench crossing ability .... 7 ft., 5 ins.
Vertical obstacle ability .... 24 ins.
Fording depth (slowest forward speed) 36 ins.
Fuel capacity—M4 .... 175 gals.
M4A3 .... 174 gals.
Cruising range—M4 .... 120 miles
M4A3 .... 130 miles

Vision and Fire Control

Commander's vision cupola 1
Periscope, M6 6
Periscope, M4, with Telescope, T73 1
Gunner's Quadrant, M1 1

Communications

Radio .... SCR-508, 528, or 538
Interphone stations 5
Flag Set M238

Battery, Voltage, total 24

Fire Protection and Decontamination

Fire Extinguisher—CO₂–10 lb. (fixed) 2
CO₄–4 lb. (hand) 2
Decontaminating Apparatus, M2, 1½ qts. .. 2

(Other characteristics same as for Medium Tanks, M4 or M4A3.)

MEDIUM TANK M4 (76 MM) SERIES

These modifications of the Medium Tank, M4, series, provide greatly increased firepower. The 76 mm gun uses 3 inch ammunition, with muzzle velocity, maximum range, and armor penetration considerably greater than that of 75 mm ammunition.

Principal armament is a 76 mm Gun, M1A1 or M1A2, with a cal. .30 Machine Gun, M1919A4 (flexible), with stabilizer, in a 360° power-operated turret. The guns may be elevated from −10° to +25°.

The 3 Inch A.P.C. Projectile, M62, fired from the 76 mm gun, has a muzzle velocity of 2,600 feet per second, and a maximum range of 16,100 yards. It will penetrate 4 inches of face-hardened armor plate at 1,000 yards.

Provision is made for fire control at 3,000 yards range, direct fire. By use of an azimuth indicator and elevation quadrant, indirect fire control can be had up to the maximum range.

A commander's vision cupola is mounted above the turret hatch. Equipped with six prismatic vision blocks of 3 inch laminated bullet-resistant glass, it affords a wide view.

Other armament and general characteristics are the same as on the respective variations of the Medium Tank, M4, series.

Water-protected ammunition racks are used. A traveling lock is provided on the front hull of the vehicle to support the gun when traveling in noncombat zones.

Medium Tank, M4 (76 mm), welded, and Medium Tank, M4A1 (76 mm), cast, are powered by Continental R975–C1 gasoline engines.

Medium Tank, M4A2, welded, is powered by a General Motors Diesel engine 6–71, 6046.

Medium Tank, M4A3, welded, is powered by a Ford GAA-III gasoline engine.

REFERENCES—OCM 18661, 18874, 20531, 20798, 22994.

MEDIUM TANK, M4 (76 MM), WITH GUN SUPPORTED BY TRAVELING LOCK

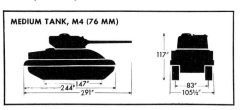

MEDIUM TANK, M4 (76 MM)

TYPICAL CHARACTERISTICS

MEDIUM TANKS, M4 (76 mm), M4A1 (76 mm)
Crew 5
Physical Characteristics
Weight (gross—approx.) ....70,000 lb.
Length—over end of gun........24 ft., 3 ins.
excluding gun (with sand
shields)....................20 ft., 4 ins.
Width............................8 ft., 9½ ins.
Height............................9 ft., 9 ins.
Ground clearance..................17⅛ ins.
Tread (center to center of tracks)......83 ins.
Ground contact length................147 ins.
Ground pressure............14.4 lb./sq. in.
Armament
76 mm Gun, M1A1 or M1A2, ⎰ In Combination
and 1 cal. .30 Machine ⎱ Gun Mount,
Gun, M1919A4 (flex.).... ⎱ M62, in turret
Elevation....................−10° to +25°
Traverse............................360°
1 cal. .30 Machine Gun,
M1919A4 (flex.) .... In ball mount on bow
1 cal. .50 Machine Gun,
M2, HB (flex.)........On turret, antiaircraft
1 Mortar, 2 In., M3
1 Tripod Mount, Cal. .30, M2
Provision for:
5 cal. .45 Submachine Guns
Ammunition, Stowage
76 mm (3 Inch, H.E., M42A1; 3 Inch,
A.P.C., M62; 3 Inch, Smoke, M8) 71 rounds
Cal. .30 ....6,250 rounds
Cal. .50 ....600 rounds
Cal. .45 ....900 rounds
Mortar, 2 Inch ....18 rounds
Grenades, Hand (Fragmentation, Mk. II, 4;
Offensive, Mk. III, w/fuze, detonation,

M6, 2; Smoke, H.C., M8, 4; Thermite,
Incendiary, 2)........................12

Armor

	Actual	Basis
Hull, Front......	2½ ins.	4 ins.
Sides.........	1½ ins.	1½ ins.
Rear......	1½ ins.	1½ ins.
Top......	¾ in.	
Bottom, Forward...	1 in.	
Rear.......	½ in.	
Turret, Front......	2½ ins.	
Sides and rear ...	2½ ins.	
Top......	1 in.	

Performance
Maximum speed on level............24 m.p.h.
Speed on 10% grade.................9 m.p.h.
Maximum grade ability................60%
Trench crossing ability.........7 ft., 6 ins.
Vertical obstacle ability.............24 ins.
Fording depth (slowest forward speed)...36 ins.
Turning radius.......................31 ft.
Fuel capacity......................175 gals.
Cruising range......................85 miles
Vision and Fire Control
Periscopes, M6..........................6
Periscope, M4, w/M47 Telescope..........1
Telescope, T92 (M71D) or M70H..........1
Telescope Mount, T82 (M57)..............1
Azimuth Indicator, M19..................1
Elevation Quadrant, M9..................1
Gunner's Quadrant, M1...................1
Pistol port.............................1
Commander's vision cupola...............1
Communications
Radio...........................SCR-508
Command tank....................SCR-506
Interphone stations......................5
Battery, Voltage, total 24

Fire Protection and Decontamination
Fire Extinguisher, CO₂-10 lb. (fixed)........2
CO₂-4 lb. (hand).....................2
Decontaminating Apparatus, M2, 1½ qts....1
Engine, Make and Model. Continental, R975-C1
(See additional engine characteristics on page 28.)
MEDIUM TANK, M4A2
Characteristics same as for Medium Tank, M4 (76 mm), except as noted:
Physical Characteristics
Weight (gross—approx.) ....72,800 lb.
Length—over end of gun........24 ft., 7 ins.
excluding gun (with sand
shields)....................20 ft., 8 ins.
Width............................8 ft., 9½ ins.
Ground pressure............14.9 lb./sq. in.
Performance
Maximum speed on level............29 m.p.h.
Speed on 10% grade................12 m.p.h.
Fording depth (slowest forward speed)...40 ins.
Fuel capacity......................148 gals.
Cruising range.....................100 miles
Engine, Make and Model........G.M. 6-71
MEDIUM TANK, M4A3
Characteristics same as for Medium Tank, M4 (76 mm), except as noted:
Physical Characteristics
Weight (gross—approx.) ....71,100 lb.
Length—over end of gun......24 ft., 6½ ins.
excluding gun (with sand
shields)....................20 ft., 7½ ins.
Width............................8 ft., 9½ ins.
Ground pressure............14.6 lb./sq. in.
Performance
Maximum speed on level............26 m.p.h.
Speed on 10% grade................10 m.p.h.
Fuel capacity......................174 gals.
Cruising range.....................100 miles
Engine, Make and Model......Ford, GAA-III

HEAVY TANKS M6, M6A1, T1E1

HEAVY TANK M6 HAD CAST HULL AND DOUBLE TRACKS AND BOGIES. 3-INCH GUN WAS MOUNTED WITH 37-MM GUN IN POWER-TRAVERSED TURRET

Heavy Tanks M6 and M6A1 were standardized in May 1942, at which time they were the largest and most powerful tanks ever built in the U. S., weighing more than 60 tons each. Shortly afterward the Ordnance Committee authorized Limited Procurement of Heavy Tank T1E1, sometimes referred to as Heavy Tank M6A2. Because of changes in tactical thinking, comparatively few of these tanks were built and in December 1944 all three models were declared obsolete.

Heavy Tank M6 had a cast hull and a cast turret. Heavy Tank M6A1 had a welded hull and a cast turret. Each was powered by a Wright G-200 gasoline engine through a hydraulic torque converter and transmission. The torque converter, transmission, and final drive were mounted directly behind the engine, connected by a flexible coupling, without the use of a propeller shaft. A pedal, placed in the position usually occupied by a clutch pedal, served as a transmission brake pedal. Two forward speeds and one reverse speed were provided.

Heavy Tank T1E1 was similar to the M6 in general design, but used an electric drive. A large direct current generator was mounted directly behind the engine. This generator converted the mechanical

output of the engine into electrical power for two traction motors, one for each track. The tank had varying speeds up to 22 m.p.h., and could turn in its own radius.

These vehicles had as their principal armament a 3-In. Gun M7 mounted with a 37-mm Gun M6. Additional firepower was provided by a cal. .30 machine gun on the turret for antiaircraft use, two cal. .50 machine guns in the bow, and a cal. .30 machine gun (flexible) in the bow. Provision was made for carrying two cal. .45 submachine guns.

The turret guns had elevations from −10° to +30° and could be traversed 360° by an electrically operated mechanism or by hand. A gyrostabilizer was provided.

The 3-In. Gun M7 was the same as used on the 3-In. Gun Motor Carriage M10, which proved so effective against Marshal Rommel's troops in North Africa. Fired from this gun, the 3-in. APC projectile had a muzzle velocity of 2,600 feet per second and at 45° elevation a maximum range of 16,100 yards. It could penetrate 3.9 inches of 20° obliquity homogeneous armor plate at 1,000 yards.

A horizontal volute spring suspension was used, with four bogie assemblies on each track. Each assembly had four bogie

wheels, two wheels riding the outside half of the track and two the inside half. Two volute springs were mounted horizontally on each bogie assembly.

Each track block consisted, in effect, of two shoes held together by connecting pins. The pins were bare between the shoes, to provide space for a center track connector. Shoes were half rubber and half steel, the steel side making contact against the ground, and the rubber side riding against the bogie wheels and idlers.

The driving sprockets were at the rear of the vehicle. In addition to the main idler, provided to adjust each track, there was an auxiliary, non-adjustable idler between the main idler and the front bogie assembly. This gave additional track support when crossing rough terrain.

Maximum armor thickness was 3¼ in., as compared to 2½ in. on Medium Tank M4. An armor plate skirting was used over each suspension.

Six periscopes were provided. There were four escape doors.

REFERENCES—TM 9–721; OCM 15842, 15946, 16040, 16200, 16297, 16477, 16655, 17812, 17906, 17952, 18059, 18283, 18544, 18984, 19199, 19625, 19981, 20034, 20680, 26039, 26357; SNL G–118, Vols. 1 and 2.

HEAVY TANK M6A1 WAS SIMILAR TO THE M6, BUT HAD A WELDED HULL. POWER WAS SUPPLIED BY WRIGHT G-200 ENGINE, THROUGH TORQUE CONVERTER

TYPICAL CHARACTERISTICS

Physical Characteristics
Weight (gross)....................126,500 lb.
Length, Gun forward............27 ft., 8 in.
   Hull only.......................24 ft., 9 in.
Width (overall)...............10 ft., 2½ in.
Height, Top of turret............9 ft., 10 in.
   Top of machine gun mount....10 ft., 7 in.
Turret ring diameter (inside)..........69 in.
Ground clearance...................20½ in.
Tread (center to center of tracks).......93 in.
Ground contact length.............186 in.
Ground pressure..........12.3 lb./sq. in.

Armament
3-In. Gun M7 and   In Combination
37-mm Gun M6   Gun Mount T49, in turret
1 Cal. .30 Machine Gun M1919A4
  (flexible)..........................In bow
1 Cal. .30 Machine Gun M1919A4
  (flexible)........................On turret
2 Cal. .50 Machine Guns M2 HB
  (fixed)...........In twin mount in bow
1 Cal. .30 Machine Gun Tripod Mount M2
Provision for:
2 Cal. .45 Submachine Guns M3

TORQUE CONVERTER AND FINAL DRIVE

Ammunition, Stowage
3-in. ....75 rounds
37-mm ....202 rounds
Cal. .50 ....5,700 rounds
Cal. .45 ....1,200 rounds
Cal. .30 ....7,500 rounds
Hand Grenades 12

Armor

	Actual	Basis
Hull, front, upper........	3¼ in.	4 in.
Lower..........	2¾–4 in.	4 in.
Sides...............	1¾ in.	1¾ in.
Rear..............	1⅝ in.	2 in.
Top..............	1 in.	
Bottom.............	1 in.	
Turret, front.............	3¼ in.	3¼ in.
Sides and rear........	3¼ in.	3¼ in.
Top.............	1 in.	

Performance
Maximum speed on level...........22 m.p.h.
Maximum grade ability...............60%
Trench crossing ability.................11 ft.
Vertical obstacle ability..............36 in.
Fording depth (slowest forward speed)..48 in.
Angle of approach....................32°
Turning diameter....................74 ft.
Fuel capacity.....................464 gal.
Cruising range (approx.)..........100 miles

Vision and Fire Control
Periscope M6 5
Periscope M8, w/Telescope M39..........1
Gunner's Quadrant M1, w/case...........1
Bore Sight, 3-inch gun.................1
Telescope M15........................1

Communications
Radio.................SCR-508, 528, or 538
   Command tank.................SCR-506
Interphone stations......................6
Battery, Voltage, total.....................24

Fire Protection and Decontamination
Fire Extinguisher
  CO_2–10 lb. (fixed) 6
  CO_2–4 lb. (hand) 2
Decontaminating Apparatus M2, 1½ qt.....4

Engine, Make and model ....Wright G-200
Type ....Radial, A.C.
No. of cylinders.........................9
Fuel (gasoline)..................80 octane
Max. governed speed..........2,300 r.p.m.
Gross hp ....800 at 2,300 r.p.m.
Max. torque.....1,850 lb.-ft. at 2,300 r.p.m.

Transmission, Type.........Torque converter
Gear ratios
  First speed 1.61:1
  Second speed 0.22:1
  Reverse 1.61:1

Gear Reduction Case, Type. Twin Disc Clutch Co.

Torque Converter, Type. Twin Disc Clutch Co.

Differential, Type................ Controlled
Gear ratio 0.62:1
Steering ratio 1.62:1

Final Drive, Gear Ratio.................5:1
Sprocket, no. of teeth................14
Pitch diameter.....................26.806

Suspension, Type.....Horizontal volute spring
Wheel or tire size................18x7x15

Idler, Type.....................Adjustable

Track, Steel bottom, rubber top, rubber bushed
Width ....25¾ in.
Pitch ....6 in.
No. of blocks per vehicle................198

HEAVY TANK M26—STANDARD

Standardization of Heavy Tank M26 in May 1945 culminated a consistent program of experimentation and development conducted over several years. Formally classified as Limited Procurement type in October 1944 and designated Heavy Tank T26E3, the vehicle embodies improvements which have been tested thoroughly on this and other tanks of the T20 series.

Compact in design, it is lower and wider than Heavy Tanks M6 and M6A1 and is not as heavy. It has greater fire power and heavier armor and has better mobility and maneuverability.

Weighing 46 tons, the vehicle has a ground pressure of 12.7 lb./sq. in. with 24-in. track and can be operated at speeds up to 25 m.p.h. Consideration is being given to reducing the unit ground pressure to 10.9 lb./sq. in. by using the T80E1 type of track with extended end connectors. It will climb a 60% grade and will cross a trench almost 8 feet wide.

Principal armament is a 90-mm Gun M3, mounted coaxially with a Cal. .30 Machine Gun M1919A4 in the turret. These guns can be depressed to −10° and elevated to +20° and can be traversed through 360°, either manually or by power. The gun is equipped with a muzzle brake.

The Shot, Fixed, HVAP-T, 90-mm, T30E16, fired from this gun, has a muzzle velocity of 3,350 feet per second. It will penetrate 7.2 inches of homogeneous armor plate at 30° obliquity at 1,000 yards.

A Cal. .30 Machine Gun M1919A4

HEAVY TANK M26, LEFT FRONT, SHOWING 90-MM GUN M3 WITH MUZZLE BRAKE

(flexible) is located in the bow. A Cal. .50 Machine Gun M2 HB (flexible) for antiaircraft use is mounted on the turret.

Provision is made for carrying five cal. .45 submachine guns and one cal. .30 carbine with grenade launcher.

The armor is placed at varying angles designed to provide the greatest possible protection against enemy projectiles. The front upper hull is 4 inches thick and has a basis of 6.9 inches. The turret front is 4 inches thick and has the additional

protection of a gun mount shield with a 4½-inch basis.

The suspension is of the individually sprung torsion bar type, with bumper springs and double-acting shock absorbers to give additional protection. Center-guided track is used.

Power is supplied by a Ford GAF gasoline engine through a torqmatic transmission and a controlled differential, the tracks being driven by sprockets at the rear.

OVERHEAD VIEW, SHOWING COMMANDER'S VISION CUPOLA AND LOADER'S HATCH ON TURRET. TURRET IS TURNED TO REAR DURING TRAVEL

The commander, gunner, and loader are seated in the rotating turret, entrance to which is through the commander's hatch or a smaller hatch over the loader. The driver and assistant driver are seated in the lower front hull, access to which is through two hatches. Two emergency exit doors are located in the floor of the hull.

The commander's hatch is surmounted by a vision cupola, equipped with six laminated glass vision blocks, permitting vision in all directions. Periscopes for all crew members and a two-way radio are provided. When traveling in non-combat areas, the turret is turned to the rear and the 90-mm gun is secured in an exterior traveling lock.

Heavy Tank M26 is an outgrowth of the Medium Tank T20 series, which included Medium Tanks T20, T22, T23, and T25, and variations. Development of these tanks started in 1942, utilizing new components and new principles of design which were tested and proved satisfactory. The original Heavy Tank T26 was designed to use an electric drive, while the Heavy Tank T26E1 utilized a torqmatic transmission. Heavy Tank T26E3 was the production model of the T26E1, incorporating many improve-

RIGHT REAR VIEW. NOTE DETAILS OF TORSION BAR SUSPENSION AND OF STOWAGE

ments which were found advisable during tests. It is being used as the basis of additional tank developments, with the purpose of providing a well-rounded combat team.

REFERENCES—TM 9–735; OCM 24277, 24619, 26038, 26282, 27123, 27536.

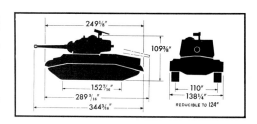

TYPICAL CHARACTERISTICS

Crew. 5

Physical Characteristics
Weight (gross). . . . . .92,000 lb.
Length, gun forward. . . . . 28 ft., 8 3/16 in.
  Gun to rear. . . . . .24 ft., 1 9/16 in.
  Hull only. . . . . .20 ft., 9 1/8 in.
Width (overall). . . . . 11 ft., 6 1/4 in.
  Reducible to. . . . . .10 ft., 4 in.
Height. . . . . 9 ft., 1 3/8 in.
Turret ring diameter (inside). . . . . .69 in.
Ground clearance. . . . . .17 3/16 in.
Tread (center to center of tracks). . . . . .110 in.
Ground contact length, right side. . .152 7/16 in.
  Left side. . . . . .148 7/16 in.
Ground pressure. . . . . .12.7 lb./sq. in.

Armament
1 90-mm Gun M3 and   } In Combination
1 Cal. .30 Machine Gun   } Gun Mount M67
  M1919A4 (flexible)   }
  Elevation. . . . . −10° to +20°
  Traverse. . . . . .360°
1 Cal. .30 Machine Gun M1919A4
  (flexible). . . . . .In bow
1 Cal. .50 Machine Gun M2 HB
  (flexible). . . . . .On turret
1 Cal. .30 Machine Gun Tripod Mount M2
Provision for:
5 Cal. .45 Submachine Guns M3
1 Cal. .30 Carbine M2 and Grenade
  Launcher M8

Ammunition, Stowage
90-mm. . . . . .70 rounds
Cal. .50. . . . . .550 rounds
Cal. .45. . . . . .900 rounds
Cal. .30. . . . . .5,000 rounds
Hand grenades 12
Signal flares 12

Armor	Actual	Basis
Hull, front, upper.	4 in.	6.9 in.
Lower.	3 in.	6.4 in.
Sides, forward.	3 in.	3 in.
Engine compartment.	2 in.	2 in.
Rear.	2 in.	2 in.
Top.	7/8 in.	
Bottom.	1 in. and 1/2 in.	
Turret, front.	4 in.	4.4 in.
Sides and rear. . .	3 in.	3 in.
Top.	1 in.	
Gun mount shield.		4 1/2 in.

Performance
Maximum speed on level. . . . . .20 m.p.h.
Maximum grade ability. 60%
Trench crossing ability. . . . . 7 ft., 11 in.
Vertical obstacle ability. . . . . .46 in.
Fording depth (slowest forward speed). .48 in.
Turning diameter. . . . . .60 ft.
Fuel capacity. . . . . .186 gal.
Cruising range (approx.). . . . . .75 miles.

Vision and Fire Control
Commander's Vision Cupola 1
Periscope M6. 6
Periscope M10F, w/Instrument Light M30. . . .1
  (1 Periscope M4A1, w/Telescope
  M77F as spare)
Telescope Mount T90. 1
Elevation Quadrant M9, w/Instrument
  Light M30. 1
Gunner's Quadrant M1. 1
Azimuth Indicator M20. 1
Aiming Post M1, w/Aiming
  Post Light M14. 2
Fuze Setter M22. 1
Pistol port. 1

Communications
Radio. . . . . .SCR–508, 528, 608B or British
  No. 19; AN/VRC–3
Interphone stations. 5

Battery, Voltage, total. 24
Fire Protection and Decontamination
Fire Extinguisher, CO₂-10 lb. (fixed). 2
  CO₂-4 lb. (hand). 2
Decontaminating Apparatus M2, 1 1/2 qt. 2
Engine, Make and model. . . . . .Ford GAF
  Type. . . . . .V–8, LC
  No. of cylinders. 8
  Fuel (gasoline). . . . . .80 octane
  Max. governed speed. . . . . .2,600 r.p.m.
  Gross hp. . . . . .500 at 2,600 r.p.m.
  Max. torque. . . . . .1,040 lb.-ft. at 2,200 r.p.m.
Transmission, Type. . . . . .Torqmatic
  Gear ratios
    First speed. 1:1
    Second speed. . . . . .1:2.337 }
    Third speed. . . . . .1:4.105 } overdrive
    Reverse. . . . . .1:1.322 }
Transfer Case
  Gear ratio, engine to transmission. 1.38:1
Torque Converter,
  Ratio. . . . . .Varies from 1:1 to 4.8:1
Differential, Type. . . . . .Controlled
  Steering ratio. 1.78:1
Final Drive
  Sprocket, No. of teeth. 13
    Pitch diameter. 25.068
  Gear ratio. 3.82:1
Suspension, Type. . . . . .Torsion bar
  Wheel or tire size. 26x6
Idler, Type. . . . . .Compensating
  Wheel or tire size. 26x6
Track, Type. . . . . .T80E1 or T81
  Width. . . . . .23 or 24 in.
  Pitch. . . . . .6 in.
  No. of shoes per vehicle. 164
Radiator, Type. . . . . .Fin and tube
Brakes, Type. . . . . . . .External-contracting
  Operation. . . . . .Manual lever

LIGHT TANK ENGINES

TYPICAL CHARACTERISTICS

	CONTINENTAL W-670-9A	GUIBERSON T-1020-4	CADILLAC Series 44†**	LYCOMING O-435-T
Type	Radial, A.C.	Radial, A.C.	V-8, L.C.	Opposed, A.C.
No. of cylinders	7	9	8	6
Cycle	4	4	4	4
Fuel, Octane or cetane	80 Octane	40 Cetane	80 Octane	80 Octane
Type	Gasoline	Diesel	Gasoline	Gasoline
Bore and stroke	5⅛ x 4⅝ in.	5⅛ x 5½ in.	3½ x 4½ in.	4⅞ x 3⅞ in.
Displacement	667 cu. in.	1,021 cu. in.	346 cu. in.	434 cu. in.
Compression	6.1:1	14.5:1	6.77:1	6.25:1
Max. governed speed	2,400 r.p.m.	2,200 r.p.m.	Not governed	2,800 r.p.m.
Gross hp.	262 at 2,400 r.p.m.	245 at 2,200 r.p.m.	148 at 3,200 r.p.m.	192 at 2,800 r.p.m.
Max. gross torque	590 lb.-ft. at 1,700 r.p.m.	645 lb.-ft. at 1,300 r.p.m.	280 lb.-ft. at 1,200 r.p.m.	360 lb.-ft. at 2,100 r.p.m.
Crankshaft rotation (facing drive end)	C'Clockwise	C'Clockwise	C'Clockwise	C'Clockwise
Length	32 in.	37 in.	65³⁄₁₆ in.	48 in.
Width	53¼ in.*	45½ in.	25⅜ in.	35½ in.
Height	42⅜ in.	45½ in.	38³⁄₃₂ in.	31¼ in.
Ignition	Magneto	Compression	Battery	Battery
Weight, Dry	1,070 lb.	700 lb.	584 lb.	1,000 lb.
Weight, Installed	1,214 lb.			

*To outside of exhaust manifold.
†Data for Series 42, used on Light Tanks M5 and M5A1, essentially same except: Length, 63 in.; Width, 27¼ in.; Height 36 in.
**Two of these engines used in each Light Tank M24.

CONTINENTAL ENGINE W-670-9A, LIGHT TANK M3 SERIES

LYCOMING GASOLINE ENGINE O-43-T USED ON LIGHT TANK T9E1

CADILLAC ENGINE SERIES 44 USED ON LIGHT TANK M24

GUIBERSON ENGINE T1020-4 USED ON LIGHT TANK M3 (DIESEL)

MEDIUM AND HEAVY TANK ENGINES

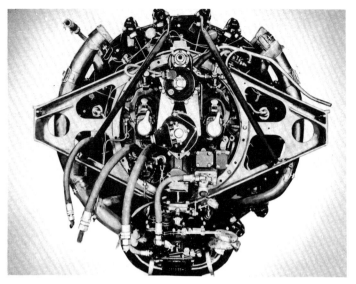

CONTINENTAL ENGINE FOR MEDIUM TANKS M4, M4A1

GENERAL MOTORS POWER UNIT FOR MEDIUM TANK M4A2

FORD GAA ENGINE IS USED IN THE MEDIUM TANK M4A3

CHRYSLER POWER UNIT FOR MEDIUM TANK M4A4

TYPICAL CHARACTERISTICS

	CONTINENTAL R-975-C1*	G.M. DIESEL 6046	FORD GAA†	CHRYSLER A-57
Type	Radial, A.C.	2-line, L.C.	V-8, L.C.	5-line, L.C.
No. of cylinders	9	12	8	30
Cycle	4	2	4	4
Fuel, Octane or cetane	80 Octane	40 Cetane	80 Octane	80 Octane
Type	Gasoline	Diesel	Gasoline	Gasoline
Bore and stroke	5 x 5½ in.	4¼ x 5 in.	5.4 x 6 in.	3⁷⁄₁₆ x 4½ in.
Displacement	973 cu. in.	850 cu. in.	1,100 cu. in.	1,253 cu. in.
Compression	5.7:1	16:1	7.5:1	6.2:1
Max. governed speed	2,400 r.p.m.	2,100 r.p.m.**	2,600 r.p.m.	2,850 r.p.m.
Gross hp.	400 at 2,400 r.p.m.	410 at 2,900 r.p.m.	500 at 2,600 r.p.m.	425 at 2,850 r.p.m.
Max. gross torque	890 lb.-ft. at 1,800 r.p.m.	885 lb.-ft. at 1,900 r.p.m.	1,040 lb.-ft. at 2,200 r.p.m.	1,060 lb.-ft. at 1,400 r.p.m.
Crankshaft rotation (drive end)	C'Clockwise	C'Clockwise‡	C'Clockwise	C'Clockwise
Length	53 in.	65⅝ in.	60⅜ in.	54⅛ in.
Width	45 in.	59⁵⁄₃₂ in.	33¼ in.	58¾ in.
Height	45 in.	46¾ in.	47½ in.	56½ in.
Ignition	Magneto	Compression	Magneto	Battery
Weight, Dry	1,137 lb.	5,110 lb.	1,560 lb.	5,400 lb.

*R-975-C4 essentially same except: Gross hp., 460 at 2,400 r.p.m.; Max. torque, 1,025 lb.-ft. at 1,800 r.p.m.; Weight, dry, 1,212 lb.
**Crankshaft speed of each 6-cylinder half of power plant.
†Characteristics of Ford GAN engine are generally similar.

‡At power take-off flange out of transfer case, which couples both halves of the power plant, steps up the shaft speed, and reverses rotation with respect to the crankshafts of each half of the power unit.

MEDIUM AND HEAVY TANK ENGINES (Continued)

The variety of medium tank engines shown here is a tribute to the resourcefulness of American industry, in cooperation with the Ordnance Department, in meeting an emergency.

When the program for the quantity production of medium tanks was inaugurated in 1940, it became necessary to find sources of sufficient engines. Medium Tank M3 used the Continental (Wright) R-975 engine, an aircraft type of engine adapted for use in tanks. Medium Tank M3 (Diesel) used the Guiberson T-1400 Diesel engine, but only a few of these were built.

To avoid conflicting with the Air Forces, whose need for engines was equally imperative, efforts were made to adapt commercial truck and passenger car engines, already in production, for use in tanks.

First such engine authorized for use as an alternate power plant was the G.M. 6046 Diesel engine, made up of two standard bus and truck type engines. In the medium tank installation, the engines, located one on either side of the engine compartment, are connected through a step-up gear and double clutch housing to a common propeller shaft. Originally authorized for use in Medium Tank M3A3 by Ordnance Committee action in December 1941, these engines are now used in Medium Tank M4A2 and in vehicles based on these tanks.

The Chrysler A-57 power unit consists of five conventional passenger car engines, geared together to operate as a single unit. Originally authorized for use in Medium Tank M3A4, it was used subsequently in Medium Tank M4A4.

The Ford GAA engine is an 8-cylinder, V-type engine designed specifically for tanks. It was introduced in Medium Tank M4A3 by Ordnance Committee action in January 1942. A modification known as the Ford GAN engine is being used in Medium Tank T23. Virtually the same engine, known as model GAF, is used in Heavy Tank T26E3.

Ordnance Committee action in May 1943 authorized the use of the RD-1820 Ordnance engine in Medium Tank M4A4 hulls, and designated this vehicle Medium Tank M4A6. This engine was formerly known as the Caterpillar D-200A engine.

Heavy Tanks M6 and M6A1 use Wright G-200 series engines, Model 781C9GC1. Heavy Tank T1E1, sometimes referred to as the M6A2, uses a modification of this engine, designated Model 795C9GC1, which is directly coupled to an electric generator.

REFERENCES—OCM 17503, 17578, 17678, 18283, 19200, 19439, 19630, 19631, 20607, 20796, 25785.

TYPICAL CHARACTERISTICS

	ORDNANCE ENGINE RD-1820	GUIBERSON T-1400	WRIGHT G-200 781C9GC1	WRIGHT G-200 795C9GC1**
Type	Radial, A.C.	Radial, A.C.	Radial, A.C.	Radial, A.C.
No. of cylinders	9	9	9	9
Cycle	4	4	4	4
Fuel, Octane and cetane	40 Cetane	40 Cetane	80 Octane	80 Octane
Type	Diesel	Diesel	Gasoline	Gasoline
Bore and Stroke	6⅛ x 6⅞ in.	5¾ x 6 in.	6⅛ x 6⅞ in.	6⅛ x 6⅞ in.
Displacement	1,823 cu. in.	1,400 cu. in.	1,823 cu. in.	1,823 cu. in.
Compression	15.5:1	14.3:1	4.92:1	4.92:1
Max. governed speed	2,000 r.p.m.*	2,400 r.p.m.	2,300 r.p.m.	1,950 r.p.m.
Gross hp.	497 at 3,000 r.p.m.†	350 at 2,400 r.p.m.	800 at 2,300 r.p.m.	675 at 1,950 r.p.m.
Max. gross torque	945 lb.-ft. at 2,100 r.p.m.†	935 lb.-ft. at 1,400 r.p.m.	1,850 lb.-ft. at 2,300 r.p.m.	1,810 lb.-ft. at 1,950 r.p.m.
Crankshaft rotation (drive end)	C'Clockwise	C'Clockwise	C'Clockwise	C'Clockwise
Length	56 in.	41½ in.	52 in.	101⅛ in.
Width	55 in.	50 in.	55 in.	64¼ in.
Height	55 in.	50 in.	55 in.	58 in.
Ignition	Compression	Compression	Magneto	Magneto
Weight, Dry	3,536 lb.	1,100 lb.	1,350 lb.	7,900 lb.
Weight, Installed			1,711 lb.	8,261 lb.

*Engine crankshaft speed.
†These data refer to power take-off flange on output shaft out of step-up gear transfer case.
**Data for this power plant take into consideration the direct-coupled main propulsion generator.

RD-1820 ORDNANCE ENGINE USED IN MEDIUM TANK, M4A6

WRIGHT G-200 SERIES ENGINE USED IN HEAVY TANKS

TANK RECOVERY VEHICLES **M31** SERIES—LIMITED STANDARD

TANK RECOVERY VEHICLE M31. RIGHT FRONT VIEW. NOTE DUMMY GUNS

LEFT REAR VIEW WITH BOOM IN TRAVELING POSITION, SHOWING TOOL BOXES

These vehicles, designed for the recovery of disabled tanks on the battlefield, are modifications of medium tanks of the M3 series.

For camouflage purposes, the normal appearance of the tank is retained as far as possible. A simulated turret without cupola is used, and dummy 75-mm and 37-mm guns are mounted in place of the real guns. Actual armament is limited to a cal. .30 machine gun in the bow and one on the turret for antiaircraft purposes. Provision is made for carrying a cal. .45 submachine gun.

The right hull plate, on which the dummy 75-mm gun is mounted, opens as a door, giving access to the crew compartment. There is no turret basket.

A 60,000-pound-capacity winch is installed in the hull directly below and on the center line of the turret. A boom is mounted on a special mounting plate which replaces the 37-mm gun plate.

The vehicle may be used to tow light, medium, and heavy tanks across country and on highways and to winch tanks out of mudholes, sand, and soft ground, and up slopes. With the winch line threaded through the turret and over the boom, it may be used for various lifting operations, including removal of turrets from medium tanks and lifting a side, front, or rear of a medium tank for work on a track or suspension.

Tank Recovery Vehicle M31 is based on Medium Tank M3 (riveted), with a Continental R-975-C1 engine.

Tank Recovery Vehicle M31B1 is based on Medium Tank M3A3 (welded), with a G.M. 6046 Diesel engine.

Tank Recovery Vehicle M31B2 is based on Medium Tank M3A5 (riveted), with a G.M. 6046 Diesel engine.

The pilot vehicle was built by the Baldwin Locomotive Works.

REFERENCES—OCM 18596, 18928, 20373, 21554, 21783.

TYPICAL CHARACTERISTICS TANK RECOVERY VEHICLE M31

Crew 6

Physical Characteristics
Weight (gross) . . . . .60,000 lb.
Length . . . . .26 ft., 5 in.
Width . . . . .8 ft., 4 in.
Height . . . . .9 ft., 9 in.
Turret ring diameter (inside) . . . . .57 in.
Ground clearance . . . . .17⅛ in.
Tread (center to center of tracks) . . . . . . .83 in.
Ground contact length . . . . .147 in.
Ground pressure . . . . .12.5 lb./sq. in.

Armament
1 Cal. .30 Browning Machine Gun
   M1919A4 (flexible) . . . . .In bow
1 Cal. .30 Browning Machine Gun
   M1919A4 (fixed) . . . . .In turret
1 Cal. .30 Tripod Mount M2
Provision for:
   1 cal. .45 submachine gun

Ammunition, Stowage
Cal. .30 .2,000 rounds
Cal. .45 . . . . .600 rounds
Grenades, Hand (Smoke, M8, 10;
   Thermite, Incendiary, 4) 14
Smoke Pots, H.C., M1 3

Performance
Maximum speed on level . . . . .25 m.p.h.
Maximum grade ability 60%
Trench crossing ability . . . . .7 ft., 5 in.
Vertical obstacle ability . . . . .24 in.
Fording depth (slowest forward speed) . . .42 in.
Turning radius . . . . .35 ft.
Fuel capacity . . . . .185 gal.
Cruising range (approx.) . . . . .110 miles

Vision
Protectoscopes and direct vision slots

Communications
Radio . . . . . .SCR-528 or 610 or British No. 19
Interphone stations 6
Flag Set M38 1

Battery, Voltage, total 24

Fire Protection and Decontamination
Fire Extinguishers, CO²–10 lb. (fixed) 2
                         CO²–4 lb. (hand) 3
Decontaminating Apparatus M2, 1½ qt. 2

(Other characteristics same as for Medium Tanks M3, M3A3, and M3A5, respectively.)

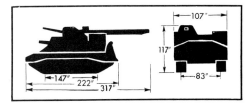

TANK RECOVERY VEHICLE M32 SERIES—STANDARD

TANK RECOVERY VEHICLE, M32, WITH BOOM RAISED

LEFT FRONT VIEW, SHOWING 81 MM MORTAR, WITH BOOM IN CARRYING POSITION

These vehicles are modifications of medium tanks of the M4 series, designed primarily for recovery of tanks from battlefields.

The boom is of the "A" frame type, of 4½ inch tubular steel approximately 18 feet long. It is mounted on the forward sides of the sponsons and is pivoted. In the carrying position, laid back over the hull and supported by the sub "A" frame in the rear, it can be used for lifting and towing purposes where it is designed to carry a portion of the towed weight. When extended to its full raised position in front, the boom is held in position by cables.

An 81 mm mortar is mounted on the front plate. Other armament includes a cal. .50 machine gun on the turret, and a cal. .30 machine gun in the bow.

A rounded front fixed turret is provided in place of the customary tank turret.

A 60,000 pound capacity winch is installed on the floor directly in back of the driver. Operation of the winch and of the "A" frame boom is controlled by the driver. The vehicle may be driven and the winch operated at the same time.

Chock blocks are supplied to keep the vehicle from moving during winching operations. Telescopic hold-off poles are furnished to keep towed vehicles from getting too close to the recovery vehicle.

Tank Recovery Vehicle, M32, is a modification of Medium Tank, M4, welded hull, with a Continental R975-C1 engine.

Tank Recovery Vehicle, M32B1, is based on Medium Tank, M4A1, cast hull, with a Continental R975–C1 engine.

Tank Recovery Vehicle, M32B2, is a modification of Medium Tank, M4A2, welded hull, powered by a GMC 6–71 6046 Diesel engine.

Tank Recovery Vehicle, M32B3, is a modification of Medium Tank, M4A3, welded hull, with a Ford GAA engine.

Tank Recovery Vehicle, M32B4, is based on Medium Tank, M4A4, welded hull, with Chrysler Multibank engine.

The pilot vehicle was built by the Lima Locomotive Works.

REFERENCES — OCM 19995, 20011, 20245, 20374, 20980, 21554, 21713.

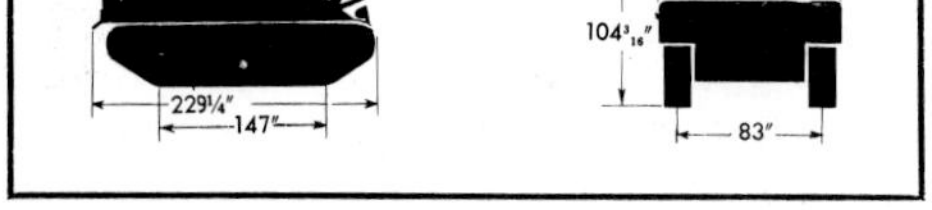

CHARACTERISTICS OF TANK RECOVERY VEHICLE, M32

Crew 4

Physical Characteristics

Weight (gross)	62,000 lb.
Length of hull	19 ft., 1¼ ins.
Width	8 ft., 7 ins.
Height	8 ft., 8³⁄₁₆ ins.
Length of boom	18 ft.
Turret ring diameter (inside)	68 ins.
Ground clearance	17⅛ ins.
Tread (center to center of tracks)	83 ins.
Ground contact length	147 ins.
Ground pressure	13.3 lb./sq. in.

Armament

1 cal. .50 Machine Gun, M2, HB,
(flexible) . . . On Ring Mount, M49, on turret
1 81 mm Mortar, M1 . . . . On front plate of hull
    Elevation . . . . +40° to +80°
    Traverse . . . . 130 mils
1 cal. .30 Machine Gun, M1919A4
(flexible) . . . . In ball mount in bow
1 81 mm Mortar Mount, M1, w/o base plate
1 Carriage and cradle assembly
1 Tripod Mount, cal. .30, M2
Provision for:
1 cal. .45 submachine gun

Ammunition, Stowage

Cal. .30	2,000 rounds
Cal. .50	300 rounds
Cal. .45	600 rounds
81 mm Mortar, W.P., M57	30 rounds
Grenades, Hand (Fragmentation Mk. II, 5; Smoke, WP, M15, 15)	20
Smoke Pots, H.C., M1	6

Armor

	Actual	Basis
Hull, Front, Upper	2 ins.	2–4 ins.
Lower	1½–2 ins.	2–2½ ins
Sides	1½ ins.	1½ ins.
Rear	1–1½ ins.	1–1½ ins.
Top	¾ in.	
Bottom	½ in.	
Turret, Front	1¼ ins.	1¼ ins.
Sides and Rear	1¼ ins.	1¼ ins.

Performance

Maximum speed on level	24 m.p.h.
Maximum grade ability	60%
Trench crossing ability	6 ft., 2 ins.
Vertical obstacle ability	24 ins.
Fording depth (slowest forward speed)	48 ins.
Turning radius	31 ft.
Fuel capacity	175 gals.
Cruising range	120 miles

Vision and Fire Control

Periscopes, M6	4
Sight, M4	1

Communications

Radio	SCR 528, 538 (less Radio Receiver BC-603), 610 or British 19
Interphone stations	4
Flag Set, M238	1

Battery, Voltage, total 24

Fire Protection and Decontamination

Fire Extinguisher, CO₂–10 lb. (fixed)	2
CO₂–4 lb. (hand)	3
Decontaminating Apparatus, M2, 1½ qts.	3

(Other characteristics same as for respective variation of Medium Tank, M4, Series.)

45-TON TANK TRANSPORTER TRUCK, TRAILER M19—LIMITED STANDARD

45-TON TANK TRANSPORTER TRUCK, TRAILER, M19, IS CAPABLE OF HAULING MEDIUM TANKS AND SIMILAR EQUIPMENT ALONG THE HIGHWAY

Manufactured originally by the Quartermaster Corps for the British, these vehicles were authorized for limited procurement and designated Substitute Standard, in September, 1942. The vehicles were reclassified as Limited Standard in June, 1943, upon standardization of the M25 vehicle.

Consisting of 12-Ton, 6x4 (4DT) Truck, M20, and 45-Ton, 12 Wheel (12DT) Trailer, M9, the complete tank transporter is approximately 52 feet, 9 inches long, and has a train weight, with 90,000 pound payload, of 160,000 pounds.

Its main use is the evacuation of heavy equipment from points along the axis of evacuation and supply. Its use in battlefield recovery is limited because it is not designed for travel over rough or muddy terrain.

References — OCM 18552, 18626, 20129, 20375, 20717.

12-TON, 6x4 (4DT) TRUCK, M20, serves as the prime mover for the tank transporter trailer, and may also be used for many independent operations.

It is powered by a Hercules DXFE Diesel engine. The main transmission has four speeds forward and one in reverse. An auxiliary transmission, for low-range driving, has three forward speed selections, and also powers the 40,000 pound capacity winch, mounted at the rear.

The winch cable may be threaded through a roller alongside the radiator for operations requiring a front winch. A torque control stops the winch if the line pull becomes excessive.

Skid pans are used to help anchor the transporter during winch operations.

TYPICAL CHARACTERISTICS

12-TON, 6x4 (4DT) TRUCK, M20
Crew...3

Physical Characteristics
Weight—empty...................26,650 lb.
   loaded............................45,000 lb.
Length.....................23 ft., 3¾ ins.
Width.........................8 ft., 4 ins.
Height........................3 ft., 4 ins.
Ground clearance...............11⅛ ins.
Wheelbase........179¼ ins. (52 in. bogie)
Tread (center to center, rear)........74 ins.
Tire equipment..........12.00 x 20, 14 ply

Performance
Maximum speed on level.........23 m.p.h.
Speed on 3% grade..............6 m.p.h.
Speed on 10% grade.............2 m.p.h.
Maximum grade ability, with towed load..25%
   without towed load................65%
Fording depth (slowest forward speed)..32 ins.
Angle of approach................40½°
Angle of departure................51°
Turning radius....................33 ft.
Fuel capacity...................150 gals.
Cruising range.................300 miles
Payload......................18,350 lb.
Max. towed load..............115,000 lb.
Winch capacity...............40,000 lb.

Battery, Voltage, total...................24

Engine, Make and Model.....Hercules, DFXE
No. of cylinders.........................6

Fuel (Diesel)...................45 Cetane
Max. governed speed...........1,600 r.p.m.
Net hp................178 at 1,600 r.p.m.
Max. torque.......685 lb.-ft. at 1,200 r.p.m.

Transmission, Gear ratios
First speed.......................5.55:1
Second speed.....................3.27:1
Third speed......................1.76:1
Fourth speed........................1:1
Reverse..........................6.58:1

Transfer Case, Gear ratios..77:1; 1:1; 1.99:1

Rear Axle, Gear ratio.................11.66:1

Brakes, Service, Type ....Air
Parking, Type....................Disk

45-TON, 12 WHEEL (12DT) TRAILER, M9
Physical Characteristics
Weight—empty (approx.).........25,000 lb.
   payload......................90,000 lb.
Length—overall (approx.).......29 ft., 8 ins.
Width.........................9 ft., 6 ins.
Height (trailer only)...........4 ft., 9½ ins.
Height of deck..................39 ins.
Ground clearance..................18 ins.
Wheelbase..........187 ins. (40 in. bogie)
Tire equipment...........8.25 x 15, 14 ply

Brakes, Service, Type....................Air
Parking, Type.............Wheel-operated

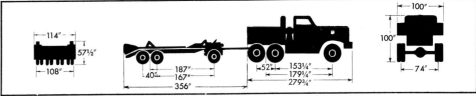

The truck has accommodations for a crew of three. Pintles are provided at the front and rear. The vehicle has air-brake controls for the trailed load.

45-TON, 12 WHEEL (12DT) TRAILER, M9, is designed to transport medium and light tanks. It may be used with the above truck, or with a tractor or similar prime mover. It is fastened behind the towing vehicle by a draw bar and safety chains.

Two ramps, hinged at the rear of the trailer, facilitate loading. Four chock blocks are provided to keep the load in position while traveling.

Air brakes, controlled from the towing vehicle, stop the trailer automatically if it breaks away.

TRACTOR TRUCKS M26—LIMITED STANDARD; M26A1—STANDARD
SEMITRAILER M15—LIMITED STANDARD
45-TON, 8-WHEEL, TRANSPORTER SEMITRAILER M15A1—SUBSTITUTE STANDARD

TRACTOR TRUCK M26 HAS ARMORED CAB WITH RING MOUNT

TRACTOR TRUCK M26A1 HAS UNARMORED, "SOFT TOP" CAB

Tractor Truck M26 and Semitrailer M15 were standardized in June 1943 as components of the 40-Ton Tank Transporter Truck-Trailer M25. In October 1944 Tractor Truck M26A1 was standardized and Tractor Truck M26 was reclassified as Limited Standard, and at the same time the practice of assigning nomenclature to the combination of tractor truck and semitrailer was discontinued. Previously the 45-Ton, 8-Wheel, Transporter Semitrailer M15A1 was classified as Substitute Standard to replace Semitrailer M15 in production, and arrangements were made to reclassify the M15 as Limited Standard when production of the M15A1 got under way.

The tractor truck and semitrailer were designed for use in combination in recovering and evacuating disabled materiel over all types of terrain, but can be used separately. When separated from the semitrailer, the tractor truck can perform most of the functions of a heavy wrecker.

REFERENCES—OCM 18047, 18079, 18319, 18552, 18732, 20129, 20676, 20680, 20717, 20802, 21002, 21008, 21871, 24053, 24938, 25029, 25258, 25332; SNL G–160.

TRACTOR TRUCK M26 is a 6x6 vehicle designed to supply the power and equipment needed for a variety of recovering and wrecking operations. It has an armored cab, all openings of which are protected against lead splash, to permit operation in combat areas. A Ring Mount M49 for a cal. .50 machine gun is mounted on the roof for protection against aircraft.

Accommodations are provided for a crew of seven, including the driver.

The vehicle uses divided rim type wheels with beadlocks. Single wheels are used at the front and dual wheels on

SEMITRAILER M15 WILL CARRY TWO LIGHT TANKS OR ONE MEDIUM TANK

SEMITRAILER M15A1 HAS RAMPS FOR LOADING HEAVY TANK OVER TIRES

the rear. Power is applied to all wheels.

A heavy duty universal type semi-automatic fifth wheel is provided for towing the semitrailer. Air brakes are provided on the four rear wheels and there is an air-brake valve connection for the semitrailer.

Power is supplied by a Hall Scott, 440, in-line, 6-cylinder, water-cooled engine. The transmission has four speeds forward and one reverse speed. In connection with an auxiliary transmission, twelve forward

speeds and three reverse speeds are available.

A front-mounted winch, controlled from the cab, has a capacity of 35,000 pounds on the first layer. Its primary purpose is the recovery of the truck and semitrailer when stuck in terrain which they cannot negotiate. It may also be used for recovery of other loads if the terrain makes the use of the rear winches unfeasible.

Two winches mounted behind the cab are controlled from the operations plat-

TRACTOR TRUCKS M26 AND M26A1—SEMITRAILERS M15 AND M15A1 (Continued)

form and have a capacity of 60,000 pounds on the first layer. These are generally used for loading and unloading the semi-trailer and for doing the bulk of the recovery work. They may be used in tandem or independently of each other.

The pilot vehicle was built by the Knuckey Truck Co. Production vehicles were built by the Pacific Car and Foundry Co.

TRACTOR TRUCK M26A1 is a modification of the M26 with an unarmored "soft top" cab. A Ring Mount M49 for a cal. .50 machine gun is provided.

SEMITRAILER M15 is an eight-wheeled semitrailer designed especially for use with the Tractor Truck M26.

It will carry loads up to 80,000 pounds.

Hinged ramps at the rear are lowered to the ground for use in loading, the winch cables from the tractor truck being threaded through rollers at the front of the trailer and to the disabled vehicle. The semitrailer wheels may be moved closer together or farther apart to accommodate vehicles of different widths.

The semitrailer may be loaded and made ready for travel in the absence of the tractor truck, inasmuch as its front end may be made to rest on skis supported by collapsible legs.

Wheel covers, skid rails, and bed rails are used to provide a smooth surface, and to protect the tires when vehicles without

wheels or tracks are winched onto the semitrailer.

The vehicle uses divided rim type wheels and has air brakes operated from the tractor.

The pilot vehicle was built by the Fruehauf Trailer Co.

45-TON, 8-WHEEL, TRANSPORTER SEMITRAILER M15A1 is a modification of Semitrailer M15 designed to accommodate Heavy Tank T26E3. The trailer bed is strengthened to support the weight of the Heavy Tank T26E3. Hinged ramps are provided over the outer wheels so the tank may be loaded over the wheels. All of the functions of the Semitrailer M15 are preserved.

TYPICAL CHARACTERISTICS

	M26	M26A1
Crew	7	7
Physical Characteristics		
Weight (gross)	48,300 lb.	45,000 lb.
Length (overall)	25 ft., 4 in.	25 ft., 7 in.
Width	10 ft., 10¾ in.	10 ft., 10½ in.
Height, To top of ring mount	10 ft., 4 in.	10 ft., 8 in.
To top of cab	9 ft., 6 in.	9 ft., 6 in.
Ground clearance	14 in.	14 in.
Tread (center to center, rear)	98½ in.	98½ in.
Wheelbase	172 in.	172 in.
Tire equipment	14.00x24, 20-ply	14.00x24, 20-ply
Armament		
Ring Mount M49	1	1
Provision for:		
Cal. .50 Machine Gun HB M2 (flexible)	1	1
Cal. .50 Tripod Mount M3	1	1
Cal. .45 submachine gun	1	1
Cal. .30 carbine		1
Ammunition, Stowage		
Cal. .50	1,500 rounds	700 rounds
Cal. .45	600 rounds	600 rounds
Grenades	24	
Armor, Actual Thickness		
Front	¾ in.	¾ in.
Sides, rear, and top	¼ in.	¼ in.
Performance		
Maximum speed on level	26 m.p.h.	26 m.p.h.
Speed on 3% grade	12 m.p.h.	12 m.p.h.
Maximum grade ability	30%	30%
Vertical obstacle ability	22 in.	22 in.
Fording depth	56 in.	56 in.
Angle of approach	35°	32°
Fuel capacity	120 gal.	120 gal.
Cruising range (approx.)	250 miles	270 miles
Maximum drawbar pull (with trailer coupled)	60,000 lb.	60,000 lb.
Payload	55,000 lb.	58,000 lb.
Normal towed load	115,000 lb.	132,675 lb.
Communications		
Flag Set M238	1	1
Battery, Voltage, total	12	12
Fire Protection and Decontamination		
Fire Extinguisher, CO$_2$–4 lb. (hand)	4	3
Decontaminating Apparatus M2, 1½ qt.	2	2

	M26	M26A1
Engine, Make and model	Hall Scott, 440	Hall Scott, 440
Type	In-line, L.C.	In-line, L.C.
No. of cylinders	6	6
Fuel (gasoline)	70–72 octane	70–72 octane
Max. governed speed	2,100 r.p.m.	2,100 r.p.m.
Net hp.	230 at 2,100 r.p.m.	230 at 2,100 r.p.m.
Max. torque	810 lb.-ft. at 1,100 r.p.m.	810 lb.-ft. at 1,100 r.p.m.
Transmission, Type	Selective sliding	Selective sliding
Gear ratios		
First speed	5.55:1	5.55:1
Second speed	3.27:1	3.27:1
Third speed	1.76:1	1.76:1
Fourth speed	1:1	1:1
Reverse	6.58:1	6.58:1
Transfer Case		
Gear ratios	0.75:1, 1:1, 2.62:1	0.75:1, 1:1, 2.29:1
Rear Axle, Gear ratio	7.69:1	
Including chain reduction		14.65:1
Brakes, Service, Type	Air	Air
Parking, Type	Drum	Drum

SEMITRAILERS

Physical Characteristics	M15	M15A1
Weight (gross, without tank load)	35,000 lb.	42,675 lb.
With load	115,000 lb.	132,675 lb.
Length	38 ft., 9 in.	39 ft., 6½ in.
Length of bed	27 ft., 5 in.	27 ft., 5 in.
Width, Normal operating	12 ft., 6½ in.	12 ft., 6½ in.
Emergency operating	10 ft., 4 in.	10 ft., 4 in.
Width of bed	10 ft., 2 in.	10 ft., 4 in.
Height (overall)	9 ft., 6 in.	9 ft., 6 in.
Height of bed	3 ft., 6 in.	3 ft., 6 in.
Ground clearance	14 in.	14 in.
Tread (center to center, rear)	131 in.	131 in.
Wheelbase (center of bogie to king pin)	372 in.	372 in.
Tire equipment	14.00x24, 20-ply	14.00x24, 20-ply
Performance		
Payload	80,000 lb.	90,000 lb.
Brakes, Type	Two-shoe, fixed anchor	Two-shoe, fixed anchor
Operation	Internal-expanding, air	Internal-expanding, air

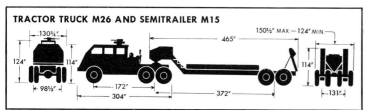

TRACTOR TRUCK M26 AND SEMITRAILER M15

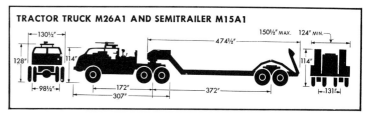

TRACTOR TRUCK M26A1 AND SEMITRAILER M15A1

75-MM GUN MOTOR CARRIAGES M3, M3A1

75-MM GUN MOTOR CARRIAGE M3, WITH MODIFIED GUNSHIELD FOR INDIRECT SIGHTING DEVICE; THE M3A1 DIFFERED ONLY IN GUN MOUNT

TYPICAL CHARACTERISTICS

Crew 5
Physical Characteristics
  Weight (gross). . . . . .20,000 lb.
  Length. .20 ft., 5½ in.
  Width. . . . . .7 ft., 1 in.
  Height. .8 ft., 2⅝ in.
  Height of center line of bore. . . . . . . .82 in.
  Ground clearance. . . . . .11³/₁₆ in.
  Tread, Front. . . . . .64½ in.
    Rear. . . . . .63¹³/₁₆ in.
  Wheelbase. . . . . .135½ in.
  Ground contact length. . . . . .46¾ in.
  Tire equipment. . . . . .8.25x20, 12-ply, combat

Armament
1 75-mm Gun M1897A4, on Mount M3 or M5
Provision for:
  1 Cal. .30 Rifle M1903
  4 Cal. .30 Carbines M1

1 Grenade Launcher. . . . . .For rifle
Ammunition, Stowage
  75-mm (H.E., Mk. 1; H.E., M48; Chem.,
    Mk. II; A.P.C., M61; A.P., M72).59 rounds
  Grenades (Hand: Fragmentation, Mk. II, 5;
    Smoke, M8, 5; Thermite, Incendiary, 2;
    Rifle: M9A1, 10). 22

Armor, Front, sides, and rear. . . . . . .¼ in.
  Windshield shield. . . . . .½ in.
  Wingshields. . . . . .¼ in.
  Top, engine compartment. . . . . .¼ in.
  Gun shield, Front. . . . . .⅝ in.
  Sides and top. . . . . .¼ in.

Performance
  Maximum speed on level. . . . . .45 m.p.h.
  Speed on 4% grade. . . . . .25 m.p.h.
  Maximum grade ability. 60%
  Vertical obstacle ability. . . . . .12 in.

Fording depth (slowest forward speed). . .32 in.
Turning radius. . . . . .30 ft.
Fuel capacity. . . . . .60 gal.
Cruising range. . . . . .200 miles

Vision and Fire Control
  Direct—Slits in windshield and wingshields
  Telescope M33. 1
  Telescope Mount M36. 1
  Instrument Light M17. 1

Communications
  Radio. .SCR 510
  Flag Set M238. 1

Fire Protection and Decontamination
  Fire Extinguisher, CO₂-2 lb. 1
  Decontaminating Apparatus M2, 1½ qt. 1

(Other characteristics same as for Half-Track Personnel Carrier M3.)

The 75-mm Gun Motor Carriage M3, the first standardized American self-propelled antitank weapon used in World War II, provided high mobility for the 75-mm gun. Standardized in November 1941, it was put into production in time to aid in the rout of Rommel's troops in North Africa.

It was reclassified as Limited Standard in March 1944 upon the standardization of 76-mm Gun Motor Carriage M18, and was declared obsolete in September 1944.

The gun was carried on Mount M3, a mount adapted from the 75-mm Gun Carriage M2A3. It could be elevated from −10° to +29° and could be traversed 19° to the left and 21° to the right.

The 75-mm Gun Motor Carriage M3A1, which was also declared obsolete in September 1944, used Gun Mount M5, adapted from Gun Carriage M2A2. Its gun could be elevated from 6½° to +29° and traversed 21° right and 21° left. Both vehicles had a gunshield that gave protection against cal. .30 armor-piercing bullets at 250 yards and overhead protection from frontal attack by aircraft. The shield traversed with the gun.

An A. P. C. projectile fired from the gun had a muzzle velocity of 2,000 feet per second, and would penetrate 3 inches of face-hardened plate at 1,000 yards.

The gun was loaded and operated from the crew compartment. Stowage space was provided for 59 rounds of ammunition and for a cal. .30 rifle and four cal. .30 carbines, which were the personal equipment of the crew.

Body armor was the same as on Half Track Personnel Carrier M3, including hinged protective shields for the windshield and doors. A detachable canvas top was provided. The vehicle was equipped with a two-way radio.

The pilot vehicle was built by the Autocar Co.

REFERENCES—TM 9–306, 9–710; M3: OCM 16970, 17054, 17377, 17450, 17878, 18072, 18160, 20680, 21002. M3A1: OCM 18682, 20253, 22918, 23202, 24942, 25260; SNL G–102, Vols. 8 and 9.

37-MM GUN MOTOR CARRIAGE M6

37-MM GUN MOTOR CARRIAGE M6 WAS BASED ON ¾-TON, 4x4, TRUCK

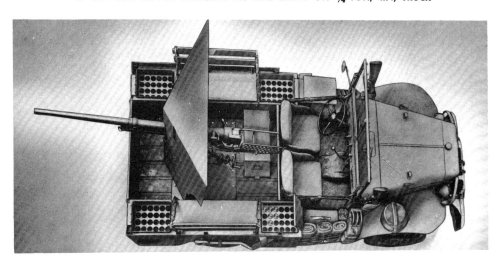

OVERHEAD VIEW, SHOWING GUN MOUNT AND STOWAGE OF AMMUNITION

TYPICAL CHARACTERISTICS

Crew 4

Physical Characteristics

Weight (gross) . . . . 7,350 lb.
Length . . . . 14 ft., 10 in.
Width . . . . 7 ft., 4 in.
Height . . . . 6 ft., 10¾ in.
Height of center line of bore . . . . . . 5 ft., 4½ in.
Ground clearance . . . . 10⅝ in.
Tread (center to center, rear) . . . . 64¾ in.
Wheelbase . . . . 98 in.
Tire equipment . . . . 9.00x16, 8-ply, combat

Armament

1 37-mm Gun M3 . . . . On Pedestal Mount
M25 or M26
Elevation . . . . −10° to +15°
Traverse . . . . 360°
Provision for:
1 Cal. .30 Rifle M1903A1
1 Grenade Launcher
3 Cal. .30 Carbines M1

Ammunition, Stowage

37-mm (A.P.C. M51B1, with tracer; H.E.
M63, with BD Fuze M58; Canister M2;
A.P. M74, with tracer) . . . . 80 rounds
Grenades (Hand: Fragmentation, 5; Smoke,
W.P., M8, 5; Thermite Incendiary, 2;
Rifle: M9A1, 10) 22

Armor

Gun shield, Front and top . . . . ¼ in.

Performance

Maximum speed on level . . . . 55 m.p.h.
Speed on 10% grade . . . . 20 m.p.h.
Maximum grade ability 60%
Vertical obstacle ability . . . . 12 in.
Fording depth (slowest forward speed) . . . 35 in.
Angle of approach . . . . 36½°
Angle of departure . . . . 31°
Turning radius . . . . 22 ft.
Fuel capacity . . . . 30 gal.
Cruising range . . . . 180 miles
Payload . . . . 1,200 lb.

Vision and Fire Control

Telescope M6 1
Telescope Mount M19 1
Bore Sight 1

Communications

Radio SCR-510
Flag Set M238 1

Battery, Voltage, total 6

Fire Protection and Decontamination

Carbon tetrachloride, 1 qt. 1
Decontaminating Apparatus M2, 1½ qt. 1

Engine, Make and model . . . . Dodge T-214
Type . . . . In-line, L
No. of cylinders 6
Fuel (gasoline) . . . . 72 octane
Net hp. . . . . 99 at 3,300 r.p.m.
Max. torque . . . . 184 lb.-ft. at 1,400 r.p.m.

(Other characteristics same as for ¾-Ton, 4x4,
Truck.)

This vehicle was standardized in February 1942, to provide greater mobility for the 37-mm antitank gun, previously used on a gun carriage towed behind a separate vehicle.

It depended on its speed to travel quickly to a point of vantage, deliver firepower sufficient to knock out a light tank, and retire before heavier firepower could be concentrated against it. It was reclassified as Limited Standard in September 1943 and was declared obsolete in January 1945.

The 37-mm Antitank Gun M3 had a muzzle velocity of 2,900 feet per second. The A. P. C. projectile fired from this gun would penetrate 1.8 inches of face-hardened armor plate at 1,000 yards.

The gun was mounted on the chassis of a standard ¾-Ton, 4x4, Truck by means of a Pedestal Mount M25 or M26 bolted to the floor. The cradle or top assembly was identical with the top carriage of 37-mm Carriage M4. The mount afforded elevations from −10° to +15° and a traverse of 360°. Normal firing was to the rear because full depression could not be obtained to the front.

A ¼-inch armor plate shield gave upper and lower frontal and partial flank protection, including overhead protection against frontal attack by low-flying aircraft.

Power was supplied by a 6-cylinder, L-head gasoline engine. A take-off from the engine supplied the power to operate the 5,000-pound-capacity winch.

Normal crew consisted of a commander, gunner, loader, and driver. The vehicle was equipped with a two-way radio. Provision was made for carrying a rifle and three carbines and also for blankets, a water bucket, and pioneer tools.

The pilot vehicle was manufactured by the Fargo Division, Chrysler Motor Co.

REFERENCES — TM 9–750A; OCM 16802, 16835, 16933, 17273, 17303, 17359, 17495, 17579, 17847, 19048, 19134, 20680, 21002, 21266, 21457, 25889, 26359.

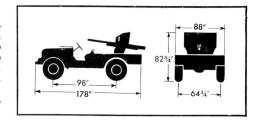

105-MM HOWITZER MOTOR CARRIAGES M7, M7B1 — SUBSTITUTE STANDARD
105-MM HOWITZER MOTOR CARRIAGE M37 — STANDARD

Standardization in January 1945 of 105-mm Howitzer Motor Carriage M37 added another vehicle to the combat team built upon the Light Tank M24 chassis and continued the line of powerful weapons started with 105-mm Howitzer Motor Carriage M7, which helped rout Rommel in Libya.

All are lightly-armored, open-top vehicles in which a 105-mm howitzer is the principal armament. The pulpit-like appearance of the machine gun compartment caused the M7 to be nicknamed "The Priest" by British troops.

105-MM HOWITZER MOTOR CARRIAGE M7 was standardized in April 1942 and was reclassified as Substitute Standard in January 1945. The vehicle is based on a Medium Tank M3 chassis which has a Continental R–975–C1 gasoline engine, syncromesh transmission, and a vertical volute spring suspension.

Principal armament is a 105-mm Howitzer M2A1 mounted at the front of the crew compartment. The howitzer can be elevated from −5° to +35° and can be traversed 30° to the right and 15° to the left. An HE shell, fired from this howitzer, has a muzzle velocity of 1,550 feet per second at an elevation of 44° and a maximum range of 12,205 yards.

A Cal. .50 Machine Gun M2 HB (flexible) on a ring mount is provided for use against low-flying aircraft. Provision is made for 3 cal. .45 submachine guns.

The crew of seven consists of the driver, chief of section, gunner, and four cannoneers. The crew compartment is protected by ½-in. armor at the front, sides, and rear, and is open at the top. The upper portion of the side and rear armor is hinged and held in position by lock pins. Grip handles, which serve as ladders leading to the crew compartment, are at both sides of the vehicle.

Direct vision for the driver is through a removable windshield and indirect vision through a protectoscope. The vehicle has five speeds forward and one reverse, the maximum speed being 24 m.p.h.

The pilot vehicle was manufactured by the American Locomotive Co.

REFERENCES—TM 9-731E; OCM 17760, 18007, 18120, 18151, 18226, 19327, 19525, 20680, 21002, 21211, 23540, 23712, 24984, 25812, 26429; SNL G–128.

105-MM HOWITZER MOTOR CARRIAGE M7B1 is based on the Medium Tank M4A3 chassis and is powered by a Ford GAA, V–8, gasoline engine. Stand-

105-MM HOWITZER MOTOR CARRIAGE M7 USES MEDIUM TANK M3 CHASSIS

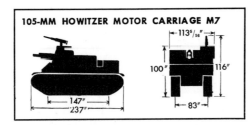

105-MM HOWITZER MOTOR CARRIAGE M7

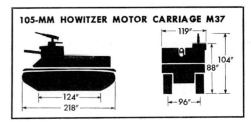

105-MM HOWITZER MOTOR CARRIAGE M37

105-MM HOWITZER MOTOR CARRIAGE M37 HAS LIGHT TANK M24 CHASSIS

ardized in September 1943, it was reclassified as Substitute Standard in January 1945.

Physical characteristics and performance of this vehicle are generally similar to those of 105-mm Howitzer Motor Carriage M7, the only difference being in the variations of the respective tanks.

REFERENCES—TM 9-749; OCM21720, 25812, 26429; SNL G–199.

105-MM HOWITZER MOTOR CARRIAGE M37 was standardized in Jan-

uary 1945. It is a lighter, more mobile, and less expensive 105-mm howitzer motor carriage than the earlier vehicles, which were based on medium tank chassis, and has better armor protection.

It is a full track-laying vehicle, with individual torsion bar suspension, driven from the front sprocket. Like the Twin 40-mm Gun Motor Carriage M19, it has a chassis similar to the Light Tank M24, forming another member of a combat team of vehicles designed for maximum interchangeability.

OVERHEAD VIEW OF THE M37, SHOWING OPEN FIGHTING COMPARTMENT

a muzzle velocity of 1,550 feet per second and at an elevation of 44°, has a range of 12,205 yards. The howitzer, which is carried on Mount M5, can be elevated from −10° to +45° and can be traversed 22½° left and 22½° right. A Cal. .50 Machine Gun M2 HB (flexible) on a concentric ring mount is provided. Provision is made for carrying one cal. .45 submachine gun and six cal. .30 carbines.

Power is supplied by twin Cadillac engines through Hydra-Matic transmissions and a transfer unit with synchronizer that provide eight forward speeds up to 35 m.p.h. and four reverse speeds up to 18 m.p.h.

Indirect vision for the driver is provided by a periscope.

Provision is made for installing a telephone and reel unit, with interphone communication for the chief of section and the driver. A British No. 19 wireless set may be installed if 24 rounds of ammunition are removed.

REFERENCES—OCM 20679, 21009, 22304, 22435, 24883, 25812, 26429.

Shorter but wider than the 105-mm Howitzer Motor Carriages M7 and M7B1, the M37 provides greater working space for the crew members and increased space for ammunition stowage. Armor plate ½ in. thick affords protection at the front, sides, and rear of the vehicle, and also over the driver's compartment.

Principal armament is a 105-mm Howitzer M4, which when firing the HE shell at

CHARACTERISTICS OF 105-MM HOWITZER MOTOR CARRIAGES M7, M7B1, M37

	M7*, M7B1**	M37†
Crew	7	7
Physical Characteristics		
Weight	50,634 lb.	40,000 lb.
Length	19 ft., 9 in.	18 ft., 2 in.
Width	9 ft., 5⁵⁄₁₆ in.	9 ft., 11 in.
Height	8 ft., 4 in.	7 ft., 4 in.
Over A. A. gun	9 ft., 8 in.	8 ft., 8 in.
Ground clearance	17⅛ in.	17 in.
Tread (center to center of tracks)	83 in.	96 in.
Ground contact length	147 in.	124 in.
Ground pressure	10.4 lb./sq. in.	10.1 lb./sq. in.
Armament		
105-mm Howitzer	M2A1 in Mount M4	M4 in Mount M5
Elevation	−5° to +35°	−10° to +45°
Traverse	30° right, 15° left	22½° right, 22½° left
1 Cal. .50 Machine Gun M2 HB (flexible)	On ring mount	On ring mount
Provision for:		
Cal. .45 submachine guns	3	1
Cal. .30 carbines	0	6
Ammunition, Stowage		
105-mm	69 rounds	90 rounds
Cal. .50	300 rounds	900 rounds
Cal. .45	1,620 rounds	600 rounds
Hand Grenades	8	8

Armor	Actual	Basis	Actual	Basis
Hull, front, upper	½ in.	½ in.	½ in.	1¼ in.
Lower	2–4¼ in.	2–4½ in.	½ in.	⅞ in.
Sides, upper	½ in.	½ in.	½ in.	½ in.
Lower	1½ in.***	1½ in.	½ in.	½ in.
Rear, upper	½ in.	½ in.	½ in.	½ in.
Lower	1½ in.***	1½ in.	½ in.	⅞ in.
Bottom, front	1 in.	1 in.	½ in.	½ in.
Rear	½ in.	½ in.	⅜ in.	⅜ in.
Top, forward			½ in.	
Gun mount shield			½ in.	½ in.

Performance	M7*, M7B1**	M37†
Maximum speed on level	25 m.p.h.	35 m.p.h.
Maximum grade ability	60%	60%
Trench crossing ability	7 ft., 6 in.	7 ft.
Vertical obstacle ability	24 in.	42 in.
Fording depth (slowest forward speed)	48 in.	42 in.
Turning diameter	62 ft.	40 ft.
Fuel capacity	179 gal.	115 gal.
Cruising range (approx.)	85–125 miles	100–150 miles

Vision and Fire Control		
Periscope M6	0	2
Protectoscope	1	0
Panoramic Telescope M12-A2, w/Instrument Light M19	1	1
On Mount M21A1, w/8-in. filler piece	1	0
On Mount T96	0	1
Telescope M76G (3-power), on Mount T95, w/Instrument Light M33	0	1
Elbow Telescope M16 or M16A1C	1	0
Telescope Mount M42	1	0
Instrument Light M36 (for M16A1C)	1	0
Aiming Post M1, w/Aiming Post Light M14	2	2
Range Quadrant M4	1	0
Range Quadrant T14, w/Instrument Light M18	0	1
Gunner's Quadrant M1	1	1
Fuze Setter M22	1	1
Communications		
Flag Set M238	1	1
Panel Set AP50A	0	1
Provision for:		
Telephone EE-8-( ) and Reel Unit RL-39	0	1
Interphone RC-99	0	1
British Wireless Set No. 19	0	1 ††
Battery, Voltage, total	24	24
Fire Protection and Decontamination		
Fire Extinguisher		
CO₂–10 lb. (fixed)	2	2
CO₂–4 lb. (hand)	2	2
Decontaminating Apparatus, 1½ qt.	3	2

*Other characteristics same as for Medium Tank M3.
**Characteristics of M7B1 same as for M7 except: weight, 50,000 lb.; length, 20 ft., 3¾ in.; ground pressure, 10.3 lb./sq. in.; maximum speed, 26 m.p.h.; fording depth, 36 in.; fuel capacity, 168 gal.
***Soft plate, minimum ballistics of ½-inch armor.
†Other characteristics same as for Light Tank M24.
††Displaces 18 rounds of 105-mm ammunition.

155 MM GUN MOTOR CARRIAGE M40 – STANDARD
8 INCH HOWITZER MOTOR CARRIAGE M43 – STANDARD

The Gun Motor Carriage M40 and Howitzer Motor Carriage M43 are essentially the same vehicles, the equipments differing only in the primary armament mounted and in the primary ammunition stowage racks. The GMC M40 mounts the 155mm Gun M1 or M2 by means of the Mount M3, while the HMC M43 mounts the 8 in howitzer M1 or M2 on Mount M17. Either weapon and mount can be interchanged with the other on any given carriage, though adjustments to the equilibrators and to the Belleville springs supporting the traversing roller path must be made, due to the differences in weight, balance and recoil force.

The GMC M40 was requested as a replacement for the GMC M12, since the

PRINCIPAL CHARACTERISTICS

Crew

Physical characteristics:
Weight (gross)
M40 . . . . 81,000 lbs.
M43 . . . . 80,000 lbs.
Length. w/o cannon . . . . 280.4 ins.
Cannon overhang
M40 . . . . 68 ins.
M43 . . . . 0 ins.
Width . . . . 124 ins.
Height . . . . 130 ins.
Ground clearance . . . . 17 ins.
Tread . . . . 101 ins.
Ground contact length . . . . 164 ins.
Ground pressure

M40 . . . . 10.7 psi
M43 . . . . 10.6 psi

Armament
Primary:
M40 . . . . 155mm Gun M1A1 or M2 in Mount M3
M43 . . . . 8in Howitzer M1 or M2 in Mount M17
Elevation . . . . –5 to +45 degrees
Traverse . . . . 36 degrees (18R to 18L)
Secondary: . . . . Provision for 8 Carbines, Cal .30, M1
. . . . and 1 Grenade Launcher M8

Ammunition stowage
M40 . . . . 155mm rounds – 20
M43 . . . . 8in rounds – 16
Both: . . . . 960 rounds .30 Cal Carbine
. . . . 12 hand grenades
. . . . 10 anti-tank grenades

supply of M1918 guns was exhausted and the M12 chassis was unsuitable for the more powerful M1 and M2 155mm guns. The GMC T83 was developed from existing M4 tank components, using a wider hull and the new horizontal volute spring suspension. The general arrangement follows that of the M12, with the driver at the front, engine behind him, and cannon compartment at the rear. The hull is open on top except for the driving compartment where access is provided by two hatches in the roof. A floor mounted escape hatch is located just behind the assistant driver's seat. A spade can be lowered at the rear to stabilize the carriage against recoil. A hinged platform is provided for the gun crew when the spade is lowered.

OCM 23279 of 18 March 1944 authorized procurement of five pilot T83 vehicles armed with 155mm guns; after trials with an 8in howitzer, OCM 25754 of November 1944 authorized development of the HMC under the designation T89. Standardization of the T83 as the M40 took place in May 1945, and that of the T89 as the M43 in November 1945.

A Cargo Carrier T30 was developed to accompany these carriages, but development was canceled and the High Speed Tractor M4 will be used to carry ammunition.

Ammunition

Ammunition for the 155mm GMC M40 is the same as that for the 155mm Gun M1 or M2. It is of the separate-loading type. The standard round is the HE Shell M101 which weighs 95 pounds, contains 15.13 pounds of TNT and can be fitted with Fuze PD M51 or Fuze MT M67; the Charge Propelling, Base and Increment, weighing 30.74 pounds of NH powder, and the Primer Percussion Mk IIA4.

Ammunition for the 8in HMC M43 is the same as that for the 8in Howitzer M2 and is also of the separate-loading type. The standard round is the HE Shell M106 weighing 200 pounds, filled with 36.98 pounds of TNT, and using Fuze PD M51 or Fuze MT M67; the Charge Propelling M1, weighing 13.19 pounds of NH powder and giving Zones 1 to 5; the Charge Propelling M2, weighing 28.19 pounds and giving Zones 5 to 7; and the Primer, Percussion, Mk IIA4

Armor . . . .**Actual** . . . .**Angle w/vertical**

Armor	Actual	Angle w/vertical
Hull, front, upper	0.5 in	58°
lower	2.0 to 4.25 in	0 to 46°
Sides, upper	0.5 in	0°
lower	1.0 in	0°
Rear	0.5 in	0°
Bottom, front	1.0 in	90°
rear	0.5 in	90°
Top	0.5 in	85°
Gun shield	0.5 in	45°

Engine

Make and model	Continental R975 C4
Type	9 cylinder, 4-cycle, radial
Cooling system	Air
Ignition	Magneto
Displacement	973 cubic ins.
Bore and stroke	5 x 5.5 ins.
Compression ratio	5.7 to 1
Net horsepower (max)	400 hp at 2400 rpm
Gross horsepower (max)	460 hp at 2400 rpm
Net Torque (max)	940 ft-lb at 1700 rpm
Gross torque (max)	1025 ft-lb at 1800 rpm
Weight	1212 lbs. dry

Power train

Clutch	Dry disc, two plate
Gear ratios:	1st 7.56:1
4th 1.11:1	
2nd 3.11:1	5th 0.73:1
3rd 1.78:1	Reverse 5/65:1
Steering	Controlled differential
Steering ratio	1.55:1
Brakes	Mechanical, external, contracting
Final drive	Herringbone gear, Ratio 2.84:1

Running Gear

Suspension	Horizontal volute spring
Wheels	12 dual in six bogies
Tire size	20.5 x 6.25 ins.
Tracks	Center guide, T66, T80 and T84:
T66:	single pin, 23 inch wide, cast steel
T80:	double pin, 23 in, rubber & steel
T84:	double pin, 23 in, rubber
Pitch	6 ins.
Shoes	172

Battery . . . . 24v DC

Communications . . . . Radio SCR610 or SCR608B
Interphone RC99 (4 stations)

Fire protection and Decontamination
Fire extinguisher, CO_2, 10lb (fixed)
Fire extinguisher, CO_2, 4lb (hand)
Decontaminating Apparatus, 1½ quarts, M2

Performance

Maximum speed on level	21 m.p.h.
Maximum grade ability	60 percent
Trench crossing ability	7.7 feet
Vertical obstacle ability	24 ins.
Fording depth	40 ins.
Turning diameter	83 feet
Fuel capacity	80 octane gasoline, 215 gallons
Cruising range, roads (approx.)	100 miles

RECONSTRUCTED PAGE 1 November 1945

75 MM HOWITZER MOTOR CARRIAGE M8—STANDARD

75 MM HOWITZER MOTOR CARRIAGE, M8, IS BASED ON LIGHT TANK, M5, CHASSIS

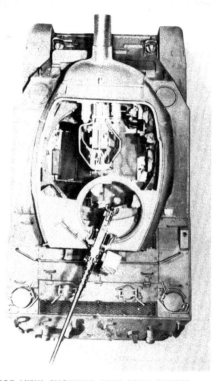

TOP VIEW, SHOWING SEMI-OPEN TURRET

This is a highly mobile 75 mm howitzer motor carriage capable of being used as assault or support artillery with full protection against small arms fire.

It is similar to Light Tank, M5, but has a redesigned turret to mount a 75 mm howitzer.

Principal armament is a 75 mm Howitzer, M2 or M3, with a rate of fire of 25 rounds per minute. Firing an H.E. shell, M48, with a muzzle velocity of 1,250 feet per second, it has a maximum range of 9,610 yards. The howitzer has an elevation of from −20° to +40°.

The turret is of welded armor, open at the top except for a partial roof to support the cal. .50 HB antiaircraft machine gun ring mount. It has a traverse of 360°.

The hull is of armor plate and is a completely welded structure except for portions of the front, top and rear which are removable for service operations.

The vehicle is powered by two Cadillac engines, each of which is connected to a Hydra-Matic transmission, providing six forward speeds and one reverse speed. It is wired for radio and for an interphone system. Four periscopes are provided.

The pilot model was manufactured by the Cadillac Motor Car Division, General Motors Corp.

REFERENCES — TM 9–732B; OCM 17236, 17315, 17966, 18049, 18098, 18188, 19368, 19398, 19979, 21838.

TYPICAL CHARACTERISTICS

Crew 4

Physical Characteristics
Weight (gross) . . . . 34,600 lb.*
Length . . . . 14 ft., 6¾ ins.
Width . . . . 7 ft., 4¼ ins.
Height . . . . 7 ft., 6½ ins.
Turret ring diameter (inside) . . . . 54½ ins.
Ground clearance . . . . 16½ ins.
Tread (center to center of tracks) . . . . . 73 ins.
Ground contact length . . . . 121 ins.
Ground pressure . . . . 11.6 lb./sq. in.

Armament
75 mm Howitzer, M2 or M3, in
   75 mm Howitzer Mount, M7
   Elevation . . . . −20° to +40°
   Traverse . . . . 360°
1 cal. .50 Machine Gun, M2,
   HB (flexible) . . . . . . On Turret (antiaircraft)
Provision for:
1 cal. .45 Submachine Gun
3 cal. .30 Carbines, M1

Ammunition, Stowage
75 mm (H.E., M48; A.P.C., M61;
   A.P., M72) . . . . 46 rounds
Cal. .50 (in 50 round boxes) . . . . . 400 rounds
Cal. .45 (in 20 or 30 round clips) . . . 600 rounds
Cal. .30 (in cartridge belts) . . . . . 735 rounds
Grenades, Hand (Fragmentation, Mk. II, 2;
   Smoke, H.C., M8, 4; Thermite,
   Incendiary, 2) 8

Armor | **Actual** | **Basis**
Hull, Front, upper . . . . . . 1⅛ ins. | 2½ ins.
   lower . . . . . . 1¾ ins. | 2½ ins.
Sides . . . . 1 in. | 1⅛ ins.
Rear . . . . 1 in. |
Top . . . . ½ in. |
Bottom . . . . ⅜–½ in. |
Turret, Front . . . . 1½ ins. |
Sides and rear . . . . 1 in. |
Top . . . . ⅜ in. |

Performance
Maximum speed on level . . . . 40 m.p.h.
Maximum grade ability 60%
Trench crossing ability . . . . . . 5 ft., 4 ins.
Vertical obstacle ability . . . . 18 ins.
Fording depth (slowest forward speed) . . 36 ins.
Fuel capacity . . . . 89 gals.
Cruising range . . . . 100 miles

Vision and Fire Control
Periscopes, M9 4
Bore Sight 1
Panoramic Telescope, M12A5 1
Telescope, M70C 1
Gunner's Quadrant, M1 1

Communications
Radio . . . . SCR–510 or 210
Interphone stations 3
Battery, Voltage, total 12

Fire Protection and Decontamination
Fire Extinguisher—CO₂–10 lb. (fixed) 1
   CO₂–4 lb. (hand) 1
Decontaminating Apparatus, 1½ qts., M2 . . 3

*With T16 Tracks.

(Other characteristics same as for Light Tank, M5.)

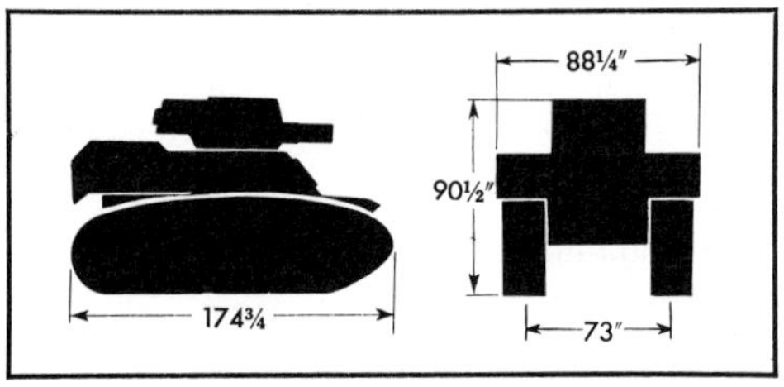

3 INCH GUN MOTOR CARRIAGES **M10, M10A1**—STANDARD

3 INCH GUN MOTOR CARRIAGE, M10A1, SHOWING CIRCULAR BOSSES ON SIDES FOR ATTACHING AUXILIARY ARMOR

This weapon, designed for use against tanks and armored vehicles, embodies heavy firepower, excellent mobility and sloping armor with good ballistic qualities.

It consists of a 3 Inch Gun, M7, mounted in a semi-open turret on a medium tank chassis.

3 Inch Gun Motor Carriage, M10, is based on a Medium Tank, M4A2, chassis, with twin General Motors Diesel engines. The pilot vehicle was manufactured by the Fisher Body Co.

3 Inch Gun Motor Carriage, M10A1, is based on a Medium Tank, M4A3, chassis, with a Ford GAA gasoline engine. The pilot vehicle was manufactured by the Ford Motor Co.

Physical characteristics and performance of the models vary only slightly, in accordance with the variations in the respective tanks.

The 3 Inch Gun, M7, is mounted in a semi-open turret, with elevations from −10° to +19°. Fired from it, the A.P.C. projectile has a muzzle velocity of 2,600 feet per second and a maximum range of 16,100 yards. It will penetrate 4 inches of face-hardened armor plate at 1,000 yards.

A cal. .50 machine gun is mounted at the rear of the turret for protection against low-flying planes.

The armor protection may be increased by attaching auxiliary armor of varying thickness to bosses on the basic armor.

REFERENCES—M10:TM 9–752A;OCM 17462, 17642, 18006, 18061, 18313, 18332, 18435, 18597, 18944, 19045, 19055, 19167, 19242, 19245, 20067, 20281, 20310, 20680, 21002, 21461. M10A1: TM 9–731G; OCM 20515.

TYPICAL CHARACTERISTICS

3 INCH GUN MOTOR CARRIAGE, M10

Crew 5

Physical Characteristics

Weight	66,000 lb.
Length	19 ft., 7 ins.
Width	10 ft.
Height	8 ft., 1½ ins.
Height of center line, 3 inch gun	82½ ins.
Turret ring diameter (inside)	69 ins.
Ground clearance	17⅛ ins.
Tread (center to center of tracks)	83 ins.
Ground contact length	147 ins.
Ground pressure	12.3 lb./sq. in.

Armament

3 Inch Gun, M7, in Mount, M5 . . . . . .In turret
  Elevation . . . .−10° to +19°
  Traverse . . . . .360°
Cal. .50 Machine Gun, M2, HB
  (flexible) . . . . .On turret (Antiaircraft)
1 Tripod Mount, cal. .50, M3
Provision for:
5 cal. .30 Carbines, M1

Ammunition, Stowage

3 inch (A.P.C., M62, and H.E.,
  M42A1) . . . . .54 rounds
Cal. .50 (in 50 round boxes) . . . . . .300 rounds
Cal. .30 (Carbine, M1) . . . . .450 rounds
Grenades, Hand (Smoke, W.P., M15, 6;
  Fragmentation, Mk., II, 6) 12
Smoke Pots, H.C., M1 4

Armor

	Actual	Basis
Hull, Front	½–2 ins.	3¼ ins.
Sides	¾–1 in.	1–1⅜ ins.
Rear	1–1½ ins.	
Top	⅜–¾ in.	
Bottom	¼ in.	
Turret, Front	2½ ins.	4½ ins.
Sides and rear	1 in.	1⅛–1¾ ins.
Top	¾ in.	

Performance

Maximum speed on level	30 m.p.h.
Speed on 3% grade	20 m.p.h.
Maximum grade ability	60%
Trench crossing ability	7 ft., 6 ins.
Vertical obstacle ability	24 ins.
Fording depth (slowest forward speed)	36 ins.
Turning radius	31 ft.
Fuel capacity	164 gals.
Cruising range (approx.)	200 miles

Vision and Fire Control

Periscopes, M6	3
Telescope, M51	1
Bore Sight	1
Gunner's Quadrant, M1	1

Communications

Radio	SCR-510 or 610 or British 19
Interphone stations	5
Flag Set, M238	1

Battery, Voltage, total 24

Fire Protection and Decontamination

Fire Extinguisher—CO₂–10 lb. (fixed) 2
  CO₂–4 lb. (hand) 2
Decontaminating Apparatus, 1½ qts., M2 . . .2

Engine, Make and Model . . . .G.M. 6-71-6046

3 INCH GUN MOTOR CARRIAGE, M10A1

Characteristics same as for 3 Inch Gun Motor Carriage, M10, except as noted:

Weight (gross)	64,000 lb.
Fuel capacity	192 gals.
Cruising range	160 miles
Engine, Make and Model	Ford GAA

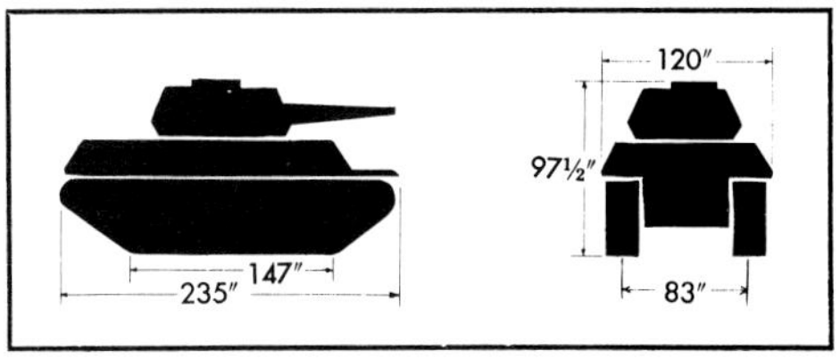

235″   147″   120″   97½″   83″

155 MM GUN MOTOR CARRIAGE **M12**—CARGO CARRIER **M30**—STANDARD

155 MM GUN MOTOR CARRIAGE, M12, WITH GUN IN TRAVELING LOCK. GUN IS ELEVATED, AND SPADE AT REAR LOWERED, WHEN FIRING

TYPICAL CHARACTERISTICS

155 mm GUN MOTOR CARRIAGE, M12
Crew......................................6

Physical Characteristics
Weight (gross)....................58,000 lb.
Length..........................22 ft., 1 in.
Width............................8 ft., 9 ins.
Height..........................8 ft., 10 ins.
Height of center line of bore....7 ft., 1½ ins.
Ground clearance................17⅛ ins.
Ground contact length...........147 ins.
Tread (center to center of tracks)......83 ins.
Ground pressure.................116 lb./sq. in.

Armament
155 mm Gun, M1918M1, M1917A1
   or M1917................On Mount, M4
   Elevation..............−5° to +30°
   Traverse...................28°
Provision for:
5 cal. .30 carbines........Equipment of crew
1 Grenade Launcher, M8........For carbine

Ammunition, Stowage
155 mm (H.E., Mk. IIIA1 or M101). 10 rounds
Grenades (Hand: Fragmentation, Mk. II, 4;
   Offensive, Mk. III, w/fuze, M6, 2;
   Smoke, WP, M8, 4; Thermite, Incendi-
   ary, 2; Rifle: M9A1, 10)................22

Armor

	Actual	Basis
Hull, Front	1½–2 ins.	3½ ins.
Sides	1 in.	1 in.
Rear	¾ in.	¾ in.
Top	½ in.	½ in.
Bottom	½–1 in.	½–1 in.
Shield	¾ in.	

Performance
Maximum speed on level..........24 m.p.h.
Maximum grade ability.............60%
Trench crossing ability.......7 ft., 6 ins.
Fording depth (slowest forward speed). 36 ins.
Fuel capacity....................200 gals.
Turning radius....................35 ft.
Cruising range (approx.).........140 miles

Vision and Fire Control
Panoramic Telescope, M6 (with Instrument
   Light, M9, and one 14-in. extension
   bar)....................................1
Telescope, M53.............................1
Telescope Mount, M40......................1
Aiming Post, M1 (with Aiming Post
   Light, M14)............................1
Gunner's Quadrant, M1, w/case.............1
Quadrant Sight, M1918A1, w/cover,
   M1918..................................1
Fuze Setter, M21 or M14..................1
Bore Sight................................1
Vision Slots..............................2

Communications
Flag Set, M113............................1

Battery, Voltage, total..................24

Fire Protection and Decontamination
CO₂—10 lb. (Fixed)........................2
Fire Extinguisher, CO₂—4 lb. (Hand).......2
Decontaminating Apparatus, M2, 1½ qts....2

Engine, Make and Model... Continental R975-C1
Type..........................Radial A.C.
No. of cylinders..........................9
Cycle.....................................4
Fuel (gasoline)...................80 octane
Max. governed speed.........2,400 r.p.m.
Net hp................353 at 2,400 r.p.m.
Max. torque.......850 lb.-ft. at 1,800 r.p.m.
(See additional engine characteristics on page
28.)

Transmission, Type..............Syncromesh
Gear ratios
   First speed....................7.56:1
   Second speed...................3.11:1
   Third speed....................1.78:1
   Fourth speed...................1.11:1
   Fifth speed......................73:1
   Reverse........................5.65:1

Differential, Type.................Controlled

Final Drive, Type.............Herringbone

Suspension, Type............Volute spring

Idler, Type.........................Fixed

Track, Type..................Rubber block

Brakes, Type..................Mechanical

CARGO CARRIER, M30
Physical Characteristics
Weight (gross)....................47,000 lb.
Length..........................19 ft., 10 ins.
Width............................8 ft., 9 ins.
Height—ring mount up, with gun........10 ft.
   ring mount, lowered, without gun. 8 ft., 6 ins.
Ground pressure.................10 lb./sq. in.

Armament
Provision for:
5 cal. .30 carbines........Equipment of crew
1 Grenade Launcher, M8........For carbine
1 cal. .50 Machine Gun, M2,
   HB (flexible)............On ring mount

Ammunition, Stowage
155 mm (H.E., Mk. IIIA1 or M101). 40 rounds
Cal. .50......................1,000 rounds
Grenades (Hand: Fragmentation, Mk. II, 4;
   Offensive, Mk. III w/fuze, M6, 2; Smoke,
   4; Thermite Incendiary, 2; Rifle: M9A1,
   10)..................................22

Vision
Protectoscopes............................2

Communications
Radio........................SCR-610

(Other characteristics same as for 155 mm Gun
Motor Carriage, M12.)

CARGO CARRIER, M30, SHOWING MACHINE GUN ON MOUNT

155 mm GUN MOTOR CARRIAGE, M12, IN FIRING POSITION

155 mm GUN MOTOR CARRIAGE, M12, provides increased mobility and maneuverability for the powerful 155 mm gun.

It is intended for use principally (a) where the tactical situation calls for quick-moving, long-range fire and (b) as a special purpose weapon for beach defense.

The weapon consists of a 155 mm Gun, M1918M1, M1917A1 or M1917, mounted on 155 mm Gun Mount, M4, on a modified Medium Tank, M3, chassis.

The 155 mm gun has an elevation from −5° to +30° and a traverse of 28°. Using a 95 pound projectile, with a muzzle velocity of 2,410 feet per second, it has a maximum range of 20,100 yards. Provisions are made for carrying five cal. .30 carbines and one cal. .30 rifle.

A spade at the rear is used to stabilize the weapon against recoil. This may be elevated out of the way when the vehicle is in motion. A hinged platform is provided for the gun crew when the spade is lowered.

Direct and indirect vision are provided for the driver and assistant driver. Seats for four other crew members are provided. Additional ammunition, and additional personnel needed to serve the gun, are carried in a companion vehicle, Cargo Carrier, M30.

The pilot model was manufactured by Rock Island Arsenal.

REFERENCES—TM9–751;OCM16859,16912, 18074, 18584, 18727, 19399, 21546, 21835.

CARGO CARRIER, M30, is the companion vehicle for 155 mm Gun Motor Carriage, M12, and like it is built on a modified Medium Tank, M3, chassis.

It is used to transport additional personnel needed to operate the 155 mm gun, and adequate ammunition and equipment for it. The tail gate may be lowered to facilitate access to the cargo.

A ring mount for a cal. .50 machine gun is provided for antiaircraft and ground protection. Provision is made for carrying a cal. .30 rifle, and four cal. .30 carbines.

The pilot vehicle was designed at Rock Island Arsenal, and built by the Pressed Steel Car Company.

REFERENCES—TM9–751;OCM18628,18731, 21444, 21628.

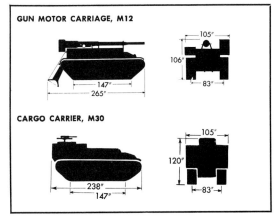

GUN MOTOR CARRIAGE, M12

105″
106″
83″
147″
265″

CARGO CARRIER, M30

105″
120″
83″
238″
147″

57 MM GUN MOTOR CARRIAGE T48—LIMITED PROCUREMENT

57 mm GUN MOTOR CARRIAGE, T48, FROM ABOVE, SHOWING GUN IN TRAVELING POSITION, GUN SHIELD, AND STOWAGE

This vehicle consists of a 57 mm Gun, M1, on 57 mm Gun Mount, T5, on a Half Track Personnel Carrier, M3.

Its development was initiated by Ordnance Committee action in April, 1942, as an expedient mounting for the 57 mm gun pending the development of a more suitable motor carriage for the weapon.

The pilot vehicle was constructed at the Aberdeen Proving Ground.

It was originally expected that the vehicle would be manufactured to fill both United States and British requirements, but later developments resulted in requirements for the British only. In accordance with requests from the British Army Staff, and in accordance with requirements of the Army Supply Program, production of the vehicles for the British was initiated. O.C.M. 19063, dated 18 October 1942, gave military characteristics as required for British use.

The 57 mm Gun, M1, has an elevation from −5° to +15° and may be traversed 27½° right and 27½° left. Using A.P. projectile, M70, with a muzzle velocity of 2,800 feet per second, it will penetrate 2.2 inches of face-hardened armor plate at 1,000 yards. Provision is made for carrying five British cal. .30 rifles.

The 57 mm gun is mounted on the center of the vehicle, immediately behind the front bulkhead, and fires to the front. A pivoted gunner's seat is provided, and swings independently of the gun.

The gun shield is of sloping, face-hardened armor plate, ⅝ inch thick at the front, and ¼ inch at the sides and overhead.

Other armor is essentially the same as on Half Track Personnel Carrier, M3. Space for the gun tube is allowed between the two windshields.

A traveling lock, with a quick release mechanism, holds the gun in place above the hood when not in use. It may be pulled away when the gun is being fired.

Removable headlights are provided, as well as removable blackout lights which may be fitted into the headlight brackets.

The vehicle is equipped with a British Wireless Set, No. 19.

REFERENCES — OCM 18099, 18149, 19063, 20680, 21002.

TYPICAL CHARACTERISTICS

Crew. 5

Physical Characteristics
Weight (gross). . . . . .19,000 lb.
Length. . . . . .21 ft., ⅝ in.
Width. . . . . .7 ft., 1 in.
Height. . . . . .7 ft.
Height—to center of gun bore . . . . 72 ins.
Ground clearance. . . . . .11¹³⁄₁₆ ins.
Wheelbase. .135½ ins.
Tread (center to center rear). . . . . . .63¹³⁄₁₆ ins.
Ground contact length—tracks. . . . . .46¾ ins.
Tire equipment. . . .8.25 x 20, 12 ply, (combat)

Armament
57 mm Gun, M1. . . . . .On mount, T5
  Elevation. . . . .−5° to +15°
  Traverse. . . . . .27½° right, 27½° left
Provision for:
5 cal. .30 Rifles, British. . . . .Equipment of crew
1 Grenade Launcher. . . . . .For rifle

Ammunition, Stowage
57 mm (A.P., M70). . . . . .99 rounds
Grenades (Hand: Fragmentation, Mk. II, 5; Smoke, M8, 5; Thermite, Incendiary, 2; Rifle: M9A1, 10). 22

Armor
Vehicle—same as Half Track Personnel Carrier, M3
Gun shield, Front. . . . . .⅝ in.
Sides and top. . . . . .¼ in.

Performance
Maximum speed on level. . . . . .45 m.p.h.
Speed on 4% grade. . . . . .25 m.p.h.
Maximum grade ability. 60%
Vertical obstacle ability. . . . . .12 ins.
Fording depth (slowest forward speed). .32 ins.
Angle of approach. . . . . .37°
Angle of departure . . . . .32°
Turning radius. . . . . .30 ft.
Fuel capacity. . . . . .60 gals.
Cruising range (approx.). . . . . .200 miles

Vision and Fire Control
Telescope, M18. 1
Telescope Mount, M24. 1
Bore Sight. 1

Communications
Radio. . . . . .British Wireless Set, No. 19
Flag Set, M238. 1

Battery, Voltage, total. 12

Fire Protection and Decontamination
Fire Extinguisher, CO₂-2 lb. (hand) 1
Decontaminating Apparatus, M2, 1½ qts. . .1

(Other characteristics same as for Half Track Personnel Carrier, M3.)

MULTIPLE GUN MOTOR CARRIAGE M15—LIMITED STANDARD
COMBINATION GUN MOTOR CARRIAGE M15A1—SUBSTITUTE STANDARD

COMBINATION GUN MOTOR CARRIAGE, M15A1, MOUNTS 37 mm GUN AND TWO CAL. .50 MACHINE GUNS, IN LOW SILHOUETTE, ROTATING TURRET MOUNT

MULTIPLE GUN MOTOR CARRIAGE, M15—LIMITED STANDARD—This highly mobile weapon, capable of a concentration of rapid fire, was designed primarily for vehicular antiaircraft column defense.

It is comprised mainly of a Half Track Personnel Carrier, M3, chassis, and the top carriage of the 37 mm Gun Carriage, M3E1 (designated Combination Gun Mount, M42), mounting a 37 mm Gun, M1A2, and two cal. .50 Machine Guns, M2, HB, and Sighting System, M6.

The mount is manually operated and has an elevation from 0° to +85° and a traverse of 360°. Depression at the front is limited to +20°.

The H.E. shell, fired from the 37 mm gun, has a maximum range, vertical, of about 6,200 yards, and, horizontal, of about 8,875 yards. The cal. .50 guns have a maximum range each of 7,200 yards.

References—TM 9–708; OCM 17313, 18152, 18477, 18698, 18957, 19087, 19115, 19198, 21281, 21563.

COMBINATION GUN MOTOR CARRIAGE, M15A1—SUBSTITUTE STANDARD—This is similar to Multiple Gun Motor Carriage, M15, but embodies several improvements. Combination Gun Mount, M54, is used. This mount consists of the top carriage of a 37 mm Gun Carriage, M3A1, mounting a 37 mm Gun, M1A2, two cal. .50 Machine Guns, M2, HB, and Sighting System, M5.

The vehicle is lighter and more stable than the M15, and is regarded as better in appearance because of its lower silhouette. It does not require gear box controls. Interference between the guns and other equipment has been eliminated at several points.

A platform is provided for a loader for the 37 mm gun and for the lead setter, and ammunition chests have been separated so as to provide sufficient room for him to stand. A rail is provided in the rear of the mount for convenience of the gun crew in getting on the mount. The lead setter's seat is raised to facilitate operation of the sight.

References — OCM 16367, 16428, 21226, 21281, 21563, 21850, 22628, 23746, 24133.

TYPICAL CHARACTERISTICS

COMBINATION GUN MOTOR CARRIAGE, M15A1

Crew................................7

Physical Characteristics

Weight (gross)	20,800 lb.
Length	20 ft., 3½ ins.
Width	7 ft., 4½ ins.
Height (overall)	7 ft., 10 ins.
Ground clearance	11³⁄₁₆ ins.
Wheelbase	135½ ins.
Tread, front	64½ ins.
rear	63¹³⁄₁₆ ins.
Ground contact length	46¾ ins.
Tire equipment	8.25 x 20, 12 ply (combat)

Armament

37 mm Gun, A.A., M1A2, and
2 cal. .50 Machine Guns, M2, HB*
          On Combination Gun Mount, M54
  Elevation....................−5° to +85°
  Traverse...........................360°
Provision for:
4 cal. .30 carbines........Equipment of crew

*With side plate triggers.

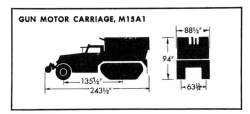

GUN MOTOR CARRIAGE, M15A1

88½" · 94" · 135½" · 243½" · 63½"

Ammunition, Stowage

37 mm (H.E., M54; A.P., M74; A.P.C., M59)	200 rounds
Cal. .50	1,200 rounds

Armor
  Chassis—Same as Half Track Personnel Carrier, M3, omitting side and rear body armor
  Gun Shield—rotating................¼ in.

Vision and Fire Control
  Computing Sight, M14................1
  Bore Sight...........................1

Communications
  Radio.........................SCR–510

Battery, Voltage, total...................12

Fire Protection and Decontamination
  Fire Extinguisher, CO₂–2 lb..............1
  Decontaminating Apparatus, M2, 1½ qts....1

(Other characteristics essentially same as for Half Track Personnel Carrier, M3.)

MULTIPLE GUN MOTOR CARRIAGE, M13, consists of a Twin cal. .50 Machine Gun Mount, M33, developed by the W. L. Maxson Co., on a modified Half Track Personnel Carrier, M3. Standardized in September, 1942, it was redesignated Substitute Standard upon standardization of Multiple Gun Motor Carriage, M16.

Principal armament is two cal. .50 Machine Guns, M2, HB (TT), in a power-operated turret. The turret has a traverse of 360° and may be elevated from −10° to +90°, except in front where depression is limited to +5° because of the projection of the cab. The guns may be elevated and traversed at infinitely variable speeds ranging from 0° to 60° per second.

Each gun will fire 400 to 500 rounds per minute, and has a maximum range of 7,200 yards. Standard ammunition feed boxes of 200 rounds capacity each are provided. Fire control is by a Navy Mark IX reflex sight. Provision is made for carrying a cal. .45 submachine gun, a cal. .30 rifle and three cal. .30 carbines.

The crew consists of a gunner, two loaders, a driver and the commander.

Armor is the same as on Half Track Personnel Carrier, M3, except that the upper sides and rear are hinged and can be folded downward to permit firing at −10°. A ¼-inch frontal armor shield is provided for the protection of the gunner.

The vehicles are manufactured by the Autocar Co., the Diamond T Motor Co. and the White Motor Co.

REFERENCES — OCM 17848, 17928, 18627, 18681, 18839, 19264, 19430.

MULTIPLE GUN MOTOR CARRIAGE, M14, consists of a twin cal. .50 Machine Gun Mount, M33, mounted on a Half

TWIN CAL. .50 MACHINE GUN MOUNT ON MULTIPLE GUN MOTOR CARRIAGE, M13 OR M14

Track Personnel Carrier, M5. It is similar to the M13, except for the variations in the basic vehicles.

It was designated Substitute Standard in October, 1942. The vehicles are manufactured by the International Harvester Co.

REFERENCES—TM 9–707; OCM 18694.

MULTIPLE GUN MOTOR CARRIAGE, M17, consists of four cal. .50 Machine Guns, M2, HB (TT), in a Multiple Mount, M45, mounted on a Half Track Personnel Carrier, M5.

It is similar to Multiple Gun Motor Carriage, M16, except for the variations in the basic vehicles.

It was designated as Substitute Standard by Ordnance Committee action in December, 1942. The vehicles are manufactured by the International Harvester Co.

REFERENCES—TM 9–707; OCM 19264, 19430.

TYPICAL CHARACTERISTICS

GUN MOTOR CARRIAGES, M13, M14

Crew 5

Armament
2 cal. .50 Machine Guns, M2, HB (TT), w/Edgewater adapter
  On Twin cal. .50 Machine Gun Mount, M33
Provision for:
1 cal. .45 Submachine Gun ⎫
1 cal. .30 Rifle, M1903   ⎬ Equipment of crew
3 cal. .30 Carbines   ⎭
1 Grenade Launcher, M1 . . . . For rifle

Ammunition, Stowage
Cal. .50 . . . . 5,000 rounds
Cal. .45 . . . . 480 rounds
Grenades (Hand: Fragmentation, Mk. II, 12; Smoke, M8, 12; Thermite, Incendiary, 2; Rifle: M9A1, 10) 36

Vision and Fire Control
Reflex Sight, Mark IX (Navy)

Communications
Radio . . . . SCR-528 or British 19
Flag Set, M238 1

GUN MOTOR CARRIAGE, M17

Crew 5

Armament
4 cal. .50 Machine Guns, M2, HB (TT), w/o Edgewater Adapter . . On Multiple cal. .50 Machine Gun Mount, M45
Provision for:
1 cal. .45 Submachine Gun ⎫
1 cal. .30 Rifle, M1903   ⎬ Equipment of crew
3 cal. .30 Carbines, M1   ⎭
1 Grenade Launcher, M1 . . . . For rifle

Ammunition, Stowage
Cal. .50 . . . . 5,000 rounds
Cal. .45 . . . . 420 rounds
Grenades (Hand: Fragmentation, Mk. II, 12; Smoke, M8, 12; Thermite, Incendiary, 2; Rifle: M9A1, 10) 36

Vision
Direct . . . . Slits in shields

Communications
Radio . . . . SCR-528 or British 19
Flag Set, M238 1

MULTIPLE CAL. .50 MACHINE GUN MOUNT, M45

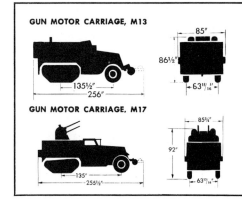

GUN MOTOR CARRIAGE, M13

85″
86½″
135½″
256″
63¹¹⁄₁₆″

GUN MOTOR CARRIAGE, M17

85¾″
92″
135″
255½″
63¹¹⁄₁₆″

MULTIPLE GUN MOTOR CARRIAGE M16—STANDARD

MULTIPLE GUN MOTOR CARRIAGE, M16, MOUNTS 4 CAL. .50 MACHINE GUNS IN MAXSON TURRET; HAS FOLDING ARMOR AT SIDES AND REAR

This weapon consists of four cal. .50 Machine Guns, M2, HB (TT), in a Multiple Mount, M45, mounted on a Half Track Personnel Carrier, M3.

The mount, known as the Maxson turret, is essentially the same as that used on Multiple Gun Motor Carriage, M13, which it replaced in production, but is modified to permit the use of four cal. .50 guns, instead of two.

Each gun will fire 400 to 500 rounds per minute, and has a maximum range of 7,200 yards. The turret may be elevated from −10° to +90°, and has a traverse of 360° at a maximum speed of 60° per second. Interrupter switches prevent firing when the guns enter the driver's compartment-area. Provision is made to align the guns with each other and with the sight by means of adjustment for vertical and horizontal alignment.

The gunner sits in a 45° reclining position on a fabric seat adjustable to his height. The seat is arranged to provide a comfortable position and to permit the gunner to rest his elbows against the seat or his body while aiming. This results in stability of control and minimum fatigue.

The sight and guns pivot about an axis running approximately through the gunner's ears. He can conveniently follow the sight in any position without moving.

Control grips are mounted on a handlebar located on a post between the gunner's knees. Each grip contains a "dead man's" switch and a trigger switch, either of which will fire all guns. Rotation of the handlebars in the vertical plane controls elevation and in the horizontal plane controls traverse. The guns may be trained precisely when following a target and yet may be slewed rapidly to pick up a new target.

The crew consists of five men, the driver and commander, two loaders, and the gunner. Provision is made for carrying one cal. .45 submachine gun, one cal. .30 rifle with grenade launcher, and three cal. .30 carbines.

The gunner is protected from the front against small arms fire by a shield of armor plate. The vehicular armor is substantially the same as on Half Track Personnel Carrier, M3. Armor at the sides and rear of the vehicle may be folded down when the guns are in use. Two cargo boxes are provided at the rear of the vehicle.

REFERENCES — OCM 17848, 17928, 17969, 18020, 18627, 18681, 18839, 18845, 18964, 19140, 19264, 19430, 20680, 20726, 21002.

TYPICAL CHARACTERISTICS

Crew 5

Physical Characteristics
Weight (gross) . . . . 19,800 lb.
Length . . . . 21 ft., 4 ins.
Width . . . . 7 ft., 1 in.
Height . . . . 7 ft., 8 ins.
Height of center line of bore . . . . . . 6 ft., 3 ins.
Ground clearance . . . . 11$\frac{3}{16}$ ins.
Tread, rear . . . . 63$\frac{13}{16}$ ins.
Wheelbase . . . . 135$\frac{1}{2}$ ins.
Tire equipment . . . . 8.25 x 20, 12 ply (combat)

Armament
4 cal. .50 Machine Guns, M2, HB (TT),
w/o Edgewater Adapter . . . On Multiple cal.
.50 Machine Gun Mount, M45
Provision for:
1 cal. .45 Submachine Gun ⎫
1 cal. .30 Rifle, M1903 ⎬ Equipment of crew
3 cal. .30 Carbines, M1 ⎭
1 Grenade Launcher, M1 . . . . For rifle

Ammunition, Stowage
Cal. .50 . . . . 5,000 rounds
Cal. .45 . . . . 420 rounds
Grenades (Hand: Fragmentation, Mk. II,
12; Smoke, M8, 12; Thermite, Incendiary, 2; Rifle: M9A1, 10) 36

Vision—Direct . . . . Slits in shields

Communications—Radio. SCR-528 or British 19
Flag Set, M238 1

Fire Protection and Decontamination
Fire Extinguisher, CO₂-2 lb. (hand) 1
Decontaminating Apparatus, M2, 1½ qts. . . . 1

(Other characteristics same as for Half Track Personnel Carrier, M3.)

76 MM GUN MOTOR CARRIAGE M18—STANDARD

76 MM GUN MOTOR CARRIAGE, M18, HAS SLOPING ARMOR AND USES TORSION BAR SUSPENSION; MOUNTS MACHINE GUN ABOVE OPEN TURRET

This is a highly mobile, low-silhouette, lightly armored 76 mm gun motor carriage designed for tank destroyer use.

It is of the full track-laying type, using a torsion bar independent suspension, front-sprocket driven. Sloping armor is used, affording good ballistic qualities.

Principal armament is a 76 mm Gun, M1A1 or M1A2, in an open-top turret with a partial turret basket. The gun can be elevated from — 10° to + 19½°. The turret can be traversed through 360°. A ring mount for a cal. .50 machine gun is provided on the top of the open turret for antiaircraft protection. Provision is made for carrying five cal. .30 carbines.

The A.P.C. projectile, M62, fired in the 76 mm gun, with a muzzle velocity of 2,600 feet per second, will penetrate 4-inch face-hardened armor plate at 1,000 yards.

Driver and assistant driver occupy seats in the hull, and the gunner, loader, and commander in the turret. Two escape hatches are in the hull roof and one in the floor. Periscopes, M6, are provided for the driver and assistant, and a Periscope, M4 or M4A1, with Telescope, M47 or M47A2, for the gunner.

Power is supplied by a Continental R975–C1 or –C4 gasoline engine. Transmission is torqmatic, with three speeds forward and one reverse.

An SCR–610 or British No. 19 Radio is provided, as well as interphone stations.

The pilot vehicle was built by the Buick Motor Division, General Motors Corp.

REFERENCES — OCM 19185, 19319, 19438, 19628, 20584, 21523, 22918, 23202.

TYPICAL CHARACTERISTICS

Crew 5

Physical Characteristics
Weight (gross, approx.)	40,000 lb.
Length—to end of gun	21 ft., 10 ins.
excluding gun	17 ft., 4 ins.
Width	9 ft., 2 ins.
Height	8 ft., 5 in. over A.A. Gun
Ground clearance	14 ins.
Tread (center to center of tracks)	95 ins.
Ground contact length	116 ins.
Ground pressure	12.5 lb./sq. in.

Armament
76 mm Gun, M1A1 or M1A2, in open top turret (with partial basket) . . . . In Mount, M1
Elevation	—10° to +19½°
Traverse	360°

1 cal. .50 Machine Gun,
M2, HB . . . . On Ring Mount
1 Tripod Mount, cal. .50, M3
Provision for:
5 cal. .30 Carbines, M1

Ammunition, Stowage
76 mm (A.P.C., M62; A.P., M79; H.E., M42A1; Smoke, M88) . . . . 45 rounds

Cal. .30 Carbine	450 rounds
Cal. .50 Machine Gun	800 rounds
Grenades, Hand (Smoke, WP, M8, 6; Fragmentation, Mk. II, 6)	12
Smoke Pots	4

Armor — Actual
Hull,
Front, sides, and rear	½ in.
Top	5/16 in.
Bottom	¼ in.

Turret
Front w/gunshield	¾–1 in.
Sides and rear	½ in.

Performance
Sustained speed on level	50 m.p.h.
Speed on 10% grade	15 m.p.h.
Maximum grade ability	60%
Vertical obstacle ability	36 ins.
Fording depth (slowest forward speed)	48 ins.
Fuel capacity	165 gals.
Cruising range	150 miles

Vision and Fire Control
Periscope, M6	2
Periscope, M4 or M4A1, w/Telescope, M47 or M47A2, and Instrument Light, M30 for M4A1	1

Telescope, M76C, w/Instrument Light,
M33, or Telescope, M70H, w/Instrument
Light, M32	1
Telescope Mount, M55	1
Elevation Quadrant, M9, w/Instrument Light, M30	1
Azimuth Indicator, M20 or M18	1

Communications
Radio	SCR–610 or British No. 19
Interphone stations	5

Battery, Voltage, total 24

Fire Protection and Decontamination
Fire Extinguisher, CO₂–10 lb. (fixed)	1
CO₂–4 lb. (hand)	1
Decontaminating Apparatus, M2, 1½ qts.	1

TWIN 40 MM GUN MOTOR CARRIAGE M19—STANDARD

TWIN 40 MM GUN MOTOR CARRIAGE, M19, SHOWING GUNS IN TRAVELING POSITION. VEHICLE USES LIGHT TANK, M24, CHASSIS

This lightly armored, low silhouette, high-speed, twin 40 mm gun motor carriage, designed for protection of armored force and motor columns against aircraft, was standardized in June, 1944, to replace Combination Gun Motor Carriage, M15A1.

It consists of one 40 mm Dual Automatic Gun, M2, on Twin 40 mm Gun Mount, M4, on a modified Light Tank, M24, chassis. The gun can be elevated from −5° to +85°, and has a traverse of 360° in a power-operated turret.

The 40 mm A.P. Shot, M81A1, fired from the gun, has a muzzle velocity of 2,870 feet per second. It has a maximum range of 9,475 yards horizontal, and will penetrate 1.6 inches of 20° obliquity face-hardened armor plate at 1,000 yards. The 40 mm H.E. Shell, Mk. II, also has a muzzle velocity of 2,870 feet per second. It has a horizontal range of 10,820 yards and a vertical range of 7,625 yards. The dual gun can be fired at the rate of 240 rounds per minute. It can be traversed at speeds up to 40° per second.

Provision is made for carrying four carbines. Sheet-metal, dust-proof and water-proof ammunition containers are furnished.

The crew consists of six men. The driver and assistant driver occupy seats in the front of the hull. The commander and gun crew members occupy seats in the semi-open turret, which is at the rear of the vehicle. A 5/16-in. belt of vertically disposed plate incloses the gun mount on all

sides. Additional ½-in. frontal shields protect the gunners.

An individually sprung, compensated torsion bar suspension is used, together with a single-pin, rubber-bushed, center guide track.

The driver and assistant driver have direct vision, and are provided with a periscope each for use in combat areas. A Computing Sight, M13, and Local Control System, M16, are furnished for use by the gun crew.

REFERENCES — OCM 19046, 19133, 19846, 20035, 20297, 20394, 20583, 20705, 22629, 20446, 21699, 23746, 24133, 24244.

TYPICAL CHARACTERISTICS

Crew..6

Physical Characteristics
Weight (gross, approx.)...........38,500 lb.
Length...................17 ft., 11 ins.
Width......................9 ft., 4 ins.
Height (overall)............9 ft., 9½ ins.
Turret ring diameter (inside)...........31 ins.
Ground clearance...............17 ins.
Tread (center to center of tracks).......96 ins.
Ground contact length.............124 ins.
Ground pressure.............9.7 lb./sq. in.

Armament
1 40 mm Dual Automatic Gun, M2, on Twin
40 mm Gun Mount, M4
Elevation....................−5° to +85°
Traverse.........................360°
Provision for:
4 cal. .30 Carbines, M1
1 Grenade Launcher for Carbine
1 cal. .45 Submachine Gun, M3

Ammunition, Stowage
40 mm.....................336 rounds
Cal. .30 carbine...............480 rounds
Grenades, Hand (Smoke, WP, M15, 6; Fragmentation, Mk. II, 6; Rifle, M9A1, 10)..........................22
Cal. .45 (in 30-rd. clips).........570 rounds

Armor
Hull, Front.....................½ in.
Sides.......................½ in.
Rear........................¼ in.
Top (over driver)................½ in.
Roof (over engine compartment).....¼ in.
Bottom, forward of 2nd suspension....½ in.
remainder...................⅜ in.
Turret, Sides...................⁵⁄₁₆ in.
Gun shields....................½ in.

Performance
Maximum speed on level..........35 m.p.h.
on 3% grade.................18 m.p.h.
on 10% grade................11 m.p.h.
Maximum grade ability.............60%
Trench crossing ability............8 ft.
Vertical obstacle ability...........40 ins.
Fording depth (slowest forward speed)..42 ins.
Turning radius.................20 ft.
Fuel capacity.................115 gals.
Cruising range (approx.)......100–160 miles
Maximum tractive effort.........26,950 lb.

Vision and Fire Control
Periscopes, M6...................2
Computing Sight, M13...............1
Local Control System, M16............1

Communications
Radio.....SCR–510 or 528 or British No. 19
Interphone stations.................4

Battery, Voltage, total.................24

Fire Protection and Decontamination
Fire Extinguisher, CO₂–10 lb. (fixed).......1
CO₂–4 lb. (hand).................2
Decontaminating Apparatus, M2, 1½ qts....3

(Other characteristics same as for Light Tank, M24.)

59

90 MM GUN MOTOR CARRIAGE M36—STANDARD

90 MM GUN MOTOR CARRIAGE, M36. RIGHT FRONT VIEW, WITH COVER OVER MACHINE GUN. WHILE TRAVELING, TURRET IS TURNED TOWARD REAR

This is a modification of the 3-Inch Gun Motor Carriage, M10A1, designed to provide a more powerful self-propelled antitank gun. It was standardized in June, 1944.

Principal weapon is the 90 mm Gun, M3, in 90 mm Gun Mount, M4, in a semi-open top turret with 360° power traverse.

The gun can be elevated from −10° to +20°. Using A. P. C. projectile, M82, with a muzzle velocity of 2,670 feet per second, it has a maximum range of 15,600 yards. This projectile is capable of penetrating 3 inches of homogeneous armor at ranges up to 4,700 yards. A cal. .50 Machine Gun, M2, HB (flexible), on a pedestal mount on the turret, is provided.

A new turret with a partial turret basket is used. Seats, traversing with the turret, are provided for the gunner, loader, and commander.

The chassis is essentially the same as that of the 3-Inch Gun Motor Carriage, M10A1. To provide for the stowage of 90 mm ammunition, the sponson stiffener brackets were moved forward. An auxiliary generator was installed in the engine compartment, and a bracket installed to hold the trunnions of the slip ring. The hull electrical installation was modified to accommodate the auxiliary generator and the slip ring. The hinging of the subfloor doors was changed, and the fixed fire extinguisher cover was modified.

Power is supplied by a Ford GAA gasoline engine.

Pilot vehicles were manufactured by the Chevrolet Division of the General Motors Corporation.

TYPICAL CHARACTERISTICS

Crew. 5

Physical Characteristics

Weight (gross). . . . . .62,000 lb.
(net). . . . . .57,000 lb.
Length. . . . . .20 ft., 2 ins.
Width. . . . . .10 ft.
Height—pedestal A. A. gun
folded. . . . . .8 ft., 11 ins.
Ground clearance. . . . . .17⅛ ins.
Tread (center to center of tracks). . . . . .83 ins.
Ground contact length. . . . . .147 ins.
Ground pressure. . . . . .12.7 lb./sq. in.

Armament

90 mm Gun, M3, in Mount, M4. . . . .In turret
Elevation. . . . .−10° to +20°
Traverse. .360°
Cal. .50 Machine Gun, M2, HB
(flexible). . . . . .On pedestal mount
1 Tripod Mount, Cal. .50, M3
Provision for:
5 cal. .30 Carbines, M1A2

Ammunition, Stowage

90 mm (H.E., M71; A.P.C., M82). .47 rounds
Cal. .50. . . . . .1,000 rounds
Cal. .30 Carbine, M1. . . . . .450 rounds
Grenades, Hand (Fragmentation, Mk. II,
6; Smoke, M15, 6). 12
Smoke Pots, H.C., M1. 4

Armor

	Actual	Basis
Hull, Front, Upper	1½ ins.	3¼ ins.
Lower	2 ins.	3¾ ins.
Sides, Upper	¾ ins.	1⅜ ins.
Lower	1½ ins.	
Rear, Upper	¾ in.	1 in.
Lower	1½ ins.	
Top, Forward	¾ in.	
Rear	⅜ in.	
Bottom	½ in.	
Turret, Front	3 ins.	
Sides	1¼ ins.	1½ ins.
Top	1⅛ ins.	
Rear	4 ins.	

Performance

Maximum speed on level. . . . . .30 m.p.h.
Speed on 3% grade. . . . . .20 m.p.h.
10% grade. . . . . .12 m.p.h.
Maximum grade ability. 60%
Trench crossing ability. . . . . . .7 ft., 5 ins.
Vertical obstacle ability. . . . . .24 ins.
Fording depth (slowest forward speed). .36 ins.
Fuel capacity. . . . . .192 gals.
Cruising range. . . . . .150 miles

Vision and Fire Control

Periscopes, M6. 3
Telescope, M71C or M76D or M76F,
w/Instrument Light, M33. 1
Telescope Mount, M64 (T92). 1
Elevation Quadrant, M9, w/Instrument
Light, M30. 1
Azimuth Indicator, M20 or M18. 1
Gunner's Quadrant, M1. 1

Communications

Radio. . .SCR-510 or 610 (with Reel Assembly,
RL-106/V1) or British No. 19
Interphone stations. 5
Flag Set, M238. 1

Fire Protection and Decontamination

Fire Extinguisher—10 lb.-CO_2 (fixed). 2
4 lb.-CO_2 (hand). 2
Decontaminating Apparatus, M2, 1½ qts.. . .1

(Other characteristics same as for Medium Tank, M4A3.)

REFERENCES—OCM 18944, 19055, 19845, 20144, 21210, 21512, 22129, 22336, 22588, 22632, 23978, 24206, 24985.

HALF TRACK 81 MM MORTAR CARRIERS M4, M4A1—LIMITED STANDARD
HALF TRACK 81 MM MORTAR CARRIER M21—STANDARD

HALF TRACK 81 MM MORTAR CARRIER, M21, HAS MORTAR MOUNTED TO FRONT

OVERHEAD VIEW, SHOWING STOWAGE

These vehicles are designed to give greater mobility to the 81 mm Mortar, M1, which can be used on the vehicle or separate from it.

HALF TRACK 81 mm MORTAR CARRIER, M4, consists of the 81 mm Mortar, M1, mounted on a Half Track Car, M2, to fire to the rear. It was designed in 1940 with provisions made to fire the weapon from the vehicle in extreme emergencies only. The traverse is limited to that contained in the bipod (130 mils). Standardized in October, 1940, it was reclassified as Limited Standard in December, 1942.

HALF TRACK 81 mm MORTAR CARRIER, M4A1, is generally the same as the Half Track 81 mm Mortar Carrier, M4, with modifications to permit the weapon to be placed in action with greater rapidity.

The 81 mm Mortar, M1, has a traverse of 600 mils, and can be elevated from +40° to +80°. It can be fired from the chassis in all ordinary firing problems. Using H.E. projectile, M43A1, with a muzzle velocity of 700 feet per second, it has a range of 3,288 yards at 45° elevation.

A cal. .30 Browning machine gun is provided, which can be used from the gun rail which surrounds the top of the body, or separate from the vehicle. Provisions are made for carrying a Rocket Launcher, A.T., 2.36", M1, and a cal. .45 submachine gun, which are the personal equipment of the crew members.

Armor is the same as on Half Track Car, M2, and performance is essentially the same.

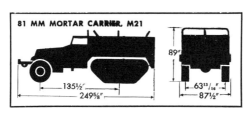

81 MM MORTAR CARRIER, M21

135½"
249⅝"
89"
63¹³/₁₆"
87½"

Standardized in December, 1942, it was reclassified as Limited Standard in July, 1943.

HALF TRACK 81 mm MORTAR CARRIER, M21, standardized in July, 1943, is based on the Half Track Personnel Carrier, M3, with winch, instead of the Half Track Car, M2, and is modified to allow the mortar to fire to the front.

Principal armament consists of the 81 mm Mortar, M1, with 81 mm Mortar Mount, M1, designed so that the base plate of the mount can be used in firing from the ground. It has an elevation of +40° to +85°, and a traverse of 60° to the front. Fire control is provided by Sight, M6.

A cal. .50 Machine Gun, M2, HB (flexible), is provided and can be used from a pedestal mount on the vehicle, or from a Tripod Mount, M3, on the ground. Provisions are made for carrying a cal. .45 submachine gun and a Rocket Launcher, M1.

Armor is the same as on Half Track Personnel Carrier, M3, and the vehicle performance characteristics are the same. A two-way radio is provided.

The pilot vehicles were manufactured by the White Motor Co.

REFERENCES—TM 9-710; OCM 16112, 16187, 18312, 18963, 19607, 19821, 19980, 20064, 20846, 21142; SNL G-102, vol. 15.

CHARACTERISTICS OF HALF TRACK 81 MM MORTAR CARRIER, M21

Crew 6
Physical Characteristics
  Weight (gross) . . . . 18,500 lb.
  Length, with winch . . . . 20 ft., 9⅝ ins.
  Width . . . . 7 ft., 3½ ins.
  Height—over bows . . . . 7 ft., 5 ins.
  Ground clearance . . . . 11³/₁₆ ins.
  Tread—front . . . . 64½ ins.
    rear . . . . 63¹³/₁₆ ins.
  Wheelbase . . . . 135½ ins.
  Ground contact length . . . . 46¾ ins.
  Tire equipment . . . . . 8.25x20, 12 ply (combat)
Armament
  81 mm Mortar, M1, with 81 mm Mortar Mount, M1 (Base plate of mount to be used in firing from ground)
    Elevation . . . . +40° to +85°
    Traverse . . . . 60° to front
  1 cal. .50 Machine Gun, M2, HB (flexible), on Pedestal Mount
  1 cal. .50 Tripod Mount, M3
  Provision for:
    1 cal. .45 Submachine Gun
    1 Rocket Launcher, M1
Ammunition, Stowage
  81 mm (H.E., M43A1; W.P., M57; or H.E., M58) . . . . 97 rounds
  Cal. .50 . . . . 400 rounds
  Cal. .45 . . . . 600 rounds
  Grenades, Hand (Offensive, Mk. III, 2; Fragmentation, Mk. II, 4; Smoke, HC, M8, 4; Thermite Incendiary, 2) 12
  Rockets, A.T., 2.36-in. 6
  Mines, A.T., M1A1 12
Fire Control
  Sight, M6 1
Communications
  Radio, SCR-509 or SCR-510, less Battery Case, CS-79 1
  Flag Set, M238 1
Fire Protection and Decontamination
  Fire Extinguisher
    CO₂-2 lb. (hand) 1
  Decontaminating Apparatus, M2, 1½ qts. . . . 3

(Other characteristics same as for Half Track Personnel Carrier, M3.)

VEHICULAR MACHINE GUN MOUNTS

Development of the machine gun mounts shown in these pages converts each vehicle so equipped into a potent weapon against aircraft and against personnel.

The principal types, as illustrated, are the pedestal truck mounts, the dash mount, and the ring mounts for trucks and other vehicles.

PEDESTAL TRUCK MOUNTS

Each mount consists essentially of a pintle or cradle-pintle assembly and a pedestal body. The pintle is rotatable in a socket of the pedestal body, and can be locked at any point of traverse by means of a clamping screw.

PEDESTAL TRUCK MOUNT M24 was designed for the ½-Ton, 4x4, Weapons Carrier Truck.

Inasmuch as the vehicle was classified as Limited Standard, Pedestal Truck Mount M24 was reclassified as Limited Standard in July 1942.

The mount is suitable for mounting the Cal. .50 Machine Gun M2 IIB, the Cal. .30 Machine Gun M1919A4, the Cal. .30 Machine Gun M1917A1, and the Browning automatic rifle. The mount is attached to the front panel of the truck body, to the rear of and between the driver's and assistant driver's seats.

REFERENCES—TM 9–224; OCM 16294, 16373, 18357, 18563; SNL A–55, Sec. 16, Add.

PEDESTAL TRUCK MOUNT M24C is the designation applied to Pedestal Truck Mount M24 when Pintle D38579 is replaced by the improved cradle, pintle, and ammunition box holder assembly E10014. The latter assembly provides for use of standard Ammunition Boxes M1 and M2, although normally only the Cal. .50 Machine Gun M2 HB will be used with this mount.

REFERENCES—OCM 24118, 24328.

PEDESTAL TRUCK MOUNT M24A1 is a modification of Pedestal Mount M24 to adapt it for use on the ¾-Ton, 4x4, Truck. Standardized in July 1942, it was reclassified as Limited Standard in December 1943.

It is suitable for mounting the Cal. .30 Machine Guns M1917A1 and M1919A4 and the Browning automatic rifle. Because of excessive dispersion, it is not suitable for the cal. .50 machine gun.

REFERENCES—TM 9–224; OCM 18357, 18563, 21990, 22263; SNL A–55, Sec. 16, Add.

PEDESTAL TRUCK MOUNT M24A2 is a redesign of Pedestal Truck Mount M24A1 strengthened for use with the cal. .50 machine gun as well as the cal. .30 machine gun. A new cradle and pintle assembly with an ammunition box holder suitable for use with standard cal. .30 and cal. .50 ammunition boxes is included. The mount is adaptable to the ¾-Ton, 4x4, and 1½-Ton, 6x6, Trucks. It was standardized in December 1943.

REFERENCES — OCM 20147, 21990, 22263.

PEDESTAL TRUCK MOUNT M25 is designed for Half-Track Personnel Carriers M3 and M5. It mounts the Cal. .30 Machine Gun M1919A4.

REFERENCES—TM 9–224; OCM 16575; SNL A–55, Sec. 17, Add.

PEDESTAL TRUCK MOUNT M31 is designed for mounting a machine gun on the ¼-Ton, 4x4, Truck. It is used by all services other than the Infantry.

It consists of a vertical pedestal, with attachments for mounting and bracing the gun, fastened to the floor by a base plate and given additional support by three steel braces. The mount is fastened at the front of the cargo compartment, with one supporting brace positioned between the two seats in the driver's compartment.

PEDESTAL MOUNT M31 ON ¼-TON TRUCK

This mount is suitable for mounting Cal. .30 Machine Guns M1917A1 and M1919A4, the Cal. .50 Machine Gun M2 HB, and the Browning automatic rifle.

One ammunition tray each for the Cal. .30 Machine Gun M1919A4 and the Cal. .50 Machine Gun M2 is supplied with each mount.

REFERENCES—TM 9–224; OCM 16805, 16914, 18338, 18479; SNL A–55, Sec. 18, Add.

PEDESTAL TRUCK MOUNT M31C is the designation applied to Pedestal Truck Mount M31 when Pintle D38579 is replaced by the improved cradle, pintle, and ammunition box holder assembly E10014. The latter assembly provides for use of standard Ammunition Boxes M1 and M2, although normally only the Cal. .50 Machine Gun M2 HB will be used with this mount.

REFERENCE—OCM 24118, 24328.

MACHINE GUN MOUNT M35 consists of a carriage and cradle assembly designed for use on skate rails, as on Scout Car

CAL. .30 MACHINE GUN MOUNT M48 ON DASH OF ¼-TON TRUCK

PEDESTAL MOUNT M24A2 WITH CAL. .50 MACHINE GUN

MACHINE GUN MOUNT M35 ON SKATE RAIL OF HALF-TRACK CAR M2

RING MOUNT M66 ON HIGH SPEED TRACTOR M4. NOTE BACK REST

M3A1, Half-Track 81-mm Mortar Carrier M4A1, Half-Track Car M2, and Landing Vehicles, Tracked. It will mount either the Cal. .50 Machine Gun M2 HB or the Cal. .30 Machine Gun M1919A4.

REFERENCES—OCM 18312; SNL A–55, Sec. 28.

MACHINE GUN MOUNT M35C is the designation applied to the M35 when Cradle Assembly D54075 is replaced by cradle, pintle, and ammunition box holder assembly E10014. The latter assembly provides for use of standard Ammunition Boxes M1 and M2, although normally only the Cal. .50 Machine Gun M2 HB will be used with this mount.

REFERENCES—OCM 24118, 24328.

DASH MOUNT

CAL. .30 MACHINE GUN MOUNT M48 is a dash mount for the Cal. .30 Machine Guns M1917A1 and M1919A4 and the Browning automatic rifle, for use on the ¼-Ton, 4x4, Truck. It was designed by the Infantry Board and revised slightly after

TRUCK MOUNT M36 ON OPEN CAB TRUCK

testing at the Aberdeen Proving Ground. The mount was standardized in March 1943 for use by the Infantry.

The mount is attachable to the extreme right side of the instrument panel of the truck, and is intended for fire against ground targets and limited use against aerial targets. It consists of a bracket employing the pintle supplied with Pedestal Truck Mounts M24, M24A1, and M31, and is attached by bolts to the dash.

By means of an adapter developed by Aberdeen Proving Ground, the Cal. .30 Ammunition Box M1 can be used with the Cal. .30 Machine Gun M1919A4 on this mount. The cradle assembly of the Tripod Mount M1917A1 will ordinarily be used in lieu of the Pintle D38579 to mount the Machine Gun M1917A1. This cradle assembly permits mounting of the Cal. .30 Ammunition Box M1 thereon, and eliminates the necessity for an adapter with this weapon.

REFERENCES—TM 9–224; OCM 18388, 18479, 19746, 19991, 20727, 21412; SNL A–55, Sec. 32.

RING MOUNTS

Each mount consists essentially of a circular track on which is mounted a carriage assembly, a cradle assembly, and an ammunition box for a machine gun.

The cradle, which allows elevations from −20° to + 85°, is rotatable in the pintle sleeve of the carriage, which is guided on the track by means of rollers, providing a traverse of 360°.

The mount is supported above a vehicle in such a manner as to permit the machine gunner to stand within the ring while operating the gun, firing against a fast-moving aerial target, without moving from his position.

The designation, Ring Mount, is applied to those components which are common to all vehicle installations without reference to the supporting structure.

REFERENCES—TM 9–224; OCM 17761, 18562, 20099, 20721, 20722, 21420, 21954, 23016, 23802, 24570, 24776; SNL A–55, Sec. 19.

RING MOUNT M49 is the basic ring mount used on truck mounts as well as on half tracks and various other vehicles.

RING MOUNT M49C designed for use on high-speed tractors, makes use of a track with a slightly different cross-section from the original ring. It is provided with a continuous flange throughout its entire circumference, to provide a seal against water and foreign matter when installed in the roof of a vehicle.

RING MOUNT M66 is a roller-bearing mount for the Cal. .50 Machine Gun M2 HB. It is similar in appearance and size to the Ring Mount M49C, but because of its roller-bearing construction the entire inner ring is turned to traverse the gun. The gun is mounted at the front of the inner ring in an equilibrated cradle assembly similar to that used on light and medium tanks. A padded back rest, which is fastened to the rear of the inner ring, enables the gunner to control the traverse of the weapon through 360° by the use of his body. This mount was standardized in August 1944 for use on the Armored Utility Car M20, 18-Ton High-Speed Tractor M4, and 38-Ton High-Speed Tractor M6.

TRUCK MOUNTS

The designation, Truck Mount, is applied to a ring mount together with the supporting structure designed for use on a particular truck. The mount is supported above the assistant driver's seat, and is manned by the assistant driver, standing on the seat cushion or on a firing platform provided by folding the seat back and down over the cushion. It is suitable for either the cal. .30 or cal. .50 machine gun.

VEHICULAR MACHINE GUN MOUNTS (Continued)

TRUCK MOUNT M32 IS USED ON 2½-TON, CLOSED CAB TRUCKS

TRUCK MOUNT M37 ON SHORT WHEELBASE, CLOSED CAB TRUCK

REFERENCES—TM 9–224; OCM 17600, 17720, 17761, 18562, 20100, 20582, 22212, 24052, 24263; SNL A–55, Sec. 19.

TRUCK MOUNT M32 is designed for 2½-ton, 6x6, long wheelbase, closed cab trucks, with conventional steel bodies.

TRUCK MOUNT M36 is designed for 2½-ton, or larger, trucks with open cabs, as follows:

2½-ton, 6x6, G.M.C., long wheelbase, short wheelbase, cab-over-engine, water tank, gasoline tank, dump, and amphibian types with open cabs.

4-ton, 6x6, Diamond T, short wheelbase, long wheelbase and wrecker, with open cabs.

4–5 ton, 4x4, open cab tractor (Federal and Autocar).

5-ton, 4x2, open cab tractors, short wheelbase, heavy duty and light duty (International).

5–6 ton, 4x4, open cab tractor (Autocar).

6-ton, 6x6, open cab prime mover (White and Corbitt).

7½-ton, 6x6, open cab prime mover (Mack).

Heavy Wrecking Truck M1A1.

10-ton, 6x4, G.S.L.C., open cab (Mack).

12-ton, 6x4, Truck M20, open cab.

TRUCK MOUNT M37 is designed for 2½-ton, 6x6, short wheelbase, closed cab trucks, with conventional steel bodies.

TRUCK MOUNT M37A1 is designed for 2½-ton, 6x6, short wheelbase, closed cab trucks, with wood bodies.

TRUCK MOUNT M37A2 is designed for 2½-ton, 6x6, long wheelbase, closed cab trucks, with wood bodies.

TRUCK MOUNT M37A3 is designed for the camouflaged 2½-ton, 6x6, 750-gallon gasoline tank truck and 700-gallon water tank truck.

TRUCK MOUNT M50 is designed for the 1½-ton, 6x6, truck.

TRUCK MOUNT M56 is designed for closed cab, 4-ton, 6x6, trucks; cargo, short wheelbase; cargo, long wheelbase; and wrecker (Diamond T).

TRUCK MOUNT M57 is designed for 6-ton, 6x6, closed cab prime mover and 2,000-gal. gasoline tank trucks (White).

TRUCK MOUNT M58 is designed for 6-ton, 6x6, closed cab, prime mover truck (Corbitt).

TRUCK MOUNT M59 is designed for 6-ton, 6x6, closed cab, bridge erecting truck (Brockway).

TRUCK MOUNT M60 is designed for 4-5 ton, 4x4, closed cab tractor truck (Federal).

TRUCK MOUNT M61 is designed for 4-5 ton, 4x4, closed cab tractor truck and 5-6 ton, 4x4, closed cab tractor truck (Autocar).

TRUCK MOUNT M56 ON 4-TON, 6 X 6, CLOSED CAB CARGO TRUCK

TRUCK MOUNT M57 ON 6-TON, 6 X 6, CLOSED CAB PRIME MOVER

ARMORED TRAILER M8—LIMITED STANDARD

ARMORED TRAILER M8, WITH PINTLE HITCH FOLDED BACK ON FRAME

TYPICAL CHARACTERISTICS

Physical Characteristics

Weight (gross)..................5,058 lb.
(Trailer, 2,640 lb.; tank hitch, 218 lb.;
payload 2,200 lb.)

Length (over front lunette and
rear pintle)..................9 ft., 10¼ in.
Width........................7 ft., 4⅝ in.
Height........................4 ft., 4¼ in.

Inside Body Dimensions
Length........................4 ft., 8 in.
Width........................5 ft., ¾ in.
Depth........................2 ft., 4½ in.
Ground clearance................16½ in.

Tread (center to center of tires)..........75 in.
Tire equipment—combat tires......9.00 x 20

Armor

Cargo body—sides and rear............⅜ in.
front and top....................¼ in.

Coupling Devices

Lunette on frame in front
Pintle on rear (for tandem use)
Pintle hitch assembly with quick release pintle
provided with trailer (carried on lunette frame
when not in use)

Brakes, Parking.....................Hand

Armored Trailer M8 is a two-wheeled, rubber-tired vehicle, designed to be towed behind tanks and other combat vehicles or trucks. Standardized in September 1942, it was reclassified as Limited Standard by Ordnance Committee action in November 1943.

It is suitable for transporting fifty-four 5-gallon Quartermaster gasoline cans or the following rounds of ammunition:

105-mm howitzer, 42 rounds;
75-mm gun, 93 rounds;
37-mm gun, 360 rounds;
Cal. .50 machine gun, 25,200 rounds;
81-mm mortar, 222 rounds.

The body is constructed of ⅜-inch armor at the sides and rear, and ¼-inch armor at the front and top. The floor is not armored, but consists of a ⅛-inch steel floor plate with an additional ⅛-inch skid plate under the frame to prevent snagging. The body is mounted on a channel iron framework to which the axle also is welded. Two hinged covers permit access to the body. Web straps, inside the body and on the covers, hold the cargo in place.

The trailer is provided with a lunette frame, for use when towed by a vehicle equipped with a pintle. To permit use of the trailer with tanks not equipped with pintles, a hitch incorporating a pintle is supplied as a part of each trailer, and may be attached to the towing lugs on the rear of any type of tank. The hitch is equipped with a cable release, operated from the towing vehicle. The hitch may be folded back on the lunette frame when not in use.

A pintle on the rear of the trailer permits towing in tandem. There is a retractable pole prop for supporting the front of the trailer when detached from the vehicle.

The vehicle is equipped with parking brakes, operated by a hand lever located on the front of the body. Standard combat zone safety lights on the rear are operated from batteries carried on the trailer.

The vehicle was manufactured by John Deere & Co.

REFERENCES—TM 9–791; OCM 17970, 18063, 18350, 18520, 18840, 19781, 19986, 22361.

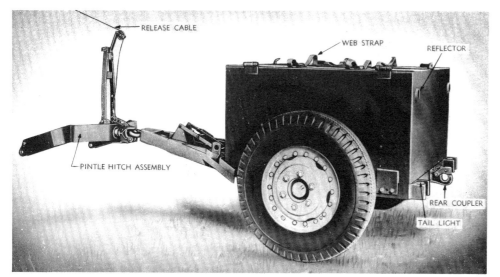

SIDE VIEW, WITH PINTLE HITCH EXTENDED FOR ATTACHING TO TANK

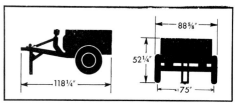

LIGHT ARMORED CAR M8—STANDARD

Light Armored Car M8 is designed as a light, highly mobile, armored reconnaissance vehicle which may also be used as a 37-mm gun motor carriage.

It consists of a welded hull and cast turret on a 6-wheel (6x6) chassis. The vehicle uses a conventional type of steering wheel and a Hercules model JXD engine.

Principal armament consists of a 37-mm Gun M6, mounted with a cal. .30 machine gun in a combination mount in the turret. The guns have an elevation from −10° to +20°. The machine gun can be removed from the combination mount and used on a Tripod Mount M2 if required.

The 37-mm gun, using A.P.C. shot M51B1 or M51B2, with a muzzle velocity of 2,900 feet per second, will penetrate 1.8 inches of face-hardened armor plate at 1,000 yards. A folding cal. .50 anti-aircraft machine gun mount is provided.

The commander and gunner occupy positions in the open-top turret, which has a traverse of 360°. Driver and assistant are seated forward in the hull. In combat zones, the direct-vision slot shutters and hatch covers can be closed, and vision afforded by protectoscopes.

The vehicle is equipped with a radio and an intracar speaking tube. It is provided with a removable folding canopy of heavy canvas for covering the turret.

LIGHT ARMORED CAR M8, WITH PEDESTAL MOUNT FOR MACHINE GUN AT REAR OF TURRET

A pintle hook is affixed to the rear of the vehicle for towing a trailer.

The pilot vehicle was manufactured by the Ford Motor Co.

REFERENCES—TM 9–743; OCM 17303, 17359, 17718, 17929, 18133, 18314, 18340, 18511, 19432, 20680, 21002, 22248, 22381, 23333, 23570; SNL G-136.

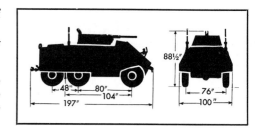

TYPICAL CHARACTERISTICS

Crew 4

Physical Characteristics
Weight (gross) . . . . 17,400 lb.
Length . . . . 16 ft., 5 in.
Width . . . . 8 ft., 4 in.
Height . . . . 7 ft., 4½ in.
Ground clearance . . . . 11½ in.
Tread (center to center of tracks) . . . . . . 76 in.
Wheelbase, front to rear axle . . . . 128 in.
   Front to intermediate axle . . . . 80 in.
Ground pressure at 3-inch
   penetration . . . . 13.6 lb./sq. in.
Tire equipment . . . . . 9.00x20, 12-ply (combat)

Armament
1 37-mm Gun M6 and
1 Cal. .30 Browning Machine Gun
   M1919A4 (flexible)
   In Combination Mount M23A1 in turret
   Elevation . . . . −10° to +20°
   Traverse . . . . 360°
1 Cal. .50 Machine Gun M2 HB (flexible)
   on turret, antiaircraft
1 Tripod Mount, Cal. .30, M2
1 Tripod Mount, Cal. .50, M3
Provision for:
   4 Cal. .30 Carbines . . . . . Equipment of crew

Ammunition, Stowage
37-mm (A.P.C., M51B1 or M51B2;
   H.E., M63; and Can., M2) . . . . . 80 rounds*
Cal. .30 carbine . . . . 400 rounds

Cal. .30 machine gun . . . . 1,500 rounds
Cal. .50 . . . . 400 rounds
Grenades, Hand (Fragmentation, Mk. II, 6;
   Smoke, WP, 6) 12
Mines, Antitank, H.E., M1A1 6
Smoke Pots M1 or M2 4

Armor
	Actual
Hull, Front, Upper	⅝ in.
Lower	¾ in.
Sides	⅜ in.
Rear	⅜ in.
Top	¼ in.
Bottom	⅛–¼ in.
Turret, Front	¾ in.
Sides and rear	¾ in.

Performance
Maximum speed on level . . . . 55 m.p.h.
Speed on 3% grade . . . . 30 m.p.h.
Maximum grade ability 60%
Vertical obstacle ability . . . . 12 in.
Fording depth (slowest forward speed) . . 24 in.
Turning radius . . . . 28 ft.
Fuel capacity . . . . 56 gal.
Cruising range . . . . 350 miles

Vision and Fire Control
Protectoscopes 2
Telescope M70D, w/Instrument Light M39C . . 1

Communications
Radio . . . . SCR-506 and/or 508, 510, 608, 610
Interphone stations 4
Flag Set M238 1

Battery, Voltage, total 12

Fire Protection and Decontamination
Fire Extinguisher, CO₂–4 lb. (hand) 1
Decontaminating Apparatus M2, 1½ qts. . . . 2

Engine, Make and model . . . . Hercules JXD
Type . . . . In-Line, "L"
No. of cylinders 6
Fuel (gasoline) . . . . 70 octane
Net hp . . . . 110 at 3,000 r.p.m.
Max. torque . . . . 238 lb.-ft. at 1,100 r.p.m.

Transmission, Type . . . . . . Selective sliding gear
Gear ratios
   First speed 6.499:1
   Second speed 3.543:1
   Third speed 1.752:1
   Fourth speed 1.000:1
   Reverse 6.987:1

Transfer Case, Gear ratios
   High gear 1.000:1
   Low gear 1.956:1

Suspension, Type . . . . Leaf springs
Wheel construction . . . . Divided rim

Master Clutch, Type . . . . Dry, single plate

Radiator, Type . . . . Tube and fin
Capacity of system . . . . 23 qt.

Brakes, Type . . . . Hydraulic

*Vehicles with two radios carry only 16 rounds of 37-mm ammunition.

ARMORED UTILITY CAR M20—STANDARD

ARMORED UTILITY CAR M20, WITH RING MOUNT M49. LATER VEHICLES USE RING MOUNT M66

TYPICAL CHARACTERISTICS

Crew..................................2 to 6

Physical Characteristics
Weight (unloaded)...............12,800 lb.
Weight (loaded—depending on use)
                       14,500 to 17,500 lb.
Length.........................16 ft., 5 in.
Width............................8 ft., 4 in.
Height...........................7 ft., 7 in.
Ground clearance...................11½ in.
Tread (center to center, rear)........76 in.
Wheelbase, front to rear axle.......128 in.
Wheelbase, front to intermediate axle...80 in.
Ground pressure at 3-in. penetration
  (depending on load).12.7 to 14.35 lb./sq. in.
Tire equipment......9.00x20, 12-ply, combat

Armament
1 Ring Mount M49 or M66 for Cal. .50
  Machine Gun M2 HB (flexible)
Provision for:
  1 Cal. .50 Machine Gun M2 HB (flexible)
  1 Cal. .50 Tripod Mount M3
  5 Cal. .30 Carbines
  1 2.36-In. Rocket Launcher M9A1

Ammunition, Stowage
Cal. .50.......................1,000 rounds
Cal. .30 carbine.................500 rounds
Grenades (Hand: Fragmentation, Mk. II, 6;
  Smoke, WP, 6; Rifle: M9A1, 3).......15
Rockets, A.T., 2.36-In., M6A3.........10
Mines, A.T., M1A1......................3
Smoke Pots M1 or M2....................4

Armor   **Actual**
Hull, Front, Upper.....................⅝ in.
         Lower.........................¾ in.
     Sides.............................⅜ in.
     Rear.............................⅜ in.
     Top..............................¼ in.
     Bottom.........................⅛-¼ in.

Performance
Maximum speed on level...........55 m.p.h.
  On 3% grade....................30 m.p.h.
Maximum grade ability...............60%

Vertical obstacle ability..............12 in.
Fording depth (slowest forward speed)...24 in.
Turning radius.......................28 ft.
Fuel capacity........................56 gal.
Cruising range (approx.)...........350 miles

Vision and Fire Control
Protectoscopes..........................2

Communications
Radio....SCR-506 and/or 508, 510, 608, 610
Flag Set M238...........................1

Battery, Voltage, total................12

Fire Protection and Decontamination
Fire Extinguisher, CO₂-4 lb. (hand)........1
Decontaminating Apparatus M2, 1½ qt.....2

Engine, Make and model........Hercules JXD
Type..........................In-line, "L"
No. of cylinders........................6
Fuel (gasoline)..................70 octane
Net hp....................110 at 3,000 r.p.m.
Max. torque........238 lb.-ft. at 1,100 r.p.m.

Transmission, Type......Selective sliding gear
Gear ratios
  First speed......................6.499:1
  Second speed.....................3.543:1
  Third speed......................1.752:1
  Fourth speed.....................1.000:1
  Reverse..........................6.987:1

Transfer Case, Gear ratios
  High gear........................1.000:1
  Low gear.........................1.956:1

Suspension, Type.............Leaf springs
Wheel construction............Divided rim

Master Clutch, Type....Dry, single plate

Radiator, Type.................Tube and fin
Capacity of system................23 qt.

Brakes, Type...................Hydraulic

This vehicle, which is based on the chassis of Light Armored Car M8, is designed to combine the functions of a command car and of a personnel and cargo carrier.

Following the standardization of Light Armored Car M8, the Tank Destroyer Command requested the development of three vehicles—a command car, a personnel and cargo carrier, and an anti-aircraft multiple machine gun mount—based on the same chassis.

Of these, it was proposed that the command car should be essentially the same as Armored Car M8, the principal change being the substitution for the 37-mm gun of a cal. .50 machine gun on a ring mount on top of the turret. The proposed personnel and cargo carrier was to be without a turret. Subsequently the Tank Destroyer Board indicated a preference for a turretless command car. This permitted the combination of the two functions in a single vehicle, with provision for stowage as required for the two different uses.

The vehicle was originally standardized in April 1943 as Armored Utility Car M10. To avoid confusion with the 3-Inch Gun Motor Carriage M10 in tank destroyer organizations, the designation was changed to Armored Utility Car M20.

A Ring Mount M49 or M66, for the Cal. .50 Machine Gun M2 HB (flexible), is provided over the rear of the open cargo compartment, for protection against low-flying aircraft. Provision is made for carrying a 2.36-in. rocket launcher and five cal. .30 carbines.

The car will accommodate two to six men, depending on the use for which it is intended. Protectoscopes and direct vision are provided for the driver and assistant driver.

Like the Armored Car M8, the vehicle is of the six-wheeled type, with power from a Hercules JXD gasoline engine being supplied to all six wheels.

The pilot vehicle was manufactured by the Ford Motor Co.

REFERENCES—TM 9-743; OCM 18314, 18390, 19347, 19431, 19993, 20077, 20203, 20363, 20446, 20680, 20982, 21002, 21178, 21339, 24570, 24776, 25471, 25641; SNL G-176.

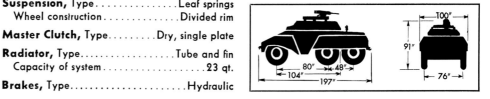

ARMORED CARS T17, T17E1, T17E2—LIMITED PROCUREMENT

As the result of reports from war areas, particularly North Africa, indicating the need for armored, wheeled vehicles for reconnaissance and combat, the Ordnance Committee, in July 1941, set forth military characteristics for medium and heavy armored cars.

In September 1941, authority was given to procure pilot models. A six-wheeled vehicle, built by the Ford Motor Co., was designated Armored Car T17, and a four-wheeled vehicle, built by the Chevrolet Motor Co., was designated Armored Car T17E1.

On 15 October 1942, a board, composed of Armored Force, Cavalry, Tank Destroyer, and Ordnance representatives was appointed to consider armored cars in production or in development. As the medium and heavy armored cars were considered too large, the contract for Armored Car T17, then in production, was reduced to 250 cars, which the British agreed to accept. None were sent overseas, however. The guns were removed, and the vehicles were assigned for military police use in this country.

Limited procurement of Armored Car T17E1 was authorized for International Aid. Ordnance Committee action in June 1943 recorded authority for procurement of a quantity of these vehicles with a Fraser-Nash turret instead of a tank type turret, and designated the modified vehicle Armored Car T17E2.

REFERENCES — OCM 16987, 17091, 17217, 17473, 18229, 19780, 20645, 20680, 21002, 22818.

ARMORED CAR T17 is a 6x6 vehicle which originally mounted a 37-mm Gun M6 and a cal. .30 machine gun (fixed) in a Combination Mount M21, with gyro stabilizer, in a tank type turret. A cal. .30 machine gun (flexible) was mounted in the bow and another was provided for antiaircraft use. Provision was made for carrying a cal. .45 submachine gun.

Power is supplied by two Hercules JXD engines, each having its own clutch and four-speed transmission. Gears are shifted by a single lever, and either transmission can be put into neutral. A transfer case provides eight forward and two reverse speeds. Steering is by means of a hydraulic-boosted, worm and roller type gear and a conventional steering wheel.

REFERENCES—TM 9–740; OCM 16987, 17091, 18229, 19780, 20680, 21002, 22818; SNL G–134.

ARMORED CAR T17E1 is a 4x4 vehicle designed for distant reconnaissance, convoy escort, and police purposes. The hull is so constructed that a frame is not required, the springs, steering gear, transfer case, and other units being attached directly to the hull.

Principal armament is a 37-mm Gun M6 and a Cal. .30 Machine Gun M1919A4 (fixed), in a combination mount in a power-operated turret. A Cal. .30 Machine Gun M1919A4 (flexible) is mounted in the bow and one on the turret.

Direct-vision doors, with protected vision slots, and six periscopes are provided. The vehicle is intended for British use, and was modified to satisfy British requirements.

REFERENCES—TM 9–741; OCM 17217, 17473, 18229, 19780, 22818; SNL G–128.

ARMORED CAR T17, WITH VISION SLOTS OPEN, SHOWING TURRET AND BOW GUNS

ARMORED CAR T17E1, HAS 37-MM AND CAL. .30 GUNS IN TURRET

ARMORED CAR T17

102″ 91″ 86″
146″ 218″

ARMORED CAR T17E1

106″ 93″ 89″
120″ 216″

ARMORED CARS T17, T17E1, T17E2 (Continued)

ARMORED CAR T17E2 HAS TWO CAL. .50 A. A. GUNS IN TURRET

ARMORED CAR T17E2 is similar to Armored Car T17E1, but has a Fraser-Nash type of power turret mounting two cal. .50 antiaircraft guns.

One thousand of these vehicles were manufactured at the request of the British.

The cal. .50 machine guns can be elevated from −10° to +75° at a speed of 30° per second, and can be traversed 360° at a rate of 43° per second.

References—TM 9–741; OCM 20645, 21848, 22203, 22818; SNL G-122.

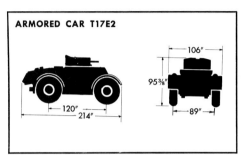

ARMORED CAR T17E2

106″
95 3/8″
120″
214″
89″

TYPICAL CHARACTERISTICS

	T17	T17E1	T17E2
Crew	5	5	3
Physical Characteristics			
Weight (gross)	32,000 lb.	30,705 lb.	26,558 lb.
Length	18 ft., 2 in.	18 ft.	17 ft., 10 in.
Width	8 ft., 6 in.	8 ft., 10 in.	8 ft., 10 in.
Height	7 ft., 7 in.	7 ft., 9 in.	7 ft., 11 3/8 in.
Ground clearance	13 1/2 in.	15 in.	15 in.
Tread	86 in.	89 in.	89 in.
Wheelbase	146 in.	120 in.	120 in.
Tire equipment (combat)	12.00 x 20	14.00 x 20	14.00 x 20
Ground pressure at 4 in. penetration	17.7 lb./sq. in.	17.95 lb./sq. in.	15.4 lb./sq. in.
Armament			
37-mm Gun M6 and Cal. .30 Machine Gun M1919A4 (fixed)	1 each, in Combination Mount M24, in turret	1 each, in Combination Mount M24A1, in turret	
Cal. .50 Machine Guns M2 HB, TT (special)			2, in Fraser-Nash turret
Elevation	−10° to +45°	−7° to +40°	−10° to +75°
Traverse	360°	360°	360°
Cal. .30 Machine Gun M1919A4 (flexible)	1, in bow 1, on turret (antiaircraft)	1, in bow 1, on turret (antiaircraft)	
Tripod Mount, cal. .30, M2	1		
2-In. Mortar M3		1	
Provision for: Cal. .45 submachine guns	1	1	1
Ammunition			
37 mm	111 rounds	103 rounds	
Cal. .30	4,750 rounds	5,250 rounds	
Cal. .45	450 rounds	450 rounds	450 rounds
Cal. .50			2,610 rounds
Grenades, Hand	12	12	12
2-In. Mortar		14 rounds	
Armor	**Actual**	**Actual**	**Actual**
Hull, Front	3/4 in.	7/8–5/8 in.	7/8–5/8 in.
Sides	3/4 in.	3/4 in.	3/4 in.
Rear	1/2 in.	3/8 in.	3/8 in.
Top	5/8 in.	1/2 in.	1/2 in.
Bottom	1/4 in.	1/2–1/4 in.	1/2–1/4 in.

	T17	T17E1	T17E2
Armor	**Actual**	**Actual**	**Actual**
Turret, Front	1 1/4 in.	1 3/4 in.	1 1/4 in.
Sides and rear	1 1/4 in.	1 1/4 in.	1 1/4 in.
Top	3/4 in.	1/2 in.	
Shield		1 in.	
Performance			
Maximum speed	60 m.p.h.	55 m.p.h.	55 m.p.h.
Speed on 3% grade	35 m.p.h.	35 m.p.h.	35 m.p.h.
Maximum grade	60%	57%	57%
Vertical obstacle	18 in.	21 in.	21 in.
Fording depth	32 in.	32 in.	32 in.
Turning radius	30 ft.	27.5 ft.	27.5 ft.
Fuel capacity	75 gal.	137 gal.	137 gal.
Cruising range	250 miles	450 miles	450 miles
Vision and Fire Control			
Direct vision slots	2	2	2
Periscope M6	6	6	3
Periscope M4, with Telescope M40	1	1	
Sight, Illuminated, Mk. IX (24-volt)			1
Communications			
Radio	British No. 19	British No. 19	British No. 19
Interphone stations	5	5	3
Flag Set M238	1	1	1
Battery, Voltage	24	24	24
Fire Protection and Decontamination			
Fire Extinguisher, CO₂ −10 lb. (fixed)	2	2	2
CO₂–4 lb. (hand)	1	1	1
Decontaminating Apparatus M2	1	1	1
Engine, Make	Hercules JXD (2)	G.M.C. 270 (2)	G.M.C. 270 (2)
Type	In-line, L, L.C.	In-line, L.C.	In-line, L.C.
No. of cylinders (each engine)	6	6	6
Fuel (gasoline)	70–80 octane	70–80 octane	70–80 octane
Displacement (each engine)	320 cu. in.	270.5 cu. in.	270.5 cu. in.
Net hp. at r.p.m. (each engine)	110 at 3,000	97 at 3,000	97 at 3,000
Max. torque at r.p.m. (each engine)	238 lb.-ft. at 1,100	216.3 lb.-ft. at 1,000	216.3 lb.-ft. at 1,000

LIGHT ARMORED CAR M38—STANDARD

Light Armored Car M38, which was standardized in March 1945, is the result of efforts to develop a 6-wheel-drive reconnaissance vehicle with superior qualities for cross-country operation.

Its excellent mobility and riding qualities are largely the result of the spacing of the axles on the chassis. Unlike Light Armored Car M8, which it is expected to replace, the M38 has axles evenly spaced from front to back to provide better distribution of weight, whereas the rear axles of the M8 are close together, as on a conventional 6-wheel-drive transport vehicle.

This improvement gives not only better flotation in soft terrain but also greater ability to cross craters and trenches and to surmount obstacles. Light Armored Car M38 can surmount a 24-in. vertical obstacle and cross a 50-in. trench; Light Armored Car M8 can surmount only a 12-in. vertical obstacle and has negligible trench-crossing ability. To prevent undue wear on the tires that would otherwise result from the even spacing of the axles, the wheels on the two forward axles pivot for steering.

Other improvements that contribute to the good riding qualities are the independent suspension of the wheels, the oversize tires (12.00x20 as against 9.00x20 on the M8), and light weight. Combat loaded, the M38 weighs approximately 2,000 lb. less than the M8.

Some of the decrease in weight has been obtained by cutting down the thickness of armor. The M38 has 3/8-in. armor on many portions of the hull and turret where the M8 has 5/8- and 3/4-in. plate. Increased angles, however, retain comparable ballistic characteristics to a large extent.

Except that the M38 has a Cadillac V-8 engine and a Hydra-Matic transmission instead of a Hercules JXD engine and selective sliding gear transmission, characteristics of the two armored cars are much the same. Principal armament of the M38 is the 37-mm Gun M6 in a combination mount with a Cal. .30 Machine Gun M1919A4 (flexible). A cal. .50 machine gun for protection against low-flying aircraft is mounted on the turret. Tripod mounts for a cal. .30 and a cal. .50 machine gun are also provided, along with adequate stowage for ammunition.

The vehicle has a top speed of 60 m.p.h. and a cruising range of 300 miles. It carries a crew of four.

The pilot vehicle was built by the Chevrolet Division, General Motors Corporation.

REFERENCES — OCM 19581, 19955, 20794, 25967, 26849.

NEW TYPE OF SUSPENSION GIVES LIGHT ARMORED CAR M38 GREAT MOBILITY

TYPICAL CHARACTERISTICS

Crew...4
Physical Characteristics
  Weight (combat loaded)........15,300 lb.
  Length.....................16 ft., 9¼ in.
  Width...............................8 ft.
  Height.......................6 ft., 6 in.
  Turret ring diameter...............56 in.
  Ground clearance................14½ in.
  Tread (center to center of tires).....80 in.
  Wheelbase (59 in. between axles).....118 in.
  Ground pressure at
    3-in. penetration...........8.1 lb./sq. in.
  Tire equipment.12.00x20, new standard combat
Armament
  37-mm Gun M6 and
  1 Cal. .30 Machine Gun M1919A4 (flexible)
  In Combination Mount M03A0, in turret
    Elevation...............—10° to +20°
    Traverse.........................360°
  1 Cal. .50 Machine Gun
    M2 HB (flexible).....On pedestal, on turret
  1 Cal. .50 Tripod Mount M3
  1 Cal. .30 Tripod Mount M2
  Provision for:
  4 Cal. .30 carbines
  1 Grenade Launcher M8
Ammunition, Stowage
  37-mm.........................93 rounds
  Cal. .50.....................440 rounds
  Cal. .30...................1,750 rounds
  Smoke pots..........................4
  Grenades (hand, 12; rifle, 6).......18

Armor	Actual	Basis
Hull, front	3/8 in.	5/8 in. and 1½ in.
Sides and rear	3/8 in.	7/16 in.
Top	1/4 in.	
Bottom, front 10 in.	3/8 in.	
Remainder	1/4 in.	
Turret, front	1/2 in.	5/8 in.
Sides	3/8 in.	7/16 in.
Rear	3/8 in.	3/8 in.
Top	Open	

Performance
  Maximum speed, on Level........60 m.p.h.
    On 3% grade..................35 m.p.h.
  Maximum grade ability...............60%
  Vertical obstacle ability...........24 in.

Trench crossing ability...............50 in.
Fording ability (slowest forward speed)..48 in.
Turning radius.......................28 ft.
Fuel capacity.......................51 gal.
Cruising range....................300 miles
Vision and Fire Control
  Periscope M6 (for driver)..............1
  Telescope M70D, w/Instrument Light M39C..1
  Auxiliary knife-blade pointing sight.......1
  Provision for:
  Observation Telescope M49
  Tripod M15
Communications
  Radio..............SCR-506 and 528 or 510
  Interphone stations....................4
Battery, Voltage, total...............12
Fire Protection and Decontamination
  Fire Extinguisher, CO₂–4 lb. (hand)......1
Engine, Make and model........Cadillac 42
  Type.........................V-8, L.C.
  Displacement...............346 cu. in.
  Fuel (gasoline).................80 octane
  Gross hp..............148 at 3,200 r.p.m.
  Max. torque........280 lb.-ft. at 1,200 r.p.m.
Transmission, Type............Hydra-Matic
  Gear ratios
    First speed....................3.92:1
    Second speed...................2.53:1
    Third speed....................1.55:1
    Fourth speed...................1.00:1
    Reverse.......................4.167:1
Transfer Case, Gear ratios...3.441:1; 1.392:1
Differential, Gear ratio.............6.667:1
Suspension, Type.Independent, swing arm, 6x6
Clutch, Type..............Fluid coupling
Radiator, Capacity of system..........38 qt.
Brakes, Type.....................Vacuum

UNIVERSAL CARRIERS T16, T16E2—LIMITED PROCUREMENT

UNIVERSAL CARRIER T16 IS MODIFICATION OF BRITISH BREN GUN CARRIER

TYPICAL CHARACTERISTICS

(UNIVERSAL CARRIER T16)

Crew...................................4

Physical Characteristics
Weight (gross w/payload, approx.).10,500 lb.
  Net (unserviced)...............8,194 lb.
Length....................12 ft., 11⅛ in.
Width......................6 ft., 11½ in.
Height.......................5 ft., 1 in.
Ground clearance.................10½ in.
Tread (center to center of tracks).....61½ in.
Ground contact length.............71 in.
Ground pressure (gross weight)...7.4 lb./sq. in.

Armament
Provision for:
1 Infantry antitank projector (PIAT)
2 Bren machine guns
1 2-inch smoke mortar
2 Service rifles

Ammunition............Supplied by British

Armor   **Actual**
Hull, front, upper.................⁷/₃₂ in.
    Lower..................⁹/₃₂ in.
  Sides, rear, and bottom..........⁹/₃₂ in.

Performance
Maximum speed on level..........30 m.p.h.
Maximum grade ability..............60%
Trench crossing ability............30 in.
Vertical obstacle ability...........18 in.
Fording depth (slowest forward speed)...Floats
Turning diameter.................32 ft.
Fuel capacity...................23.6 gal.
Cruising range (approx.).......100-150 miles
Payload.......................1,200 lb.

Vision.....................3 vision slots

Communications
Provision for British Wireless
  Set No. 19........................1

Battery, Voltage, total.................12

Fire Protection
Fire Extinguisher, Carbon Tetrachloride,
  1 qt.............................3

Engine, Make and model.....Ford V-8, GAU
  Type...................90°, L-head
  No. of cylinders...................8
  Fuel (gasoline)............70 octane
  Displacement............239 cu. in.
  Max. governed speed.........3,300 r.p.m.
  Net hp..........102.5 at 4,000 r.p.m.
  Max. torque......176 lb.-ft., at 2,000 r.p.m.

Transmission, Type.............Spur gear
  Gear ratios
    First speed.................6.40:1
    Second speed...............3.09:1
    Third speed................1.69:1
    Fourth speed...............1.00:1
    Reverse....................7.82:1

Differential, Type.............Controlled
  Gear ratio (ring gear to pinion).......5.83:1
  Steering ratio..................1.8:1

Final Drive
  No. of teeth in sprocket.............35
  Pitch diameter of sprocket..........19.4 in.

Suspension, Type.............Coil spring

Idler, Type............Fixed, front-mounted

Track, Type...........T79, cast steel
  Width.........................10 in.
  Pitch........................1.75 in.
  No. of shoes per vehicle............348

Clutch, Type...........Dry, single-plate

UNIVERSAL CARRIER T16E2

Characteristics same as for Universal Carrier T16 except:

Length...................13 ft., 6 in.
Ground contact length............77 in.
Ground pressure (gross weight).....6.8 lb./sq. in.
Armor, hull, front...........⁹/₃₂ and ²⁵/₆₄ in.
Fuel capacity..................27.8 gal.

These are full-track, high-speed cargo carriers, designed to transport personnel, ammunition, and accessories. They are produced for the British only.

Universal Carrier T16 is a modification of the so-called Bren gun carrier, widely used by the British. The principal changes in design provide for the use of the controlled differential steering system, Ford Mercury engine, two two-wheeled bogies on each side, a redesigned and simplified welded hull structure, and for refinement of the track and suspension.

The original vehicle was designated Cargo Carrier T16, but was redesignated Universal Carrier T16 for the sake of uniformity with British nomenclature. Production of 30,000 for the British was authorized by agreement of the Joint British Tank Mission and the U. S. Tank Committee.

Universal Carrier T16E2, authorized to replace the T16 in production in 1945, is an elongated vehicle designed for improved stability and better bogie loading without major change in the spare parts required. The front bogie was moved back 6 in., the rear bogie was moved back 9 in. and reversed, and the drive axle was moved back 8 in.

Each vehicle has accommodations for a crew of four men, including the driver, and is armored at the front, sides, rear, and bottom, but is open at the top.

Sustained speed on improved level roads is 30 m.p.h. The vehicles will float with a partial load, propelling themselves by the action of the tracks in the water.

REFERENCES—TM 9–746, 9–1746A, 9–1746B; OCM 16635, 16727, 18229, 18434, 18598, 19782, 20576, 23959, 24491, 25361, 26380; SNL G–166.

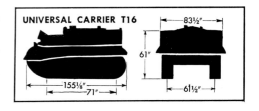

UNIVERSAL CARRIER T16
83½"
61"
155⅛"
71"
61½"

CARGO CARRIERS M28—LIMITED STANDARD; M29, M29C—STANDARD

Designed originally for use over snow and ice, Cargo Carriers M28 and M29 have proved useful wherever small, speedy vehicles with very low ground pressures have been required. Cargo Carrier M29C is an amphibian vehicle.

Power is supplied by a liquid-cooled, six-cylinder engine. The flywheel end of the engine is connected by means of a single-plate clutch, a conventional transmission, a propeller shaft, and two needle-bearing type universal joints to a controlled differential and the driving axle. The axle is of the planetary, two-speed type.

Vehicles are fully suppressed for radio installation. Except for various covers which are removable to facilitate maintenance and inspection operations, the hulls are of welded sheet steel. Plugs and a plate are provided for draining purposes.

CARGO CARRIER M28—LIMITED STANDARD—This vehicle has accommodations for a crew of two and for 800 pounds of equipment, including skis, ski poles, snowshoes, rucksacks, mountain-climbing axes, and other items essential for operations in snowy country. It was classified as Limited Standard by Ordnance Committee action in September 1943.

The engine is at the rear of the hull, and the driving axle at the front of the vehicle. The rear and side walls of the rear air duct and the front wall of the cargo boxes are of armor plate.

The track, designed especially for use on snow, is 18 inches wide. The track shoes are rubber covered.

There are two sets of bogie suspensions on each track, each with a semielliptic, three-section spring. Two rubber-tired bogie wheels are at each end of the spring, one riding each belt band. Two guide wheels on each side support and guide the track. Proper tension on the track is maintained by the spring-loaded rear idler.

A windshield defroster with an electric heating element is supplied. A pump-type primer aids in starting the engine when cold.

Towing eyes are mounted at the front of the vehicle and a pintle at the rear. Provision is made for carrying the armament of the crew members and the necessary ammunition.

REFERENCES—TM 9–893; OCM 18436, 19138, 19819, 19820, 19989, 20976, 21397, 21627, 23957; SNL G–154.

CARGO CARRIER M29—STANDARD—This vehicle, standardized in September 1943, is basically similar to Cargo Carrier M28, but has a rear drive. The change in design moved the center of gravity forward and also resulted in a more desirable arrangement of engine, crew, and cargo. The revised suspension,

CARGO CARRIER M28 HAS ENGINE AT REAR AND DRIVING AXLE AT FRONT

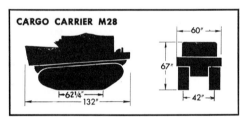

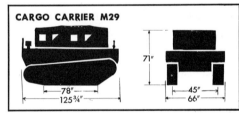

CARGO CARRIER M29 HAS DRIVING AXLE AT REAR, USES MORE BOGIES

which has transverse springs and twice the number of bogie wheels, provides improved riding characteristics.

The engine, engine accessories, fuel tank, driver's seat, vehicle controls, etc., are in the front of the vehicle. The rear houses the radio equipment and has seating capacity for the assistant driver and two extra passengers, or space for approximately 1,000 pounds of miscellaneous equipment. A track guard and step plates are on each side of the vehicle. An A-frame towing hitch permits use of the vehicles in tandem.

The transmission has three speeds forward and one reverse. A transfer unit provides a total of six speeds forward and two reverse.

First production vehicles were provided with 15-inch tracks, but later models have 20-inch tracks. A 40-ampere generator is furnished. When the vehicle uses a radio set with a drain in excess of 40 amperes, a 55-ampere generator can be installed by means of a conversion kit.

REFERENCES—TM 9–772; OCM 20976, 21397, 21627, 22590, 22704, 22753, 22851, 23077, 23652, 23956, 24274, 25472, 25697; SNL G–179.

CARGO CARRIER M29C—STANDARD

—This is a modification of Cargo Carrier M29 adapted for amphibious operation. Watertight cells are added at the front and rear of the vehicle for buoyancy. Openings in the top of these cells permit bilge water to be pumped out. A surf guard on the forward edge of the front cell reduces the amount of water that is shipped.

The vehicle is propelled by its tracks, in water as well as on land.

Aprons fastened over the upper portion of the tracks facilitate the forward motion of the vehicle in water. Twin rudders are provided at the stern. Special equipment includes a fixed mounted driving light on the front deck, a signal spotlight and reel, and a capstan on the front deck.

The basic Cargo Carrier M29 is so designed that it can be converted in the field for amphibious use if required.

REFERENCES—TM 9–772; OCM 22590, 22851, 23331, 23574, 23652, 23956; SNL G–179.

CARGO CARRIER M29C, SHOWING SEATING ARRANGEMENT

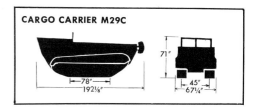

CARGO CARRIER M29C

TYPICAL CHARACTERISTICS

	Cargo Carrier M28	Cargo Carrier M29	Cargo Carrier M29C
Crew	2	2 to 4	2 to 4
Physical Characteristics			
Weight (gross)	4,650 lb.	5,425 lb.	6,000 lb.
Length (overall)	11 ft.	10 ft., 5¾ in.	16 ft., ⅛ in.
Width, With 15-in. track	5 ft.	5 ft.	
With 20-in. track		5 ft., 6 in.	5 ft., 7¼ in.
Height (overall)	5 ft., 7 in.	5 ft., 11 in.	5 ft., 11 in.
Top & windshield folded	4 ft., 8 in.	4 ft., 5¾ in.	4 ft., 7⅝ in.
Ground clearance	11 in.	11 in.	11 in.
Tread (center to center of tracks)	42 in.	45 in.*	45 in.*
Center of gravity, From front	62¾ in.	64 in.	83 in.
Below deck line	22 in.	19 in.	21⅜ in.
Ground contact length at 0 penetration	62¼ in.	78 in.	78 in.
Ground pressure at 0 penetration, With 15-in. track	2.15 lb./sq. in.	2.3 lb./sq. in.	
With 20-in. track		1.7 lb./sq. in.	1.9 lb./sq. in.
Freeboard in deep water			8–10 in.
Performance			
Maximum speed on hard-surfaced road, at 3,000 ft. altitude	35 m.p.h.	36 m.p.h.	36 m.p.h.
Maximum speed in water			4 m.p.h.
Maximum grade ability on hard surface	100%	100%	100%
Trench crossing ability	3 ft.	3 ft.	3 ft.
Angle of approach		90°	47°
Angle of departure		60°	36°
Turning diameter	24 ft.	24 ft.	24 ft.
Fuel capacity	25 gal.	35 gal.	35 gal.
Cruising range (approx.)	115 miles	175 miles	175 miles
Maximum drawbar pull		3,800 lb.	4,200 lb.
Payload	1,260 lb.	1,200 lb.	1,200 lb.

	Cargo Carrier M28	Cargo Carriers M29, M29C
Communications		
Radio	As specified	As specified
Battery, Voltage, total	12	12
Fire Protection and Decontamination		
Fire Extinguisher, CCl₄, 1 qt.	1	1
Engine, Make and model	Studebaker 6–170	Studebaker 6–170
Type	L-head, In-line, L.C.	L-head, In-line, L.C.
No. of cylinders	6	6
Fuel (gasoline)	80 octane at sea level 70 octane at 3,000 ft.	80 octane at sea level 70 octane at 3,000 ft.
Displacement	169.6 cu. in.	169.6 cu. in.
Compression ratio	7:1	7:1
Net hp.	65 at 3,600 r.p.m.	65 at 3,600 r.p.m.
Max. torque	125 lb.-ft. at 1,600 r.p.m.	125 lb.-ft. at 1,600 r.p.m.
Transmission		
Gear ratios		
First speed	2.66:1	2.66:1
Second speed	1.49:1	1.56:1
Third speed	1.00:1	1.00:1
Reverse	3.55:1	3.55:1
Transfer Case		
Gear ratios	1.154:1; 2.294:1	0.866:1; 2.74:1
Differential, Type	Controlled	Controlled
Gear ratio	5.857:1	4.87:1
Steering ratio	1.73:1	1.73:1
Final Drive		
Sprocket, No. of teeth	9	9
Suspension, Type	Semielliptic	Transverse, leaf spring
Idler		
Wheel or tire size	17x7¼	11¾x7
Track, Type	T77	T76E1
Width	18 in.	20 in.
Pitch	6 in.	4½ in.
No. of shoes per vehicle	82	112

*With 20-in. track.

SNOW TRACTOR M7—LIMITED STANDARD
1-TON SNOW TRAILER M19—LIMITED STANDARD

SNOW TRACTOR M7, SHOWN WITH WHEELS ON FRONT AND TOP REMOVED

TRAILER, ON SKIS, CARRYING TWO LITTERS

Designed to provide a light vehicle and trailer for transportation on snow, Snow Tractor M7 and 1-Ton Snow Trailer M19 are characterized by the fact that their wheels may be replaced by skis for use in deep snow. Standardized in August 1943, they were reclassified as Limited Standard in November 1944.

The pilot tractors and trailers were built by the Allis-Chalmers Manufacturing Co.

REFERENCES—OCM 18480, 19138, 19632, 20202, 20772, 21003, 21395, 21629, 24606, 25473, 25642; SNL G–194, G–195.

SNOW TRACTOR M7 is a half-track type high-speed vehicle. For negotiating deep snow, the front wheels may be replaced with skis. When not in use, the skis are carried at the side of the hood, serving as mudguards. The crew consists of two men, including the driver, one seated behind the other.

Grade ability is dependent upon shear strength of the snow; however, under extremely soft snow conditions the vehicle has negotiated a 38% grade with the driver only. It will climb a 60% grade if traction is available.

Power is supplied by a Willys MB four-cylinder liquid-cooled engine, similar to that used on the ¼-Ton, 4x4, Truck.

The transmission has three speeds forward and one reverse speed.

The steering mechanism is of the roller and segment type.

A six-volt ignition system suppressed for 30 meters is provided.

The vehicle has a towing pintle on the rear. Standard ¼-Ton, 4x4, Truck cold starting equipment is installed. Other equipment includes a removable canopy top and side curtains, a ten-foot tow chain, and a set of tools. Two spare skis are carried on each tractor.

1-TON SNOW TRAILER M19 is an unsprung light-weight trailer for use in towing equipment and supplies behind the Snow Tractor M7 or other suitable prime mover either on snow or over ground for limited distances.

For operation in deep snow, the wheels may be replaced by skis. A drop pole is provided for balancing the trailer when separated from the tractor.

Space is provided for carrying two litters, one above the other. When desired, the litters may be removed, and the trailer used to carry one C13 gasoline-electric generator set and cold starting equipment designed in accordance with Army Air Forces specifications. A pintle is provided on the rear of the trailer to permit towing of trailers in tandem.

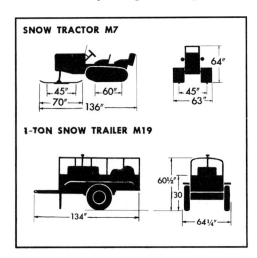

SNOW TRACTOR M7

45″ 60″
70″
136″
64″
45″
63″

1-TON SNOW TRAILER M19

134″
60½″
30
64¼″

TYPICAL CHARACTERISTICS
SNOW TRACTOR M7

Crew	2
Physical Characteristics	
Weight (gross)	3,049 lb.
Length (overall from tip of skis to end of pintle hook—approx.)	11 ft., 4 in.
Width	5 ft., 3 in.
Height (to top of windshield)	5 ft., 4 in.
(to top of windshield lowered)	3 ft., 7 in.
Ground clearance (approx.)	12¾ in.
Tread (center to center of tracks)	45 in.
Ground contact length at 3-in. penetration—track	60 in.
—skis	45 in.
Ground pressure	0.75 lb./sq. in.
Tire equipment	4.00x15
Performance	
Maximum speed at 2,400 r.p.m.	40 m.p.h.
Maximum grade ability (with driver only)	60%
—in deep soft snow	38%
Fording depth (slowest forward speed)	30 in.
Turning radius (approx.)	15 ft.
Angle of approach, w/skis	40°
w/wheels	60°
Angle of departure	60°
Fuel capacity	10½ gal.
Cruising range (approx.)	160 miles
Normal towed load	2,000 lb. plus trailer
Payload	500 lb.
Battery, Voltage, total	6
Suspension, Type,	
Rear	Unsprung walking beam
No. of wheels	10
Wheel size	8x1¼ in.
Track, Type	Endless band
Width	18 in.
Pitch	3 in.
No. of shoes per vehicle	66
Skis	Interchangeable with front wheels
Width	9 in.
Length, overall	70 in.

1-TON SNOW TRAILER M19

Physical Characteristics	
Weight (net with skis)	640 lb.
Length (overall—approx.)	11 ft., 2 in.
Width—with wheels	5 ft., 4¼ in.
—with skis	5 ft., 4¼ in.
Ground clearance	16 in.
Tread	58 in.
Payload (maximum)	2,000 lb.
Skis	Same as provided on Snow Tractor M7

SCOUT CAR M3A1—STANDARD

This vehicle, designed for high-speed scouting duty, consists of a specially designed, commercial type, 4-wheel truck chassis, surmounted by an armored body mounted on a double-drop type, channel section frame. It can attain a maximum road speed of 55 m.p.h. It was standardized in June 1939.

Seats are provided in the driver's compartment for the driver and the observation commander, and in the personnel compartment for six additional riders.

Armament consists of a cal. .50 and a cal. .30 machine gun. These can be fired from the skate rail which encircles the body interior and permits the gunners to aim in any direction, or on tripod mounts independently of the vehicle.

The body is protected by ¼-inch armor on the sides and rear. Top and side protection for the engine is provided by the armored hood. Armored shutters, controlled from within the driver's compartment, protect the radiator.

The windshield is of shatter-proof glass. An armor plate windshield shield, ½-inch thick, with direct-vision slots, is hinged above the windshield, and other armor plate shields are hinged above the doors. These can be swung into position to provide additional protection in combat areas.

The detachable canvas top is supported by three removable bows and the wind-shield frame. Side curtains are of canvas with pyralin windows.

Ammunition racks are located at both sides of the personnel compartment, and space is provided between the front seats for additional ammunition or a radio set. The radio mast is mounted inside the body. Smaller sections for ammunition and water chests and a tool box are behind the front seats.

The vehicle is powered by a 6-cylinder Hercules 110 hp. gasoline engine. The pilot vehicle was built by the White Motor Co.

REFERENCES — TM 9–705, 9–1706, 9–1709; OCM 13253, 13578, 13997, 14321, 14386, 14965, 15064, 15948, 17919, 17952, 18312, 20483, 20680, 20723, 21002; SNL G–67.

SCOUT CAR M3A1 WITH TOP UP AND RADIATOR SHUTTERS CLOSED

TYPICAL CHARACTERISTICS

Crew 8

Physical Characteristics
Weight (gross) . . . . 12,400 lb.
Length . . . . 18 ft., 5½ in.
Width . . . . 6 ft., 8 in.
Height . . . . 6 ft., 6½ in.
Ground clearance . . . . 15¾ in.
Center of gravity, Above ground . . . . . 33.9 in.
   Rear of center line of front axle . . . . . . 81 in.
Tread (center to center, rear) . . . . . . 65¼ in.
Wheelbase . . . . 131 in.
Ground pressure . . . . 60 lb./sq. in.
Tire equipment . . . . 8.25x20, combat

Armament
1 Cal. .50 Browning Machine Gun M2
  HB (flexible) . . . . Skate rail mount
1 Cal. .30 Browning Machine Gun
  M1919A4 (flexible) . . . . . . Skate rail mount
1 Cal. .30 Tripod Mount M2
1 Cal. .50 Tripod Mount M3
2 Cal. .30 or cal. .50 carriage assemblies
1 Cal. .50 cradle assembly
Provision for:
1 Cal. .45 submachine gun

Ammunition, Stowage
Cal. .50 . . . . 750 rounds
Cal. .45 . . . . 540 rounds
Cal. .30 . . . . 8,000 rounds

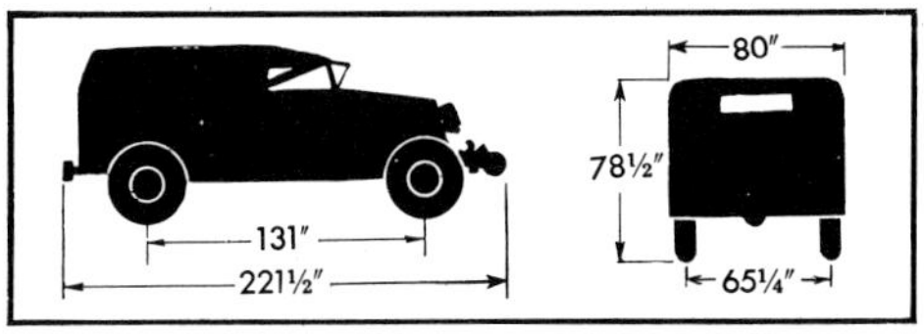

Armor   **Actual**
Windshield shield . . . . ½ in.
Engine compartment . . . . ¼ in.
Sides and rear . . . . ¼ in.

Performance
Maximum speed on level . . . . 50 m.p.h.
Maximum grade ability 60%
Vertical obstacle ability . . . . 12 in.
Fording depth (slowest forward speed) . . 28 in.
Angle of approach . . . . 37°
Angle of departure . . . . 35°
Turning diameter . . . . 28½ ft.
Fuel capacity . . . . 30 gal.
Cruising range . . . . 250 miles
Maximum drawbar pull . . . . 6,155 lb.

Vision—Direct . . . . Slits in shields

Communications
Radio . . . . SCR–506, 508, or 510

Battery, Voltage, total 12

Fire Protection and Decontamination
Fire Extinguisher, CO₂–2 lb. (hand) 1
Decontaminating Apparatus M2, 1½ qt. 1

Engine, Make and model . . . . Hercules JXD
Type . . . . In–line, L.C.
No. of cylinders 6
Displacement . . . . 320 cu. in.
Fuel (gasoline) . . . . 70–80 octane
Net hp. . . . . 87 at 2,400 r.p.m.
Max. torque . . . . 220 lb.-ft. at 1,150 r.p.m.

Transmission, Type . . . Combination sliding and constant mesh
Gear ratios
  First speed 5.00:1
  Second speed 3.07:1
  Third speed 1.71:1
  Fourth speed 1.00:1
  Reverse 5.83:1

Transfer Case, Gear ratios 1.00:1; 1.87:1
Steering, Type . . . . Cam and twin lever
Differential, Gear ratio 5.14:1
Suspension, Type . . . . . Semi-elliptic leaf springs
Clutch, Type . . . . Dry, single-plate
Fan, Type 6-blade
Radiator, Type . . . . Fin and tube
  Capacity of system . . . . 19 qt.
Brakes, Type . . . . Internal-expanding
  Operation . . . . Hydraulic
Brakes, Parking, Type . . . . Disk
  Location . . . . Rear of transfer case

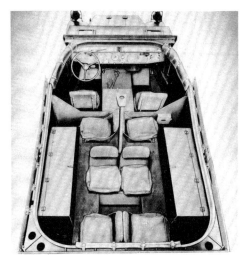

OVERHEAD VIEW, SHOWING SEATING

80"
78½"
131"
221½"
65¼"

HALF-TRACK CARS M2, M2A1—LIMITED STANDARD
HALF-TRACK PERSONNEL CARRIERS M3, M3A1—LIMITED STANDARD
HALF-TRACK CAR M3A2—STANDARD

Half-Track Car M2 and Half-Track Personnel Carrier M3, the basic half-track vehicles, were standardized in 1940 and used throughout 1941 and 1942. With the addition of ring mounts for antiaircraft use and with other modifications, their designations were changed to M2A1 and M3A1 respectively. All of these vehicles are now classified as Limited Standard and will be replaced in production by Half-Track Car M3A2.

Consisting of a specially designed, commercial-type, front-and-rear drive truck chassis with an armored hull, the half-track vehicle can attain a maximum road speed of 40 m.p.h. Because of its endless-band track-laying rear drive, however, it can be used over rough terrain. It will cross ditches which are not sufficiently deep to cause the front or rear to become embedded. Some models are provided with a roller at the front to assist in climbing out of ditches. On other models, the roller is replaced by a winch for use in towing the vehicle out of soft terrain.

The body is protected by ¼-in. armor at the sides and rear. Top and side protection is given the engine by the armored hood. The radiator is protected by armored shutters which can be opened or closed or set in three intermediate positions from within the driver's compartment. The windshield is of shatter-proof glass.

For further protection, a ½-in. armored shield is hinged above the windshield frame, held open by three supports, and additional armored shields are hinged to the doors. In combat zones, the windshield can be removed and these shields swung into place. They are provided with direct-vision slots.

The detachable top is of canvas and is supported by three removable bows and the windshield frame. Removable side curtains with transparent windows also are provided. Mine racks are mounted on the sides of late production models.

Power is supplied by a White 160AX gasoline engine.

HALF-TRACK CAR M2—LIMITED STANDARD, has seats for a crew of ten. A skate rail surrounds the interior of the vehicle. By the use of two carriage mounts, a cal. .30 and a cal. .50 machine gun can be moved along this rail and fired in any direction.

This vehicle can be used as a prime mover for the 105-mm howitzer.

HALF-TRACK CAR M2 HAS GUN RAIL AROUND INTERIOR

HALF-TRACK CAR M2A1 HAS RING MOUNT FOR MACHINE GUN

HALF-TRACK PERSONNEL CARRIER M3 HAS PEDESTAL MOUNT

HALF-TRACK PERSONNEL CARRIER M3A1 WITH WINCH AT FRONT

HALF-TRACK CAR M2A1—LIMITED STANDARD, is similar to the M2 but has an M49 ring mount for cal. .50 machine gun over the assistant driver's seat. By use of this mount the cal. .50 HB machine gun can be traversed 360° from a single position, permitting rapid fire against low-flying aircraft as well as against ground targets. It can be elevated from −15° to +85°.

Three fixed pintle sockets are mounted, one on each side and one on the rear of the body, permitting the use of a cal. .30 machine gun.

HALF-TRACK PERSONNEL CARRIER M3—LIMITED STAND-ARD, is generally similar to the M2 but has seating accommodations for 13 men. The body is about 10 inches longer than on the M2 and has a door at the rear. Instead of a skate rail, the vehicle has an M25 pedestal mount for a cal. .30 machine gun, which is secured to the floor of the personnel compartment.

TYPICAL STOWAGE ARRANGEMENT OF HALF-TRACK CAR M3A2

This half-track, with modifications, is used as the chassis for several gun motor carriages.

HALF-TRACK PERSONNEL CARRIER M3A1—LIMITED STANDARD, is similar to the M3 but has an M49 ring mount for a cal. .50 machine gun over the assistant driver's seat.

Three pintle sockets are mounted, one on each side and one on the rear of the body.

HALF-TRACK CAR M3A2—STANDARD, is a modification of the Half-Track Personnel Carrier M3A1 designed to take the place of Half-Track Personnel Carriers M3 and M3A1, and Half-Track Cars M2 and M2A1.

Variations in stowage arrangements, through the use of suitable boxes, give the vehicle a variety of uses. Crews range from 5 to 12 men, depending on the amount of stowage carried and the tactical purpose intended.

Normally the vehicle mounts one cal. .50 machine gun or one cal. .30 machine gun, together with the required vehicular accessories, tools, spare parts, and equipment which are provided for all half-tracks. Under such circumstances, a crew of 12 can be carried. Three pintle sockets are provided to accommodate additional machine guns when authorized.

When the vehicles carry special loadings or have radios installed, personnel are displaced. As an example, if an SCR-508 radio is installed, the crew is reduced by two men.

The basic vehicle is equipped to stow and carry 330 rounds of cal. .50 ammunition and 2,000 rounds of cal. .30 ammunition. When used as a machine gun squad carrier, however, additional ammunition is carried in place of two of the seat positions. When used by a heavy machine gun squad armed with water-cooled machine guns, these guns and their accessories are substituted for the air-cooled cal. .30 machine gun.

HALF-TRACK CAR M3A2 WITH FRONT ROLLER. VEHICLE HAS RING MOUNT AND THREE PINTLE MOUNTS FOR MACHINE GUNS. IT SEATS 5 TO 12 MEN

Miscellaneous equipment boxes are provided for carrying additional stowage items pertaining to special loading of different organizations. When the vehicle is used to carry cargo in considerable quantity, fewer personnel are carried.

Half-Track Car M3A2 is intended for manufacture by the Autocar Co., the Diamond T Motor Co., and the White Motor Co.

A Ring Mount M49, for a cal. .50 machine gun, is erected above the assistant driver's seat, for use against low-flying aircraft. A one-piece armor shield protects the machine gunner.

REFERENCES—TM 9–710, 9–710A; OCM 16112, 16187, 16410, 16679, 17952, 18312, 18394, 20070, 20368, 20438, 20680, 21002, 21501, 21782; SNL G–102, Vols. 1, 2, 3, 4.

TYPICAL CHARACTERISTICS

	M2	M2A1	M3	M3A1	M3A2
Crew	10	10	13	13	5 to 12
Physical Characteristics					
Weight (gross)	19,800 lb.	19,600 lb.	20,000 lb.	20,500 lb.	21,200 lb.
Length—with roller	19 ft., 6¾ in.	19 ft., 6¾ in.	20 ft., 3½ in.	20 ft., 3½ in.	20 ft., 3½ in.
with winch	20 ft., 1⅝ in.	20 ft., 1⅝ in.	20 ft., 9⅝ in.	20 ft., 9⅝ in.	20 ft., 9⅝ in.
Width—without mine racks	6 ft., 5¼ in.	6 ft., 5¼ in.	6 ft., 5¼ in.	6 ft., 5¼ in.	6 ft., 5¼ in.
with mine racks	7 ft., 3½ in.	7 ft., 3½ in.	7 ft., 3½ in.	7 ft., 3½ in.	7 ft., 3½ in.
Height—overall	7 ft., 5 in.	7 ft., 5 in.	8 ft., 10 in.	8 ft., 10 in.	8 ft., 10 in.
Ground clearance	11³⁄₁₆ in.	11³⁄₁₆ in.	11³⁄₁₆ in.	11³⁄₁₆ in.	11³⁄₁₆ in.
Tread—front	64½ in.	64½ in.	64½ in.	64½ in.	64½ in.
rear	63¹³⁄₁₆ in.	63¹³⁄₁₆ in.	63¹³⁄₁₆ in.	63¹³⁄₁₆ in.	63¹³⁄₁₆ in.
Wheelbase	135½ in.	135½ in.	135½ in.	135½ in.	135½ in.
Ground contact length	46¾ in.	46¾ in.	46¾ in.	46¾ in.	46¾ in.
Tire equipment (combat, 12-ply)	8.25 x 20	8.25 x 20	8.25 x 20	8.25 x 20	8.25 x 20
Armament					
Cal. .50 Machine Gun M2, HB (flexible)	1	1		1	1
Cal. .30 Browning Machine Gun M1919A4 (flexible)	1	1	1	1	1
Pedestal Mount M25			1		
Ring Mount M49 for cal. .30 or cal. .50 Machine Gun		1		1	
Carriage assembly		1		1	
Cradle assemblies		2	1	2	
Cal. .50 Tripod Mount M3	1	1		1	1
Cal. .30 Tripod Mount M2	1	1	1	1	1
Machine Gun Mounts M35	2				
Provision for:					
Rocket Launcher, AT, 2.36-in., M9 or M1A1					1
Cal. .45 Submachine Gun M3 or M1928A1	1	1	1	1	1
Cal. .30 Rifles M1 or Carbines M1			12	12	12
Ammunition, Stowage					
Cal. .50	700 rounds	700 rounds	700 rounds	700 rounds	330 rounds*
Cal. .30	7,750 rounds	7,750 rounds	4,000 rounds	7,750 rounds	2,000 rounds*
Cal. .45	540 rounds	540 rounds	540 rounds	540 rounds	180 rounds
Rockets, Grenade, AT, 2.36-in., M6					6
Grenades, Hand (Fragmentation, Mk. II; Smoke, WP, M15; Smoke, Colored, M6 or M18)	10	10	22	22	24
Mines, AT, H.E., w/Fuze M1	14	14	24	24	24

Armor—Front .... ¼ in.
Sides and rear .... ¼ in., F.H.
Windshield protective plate ...... ½ in.

Performance
Maximum speed on level ...... 40 m.p.h.
Maximum grade ability 60%
Vertical obstacle ability ...... 12 in.
Fording depth (slowest forward speed) .. 32 in.
Turning radius .... 30 ft.
Fuel capacity .... 60 gal.
Cruising range (approx.) ...... 175 miles

Vision
Driver ...... Slits in windshield and wingshield

Communications
Radio .. SCR–193 or 506, and 508 and 593; 284 and 508 and 593; 193 or 506, and 508 or 528 or 510 or 608 or 610 or 628. (Or any of these individually)

Battery, Voltage, total 12

Fire Protection and Decontamination
Fire Extinguisher, CO₂–4 lb. (hand) 1
Decontaminating Apparatus M2, 1½ qt. ... 3

Engine, Make and model ...... White 160AX
Type .... In-line, "L"
No. of cylinders 6

Cycle 4
Fuel (gasoline) .... 80 octane
Bore and stroke .... 4 x 5⅛ in.
Displacement .... 386 cu. in.
Compression 6.3:1
Net hp. .... 128 at 2,800 r.p.m.
Max. torque ...... 300 lb.-ft. at 1,200 r.p.m.
Crankshaft rotation .... C'Clockwise
Length .... 52¼ in.
Width .... 26 in.
Height .... 37 in.
Ignition .... Battery
Weight, dry .... 1,015 lb.
Weight, installed .... 1,207 lb.

Transmission, Gear ratios
First speed 4 92:1
Second speed 2.60:1
Third speed 1.74:1
Fourth speed 1.00:1
Reverse 4.37:1

Transfer Case
Gear ratios 1.00:1; 2.48:1

Differential, Track Drive, Gear ratio .. 4.444:1
Ring gear, No. of teeth 40
Pinion, No. of teeth 9

Differential, Front Axle, Gear ratio 6.8:1
Ring gear, No. of teeth 34

Pinion, No. of teeth 5
Steering ratio 23.4; 19.5; 23.4:1

Final Drive
Sprocket, No. of teeth 18
Pitch diameter .... 22.918 in.

Suspension, Track, Type ...... Volute spring
Wheel or tire size ...... 12 x 4⅛ dual

Suspension, Front
Type (longitudinal leaf) ...... Semi-elliptic
Wheel or tire size .... 8.25 x 20
Wheel construction ...... Ventilated disk

Idler, Wheel size .... 12½ x 9⅜

Track, Type .... Endless band
Width .... 12 in.
Pitch .... 4 in.

Master Clutch, Type ...... Dry, single plate

Radiator, Type .... Fin and tube
Capacity of system .... 26 qt.

Brakes, Type ..... Internal expanding
Operation .... Hydraulic

Brakes, Parking, Type .... Disk

*When organizational use of vehicle requires it, 600 rounds of additional cal. .50 ammunition or 6,000 rounds of additional cal. .30 ammunition are carried, and personnel capacity is reduced by two men.

HALF-TRACK CAR M9A1—LIMITED STANDARD
HALF-TRACK PERSONNEL CARRIERS M5, M5A1—LIMITED STANDARD
HALF-TRACK CAR M5A2—SUBSTITUTE STANDARD

These vehicles are generally similar to Half-Track Car M2A1, Half-Track Personnel Carriers M3 and M3A1, and Half-Track Car M3A2, respectively, but they were manufactured by the International Harvester Co., and contain that company's component parts.

Each is powered by an International RED 450B 6-cylinder, 4-cycle, in-line gasoline engine. Body armor is of homogeneous armor plate. The windshield protective plate is ⅝ in. thick and the other armor ⁵⁄₁₆ in.

REFERENCES—TM 9–707; OCM 18370, 18509, 20070, 20368, 21501, 21782, 21847; SNL G–147.

HALF-TRACK CAR M9A1—This corresponds to Half-Track Car M2A1, and has seats for ten men. It is provided with a Ring Mount M49 for a cal. .50 antiaircraft machine gun and has three fixed pintle sockets, permitting the use of a cal. .30 machine gun.

HALF-TRACK PERSONNEL CARRIER M5A1—This corresponds to Half-Track Personnel Carrier M3A1 with seats for 13. It has a Ring Mount M49 for a cal. .50 antiaircraft machine gun and three fixed pintle sockets, permitting the use of a cal. .30 machine gun.

HALF-TRACK CAR M5A2—This corresponds to Half-Track Car M3A2, with the same stowage arrangements and with accommodations for crews varying from 5 to 12 men. It has a Ring Mount M49 and three pintle sockets. It is intended for International Aid Requirements only.

HALF-TRACK CAR M9A1 FROM ABOVE, SHOWING RING MOUNT AND PINTLE MOUNTS

HALF-TRACK CAR M5A2 SHOWING STOWAGE ON LEFT SIDE AND ON REAR

TYPICAL CHARACTERISTICS

Physical Characteristics
Weight (gross)—M9A1	21,200 lb.
M5	20,500 lb.
M5A1	21,500 lb.
M5A2	22,500 lb.
Length—with roller	20 ft., 2³⁄₁₆ in.
with winch	20 ft., 9¹⁄₁₆ in.
Width—over mine racks	7 ft., 2⅞ in.
Height—over bows	7 ft., 7 in.
Top of A.A. gun (M49 Mount)	9 ft.
Ground clearance	11³⁄₁₆ in.
Tread—front	66½ in.
rear	63¹³⁄₁₆ in.
Wheelbase	135½ in.
Tire equipment	9.00 x 20 (combat)

Armor—Front, sides, and rear....⁵⁄₁₆ in. homo.
Floor	⁵⁄₁₆ in.
Windshield protective plate	⅝ in.

Performance
Maximum speed on level	38 m.p.h.
Maximum grade ability	60%
Vertical obstacle ability	12 in.
Fording depth	32 in.
Angle of approach—with roller	40°
with winch	36°
Angle of departure	32°
Fuel capacity	60 gal.
Cruising range (approx.)	125 miles
Normal towed load	4,500 lb.

Engine, Make
Make	International
Model	RED 450B
Type	In-line, L.C.
Number of cylinders	6
Cycle	4
Fuel (gasoline)	80 octane
Max. governed speed	2,700 r.p.m.
Net hp.	143 at 2,700 r.p.m.
Max. torque	348 lb.-ft. at 800 r.p.m.

Radiator, Capacity....................31 qt.

Other characteristics same as for corresponding models in Half Track M2 and M3 series.

ARMORED UTILITY VEHICLE T41—LIMITED PROCUREMENT

This vehicle is a modification of the 76-mm Gun Motor Carriage M18 designed in order to provide a prime mover equal to the M18 in performance.

As compared to the gun motor carriage, the turret is omitted and certain components are rearranged to provide better stowage. Limited procurement of the vehicles was authorized in June 1944.

The vehicle has stowage and accessory equipment for use as a prime mover for the 3-Inch Gun Carriage M6. It is capable of carrying the crew members and initial rounds of ammunition for the gun.

The vehicle is of the full track-laying type, using an independently sprung torsion bar suspension, driven from the front sprocket. It will accommodate a crew of nine men, including the driver and assistant driver.

Armament consists of a Cal. .50 Machine Gun M2 HB (flexible), mounted on a concentric ring in the forward part of the crew compartment, and a Cal. .50 Tripod Mount M3. Provision is made for carrying two Cal. .30 Carbines M1, and additional carbines may be carried by crew members.

Armor at the front, sides, and rear is ½ inch, with additional ⅝-inch armor applied locally at the front. Top armor is $\frac{5}{16}$ inch, and bottom armor ¼ inch.

The vehicle will attain a speed of 50 miles per hour or better, and will climb grades up to 60%.

Power is supplied by a Continental R-975–C1 or C4 engine.

Hatches for the driver and assistant driver are provided with periscopes for vision in combat areas. An additional escape hatch is in the floor of the hull. The crew compartment is open at the top but has a detachable canvas cover for protection against inclement weather. The vehicle is equipped with a two-way radio.

REFERENCES—OCM 24056, 24262.

TYPICAL CHARACTERISTICS

Crew..................................9

Physical Characteristics
Weight (gross)....................35,000 lb.
Length.........................17 ft., 4 in.
Width........................9 ft., ½ in.
Height—over antiaircraft gun.......6 ft., 7 in.
  over crew compartment ...5 ft., 11 in.
Ground clearance.....................14 in.
Tread (center to center of tracks)......94¼ in.
Ground contact length................116 in.

Armament
1 Cal. .50 Machine Gun M2 HB
  (flexible) on ring mount, antiaircraft
1 Tripod Mount, Cal. .50, M3
Provision for:
2 Cal. .30 Carbines M1

Ammunition, Stowage
3-in..........................42 rounds
Cal. .50......................900 rounds
Cal. .30 Carbine.............1,620 rounds
Grenades, Hand (Fragmentation,
  Mk. II, 6; Smoke, W.P., 6)..............12
Smoke Pots...........................4

Armor   **Actual**
Hull, Front.......................½ in.
  Sides and rear.....................½ in.
    additional, frontal, local...........⅝ in.
  Top.............................$\frac{5}{16}$ in.
  Bottom...........................¼ in.

Performance
Maximum speed on level...........50 m.p.h.
Speed on 10% grade..............15 m.p.h.
Maximum grade ability................60%
Trench crossing ability..........6 ft., 2 in.
Vertical obstacle ability..............36 in.
Fording depth (slowest forward speed)...48 in.
Cruising range (approx.)...........150 miles

Vision and Fire Control
Periscopes M6..........................2

Communications
Radio.........................SCR–610

Battery, Voltage, total....................24

Fire Protection and Decontamination
Fire Extinguisher, CO₂–10 lb. (fixed)........2
  CO₂–4 lb. (hand)......................1
Decontaminating Apparatus M2, 1½ qts....1

Other characteristics same as 76-mm Gun Motor Carriage M18.

ARMORED UTILITY VEHICLE T41 IS PRIME MOVER FOR 3-INCH GUN CARRIAGE

VEHICLE ALSO CARRIES CREW MEMBERS AND AMMUNITION FOR TOWED GUN

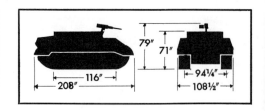

FULL-TRACK PRIME MOVERS M33, M34, M35—SUBSTITUTE STANDARD

These prime movers for 240-mm howitzer and 8-in. gun materiel were designed as expedients pending production in quantity of the 38-ton High Speed Tractor M6. They are Substitute Standard.

REFERENCES—OCM 23183, 23571.

FULL-TRACK PRIME MOVER M33 is a modification of Tank Recovery Vehicle M31 and has a riveted hull. The turret, turret ring, and boom assembly, and certain other parts peculiar to the tank recovery vehicle, were removed, as were also the cal. .30 bow and turret machine guns and the cal. .30 machine gun tripod mount. An air compressor and rear outlet lines for operation of brakes on the towed load were added, as well as an electric outlet for stop and tail lights on the trailed load. A cal. .50 machine gun mount for anti-aircraft use was supplied. Canvas covers are furnished for the turret and machine gun mount openings.

FULL-TRACK PRIME MOVER M34 is a conversion of Tank Recovery Vehicle M32B1 and has a cast hull. The 81-mm mortar and mount, the cal. .50 machine gun, and the cal. .30 machine gun and tripod mount were removed, as were also the boom assembly and miscellaneous stowage items and accessories. An air compressor and lines for operation of towed load brakes were added, with outlets front and rear, together with an electric outlet for stop and tail lights on the trailed load, and necessary stowage.

FULL-TRACK PRIME MOVER M35 is a modification of 3-in. Gun Motor Carriage M10A1 with a welded hull. The turret, including the 3-in. Gun M7 and cal. .50 machine gun, and the cal. .50 tripod mount were removed, as were also the rear pintle, the pioneer compass, and miscellaneous stowage items. An air compressor unit and lines, with outlets front and rear, were added. Pintle assemblies, similar to those on the Tank Recovery Vehicle M32 series, were supplied at front and rear. Four seats were installed in the crew compartment. An electric outlet for the towed load stop and tail lights and various stowage items were added.

FULL-TRACK PRIME MOVER M33 HAS RIVETED HULL

FULL-TRACK PRIME MOVER M34 HAS CAST HULL

TYPICAL CHARACTERISTICS

	Prime Mover M33	Prime Mover M34	Prime Mover M35
Crew	6	6	6
Physical Characteristics			
Weight (gross)	60,000 lb.	63,000 lb.	55,000 lb.
Length	18 ft., 6 in.	19 ft., 1¼ in.	19 ft., 7 in.
Width	8 ft., 11 in.	8 ft., 7 in.	10 ft.
Height	7 ft., 3 in.	8 ft., 8³⁄₁₆ in.	5 ft., 10 in.
Ground clearance	17⅛ in.	17⅛ in.	17⅛ in.
Tread (center to center of tracks)	83 in.	83 in.	83 in.
Ground contact length	147 in.	147 in.	147 in.
Ground pressure	12.3 lb./sq. in.	13.0 lb./sq. in.	11.3 lb./sq. in
Armor, Actual			
Hull, Front, Upper	2 in.	2 in.	½-2 in.
Lower	1½-2 in.	1½-2 in.	1 in.
Sides	1½ in.	1½ in.	¾-1 in.
Rear	1-1½ in.	1-1½ in.	1-1½ in.
Top	½ in.	¾ in.	⅜-¾ in.
Bottom	½-1 in.	½-1 in.	¼ in.
Performance			
Maximum speed on level	25 m.p.h.	24 m.p.h.	30 m.p.h.
Maximum grade ability	60%	60%	60%
Trench crossing ability	7 ft., 5 in.	6 ft., 2 in.	7 ft., 6 in.
Vertical obstacle ability	24 in.	24 in.	24 in.
Fording depth (slowest forward speed)	42 in.	48 in.	36 in.
Turning radius	35 ft.	31 ft.	31 ft.
Fuel capacity	185 gal.	175 gal.	192 gal.
Cruising range (approx.)	150 miles	120 miles	160 miles
Vision and Fire Control			
Periscope M6		5	3
Protectoscopes and direct vision slots	4		

Other characteristics same as for Medium Tank M3, Medium Tank M4A1, Gun Motor Carriage M10A1.

FULL-TRACK PRIME MOVER M35 HAS WELDED HULL

TRUCK MOUNTED CRANE M2; CLAMSHELL TRAILER M16—STANDARD

TRUCK MOUNTED CRANE, M2, WITH BOOM IN TRAVELING POSITION, TOWING CLAMSHELL TRAILER, M16, CARRYING ⅝ YARD CLAMSHELL BUCKET

TRUCK MOUNTED CRANE, M2, is designed to handle 240 mm howitzer matériel and 8 inch gun matériel in the field. It was developed in connection with design and development of the 240 mm howitzer matériel, M1918A2 and M1, to handle components of the matériel when changing from traveling to firing position and vice versa. It was standardized in September, 1942.

The cradle recoil mechanism and tube (approximately 36,000 pounds for the heaviest weapon) are carried as one load and the carriage (approximately 33,000 pounds for the heaviest weapon) as another load on transport wagons. Truck Mounted Crane, M2, is used to remove the matériel from the transport wagons and to set it up in firing position.

Basis of issue is one per firing battery armed with 240 mm Howitzer, M1918M1, on 240 mm Howitzer Carriage, M1918A2; 240 mm Howitzer and Carriage, M1; and 8 inch Gun, M1, on 8 inch Gun Carriage, M2.

The crane is capable of accompanying the transport wagons in convoy at a maximum speed of about 30 miles per hour, with road ability and cross country ability comparable to the prime mover towing the trailed loads. The crew consists of the chassis operator and the crane operator. In addition to these particular uses, the crane may be employed for many other purposes by field maintenance and depot organizations.

The chassis is of special construction for full revolving crane service, and is equipped with screw type extension outrigger beams and floats.

It is of the six-wheeled type, with power supplied to all six wheels. Four of the wheels are dual tired. A ⅝ yard clamshell bucket is provided with each

crane. The entire crane cab may be closed and locked. Windows are provided with shatterproof glass. Tow hooks are provided at the front and a pintle at the rear. The vehicle is manufactured by the Thew Shovel Co.

REFERENCES — OCM 16600, 17111, 17178, 17240, 18648, 18863.

TYPICAL CHARACTERISTICS

TRUCK MOUNTED CRANE, M2
Crew......................................2

Physical Characteristics
Weight (gross)....................54,760 lb.
Length, over-all (boom in traveling
position)....................33 ft., 7 ins.
Length of truck................25 ft., 7 ins.
Width.......................9 ft., ½ in.
Height.....................11 ft., 8 ins.
Ground clearance.................17½ ins.
Tread (center to center, rear)..........78 ins.
Wheelbase......................168¾ ins.
Tire equipment.................12.00 x 20
(mud and snow type)
Ground contact at 4 in.
penetration..................3,100 sq. ins.
Ground pressure............17.6 lb./sq. in.

Performance
Lifting capacities with 22 ft. boom
at 11 ft. radius
—with outriggers set...........40,000 lb.*
—over back without outriggers..24,500 lb.*
—over side without outriggers...21,850 lb.*
Maximum speed on level..........30 m.p.h.
Cross country speed..............5 m.p.h.
Maximum grade ability.............40%
Trench crossing ability..............3 ft.
Turning radius................47 ft., 2 ins.
Fuel capacity..................100 gals.
Cruising range..................150 miles
Maximum drawbar pull..........29,000 lb.

*Includes weight of hooks, blocks, slings, etc.

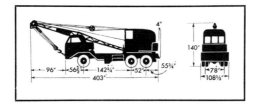

Battery, Voltage, total......................12
Engine, Make and Model
(Crane Carrier)................Hercules HXC
Type............................L head
No. of cylinders.......................6
Fuel (gasoline)..................70 octane
Displacement.................779 cu. ins.
Rated hp..........179 at 2,200 r.p.m.
Max. torque....555 lb.-ft. at 900 r.p.m.
Engine, Make and Model
(Crane)................Waukesha 6 MZR
Type............................L head
No. of cylinders.......................6
Fuel (gasoline)..................70 octane
Displacement.................404 cu. ins.
Rated hp..........82 at 1,600 r.p.m.
Weight without accessories........920 lb.
Transmission, Type..........Constant mesh
Gear ratios
First speed......................6.54:1
Second speed....................3.27:1
Third speed......................1.76:1
Fourth speed....................1.00:1
Reverse........................7.24:1
Suspension, Type, Front.........Semi-elliptic
Rear......................Steel beams
Master Clutch, Type.............Single plate
Radiator, Type..............Fin and tube
Capacity of system..............14 gals.
Brakes, Type........Internal-expanding, air
Brakes, Parking..............Ventilated disk

CLAMSHELL TRAILER, M16
Physical Characteristics
Weight—empty (approx.)..........2,425 lb.
loaded (approx.)..............8,240 lb.
Length—empty............13 ft., 3 ins.
loaded..................14 ft., 3 ins.
Width...........................9 ft.
Height—empty..........4 ft., 1½ ins.
loaded..................10 ft., 4 ins.
Ground clearance..................20 ins.
Tread (center to center)..............96 ins.
Tire equipment........12.00 x 20 (highway)

CLAMSHELL TRAILER, M16, is designed to be towed by the Truck Mounted Crane, M2, to carry the clamshell bucket, and the ten 3″x24″x10′ timbers required for use where operations are on soft or marshy ground. It was standardized July, 1943.

7-TON HIGH-SPEED TRACTOR M2—STANDARD

7-TON HIGH-SPEED TRACTOR, M2, IS USED TO TOW HEAVY AIRCRAFT

TYPICAL CHARACTERISTICS

Crew.................................3

Physical Characteristics
Weight (gross)....................15,000 lb.
Length.......................13 ft., 10 ins.
Width..........................5 ft., 10 ins.
Height...........................5 ft., 8 ins.
Height of hitch....................20 ins.
Ground clearance...................19 ins.
Center of gravity above ground.......31 ins.
Tread (center to center of tracks)......52 ins.
Ground contact length.............63 ins.
Ground pressure............8.5 lb./sq. in.

Performance
Maximum speed on level..........22 m.p.h.
Maximum grade ability.................60%
Trench crossing ability..............5 ft.
Vertical obstacle ability............20 ins.
Fording depth (slowest forward speed)..32 ins.
Angle of approach.....................45°
Angle of departure....................41°
Turning radius....................10½ ft.
Fuel capacity...................33 gals.
Cruising range (approx.)...........100 miles
Maximum drawbar pull...........9,000 lb.
Normal towed load........Heavy aircraft
Winch capacity.................10,000 lb.

Vision.....................Open vehicle

Battery, Voltage, total 12

Fire Protection and Decontamination
Fire Extinguisher, CO₂—15 lb. (hand).......1
Decontaminating Apparatus, M2, 1½ qts....1

Engine, Make and Model....Hercules WXLC3
Type......................In-line "L"
No. of cylinders....................6
Fuel (gasoline)...............70 octane
Max. governed speeds. 2,500 and 3,280 r.p.m.
Net hp.............150 at 3,000 r.p.m.
Max. torque.......312 lb.-ft. at 1,200 r.p.m.

Transmission, Type...............Selective
Gear ratios
First speed.....................2.37:1
Second speed...................1.16:1
Third speed......................80:1
Fourth speed.....................49:1
Reverse........................1.92:1

Differential, Type...............Controlled
Gear ratio.......................3.5:1
Steering ratio....................1.8:1

Final Drive, Type...............Spur Gear
Gear ratio.......................6.61:1
Sprocket, no. of teeth..............20
Pitch diameter................25.468 ins.

Suspension, Type.............Volute spring
Wheel or tire size.........14 x 4⅛ ins.

Track, Type................Band block
Width.......................13⅝ ins.
Pitch.............................4 ins.
No. of shoes per vehicle..........148

Master Clutch, Type...........Double plate

Radiator, Type.............Tube and fin
Capacity of system...............37 qts.

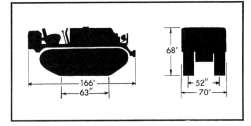

The 7-Ton High-Speed Tractor, M2, is the first of several tractors, built to Ordnance specifications, and combining speed with great pulling power. It was standardized in February, 1941, as Medium Tractor, M2.

Based on a commercial tractor, modified in accordance with military requirements, it is used for towing aircraft of the heavy bombardment type and for general utility use on flying fields.

Low enough to drive under the wings of a big plane, the tractor can be used as a platform for servicing operations.

Special equipment includes a three-stage air compressor driven by the tractor engine for inflation of landing-gear shock struts. The compressor operates at 16.7 cubic feet per minute, with a maximum pressure of 2,000 pounds per square inch. It is equipped with pressure outlets reducible to 100 pounds per square inch. A 3KW, 100-volt, DC auxiliary generator is driven by a V-belt from the tractor engine.

Power is supplied by a Hercules WXLC3 in-line, L-type, 6-cylinder gasoline engine. The selective type transmission provides four speeds forward, ranging from 2½ to 22 m.p.h., and a reverse. Normal high speed is 15 m.p.h. Steering is by a controlled differential. Drive sprockets are at the rear to provide steering characteristics desired for handling airplanes.

The vehicle is capable of starting and turning without jerking, of negotiating marshy terrain and of starting from a dead stop in the same terrain. It is designed to turn on a radius of 11 feet without excessive disturbance of turf, and to maneuver easily in close quarters. Continuous rubber track, with detachable rubber blocks, is used.

Upholstered seats are provided for a crew of three. The front-mounted winch, which is operated from the side of the tractor, has a pull of 10,000 pounds on the first layer, and a line speed of approximately 65 feet per minute. The winch drum has a capacity of 300 feet of ⅜ inch cable.

A quickly detachable, spring-type swinging hitch is supplied, together with a standard Ordnance pintle. An extra set of steel-backed rubber blocks, and an extra set of steel grousers, are furnished with each tractor. Special equipment includes a channel type front bumper with wood filler, an air cleaner, and an oil filter.

The vehicle is manufactured by the Cleveland Tractor Co.

REFERENCES — OCM 16409, 16521, 21220.

18-TON HIGH-SPEED TRACTOR M4—STANDARD

This prime mover is designed for artillery loads of from 18,000 to 30,000 pounds weight, and is capable of transporting personnel, ammunition, and accessories pertaining to the section.

It can be used for the following types of matériel:

3 inch A.A. Gun Mount, M2A2
90 mm A.A. Gun Mounts, M1A1, M2
155 mm Gun Carriages, M1, M2 and M3
8 inch Howitzer Carriage, M1
240 mm Howitzer Carriage, M1918

It is designated Class A when carrying an ammunition box with shell racks for 3 inch and 90 mm ammunition, and Class B when carrying a cargo box, with shell racks and hold-down plates suitable for 155 mm howitzer, 8 inch howitzer, and 240 mm gun ammunition. A special swing crane with trolley hoist is provided with each cargo box for hoisting shells into the box.

The cab is divided into two compartments, with seating room for the driver and two men in the front compartment, and double seats accommodating eight additional men in the rear compartment. Back cushions are leather covered, and canvas zipper bags padded with blankets serve as seat cushions.

The winch, equipped with 300 feet of ¾ inch wire cable, has a maximum pull of 30,000 pounds.

A Ring Mount, M49C, for a cal. .50 Machine Gun, M2, HB, is provided for protection against aircraft. The gun has an elevation from —20° to +80°. However, full depression is not obtainable to the front and rear.

The tractor is equipped with complete controls and operating mechanism for both air brakes and electric brakes for the trailer. A tire inflation hose is part of the equipment.

The vehicle is powered by a Waukesha, 145GZ, in-line, 6 cylinder, 4 cycle gasoline engine.

The tractor is manufactured by the Allis-Chalmers Manufacturing Co.

References—TM 9-785; OCM 16726, 16806, 17816, 17925, 18583, 18730, 19365, 19458, 20208, 21220.

18-TON HIGH-SPEED TRACTOR, M4, HAS RING MOUNT FOR MACHINE GUN ON TOP

TYPICAL CHARACTERISTICS

Crew 11

Physical Characteristics
Weight (gross) . . . . 31,500 lb.
Length—Class A . . . . 17 ft., 2 ins.
    Class B . . . . 16 ft., 11 in.
Width . . . . 8 ft., 1 in.
Height, to top of cab . . . . 7 ft., 10 ins.
    to top of gun mount . . . . 8 ft., 3 ins.
Turret ring diameter (inside) . . . . 42 ins.
Height of pintle . . . . 29 ins.
Ground clearance . . . . 20 ins.
Tread (center to center of tracks) . . . . . . 80 ins.
Ground contact length . . . . 124 ins.
Ground pressure (with 90 mm gun)
                           7.6 lb./sq. in.

Armament
Ring Mount, M49C, for cal. .50 machine gun
1 Tripod Mount, cal. .50, M3
1 Carriage assembly
1 Cradle assembly
Provision for:
1 cal. .50 Machine Gun, M2, HB (flexible)

Ammunition
Cal. .50 . . . . 500 rounds
One of the following, depending on
    artillery towed:
90 mm A.A. 54 rounds
3 inch A.A. . . . . 54 rounds
155 mm Gun . . . . 30 rounds
8 inch Howitzer . . . . 20 rounds
240 mm Howitzer . . . . 12 rounds

Performance
Maximum speed towing 90 mm A.A. gun
    On level . . . . 33 m.p.h.
    On 3% grade . . . . 20 m.p.h.
Maximum grade ability 60%
Trench crossing ability . . . . 5 ft.
Vertical obstacle ability . . . . 29 ins.
Fording depth (slowest forward speed) . . 41 ins.
Turning radius . . . . 18 ft., 6 ins.
Fuel capacity . . . . 125 gals.
Cruising range (approx.) . . . . 180 miles
Maximum drawbar pull . . . . 38,700 lb. at stall
                       13,000 lb. at 4 m.p.h.
Winch capacity . . . . 30,000 lb.

Battery, Voltage, Total 12

Fire Protection and Decontamination
Fire Extinguisher, CO₂—4 lb. (hand) 2
Decontaminating Apparatus, M2, 1½ qts. . . . 2

Engine, Make and Model . . . Waukesha 145GZ
Type . . . . In-line
No. of cylinders 6
Fuel (gasoline) . . . . 70 octane
Max. governed speed . . . . 2,100 r.p.m.
Net hp. . . . . 210 at 2,100 r.p.m.
Max. torque . . . . . . 528 lb.-ft. at 1,680 r.p.m.

Transmission, Type . . . . Selective
Gear ratios—First speed 2.166:1
    Second speed 1.555:1
    Third speed 0.437:1
    Reverse 1.822:1

Torque Converter, Gear ratio 1.372:1

Differential, Type . . . . Controlled
Gear ratio 2.666:1
Steering ratio 1.747:1

Suspension, Type . . . . . Horizontal volute spring
Wheel or tire size . . . . 20 x 9

Idler, Type . . . . Trailing
Wheel or tire size . . . . 32 x 9

Track, Type . . . . Steel Block, Rubber Bushed
Width . . . . 16⁹⁄₁₆ ins.
Pitch . . . . 6 ins.
No. of shoes per vehicle 130

Master Clutch, Type . . . Spring loaded, dry disk

Final Drive, Type . . . . Spur gear
Sprocket, no. of teeth 13
    Pitch diameter . . . . 25.038 ins.
Gear ratio 2.764:1

Radiator, Type . . . . Fin and tube
Capacity of system . . . . 72 qts.

Brakes, Type . . . . Mechanical on controlled
                                 differential

Brakes, Trailer, Type . . . . Air and/or electrical

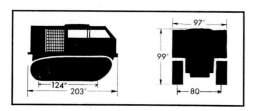

13-TON HIGH-SPEED TRACTOR M5—STANDARD

13-TON HIGH-SPEED TRACTOR, M5, WITH RING MOUNT, M49C, FOR CAL. .50 MACHINE GUN

TYPICAL CHARACTERISTICS

Crew......................................9

Physical Characteristics
Weight (gross)...................28,300 lb.
Length........................15 ft., 11 ins.
Width...........................8 ft., 4 ins.
Height
   Top of windshield lowered......6 ft., 8 ins.
   Top of canopy top.............8 ft., 8 ins.
Height of pintle...................28¼ ins.
Ground clearance...................20 ins.
Tread (center to center of tracks).....83 ins.
Ground contact length...........108½ ins.
Ground pressure.............11.1 lb./sq. in.

Armament
Ring Mount, M49C, for Cal. .50 Machine Gun
1 Tripod Mount, Cal. .50, M3
1 Elevator Cradle, M1

Provision for:
1 Cal. .50 Machine Gun, HB, M2
  (flexible)
9 cal. .30 rifles or } ....Equipment of crew
9 cal. .30 carbines }

Ammunition, Stowage
Cal. .50.........................400 rounds
One of the following:
  105 mm Howitzer...............56 rounds
  4.5 inch Gun..................38 rounds
  155 mm Howitzer...............24 rounds

Performance
Maximum speed towing 155 mm howitzer
  carriage, on level.............35 m.p.h.
Speed on 3% grade.............20 m.p.h.
Maximum grade ability, with towed load.50%
               without towed load.72%
Trench crossing ability..........5 ft., 6 ins.
Vertical obstacle ability............18 ins.
Fording depth (slowest forward speed)..53 ins.
Turning radius....................18 ft.
Fuel capacity...................100 gals.
Cruising range (approx.).........125 miles

Maximum drawbar pull..........20,300 lb.
Payload........................5,000 lb.
Winch capacity................17,000 lb.

Battery, Voltage, total...................12

Fire Protection and Decontamination
Fire Extinguisher, CO₂—4 lb. (hand)........1
Decontaminating Apparatus, M2, 1½ qts....1

Engine, Make and Model..Continental, R6572
Type...........................In-line
No. of cylinders.....................6
Fuel (gasoline)...................70 octane
Displacement.................572 cu. ins.
Max. governed speed..........2,900 r.p.m.
Net hp................235 at 2,900 r.p.m.
Max. torque......475 lb.-ft. at 1,600 r.p.m.

Transmission, Type............Constant mesh
Gear ratios
  First speed.....................5.43:1
  Second speed...................3.20:1
  Third speed....................1.71:1
  Fourth speed...................1.00:1
  Reverse......................5.36:1

Transfer Case, Gear ratios..1.00:1 and 1.71:1

Differential, Type................Controlled
Gear ratio......................2.60:1
Steering ratio...................1.844:1

Final Drive, Type.............Spur gear
Sprocket, no. of teeth................14
Pitch diameter................24.56 ins.
Gear ratio......................2.35:1

Suspension, Type............Volute spring
Wheel or tire size.................20x6

Track, Type........Same as Light Tank, M3

Idler, Type.....................Trailing
Wheel or tire size.................28x6

The 13-Ton High-Speed Tractor, M5, is a prime mover for artillery loads weighing up to 16,000 pounds, and for transporting the personnel, ammunition, and accessories pertaining to the section. It was standardized in October, 1942, as Medium Tractor, M5.

It is used as a prime mover for:
   105 mm Howitzer Carriage, M2;
   4.5 inch Gun Carriage, M1;
   155 mm Howitzer Carriages, M1, M1917A4, or M1918A3.

The vehicle uses Light Tank, M3, tracks, and modified suspension.

Power is supplied by a Continental R6572, in-line, 6-cylinder, 4-cycle gasoline engine. Eight forward speeds and two reverse speeds are provided through the transmission, in conjunction with a dual-range clutch and gear reduction unit.

While towing a 155 mm Howitzer Carriage, the tractor can attain a maximum speed of 35 m.p.h. on level roads and 20 m.p.h. on a 3% grade. It has a cruising range of approximately 125 miles.

The dual-range clutch is operated by air pressure or by hand and permits changing the drive one full gear ratio by pushing the service clutch pedal to the toeboard, past the neutral position.

The front-mounted winch has two wind and two unwind speeds, which are controlled by a lever below the driver's seat and the dual-range engine clutch. A roller located below the winch permits pulling from the rear of the tractor, if required.

The vehicle is equipped with air couplers at the front and rear, and an electric brake connection for the towed load. A folding top with side curtains is provided.

Ordnance Committee action in February, 1944, approved the inclusion of a Ring Mount, M49C, for a cal. .50 machine gun.

The vehicle is manufactured by the International Harvester Co.

REFERENCES—OCM 17512, 17538, 18887, 19038, 19874, 21220, 21524, 22663, 22803.

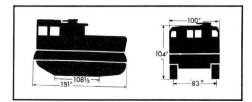

38-TON HIGH-SPEED TRACTOR M6—STANDARD

Development of high-speed fulltrack prime movers for the 240 mm Howitzer, M1, 8 inch Gun, M1, and 4.7 inch Antiaircraft Gun, T1, was authorized by Ordnance Committee action in February, 1942. Heavy Tractor, T22, was developed as the prime mover for the 240 mm Howitzer, M1, and 8 inch Gun, M1, matériel, and Heavy Tractor, T23, for the 4.7 inch Antiaircraft Gun, T1.

Heavy Tractor, T22, was designed with a fifth wheel for semi-trailing the Trailers, T29, T30 and T31, and with heavy-duty pintles for full-trailing the transport wagons for this matériel. Heavy Tractor, T23, was identical, except that the fifth wheel was omitted, allowing the installation of a cargo box on the rear of the tractor for ammunition and equipment pertaining to the section.

Decision of the Field Artillery Board to carry the 240 mm Howitzer, M1, and 8 inch Gun, M1, matériel on full-trailed transport wagons, rather than on trailers, eliminated the necessity for a prime mover, with a fifth wheel arrangement.

38-Ton High-Speed Tractor, M6, standardized in June, 1943, as Heavy Tractor, M6, represents a combination of the two pilot models. It provides a track-type prime mover for artillery loads of approximately 30,000 to 60,000 pounds, and is capable of transporting personnel, ammunition and accessories pertaining to the section.

The tractor consists of a personnel compartment, accommodating eleven men in two rows of seats, an engine compartment, and a cargo compartment, mounted on a high-speed, fulltrack-laying hull and suspension.

Power is supplied by two Waukesha 145 GZ gasoline engines, through torque converters and a constant mesh transmission which provides two speeds forward and one reverse.

A Ring Mount, M49C, for a cal. .50 machine gun, is provided on the roof for antiaircraft and ground use. Stowage is provided for 600 rounds of cal. .50 ammunition, as well as for ammunition for the gun being towed.

The vehicle is provided with a 60,000 pound capacity winch. It is equipped with air and electric brake-controls for the towed loads.

The pilot vehicles were built by the Allis-Chalmers Co.

REFERENCES — OCM 17247, 17302, 17388, 17569, 17646, 17744, 17823, 18596, 18928, 20398, 20715, 21220.

38-TON HIGH-SPEED TRACTOR, M6, IS A PRIME MOVER FOR HEAVY ARTILLERY

TYPICAL CHARACTERISTICS

Crew..11

Physical Characteristics
Weight (gross)........................75,000 lb.
Length............................21 ft., 6 ins.
Width...........................10 ft., ½ in.
Height, to top of cab............8 ft., 1 in.
  to top of gun mount.........8 ft., 7 ins.
Ground clearance.....................20 ins.
Tread (center to center of tracks).....98½ ins.
Ground contact length................172 ins.
Ground pressure.................9.9 lb./sq. in.

Armament
Cal. .50 Machine Gun, M2, HB
  (flexible)...........On Ring Mount, M49C
  Elevation.................−10° to +85°
  Traverse............................360°
Provision for:
1 cal. .30 Rifle, M1, for driver

Ammunition, Stowage
Cal. .50..........................600 rounds
One of the following:
  4.7 in. A.A.......................24 rounds
  240 mm Howitzer, M1............20 rounds
  8 in. Gun, M1....................24 rounds

Performance
Maximum speed on improved road towing
  240 mm Howitzer, M1, tube
  Level............................20.5 m.p.h.
  2½ grade..........................18 m.p.h.
  5% grade..........................14 m.p.h.
  20% grade.........................3½ m.p.h.
Maximum grade ability.................60%
Trench crossing ability..................8 ft.
Vertical obstacle ability.............30 ins.
Fording depth (slowest forward speed)..54 ins.
Angle of approach and departure.......30°
Turning radius........................14 ft.
Fuel capacity......................250 gals.
Cruising range (approx.).........110 miles
Winch capacity.................60,000 lb.

Battery, Voltage, Total.....................12

Fire Protection and Decontamination
Fire Extinguisher, CO₂–4 lb. (hand)........2
(Fixed engine compartment installation)

Engine, Make and
  Model..........Waukesha 145 GZ (two)
Cycle..................................4
No. of cylinders.......................12
Fuel (gasoline)..................80 octane
Net hp...............191 at 2,100 r.p.m.
Max. torque.......539 lb.-ft. at 1,500 r.p.m.

Transmission, Type..Constant mesh (with
Gear ratios   {torque
  First speed.....2.12:1 {converters
  Second speed...1.05:1
  Reverse......2.76:1

Torque Converter, Gear ratio...........4.5:1

Differential, Type..................Controlled
Steering ratio......................1.6:1

Final Drive, Type................Herringbone
Sprocket, No. of teeth..............13
Pitch diameter................25.04 ins.
Gear ratios.....................3.06:1

Suspension, Type.....Horizontal volute spring
Wheel or tire size................20 x 9

Idler, Type............................Trailing

Track, Type..................Center guide
Width......................21 9/16 ins.
Pitch...............................6 ins.
No. of shoes per vehicle..............336

Master Clutch, Type...Dry disk, spring-loaded

Brakes, Type.................Self-energized
Operation.........................Levers

TRACKED LANDING VEHICLES

LVT (A) (1) IS ARMORED AND MOUNTS 37 MM GUN

LVT (2) WILL CARRY 30 MEN, FULLY EQUIPPED

Designed originally for rescue work in the Everglades, these vehicles have proved effective in landings on enemy beaches.

There are two general types which are supplied by the U. S. Navy and stored, issued, and maintained by the Chief of Ordnance.

The original type, nicknamed "the Alligator," represented by Landing Vehicle, Tracked (Unarmored), Mk. I, LVT (1), is now Limited Standard. It is powered by a Hercules WLXC3, 6-cylinder, in-line gasoline engine. An angle drive and right and left reverse transmissions transmit power from the main transmission to silent chains, which operate the final drive sprocket, which, in turn, operates the tracks. Steering is by clutches and brakes.

Present standard type is the so-called "Water Buffalo," represented by Landing Vehicles, Tracked (Armored), Mk. I, LVT (A) (1); Mk. II, LVT (A) (2); and Mk. IV, LVT (A) (4); and Landing Vehicles, Tracked (Unarmored), Mk. II, LVT (2); and Mk. IV, LVT (4).

These vehicles are longer and wider than the LVT (1) and incorporate a number of improvements. Power is supplied by a Continental W670–9A, 7-cylinder gasoline engine, this and the power train being the same as used in the Light Tank, M3, Series. Steering is by a controlled differential.

The vehicles employ a bogie system of an entirely new design, with eleven single-wheeled, rubber-tired bogie assemblies on each side. The torsional effect of a shaft floating in rubber is utilized to cushion and support the vehicle. A hollow shaft, welded to the hull on a spring-end bracket, is placed inside another hollow shaft of larger diameter, to which is welded the bogie wheel arms and bogie wheel. Rubber is vulcanized between the shafts. Thus, as the vehicle negotiates irregular terrain, the outer shaft twists on the inner shaft. The natural resistance of the rubber serves to cushion the upward and downward movement of the bogie wheel, providing firm but flexible support.

These vehicles were originally designated as amphibian tractors. The nomenclature was changed to conform with designations of the U. S. Navy and the British.

The vehicles are manufactured by the Food Machinery Co.

REFERENCES — OCM 19108, 19367, 19992.

LANDING VEHICLE, TRACKED (UNARMORED), MK. I, LVT (1), LIMITED STANDARD—Formerly known as Amphibian Tractor, T33, this vehicle is now Limited Standard. It is shorter and narrower than later models, and has higher side pontoons, which cover the suspension except for the tracks. Track grousers are of a curved blade design. The cargo compartment provides space for 24 men with packs and rifles or 4,500 pounds of matériel. Machine gun rails are provided at the sides and rear of the cargo compartment.

The vehicle is of arc-welded sheet steel construction, without armor. The driver's cab has three front windows, the center of which may be opened for ventilation or escape. It also has a sliding window on each side. Seats with safety belts are provided for a crew of three.

REFERENCE—TM 9–784.

LANDING VEHICLE, TRACKED (ARMORED), MK. I, LVT (A) (1)—STANDARD—This vehicle is, in effect, an amphibian tank, with a light tank turret mounted to the rear of the driver's cab.

Principal armament consists of a 37 mm Gun, M6, with a cal. .30 Machine Gun, M1919A5, in a Combination Gun Mount, M44. The guns may be elevated from —10° to +25°. A gyrostabilizer is provided. The turret may be traversed by a hydraulic apparatus or by hand. There are two entrance hatches in the roof of the turret. Two periscopes are provided for the commander. A gunner's periscope with telescopic sight is connected with the gun mount.

Two manholes in the rear of the turret are equipped with scarf mounts for cal. .30 machine guns.

A direct vision window in front of the driver is provided with an armored cover which may be kept closed in combat areas. There are two escape hatches in the top of the cab, each equipped with a rotating periscope.

REFERENCE—TM 9–775.

LANDING VEHICLE, TRACKED (UNARMORED), MK. II, LVT (2)—STANDARD—The basic hull design and major vehicular components of this vehicle are the same as on the LVT (A) (1). Construction is of sheet steel.

This vehicle has no turret. The space between the driver's cab and the engine

LVT (4) HAS RAMP AT REAR FOR LOADING VEHICLES

LVT (A) (4) MOUNTS 75 MM HOWITZER IN TURRET

compartment is used for transporting cargo and personnel. Propeller shafts, leading from the engine to the transmission, and connected at the center by a power take-off, are encased in a control tunnel which extends through the center of the cargo compartment.

Machine gun rails are provided at the front of the cargo compartment, and along the sides and rear, permitting fire in any direction.

The cab has two front escape windows, which hinge downward and may be opened for ventilation. There is also a small window on each side. All windows are constructed of safety glass.

REFERENCE—TM 9–775.

LANDING VEHICLE, TRACKED (ARMORED), MK. II, LVT (A) (2)—STANDARD—This vehicle is generally similar to the LVT (2), but is constructed of armor plate instead of sheet steel.

The cab is similar to that used on LVT (A) (1). The single window at the front is provided with a hinged armor plate cover. Two escape hatches, with rotating periscopes, are in the roof of the cab.

REFERENCE—TM 9–775.

LANDING VEHICLE, TRACKED (UN-ARMORED), MK. IV, LVT (4)—STANDARD—This vehicle is similar in general characteristics to the LVT (2) but is provided with a ramp at the rear. The engine compartment occupies a position directly in back of the driver's cab. The

cargo compartment is in the rear. The cab and the ramp are armored. The vehicle will transport a ¼-ton, 4x4, Truck with a 37 mm Gun Carriage, M4A1; or a 57 mm gun carriage or a 75 mm or 105 mm howitzer carriage. Two swinging mounts and two stationary mounts are provided for cal. .30 or cal. .50 machine guns.

LANDING VEHICLE, TRACKED, (ARMORED), MK. IV, LVT (A) (4)—STANDARD—This vehicle is generally similar to the LVT (A) (1) but is provided with an open-top turret similar to that on 75 mm Howitzer Motor Carriage, M8. Principal armament is a 75 mm Howitzer, M2 or M3. A cal. .50 Machine Gun, M2, HB, is mounted at the rear of the turret.

LANDING VEHICLE, TRACKED (ARMORED), MK. I, LVT (A) (1)

Crew 6

Physical Characteristics
Weight (gross) . . . . 32,800 lb.*
Length . . . . 26 ft., 1 in.
Width . . . . 10 ft., 8 ins.
Height . . . . 10 ft., 1 in.†
Ground clearance . . . . 18 ins.
Draft . . . . 4 ft., 2 ins.
Tread (center to center of tracks) . . . . 113½ ins.
Ground contact length . . . . 126½ ins.
Ground pressure—at 4 in.
penetration . . . . 8.7 lb./sq. in.

Armament
37 mm Gun, M6, with
1 cal. .30 Machine Gun,
M1919A5 . . . . } In Combination Gun Mount, M44
2 cal. .30 Machine Guns,
M1919A4 . . . . . . On Scarf Mounts, Mk. 21
1 cal. .50 Machine Gun,
M2, HB . . . . On Mount, M35

Ammunition, Stowage‡
37 mm . . . . 104 rounds
Cal. .30 . . . . 6,000 rounds

Armor, Actual
Hull . . . . ¼ in.
Cab, Front . . . . ½ in.
Sides . . . . ¼ in.
Turret, Side . . . . ½ in.
Top . . . . ¼ in.

Performance
Maximum speed on land . . . . 25 m.p.h.
Maximum speed in water . . . . 6½ m.p.h.
Maximum grade ability 60%
Angle of approach . . . . 35°
Angle of departure . . . . 30°
Fuel capacity . . . . 106 gals.
Cruising range—land . . . . 125 miles
water . . . . 75 miles
Maximum drawbar pull . . . . 18,000 lb.
Payload . . . . 1,000 lb.

Vision and Fire Control
Periscopes, M6 4
Periscope, M4, w/ Telescope, M40 1
Bore Sight 1

Communications—Radio . . . . TCS
Interphone stations 6

Battery, Voltage, total 12

LVT (A) (1)

126½" · 313" · 121" · 113½" · 128"

Fire Protection
Fire Extinguisher, CO₂–10 lb. (fixed) 2
CO₂–15 lb. (hand) 1

Engine, Make and Model . . . . Continental W670–9A
Type . . . . Radial AC
No. of cylinders 7
Fuel (gasoline) . . . . 80 octane
Net hp . . . . 250 at 2,400 r.p.m.
Max. torque . . . . . . 584 lb.-ft. at 1,800 r.p.m.
(See additional engine characteristics on page 27.)

Transmission, Type . . . . Syncromesh (Light Tank, M3)

Differential, Type . . . . Controlled (Light Tank, M3)

Final Drive, Type . . . . (Light Tank, M3)

Track, Type . . . . . . Steel, with extruded cleats
Width . . . . 14¼ ins.
No. of shoes per vehicle 146

*LVT (2), 30,900 lb., LVT (A) (2), 32,000 lb., LVT (4), 33,350 lb., LVT (A) (4), 40,000 lb.

†LVT (2), LVT (A) (2), LVT (4), 8 ft., 1 in., LVT (A) (4), 10 ft., 5 ins.

‡LVT (2), LVT (A) (2), LVT (4), cal. .30, 2,000 rounds, cal. .50, 1,000 rounds, LVT (A) (4), 75 mm, 100 rounds, cal. .50 400 rounds.

BOMB SERVICE TRUCK M6—STANDARD
BOMB LIFT TRUCK M1—STANDARD

BOMB SERVICE TRUCK, M6, SHOWING COLLAPSIBLE TOP AND BOMB HOIST

TYPICAL CHARACTERISTICS

BOMB SERVICE TRUCK, M6

Crew.............................5

Physical Characteristics
Weight (gross)....................8,325 lb.
Length.......................18 ft., 5 ins.
Width..............................6 ft.
Height....................7 ft., 7½ ins.
Ground clearance..................9⅞ ins.
Wheelbase.......................125 ins.
Center of gravity above ground.......31 ins.
Tread, front.....................60½ ins.
      rear........................57¼ ins.
Ground contact..................35 sq. ins.
Ground pressure.............64 lb./sq. in.
Tire equipment..7.50x20, 8 ply (mud and snow)

Performance
Maximum speed on level...........55 m.p.h.
Maximum grade ability.............65%
Fording depth (slowest forward speed)..32 ins.
Angle of approach.....................45°
Angle of departure....................38°
Turning radius.....................26 ft.
Fuel capacity.....................48 gals.
Cruising range (approx.)..........250 miles
Payload.......................2,000 lb.

Vision..........................Windshield
Battery, Voltage.........................6
Fire Protection...................CO_2, 2 lb.
(Other characteristics same as for 1½-ton, 4 x 4, Truck.)

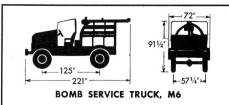

BOMB SERVICE TRUCK, M6

BOMB LIFT TRUCK, M1

Physical Characteristics
Weight........................290 lb.
Length (handle extended).........7 ft., 1 in.
Width......................2 ft., 9 ins.
Height (platform raised)...........13 ins.
Height (platform lowered)..........7 ins.
Tire equipment....................5.00x4

BOMB SERVICE TRUCK, M6, is used to load, unload, and tow bomb trailers.

It consists of a specially designed Chevrolet 1½-ton, 4x4, truck with an open body and a platform on which is mounted a hoist for loading and unloading the bomb trailer.

The hand-operated hoist has a capacity of 4,000 pounds.

The vehicle was designed for a low silhouette, short wheelbase and a short turning radius. Provision is made for the use of dual tires, front or rear, when required.

A removable top over the front seat provides protection during road marches in inclement weather or when the vehicle is stored in the open. Seats are provided in the front for two men, and in the rear for three additional men.

Power is supplied by a six-cylinder valve-in-head engine. A single plate dry disk clutch with a diaphragm spring is used. A selective sliding gear type transmission supplies four forward speeds and one reverse speed.

The truck is equipped with controls for electric brakes and a stop light on a trailer.

A pintle hook is provided at the rear and two pull hooks on the front of the vehicle.

The truck is manufactured by the Chevrolet Motor Division, General Motors Corporation.

REFERENCES—TM 9–765; OCM 15077, 15179, 16969, 17116.

BOMB LIFT TRUCK, M1, was designed to lift bombs weighing from 500 pounds to 2,000 pounds, with the bomb stand, from the ground and place them under the bomb bays of airplanes. From this point they can be loaded by the airplane hoisting gear.

It is a low three-wheeled, modified, standard shop lift truck, with a hydraulic-operated lifting platform and pneumatic tires.

The truck is used as an accessory to Bomb Service Truck, M6, and also is used separately in some branches.

REFERENCES—OCM 15970, 16969, 20517.

BOMB LIFT TRUCK, M1, WITH PLATFORM LOWERED, AND HANDLE BACK

2½-TON, 6x6 (4DT), BOMB SERVICE TRUCK, M27, SHOWING BOMB ABOUT TO BE LOWERED TO DOLLY ON TRACK FOR TRANSFER TO AIRPLANE

This vehicle was designed at the request of Headquarters, Army Air Forces, for handling the 4,000 pound bomb.

It consists of a 2½-Ton, 6x6 (4dt), Cargo Truck, L.W.B. w/winch, less troop seats, on which is mounted a specially designed, power-operated bomb-lift mechanism, consisting of a steel superstructure built over the body, and independently controlling hoisting and traversing mechanisms driven from the vehicle power takeoff. This enables the unit to lift the bomb, carry it into the cargo body for transporting to position near an airplane, and lower it onto a dolly and track on which it may be pushed to a position beneath the bomb bay of the airplane.

A Dolly and Track Set, 2-Ton, consisting of two dollies and five track sections, is part of the equipment of the truck, and is carried inside the cargo body. During local operations, straight sections are carried on brackets on the sides of the body. The track, which has one curved section and a total length of 50 feet, provides considerable flexibility of operation and makes it possible to manhandle the bomb over soft and uneven terrain which would be impassable to the Bomb Lift Truck, M1. The dolly has dual, concave bomb cradles which provide adequate stability even though the track is not level, and operates with minimum rolling resistance.

The truck superstructure is constructed to permit its disassembly when necessary to conserve shipping space. Bows and tarpaulins are provided and give the vehicle an appearance similar to that of the standard 2½-ton cargo truck. The hoisting mechanism is equipped with an automatic overload slip clutch to prevent cable breakage. Bomb Service Kit, for 2½-Ton, 6x6, Cargo Truck contains all material necessary for field conversion of the standard truck to Bomb Service Truck, M27.

Basis of issue for the truck is one to each fighter squadron and fighter-bomber squadron, two to each bomber squadron, medium and heavy, and each Ordnance Am. Co. Aviation, and one to each Ordnance S. & M. Co.-Aviation. Basis of issue for the Dolly and Track Set is one to each Truck, Bomb Service, M27, and two additional to each Ordnance section of bombardment squadrons and Ordnance S. & M. Co.-Aviation.

REFERENCES — OCM 20964, 21256, 21499, 21787, 22150, 23148.

TYPICAL CHARACTERISTICS

Crew 2
Physical Characteristics
Weight (gross) . . . . .17,880 lb.*
Length (overall) . . . . .29 ft., 10 ins.
Length (frame and body only) . .22 ft., 5⅜ ins.
Width .7 ft., 4 ins.
Height . . . . .10 ft., 6 ins.
Inside body length . . . . .12 ft.
Inside body width . . . . .6 ft., 8 ins.
Ground clearance . . . . .10 ins.
Tread (center to center, rear) . . . . . .67¾ ins.
Wheelbase . . . . .164 ins.
Ground contact, front . . . . .90 sq. ins.
　rear . . . . .240 sq. ins.
Ground pressure, front . . . . .62 lb./sq. in.
　rear . . . . .52 lb./sq. in.
Tire equipment . . . . .7.50 x 20, 8 ply

Performance
Maximum speed on level . . . . .45 m.p.h.
Maximum grade ability 65%
Vertical obstacle ability . . . . .10 ins.
Fording depth (slowest forward speed) . .30 ins.†
Angle of approach . . . . .31°
Angle of departure . . . . .36°
Turning radius . . . . .35 ft.
Fuel capacity . . . . .40 gals.

Cruising range (approx.) . . . . .240 miles
Payload . . . . .4,000 lb.
Normal towed load . . . . .7,200 lb.
Winch capacity . . . . .10,000 lb.
(Other characteristics same as for 2½-ton, 6x6, Cargo Truck.)

Dolly, Type . . . . .Welded Sheet Steel
Weight . . . . .85 lb.
Length . . . . .28 ins.
Width .25½ ins.
Height .6⅝ ins.
Wheelbase . . . . .21 ins.
Crosstie clearance—Dolly . . . . .1¹⁄₁₆ ins.
Rail Side Clearance . . . . .⁷⁄₁₆ in.
Wheel type . . . . .Cast Steel, Flanged
Wheel diameter . . . . .5 ins.

Track, Type . . . . .All Steel
Gage (Ctr. to ctr. of rails) . . . . .21 ins.
Length—Straight rail . . . . .135½ ins.
Weight—Straight section . . . . .130 lb.
Curvature—Curved section . . . . .45°
Radius of curve—Inside rail . . . . .8 ft.
Weight—Curved section . . . . .85 lb.

*Including: Payload, 4,000 lb.; Dolly and Track Set, 780 lb.
†With fording equipment, 60 ins.

LIFT TRUCK M22—STANDARD
BOMB TRAILER M5—STANDARD

LIFT TRUCK, M22, IS USED IN HANDLING BOMBS AND TORPEDOES

TYPICAL CHARACTERISTICS

LIFT TRUCK, M22

Physical Characteristics

Weight (without cradle)	950 lb.
Weight (with cradle)	1,400 lb.
Length (excluding tongue)	10 ft., 3 ins.
Width	4 ft., 10 ins.
Height (cradle lowered)	18½ ins.
Height (cradle raised)	42 ins.
Over-all height (cradle lowered, with bomb adapter)	32 ins.
Over-all height (cradle raised, with bomb adapter)	56 ins.
Wheelbase	97 ins.
Tread (center to center) front	40 ins.
rear	50 ins.
Ground clearance	4 ins.
Tire equipment	5.50x18, 6 ply

Lift Characteristics

Range of lift (with cradle without adapter)	9 ins. to 33 ins.
Range of lift (with cradle with adapter)	25½ ins. to 49½ ins.
Angles of lift tilt	−15° to +15°

Performance

Angle of departure	24°
Turning radius	14 ft.
Payload	5,000 lb.

BOMB TRAILER, M5

Physical Characteristics

Weight empty	2,000 lb.
Weight loaded	7,000 lb.
Length overall	17 ft., 11 ins.
Length of deck	11 ft., 3 ins.
Width overall	7 ft., 4 ins.
Width of deck	5 ft., 9 ins.
Height	3 ft., 9 ins.
Height of deck loaded	21½ ins.
Wheelbase	102¾ ins.
Ground clearance	9 ins.
Tread (center to center, rear)	80½ ins.
Tire equipment, rear	7.50x18–8 ply
front	6.50x10–6 ply

Performance

Maximum speed on level	45 m.p.h.
Cross country speed	20 m.p.h.

Battery, Voltage 6

LIFT TRUCK, M22, is used to carry the 4,000 lb. Bomb, AN-M56, and the 2,000 lb. Torpedo, Mk. XIII, Mod. 1 or 2, placing them in a position from which they can be loaded onto bombardment aircraft.

Two hand-operated, piston-type pumps are connected to the forward frame for raising and lowering the cradle.

The cradle assembly consists of a cradle body, folding jack legs and radius rods which can be raised by means of hydraulic jacks.

Normal range of lift is from 9 inches to 33 inches. A removable adapter is provided for lifting the 4,000 lb. bomb, by which the range of lift is changed from 25½ inches to 49½ inches.

A tongue on the front with lunette eye and handles permits towing behind a vehicle or pulling by the crew. Ball rollers on the truck bed facilitate shifting the position of the bomb or torpedo. Chock blocks and chain ties to position loads are provided. The truck is equipped with a pintle at the rear.

REFERENCES — TM 9–762; OCM 15970, 17947, 18019, 18819, 19428.

BOMB TRAILER, M5, is a castered third-wheel trailer for transporting bombs between munitions dumps and airfields, and is designed to meet requirements of low loading and ease of handling.

Trailers may be connected in trains behind a prime mover for operation at fairly high speed. The front caster unit permits a turning radius about equal to the wheelbase.

The front of the hitch yoke is provided with a reversible lunette which may be attached to the rear pintle of another trailer or a prime mover. The electric brakes and the lighting system are controlled by the driver of the prime mover by means of an electric connecting cable. A safety switch applies the brakes automatically in case the towing connection between the trailer and the prime mover is broken.

A stabilizer mechanism minimizes the tendency for the vehicle to "pitch" on rough roads.

Deck channels are provided to hold the bombs securely. A loading ramp and a supporting stand are furnished with each trailer to aid in loading. The ramp is equipped with hooks for engaging the pins on the side of the deck chamber.

REFERENCES—TM 9–760; OCM 13181, 13287, 14097, 15077, 15179, 16430.

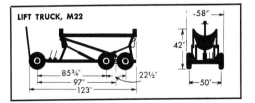

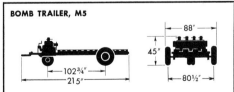

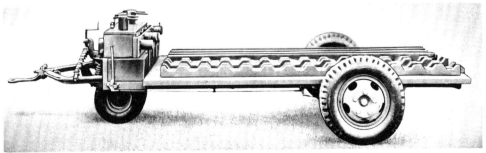

BOMB TRAILER, M5, TRANSPORTS BOMBS FROM DUMPS TO AIRFIELDS

GENERATOR TRAILER M7—STANDARD
DIRECTOR TRAILERS M13, M14—LIMITED STANDARD; M22—STANDARD
MOUNT TRAILER M17—STANDARD; TRAILER M18—STANDARD

These 4-wheel, short wheelbase vehicles use the same basic chassis, modified for particular purposes.

GENERATOR TRAILER M7, STANDARD, was designed specifically to transport an engine generator set and to give it a solid, level foundation when in use at a halt. It is now being used also by the Chemical Warfare Service for transporting smoke-generating equipment. Four built-in corner-lift jacks permit the lifting of body weight off springs and tires. The trailer, which has a welded-steel pick-up body and an adjustable tongue mounted in an A-frame, can be coupled quickly to any vehicle equipped with a pintle. Understructure is of the rocker-arm type, assuring 4-wheel ground contact.

DIRECTOR TRAILER M13, LIMITED STANDARD, is a modification of Generator Trailer M7. It is designed to transport Directors M9 and M10 and to give them a level operating foundation. It has a steel pick-up body that extends slightly higher than that of the basic trailer and is equipped with bows and a canvas top.

DIRECTOR TRAILER M14, LIMITED STANDARD, is a more durable modification of Generator Trailer M7 and also is designed for transporting Directors M9 and M10. It has a solid steel body with rigid top or superstructure. Double top and side walls are separated by insulation 1¾ inches thick. A gasoline heating system is mounted inside the trailer and an electric ventilating blower is installed in the superstructure. There are five windows, all equipped with sliding blackout panels.

DIRECTOR TRAILER M22, STANDARD, is a modification of Director Trailer M14 embodying improvements requested by the Antiaircraft Artillery Board.

MOUNT TRAILER M17, STANDARD, is the designation given to Generator Trailer M7 as modified to mount Multiple Cal. .50 Machine Gun Mount M45, the combination being designated Multiple Cal. .50 Machine Gun Carriage M51.

TRAILER M18, STANDARD, is Generator Trailer M7 modified by the addition of a winch. It is used in transporting generating units mounted on skids.

REFERENCES—TM 9–881, 9–881 (C1), 9–2800; OCM 16869, 19740, 19905, 20142, 20276, 21125, 21326, 21565, 22696, 23544, 23921, 24210; SNL G–221.

GENERATOR TRAILER M7 IS DESIGNED TO TRANSPORT AN ENGINE GENERATOR SET

DIRECTOR TRAILER M14, ON SAME CHASSIS, TRANSPORTS DIRECTORS M9, M10

TYPICAL CHARACTERISTICS

Physical Characteristics	Generator Trailer M7	Director Trailer M13	Director Trailers M14, M22
Weight (net)	4,500 lb.	4,800 lb.	5,800 lb.
Length (overall)	16 ft.	16 ft.	16 ft.
Width	8 ft.	8 ft.	8 ft.
Height	3 ft., 9 in.	8 ft.	8 ft., 2 in.
Ground clearance	4½ in.	4½ in.	4½ in.
Tread (center to center, rear)	83¾ in.	83¾ in.	83¾ in.
Wheelbase	40 in.	40 in.	40 in.
Ground pressure (empty)	28 lb./sq. in.	30 lb./sq. in.	36 lb./sq. in.
(loaded)	53 lb./sq. in.	51 lb./sq. in.	57 lb./sq. in.
Tire equipment	7.50 x 20, 8-ply	7.50 x 20, 8-ply	7.50 x 20, 8-ply
Performance—Payload	4,000 lb.	3,400 lb.	3,400 lb.
Brakes, Type	Electric	Electric	Electric

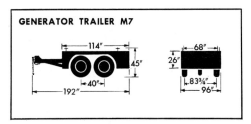

GENERATOR TRAILER M7

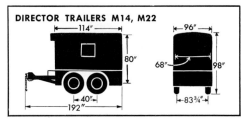

DIRECTOR TRAILERS M14, M22

4-TON, 2-WHEEL AMMUNITION TRAILER M21—STANDARD
1-TON, 2-WHEEL AMMUNITION TRAILER M24—STANDARD

4-TON, 2-WHEEL AMMUNITION TRAILER M21 CARRIES AMMUNITION, FUZES, AND PRIMERS

1-TON, 2-WHEEL AMMUNITION TRAILER M24

4-TON, 2-WHEEL AMMUNITION TRAILER M21, STANDARD, is a single-axle, sprung trailer, designed to transport 72 complete rounds of 155-mm howitzer ammunition or 108 complete rounds of 4.5-inch gun ammunition. A box is provided for fuzes and primers.

Brakes, operated by compressed air and controlled from the towing vehicle, are automatically applied if the trailer is accidentally disconnected. A hand brake is provided.

Brake parts and wheel bearings are interchangeable with those of the 4-Ton, 6x6, Truck. The lunette and the wheels, tires, and tubes are interchangeable with those of the 4.5-inch gun and the 155-mm Howitzer Carriage M1.

The body is built as an integral part of the trailer frame. A paulin, lashing hooks, hold-down straps for propelling charges, and ammunition racks are provided.

REFERENCES—OCM 18048, 20921, 21991, 22264.

1-TON, 2-WHEEL AMMUNITION TRAILER M24, STANDARD, is a modification of the 1-Ton, 2-Wheel Cargo Trailer designed to carry additional ammunition for Combination Gun Motor Carriage M15A1. The interior of the body is fitted with metal stowage boxes. Two lockers, each having two compartments, are bolted to the floor on the left side. The first three compartments (back to front) are each designed to carry nine Cal. .50 Ammunition Boxes M2, a total of 2,700 rounds, and the fourth compartment is intended to carry any articles desired. Outsides of the lockers are fitted with clamps to carry six machine gun barrels.

On the right side are five removable metal boxes fitted with spacers for carrying 350 rounds of 37-mm ammunition. Each box will carry seven clips of ten rounds each. The boxes are secured to the floor by spring clamps. A rainproof stowage compartment is at the front of the trailer.

REFERENCES—TM 9–883; OCM 24117, 24456.

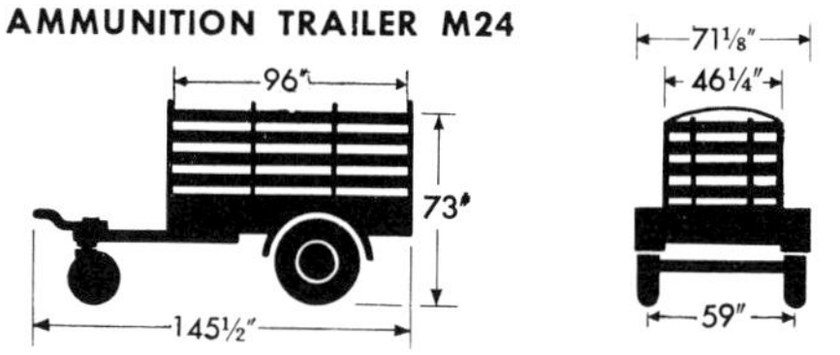

TYPICAL CHARACTERISTICS

AMMUNITION TRAILER M21

Physical Characteristics

Weight (gross)	13,056 lb.
Length (over front lunette and rear towing hooks)	12 ft., 2½ in.
Width	8 ft., ¾ in.
Height	6 ft., 11⅛ in.
Ground clearance	13½ in.
Tread (center to center of tires)	82¾ in.
Tire equipment (may be changed to heavy-duty type)	14.00 x 20, highway

Body (inside dimensions)

Length	6 ft., 10½ in.
Width	7 ft., 2½ in.
Height	3 ft., 4⅞ in.
Brakes, Service	Air
Brakes, Parking	Hand

AMMUNITION TRAILER M24

Physical Characteristics

Weight (gross)	3,600 lb.
Length (overall)	12 ft., 1½ in.
Length (inside body)	8 ft.
Width (overall)	5 ft., 11⅛ in.
Width (inside body)	3 ft., 10¼ in.
Height (overall, top up)	6 ft., 1 in.
Height (inside body, top up)	3 ft., 7 in.
Ground clearance	16¼ in.
Tread (center to center of tires)	59 in.
Tire equipment	7.50 x 20, 8-ply, mud and snow
Desert	11.00 x 18, 10-ply

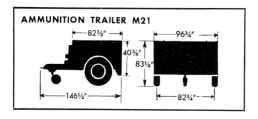

8-TON, 4-WHEEL, AMMUNITION TRAILER M23, ¾ FRONT VIEW

OVERHEAD VIEW, SHOWING RACKS FOR POSITIONING AMMUNITION

This trailer, designed to transport 240-mm howitzer ammunition, 8-in. howitzer and gun ammunition, and 155-mm gun ammunition, was standardized in April 1944.

It is an 8-ton payload, 4-wheel trailer with walking beam axle. It can be used with Heavy Carriage Limber M5, which serves as a trailer dolly, as a trailed load for 18-Ton High-Speed Tractor M4 and 38-Ton High-Speed Tractor M6, or without limber as a trailed load behind the 7½-Ton, 6x6, Truck. In the latter case the trailer is attached by means of the universal pintle coupling installed on the truck.

The body, which is of steel construction, is an integral part of the trailer frame, and is provided with paulin, lashing hooks, hold-down straps for propelling charges, and ammunition racks. Stowage is provided for approximately 32 complete rounds of 240-mm howitzer ammunition, 60 complete rounds of 8-in. howitzer ammunition, 96 complete rounds of 155-mm ammunition, or 33 complete rounds of 8-in. gun ammunition up to the maximum payload of 16,000 lb.

The vehicle is capable of being towed at speeds up to 35 miles per hour on smooth concrete roadway and up to 20 miles per hour cross country. Tire and wheel assemblies are interchangeable with those of the 155-mm Gun, 8-In. Howitzer Carriage M1, and Heavy Carriage Limber M5.

Air brakes, which operate on all four wheels of the walking beam axle, can be controlled from the towing vehicle. Hand-operated parking brakes located on the right and left sides of the trailer can be applied independently to a wheel on either side of the walking beam axle.

U. S. Army standard combat-zone lighting is provided, with current supplied from the towing vehicle. Reflectors conform to I.C.C. regulations. A retractable landing-wheel assembly is furnished.

The rear pintle is interchangeable with that on the 18-Ton High-Speed Tractor M4. The vehicle is equipped with towing hooks on the two rear corners and lifting eyes on the front and rear corners of the body.

REFERENCES—OCM 18048, 20921, 21741, 21944, 23262, 23569.

TYPICAL CHARACTERISTICS
8-TON, 4-WHEEL, AMMUNITION TRAILER M23

Physical Characteristics

Weight (gross)—Trailer only	26,000 lb.
Trailer and Limber	28,000 lb.
Weight (net)—Trailer only	10,460 lb.
Trailer and Limber	12,350 lb.
Length—center of bogie to center of lunette (coupling) eye	14 ft., 4½ in.
Length—overall	18 ft., 7 in.
Width	8 ft., 8½ in.
Height	6 ft., 11 in.
Ground clearance	16¾ in.
Tread (center to center of tires)	88¾ in.
Wheelbase—center of bogie to center of limber axle	170¼ in.
Tire equipment	11.00 x 20, 12-ply

Body—Inside dimensions

Propelling charge section
Length . . . . 11 ft., 8 in.

Width	8 ft., 4 in.
Ammunition well	
Length	11 ft., 8 in.
Width	4 ft., 2 in.

Fuze Box—Inside dimensions

Length	4 ft., 11 in.
Depth	1 ft., 7½ in.
Width	1 ft., 4½ in.

Performance

Maximum speed on level	35 m.p.h.
Angle of departure	90°
Payload	16,000 lb.
Brakes, Type	Air
Brakes, Parking, Type	Hand

HEAVY CARRIAGE LIMBER M5

Physical Characteristics

Weight (net)	1,890 lb.
Length—overall	8 ft., 1½ in.
Ground clearance	11¾ in.
Tread (center to center of tires)	82 in.
Tire equipment	11.00 x 20, 12-ply

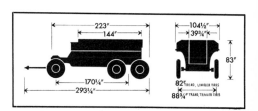

AMMUNITION TRAILER M23 USED AS SEMITRAILER WITH HEAVY CARRIAGE LIMBER M5

HEAVY WRECKING TRUCK M1A1 WITH OPEN CAB, SHOWING CRANE IN TRAVELING POSITION

These vehicles are used for towing, salvaging, and recovering operations, as well as for numerous repair operations away from base repair shops, where heavy hoist and winch equipment is needed.

Heavy Wrecking Truck M1, standardized in July 1937, is now classified as Limited Standard.

Heavy Wrecking Truck M1A1, standardized in March 1944, is generally similar to the M1, but has an open cab, an improved crane assembly, and other improvements. It will tow vehicles weighing up to 60,000 pounds.

It consists of a 6x6 truck, with a payload of 8,000 pounds, on which is mounted a heavy crane assembly, rear winch assembly, and other equipment. The winches are operated by power through power take-offs mounted on the transfer case and the transmission. Body jacks, telescoping boom jacks, outriggers, and ground spades are provided to take the strain off the truck and the crane when heavy loads are lifted.

The crane can be used at the rear or at the side of the truck. Its capacity varies according to the elevation of the boom and the position of the boom hook line. It has a maximum capacity of 16,000 pounds on the inner sheave only when used with boom jacks at a jack height of 10 feet, 10 inches.

The rear winch is used for straight recovery, heavy recovery, and angle recovery operations, using a one-, two-, three-, or four-part line as required. Using one cable, it has a maximum direct pull of 37,500 pounds.

The front winch, used primarily for recovering the wrecker itself if mired or for anchoring it for rear-winch operations, has a direct-pull capacity of 20,000 pounds with one cable.

The vehicle carries welding and cutting equipment, an 8-ton and a 30-ton jack, tow chains, a towbar and a whiffletree assembly, and other necessary equipment.

Compressed-air brakes are provided, with trailer air connections at both the front and rear. A double check valve permits operation of the wrecker brakes from a vehicle ahead of the wrecker.

Provision is made for stowing two cal. .30 carbines.

Bows and paulins for camouflage are furnished. These give the wrecker the appearance of a cargo vehicle and make it a less conspicuous target from the air. Two floodlights on top of the crane A-frame furnish light for night work.

The vehicles are manufactured by the Ward La France Truck Division and the Kenworth Motor Truck Corp.

REFERENCES—TM 9–796; OCM 17983, 18100, 18153, 18371, 18806, 19036, 19107, 20442, 20511, 21812, 21954, 22853, 23130, 23146, 23504; MCM 25; SNL G–116.

TYPICAL CHARACTERISTICS

Crew 2
Physical Characteristics
    Weight (gross)—M1 . . . . 38,500 lb.
       M1A1 . . . . 40,500 lb.
    Length . . . . 23 ft., 5 in.
    Width . . . . 8 ft., 4¾ in.
    Height . . . . 10 ft.
    Ground clearance . . . . 11 in.
    Tread (center to center, rear) . . . . 88¾ in.
    Wheelbase . . . . 181 in.
    Tire equipment . . . . 11.00 x 20, 12-ply,
                       mud and snow
    Provision for:
    2 cal. .30 carbines
Ammunition, Stowage
    Cal. .30 (carbine) . . . . 640 rounds
Performance
    Maximum speed on level . . . . 45 m.p.h.
    Maximum grade ability 65%
    Fording depth (slowest forward speed) . . . . 48 in.
    Angle of approach . . . . 55½°
    Angle of departure . . . . 55°
    Turning radius . . . . 38 ft.
    Fuel capacity . . . . 100 gal.
    Cruising range (approx.) . . . . 250 miles
    Payload . . . . 8,000 lb.
Communication—Flag Set M238 1
Battery, Voltage, total 12
Fire Protection and Decontamination
    Fire Extinguisher, CO.-2 lb. (hand) 3
    CCL.-1 qt. 1
    Decontaminating Apparatus M2, 1½ qts. 2
Engine, Make and model . . . . . Continental, 22R
    Type . . . . In-line, valve-in-head
    No. of cylinders 6
    Fuel (gasoline) . . . . 70 octane
    Displacement . . . . 501 cu. in.
    Max. governed speed . . . . 2,400 r.p.m.
    Net hp. . . . . 133 at 2,400 r.p.m.
    Max. torque . . . . 365 lb.-ft. at 1,200 r.p.m.
    Width . . . . 34 in.
    Height . . . . 52 in.
    Weight . . . . 1,650 lb.
Transmission, Gear ratios
    First speed 7.07:1
    Second speed 3.50:1
    Third speed 1.72:1
    Fourth speed 1.00:1
    Fifth speed 0.776:1
    Reverse 7.11:1
Transfer Case
    Gear ratio 1.00:1, 2.55:1
Steering Ratio 25:1
Rear Axle, Gear ratio 8.27:1
Brakes, Service, Type . . . . Compressed air
Brakes, Parking, Type . Ventilated, disk, 4-shoe

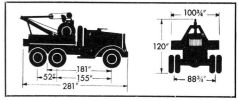

ORDNANCE MAINTENANCE TRUCKS, 2½-TON, 6x6 (4DT)

Artillery Repair M9A1

Automotive Repair M8A1

Electrical Repair M18A2

Instrument Repair M10A1, Load A

Instrument Bench M23

Machine Shop M16A2, Load A

Machine Shop M16A1, Loads B, B1, B2

Signal Corps General Repair M31

Signal Corps Repair M30

Small Arms Repair M7A2

Tire Repair M32

ORDNANCE MAINTENANCE TRUCK WITH ST-6 BODY, SHOWN ASSEMBLED

These are Mobile Shop Trucks, used for Ordnance maintenance, mounted on 2½-ton, 6x6 (4dt) truck chassis of 164-in. wheelbase. Bodies are all metal, completely inclosed. The same body is used for all the various models. They differ only in the various tools and equipment mounted or carried within them.

The present production model of the body is known as Model ST-6. This body incorporates a collapsible feature which permits the rear doors, front and rear belt panels, windows and other allied equipment to be removed and the top lowered approximately 24 inches. The mounted equipment remains intact and the disassembled parts can then be packed inside the collapsed body so as to form a compact item for shipping and thereby conserve shipping space.

The ST-6 Body is 148 inches long, 96 inches wide, and 81⅝ inches high, outside dimensions. Six windows are provided on each side, as well as a small window in the front and two windows in the doors. They are all protected by heavy brush guards and screen wire, so as to break up light reflection. Side windows can all be opened and all windows are provided with blackout curtains. A heating and ventilating unit is provided so that the truck can be used under all climatic conditions.

Standard equipment for the various models of the trucks includes a safety ladder for access to the rear of the unit

SAME TRUCK, WITH BODY COLLAPSED FOR SHIPMENT OVERSEAS

and an electric light system having a blackout arrangement which automatically turns off the lights when the doors are opened. The equipment and tools furnished in the various loads are interchangeable to a great extent and are also to be found in common items for shop use.

Earlier models of Mobile Shop Trucks used a Model ST-5 Body, which lacked the collapsible feature. They were classified as Limited Standard by Ordnance Committee action in November 1942 and February 1943. They were:

Artillery Repair M9; Automotive Repair M8, Loads A and B; Electrical Repair M18; Instrument Repair M10, Loads A and B; Machine Shop Repair M16, Loads A, B, C, D, and F; Small Arms Repair M7; Spare Parts M14, Loads A and B; Tool and Bench M13; Welding Repair M12.

REFERENCES—TM 9–801; OCM 16017, 17890, 18115, 18392, 19230, 19392, 19722, 20249, 20513, 21555, 21876, 22195, 22213, 23486, 23999.

TYPICAL CHARACTERISTICS

Crew (for transport)................2
Physical Characteristics
Weight (without load)..........12,270 lb.
Length.......................21 ft., 3 in.
Width...........................8 ft.
Height..................9 ft., 9½ in.
Ground clearance....................10 in.
Tread (center to center, rear)........67¾ in.
Wheelbase.....................164 in.
Tire equipment............7.50 x 20, 8-ply
Performance
Maximum speed on level...........45 m.p.h.
Maximum grade ability................65%
Angle of approach.....................54°
Angle of departure...................36°
Turning radius......................35 ft.
Fuel capacity.....................40 gal.
Cruising range (approx.)..........240 miles
Battery, Voltage, total.................6
Engine, Make and model........G.M.C. 270
Type...........................In-line
Number of cylinders...................6
Displacement................269.5 cu. in.
Fuel (gasoline)................70 octane
Radiator, Type...............Fin and tube
Capacity.....................19 qt.
Brakes, Type...................Hydraulic
Other characteristics same as for 2½-ton, 6 x 6 (4DT) Truck.

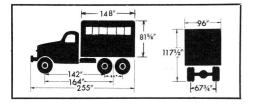

ARTILLERY REPAIR TRUCK M9A1, STANDARD, is intended for maintenance of various artillery items by the Heavy Maintenance Companies.

Each truck carries a workbench with drawers, as well as tackle blocks, rope, chain hoists, a 1-ton collapsible tripod, electrical cords and connections, portable electric drill, a vise, and allied equipment. Special artillery tools are added by the using organizations according to their assignments. The artillery mechanic's tool kits that are furnished include such items as chisels, drifts, files, hammers, punches, screwdrivers, sharpening stones, and wrenches.

Electric power is not available within this truck itself but is obtained from another unit within the company.

A similar set of equipment, known as "Ordnance Maintenance Set F," is furnished to Medium Maintenance Companies. This unit is carried in a standard 2½-ton, l.w.b. cargo truck.

REFERENCES—SNL G-140; OCM 15100, 18115, 19722, 21555, 21892.

AUTOMOTIVE REPAIR TRUCK M8A1, LOAD A, STANDARD, contains tools and equipment needed for general automotive repair work. It is used primarily by the Air Force for airfield vehicle maintenance.

The load consists of such items as general automotive tools, including a hydraulic portable press, drill sets, extractor sets, hammers, pliers, sledge, vises, test sets (both high and low tension and compression), pneumatic nut runner set, pneumatic chisel set, tube vulcanizer, socket wrench sets of various sizes, and automotive mechanic's tool kits with the individual mechanic's chisels, files, hammers, screwdrivers, etc.

Electric power for this unit is furnished from a combination air compressor and generator engine-driven set. The air compressor has a 60-cu.-ft. capacity. The generator can furnish 5-k.w., 110-v., alternating current.

REFERENCES—SNL G-139, Vol. 1; OCM 15100, 18115, 19722, 22362, 22569.

ELECTRICAL REPAIR TRUCK M18A2, STANDARD, is intended for use as a test and repair station for various automotive types of electrical equipment.

Its major items of equipment and its tools are an electrical test bench, magneto test stand, magnet charger, and other similar electrical test equipment. Repair tools and equipment include such items as

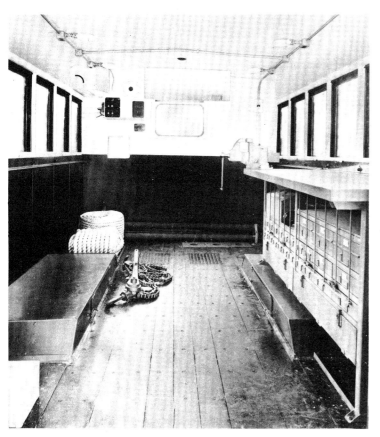

ARTILLERY REPAIR TRUCK M9A1, INTERIOR VIEW

INSTRUMENT REPAIR TRUCK M10A1, SHOWING INTERIOR

standard tools, a vise, hammers, chisels, pliers, wrenches, and automotive mechanic's tool kits.

A portable gasoline-engine-driven battery-charging generator is furnished, along with allied test and repair equipment. The unit has its own source of power in a 10-k.w., 115/230-v., a.c., engine-driven generator set.

REFERENCES—SNL G-149; OCM 18115; 18392, 19722, 23486, 23999.

INSTRUMENT BENCH TRUCK M23, STANDARD,

is primarily intended to maintain and repair special fire-control equipment, such as antiaircraft directors and range and height finders. The truck body is ideally suited for this type of work in that the heater ventilation system is 97% efficient in removing all dust and foreign particles from the air.

Essential equipment consists of one bench across the front of the truck and two collapsible tables, which can be used within the truck or set up on the ground. In this manner, considerable space is made available for the setting up of the instruments to be worked upon. A special tripod is furnished for the Directors M5 and M6. Special harnesses are furnished for strapping down the directors should it be necessary to move a truck with the directors inside.

Small tools are furnished, as well as Instrument Repairmen's Kits. A set of outrigger jacks is provided to help stabilize the truck.

This unit has no power of its own, but connections are furnished so that it can obtain power from the generator normally used with the directors or from one of the other mobile shop trucks.

REFERENCES—SNL G-178; OCM 19230, 19392.

INSTRUMENT REPAIR TRUCK M10A1, LOAD A, STANDARD,

is intended for repair and maintenance of optical instruments and equipment.

For major repair work, a standard 10-in. precision bench lathe, a ¼-in. precision drill press, a ½-ton arbor press, and an electric bench grinder are furnished.

Standard tools and equipment include surface plates with leveling screws, mandrel sets, drill sets, drifts, clamps, chisels, files, stud extractors, gages, hammers, pliers, reamers, rules, sharpening stones, threading sets (both U. S. standard and metric), vises, and wrenches.

Each truck is furnished with several Instrument Repairmen's Kits. These are equipped with forceps, gravers, hammers, watchmaker's loups, oilers, adjusting pins, punches, scrapers, scribers, special wrenches, etc.

A Leatherworker's Kit is included for repair of the leather cases normally found with optical instruments. This kit has such items as awls, saddler's carriage, leather creaser, leather knives, needles, sailmaker's palm, punches, rivet set, and saddler's tools.

Special tools, fixtures, etc. are furnished to the using organizations for this truck in relation to the work assigned.

Outrigger jacks are provided to stabilize the truck for the delicate repair operations.

Normally this truck obtains its electric power from another truck or a commercial source. However, it has a 2-k.w., 115-v., a.c., engine-driven generator (portable) that can be set up on the ground so as not to cause vibrations within the truck.

REFERENCES—SNL G-141, Vol. 1; OCM 18115, 19722.

MACHINE SHOP TRUCK M16A1, M16A2, STANDARD.

These units are intended for basic machine-shop work and are equipped for almost any general kind of machine-shop work encountered in the field. They are all equipped with an engine-driven, 10-k.w., 115/230-v., a.c., single-phase generator set.

MACHINE SHOP TRUCK M16A2, LEFT SIDE INTERIOR

SIGNAL REPAIR TRUCK M30, INTERIOR VIEW

M16A2, LOAD A—This unit is built around a standard 10-in. bench lathe with complete set of tools and accessories, electric bench grinder, a 7-in. bench shaper, a 10-ton hydraulic press, a milling head attachment for the lathe, and a special ½-in. drill press that is very much like a radial drill. A complete set of hand tools, gages, calipers, extractors, drill sets, threading sets (U. S. standard as well as metric), etc., are furnished to complement the basic machine tools.

M16A1, LOAD B—This is basically a heavy lathe truck. Load B is equipped with a 14–21-in. gap lathe, as well as a 1¼-in. portable electric drill with stand and a drill grinder. A few hand tools and drill sets are furnished with this load to supplement the Load A and to make the lathe as useful as possible.

M16A1, LOAD B1—This unit is much the same as the Load B, except that it has a 16-in.-swing lathe and a milling head attachment.

M16A1, LOAD B2—This unit is essentially the same as the Load B, except that it has an extension-gap lathe of 14–29-in. swing capacity. The gap can be extended to 19 inches.

REFERENCES—SNL G-146, Vols. 1 and 2; OCM 15053, 16017, 18115, 19722, 22195, 22536, 23486, 23999.

SIGNAL CORPS GENERAL REPAIR TRUCK M31, STANDARD. This unit is a redesignation of the former Small Arms Repair Truck M7 (Signal Corps). It is used by the Signal Corps for various repair functions of radio, wireless, etc. Its basic equipment includes two long benches, a bench grinder, a portable drill, drill sets, extension cords, spare parts boxes, and other similar equipment.

It obtains its power from an outside source.

REFERENCES—SNL G-138, Vol. 2; OCM 15100, 16017, 18115, 19722, 23486, 23999.

SIGNAL CORPS REPAIR TRUCK M30, STANDARD. This unit is equipped with a basic set of equipment for issuance to the Signal Corps for their use in repairing various radio, wire, and radar equipment. It is essentially the same as the Signal Corps General Repair Truck M31, except that it has additional equipment, such as a shockproof shelf for carrying the delicate test equipment, a small air compressor for cleaning purposes, a 12-volt battery, a battery charger, and special 6-, 12-, and 24-volt d.c. circuit. Many additional convenience outlets are furnished in order to permit testing and repairing of numerous pieces of equipment at the same time.

The unit obtains its electric power from an outside source.

REFERENCES—SNL G-138, Vol. 2; OCM 15100, 16017, 18115, 19722, 23486, 23999.

SMALL ARMS REPAIR TRUCK M7A2, STANDARD, is intended for inspection, maintenance, and repair of small arms.

The benches furnished provide space for the tools and the armorer's tool kits, and also for kits carrying spare parts for the individual weapons. Common tools, such as a ⅜-in. portable electric drill with stand, electric bench grinder, vises, drill sets, hack saws, hammers, reamers, cleaning rods, gasoline torches, trigger weights, are supplied. The armorer's tool kits are equipped with common hand tools and also special tools needed in small-arms repair work, such as cartridge extractors and oil stones.

A portable rifle rack is furnished for storing rifles under examination or repair. A portable table is also furnished to give additional work space outside the vehicle.

Electric power normally is furnished from one of the other mobile shop trucks, but the truck can get its own power from a portable, gasoline-engine-driven generator of 2-k.w. capacity.

REFERENCES—SNL G-138, Vol. 1; OCM 15100, 16017, 18115, 19722, 23486, 23999.

TIRE REPAIR TRUCKS M32, STANDARD. This unit consists of two trucks, Load A and Load B, and two 1-Ton, 2-Wheel, Tire Repair Trailers M25, Load A and Load B. The complete unit is used for sectional tire repair and tube work.

LOAD A—This unit carries all of the electric mold equipment, including an electric steam generator, some of the air bags, molds, matrices, and repair equipment.

LOAD B—This unit is primarily an inspection and work unit. Its equipment consists of a bench with tire mandrel and electrically driven air compressor, tire spreaders of three different sizes and types, tube inspection tank, some matrices, bead plates, air bags, and repair supplies and equipment.

TRAILER, LOAD A—The trailer loads are carried in the standard 1-ton cargo trailers. This load consists only of a 25-k.w., 115/230-v., a.c., 3-phase, engine-driven generator set. It furnishes all power needed for the complete unit.

TRAILER, LOAD B—This trailer carries additional equipment and accessories needed for the operation of the complete unit. Some of these items are buffing machines, additional matrices, bead plates, air bags, extra gasoline and water cans, supplies, and company equipment.

REFERENCES — OCM 18803, 23041, 23282, 24302.

SMALL ARMS REPAIR TRUCK M7A2, SHOWING RIGHT SIDE INTERIOR

5 PASSENGER LIGHT SEDANS (4x2)

Passenger cars for Army use are purchased from the regular stocks of the manufacturers, and differ from privately owned passenger cars of the same manufacturers principally in the fact that they are painted with U. S. Army standard dull-finish paint and equipped with black-out light equipment. This is done to reduce reflection of light to the minimum practicable.

Military characteristics for light sedans are described in MCM 17. Military equipment includes sturdy bumpers at the front and rear, and approved combat-zone safety lighting. All wheels are interchangeable at the hub. One spare wheel and tire assembly is mounted in the luggage compartment. Suitable motor vehicle tool equipment is provided. Equipment includes an oil-bath type air-cleaner, an oil filter with a minimum efficiency life of 120 hours and shock absorbers on both axles.

Military service requirements call for a brake mechanism so designed as to per-

CHEVROLET, 5 PASSENGER, LIGHT SEDAN

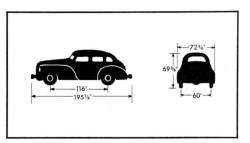

CHEVROLET

FORD, 5 PASSENGER, LIGHT SEDAN

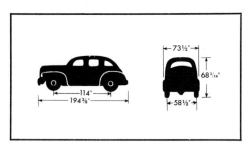

FORD

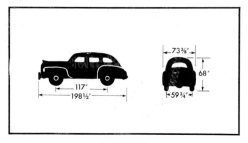

PLYMOUTH

PLYMOUTH, 5 PASSENGER, LIGHT SEDAN

100

5 PASSENGER LIGHT SEDANS (4X2) (Continued)

mit ready external adjustment. Headlights are "sealed beam" construction, properly positioned. Ignition is suppressed to prevent radio interference, but vehicles are not otherwise equipped for radio transmitter installation.

Body is the manufacturer's standard commercial four-door, seven-window sedan.

The cars are required to be able to operate over unimproved roads, trails and open, rolling and hilly cross country, and must be able to attain a speed not less than 50 m.p.h. on smooth concrete highway.

Cars acceptable under this classification are: Chevrolet, 1,500 and 2,000 series, 1942; Ford, Model 2 GA–73B, 1942; and Plymouth, Model P–11, 1941.

REFERENCES—OCM 19107; MCM 17.

CHARACTERISTICS, LIGHT SEDAN

Physical Characteristics	CHEVROLET	FORD	PLYMOUTH
Weight (gross)	4,075 lb.	4,100 lb.	3,190 lb.
Length	16 ft., 3⅞ ins.	16 ft., 2⅜ ins.	16 ft., 6½ ins.
Width	6 ft., ¾ in.	6 ft., 1½ ins.	6 ft., 1⅜ ins.
Height	5 ft., 9⅜ ins.	5 ft., 8³⁄₁₆ ins.	5 ft., 8 ins.
Ground clearance	8½ ins.	7⅝ ins.	7⅛ ins.
Wheelbase	116 ins.	114 ins.	117 ins.
Tread (center to center)	60 ins.	58½ ins.	59¾ ins.
Tire equipment	6.00x16, 6 ply, Highway tread	6.00x16, 6 ply, Highway tread	6.00x16, 6 ply, Highway tread
Performance			
Maximum speed on level	80 m.p.h.	80 m.p.h.	70 m.p.h.
Maximum grade ability	38.3%	35%	30%
Fording depth	16½ ins.	18 ins.	18 ins.
Fuel capacity	16 gals.	17 gals.	17 gals.
Cruising range	224 miles	240 miles	238 miles
Payload	800 lb.	800 lb.	800 lb.
Angle of approach	25°	21°	28.5°
Angle of departure	15°	23°	15.5°
Turning radius	20½ ft.	21 ft.	20½ ft.
Engine, Make and Model	Chevrolet 2AA or BA	Ford, 2GA	Plymouth
Type	In line	In line	In line
No. of cylinders	6	6	6
Cycle	4	4	4
Displacement	216.5 cu. ins.	226 cu. ins.	201.3 cu. ins.
Fuel (gasoline)	70 octane	70 octane	70 octane
Cooling System, Type	Liquid	Liquid	Liquid
Capacity	15 qts.	17½ qts.	14 qts.
Battery, Voltage	6	6	6
Brakes, Type	Hydraulic	Hydraulic	Hydraulic

5 PASSENGER MEDIUM SEDAN (4 x 2)

This car, which is larger and roomier than the light sedans, and which has a higher speed and greater cruising range, is provided for the transportation of staff officers.

Military characteristics, as given in MCM 18, provide for a minimum weight of 4,000 pounds, and for a vehicle with not less than 8 cylinders. Military equipment and military service requirements are the same as for the light sedans.

The car selected under this classification is the Packard, Model 2001, 1942. The manufacturer's standard commercial four-door, seven-window sedan is used. The vehicle is painted with U. S. Army standard dull-finish paint.

The car is equipped with an overdrive feature, which permits greater speed and fuel economy. Normal maximum speed is 90 m.p.h. At 40 m.p.h., the vehicle will average about 18.4 miles per gallon, with a cruising range of approximately 312 miles. With the overdrive, maximum speed may be increased to 95 m.p.h. At 40 m.p.h., mileage is increased to 20.9 miles per gallon, with a cruising range of approximately 355 miles.

REFERENCES—OCM 19107; MCM 18.

PACKARD, 5 PASSENGER, MEDIUM SEDAN

CHARACTERISTICS, MEDIUM SEDAN, PACKARD

Physical Characteristics	
Weight (gross)	4,400 lb.
Length	17 ft., 4½ ins.
Width	6 ft., 4⅛ ins.
Height	5 ft., 3½ ins.
Ground clearance	6¹¹⁄₁₆ ins.
Wheelbase	120 ins.
Tread (center to center)	60½ ins.
Tire equipment	6.50x15, 4 ply, Highway tread
Performance	
Top speed, without overdrive	90 m.p.h.
with overdrive	95 m.p.h.
Maximum grade ability	25%
Fording depth	18¾ ins.
Fuel capacity	17 gals.
Cruising range, with overdrive	355 miles*
without overdrive	312 miles*
Payload	800 lb.
Angle of approach	15°
Angle of departure	16°
Turning radius	21 ft.

*At 40 m.p.h.

Engine, Make and Model	Packard, 2001
Type	In line
No. of cylinders	8
Cycle	4
Displacement	282 cu. ins.
Fuel (gasoline)	70 octane
Cooling System	Liquid
Capacity	17 qts.
Battery, Voltage	9
Brakes, Type	Hydraulic

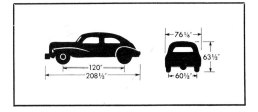

CHAIN DRIVE SOLO MOTORCYCLE—STANDARD
EXTRA LIGHT SOLO MOTORCYCLE M1—STANDARD

TYPICAL CHARACTERISTICS

Physical Characteristics	Solo	Extra Light Solo
Weight (with gas, oil and accessories)	576 lb.	241 lb.
Length	7 ft., 4 in.	6 ft., 5½ in.
Width	3 ft., ¼ in.	2 ft., 4 in.
Height	3 ft., 5 in.	3 ft., ¼ in.
Ground clearance (amidships)	4 in.	5½ in.
Wheelbase	59½ in.	50 in.
Tire equipment	4.00x18, 4-ply	3.00x18, 4-ply
Desert	5.50x16, 4-ply	
Performance		
Maximum allowable speed	65 m.p.h.	45 m.p.h.
Maximum grade ability	30%	25%
Fording depth	12 in.	12 in.
Turning diameter	15 ft.	10 ft., 8 in.
Fuel capacity	3⅜ gal.	2½ gal.
Cruising range (approx.)	125 miles	250 miles
Engine, Make and model	Harley-Davidson, WLA	Indian, Model 144
Type	L-head, V, A.C.	L-head, A.C.
No. of cylinders	2	1
Cycle	4	4
Displacement	45.12 cu. in.	13.50 cu. in.
Bore and stroke	2¾x3 13/16 in.	2½x2¾ in.
Gross horsepower	23	6.2 at 4,700 r.p.m.
Max. torque	28 lb.-ft. at 3,000 r.p.m.	8.1 lb.-ft. at 3,600 r.p.m.
Sprockets, No. of teeth		
Engine	30	15
Clutch	59	38
Countershaft	17	17
Rear wheel	41	43
Transmission, Type	Constant mesh	Constant mesh
Gear ratios		
First speed	11.71:1	18.2:1
Second speed	7.45:1	10.4:1
Third Speed	4.74:1	6.4:1

CHAIN DRIVE SOLO MOTORCYCLE, SUPPLIED TO ALL ARMS AND SERVICES

EXTRA LIGHT SOLO MOTORCYCLE M1, DEVELOPED FOR AIRBORNE USE

CHAIN DRIVE SOLO MOTORCYCLE—STANDARD—Except for special military equipment, the standard solo motorcycle is similar to the familiar 2-cylinder motorcycles used by police and civilians. It is used by the Army for reconnaissance, messenger service, and police operations, and can be supplied to all arms and services. In addition to conventional equipment, it has a box for submachine gun ammunition, a bracket for carrying a submachine gun, and combat zone safety lighting.

For special operations, 5.50x16 desert tires can be provided in place of the standard 4.00x18 tires, in which case the rear wheel is fitted with a beadlock to prevent creeping of the tire at the low inflation needed on soft terrain.

The manufacturer is the Harley-Davidson Motor Co. A somewhat similar machine made by the Indian Motorcycle Co. also meets the specifications for the Chain Drive Solo Motorcycle.

REFERENCES—TM 9–879, MC 9c; OCM 19107, 20341, 21016, 21221, 21809, 22019.

EXTRA LIGHT SOLO MOTORCYCLE M1—STANDARD—This motorcycle was developed especially for airborne troops, but it can be used by other services requiring lightweight motorcycle equipment. It was standardized in December 1944.

Although its weight is only 241 lb., less than half that of the standard heavy motorcycle, tests have shown that it is a rugged and versatile vehicle. It can operate successfully off the road, in mud or sand, or in water a foot deep. In tests, its operation was not affected when it was dropped 800 feet by parachute from an airplane traveling at a ground speed of 100 m.p.h. Because the engine has magneto ignition, the generator, battery, and the lights can be removed. The weight can thus be reduced to 224 lb.

The motorcycle is of clean design and free of projections and snares that might entange parachute or rigging. It has a non-spillable, 10-ampere-hour storage battery, a non-spillable, oil-bath air cleaner, and rings for attaching a parachute and a paracrate into which the wheels fit for protection when the motorcycle is dropped by parachute. There is a pintle hook at the rear for towing a lightweight utility cart.

The machine is manufactured by the Indian Motorcycle Co.

REFERENCES — OCM 24145, 24276, 25611, 26057.

SOLO, CHAIN DRIVE

59½″ / 88″ / 41″ / 36¼″

SOLO, EXTRA LIGHT

50″ / 77½″ / 36¼″ / 28″

MEN'S AND WOMEN'S BICYCLES—STANDARD

MEN'S BICYCLE, DESIGNED FOR ALL ARMS AND SERVICES

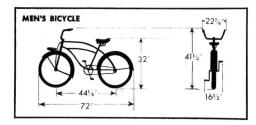

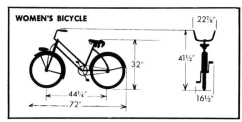

WOMEN'S BICYCLE, DESIGNED FOR THE WOMEN'S ARMY CORPS

MEN'S BICYCLES, although previously in Army use for administrative purposes, were not standardized until October 1942. The standard bicycle is designed for all arms and services.

The machine has a men's type of frame and leather seat, and a sprocket ratio of 26 to 10. Tires are size 2⅛x26, 2-ply, balloon, with heavy duty inner tubes, mounted on drop-center rims that are integral with the wheel.

Equipment includes a tool bag and tools, tire pump, bell, an electric headlight operated by dry cells, a reflector tail light, coaster brake, front and rear fenders, chain guard, and kick stand. The finish is non-reflecting paint.

The men's bicycles are made by the Huffman Manufacturing Co. and the Westfield Manufacturing Co.

REFERENCES—MCM 32; OCM 18948, 19039, 20395, 20734.

WOMEN'S BICYCLES, developed at the request of the Women's Army Corps after that organization had been set up, were standardized in February 1943.

The women's bicycle has the typical open frame and a lower sprocket ratio than the men's. Except for the frame, chain, front sprocket, and seat, all parts for both men's and women's bicycles are interchangeable, and the equipment and finish are the same.

Women's bicycles are also made by the Huffman Manufacturing Co. and the Westfield Manufacturing Co.

REFERENCES—MCM 32; OCM 19423, 19548, 19770, 20395, 20734.

TYPICAL CHARACTERISTICS

Physical Characteristics

Weight (net)	55 lb.
Length, overall	6 ft.
Width, over handle bars	1 ft., 10⅞ in.
Over pedals	1 ft., 4½ in.
Height, top of handle bars	3 ft., 5½ in.
Less handle bars	2 ft., 8 in.
Wheelbase	44¼ in.
Tire equipment	2⅛x26, 2-ply, balloon
Sprocket ratio	
Men's	26:10 (for 1-in. pitch chain)
Women's	22:10 (for 1-in. pitch chain)

Performance

Payload	200 lb.

MOTOR SCOOTERS AND MOTOR-DRIVEN BICYCLES

STANDARD 3-WHEEL MOTOR SCOOTER WITH SIDE CAR

2-WHEEL MOTOR SCOOTER PROCURED FOR AIRBORNE USE

3-WHEEL MOTOR SCOOTER WITH SIDE CAR—STANDARD
—Standardized in November, 1943, this vehicle is used principally for messenger use. It has a payload of 375 pounds.

Power is supplied by a one-cylinder, four-cycle gasoline engine of 4 hp. A kick starter and an A.C. type generator are provided. A spring type, imitation leather, driver's seat; a headlight and tail light, tools, a gasoline filter, and an air cleaner are furnished.

The vehicle is manufactured by the Cushman Motor Works.

REFERENCES—MCM 109; OCM 20313, 21805, 21517, 21673, 22018.

2-WHEEL AIRBORNE MOTOR SCOOTER—STANDARD—
This vehicle was standardized in March, 1944.

It has two speeds, with a maximum speed of approximately 40 m.p.h. Parachute-attaching rings are mounted at two balanced points. A small pintle hook is mounted on the rear. Payload is 250 pounds, including the driver.

Military equipment includes a motorcycle type leather driver's seat, tools, a gasoline filter, and an air cleaner.

The vehicle is manufactured by the Cushman Motor Works.

REFERENCES—MCM 41; OCM 21934, 22139, 23182.

MOTOR-DRIVEN BICYCLE—Limited procurement of these vehicles, was authorized in April, 1943.

Power is carried to the rear wheel through two V-belts. High and low ratio are obtained by actuating a foot lever, which, in turn, tightens, or loosens the V-belt in the pulley, causing the

MOTOR-DRIVEN BICYCLE PROCURED FOR AIRBORNE USE

belts to move higher or lower in their pulleys. The machine is started by pushing. It has a maximum speed of 30 m.p.h.

Fuel is fed by gravity to a carburetor, and from there through a rotary valve carrying mixed oil and gasoline into the crankcase.

Equipment includes a spring type leather driver's saddle; a headlight, combat zone lighting, a tool bag and tools, a gasoline filter and an air cleaner, front and rear fenders, a luggage carrier, a jiffy stand, and a speedometer.

The vehicles are manufactured by the Simplex Mfg. Co.

REFERENCES—MCM 35; OCM 20250, 21421, 21674, 21893.

TYPICAL CHARACTERISTICS

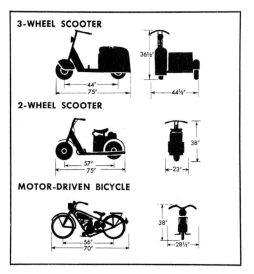

Physical Characteristics	3-Wheel Scooter	2-Wheel Scooter	Motor-Driven Bicycle
Weight (gross)	735 lb.	499 lb.	365 lb.
Length	6 ft., 3 ins.	6 ft., 3 ins.	5 ft., 10 ins.
Width	3 ft., 8½ ins.	1 ft., 11 ins.	2 ft., 4½ ins.
Height	3 ft., ½ in.	3 ft., 2 ins.	3 ft., 2 ins.
Ground clearance	4 ins.	6¾ ins.	5½ ins.
Wheelbase	44 ins.	57 ins.	56 ins.
Tire equipment	4.00 x 8, 4 ply	6.00 x 6, 4 ply	2.25 x 26, 2 ply
Performance			
Maximum speed	25 m.p.h.	40 m.p.h.	30 m.p.h.
Maximum grade ability	5%	30%	15%
Fording depth	10 ins.	12 ins.	12 ins.
Fuel capacity	1¼ gals.	2 gals.	2½ gals.
Cruising range	50 miles	100 miles	
Payload (incl. driver)	375 lb.	250 lb.	200 lb.
Engine			
Make and Model	Cushman	Cushman	Servi-Cycle
No. of cylinders	1	1	1
Cycle	4	4	2
Fuel (gasoline)	70 octane	70 octane	70 octane
Brake hp.	4 at 3,500 r.p.m.	4 at 3,500 r.p.m.	1.6 at 2,000 r.p.m.

¼-TON, 4X4, TRUCK—STANDARD

This vehicle, popularly called the "jeep," is one of the outstanding automotive developments of this war. Developed by the Quartermaster Corps, it and other motor transport vehicles were transferred to the Ordnance Department in August, 1942.

It has been found useful in a variety of ways, and despite its light weight has been able to function under rigorous conditions. Operated by a crew of two, it has a space for equipment or additional personnel.

The truck is capable of operation over unimproved roads, trails, and open, rolling, and hilly cross country. It will climb a 60% grade, and will operate at a speed of 65 m.p.h. on level highways. It can ford a stream 18 inches deep, while fully equipped and loaded. It has a cruising range of approximately 300 miles on 15 gallons of gasoline.

Towing a 37 mm antitank gun, it will climb a 7% grade, and can achieve a speed of 20 m.p.h. on a level highway.

Power is supplied by a four-cylinder L head gasoline engine equipped with a counter-balanced crankshaft. The clutch is a single-plate, dry-disk type. The transmission is of the three-speed, syncromesh type, which, through a transfer case, provides six speeds forward and two reverse.

The vehicle has internal-expanding, hydraulic four-wheel brakes and a mechanical handbrake.

A base plate is provided for a pedestal mount for a cal. .30 or a cal. .50 machine gun. The infantry uses the Cal. .30 Machine Gun Mount, M48, on the dash, and other arms use the Pedestal Truck Mount, M31.

Provision is made for a lighting socket connection for a trailer, and for a radio outlet. The windshield may be folded down over the hood when desired. A removable canvas top is provided.

Desert equipment includes a radiator surge tank, a power-driven air compressor, a low-pressure tire gage, a 3-inch copper fin radiator, and a fuel filter, relocated to minimize vapor lock.

A tandem hitch makes it possible to use two of these vehicles for emergency towing of a 155 mm howitzer. When used in this way, speed is limited to 30 m.p.h. on level highway, and 10 m.p.h. down hill.

The vehicles are produced, to identical specifications, by the Willys-Overland Motors, Inc., and the Ford Motor Co.

REFERENCES—MCM 8e; TM 10-1207, 10-1349; OCM 19107, 19549, 21179, 21221, 21590, 21788.

THE POPULAR "JEEP" TRANSPORTS PERSONNEL AND CARGO; TOWS GUNS OR ¼-TON TRAILER

TYPICAL CHARACTERISTICS

Crew 2
Physical Characteristics
  Weight (gross) . . . . 3,253 lb.
  Length . . . . 11 ft., ¼ in.
  Width . . . . 5 ft., 2 ins.
  Height—top of cowl . . . . 3 ft., 4 ins.
    top of steering wheel . . . . 4 ft., 4 ins.
    with top up . . . . 5 ft., 9¾ ins.
  Ground clearance . . . . 8¾ ins.
  Wheelbase . . . . 80 ins.
  Tread (center to center of tires) . . . . 49 ins.
  Ground pressure . . . . 20.8 lb./sq. in.
  Tire equipment. 6.00x16, 6 ply (mud and snow)
Armament
  Provision for one cal. .30 or cal. .50 machine
  gun
Performance
  Maximum speed on level . . . . 65 m.p.h.
    with towed load . . . . 20 m.p.h.
  Maximum grade ability 60%
    with towed load 45%
  Angle of approach . . . . 45°
  Angle of departure . . . . 35°
  Fording depth . . . . 18 ins.
  Fuel capacity . . . . 15 gals.
  Cruising range (approx.) . . . . 300 miles
    with towed load . . . . 260 miles
  Normal towed load (37 mm gun carriage
    or ¼-ton, 2-wheel, cargo trailer) . . . 1,000 lb.
  Payload (including driver and assistant). 800 lb.
  Turning radius . . . . 17½ ft.
Communication . . . . Radio outlet
Battery, Voltage 6-12
Engine, Type . . . . "L" head
  No. of cylinders 4

Cycle 4
Fuel (gasoline) . . . . 68 octane
Bore and stroke . . . . 3⅛ x 4⅜ ins.
Displacement . . . . 134.2 cu. ins.
Compression ratio 6.48:1
Net h.p. . . . . 54 at 4,000 r.p.m.
Max. torque . . . . 105 lb.-ft. at 2,000 r.p.m.
Crankshaft rotation . . . . C'Clockwise
Length . . . . 27 ins.
Width . . . . 22½ ins.
Height . . . . 26¾ ins.
Ignition . . . . Battery
Weight . . . . 355 lb.

Master Clutch, Type . . . . Dry, single plate
Radiator, Type . . . . Fin and tube
  Capacity of system . . . . 11 qts.
Transmission, Gear ratios
  First speed 2.67:1
  Second speed 1.56:1
  Third speed 1.00:1
  Reverse 3.55:1
Transfer case, Gear ratio, Low 1.97:1
  High 1.00:1
Differential, Gear ratio 4.88:1
  Type of drive . . . . Hypoid bevel
Steering ratio 14, 12, 14:1
Suspension, Type . . . . Semi-elliptic
  Wheel construction . . . . Divided
Brakes, Type . . . . Internal Hydraulic
Brakes, Parking, Type . . . . External Contracting
Front Axle, Type . . . . Full floating
Rear Axle, Gear ratio 4.88:1

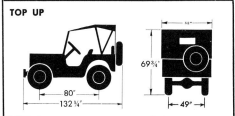

TOP UP

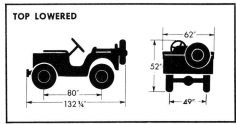

TOP LOWERED

¼-TON AMPHIBIAN TRUCK—STANDARD

This is a modification of the ¼-Ton, 4 x 4 Truck, designed for use on water as well as on land. It was standardized in February, 1943.

Power plant, transmission and many other components are the same as on the non-amphibious truck. The body is in the form of a waterproof hull, with special equipment required for operation on water.

Military characteristics, as given in MCM 26, provide for a vehicle with a payload of 800 pounds and a towing capacity of 1,000 pounds.

The vehicle has a grade ability of 45% without towed load, in transmission lowest forward gear and transfer case low range. It is capable of operation over unimproved roads, trails, and open, rolling and hilly cross country, and on water.

Maximum speed on land is 55 miles per hour, and on water is 5½ miles per hour.

Tires are 6.00 x 16, 6 ply, mud and snow tread, with heavy-duty type inner tubes. Wheels are standard divided type, single front and rear. One spare wheel and tire assembly is furnished.

Military equipment includes a towing eye at the front, a brush guard and a rear pintle. Sealed beam type headlights are supplemented by combat-zone safety lighting. A trailer lighting socket and a radio terminal box are provided.

A power take-off aperture at the rear of the transfer case is designed to supply power with the vehicle moving or at a standstill. A folding windshield is provided. An engine-operated power capstan of 3,500 pounds direct pull is installed at the bow centerline.

The vehicle has a marine rudder and controls, and a propeller. Five chocks and four lifting eyes are provided. Five life preservers are carried.

A 12 volt electrical system for radio is used. The vehicle will tow a ¼-Ton Trailer, which also will float with its rated payload.

The truck is manufactured by the Ford Motor Car Co.

REFERENCES—MCM 26; OCM 19107, 19487, 19771, 20771, 21010.

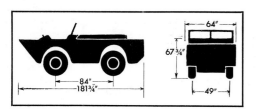

THE ¼-TON, 4 x 4, AMPHIBIAN TRUCK, TRAVELS ON LAND AT 55 M.P.H.

WATERPROOF HULL, PROPELLER AND RUDDER PERMIT TRAVEL IN WATER

TYPICAL CHARACTERISTICS

Crew 4

Physical Characteristics
Weight (gross) . . . . 4,300 lb.
Length . . . . 15 ft., 1¾ ins.
Width . . . . 5 ft., 4 ins.
Height, w/o top . . . . 5 ft., 7¾ ins.
Height of pintle . . . . 28¼ ins.
Ground clearance . . . . 8 ins.
Freeboard, loaded—front . . . . 17 ins.
            —rear . . . . 9½ ins.
Draft, loaded, to underside of tires . . . 33½ ins.
Ground clearance . . . . 8 ins.
Tread (center to center) . . . . 49 ins.
Wheelbase . . . . 84 ins.
Tire equipment . 6.00 x 16, 6 ply (mud and snow)

Performance
Maximum speed on land . . . . 55 m.p.h.
  —with towed load . . . . 35 m.p.h.
Maximum speed in water . . . . 5½ m.p.h.
Maximum grade ability 45%
Angle of approach . . . . 39°
Angle of departure . . . . 37°
Turning radius . . . . 18 ft.
Fuel capacity . . . . 15 gals.
Cruising range—land . . . . 250 miles
  —with towed load . . . . 200 miles
  —in water . . . . 35 miles

Normal towed load . . . . 1,000 lb.
Payload (including personnel) . . . . 800 lb.
Battery, Voltage, total 12
Fire Protection, Fire Extinguisher 1
Life Preservers 5
Engine, Type . . . . L head
No. of cylinders 4
Cycle 4
Bore and Stroke . . . . 3⅛ x 4⅜ ins.
Fuel (gasoline) . . . . 68 octane
Displacement . . . . 134.2 cu. ins.
Weight . . . . 355 lb.
Compression . . . . 111 at 185 r.p.m.
Net hp. . . . . 54 at 4,000 r.p.m.
Max. torque . . . . 105 lb.-ft. at 2,000 r.p.m.
Crankshaft rotation . . . . C'Clockwise
Transmission, Gear ratios
First speed 2.675:1
Second speed 1.564:1
Third speed 1.00:1
Reverse 3.55:1
Transfer Case, Gear ratios 1.97:1; 1.00:1
Front Axle, Type . . . . Full floating
Rear Axle, Gear ratio 4.88:1
Brakes, Type . . . . Hydraulic
Brakes, Parking, Type . . . . External Contracting

¾-TON, 4 x 4, TRUCKS AND AMBULANCE—STANDARD

Standard vehicles in the ¾-ton, 4 x 4, class are the Weapons Carrier and Telephone Installation Trucks, and the Ambulance. The ¾-ton Carryall Truck and ¾-ton Command and Reconnaissance Truck are Limited Standard.

The vehicles have top governed speeds of 54 miles per hour. They are capable of operation over unimproved roads, trails and open, rolling and hilly cross country with a towed load. Wheels are equipped with 9.00 x 16, 8-ply tires.

The engine is of the liquid-cooled, 6-cylinder, L-head type, and clutch is of the single dry-plate type. Power is transmitted from the four-speed selective gear transmission through a short propeller shaft to the transfer case, and thence to both front and rear axles. The vehicles may be driven with all four wheels, or with the rear wheels only.

A power take-off is provided on vehicles equipped with a winch.

Service brakes are hydraulic, internal-expanding, and handbrakes are mechanical, external-contracting. Wheel and tire assemblies are interchangeable, front and rear.

Desert equipment includes a radiator surge tank of at least four quart capacity; a power driven air compressor with sufficient hose to inflate all tires; a radiator with shroud ring for those vehicles not already equipped; and a low pressure tire gage.

Pioneer tools, two five-gallon liquid containers and a fire extinguisher are furnished with each truck.

These vehicles are manufactured by the Fargo Motor Corporation.

REFERENCES—MCM12B; OCM 18758, 18986, 19060, 19107, 20486, 20735, 21011, 21221, 21853, 22504, 23100; TM 9–808.

¾-TON, 4 x 4, COMMAND AND RECONNAISSANCE TRUCK

—This vehicle, used to provide transportation for staff officers in the field, is classified Limited Standard. The body is the U. S. Army standard phaeton type with folding windshield. The vehicle is adapted for radio installation, including a 12-volt electrical system and U. S. Army standard 55-ampere output generator. Provisions are made for an antenna mount. The truck is available with or without a winch.

¾-TON, 4 x 4, WEAPONS CARRIER TRUCK

—This truck, designed for all arms and services, is used to transport weapons, tools and equipment. The body is of the commercial pickup type, with a removable canvas top mounted on three bows. Troop seats are provided within the body. Inside body dimensions are 72 x 48¼ inches. In lieu of a driver's cab, the vehicle has a seat box on which are mounted two bucket seats. A removable canvas top and a folding windshield are provided. The truck is available with or without a winch. It has a 12-volt electrical system.

GENERAL CHARACTERISTICS

Performance
Maximum speed on level	54 m.p.h.
Maximum grade ability—Weapons Carrier and Telephone	60%
—Ambulance	55%
—with towed load—Weapons Carrier and Telephone	50%
—Ambulance	48%
Fording depth (slowest forward speed)	34 ins.
Angle of approach, without winch	53°
—with winch	36½°
Angle of departure—Weapons Carrier	31°
—Telephone	29°
—Ambulance	24°
Turning radius—Weapons Carrier and Ambulance	22 ft.
—Telephone	27 ft.
Fuel capacity	30 gals.
Cruising range	240 miles
—with towed load	210 miles
Normal towed load	1,000 lb.
Payload (including personnel)—Weapons Carrier and Ambulance	1,800 lb.
—Telephone	1,300 lb.
Winch capacity	5,000 lb.
Battery, Voltage, total—Weapons Carrier	12
—Telephone and Ambulance	6
Engine, Make and Model	Dodge T-214
Type	In line, liquid cooled

No. of cylinders	6
Cycle	4
Fuel (gasoline)	70 octane
Bore and stroke	3¼ x 4⅝ ins.
Displacement	230.2 cu. ins.
Compression, ratio	6.7:1
Net hp.	76 at 3,200 r.p.m.
Max. torque	176 lb.-ft. at 1,000 r.p.m.
Crankshaft rotation	C'Clockwise
Length	37½ ins.
Width	24 ins.
Height	30 ins.
Weight, dry	603 lb.

Transmission, Gear ratios
First speed	6.40:1
Second speed	3.09:1
Third speed	1.69:1
Fourth speed	1.00:1
Reverse	7.82:1
Transfer Case, Gear ratio	1.00:1
Suspension, Type	Semi-elliptic
Master Clutch, Type	Single dry plate
Radiator, Type	Fin and tube
Capacity of system	17 qts.
Brakes, Type	Internal hydraulic
Brakes, Parking, Type	External contracting
Front Axle, Type	Full floating
Rear Axle, Gear ratio	5.83:1

Physical Characteristics
Weight—without winch	7,050 lb.
—with winch	7,350 lb.
Length—without winch	13 ft., 10⅞ ins.
—with winch	14 ft., 8½ ins.
Width	6 ft., 10¾ ins.
Height	6 ft., 9⅞ ins.
—with top lowered	5 ft., 2¼ ins.
Ground clearance	10⅝ ins.
Tread (center to center, rear)	64¾ ins.
Wheelbase	98 ins.
Ground pressure	33.8 lb./sq. in.
Ground contact	208 sq. ins.
Tire equipment (mud and snow type)	9.00 x 16, 8 ply

¾-TON, 4 x 4, WEAPONS CARRIER TRUCK, WITH WINCH, SHOWING TOP RAISED

¾-TON, 4 x 4, TRUCKS AND AMBULANCE (Continued)

¾-TON, 4 x 4, TELEPHONE INSTALLATION AND MAINTENANCE TRUCK, K-50

This vehicle, designed for the Signal Corps, has an open cab, with a folding windshield and a folding canvas top, and a steel body containing trays, drawers and various shaped storage spaces for tools and equipment used in maintaining communications systems. The body has two doors at the right side and two doors at the rear. A 24 foot extension ladder is mounted on the left side of the body.

¾-TON, 4 x 4, AMBULANCE, KD

Designed for the Medical Corps, this vehicle is used for the transportation of sick and wounded personnel. Present standard body is of knock-down wood and steel construction and is equipped to carry four litter patients or eight seated patients, with attendant. It is insulated, with provisions for heating and ventilating. It has an open cab. A special spring and shock absorber design provides improved riding characteristics.

The body is painted conspicuously with the Red Cross and the insignia of the Medical Corps. No winch is supplied with this model. The vehicle has a 6-volt electrical system and a U. S. Army standard 40-ampere output generator.

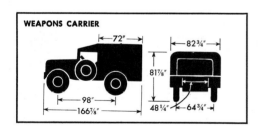

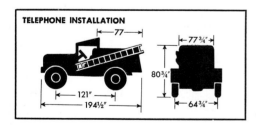

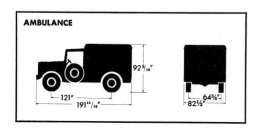

¾-TON, 4 x 4, TELEPHONE INSTALLATION AND MAINTENANCE TRUCK, K-50

Physical Characteristics

Weight	6,700 lb.
Length	15 ft., 11½ ins.
Width	6 ft., 5¾ ins.
Height	6 ft., 8¾ ins.
Ground clearance	10⅝ ins.
Tread (center to center, rear)	64¾ ins.
Wheelbase	121 ins.
Ground contact	208 sq. ins.
Ground pressure	31.7 lb./sq. in.
Tire equipment (mud and snow type)	9.00 x 16, 8 ply

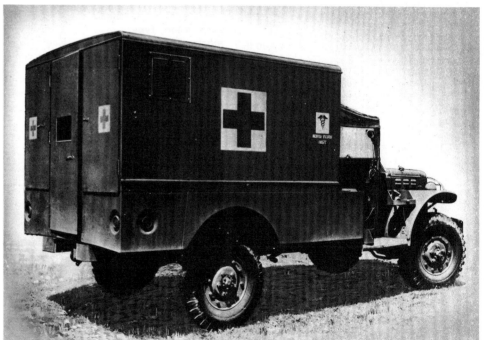

¾-TON, 4 x 4, AMBULANCE, WITH OPEN CAB. EARLIER MODEL HAD CLOSED CAB

Physical Characteristics

Weight	8,046 lb.
Length	15 ft., 11¹³⁄₁₆ ins.
Width	6 ft., 10½ ins.
Height	7 ft., 8⁵⁄₁₆ ins.
Ground clearance	10⅝ ins.
Tread (center to center, rear)	64¾ ins.
Wheelbase	121 ins.
Ground contact	208 sq. ins.
Ground pressure	38.6 lb./sq. in.
Tire equipment (mud and snow type)	9.00 x 16, 8 ply

1½-TON, 4x4 (2DT) TRUCKS—STANDARD

These trucks have payloads of 3,000 pounds each, and will tow a load of 4,000 pounds. The truck tractor has a payload of 4,500 pounds and will tow a semi-trailer weighing 12,000 pounds gross.

The trucks are available in several standard body styles or a chassis upon which may be placed special bodies required by the various services. Wheelbase is 145 inches or 175 inches.

The vehicle has a maximum grade ability of 65% and is capable of operation over unimproved roads, trails, rolling and hilly cross country. It has a top governed speed of 48 miles per hour. Cruising range is approximately 270 miles.

The truck has four wheels, including two dual-tire wheels, using 7.50 x 20, 8 ply tires. Power is supplied to all four wheels, with a declutching control for the front axle.

The engine is a six-cylinder valve-in-head type, equipped with a counter-balanced crankshaft. A single plate dry disk type clutch is used. The four-speed transmission is a heavy-duty type of sturdy construction. A two-speed transfer case connects the transmission with the front and rear axles.

Wheels are interchangeable front and rear. Dual wheels can be installed on the front wheels, as well as on the rear wheels, without changing the wheel mounting.

The braking system combines hydraulically operated service brakes, a hydro-vac booster system, a mechanically operated parking brake, and an electric controller for trailer brakes.

A power-operated winch, with a 10,000 pound capacity, is mounted on the front end of some of the cargo trucks.

Military characteristics call for open cabs. At present, however, only closed cab models are being produced.

Desertization equipment includes size 11.00 x 18, 10 ply, tires, with heavy duty tubes; army combat wheels with bead-lock, size 8.00CV x 18, single front and rear, and one spare tire and wheel assembly with carrier. A radiator surge tank of at least 4 quart capacity, a power driven air compressor with hose to permit inflation of all tires, a low pressure-tire gage, tire chains for driving wheels, a speedometer correction adapter and a six bladed fan are also included. Winterization kits are supplied for those trucks whose use will require them.

The vehicles are manufactured by the Chevrolet Motor Div., General Motors Corp.

REFERENCES— MCM2c and 23; OCM 19107, 21221.

1½-TON, 4x4 CHASSIS IS USED FOR VARIETY OF SPECIAL PURPOSE VEHICLES

TRUCK, 1½-TON, 4x4 (4DT) CHASSIS—STANDARD—This is the basic chassis for all 1½ ton, 4x4 Army trucks, including not only the standard body styles shown herewith, but also a number of vehicles for special purposes. Among these are the Signal Corps Telephone Maintenance Truck, K–43; the Signal Corps Earth Borer and Pole Setter Truck, K–44; and the Air Corps Field Lighting truck.

REFERENCE—MCM 2c.

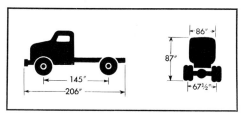

TYPICAL CHARACTERISTICS

Physical Characteristics
Weight (dry chassis)	4,500 lb.
Length	17 ft., 2 ins.
Width	7 ft., 2 ins.
Height	7 ft., 3 ins.
Ground clearance	9⅞ ins.
Tread (center to center, rear)	67½ ins.
Wheelbase	145 or 175 ins.
Ground contact	243.6 sq. ins.
Ground pressure	18.4 lb./sq. in.
Tire equipment	7.50 x 20, 8 ply (mud and snow)
desert	11.00 x 18, 10 ply

Performance
Maximum speed on level	48 m.p.h.
Maximum grade ability	65%
Fording depth (slowest forward speed)	32 ins.
Angle of approach, with winch	39°
without winch	45°
Angle of departure	30°
Turning radius	30 ft.
Fuel capacity	30 gals.
Cruising range	270 miles
with towed load	195 miles
Maximum drawbar pull	10,000 lb.

Normal towed load	4,000 lb.
Winch capacity	10,000 lb.

Battery, Voltage, total | 6

Fire Protection—Fire Extinguisher

Engine, Make and
Model	Chevrolet BV-1001 UP
Type	Valve-in-head
No. of cylinders	6
Cycle	4
Fuel (gasoline)	70 octane
Bore and stroke	3⁸⁄₁₆ x 3¹⁵⁄₁₆ ins.
Displacement	235.5 cu. ins.
Compression	110 at 210-220
Max. governed speed	3,100 r.p.m.
Net hp.	83.5 at 3,000 r.p.m.
Max. torque	189 lb.-ft. at 1,600 r.p.m.
Crankshaft rotation	C'Clockwise
Length	40 ins.
Width	22 ins.
Height	28 ins.
Ignition	Battery
Weight, dry	574 lb.

Transmission—Gear ratios
First speed	7.06:1
Second speed	3.48:1
Third speed	1.71:1
Fourth speed	1.00:1
Reverse	6.98:1

Transfer Case, Gear ratios | 1.94:1; 1.00:1

Differential, Type | Hypoid
| Gear ratio | 6.67:1 |

Suspension, Type | Semi-elliptic
| Wheel size | 20 x 7 |
| Wheel construction | Pierced disk |

Master Clutch, Type | Single dry plate

Radiator, Type | Fin and tube
| Capacity of system | 17¼ qts. |

Steering Ratio | 23.6:1

Brakes, Type | Internal Hydraulic

Brakes, Parking, Type | External Band

Front Axle, Type | Full floating

Rear Axle, Gear ratio | 6.67:1

1½-TON, 4x4 (2DT) CARGO TRUCK STANDARD

This truck, designed for use by all arms and services, has the U. S. Army standard cargo body, with troop seats with lazy backs. A detachable canvas top is supported by five bows, and is provided with roll-up straps arranged to permit ventilation in the body. The top is equipped with front and rear curtains with window flaps. Inside dimensions are approximately 70 x 108 inches. It has a payload of 2,320 lb. Wheelbase is 145 inches.

Present military characteristics call for the U. S. Army standard open type cab with collapsible top and folding windshield.

The vehicle is available with or without a winch, of 10,000 pounds capacity.

REFERENCES—TM 10–1127, 10–1438.

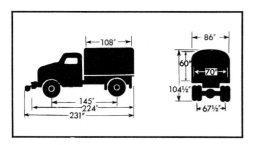

CARGO TRUCK, WITH TOP UP. TROOP SEATS ARE PROVIDED IN THE BODY

Physical Characteristics

Weight, without winch	10,865 lb.	Ground clearance	9⅞ ins.
with winch	11,535 lb.	Wheelbase	145 ins.
Length, without winch	18 ft., 8 ins.	Tread (center to center, rear)	67½ ins.
with winch	19 ft., 3 ins.	Tire equipment	7.50 x 20, 8 ply (mud and snow)
Width	7 ft., 2 ins.	Ground contact	243.6 ins.
Height	8 ft., 8½ ins.	Ground pressure per sq. in.	43.4 lb.
with bows removed	7 ft., 3 ins.		

1½-TON, 4x4 (2DT) STAKE AND PLATFORM TRUCK—STANDARD

This truck, designed for the Signal Corps, has a body of the commercial stake and platform type. It is used to transport general cargo. The outside dimensions are approximately 96 x 192 inches, with 42 inch stakes. It has a payload of 2,300 lb.

Present military characteristics call for the U. S. Army standard Cab-over-Engine open type cab with collapsible top and folding windshield.

No winch is furnished with this vehicle.

REFERENCES—TM 10–1130, 10–1131.

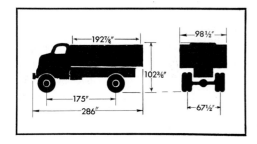

1½-TON, 4x4, STAKE AND PLATFORM TRUCK IS USED BY THE SIGNAL CORPS

Physical Characteristics

Weight (gross)	11,570 lb.	Wheelbase	175 ins.
Length	23 ft., 10 ins.	Tread (center to center, rear)	67½ ins.
Width	8 ft., 2½ ins.	Tire equipment 7.50 x 20, 8 ply (mud and snow)	
Height	8 ft., 6⅜ ins.	Ground contact	243.6 sq. ins.
Ground clearance	10 ins.	Ground pressure per sq. in.	47.4 lb.

1½-TON, 4x4 (2DT) TRUCKS (Continued)

PANEL DELIVERY TRUCK HAS CLOSED CAB INTEGRAL WITH THE BODY

1½-TON, 4x4 (2DT) PANEL DELIVERY TRUCK—STANDARD—This vehicle, designed for all arms and services, has the U. S. Army standard panel delivery body, and a cab that is integral with the body. The truck is used to transport light general cargo, and also to transport Signal Corps radio equipment. It has a payload of 3,320 pounds. Two rear doors facilitate loading and unloading.

No winch is furnished with this model.

REFERENCES—TM 10–1127, 10–1438, 10–1461.

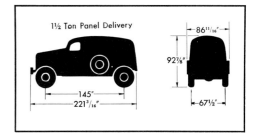

Physical Characteristics

Weight (gross)	10,080 lb.	Wheelbase	145 ins.
Length	18 ft., 5³⁄₁₆ ins.	Tread (center to center, rear)	67½ ins.
Width	7 ft., 2¹¹⁄₁₆ ins.	Tire equipment 7.50 x 20, 8 ply (mud and snow)	
Height	7 ft., 6⅞ ins.	Ground contact	243.6 sq. ins.
Ground clearance	9⅞ ins.	Ground pressure per sq. in.	40 lb.

1½-TON 4x4 TRACTOR TRUCK WILL TOW SEMI-TRAILERS TO 6 TONS

1½-TON, 4x4 (2DT) TRACTOR TRUCK—STANDARD—This truck, designed for all arms and services, is used for towing semi-trailers with a gross weight up to 12,000 pounds. It has a payload of 4,820 pounds, consisting of the weight imposed by the semi-trailer on the fifth wheel and the weight of the lower half of the fifth wheel, but exclusive of the driver.

The fifth wheel is of the U. S. Army standard universal type. An electric-brake hand controller on the truck steering column permits independent operation of the semi-trailer brakes.

No winch is provided with this model and rear bumperettes are omitted.

Present military characteristics call for the U. S. Army standard open type cab with collapsible top and folding windshield.

REFERENCE—MCM 23.

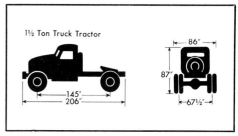

Physical Characteristics

Weight (gross)	10,885 lb.	Wheelbase	145 ins.
Length	17 ft., 2 ins.	Tread (center to center, rear)	67½ ins.
Width	7 ft., 2 ins.	Tire equipment 7.50 x 20, 8 ply (mud and snow)	
Height	7 ft., 3 ins.	Ground contact	243.6 sq. ins.
Ground clearance	9⅞ ins.	Ground pressure per sq. in.	43.4 lb.

1½-TON, 6x6, CARGO TRUCK—STANDARD

TYPICAL CHARACTERISTICS

Physical Characteristics
Weight (gross) without winch....... 10,225 lb.
   with winch.................... 10,525 lb.
Length, without winch .... 17 ft., 10⅞ ins.
   with winch.............. 18 ft., 8½ ins.
Width.................... 6 ft., 10¾ ins.
Height, without Truck Mount....... 7 ft., ¾ in.
   —with Truck Mount.......... 7 ft., 5¾ ins.
Ground clearance.................... 10⅝ ins.
Tread (center to center, rear)........ 64¾ ins.
Wheelbase.......................... 125 ins.
Ground contact.................. 312 sq. ins.
Ground pressure... 32.7 lb./sq. in.
Tire equipment.. 9.00x16, 8 ply (mud and snow)

Armament
Truck Mount, M50, or Pedestal Mount, M24A2,
  for cal. .50 Machine Gun, M2, HB (flex.)
  (On one vehicle in each four)

Performance
Maximum speed on level.......... 50 m.p.h.
Maximum grade ability............. 60%
  —with towed load............. 44%
Fording depth (slowest forward speed).. 34 ins.
Angle of approach, without winch....... 54°
  with winch........................ 37°
Angle of departure.................... 33°
Turning radius.................. 26½ ft.
Fuel capacity.................... 30 gals.
Cruising range.................. 240 miles
  —with towed load............ 210 miles
Normal towed load............... 3,500 lb.
Payload (including personnel)...... 3,300 lb.
Winch capacity.................. 7,500 lb.

Battery, Voltage, total 6

Fire Protection—Fire Extinguisher

Engine, Make and Model...... Dodge T-214
Type..................... In-line, liquid-cooled
No. of cylinders...................... 6
Cycle............................... 4
Fuel (gasoline)................... 70 octane
Bore and stroke............ 3¼ x 4⅝ ins.
Di placement................ 230.2 cu. ins.
Compression.............. 108–118 at c.s.
Net hp.............. 76 at 3,200 r.p.m.
Max. torque....... 184 lb.-ft. at 1,400 r.p.m.
Crankshaft rotation .... C'Clockwise
Length.......................... 37½ ins.
Width........................... 24 ins.
Height.......................... 30 ins.
Ignition........................ Battery
Weight, dry...................... 603 lb.

Transmission—Gear ratios
First speed...................... 6.40:1
Second speed.................... 3.09:1
Third speed..................... 1.69:1
Fourth speed................... 1.00:1
Reverse........................ 7.82:1

Transfer Case—Gear ratios.... 1.50:1; 1.00:1
Steering Ratio..................... 23.2:1
Suspension, Type.............. Semi-elliptic
  Wheel construction............ Divided rim
Master Clutch, Type........ Single dry plate
Radiator, Type................. Fin and tube
  Capacity of system................ 17 qts.
Brakes, Type............. Internal hydraulic
Brakes, Parking, Type.... External contracting
Rear Axle, Type.............. Full floating
Front Axle, Gear Ratio............. 5.83:1

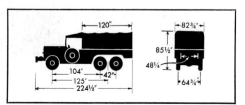

1½-TON, 6x6, CARGO TRUCK, SHOWING TRUCK MOUNT, M50, FOR CAL. .50 MACHINE GUN

This truck was designed as a substitute in certain instances for the 2½-Ton, 6x6, Truck, in which size a heavy production demand exists.

It is manufactured by using, as far as possible, those units found in the standard ¾-ton, 4x4, Truck. The principal changes are the addition of the extra bogie axle and lengthening of the frame and body, thus raising the load capacity to 3,000 pounds.

Military characteristics, as given in MCM No. 28a, call for a minimum dry chassis weight of 4,500 pounds and a towed load ability of 3,500 pounds. Wheelbase is 125 inches.

It is capable of operation over unimproved roads, trails, and open, rolling, and hilly cross country. It has a top governed speed of 54 miles per hour. Cruising range is approximately 240 miles.

The truck has six wheels, using 9.00 x 16, 8-ply tires. Power is supplied to all six wheels. The power to the front axle can be disengaged in the driver's compartment by a control.

Power is supplied by a liquid-cooled, L-head type, 6-cylinder gasoline engine. It is transmitted from the four-speed sliding-gear type transmission through a short propeller shaft to the transfer case, and thence to both front and rear axles. The vehicle may be driven with power on all six wheels or with the four rear wheels only.

Foot brakes are of the hydraulic internal-expanding four-wheel type. Hand brakes are mechanical, external-contracting.

Wheel and tire assemblies are interchangeable, front and rear.

The body is of the U. S. Army standard cargo type, with troop seats with lazy backs. A detachable canvas top is supported by five bows, and is provided with roll-up straps arranged to permit ventilation in the body. The top is equipped with front and rear curtains with window flaps. Inside dimensions are approximately 89 x 120 inches. There are two rows of seat boxes, with a space 48 inches wide between. The seat boxes are 14 inches deep.

The vehicle has an open cab. A Truck Mount, M50, or a Pedestal Mount, M24A2, is supplied on some vehicles.

The truck is supplied with or without a winch, of 7,500 pound capacity.

Desertization equipment includes a 4-pound pressure cap for the radiator surge tank, a power-driven air compressor with hose to permit inflation of all tires, and a low-pressure tire gage.

The vehicle is manufactured by the Fargo Motor Corporation.

REFERENCES—MCM 28a; TM 9–810A; OCM 18785, 19049, 19181, 19701, 19877, 19924, 20147, 20251, 20440, 20521, 20728, 20804, 21221, 21990.

2½-TON, 6x6 (4DT) TRUCKS—STANDARD

With its payload of 5,350 pounds, and with a towing capacity of 4,500 pounds, the 2½-ton, 6 x 6 (4DT) Truck has become one of the most versatile of Army vehicles.

It is available in a number of standard body styles and as a standard chassis upon which may be placed special bodies required by the various services. Wheelbase is 164 inches or 145 inches.

The truck has six wheels including four dual-tire wheels, using 7.50 x 20, 8 ply tires. Power is supplied to all six wheels with driver control for declutching the front axle.

Power is supplied by a G.M.C. six-cylinder, valve-in-head type gasoline engine. The clutch is a single-plate dry disk type. The selective, sliding gear transmission has five speeds forward and one reverse. Transmission is direct drive in the fourth speed, and over-drive in the fifth speed. The transfer case is essentially a two-speed auxiliary unit with three power take-off shafts, one

for front axle and two for rear axles.

The brakes are hydraulic, supplemented by a Hydrovac unit which utilizes atmosphere and engine manifold vacuum to assist the driver in the application of the brakes.

The axles may be "split" or "banjo" type. The type of axles used determines the type of transfer case and propeller shaft arrangement.

A 10,000 pound capacity winch, supplied on some models, is power driven by a drive shaft connected between the winch and the power take-off on the transmission. It has two speeds forward and a reverse. Winch operation is controlled by a manual shift lever in the cab and a jaw clutch at the winch.

Early production vehicles had closed cabs. Provision was made to supply a Truck Mount, M32, for a cal. .50 machine gun, with one in each four trucks, long wheelbase, and a Truck Mount, M37, with one in each four trucks, short wheelbase. Present production calls for

U. S. Army standard open type cabs, with collapsible tops and folding windshields. One vehicle in each four is provided with a Truck Mount, M36 or M37A3, for a cal. .50, HB, machine gun for antiaircraft protection.

Desertization equipment includes size 11.00 x 18, 10 ply, tires with heavy-duty tubes; army combat wheels with beadlock, size 8.00 CV x 18, single front and rear, and one spare tire and wheel assembly with carrier. A radiator surge tank of at least four-quart capacity, a power-driven air compressor with hose to permit inflation of all tires, a low-pressure gage, a speedometer correction adapter, and a five-bladed fan are also included. Winterization kits are supplied for those trucks whose use will require them.

REFERENCES—MC3C; OCM 19107, 19303, 19304, 19427, 19547, 19817, 19923, 20099, 20100, 20152, 20606, 20938, 20964, 21221, 21933, 22141, 22883, 22920.

2½-TON, 6x6 (4DT) TRUCK CHASSIS

—This rugged chassis is used for all 2½-ton, 6 x 6, G.M.C. trucks, including not only the standard body styles shown herewith, and the standard ordnance maintenance trucks shown elsewhere in these pages, but also a number of vehicles for special purposes. Among these are Chemical Service Truck, M1; Van, K-57; an air compressor truck, a decontamination truck, an engineer shop truck, and a water purification truck.

CHASSIS OF 2½-TON, 6x6 (4DT) TRUCK, SHOWING PRESENT PRODUCTION STYLE OPEN CAB

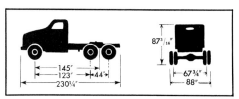

Physical Characteristics

Weight (curb)	6,000 lb.
Length, long wheelbase	21 ft., 3 ins.
short wheelbase	19 ft., 2¼ ins.
Width	7 ft., 4 ins.
Height	7 ft., 3³⁄₁₆ ins.
Ground clearance	10 ins.
Tread (center to center, rear)	67¾ ins.
Wheelbase, long wheelbase	164 ins.
short wheelbase	145 ins.
Ground contact	406 sq. ins.
Ground pressure	14.7 lb./sq. in.
Tire equipment	7.50 x 20, 8 ply
desert	11.00 x 18, 10 ply

Armament
Truck Mount, M32, M36, M37, or M37A3, for cal. .50 Machine Gun, M2, HB (Supplied with one vehicle in four)

Performance

Maximum speed on level	45 m.p.h.
Maximum grade ability	65%
Vertical obstacle ability	10 ins.
Angle of approach—w/o winch	54°
cab-over-engine model	45°
Angle of approach—with winch	31°
Angle of departure	
long wheelbase models	36°

short wheelbase models	44°
cab-over-engine model	32½°
Turning radius	32 ft.
Fuel capacity	40 gals.
Cruising range (approx.)	220 miles
with towed load	190 miles
Maximum drawbar pull	13,063 lb.
Normal towed load	4,500 lb.
Payload (including personnel)	5,350 lb.
Winch capacity	10,000 lb.

Battery, Voltage, total ... 6
Fire Protection ... Fire Extinguisher
Engine, Make and Model ... G.M.C. 270

Type	In-line, liquid-cooled
No. of cylinders	6
Cycle	4
Fuel (gasoline)	70 octane
Bore and stroke	3 25/32 x 4 ins.
Displacement	269.52 cu. ins.
Compression	130 lb. at C.S.
Max. governed speed	2,750 r.p.m.
Net hp.	94 at 3,000 r.p.m.
Max. torque	217 lb.-ft. at 1,600 r.p.m.
Crankshaft rotation	C'Clockwise
Length	41¼ ins.
Width	22½ ins.
Height	32 ins.

Ignition	Battery
Weight, dry (less accessories)	535 lb.

Transmission, Gear ratios

First speed	6.06:1
Second speed	3.50:1
Third speed	1.80:1
Fourth speed	1.00:1
Fifth speed	0.799:1
Reverse	6.00:1

Transfer Case, Gear ratios

(G.M.C. model)	1.16:1; 2.63:1
(Timken model)	1.16:1; 2.61:1

Differential, Type ... Spiral bevel

Gear ratio	6.6:1
Steering ratio	23.6:1

Suspension, Type ... Semi-elliptic

Wheel size	20 x 7
Wheel construction	Disk

Master Clutch, Type ... Dry, single plate
Radiator, Type ... Fin and tube

Capacity of system	19 qts.

Brakes, Type ... Internal hydraulic
Brakes, Parking, Type ... Band
Front Axle, Type ... Banjo or split
Rear Axle, Gear ratio ... 6.6:1

2½-TON, 6x6 (4DT) TRUCKS (Continued)

2½-TON, 6x6 (4DT) CARGO TRUCK—STANDARD—Designed for all arms and services, this 164 inch wheelbase truck has the U. S. Army standard cargo body, with troop seats with lazy backs. The seats may be folded up out of the way when desired, in order to provide additional cargo space. A detachable canvas top is supported by five bows, and is provided with roll-up straps arranged to permit ventilation in the body. The top is equipped with front and rear curtains with window flaps. Inside dimensions are approximately 80 inches by 144 inches. The truck has a payload of 5,000 pounds. A spare tire rack is mounted underneath the body.

The vehicle is available with or without a winch.

REFERENCE—TM 9–801.

164 INCH WHEELBASE CARGO TRUCK HAS SPARE TIRE BRACKET BENEATH THE BODY

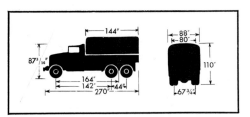

Physical Characteristics

Weight, without winch	15,450 lb.
with winch	16,450 lb.
Length, without winch	21 ft., 4 ins.
with winch	22 ft., 6 ins.
Width	7 ft., 4 ins.
Height, over bows	9 ft., 2 ins.
over cab	7 ft., 3 3/16 ins.
reducible to	6 ft., 2¼ ins.
Ground clearance	10 ins.
Tread (center to center, rear)	67¾ ins.
Wheelbase	164 ins.
Ground contact	406 sq. ins.
Ground pressure	38 lb./sq. in.

2½-TON, 6x6 (4DT) SHORT WHEELBASE CARGO TRUCK—STANDARD—This is similar to the preceding model, but is built on a chassis with 145 inch wheelbase, and is designed for use as a prime mover. The body is the same in style, but has inside dimensions approximately 80 inches by 108 inches. The vehicle has a payload of 5,350 pounds. It is supplied with or without a winch. Brackets for two spare tires are mounted in back of the cab.

Limited procurement of kits to modify this truck for airborne transportation was authorized by Ordnance Committee action in February, 1944. The truck is split into two sections, each carried in a separate plane, and is reassembled at the destination.

REFERENCE—TM 9–801.

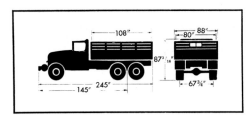

SHORT WHEELBASE CARGO TRUCK HAS SPARE TIRE BRACKETS IN BACK OF CAB

Physical Characteristics

Weight, without winch	15,350 lb.
with winch	16,350 lb.
Length, without winch	19 ft., 3 ins.
with winch	20 ft., 5 ins.
Width	7 ft., 4 ins.
Height, over bows	9 ft., 2 ins.
over cab	7 ft., 3 3/16 ins.
reducible to	6 ft., 2¼ ins.
Ground clearance	10 ins.
Tread (center to center, rear)	67¾ ins.
Wheelbase	145 ins.
Ground contact	406 sq. ins.
Ground pressure	37.8 lb./sq. in.

2½-TON, 6x6 (4DT) TRUCKS (Continued)

15 FOOT CARGO TRUCK IS CAB-OVER-ENGINE TYPE, HAS LARGEST CARGO SPACE

Physical Characteristics

Weight (gross)	14,760 lb.	Ground clearance	10 ins.
Length	22 ft., 2¼ ins.	Tread (center to center, rear)	67¾ ins.
Width	7 ft., 4 ins.	Wheelbase	164 ins.
Height, over bows	8 ft., 10 ins.	Ground contact	406 sq. ins.
over cab	8 ft., 4 ins.	Ground pressure	36.3 lb./sq. in.

2½-TON, 6x6 (4DT) 15 FT. CARGO TRUCK—STANDARD—This is a 164 inch wheelbase truck, which, because of its cab-over-engine design, provides more cargo space than the vehicle with engine in front. It has inside body dimensions of approximately 80 inches by 180 inches, and is equipped with cargo racks. The vehicle has a payload of 3,950 pounds, including personnel. Intended primarily for hauling general cargo, ammunition, and equipment, it may also be used as a prime mover for guns and trailers.

A detachable canvas top is supported by six bows, and is provided with roll-up straps to permit ventilation in the body. The top is equipped with front and rear curtains with window flaps.

No winch is supplied with this model.

REFERENCE—TM 9–809.

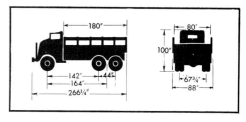

2½-TON, 6x6 (4DT) DUMP TRUCK—STANDARD—Designed for the Corps of Engineers, this vehicle is a combination cargo and dump truck. The body is equipped with troop seats, removable front rack, an adjustable cab protector, and bows and tarpaulins, and when so equipped resembles other cargo trucks.

For use as a dump truck, this equipment is removed. A hinged partition, which is in a horizontal position as a part of the cargo floor, can be raised and backed in a vertical position to provide a dump body of approximately 2½ yards capacity. The body is attached to a hoist subframe by means of two hinges and can be elevated by an underbody hydraulic arm type hoist.

The double-acting tail gate may be hinged at either the bottom, for use as a cargo truck, or at the top, to serve as a spreader when used as a dump truck.

REFERENCE—TM 9–801.

2½-TON DUMP TRUCK MAY ALSO BE USED AS CARGO AND PERSONNEL CARRIER

Physical Characteristics

Weight (gross)	16,850 lb.	Ground clearance	10 ins.
Length	22 ft., 8¾ ins.	Tread (center to center, rear)	67¾ ins.
Width	7 ft., 4 ins.	Wheelbase	164 ins.
Height, over bows	9 ft., 2 ins.	Ground contact	406 sq. ins.
over apron	8 ft., 3⅝ ins.	Ground pressure	41.5 lb./sq. in.
over cab	7 ft., 3 3/16 ins.		

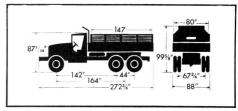

2½-TON, 6x6 (4DT) GASOLINE TANK TRUCK, 750 GALLON—STANDARD—

Designed for all arms and services, this vehicle consists of a 164 inch wheelbase chassis on which are mounted two U.S. Army standard elliptical gasoline tanks of 375 gallons each. Each section is 61 inches long by 54½ inches wide by 34 inches high. Manholes, flanges, piping, valves, running-boards, and equipment compartments are provided.

Bows and tarpaulins are furnished for camouflage, giving the vehicle the appearance of a cargo truck, and thus making it a less distinctive target from the air.

No winch is supplied with this model.

REFERENCE—TM 9–801.

750 GALLON GASOLINE TANK MAY BE CAMOUFLAGED TO RESEMBLE CARGO BODY

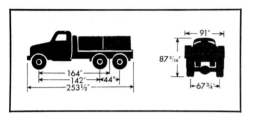

Physical Characteristics

Weight (gross)	15,450 lb.	Ground clearance	10 ins.
Length	21 ft., 1½ ins.	Tread (center to center, rear)	67¾ ins.
Width	7 ft., 7 ins.	Wheelbase	164 ins.
Height, over bows	9 ft., 2 ins.	Ground contact	406 sq. ins.
over cab	7 ft., 3 3/16 ins.	Ground pressure	38 lb./sq. in.

2½-TON, 6x6 (4DT) WATER TANK TRUCK, 700 GALLON—STANDARD—

This vehicle, designed for all arms and services, consists of a 164 inch wheelbase truck on which is mounted a U. S. Army standard elliptical tank of 700 gallon capacity. The tank is 136½ inches long, 52 inches wide, and 34 inches high. It is complete with manholes, flanges, a heater aperture, piping, valves, running-boards, equipment compartments, an auxiliary gasoline engine driven pump, and a hose.

Like the gasoline truck, it is provided with bows and tarpaulins for camouflage, giving it the appearance of a cargo truck, and making it a less conspicuous target for enemy planes.

REFERENCE—TM 9–801.

700 GALLON WATER TANK ALSO IS CAMOUFLAGED IN COMBAT ZONES

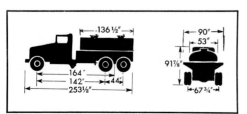

Physical Characteristics

Weight (gross)	17,690 lb.	Ground clearance	10 ins.
Length	21 ft., 1½ ins.	Tread (center to center, rear)	67¾ ins.
Width	7 ft., 6 ins.	Wheelbase	164 ins.
Height, over bows	9 ft., 2 ins.	Ground contact	406 sq. ins.
over body	7 ft., 7⅞ ins.	Ground pressure	43.5 lb./sq. in.

2½-TON, 6X6, AMPHIBIAN TRUCK—STANDARD

2½-TON, 6x6, AMPHIBIAN TRUCK, "THE DUCK," IS USEFUL IN LANDINGS ON ENEMY BEACHES. TRUCK MOUNT, M36, IS PROVIDED ON ONE VEHICLE IN FOUR.

Standardized in October, 1942, this vehicle has proved its usefulness in operations against enemy beaches, and is at home on water as well as on land. It is nicknamed "the Duck," from its official nomenclature as DUKW–353.

The vehicle was developed for the military service by the National Defense Research Committee in accordance with a directive issued by the Commanding General, Services of Supply, through the Quartermaster General.

Based on the standard 2½-ton, 6x6, Truck, it is equipped with an integral watertight hull designed in such a manner that truck chassis and drive units are attached to and in the body of the hull.

For land operation, the vehicle utilizes its six driving wheeels and conventional steering-gear assembly. In water, it is propelled with a water propeller, and is steered by the combined use of the front wheels and a rudder which is interconnected to and operated by the steering-gear column.

Springs and driving axles are attached to the bottom of the hull and suspend in water when the vehicle is in use as a boat. The welded steel hull is decked forward of the driver's compartment, to the rear of the rear wheels, and along both sides. A crash rail is installed all around the hull at deck height.

The driver's compartment is of the open type, with removable canvas top and open back, and removable side curtains. The windshield may be folded forward, or tilted upward and outward. One vehicle in each four is provided with a Truck Mount, M36, for an antiaircraft machine gun.

The cargo compartment will accommodate approximately 25 men and equipment or approximately 5,000 pounds payload for land operation. Hatches in the rear deck and floor provide access to tool and storage holds and to the rudder-operating mechanism and rear winch shaft. Two hatches in the bow facilitate access to the engine, accessories, and forward compartment.

A two-speed transfer case permits drive of both front and rear axles, or only the rear axle, as required. The water propeller transfer case, mounted in drive line between transmission and transfer case, permits engagement or disengagement of the water propeller.

A 10,000 pound capacity winch is mounted at the rear. Cable guides are provided to permit operation at either the front or the rear.

A marine rudder and controls and a propeller are provided for use in water. An anchor with shackle is furnished. One ring type life preserver and three life preserver jackets are supplied. Mooring eyes, suitable davit eyes and fender eyes for rope fenders are provided.

A 60 gallon per minute rotary pump and a 260 gallon per minute centrifugal pump are used to pump water out of the hull. A 50 gallon per minute hand pump is furnished for emergency use.

The vehicles are manufactured by the Yellow Truck and Coach Manufacturing Co.

REFERENCES—MCM 27; TM 9–802; OCM 18950, 19059, 19817, 19876, 19923, 20100, 20514, 20633, 21166, 21419, 22074, 22196.

CHARACTERISTICS

Crew (operating)........................1

Physical Characteristics

Weight	19,570 lb.
Length	31 ft.
Width	8 ft., 2⅞ ins.
Height (top up)	8 ft., 9½ ins.
(top down)	7 ft., 1⅜ ins.
Ground clearance	10½ ins.
Tread (center to center)	63⅝ ins.
Wheelbase	164 ins.
Loaded freeboard—to deck—front	24 ins.
to deck—rear	16 ins.
to coaming—front and rear	29 ins.
Loaded draft—to under side of tires	51 ins.
Tire equipment	11.00 x 18, 10 ply (desert)

Armament

Truck Mount, M36, for cal. .50 Machine Gun (On one vehicle in each four)

Performance

Maximum speed on land	45 m.p.h.
Maximum speed in water	6.3 m.p.h.
Maximum grade ability	60%
Vertical obstacle ability	18 ins.
Angle of approach	38°
Angle of departure	26½°
Turning radius—land	36 ft.
water	20 ft.
Fuel capacity	40 gals.
Cruising range—land	220 miles
water	50 miles
Payload	5,350 lb.
Winch capacity	10,000 lb.

Battery, Voltage, total....................6

(Other characteristics same as for 2½-Ton, 6x6, Cargo Truck.)

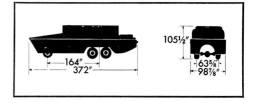

4-TON, 6x6 (4DT) TRUCKS—STANDARD

These vehicles have payloads of 8,000 pounds each and will tow a 12,000 pound trailer. Body styles are cargo, cargo long wheelbase, wrecker, and dump. In addition, the chassis is supplied to the Corps of Engineers for use with various special bodies.

The vehicles are capable of operations over unimproved roads, trails and open, rolling hilly cross country at gross weight with towed load. Maximum speed at gross weight with towed load on smooth concrete roadway is 40 miles per hour. Maximum grade ability is 65%.

Wheelbase is in two sizes, 151 and 172 inches. Tires are 9.00 x 20, 10 ply, mud and snow tread.

Military equipment includes towing hooks on the two front corners, brush guards, a sturdy front bumper and U. S. Army standard rear bumperettes. Sealed beam type headlights are used, as well as U. S. Army standard combat-zone safety lighting. A trailer light socket is provided. Brakes are air operated and have a foot valve and hand controller for independent operation of the airbrakes on the trailer

load. Four air connections for towed vehicles are provided.

The vehicle is powered with a 131.5 horsepower gasoline engine of L-head design. The clutch is a single plate dry disk type. The transmission has five forward speeds, with fifth speed overdrive and one reverse. Constant mesh helical gears are used in the three top speeds for quiet operation. The first, second, and reverse speed gears are spur cut.

Power is delivered to the front and rear axles through the transfer case, which is offset to permit the forward propeller shaft to clear the engine crankcase. A speed reduction, independent of the transmission, is provided in the transfer case. A control lever in the cab permits disengagement of the front axle if desired.

The wrecker transfer case is equipped with a power take-off which operates the wrecker winches. This take-off is mounted at the rear end of the transfer case drive shaft and transmits its power to the winches through a chain drive.

Steering gear is of the cam and twin-lever type which automatically provides

a variable gear ratio for ease of steering.

Present production calls for open cabs, with folding canvas tops. One vehicle in four is provided with a Truck Mount, M36, for an antiaircraft machine gun. Earlier production models have closed cabs, and one vehicle in four is provided with a Truck Mount, M56.

Desertization equipment includes size 14.00 x 20, 12 ply tires with heavy-duty tubes; army combat wheels with bead-lock, size 10CW x 20, single front and rear, and one spare tire and wheel assembly with carrier. A low-pressure tire gage, tire chains for driving wheels, a speedometer correction adapter, a packless type water pump, and front wheel stops and rear axle stops are also included.

The vehicles are manufactured by the Diamond T Motor Car Co.

References—TM 10–1533; MCM 4d; OCM 18888, 19107, 19436, 19676, 20100, 20340, 20512, 20580, 21221, 21872, 22212, 22332, 23565; SNL G–509.

GENERAL CHARACTERISTICS

Performance

Maximum speed on level	40 m.p.h.
Maximum grade ability	65%
with towed load	57%
Vertical obstacle ability	12 ins.
Fording depth (slowest forward speed)	24 ins.
Angle of approach	35°
Angle of departure	From 35° to 45°
Turning radius	36 ft.
Fuel capacity	60 gals.
Cruising range (approx.)	175 miles
with towed load	150 miles
Maximum drawbar pull	21,550 lb.
Normal towed load	11,000 lb.
Payload	8,000 lb.
Winch capacity	15,000 lb.

Battery, Voltage, total	6–12
Fire Protection	Fire Extinguisher
Engine, Make and Model	Hercules RXC
Type	L-head
No. of cylinders	6
Cycle	4
Fuel (gasoline)	70 octane
Bore and stroke	4⅝ x 5¼ ins.
Displacement	529 cu. ins.
Compression	110 lb. at C.S.
Net hp.	119 at 2,200 r.p.m.
Max. torque	395 lb.-ft. at 1,000 r.p.m.
Crankshaft rotation	C'Clockwise
Length	50½ ins.
Width	32 ins.
Height	44½ ins.
Ignition	Battery
Weight, dry	1,395 lb.

Transmission, Gear ratios	
First speed	7.08:1
Second speed	3.82:1
Third speed	1.85:1
Fourth speed	1.00:1
Fifth speed	0.768:1
Reverse	7.08:1
Transfer Case, Gear ratios	1.72:1, 1.00:1
Steering Ratio	22, 18, 22:1
Suspension, Type	Semi-elliptic
Wheel size	20 x 8
Master Clutch, Type	Single plate dry disk
Radiator, Type	Fin and tube
Capacity of system	48 qts.
Brakes, Type	Air
Brakes, Parking, Type	Disk
Front Axle, Type	Double reduction
Rear Axle, Gear ratio	8.435:1

4-TON, 6x6 (4DT) TRUCK CHASSIS—STANDARD—This chassis is supplied to the Corps of Engineers for use for various special purpose vehicles, including a bituminous supply truck, water distributor truck, and bituminous distributor truck. No winch is supplied. The vehicle is provided with or without a rear mounted pintle, depending on its intended use.

References—OCM 18888, 19463.

CHASSIS IS USED AS A BASIS OF SPECIAL VEHICLES FOR CORPS OF ENGINEERS

Physical Characteristics

Weight (dry chassis)	11,500 lb.	Ground contact	496 sq. ins.
Ground clearance	11 ins.	Ground pressure	23.1 lb./sq. in.
Tread (center to center, rear)	72 ins.	Tire equipment	9.00 x 20, 10 ply
Wheelbase	151 ins.		(mud and snow)

4-TON, 6x6 (4DT) CARGO TRUCK—STANDARD—This vehicle, designed for all arms and services, for hauling general cargo and personnel, has the U. S. Army standard cargo body with troop seats with lazy backs. It has a detachable canvas top, with roll-up straps to permit ventilation in the body, and front and rear curtains with window flaps. The inside dimensions are approximately 88 x 132 inches.

An open cab, with folding windshield, is provided.

The vehicle has a payload of 8,300 pounds. It is equipped with a winch.

REFERENCES—TM 10–1600 with supplement, 10–1607, 9–1811A.

CARGO BODY, WITH WINCH, SHOWING PAULINS OVER BOWS, ON OPEN CAB VEHICLE

Physical Characteristics

Weight (gross)..................26,400 lb.	Tread (center to center, rear)........72 ins.
Length.................22 ft., 4½ ins.	Wheelbase.....................151 ins.
Width...........................8 ft.	Ground contact................496 sq. ins.
Height...........9 ft., 10¼ ins.	Ground pressure...........53.2 lb./sq. in.
reducible to..............8 ft., 3⅝ ins.	Tire equipment..........9.00 x 20, 10 ply
Ground clearance.................11 ins.	(mud and snow)

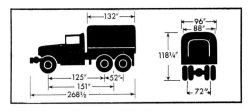

4-TON, 6x6 (4DT) CARGO TRUCK, LWB — STANDARD — Designed for the Corps of Engineers, for transporting ponton bridge equipment, this truck has a U. S. Army standard cargo body. Inside dimensions are approximately 88 x 147 inches. It has a payload of 8,300 pounds.

It has a detachable canvas top, with roll-up straps to permit ventilation in the body, and front and rear curtains with window flaps. An open cab, with folding windshield, is furnished. A front-mounted winch is provided.

REFERENCES—TM 10–1532, 10–1533, 10–1604 with supplement, 10–1605, 10–1606 with supplement, 10–1607, 9–1811A.

THIS LONG WHEELBASE CARGO TRUCK TRANSPORTS PONTON BRIDGE EQUIPMENT

Physical Characteristics

Weight (gross)..................26,800 lb.	Tread (center to center, rear)........72 ins.
Length.................24 ft., 8⅝ ins.	Wheelbase.....................172 ins.
Width...........................8 ft.	Ground contact................496 sq. ins.
Height...........9 ft., 8 3/16 ins.	Ground pressure...............54 lb./sq. in.
reducible to..............8 ft., 3⅝ ins.	Tire equipment..........9.00 x 20, 10 ply
Ground clearance.................11 ins.	(mud and snow)

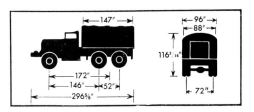

4-TON, 6x6 (4DT) TRUCKS (Continued)

4-TON, 6x6 (4DT) DUMP TRUCK—STANDARD—This vehicle is supplied to the Corps of Engineers to haul and dump earth, sand, gravel, etc. It has the U. S. Army standard dump type body with a hydraulic hoist. The inside body dimensions are approximately 80 x 120 inches. An open cab, with folding windshield, is provided. A winch is provided with present production models.

This vehicle has a steel shield over the driver's cab for protection from heavy objects.

REFERENCES—TM 9–811A, 9–1811A.

DUMP TRUCK, SHOWING STEEL SHIELD TO PROTECT DRIVER'S COMPARTMENT

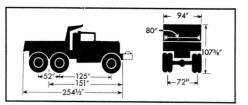

Physical Characteristics

Weight (gross)	26,400 lb.	Tread (center to center, rear)	72 ins.
Length	21 ft., 2½ ins.	Wheelbase	151 ins.
Width	7 ft., 10 ins.	Ground contact	496 sq. ins.
Height	8 ft., 11⅜ ins.	Ground pressure	53.2 lb./sq. in.
Ground clearance	11 ins.	Tire equipment	9.00 x 20, 10 ply
			(mud and snow)

4-TON, 6x6 (4DT) WRECKER TRUCK—STANDARD—Designed for all arms and services, this wrecker is used primarily for light recovery operations of wheeled vehicles. A frame just behind the cab supports two manually operated booms, one at each corner, each equipped with a winch and arranged to swing in a 90° arc over its respective side of the vehicle. Each winch may be used separately or in conjunction with the other. An additional winch is mounted on the front of the truck, for use as an anchor or for recovering the wrecker itself.

Bows and paulins for camouflage, giving the appearance of a cargo vehicle, are provided, in order that the wrecker will present a less conspicuous target to observers from the air.

REFERENCES—TM 10–1606, 10–1607; OCM 21872, 22140.

THIS WRECKER TRUCK MAY BE CAMOUFLAGED TO RESEMBLE CARGO VEHICLE

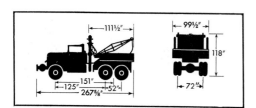

Physical Characteristics

Weight (gross)	21,700 lb.	Tread (center to center, rear)	72 ins.
Length	22 ft., 3⅝ ins.	Wheelbase	151 ins.
Width	8 ft., 3½ ins.	Ground contact	496 sq. ins.
Height	9 ft., 10 ins.	Ground pressure	43.8 lb./sq. in.
reducible to	8 ft.	Tire equipment	9.00 x 20, 10 ply
Ground clearance	11 ins.		(mud and snow)

4-5 TON, 4X4 (2DT), TRACTOR TRUCK—STANDARD

This vehicle is furnished to the Air Corps for towing its Fuel Servicing Semi-trailer, and to the Quartermaster Corps for towing 6 ton cargo semi-trailers. It is of the cab-over-engine type.

No body is required. A tread plate platform is provided across the top of the frame, extending from the rear of the cab to a line representing the front edge of the lower fifth wheel.

Two spare wheel and tire assemblies are mounted on a split type carrier behind the cab. A hand control valve is provided for independent operation of the semi-trailer brakes. Three trailer air-hose assemblies and four trailer air connections are furnished.

When furnished to the Air Corps, the vehicle is finish painted in Army yellow, dull and lusterless, if specified. For the Quartermaster Corps, the finish is Army olive drab, dull and lusterless.

Single wheels are used at the front and dual wheels at the rear. Tires are 9.00 x 20, 10 ply, balloon, mud and snow tread, with heavy-duty tubes.

Military equipment includes towing hooks on the two front corners, a brush guard, a front bumper, a rear bumper when specified and a military type pintle. Approved combat-zone lighting is used.

Desertization equipment includes size 14.00 x 20, 12 ply tires with heavy-duty tubes; army combat wheels with bead-lock, size 10.00CW x 20, single front and rear, and one spare tire and wheel assembly with carrier. A special radiator with built-in overflow return, a low-pressure tire gage, tire chains for driving wheels, a packless type water pump, and a speedometer correction adapter are also included.

Power is supplied by a Hercules RXC in-line, liquid-cooled gasoline engine. The clutch, of the single disk type, is designed for non-shock loading and automatic compensation for loss of spring pressure.

The transmission has five speeds forward and one reverse, and is equipped with silent helical gears running in constant mesh in third speed and overdrive. Fourth speed is direct drive and fifth speed is overdrive.

Power is supplied to all four wheels through a two-speed transfer case. A lever in the driver's cab permits de-clutching of the front wheels when not required. The vehicle has air-brakes, with connections for braking the trailer.

Present production calls for open cabs. One vehicle in four is provided with a Truck Mount, M36, for a cal. .50, HB, machine gun. Earlier production vehicles have closed cabs, with provision for use of a Truck Mount, M60 or M61, on one in each four.

The vehicles are manufactured by Autocar Co. and Federal Motor Truck Co.

REFERENCES—TM 10-1116, 10-1117, 10-1458, 10-1459; MCM 14a; OCM 19107, 20100, 21221, 22212; SNL G-510, G-513, G-691.

4-5 TON, 4x4, TRACTOR TRUCK, SHOWING OPEN CAB AND TRUCK MOUNT FOR MACHINE GUN

TYPICAL CHARACTERISTICS

Crew...................................2

Physical Characteristics
Weight (gross)...................21,010 lb.
Length.....................16 ft., 11½ ins.
Width..........................7 ft., 11 ins.
Height.......................9 ft., 4¾ ins.
  reducible to.............7 ft., 11½ ins.
Ground clearance...............11¾ ins.
Tread (center to center, rear)......72 ins.
Wheelbase......................134½ ins.
Tire equipment
        9.00 x 20, 10 ply (mud and snow)

Armament
Truck Mount, M36, M60, or M61, for cal. .50 Machine Gun, M2, HB

Performance
Maximum speed on level..........41 m.p.h.
Maximum grade ability.............65%
  with towed load...............57½%
Trench crossing ability............20 ins.
Fording depth (slowest forward speed).24½ ins.
Angle of approach.................54°
Angle of departure................50°
Turning radius....................30 ft.
Fuel capacity.....................60 gals.
Cruising range (approx.).........180 miles
Payload........................9,350 lb.
Normal towed load.............20,000 lb.
Battery, Voltage, total.............6-12
Fire Protection............Fire extinguisher

Engine, Make and Model.......Hercules RXC
  Type................In-line, liquid-cooled
  No. of cylinders.....................6
  Cycle...............................4
  Fuel (gasoline)...............68 octane
  Bore and stroke.........4⅝ x 5¼ ins.
  Displacement...............529 cu. ins.
  Compression ratio..........110 at C.S.
  Net hp............112 at 2,200 r.p.m.
  Max. torque.......395 lb.-ft. at 1,000 r.p.m.
  Crankshaft rotation.........C'Clockwise
  Length.......................50½ ins.
  Width...........................32 ins.
  Height........................44½ ins.

Transmission, Gear ratios
  First speed...................5.90:1
  Second speed..................3.60:1
  Third speed...................1.84:1
  Fourth speed..................1.00:1
  Fifth speed.....................75:1
  Reverse......................7.37:1
Transfer Case, Gear ratios....1.72:1; 1.00:1
Steering Ratio............22, 18, 22:1
Suspension, Type.........Semi-elliptic
  Wheel construction..............Disk
Master Clutch, Type........Single disk
Radiator, Type.........Fin and tube
  Capacity of system............38 qts.
Brakes, Type............Internal, air
Brakes, Parking, Type...........Disk
Front Axle, Type......Double reduction
Rear Axle, Gear ratio..........8.43:1

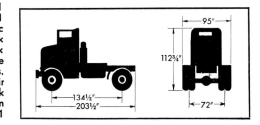

5-6 TON, 4x4 (2DT) TRACTOR AND VAN TRUCKS—STANDARD

5-6 TON, 4x4 (2DT) TRACTOR TRUCK, USED BY CORPS OF ENGINEERS

5-6 TON, 4x4 (2DT) VAN TRUCK, HAULS SIGNAL CORPS EQUIPMENT

These cab-over-engine vehicles are similar in many respects to the 4–5 Ton, 4x4, Tractor Truck.

Present production calls for open cabs, with folding windshields. One vehicle in four is provided with a Truck Mount, M36, for a machine gun.

Tires are 12.00 x 20, 14 ply, mud and snow tread, with heavy-duty tubes. Dual rear wheels are provided.

Desertization equipment includes size 14.00 x 20, 12 ply tires with heavy-duty tubes; army combat wheels with beadlock, size 10.00 CW x 20, single front and rear, and one spare tire and wheel assembly with carrier. A special radiator with built-in overflow return, a low-pressure tire gage, tire chains for driving wheels, a packless type water pump, and a speedometer correction adapter are also included.

References—TM 9–817; MCM 10b; OCM 18889, 19107, 20100; SNL G–511.

5–6 TON, 4x4 (2DT) TRACTOR, PONTON TRUCK—STANDARD—This vehicle, supplied to the Corps of Engineers, is used to tow a semi-trailer with ponton bridge equipment. A 48-inch tool chest is mounted on the off-road side. A tread plate platform is provided across the top of the frame.

A winch of 15,000-pound capacity is mounted at the front of the vehicle. It is supported between the two side-frame rails. Power for operating the winch is transmitted from the main transmission through the power take-off unit and driveshaft unit to the worm shaft of the winch. It is controlled by a power take-off shift lever in the cab.

5–6 TON, 4x4 (2DT), VAN TRUCK—STANDARD—This vehicle, supplied to the Signal Corps, is used to house and transport Signal Corps field installations. No winch is furnished with this model.

TYPICAL CHARACTERISTICS OF TRACTOR

Physical Characteristics

Weight (gross)	27,120 lb.
Length	20 ft., 6½ ins.
Width	8 ft., 1½ ins.
Height	9 ft., 6½ ins.
reducible to	8 ft., 1 in.
Ground clearance	10¾ ins.
Tread (center to center)	72¼ ins.
Wheelbase	163½ ins.
Tire equipment	12.00 x 20, 14 ply (mud and snow)
desert	14.00 x 20, 12 ply

Armament

Truck Mount, M36 or M61, for cal. .50 Machine Gun, M2, HB (On one vehicle in each four)

Performance

Maximum speed on level	47 m.p.h.
Maximum grade ability	65%
with towed load	40%
Trench crossing ability	1 ft., 10 ins.
Fording depth (slowest forward speed)	35½ ins.
Angle of approach	32½°
Angle of departure	54°
Turning radius	35 ft.
Fuel capacity	90 gals.

Cruising range (approx.)	270 miles
Maximum drawbar pull	14,360 lb.
Normal towed load	20,000 lb.
Payload	10,910 lb.
Winch capacity	15,000 lb.
Battery, Voltage, total	6–12
Fire Protection	Fire Extinguisher
Engine, Make and Model	Hercules RXC (See page 108.)

Transmission, Gear ratios

First speed	5.90:1
Second speed	3.60:1
Third speed	1.84:1
Fourth speed	1.00:1
Fifth speed	.75:1
Reverse	7.08:1
Transfer Case, Gear ratios	1.72:1; 1.00:1
Steering Ratio	27, 23, 27:1
Suspension, Type	Semi-elliptic
Wheel construction	Disk
Radiator, Type	Fin and tube
Capacity of system	38 qts.
Brakes, Type	Internal, Air
Brakes, Parking, Type	Disk
Front Axle, Type	Double reduction
Rear Axle, Gear ratio	8.15:1

TYPICAL CHARACTERISTICS OF VAN

Physical Characteristics

Weight (gross)	28,330 lb.
Length	24 ft., 8¾ ins.
Width	8 ft., 1½ ins.
Height	10 ft., 10¾ ins.
reducible to	8 ft., 13/16 in.
Ground clearance	10¾ ins.
Tread (center to center)	72¼ ins.
Wheelbase	163½ ins.
Tire equipment	12.00 x 20, 14 ply (mud and snow)

Performance

Maximum speed on level	47 m.p.h.
Maximum grade ability	60%
Fording depth (slowest forward speed)	35½ ins.
Angle of approach	57°
Angle of departure	17°
Turning radius	35 ft.
Fuel capacity	90 gals.
Cruising range (approx.)	270 miles
Payload	11,150 lb.

(Other characteristics same as for 5–6 Ton, 4x4 Tractor Truck.)

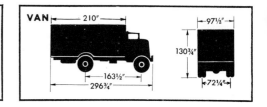

6-TON, 6x6 (4DT) TRUCK—STANDARD

6-TON, 6x6, PRIME MOVER TRUCK WILL TOW HEAVY ARTILLERY AND CARRY PERSONNEL

These trucks have a payload without towed load of 12,350 pounds, including personnel, or of 7,000 pounds with a towed load. The prime mover will pull a trailer with a gross weight of 16,500 pounds.

Military mud and snow tread tires and heavy-duty tubes are used. Wheels are of the U. S. Army standard type, single at the front and dual at the rear. One spare wheel and tire assembly is carried.

The engine is of a four-cycle, six-cylinder, in-line, liquid-cooled type. The single disk type clutch has non-shock loading and has an automatic adjustment for loss of spring pressure caused by wear.

Transmission is of selective gear type, with four speeds forward and one reverse. First and reverse gears are of spur gear type. Second, third, and fourth speeds have constant mesh helical gears, and are engined by sliding clutches. Provision is made for power take-off on both sides.

A two-speed transfer case is used to transfer power to the front and rear axles and the winch. Levers in the driver's cab permit selection of direct or low transfer case speed, and also permit de-clutching the front wheels when advisable.

The truck is equipped with air-controlled service brakes on all six wheels, and has hose connections at both front and rear for towing purposes.

Present production calls for open cabs, with folding windshields and canvas, folding-type tops with side curtains. One vehicle in each four is provided with a Truck Mount, M36, for a cal. .50 Machine Gun, M2, HB. Earlier production models had closed cabs, with provision for Truck Mount, M57, M58, or M59, for one vehicle in each four.

Desertization equipment includes size 14.00 x 20, 12 ply tires with heavy-duty tubes; army combat wheels with bead-lock, size 10.00 CW x 20, single front and rear, and one spare tire and wheel assembly with carrier. Military equipment also includes a low-pressure tire gage, tire chains for driving wheels, a packless water pump and a speedometer correction adapter.

RFERENCES—TM 10–1220, 10–1221, 10–1528, 10–1529; MCM 5e; OCM 17600, 18748, 18916, 19002, 19107, 19180, 19277, 20100, 20511, 20578, 20733, 21221, 22212, 22695, 23332, 23565.

6-TON, 6x6 (4DT) TRUCK, PRIME MOVER (AA)—STANDARD—Designed for the Coast Artillery, this vehicle is used to transport heavy artillery and general cargo or personnel. It has the Army flat-bed cargo type body, with troop seats and lazy backs, and will accommodate 16 men with full field packs.

A detachable canvas top is mounted on removable bows, and is provided with roll-up straps to permit ventilation in the body, and with front and rear curtains with window flaps. The inside body dimensions are approximately 88 by 132 by 37 inches.

The wheelbase is approximately 185 inches. Tires are 10.00 x 22, 12 ply.

A winch is mounted midship. Two U. S. Army standard pintles are mounted, one on the front and one on the rear, with provisions for mounting a Universal joint type on the rear pintle mounting bracket.

The vehicle is manufactured by the White Motor Co., the Mack Mfg. Corp., and the Corbitt Company.

REFERENCES—TM 10–1220, 10–1221; MCM 5e; SNL G–512, G–526, G–535.

TYPICAL CHARACTERISTICS OF PRIME MOVER

Crew 5

Physical Characteristics
Weight (gross), closed cab . . . . 35,250 lb.
Length . . . . 24 ft., 1 in.
Width . . . . 8 ft.
Height . . . . 9 ft., 6 ins.
reducible to . . . . 7 ft., 5 ins.
Ground clearance . . . . 10¾ ins.
Tread (center to center, rear) . . . . . . 72¼ ins.
Wheelbase . . . . 185 ins.
Tire equipment . . . . 10.00 x 22, 12 ply
(mud and snow)

Armament
Truck Mount, M36, M57, or M58, for cal. .50 Machine Gun, M2, HB
(On one vehicle in each four)

Performance
Maximum speed on level . . . . 35 m.p.h.
Maximum grade ability 65%
Fording depth (slowest forward speed) . . 24 ins.
Angle of approach . . . . 59°
Angle of departure . . . . 47°
Turning radius . . . . 41 ft.
Fuel capacity . . . . 80 gals.

Cruising range (approx.) . . . . 300 miles
with towed load . . . . 250 miles
Normal towed load . . . . 16,500 lb.
Winch capacity . . . . 25,000 lb.
Battery, Voltage, total 6–12
Fire Protection . . . . Fire Extinguisher
Engine, Make and Model . . . . . . Hercules HXD
Type . . . . In-line, liquid-cooled
No. of cylinders 6
Cycle 4
Fuel (gasoline) . . . . 70 octane
Bore and stroke . . . . 5¼ x 6 ins.
Displacement . . . . 779 cu. ins.
Compression ratio 5.69:1

Net hp. . . . . 180 at 2,150 r.p.m.
Max. torque . . . . . . 556 lb.-ft., at 1,000 r.p.m.
Crankshaft rotation . . . . C'Clockwise
Length . . . . 55½ ins.
Width . . . . 26½ ins.
Height . . . . 39 ins.
Weight, dry . . . . 2,465 lb.

Transmission, Gear ratios
First speed 6.54:1
Second speed 3.27:1
Third speed 1.76:1
Fourth speed 1.00:1
Reverse 7.24:1

Transfer Case, Gear ratios 2.55:1; 1.00:1

Suspension, Type . . . . Semi-elliptic
Wheel construction . . . . Disk

Master Clutch, Type . . . . Single plate

Radiator, Type . . . . Fin and tube
Capacity of system . . . . 80 qts.

Brakes, Type . . . . Internal, air

Brakes, Parking, Type . . . . Disk

Front Axle, Type . . . . Double reduction

Rear Axle, Gear ratio 7.33:1

6-TON, 6x6 (4DT) TRUCK (Continued)

6-TON, 6x6 (4DT) TRUCK CHASSIS, SIGNAL CORPS—STANDARD—This chassis is supplied to the Signal Corps, and is used for mounting the Communication Van body, K-56. The chassis is the same as that used for the Truck, 6-ton, 6x6 Prime Mover. Wheelbase is 185 inches. Tires are 10.00 x 22, 12 ply. No winch is required. A pintle is mounted at the rear.

The chassis is manufactured by the White Motor Co., the Mack Mfg. Corp., and the Corbitt Company.

REFERENCES—TM 10–1220, 10–1221; MCM 5e.

6-TON, 6x6 TRUCK CHASSIS, CORPS OF ENGINEERS—STANDARD—This chassis is supplied to the Corps of Engineers and is used for mounting its Bridge-Erecting body. The completed vehicle is provided with a rear-mounted derrick operated by hydraulic hoists. Metal bridge sections can be quickly moved into position directly from the truck by use of the derrick.

The chassis has a wheelbase of 220 inches, and has a winch mounted at the front and a pintle at the rear. Tires are 12.00 x 20, 14 ply. Two air compressors are provided, one for the airbrakes and the other for ponton inflation.

Because the completed vehicle is so conspicuous from the air, bows and tarpaulins are provided for camouflage, and give it an appearance similar to that of a cargo truck.

The vehicle is manufactured by the Brockway Co.

REFERENCES—TM 10–1528, 10–1529; MCM 5e; OCM 20511.

CHASSIS AS SUPPLIED TO SIGNAL CORPS, SHOWN WITH OPEN CAB AND TRUCK MOUNT

CHASSIS, SIGNAL CORPS

Physical Characteristics

Length	23 ft.
Width	8 ft.
Height	9 ft., 6 ins.
reducible to	7 ft., 5 ins.
Ground clearance	10¾ ins.
Tread (center to center, rear)	72¼ ins.
Wheelbase	185 ins.

TRUCK, CORPS OF ENGINEERS

Physical Characteristics (including body)

Weight	38,850 lb.
Length (overall)	30 ft., 10 ins.
Width	8 ft., 4 ins.
Height	9 ft.
reducible to	8 ft., 8½ ins.
Ground clearance	10¾ ins.
Tread (center to center, rear)	74 ins.
Wheelbase	220 ins.

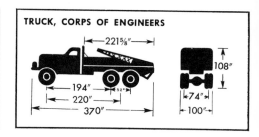

ORDNANCE DEPARTMENT SUPPLIES CHASSIS FOR ENGINEERS' BRIDGE-ERECTING TRUCK, CARRYING BRIDGE SECTIONS AND DERRICK FOR LIFTING THEM

7½-TON, 6x6 (4DT) PRIME MOVER TRUCK—STANDARD

This vehicle is used as a prime mover for heavy artillery and as a cargo and personnel carrier.

It has a payload of 15,450 pounds without towed load, and of 5,000 pounds with a towed load.

It will tow the 8 inch Howitzer, M1, with a traveling weight of 32,000 pounds, or the 155 mm Gun, M1, with a traveling weight of 31,000 pounds.

It has a maximum grade ability of 65% without towed load. The vehicle is capable of operation over unimproved roads, trails and open, rolling and hilly cross country with its towed load. It has a maximum speed of 31½ miles an hour with a towed load on a smooth concrete highway.

Body is of the U. S. Army standard cargo type, with inside body dimensions approximately 94 x 140 inches. Present production calls for an open type cab, with removable top and removable windshield. The left half of the windshield is hinged to swing out and fold over the right half. A Truck Mount, M36, for a cal. .30 or cal. .50 machine gun is provided with one vehicle in each four.

Tires are 12.00 x 24, 14 ply, mud and snow tread, and use heavy-duty type inner tubes. Wheels are U. S. Army standard type. Dual wheels are used at the rear. Two spare wheels and tire assemblies are provided.

Military equipment includes towing shackles on the two front corners, a brush guard and a sturdy front bumper. An Ordnance pintle, Model M–5, is furnished, together with special coupling attachments for the 8 inch Howitzer, M1, and the 155 mm Gun, M1. A special superstructure and chain fall is provided for raising and lowering gun trails to and from the coupling.

The vehicle has sealed beam type headlights and U. S. Army standard combat-zone safety lighting, together with a lighting socket for the towed load.

The front-mounted winch has a line pull capacity of 40,000 pounds.

Power is supplied by a six-cylinder, in-line, gasoline engine. A single dry disk clutch is used. The transmission has five speeds forward and one reverse, in which fifth speed is direct drive. Helical gears are used for the constant mesh, intermediate and high gears. The lower speeds employ spur gears.

A two-speed transfer case receives power from the transmission and divides it between the front and two rear axle driving units. Levers in the driver's compartment permit change of the transfer case gear ratio, and also permit declutching of the front wheels when advisable.

The vehicle has airbrakes, with a hand air-controller for the trailer brakes.

The truck is manufactured by the Mack Manufacturing Corp.

REFERENCES—TM 10–1478, 10–1479; MCM No. 19; OCM 19107, 20100.

THIS 7½-TON PRIME MOVER IS USED TO TOW HEAVY ARTILLERY AND CARRY CARGO OR PERSONNEL

TYPICAL CHARACTERISTICS

Crew 2
Physical Characteristics
  Weight (gross) . . . . 43,570 lb.
  Length . . . . 24 ft., 8⅝ ins.
  Width . . . . 8 ft., 5¾ ins.
  Height . . . . 10 ft., 3 ins.
    reducible to . . . . 7 ft., 10 ins.
  Ground clearance . . . . 13½ ins.
  Tread (center to center) . . . . 76¼ ins.
  Wheelbase . . . . 156 ins.
  Tire equipment . . . . 12.00 x 24, 14 ply
    (mud and snow)

Armament

  Truck Mount, M32 or M36, for cal. .50
    Machine Gun, M2, HB
  (On one vehicle in each four)

Performance
  Maximum speed on level . . . . 31½ m.p.h.
  Maximum grade ability 65%
  Angle of approach . . . . 35°
  Angle of departure . . . . 45°
  Turning radius . . . . 34 ft.
  Fuel capacity . . . . 160 gals.
  Cruising range (approx.) . . . . 400 miles
    with towed load . . . . 240 miles
  Maximum drawbar pull . . . . 43,200 lb.
  Normal towed load . . . . 32,000 lb.
  Payload . . . . 15,450 lb.
  Winch capacity . . . . 40,000 lb.

Battery, Voltage, total 6–12

Engine, Make and Model . . . . Mack, EY

Type . . . . In-line
No. of cylinders 6
Cycle 4
Fuel (gasoline) . . . . 70 octane
Displacement . . . . 707 cu. ins.
Bore and stroke . . . . 5 x 6 ins.
Compression . . . . 106 at C.S.
Net hp. . . . . 156 at 2,100 r.p.m.
Max. torque . . . . 550 lb.-ft. at 750 r.p.m.
Crankshaft rotation . . . . C'Clockwise
Length . . . . 53 ins.
Width . . . . 29½ ins.
Height . . . . 46 ins.

Transmission, Gear ratios
  First speed 8.05:1
  Second speed 4.57:1
  Third speed 2.61:1
  Fourth speed 1.45:1
  Fifth speed 1.00:1
  Reverse 8.13:1

Transfer Case, Gear ratios 2.50:1; 1.00:1

Steering Ratio 27, 23, 27:1

Suspension, Type . . . . Semi-elliptic
  Wheel size . . . . 24 x 11

Brakes, Type . . . . Internal, air

Brakes, Parking, Type . . . . Disk

Front Axle, Type . . . . Front drive

Rear Axle, Gear ratio 9.02:1

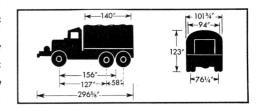

¼-TON, 2-WHEEL, AMPHIBIAN CARGO TRAILER—STANDARD

This is an all-steel, flat-bed cargo type trailer, designed to be towed by the ¼-ton, ½-ton and ¾-ton trucks, including the ¼-ton amphibian truck.

It has a gross weight of 1,050 pounds and a payload of 500 pounds. At gross weight, the trailer is capable of being towed behind a motor truck for indefinite periods, under all conditions of terrain and speeds encountered in military operations. The body is water-tight, and the trailer, with 500 pound load, will float with 6 inches freeboard.

Tires, tubes, rims and wheels are identical with those on the ¼-ton, 4x4, Truck. Approved combat-zone safety lighting is provided, current being furnished from the towing vehicle by a lighting plug connection with cable assembly.

A military type lunette, mounted at the front, is used to attach the trailer to the pintle on the towing vehicle.

THE ¼-TON CARGO TRAILER WILL FLOAT IN WATER WITH 500 LB. LOAD

The drawbar and support assembly is adjustable in the support bracket to three positions, namely, horizontal when fully retracted, vertical when the trailer is detached, and intermediate (45°) when the angle is used as a skid. A tarpaulin cover is furnished. The trailer has a hand brake.

These trailers are manufactured by the Willys Overland Motors Co. and the American Bantam Car Co.

REFERENCES—MCM 24a; TM 10–1230; OCM 18947, 19307.

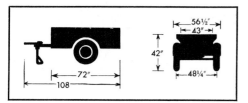

Physical Characteristics

Weight (gross)	1,050 lb.
Length (overall)	9 ft.
Length (inside body)	6 ft.
Width (overall)	4 ft., 8½ ins.
Width (inside body, top)	3 ft., 10 ins.
Height (overall)	3 ft., 6 ins.
Height (inside body)	16 ins.
Ground clearance	12½ ins.
Tread (center to center)	48¼ ins.
Tire equipment	6.00 x 16, 6 ply

Performance

Payload	500 lb.
Angle of departure	35°

2-WHEEL, 2-HORSE, VAN TRAILER—STANDARD

This is a van type, 2-wheel trailer, designed for the transportation of horses. The body, of wooden construction, is subdivided into three compartments, consisting of two longitudinal horse stalls at the rear, and a transverse groom and tack compartment at the front.

There is one door in the groom and tack compartment on the right side of the trailer, and one window in the front end of the trailer. The tail gate is designed to be usable as a ramp.

One spare wheel and tire assembly is mounted inside the body.

Electrically operated brakes are controlled from the towing vehicle.

U. S. Army standard combat-zone lighting is provided, with current supplied from the towing vehicle by means of a trailer lighting cable assembly.

The vehicles are manufactured by the Bartlett Trailer Co., the Schult Co., A. J. Miller Auto Cruiser Co., and the Porto Products Co.

REFERENCES—MCM 16a; OCM 19107.

THIS TRAILER IS DESIGNED TO TRANSPORT TWO HORSES AND EQUIPMENT

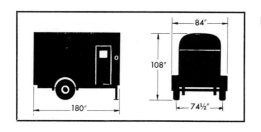

Physical Characteristics

Weight (gross)	4,700 lb.
Length (overall)	15 ft.
Length (inside body)	12 ft., 8 ins.
Width (overall)	7 ft.
Width (inside body)	4 ft., 10 ins.
Height (overall)	9 ft.
Ground clearance	13½ ins.
Tread (center to center)	74½ ins.
Tire equipment	7.50 x 16, 8 ply (highway)

Performance—Payload 2,400 lb.

Brakes, Parking, Type Electric

1-TON, 2-WHEEL TRAILERS—STANDARD

These trailers, with payloads of 2,000 pounds each, are capable of being towed over unimproved roads, trails, and open, rolling, and hilly cross country. They can be towed at speeds up to 18 miles per hour on average cross-country terrain, and to 50 miles per hour on smooth concrete roadway.

Tires are 7.50 x 20, mud and snow tread, using heavy-duty type tubes. Wheels are single, U. S. Army standard type, with integral rims.

A parking brake, operated by a hand-lever, is located on the right side of the trailer. U. S. Army standard combat-zone safety lighting is used.

The trailer has a standard type lunette for attaching it to the pintle of the towing vehicle. It has a detachable "A" type drawbar frame, and a standard retractable landing-wheel assembly, with a steel wheel. Fenders are provided.

Desertization equipment includes size 11.00 x 18, 10 ply tires with heavy-duty tubes, and army combat wheels with beadlocks, size 8.00 CV x 18. No fenders are required.

THIS 1-TON, 2 WHEEL, CARGO TRAILER HAS ALL WOOD BODY

THE WATER TANK MAY BE CAMOUFLAGED AS A CARGO TRAILER

1-TON, 2-WHEEL, CARGO TRAILER —STANDARD—Present production vehicles have flat-bed cargo type bodies of all-wood construction, with wooden side and end stakes. Bows and paulins are provided for covering the vehicles. Approximate inside dimensions are 45 x 96 inches, with 18 inch high wood sides and beds.

A hinged tail gate is provided at the rear of the vehicle.

These trailers are manufactured by the American Bantam Car Co., Ben Hur Mfg. Co., Century Boat Works, Checker Cab Mfg. Co., Dorsey Brothers, Gerstenlager Co., Henney Motor Co., Hercules Body Co., Highland Body Co., J. W. Hobbs Corp., Mifflinburg Body Co., W. C. Nabors Co., Nash-Kelvinator Corp., Omaha Standard Body Corp., Pike Trailer Co., Queen City Mfg. Co., Redman Trailer Co., Steel Products Co. Inc., Strick Co., Transportation Equipment Co., Truck Engineering Corp., Willys-Overland Motors Co., Winter-Weiss Co.

REFERENCES—TM 9–883; MCM 6c; OCM 19745, 19921, 20148, 20850, 21141, 21711, 21906, 22214, 22584.

1-TON, 2-WHEEL, WATER TANK TRAILER, 250-GALLON — STANDARD —The body of this trailer consists of a standard elliptical steel tank of 250 gallon capacity. It is complete with manhole, inlet and outlet plugs, a pump, a suction hose 25 feet long, a suction hose strainer, one large and two small self-closing faucets on each side, faucet protection boxes, and necessary piping. The pump has a capacity to permit filling the tank in 20 minutes, and is of such construction that nonuse will not affect its serviceability. Bows and paulins for camouflage are provided, to give the appearance of a cargo vehicle.

The vehicles are manufactured by the Ben Hur Mfg. Co., the Checker Cab Co., and the Springfield Auto Works.

REFERENCES—TM 10–1464; MCM 6d; OCM 20252, 21463, 21588, 21754, 22382, 22702.

TYPICAL CHARACTERISTICS

1-TON CARGO TRAILER
Physical Characteristics

Weight (gross)	3,460 lb.
Length, overall	12 ft., 1½ ins.
Length, inside body	8 ft.
Width, overall	5 ft., 11⅛ ins.
Width, inside body	3 ft., 10¼ ins.
Height, overall, top up	6 ft., 1 in.
Height, inside body, top up	3 ft., 7 ins.
Ground clearance	16¼ ins.
Tread (center to center)	59 ins.
Tire equipment	7.50 x 20, 8 ply (mud and snow)
desert	11.00 x 18, 10 ply

Performance

Payload	2,000 lb.
Angle of departure	50°

Brakes, Parking, Type | Hand

1-TON WATER TANK TRAILER
Physical Characteristics

Weight (gross)	3,390 lb.
Length, overall	11 ft., 4½ ins.
Length, inside body	5 ft., 1½ ins.
Width, overall	5 ft., 11⅛ ins.
Width, inside body	3 ft., 10 ins.
Height	5 ft., 3⅝ ins.
Ground clearance	16¼ ins.
Tread (center to center, rear)	59 ins.
Tire equipment	7.50 x 20, 8 ply (mud and snow)
desert	11.00 x 18, 10 ply

Performance

Payload	2,000 lb.
Angle of departure	50°

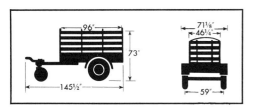

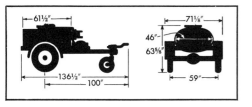

3- AND 3½-TON, 2-WHEEL (2DT) SEMI-TRAILERS—STANDARD

Military characteristics for the 3- and 3½-Ton, 2-Wheel (2dt) Semi-trailers call for minimum chassis weights of 2,400 pounds, and maximum fifth wheel loads, with the trailers loaded, of 4,500 pounds each.

The trailers, fully equipped and loaded, are capable of being towed over hard-surfaced roads at speeds up to 45 miles per hour. They are designed so that in any position, loaded or empty, the tractor-truck may assume a 90° angle to the semi-trailer without interference.

Tires are 7.50 x 20, truck and bus balloon, with heavy-duty tubes. Ventilated disk dual wheels are used, and are interchangeable with the wheels of the tractor-truck. Standard commercial rims are used. One spare wheel and tire assembly is carried on a bracket beneath the body.

The electrically operated brakes are controlled from the towing vehicle, and are provided with safety controls which automatically apply the brakes if the trailer is accidentally disconnected from the towing vehicle.

Current for the lights is obtained from the towing vehicle, by means of a U. S. Army standard trailer lighting cable assembly. A lower fifth wheel is supplied when specified. Support legs of either the hinge or vertical type are required. A sturdy rear bumper is provided.

REFERENCES — MCM 104b; OCM 19107, 21341, 21519.

3½-TON, 2-WHEEL STAKE AND PLATFORM SEMI-TRAILER — STANDARD — This semi-trailer, designed for all arms and services, has a stake and platform type body with removable sides and ends, mounted on a steel frame. Inside body dimensions are 79½ x 190 inches. Payload is 7,000 pounds.

Semi-trailers, conforming generally to these characteristics, are manufactured by the Black Diamond Trailer Co., Dorsey Bros., Highway Trailer Co., Hobbs Mfg. Co., Kingham Trailer Co., Strick Co., Utility Trailer Mfg. Co., Truck Engineering Corp., Winter-Weiss Co.

REFERENCES—TM 9–866A; TM 10–1391; MCM 104b.

3-TON, 2-WHEEL (2DT) VAN SEMI-TRAILER — STANDARD — Designed for all arms and services, this semi-trailer has a van type body, and has a payload of 6,000 pounds. Minimum inside dimensions are: width, 78 inches; height, 76 inches; length, 216 inches.

The vehicles are manufactured by the Black Diamond Trailer Co., Carolina Trailer Co., Checker Cab Mfg. Co., Highway Trailer Co., Kingham Trailer Co., A. J. Miller Auto Cruiser Trailer Co., Steel Products Co., Strick Co., Truck Engineering Corp.

REFERENCE—MCM 104b.

3½-TON, 2-WHEEL, STAKE AND PLATFORM SEMI-TRAILER HAS REMOVABLE SIDES

3-TON, 2-WHEEL VAN SEMI-TRAILER ON FOLDING FRONT SUPPORT LEGS

TYPICAL CHARACTERISTICS

STAKE AND PLATFORM	VAN
Physical Characteristics	**Physical Characteristics**
Weight (gross)...................11,440 lb.	Weight (gross)...................11,810 lb.
Length........................16 ft., 7 ins.	Length........................18 ft., 4 ins.
Width.........................7 ft., 3 ins.	Width.........................6 ft., 11½ ins.
Height............................8 ft.	Height........................10 ft., 7¼ ins.
Ground clearance..............15½ ins.	Ground clearance..............15½ ins.
Tread (center to center).........65¼ ins.	Tread (center to center).........65¼ ins.
Wheelbase—fifth wheel to rear axle..145 ins.	Wheelbase—fifth wheel to rear axle.162¾ ins.
Tire equipment....7.50 x 20, 8 ply (highway)	Tire equipment....7.50 x 20, 8 ply (highway)
Performance	**Performance**
Maximum towing speed..........45 m.p.h.	Maximum towing speed..........45 m.p.h.
Payload.......................7,000 lb.	Payload.......................6,000 lb.
Brakes, Type........................Electric	**Brakes,** Type........................Electric

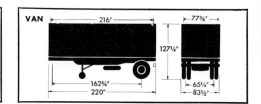

6-TON, 2-WHEEL (2DT), SEMI-TRAILERS—STANDARD

THIS VAN TYPE BODY CAN BE DISASSEMBLED FOR SHIPPING

THIS 6-TON SEMI-TRAILER CARRIES MOBILE RECORDS UNITS

These semi-trailers have payloads of 12,000 pounds each, and gross weights of approximately 20,000 pounds.

They are capable of being towed over unimproved roads, trails, and open, rolling, and hilly cross country, and can be towed on smooth concrete roadway at speeds up to 50 miles per hour.

They are so designed that when in the level and loaded position, the tractor-truck may assume a 90° angle to the semi-trailer without interference.

Tires are 9.00 x 20, 10 ply, U. S. Army standard mud and snow tread. Heavy-duty type tubes are furnished. The vehicle uses Army standard dual wheels. Rims are an integral portion of the wheels.

Compressed air operated brakes are controlled from the towing vehicle. They are provided with safety controls which will automatically apply the brakes if the trailer is accidentally disconnected from the towing vehicle.

The fifth wheel is of the semi-automatic type. Screw type support legs with hinged wheel supports and steel wheels are provided.

Desertization equipment includes size 14.00 x 20, 12 ply tires with heavy-duty tubes, and army combat wheels with beadlocks, size 10.00 CW x 20.

REFERENCES — OCM 18985, 19107, 19136, 21221, 21722; MCM 11c.

6-TON, 2-WHEEL (2DT), VAN SEMI-TRAILER — STANDARD
—Designed for the Quartermaster Corps, this semi-trailer

TYPICAL CHARACTERISTICS

Physical Characteristics	Van	Mobile Records	Animal & Cargo
Weight (gross)	19,450 lb.	21,000 lb.	20,820 lb.
Length	20 ft., 8¾ ins.	22 ft., 6 ins.	24 ft., 1³⁄₁₆ ins.
Width	8 ft.	8 ft.	8 ft.
Height	10 ft., 9¾ ins.	11 ft., 3 ins.	10 ft., 6 ins.
Ground clearance	14 ins.	16½ ins.	14 ins.
Tread (center to center)	72 ins.	69 ins.	72 ins.
Wheelbase—fifth wheel to axle	193½ ins.	197 ins.	193½ ins.
Tire equipment	9.00 x 20, 10 ply (mud and snow)	9.00 x 20, 10 ply (mud and snow)	9.00 x 20, 10 ply (mud and snow)
Performance			
Angle of departure	45°	50°	50°
Payload	12,000 lb.	12,000 lb.	12,000 lb.

is used to transport general cargo. It has a van type body, with inside body dimensions of: length, 240 inches; width, 89 inches; height, 78 inches. One spare wheel and tire assembly is provided. The vehicle is equipped with a sturdy rear bumper.

These semi-trailers are manufactured by the American Body and Trailer Co., Dorsey Brothers, Gramm Truck and Trailer Corp., Highway Trailer Co., Kentucky Mfg. Co., Olson Mfg. Co., Strick Co., Timpte Brothers, Trailer Company of America, Carter Mfg. Co., and Utility Trailer Mfg. Co.

REFERENCES — TM 10–1169; MCM 11b; OCM 19107, 21722.

6-TON, 2-WHEEL (2DT), COMBINATION ANIMAL AND CARGO CARRIER —STANDARD
—This semi-trailer is designed to transport eight men and eight horses, with equipment for both, including rifle and saddle racks. It is for all arms and services. Inside body dimensions are: length, 281 inches; width, 90 inches; height, 88 inches.

The vehicle is manufactured by the Highway Trailer Co. and Gramm Motor Truck and Trailer Corp.

REFERENCES—MCM 21a; TM 10–1372; OCM 19107.

6-TON, 2-WHEEL (2DT), MOBILE RECORDS SEMI-TRAILER—STANDARD
—This is a modification of the 6-Ton, 2-Wheel Van, Semi-trailer. It was designed for the Adjutant General's Office for mounting machine record units to be used in the theater of operations for tabulating military records. It has a van type body with minimum inside dimensions: length, 264 inches; width, 90 inches; height, 78 inches. The payload is 12,000 pounds. No spare wheel or tire is furnished.

The vehicle is manufactured by the Lufkin Foundry & Machine Co. and the Watson Automotive Equipment Co.

REFERENCES—MCM 11b; OCM 18985, 19107, 19136, 21221, 21722.

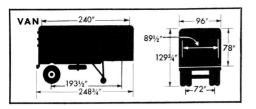

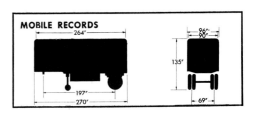

FORDING EQUIPMENT FOR VEHICLES

Successful use of fording kits for Medium Tank M4A1 and Light Tank M5 during the North African invasion prompted the development of similar kits for other vehicles normally used in landings upon enemy beaches.

By the use of these kits, the vehicles can be waterproofed to operate satisfactorily in water deeper than otherwise would be possible, permitting them to wade in from landing craft at greater distances offshore. Special attachments permit rapid jettisoning of any waterproofing equipment which interferes with satisfactory operation of the vehicles on shore.

Tanks and Tank-Like Vehicles

In sealing tanks and tank-like vehicles, all unvented openings are sealed with tape and sealing compound to render the hull watertight, after which all vented openings are extended by use of stacks and adapters.

TANK FORDING KIT T-O—This is a universal kit, containing all common materials, such as tape, paint, sealing compound, brushes, welding rod, etc., for sealing holes and cracks. It is used in connection with specialized adapter and stack fording kits.

ADAPTER AND STACK FORDING KITS LT-3 AND LT-5—These kits consist of metal adapters and stacks as required for sealing of the exhaust system and engine compartment, and canvas for sealing the air intake of particular vehicles. Kit LT-3 is used for Light Tank M3A1, and Kit LT-5 for Light Tank M5A1 and 75-mm Howitzer Motor Carriage M8. They are used in connection with the Tank Fording Kit T-O.

STACK FORDING KIT MT-S contains standard stacks and stack covers suitable for use on all M4 series medium tanks and other vehicles built on similar chassis. They are used in connection with the Tank Fording Kit T-O and an adapter fording kit or an adapter and stack fording kit.

ADAPTER FORDING KITS MT-1, MT-2, MT-3, MT-4 contain special metal adapters for attaching stacks to engine compartments of Medium Tanks M4A1, M4A2, M4A3, and M4A4 respectively.

ADAPTER AND STACK FORDING KITS SPA-7, SPA-10, AND SPA-70 contain metal adapters for attaching stacks to the engine compartments of 105-mm Howitzer Motor Carriage M7, 3-In. Gun Motor Carriage M10, and 76-mm Gun Motor Carriage M18 (T70), respectively.

Wheeled and Half-Track Vehicles; Tractors

Wheeled and half-track vehicles and tractors are prepared for fording by seal-

MEDIUM TANK WITH OPENINGS SEALED AND STACKS INSTALLED FOR FORDING

EXHAUST PIPE IN ¾-TON, 4 x 4, TRUCK

EXHAUST PIPE INSTALLED ON HALF TRACK

ing the individual components and extending air and exhaust vents above the water level.

FORDING KIT WV-6—This is a universal kit for ¼-ton to 2½-ton trucks. It contains all necessary materials such as tape, paint, flexible tubing, sealing compound, air intake hose, etc.

FORDING KIT WV-7 is a universal kit for 4-ton to 10-ton trucks.

FORDING KIT HT-1 is a universal kit for all half-track vehicles, scout cars, Light Armored Car M8, and Armored Utility Car M20.

FORDING KIT T-AC-M4 is for use on High-Speed Tractor M4.

FORDING KIT T-IHC-M5 is for use on High-Speed Tractor M5.

FORDING KIT T-AC-M6 is for use on High-Speed Tractor M6.

FORDING KIT TRV-1 contains special metal adapter and attaching parts for attaching stacks to engine exhaust system on Tank Recovery Vehicles M32 and M32B1. This kit is used in connection with T-O Fording Kit and TRV-S Fording Kit.

FORDING KIT TRV-3 contains special metal adapter and attaching parts for attaching stacks to engine exhaust system on Tank Recovery Vehicle M32B3. It is used in connection with Fording Kits T-O and TRV-S.

FORDING KIT TRV-S contains standard exhaust stacks suitable for use on Tank Recovery Vehicles M32, M32B1 and M32B3. This kit is used in connection with T-O Fording Kit and TRV-1 and TRV-3 Adapter Kits.

REFERENCES — TM 9-2853; OCM 20150, 20977, 21814, 21955, 23290, 23515.

KITS FOR AIRBORNE PREPARATION OF TRUCKS—STANDARD

1½-TON, 4x4, BOMB SERVICE TRUCK M6 COMPLETELY DISASSEMBLED AND READY FOR STOWING IN CARGO PLANE

REASSEMBLED BOMB SERVICE TRUCK, SHOWING SPLICE ON FRAME

CHASSIS OF 1½-TON, 6x6, TRUCK LOADED IN CARGO COMPARTMENT

Kits to permit the ready disassembly and reassembly of certain trucks for air transportation in C-47A airplanes to advanced bases were standardized in October 1944 following the completion of a development program based on a procedure first employed in the South Pacific theaters of war.

When these kits are used, the chassis of trucks larger than the ¾-Ton Weapons Carrier are cut at a point behind the cab, and fishplates with bolting flanges are welded to the frame where the cut has been made. The chassis can then be loaded into cargo planes and reassembled at their destination. The wood or steel bodies are also cut and are spliced together later with material provided in the kits.

In the case of trucks with closed cabs, the upper part of the cab, including the windshield, must be removed to the belt line. The windshield is then reinstalled by means of flanges welded to the pillar posts. It can thus be removed for loading.

To load the ¾-Ton, 4x4, Weapons Carrier Truck, no cutting is required except for the removal of a triangular section of metal from the platform of the driver's seat. Removal of the rear assembly, body, running-boards, and right bumperette permits this vehicle to be loaded into one airplane. Two 1½-ton trucks require three airplanes: one airplane for each chassis and a third for the two bodies. The 2½-ton trucks are divided into two loads, each carried in a separate airplane.

In addition to the fishplates and splicing material, each kit contains a valve and coupling unit, consisting of two valves, one union, and the necessary nipples, to prevent loss of hydraulic fluid when the brake line is separated. Each kit likewise contains tubing to connect the fuel line of the engine with a standard 5-gallon gasoline can, which serves as an auxiliary tank when the front section of a truck is being maneuvered into a plane under its own power, and also a small, single-wheel dolly to support the rear of the front section when it is being loaded in this manner. No special equipment is required for disassembly of the driveshaft.

KIT FOR ¾-TON, 4x4, WEAPONS CARRIER TRUCK contains a valve and coupling unit for sealing the brake line when the rear axle is removed and a single-wheel, pneumatic-tired loading dolly.

KIT FOR 1½-TON, 4x4, CARGO TRUCK OR BOMB SERVICE TRUCK M6 contains universal fishplates for reassembling the frame, splicing material for wood or steel bodies, a valve and coupling unit to seal the brake line, tubing to connect the engine fuel line with an auxiliary fuel supply, and a single-wheel loading dolly.

KIT FOR 1½-TON, 6x6, CARGO TRUCK contains fishplates with bolting flanges, body splicing material, a valve and coupling unit for sealing the brake line, rubber tubing for the fuel line, and a loading dolly.

KITS FOR 2½-TON, 6x6, TRUCKS, CARGO (LWB OR SWB) OR DUMP (LWB) contain universal fishplates with bolting flanges, body splicing material, a valve and coupling unit for the brake line, tubing for the fuel line, and a loading dolly. Each kit also contains a device for compressing the right front spring.

References — OCM 21933, 22141, 22883, 23224, 23503, 25116, 25362.

2
ARTILLERY

Mobile Artillery, 133

Railway and Seacoast Artillery, 169

Tank Armament, 177

Antiaircraft Artillery, 184

Sub Caliber Guns, 199

Harbor Defense Mines, 208

Aircraft Armament, 213

60 MM MORTAR M2—MOUNT M2—STANDARD

The 60 mm Mortar, M2, is of French origin, developed by the Edgar Brandt Company, but manufactured in the United States under rights purchased from the Brandt organization. Its design has been altered and improved to conform to our standards. In addition to its normal function, it is now utilized as a projector for the illuminating shell, M83, employed to disclose aerial targets at night.

MORTAR, M2—The mortar consists of the barrel, base cap and firing pin. The base cap, ending in a spherical projection which fits into a socket in the base plate, is screwed to the breech end of the smooth-bored barrel. The firing pin fits in the base cap, which is bored and threaded axially to receive it.

MOUNT, M2—The bipod mount comprises the leg, elevating mechanism and traversing mechanism assemblies. The leg assembly consists of two tubular steel legs connected by a clevis joint attached to the elevating screw guide tube. Spread of the legs is limited by the clevis joint, which is provided with a spring latch to lock the legs in the open position. The legs terminate in spiked feet. The left leg has a cross-leveling mechanism consisting of a sliding bracket connected by a link to the elevating screw guide tube.

The elevating mechanism assembly consists mainly of an elevating screw nut which moves vertically on a screw within a guide tube, the elevating screw being actuated by a crank attached to its lower end.

The traversing mechanism consists of a horizontal screw operating in a yoke and actuated by a traversing handwheel.

The sight bracket fits in a dovetail slot provided in the yoke.

The barrel is clamped to the bipod by means of a clamping collar and saddle, shock absorbers being used to stabilize the mortar and mount during firing.

The base plate consists of a pressed steel body to which are welded a series of ribs and braces, a front flange and a socket. A locking lever fastens the spherical projection of the base cap in the socket.

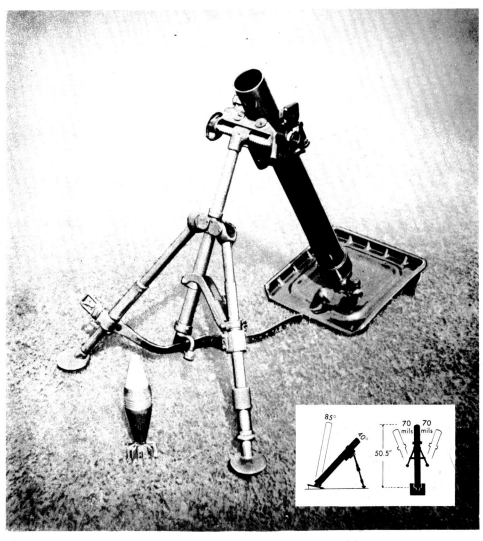

60 mm MORTAR, M2, IN FIRING POSITION, WITH SHELL, M49A2

Sighting and Fire Control Equipment

Sight (Collimator), M4

Ammunition

Projectile and propelling charge are in one unit constituting a complete round. The shell is furnished with stabilizing fins and a nose fuze. Propelling charges are divided into parts to provide for zone firing.

REFERENCES—TM 9–2005, v.3; FM 23–85.

PRINCIPAL CHARACTERISTICS

MORTAR, M2

Weight of Mortar, M2, and Mount, M2	42.0 lb.
Weight of mortar	12.8 lb.
Overall length of mortar	28.6 ins.
Diameter of bore	2.36 ins.
Rate of fire, maximum	30 to 35 rds./min.
Rate of fire, normal	18 rds./min.

MOUNT, M2

Weight of mount	29.2 lb.
Weight of bipod	16.4 lb.
Weight of base plate	12.8 lb.
Elevations, approximate	40° to 85°
Mortar clamp position A	40° to 65°
Mortar clamp position B	45° to 70°
Mortar clamp position C	50° to 85°
Maximum traverse, right	70 mils
Maximum traverse, left	70 mils

AMMUNITION

Shell	Range, Approximate
H.E., M49A2	100 to 1,985 yds.
Illuminating, M83	
Training, M69	

81 MM MORTAR M1—MOUNT M1—STANDARD

During the first World War, the standard mortar adopted by the U. S. Army for infantry use as an indirect fire weapon was the British 3″ Stokes trench mortar, Mk. I. Designs for a new mortar were started in 1920, but were abandoned in favor of attempts to improve bomb vanes in an effort to attain greater accuracy. While these tests were under way, the French firm of Edgar Brandt succeeded in developing a refined version of the Stokes mortar, together with suitable ammunition, which satisfied the requirements of the U. S. War Department. After tests of the Stokes-Brandt mortar and mount were completed successfully by the Ordnance Department, and the using arms, manufacturing rights were purchased from the Brandt Company.

The 81 mm Mortar, M1, has a heavier barrel than the Stokes, Mk. I, and a heavier base plate of new design. It also has a greater range and a higher rate of fire.

MORTAR, M1—The complete weapon consists of a barrel, bipod and base plate. The barrel is demountable from the bipod to form one load, while the bipod and base plate comprise two loads. Each load is light enough to be carried by one man. The smooth-bore muzzle-loading barrel is a seamless drawn-steel tube fitted at the breech end with a base cap within which is secured a firing pin protruding into the barrel.

MOUNT, M1—The mount consists of a base plate and a tubular steel bipod formed by two legs attached to a center trunnion by means of a compass joint. The left leg carries a cross-leveling mechanism which consists of a sliding bracket connected with the guide tube by a connecting rod. The mortar clamp, in two sections, clamps the barrel to the bipod and can be adjusted to three positions on the barrel.

The base plate is a rectangular pressed-steel body to which are welded a series of ribs and braces, a front flange, three loops, two handle plates and a socket for the spherical end of the tube base cap.

Sighting and Fire Control Equipment

Each mortar is equipped with a sight which includes a collimator, elevating and lateral deflection mechanisms, and longitudinal and cross-levels. The sight

81 mm MORTAR, M1, IN FIRING POSITION, WITH SHELLS, M43 AND M56

mechanism, supported by a bracket fitted into the mortar yoke, provides accurate laying for elevation and deflection.

Sight, M4, and Aiming Posts, M7, M8 and M9, are used with the 81 mm mortar.

Transportation

The 81 mm mortar can be carried by two men or can be transported on Hand Cart, M6A1. It is also part of the armament of the Half Track 81 mm Mortar Carrier, M4.

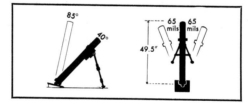

Ammunition

Stabilization in flight is obtained by fins on the shell which cause the projectile to strike nose first. A point-detonating impact type of fuze is fitted to the nose of the shell. The propelling charge attached to the base end of the projectile consists of an ignition cartridge and propellant increment. The increments of the charge are removable to provide for zone firing.

REFERENCES—TM 9–2005, v.3; TM 9–1260.

PRINCIPAL CHARACTERISTICS

MORTAR, M1

Weight of Mortar, M1, and Mount, M1	136.0 lb.
Weight of mortar	44.5 lb.
Overall length of mortar	49.5 ins.
Diameter of bore	3.2 ins.
Rate of fire, maximum	30 to 35 rds./min.
Rate of fire, normal	18 rds./min.

MOUNT, M1

Weight of mount	91.5 lb.
Weight of bipod	46.5 lb.
Weight of base plate	45.0 lb.
Elevations, approximate	40° to 85°
Mortar clamp position A	40° to 70°
Mortar clamp position B	50° to 80°
Mortar clamp position C	55° to 85°
Maximum traverse, right	65 mils
Maximum traverse, left	65 mils

AMMUNITION

Weight	Ranges, Approximate
H.E. shell, M43A1, 6.87 lb.	100 to 3,290 yds.
M36, 10.62 lb.	300 to 2,558 yds.
Chemical shell, M57, 10.75 lb.	300 to 2,470 yds.

HAND CART, M6A1 STANDARD

The Hand Cart, M6A1, is a utility vehicle which differs from the basic Hand Cart, M3A4, only in the addition of suitable brackets and straps to adapt it for transport of the 81 mm mortar. It can also be used as an ammunition cart for the 37 mm Gun, M3A1, the 60 mm mortar, or the 81 mm mortar.

CHARACTERISTICS

Overall length (including pole)	69.5 ins.
Dimensions of body	24 ins. x 32 ins. x 5 ins.
Overall width	39.1 ins.
Weight	70.8 lb.
Tire Size	4 ins. x 12 ins.

HAND CART, M6A1

MULTIPLE CAL. .50 MACHINE-GUN CARRIAGE M51—STANDARD

MULTIPLE CAL. .50 MACHINE-GUN CARRIAGE, M51 (MULTIPLE CAL. .50 MACHINE-GUN MOUNT, M45, ON TRAILER MOUNT, M17)

Mobile and semi-mobile automatic weapons battalions armed with the Caliber .50 Machine Gun, M2, on the Mount, M3, lacked firepower for effective action against enemy attack aviation. In order to provide an antiaircraft weapon of concentrated firepower which could be used for convoy defense, the Multiple Caliber .50 Machine-Gun Carriage, M51, was designed and standardized.

The Multiple Machine-Gun Carriage, M51, is composed of the Multiple Caliber .50 Machine-Gun Mount, M45, with four Caliber .50 Browning Machine Guns, HB, M2, on the Mount, Trailer, M17. The carriage is drawn by a prime mover.

The Mount, M45, is a power-driven, armored gun mount with a self-contained power unit. It can be traversed through 360°, and elevated from −10° to +90°. Firing of the guns and movement of the mount are controlled from a pair of hand grips in front of the gunner's seat within the mount.

All the rotatable elements of the mount are located in a turret which rests on a welded steel base plate anchored to the floor of the trailer. A centrally located gunner's seat is situated between two trunnion sectors which carry the guns and ammunition chests. A sight base—in the center of which is the Navy Reflector Sight, Mk. IX, the control handle, and the firing switch—extends over the gunner's head from one trunnion to the other and moves with the trunnions.

Two Caliber .50 Browning Machine Guns, HB, M2, are mounted outboard on each trunnion. An ammunition Chest, M2, with a capacity of 200 rounds, is mounted outboard of each gun. The guns are normally fired electrically by solenoids, but may be fired by a hand-firing mechanism on each gun in the event of power failure.

A variable speed drive unit beneath the mount turntable drives the mount in elevation and azimuth at speeds from 0° to 60° per second. The variable speed drive obtains its power from two heavy-duty 6-volt storage batteries in the rear of the mount. These batteries are charged by a 300-watt, 12-volt, gasoline motor-driven charger located beside the batteries.

PRINCIPAL CHARACTERISTICS OF MOUNT, M45

Weight, without armor, guns, ammunition chests, fuel, and operator	1,468 lb.
Weight, fully equipped, including gunner (approx.)	2,396 lb.
Weight of armor	132 lb.
Overall width	79½ ins.
Overall height (guns level)	4 ft., 7 ins.
Power drive	Maxson Var. Speed Drive, Model 120A with 1-hp., 12-volt, 90-amp. electric motor
Weight of power drive	139 lb.
Power charger	Briggs & Stratton, Model 304, type 25592, driven by a 1-cylinder, 4-cycle gasoline motor
Charger output	300 watts, 15 volts
Weight of power charger	75 lb.
Batteries, storage, lead, acid, 3-cell, 17 plates per cell (6 volts each)	2
Armament, Cal. .50, HB, M2, Fixed Browning Machine Guns, mounted outboard on right and left trunnions	4
Ammunition	Cal. .50, 800 rounds (200 rounds each in Cal. .50 Ammunition Chests, M2, mounted outboard on guns)
Azimuth speed	0° to 60° per sec.
Elevation speed	0° to 60° per sec.

A removable shield of armor plate, with hinged doors on the top, fits between the trunnion to provide protection for the gunner and the driving mechanisms.

The Trailer Mount, M17, is a short coupled, 4-wheel type vehicle. It is a modification of the General Trailer, M7, used to transport Generating Unit, M7, in Antiaircraft Gun Battalions. Jacks at each corner of the trailer allow it to be emplaced firmly for firing.

REFERENCES—OCM 17969; OCM 18020; OCM 18845; OCM 18964; OCM 19140; TM 9–222.

MULTIPLE CALIBER .50 MACHINE-GUN TRAILER MOUNT, M55, IN TRAVELING POSITION ATTACHED TO ¼-TON 4 X 4 TRUCK

The Multiple Caliber .50 Machine-Gun Trailer Mount, M55, was designed as an antiaircraft ground mount to be transported by airplane. It consists of the Multiple Caliber .50 Machine-Gun Mount, M45C, mounted on the Trailer Mount, M20.

The Multiple Caliber .50 Machine-Gun Mount, M45C, is identical with the Multiple Caliber .50 Machine-Gun Mount, M45, used with the Multiple Caliber .50 Machine-Gun Carriage, M51, except for a special armor shield protecting the mechanism and the gunner.

Armament consists of 4 Browning Caliber .50 Machine Guns, HB, M2, with a rate of fire of 450 to 575 rounds per minute for each gun. Two guns with their ammunition chests are mounted outboard of each trunnion. The gunner sits between the trunnions, from which position he controls the movement of the mount and the firing of the guns through the medium of a handlebar control.

Elevation is from −9° to +90°. A continuous traverse of 360° is possible for the power-operated turret. Power for the elevating and traversing mechanisms is supplied by two truck type 6-volt storage batteries connected in series to furnish 12 volts to the constant speed drive motor. Two differentials, each driven by two Reeves split pulley variable speed drives, permit variation in speed of the elevation and traverse gears. Deflection of the handlebar control governs the speed of the pulleys. Movement of the output shaft of the differential is in proportion to the amount of speed change of the pulleys. Rates of tracking in both elevation and traverse are from a minimum of ¼° per second to a maximum of 60° per second.

The Trailer Mount, M20, is a portable two-wheeled mount that may be moved for short distances by hand or by a prime mover. It is capable of stowage in a CG–4A Glider or a C47 Transport Airplane. The removable pneumatic-tired wheels are equipped with hydraulic brakes. Mechanical jacks allow the mount to be emplaced and leveled in firing position when the wheels are removed. A steel pole extends from the front of the mount and ends in a lunette for attachment to the pintle of a prime mover. Tow ropes are supplied for aid in manual manipulation of the mount.

REFERENCES—OCM 22521; OCM 22117; OCM 21716; OCM 20241; OCM 20025.

PRINCIPAL CHARACTERISTICS

Weight of gun .... 191lbs.
Weight of gun and carriage .... 950 pounds (travel order)
.... 912 pounds (firing order)
Length of gun .... 82.5 ins.
Rifling:
    Grooves 12
    Twist .... Uniform right-hand, one turn in 25 calibers
Type of breech mechanism .... Vertical sliding wedge, manual
Type of recoil mechanism .... Hydro-spring, constant length
Recoil length .... 20 inches
Maximum elevation .... +15 degrees
Maximum depression .... −10 degrees
Traverse .... 60 degrees (30R to 30L)
Weight of APC shot .... 1.92 pounds
Weight of propelling charge .... 0.53 pound FNH
Weight of complete round .... 3.36 pounds
Muzzle velocity .... 2900 feet per second
Maximum range .... 12,800 yards (HE); 7500 yards (APC)
Armor penetration .... 2.4 inches at 500 yards range
Rate of fire .... 15/20 rounds per minute

RECONSTRUCTED PAGE 1 June 1944

The 37mm Gun M3 is a highly mobile light anti-tank weapon. Development began in 1937, authorized by OCM 13348 of 14 January 1937, and resulted in the 37mm Gun T10 which was standardized as the 37mm Gun M3 in October 1938. Production at Watervliet Arsenal began in November 1938 and the first guns were delivered early in 1940. In June 1940 large production orders were given, and by the spring of 1941 production had reached 150 guns per month. Production was terminated in the summer of 1943, all necessary stocks having been provided and the 57mm Gun M1 having been standardized as a replacement. The Gun M3 is now Limited Standard.

THE 37MM GUN M3A1 is the Gun M3 with the muzzle threaded to accept a five-port Solothurn-type muzzle brake. Combat experience indicated that this brake was not necessary and they have been removed from service, but all M3A1 guns retain the threaded muzzle.

The gun is a monobloc, auto-frettaged tube carrying a vertical sliding wedge breech block, manually operated. A pull-type percussion firing mechanism is fitted into the breech block.

37 MM GUN M3A1 ON CARRIAGE M4A1— STANDARD

THE CARRIAGE M4 is a split trail carriage with shield, and with a shoulder guard which protects the gunner from the recoiling parts. It uses a hydro-spring recoil mechanism giving a constant-length recoil stroke at all angles of elevation. The M4 carriage was declared Limited Standard in January 1944.

THE CARRIAGE M4A1 is the M4 carriage with modifications to the traversing mechanism to permit the traversing handwheel gear to be thrown out of engagement so as to allow the gunner to make a quick traverse switch between targets by pushing or pulling on the shoulder guard to move the upper carriage. The traversing gear can then be reconnected to permit fine adjustment on to the target. The Carriage M4A1 was authorized as Standard in January 1944.

Ammunition

The 37mm Gun M3A1 fires fixed rounds of ammunition using AP, APC, HE and Canister projectiles. The AP Shot M74 is a solid steel shot carrying a tracer in the base. It weighs 1.92 pounds and can penetrate 1.42 inches of armor plate at 500 yards range. The HE Shell M63 is a pointed steel shell fitted with Fuze B D M58 and filled with 1.36 ounces of flaked TNT. The APC Shot M51B1 or M51B2 weighs 1.92 pounds and is a pointed steel shot with piercing and ballistic caps. It carries a base tracer and can penetrate 2.40 inches of armor at 500 yards range. The Canister Shot M2 is a terne-plate cylinder containing 122 3/8 inch steel balls packed in resin. When fired, the casing breaks and the balls are ejected from the gun in the manner of a shotgun charge, to a maximum effective range of about 250 yards.

REFERENCES—OCM 13348; FM 23-70; SNL A-44

138

The 57mm Gun M1 was developed in response to a demand for a light anti-tank gun of greater power than the 37mm Gun M1. The design originated in Britain where it is known as the '6-Pounder' anti-tank gun. Drawings of the 6-Pounder Mark 2 gun were received in the U.S.A. in early 1941 and were converted to U.S. standard dimensions, tolerances and threads by authority of OCM 16489 of 20 February 1941. A test model Gun T2 on Carriage T1 was tested and standardized as the Gun M1 on Carriage M1 by OCM 16722 of 15 May 1941. The only major difference between the British and American guns is that the American gun is 16 inches longer and has a muzzle velocity about 100 feet per second greater.

THE 57 MM GUN M1 is a monobloc auto-frettaged tube with a semi-automatic vertical sliding wedge breech-block. The block is opened manually and is held open against a spring by the extractors. On loading a fixed round the rim of the cartridge forces the extractors forward and the breech-block is free to close automatically under the spring action. On recoil and run-out the breech-block is opened by a cam on the cradle and the empty cartridge case is ejected. The gun returns to battery with the breech open ready for reloading. The firing mechanism is automatically cocked during the opening movement of the breech-block.

THE CARRIAGE M1 is the British carriage with changes in dimensions, clearances and threads to facilitate manufacture by U.S. standard methods. It is a two-wheel, split-trail type with curved shield, using handwheel traversing and elevating gears, and is fitted with commercially available wheels and tires. The Carriage M1 is classified as Limited Standard.

THE CARRIAGE M1A1 is the M1 carriage but with combat wheels and tires. It is classified Limited Standard

THE CARRIAGE M1A2 has the traversing handwheel and gear mechanism removed and can be freely traversed around its pintle by the gunner pulling and pushing on his shoulder-piece. The Carriage M1A2 is classified as Substitute Standard.

THE CARRIAGE M1A3 has a modified lunette and trail lock so as to reduce the turning circle when being towed. The Carriage M1A3 is classified Standard.

CHARACTERISTICS

Weight of gun	755lbs.
Weight of gun and carriage	2810lbs.
Length of gun	117ins.
Length of Bore	112.2ins.
Diameter of bore	57mm (2.244ins.)
Rifling:	
grooves	24
twist	Uniform, right-hand, one turn in 30 calibers
Chamber volume	100 cubic inches
Type of breech mechanism	Vertical sliding block, semi-automatic
Type of recoil mechanism	Hydro-spring, constant length
Length of recoil	29.75 inches
Maximum elevation	+15°
Maximum depression	−5°
Traverse	90 degrees (45R to 45L)
Weight of APC shell	7.30lbs.
Weight of powder charge	2.25 pounds FNH
Weight of complete round	12.56 pounds
Maximum range	10,620 yards
Muzzle velocity	2800 feet per second
Chamber pressure	41,200 pounds per square inch
Armor penetration	3.11 inches at 1000 yards
Rate of fire	12/15 rounds per minute

Ammunition
The 57mm Gun M1 fires fixed ammunition. The APC projectile M86 is a pointed, capped shell filled with 1.2 ounces of Explosive D and with Fuze BD M72. It can penetrate 2.87 inches of homogenous armor or 3.1 inches of face-hardened armor at 1000 yards range.

REFERENCES—OCM 16489; OCM 16722; TM 9-303; SNL C-36; OS 9-20

RECONSTRUCTED PAGE 1 November 1944

3 INCH GUN M5 ON CARRIAGE M1, M1A1 OR M6 — STANDARD

CHARACTERISTICS

Weight of gun . . . . 2300lbs.

Weight of gun and carriage . . . . 4875lbs.

Length of gun . . . . 158.4ins.

Length of bore . . . . 150ins.

Rifling;

    grooves 28

    twist . . . . Uniform right-hand, 1 turn in 25 calibers

Type of breech mechanism . . . . Horizontal sliding wedge, hand operated

Type of recoil mechanism . . . . Hydro-pneumatic, constant length

Length of recoil . . . . 42ins.

Maximum elevation . . . . + 30°

Maximum depression . . . . − 5°

Traverse . . . . 45 degrees (22½ R to 22½ L)

Weight of APC shell . . . . 15.44lbs.

Weight of complete round . . . . 27.24lbs.

Weight of powder charge . . . . 4.62lbs. FNH

Muzzle velocity . . . . 2800 feet per second

Maximum range . . . . 15,400 yards

Armor penetration . . . . 3.93 inches at 1000 yards

The 3 inch Gun M5 is a heavy anti-tank gun. Development of this weapon began in September 1940 with a demand for a gun capable of stopping any tank then known. In order to speed development it was decided to adapt various items in current supply or manufacture, and it was recommended that the barrel of the 3 inch AA gun M3 be fitted to the breech of the 105mm Howitzer M1 and that the 105mm Howitzer Carriage M2 be adapted to take the gun assembly. The resulting weapon was standardized as the 3 inch Gun M5 in December 1941. Production was then held in abeyance because of Tank Destroyer Command expressing a preference for a self-propelled equipment, but this design failed approval and the 3 inch Gun M5 was then put into production late in 1942.

THE 3 INCH GUN M5 is a built-up gun using a loose liner. The breech mechanism is a horizontal sliding block, hand operated, with a self-cocking percussion mechanism in the block; it is the same mechanism as used on the 105mm Howitzer M1.

3 INCH GUN M5 ON CARRIAGE M1, M1A OR M6 — STANDARD

THE CARRIAGE M1 is the standard 105mm Howitzer Carriage M2 with slight modification to the cradle to accept the 3 inch gun tube. It is a split trail, two-wheel carriage with a vertical shield. The Carriage M1 is classified Limited Standard.

THE CARRIAGE M1A1 is the M1 carriage with the shield modified to the requirements of the Tank Destroyer Board. It is now sloped backwards, and axle stops and firing segments are fitted. The Carriage M1A1 is classified as Standard.

THE CARRIAGE M2 is exactly the same pattern as the Carriage M1A1 but is of new manufacture instead of being a modified M1 carriage. The Carriage M2 is classified Standard.

Ammunition

The 3 inch Gun M5 fires a fixed round of ammunition. The HE shell M42A1 weighs 12.87 pounds and is fitted with the Fuze PD M48A1. The AP Shot M79 is a solid steel shot with base tracer, weighing 15 pounds. It will penetrate 3.93 inches of homogenous steel armor at 1000 yards range. The APC Projectile M62A1 is a pointed shell with piercing and ballistic caps, filled with 2.3 ounces of Explosive D and with a Fuze BD M66A1.

REFERENCES—TM 9-322; SNL C-40

75 mm PACK HOWITZER, M1A1, ON CARRIAGE, M1

The 75 mm pack howitzer was originally designed for pack transport, animal draft, and low-speed towing. Animal draft has been discontinued and the special accessories made obsolete. In modified form it has been adopted for many uses.

Development of the weapon, begun in 1920, culminated in standardization of the M1 in 1927. Slight changes in the M1 were made later, and the new model given the designation of M1A1. The primary use of this howitzer was for operation in mountainous terrain. With the round H.E., A.T., M66, the M1A1 howitzer is capable of engaging antitank targets, as the projectile will penetrate 3 inches of armor plate at howitzer range.

HOWITZER, M1—The Howitzer, M1, consists of a tube assembly and a breech mechanism, joined by interrupted threads for rapid assembly and disassembly. The breechblock is of the hand-operated, sliding-wedge type. Firing is accomplished by a continuous-pull mechanism known as Firing Lock, M13. The tube and breech mechanism comprise two loads for transport.

HOWITZER, M1A1—This howitzer differs from the M1 only in slight modifications of the breech ring and the breechblock. These parts are not interchangeable in the two models.

PACK HOWITZER CARRIAGE, M1—This carriage is separated into six loads

PRINCIPAL CHARACTERISTICS OF 75 mm PACK HOWITZER, M1A1, AND CARRIAGE, M1

HOWITZER

Caliber	75 mm
Weight	341 lb.
Overall length	52 ins.
Length of bore	15.93 cals.
Muzzle velocity	700, 810, 950, 1,250 f./s.
Volume of chamber	57.3 cu. ins.
Travel of projectile in bore	39.2894 ins.
Maximum powder pressure	26,000 lb./sq. in.
Type of block mechanism	Sliding block
Rate of fire	6 rds./min.
Range, Shell, M41A1	9,760 yds.

RECOIL MECHANISM

Type	Hydropneumatic
Weight	211 lb.

Normal recoil	32 ins.
Maximum recoil	33.65 ins.
Maximum piston-rod pull	5,188 lb.

CARRIAGE, M1

Total weight without howitzer	927 lb.
Length of carriage (muzzle to spade)	144 ins.
Width over hub caps	47 ins.
Maximum height at 0°	35 ins.
Type box trail	Axle traverse
Elevation (maximum)	45°
Depression (maximum)	−5°
Traverse (right)	3°
Traverse (left)	3°
Total weight of howitzer, recoil mechanism, and carriage in firing position	1,269 lb.

AMMUNITION

	M41A1	M48	H.E., A.T., M66
Weight of complete rounds	17.32 lb.	18.12 lb.	16.3 lb.
Weight of projectile	13.76 lb.	14.60 lb.	13.27 lb.
Weight of projectile explosive charge	1.11 lb.	1.47 lb.	1 lb.
Weight of propelling charge		.92 lb.	.41 lb.
Type of ammunition			semi-fixed

for pack transport. It has a hydropneumatic recoil system composed of a recoil cylinder and a recuperator cylinder connected with the bottom sleigh which forms a seat for the howitzer and maintains alinement of the tube and breech ring when assembled. A top sleigh covers the howitzer and retains it in the bottom

sleigh. Steps on the bottom sleigh are fitted to ways on the cradle, and the recoil-cylinder piston rod is connected to the cradle by means of the piston rod latch. In recoil and counterrecoil, the cylinders and bottom sleigh move with the howitzer, while the cradle remains stationary.

Traverse is along the axle, accomplished by a traversing nut operated by a handwheel.

Rockers, which pivot on trunnion pins, are located on either side of the cradle.

The box trail is divided into two groups, the front trail and the rear trail, fastened together by fittings strong enough to withstand firing stress. The elevating mechanism, rockers, and equilibrators are assembled to the front trail and are carried with it in the pack. The wheels are of wood with steel tires.

AMMUNITION—Ammunition for the 75 mm Pack Howitzer, M1A1, is in the form of semi-fixed rounds. It consists of H.E. Shell, M41A1, with P.D. Fuze, M48; H.E. Shell, M48, with P.D. Fuze, M48, and T. & S.Q. Fuze, M54; and H.E., A.T. Shell, M66, with B.D. Fuze, M62.

Sighting and Fire Control Equipment

On Carriage Equipment
Panoramic Telescope, M1
Telescope Mount, M3

Off Carriage Equipment
Bore Sight
Gunner's Quadrant, M1
Aiming Circle, M1
Compass, M2
1-Meter-Base Range Finder, M7 or M1916
B.C. Telescope, M65 or M1915A1

Trainer

The 37 mm Subcaliber Gun, M1916, and Subcaliber Mount, M5, are used for practice in laying and firing the 75 mm Pack Howitzers, M1 and M1A1.

REFERENCES—TM 9-2005, v.3; TM 9-320; TM 9-1320.

CARRIAGE (AIRBORNE), M8—The 75 mm Pack Howitzer Carriage, M8, was developed to provide airborne troops with a light, powerful weapon which could be transported as a unit to the combat area by glider or airplane. When the airplane lands at its destination the howitzer and carriage can be unloaded and maneuvered into position by hand or be towed by a prime mover. The howitzer and carriage can also be disassembled, packed in paracrate loads, and dropped by parachutes from an airplane in flight. When the paracrates reach the ground the individual loads are unpacked and the howitzer and carriage are assembled for action.

The standard 75 mm Pack Howitzer, M1A1, is mounted on the Carriage, M8. This carriage is identical to the 75 mm Pack Howitzer Carriage, M1, except for the substitution of steel disk and rim type wheels equipped with 6.00 x 16 pneumatic tires in place of the 29 inch wooden wheels used on the M1 carriage.

REFERENCES—OCM 20196; TM 9-319.

Sighting and Fire Control Equipment

On Carriage Equipment
Telescope Mount, M3
Telescope Adapter, M9
Elbow Telescope, M62

Off Carriage Equipment
Gunner's Quadrant, M1
Aiming Circle, M1
Hand Fuze Setter, M1912A4, M15, or M16

75 mm PACK HOWITZER, M8, FOR AIRBORNE USE

PARACRATES M1, M2, M3, M4, M5, M6, M7, PARA-CHEST M8, PARA-CAISSON M9

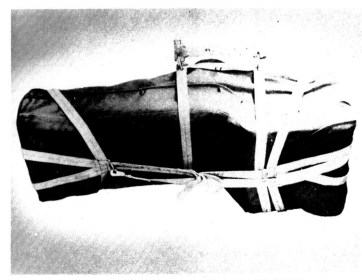

PARACRATE, M1 (FRONT TRAIL), CRATE SUSPENDED

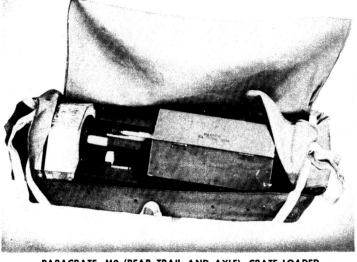

PARACRATE, M2 (REAR TRAIL AND AXLE), CRATE LOADED

In order that the disassembled 75 mm Pack Howitzer, M1A1, and Carriage, M8, together with fire control instruments, and accessories, could be safely delivered by parachute from an airplane in flight, a series of containers known as paracrates, parachest, and paracaisson, were evolved to hold the nine loads to be dropped. Fabrication of these containers was begun in September, 1942, and they were standardized in May, 1943, as Paracrates, M1 to M7, Parachest, M8, and Paracaisson, M9.

Paracrates, M1 to M7, are constructed of plywood, each paracrate being designed to accommodate a specific load. When the load is packed it is secured to

bomb shackle and parachute harnesses by means of a quick-release fastening. A standard 24-foot cargo parachute is attached to each load, the parachutes being colored to differentiate between the loads and hasten identification.

Paracrate Loads, M1 to M5, together with Paracrate Load, M9, are fastened to and dropped from parachute pack racks beneath the airplane. Paracrate Loads, M6 and M8, are carried as a daisy-chain load inside the fuselage, from which they are pushed out through the doorway of the airplane.

PARACRATE, M1—This paracrate consists of front and rear reinforces and a wooden brace for the howitzer front trail

assembly, together with a canvas paracrate cover with parachute harness attached. When packed it holds the front trail and a lifting bar.

PARACRATE, M2—Paracrate, M2, includes a canvas cover with parachute harness attached, wooden supports, and a wooden hexagonal reinforcing housing. The load comprises the howitzer rear trail, axle and traversing mechanism assembly, trail handspike, sponge staff, aiming post sleeves, and a box containing spare parts and tools.

PARACRATE, M3—This paracrate is in the form of a plywood box with pentagonal ends and a hinged cover. The load

PARACRATE, M4 (CRADLE AND TOP SLEIGH), CRATE LOADED

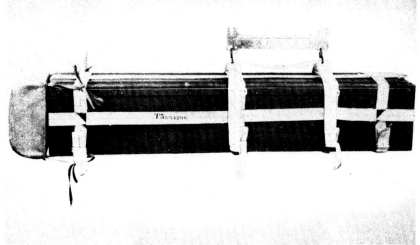

PARACRATE, M5 (TUBE), CRATE SUSPENDED

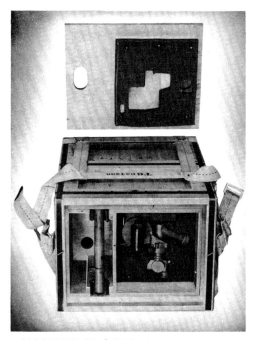

PARACRATE, M6 (BREECHBLOCK AND SIGHT), CRATE LOADED

PARACRATE, M7 (WHEELS), CRATE SUSPENDED

consists of the howitzer bottom sleigh and recoil mechanism, a lifting bar, an aiming circle with case, circular wooden supports, a shock block, and a shock pad.

PARACRATE, M4—Paracrate, M4, is similar in shape to Paracrate, M3. The load is made up of the top cradle and sleigh of the howitzer, a shock block, and a shock pad. Paracrates, M3 through M6, have the bomb shackle and parachute harnesses separated from the paracrates.

PARACRATE, M5—This paracrate is a rectangular plywood box with a hinged lid. Its load is composed of the howitzer tube, a muzzle cover, a tube thread cover, a lifting bar, lifting straps, a shock block, and a shock pad.

PARACRATE, M6—Paracrate, M6, is a rectangular plywood box with a detachable padded lid. The load consists of the howitzer breech mechanism, the hub caps, the panoramic telescope and telescope mount in a special container, the telescope mount support, and a lifting strap.

PARACRATE, M7—Paracrate, M7, consists of a square wooden frame, the inner sides of which are beveled. The parachute harness is attached to the frame. The load is composed of the howitzer wheels and hub plugs.

PARACHEST, M8—This parachest is made of plywood, and consists of a large section to which a slightly smaller section is added as a continuation. The cross section of each portion is six-sided, in the form of a square on which is imposed a truncated triangle. The front end of the large section is hinged, so that it can be opened for loading. The parachute harness is separate and when assembled on the parachest has skids lashed to it to facilitate landing. The load is composed of ten complete rounds of 75 mm howitzer ammunition, each of which is packed in a fiber container.

PARACAISSON, M9—Paracaisson, M9, is a manually drawn, knockdown cart with a plywood body of hexagonal cross section, demountable steel wheels, and an axle assembly, drawbar, tongue,

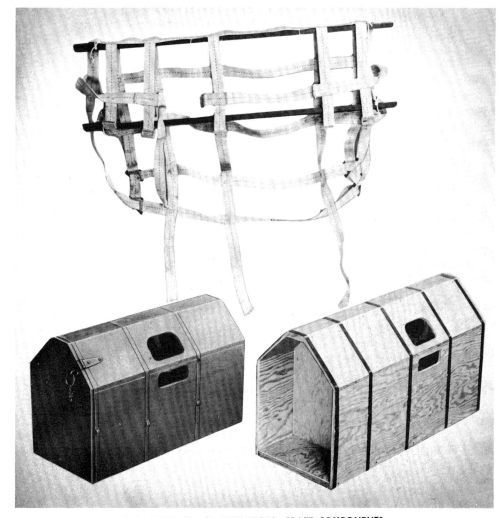

PARACHEST, M8, (AMMUNITION), CRATE COMPONENTS

PARACAISSON, M9 (AMMUNITION CART), CART ASSEMBLED

and drawlines, all of which can be packed in the body when the paracaisson is disassembled for transport. A wheel spacer, a brace support, a drawbar tray, an axle tray, tray side braces, and tray top braces are utilized in packing the components of the paracaisson. The bomb shackle and parachute harness are separate.

The paracaisson is used to transport ammunition, eight complete rounds in individual fiber containers constituting a full load. When assembled, the paracaisson is normally pulled by two men who grasp the drawbar at the free end of the tongue. When it is necessary for four men to tow the cart two drawlines are attached to the axle by means of drawline hooks which hook through holes in the axle.

The howitzer, caisson and cart, with ammunition, are packed in nine paracrate loads having a total weight of 2,571 pounds. The component parts of these loads and the equipment required for assembling them are as follows:

Paracrate Load, M1

Front trail	236 lb.
Paracrate, M1, including cover, front reinforce, rear reinforce and wooden brace	58 lb.
Lifting bar	9 lb.
Parachute	23 lb.
Total weight	326 lb.

Paracrate Load, M2

Rear trail	95 lb.
Axle	65 lb.
Trail handspike	7 lb.
Sponge staff	6 lb.
Spare parts and tool box	40 lb.
Paracrate, M2, including cover, wooden supports, and wooden hexagonal housing	38 lb.
Parachute	23 lb.
Total weight	274 lb.

Paracrate Load, M3

Bottom sleigh and recoil mechanism	203 lb.
Aiming circle with case	18 lb.
Paracrate, T3	73 lb.
Lifting bar	9 lb.
Parachute	23 lb.
Total weight	326 lb.

Paracrate Load, M4

Cradle	100 lb.
Top sleigh	121 lb.
Paracrate, M4	87 lb.
Parachute	23 lb.
Total weight	331 lb.

Paracrate Load, M5

Tube	221 lb.
Paracrate, M5	49 lb.
Lifting bar	9 lb.
Parachute	23 lb.
Total weight	302 lb.

Paracrate Load, M6

Breech assembly	121 lb.
Paracrate, M6	13 lb.
Telescope panoramic w/mount	45 lb.
Parachute	23 lb.
Total weight	202 lb.

Paracrate Load, M7

Wheels (two)	180 lb.
Paracrate, M7	14 lb.
Parachute	23 lb.
Total weight	217 lb.

Paracrate Load, M8

Ammunition, 10 rounds in indiv. fiber cont.	220 lb.
Parachest, M8	47 lb.
Parachute	23 lb.
Total Weight	290 lb.

Paracrate Load, M9

Paracrate cart	105 lb.
Ammunition, 8 rounds in indiv. fiber cont.	176 lb.
Parachute	23 lb.
Total weight	304 lb.

LEFT FRONT VIEW OF 75 mm FIELD HOWITZER, M1A1, ON CARRIAGE, M3A3, SHOWING SHIELD AND COMBAT TIRES

PRINCIPAL CHARACTERISTICS OF 75 mm FIELD HOWITZER, M1A1, AND CARRIAGE, M3A3

HOWITZER, M1A1

Caliber	75 mm
Weight	341 lb.
Overall length	52 ins.
Length of bore	15.93 cals.
Muzzle velocity	700, 810, 950, 1,250 f./s.
Volume of chamber	57.3 cu. ins.
Travel of projectile in bore	39.2894 ins.
Maximum powder pressure	26,000 lb./sq. in.
Type of block mechanism	Sliding block
Rate of fire	6 rds./min.
Range, M41A1 Shell	9,760 yds.

RECOIL MECHANISM

Type	Hydropneumatic
Weight	211 lb.

Normal recoil	32 ins.
Maximum recoil	33.65 ins.
Maximum piston-rod pull	5,188 lb.

CARRIAGE, M3A3

Total weight without howitzer	1,818 lb.
Length of carriage (muzzle to spade)	152.5 ins.
Width over hub caps	68 ins.

Maximum height at 0°	38 ins.
Type of trail	Split trail
Elevation (maximum)	50°
Depression (maximum)	−9°
Traverse (right)	22½°
Traverse (left)	22½°
Total weight of howitzer, recoil mechanism and carriage in firing position	2,160 lb.

AMMUNITION	M41A1	M48	H.E., A.T., M66
Weight of complete rounds	17.32 lb.	18.12 lb.	16.3 lb.
Weight of projectile	13.76 lb.	14.60 lb.	13.27 lb.
Weight of projectile explosive charge	1.11 lb.	1.47 lb.	1 lb.
Weight of propelling charge		.92 lb.	.41 lb.
Type of ammunition			Semi-fixed

The 75 mm field howitzer is a light artillery piece used by horse artillery and is similar to the 75 mm pack howitzer except for the carriage. With the shell, H.E., A.T., M66, it can be employed as an antitank weapon at normal battle ranges.

CARRIAGE, M3A1—Designed for towing at high speed, this carriage is a redesign of the Pack Howitzer Carriage, M1. The M1 recoil mechanism, top and bottom sleighs are utilized. A split trail and pneumatic-tired wheels mounted on spindles which can be rotated, permit the carriage to rest on a firing base and the trails. This three-point suspension gives great stability during firing. Internal-expanding brakes are used on this carriage. The M3A1 carriage is now classified as Limited Standard.

CARRIAGE, M3A2—Addition of shields to Carriage, M3A1, in accordance with O.C.M. 17990 changes the model designation of the carriage to M3A2. It is now classified as Standard.

CARRIAGE, M3A3—When Carriages, M3A1 or M3A2, are equipped with combat tires and wheels with divided rims, the designation of either carriage becomes M3A3 (O.C.M. 18154). This carriage is classified as Standard.

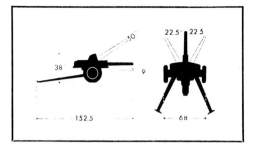

Sighting and Fire Control Equipment

On Carriage Equipment

Panoramic Telescope, M1
Telescope Mount, M16
Range Quadrant, M3
Elbow Telescope, M5

Off Carriage Equipment

Bore Sight
Gunner's Quadrant, M1
Aiming Circle, M1
Compass, M2
1-Meter-Base Range Finder, M7 or M1916
B. C. Telescope, M65 or M1915A1
Bracket Fuze Setter, M1916A2
Hand Fuze Setter, M15 or M16

Ammunition

Ammunition for the 75 mm Field Howitzer, M1, is in the form of semi-fixed rounds. It consists of H.E. Shell, M41A1, with P.D. Fuze, M48, and T.-S.Q. Fuze, M54; H.E. Shell, M41, with P.D. Fuze, M48; H.E. Shell, M48, with P.D. Fuze, M48, and T.-S.Q. Fuze, M54.

Trainer

The 37 mm Gun, M1916, with Mount M5, is used for training in laying and firing the 75 mm Howitzer, M1A1. The 37 mm Gun, M1916, and its recoil mechanism are fastened to the 37 mm Subcaliber Mount, M5, which is in turn fastened to the bottom sleigh after removal of the top sleigh for training purposes.

Light Limber, M2

This is a two-wheeled vehicle to which the trail of the howitzer carriage is connected to form a four-wheeled unit when traveling. It is equipped with pneumatic-tired disk and rim type wheels for high-speed transport. The limber chest has a capacity of 22 rounds of ammunition. The weight of the limber is 770 pounds when empty and 1,245 pounds with full ammunition load. Classification of this limber is Limited Standard. The model M4 is Standard.

Light Caisson, M1

Designed primarily to carry ammunition, this is a two-wheeled vehicle equipped with pneumatic tires and standard automobile internal-expanding brakes. It weighs 860 pounds when empty and 1,965 pounds with 52 rounds of ammunition in the caisson chest. It is now classified as Substitute Standard. The model M2 is Standard.

REFERENCES—TM 9-2005, v.3; TM 9-320; TM 9-1320; FM 6-110; FM 6-70.

LIGHT LIMBER, M4, AND LIGHT CAISSON, M2, WITH EXPERIMENTAL COUPLER, FOR 75 mm HOWITZER TRANSPORT

75 mm GUN, M1897A2, ON CARRIAGE, M2A3, IN FIRING POSITION

These weapons are modernizations of the 75 mm Gun, M1897. The M1897A2 is standard for the manufacture of the complete gun, while the M1897A4 is standard for conversion of existing M1897 guns (O.C.M. 14510).

In 1917 the A.E.F. in France and certain regiments in the United States were equipped with the French 75 mm M1897 gun as the standard for light field artillery matériel. The performance of this gun in battle was such that it was considered the most effective light field gun used in World War I. A considerable number of these guns were purchased from France, while similar guns were manufactured in the United States. The parts of the American and French manufactured guns are identical and interchangeable.

As mounted on modernized carriages which may be towed at any speed, the 75 mm gun is today a far more formidable weapon than was its counterpart in the last war. New ammunition, including armor-piercing projectiles, has been developed to give greatly increased range. These guns are now being withdrawn from service to be placed on self-propelled mounts. No further production of these guns has been undertaken.

GUN, M1897—This gun and its variations are of built-up construction with breechblocks of the cylindrical Nordenfeld eccentric screw type threaded on the exterior to fit the breech recess. The breechblock is opened by rotating 120° around its axis and automatically ejects the empty

PRINCIPAL CHARACTERISTICS OF 75 mm GUN, M1897A2, AND CARRIAGE, M2A3

GUN, M1897A2
Caliber. . . . . .75 mm
Weight. . . . . .1,026 lb.
Overall length. . . . . .107.125 ins.
Length of bore. . . . . .34.5 cals.
Muzzle velocity. . . . . .1,778, 1,950, 2,000 f./s.
Volume of chamber (M61, A.P.C.).88.05 cu. ins.
Travel of projectile in bore
  (M61, A.P.C.). . . . . .88.99 ins.
Maximum powder pressure
  (M61, A.P.C.). . . . . .38,000 lb./sq. in.
Type of block mechanism. Nordenfeld screw block
Rate of fire. . . . . .6 rds./min.
Range (M61, A.P.C.). . . . . .13,870 yds.

RECOIL MECHANISM
Type. .Hydropneumatic
Weight. . . . . .237.21 lb.
Normal recoil. . . . . .44.9 ins.
Maximum recoil. . . . . .48 ins.
Maximum piston-rod pull. . . . . .11,250 lb.

CARRIAGE, M2A3
Total weight without gun. . . . . .2,338 lb.
Height of lunette (limbered position). . . . .29 ins.
Length of carriage (muzzle to lunette). .220.5 ins.
Width over hub caps. . . . . .80 ins.
Tread width (c/—c/ of wheels). . . . . .70 ins.
Height in traveling position. . . . . .56 ins.

Trail spread (included angle). . . . . .60°
Elevation (maximum) (on wheels). . . . . . . .45°30'
Depression (maximum) (on wheels). . . . . .—9°14'
Traverse (maximum, right) (on wheels). . . . .30°9'
Traverse (maximum, left) (on wheels). . . . .30°15'
Total weight of gun, mechanism, and
  carriage. . . . . .3,400 lb.

AMMUNITION

	M48, H.E.	M72, A.P.	M61, A.P. C.
Weight of complete round	19.49 lb.	18.80 lb.	19.98 lb.
Weight of projectile	14.60 lb.	13.93 lb.	14.92 lb.
Weight of projectile explosive charge	1.47 lb.		.17 lb.
Weight of propelling charge	1.93 lb.	1.90 lb.	2.16 lb.
Type of ammunition	Fixed	Fixed	Fixed

Armor penetration—homogeneous plate
20° from normal—			
500 yds.		3.2 ins.	2.8 ins.
1,000 yds.		2.7 ins.	2.5 ins.
2,000 yds.		2.1 ins.	2.1 ins.

cartridge case. The normal life of the gun is approximately 10,000 rounds.

GUN, M1897A4—Rollers, sweeper plates with felt pads and part of the jacket are removed from the M1897 gun and replaced by steel rails and bronze strips attached to supports on the gun.

GUN, M1897A2—This gun is identical with the M1897A4 and is standard for new manufacture.

CARRIAGE, M1897—About 2,800 of the French-manufactured M1897 carriages were purchased. They were issued and stored without distinction as to their source. The gun slides on a steel-forged cradle trunnioned on a rocker assembly enabling changes of elevation to be made without disturbing the angle-of-site setting. The rocker is trunnioned on a single trail supported by the axle housing. The hydropneumatic (Puteaux) recoil system assures constant recoil. The carriage has steel-tired wheels and is equipped with a combination road brake and firing support.

CARRIAGE, M1897M1—This is the American manufactured version of Carriage, M1897, differing from the M1897 in the recuperator system which has a respirator assembly instead of a front plug, shields, lunette, wheels, wheel guards, spares and accessories. Parts of this carriage are not interchangeable with those of the M1897.

CARRIAGE, M1897A2—When equipped with a handspike, the M1897 takes the designation M1897A2.

CARRIAGE, M1897M1A2—This is the M1897M1 equipped with a handspike.

CARRIAGE, M1897A4—Fitting high-speed adapters to the M1897, M1897A2, M1897M1 and M1897M1A2 changes the model designation of any of these carriages to M1897A4. The modification consists essentially of a high-speed adapter, the substitution of pneumatic tires on disk and rim wheels in place of steel- or rubber-tired wheels and the replacement of the former brake system by one using internal-expanding brakes.

All modifications of the M1897 carriage through M1897A4 possessed the inherent disadvantages of limited elevation and traverse, with a maximum normal gun range of only 6,930 yards. By burying the trail, it was possible to obtain a range of 9,200 yards. It was, therefore, considered essential to design a new carriage to mount the M1897 gun which would overcome these handicaps. This was done in 1934,

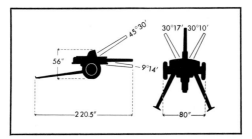

when the first of a new M2 series was originated.

CARRIAGES, M2A1 AND M2A2—A distinguishing feature of these carriages is the split trail which permits an elevation of +45°, resulting in approximately 39% greater range than that obtained in earlier models with a solid trail. For high-speed transport, the carriages are equipped with pneumatic-tired disk and rim wheels with internal-expanding brakes. Equilibrators neutralize unbalanced weight in the gun and recoil system. Traverse is increased to 85°. In firing position with the trails spread, an adjustable jack may be used to support the carriage weight, thus forming a three-point support consisting of the jack and spades. On level ground the gun may be fired safely from the wheels with the trails in either of the spread positions.

CARRIAGE, M2A3—The carriage is a modification of the Carriage, M2. It is of the split trail type, equipped with a drawbar for use with a motorized unit. The lower part of the top carriage is modified to provide clearance for the pivoted axle. The trails and spades are 19 inches shorter than those of the M2. The firing jack is replaced by segments, and the carriage has a pivoted axle which automatically adjusts itself to permit laying the piece with the wheels at an angle of up to 10° to the horizontal. The Recoil Mechanism,

M2, combines the cradle, recoil and recuperator cylinders which check movement in recoil and counter recoil gradually to prevent displacement of the carriage.

Sighting and Fire Control Equipment for Carriage, M2A3

On Carriage Equipment
Panoramic Telescope, M12A1, on Telescope Mount, M22
Elbow Telescope, M14, on Telescope Mount, M23
Range Quadrant, M5

Off Carriage Equipment
Aiming Post, M1
Gunner's Quadrant, M1
Bore sight
Aiming Circle, M1
Compass, M2
1-Meter-Base Range Finder, M7 or M1916
B. C. Telescope, M65 or M1915A1

Ammunition

Ammunition for the 75 mm Guns, M1897A2 and M1897A4, is in the form of fixed rounds. It consists of H.E. Shell, Mk. I, with P.D. Fuzes, M46 and M47; H.E. Shell, M48, with P.D. Fuze, M48, and T.-S.Q. Fuze, M54; chemical Shell, Mk. II, with P.D. Fuze, M46; Shrapnel, Mk. I, with 21-second Combination Fuze, '07M; A.P. Shot, M21, and semi-A.P. Shot, M72.

Trainer

For training purposes only, the 37 mm Subcaliber Gun, M1916, is used to provide practice in laying and firing the 75 mm matériel. The 37 mm Subcaliber Mount, M2, is used on 75 mm Gun Carriage, M1897, only. The 37 mm Subcaliber Mount, M8, is used on Carriages, M1897M1A2 and M1897A4. The 37 mm Subcaliber Mount, M7, is used on 75 mm Gun Carriages, M2, M2A1, M2A2 and M2A3.

REFERENCES—TM 9–2005, v.3; TM 9–1305.

Comparison of Gun Carriages

	M1897	M1897M1A2	M1897A4	M2A1	M2A2	M2A3
Weight of gun and carriage complete (in pounds)	2,657	2,657	3,007	3,675	3,675	3,400
Length of recoil (in inches)	44.9	44.9	44.9	41.5-46	41.5-46	44.9
Height of axis from ground (in inches)	40.4	40.4	44.4	47	47	47
Maximum elevation	19°	19°	19°	46°	46°	49°30'
Maximum depression	10°	10°	10°	10°	10°	9°15'
Maximum traverse, right	3°	3°	3°	45°	45°	30°9'
Maximum traverse, left	3°	3°	3°	40°	40°	30°15'
Muzzle velocity (f./s.)	1,955	1,955	1,955	1,955	1,955	1,778 1,950 2,000
Maximum range (in yards)	9,200	9,200	9,200	12,780	12,780	13,950

ARTILLERY REEL M1909M1—STANDARD
BATTERY REEL M1917A2—STANDARD

ARTILLERY REEL, M1909M1

BATTERY REEL, M1917A2

ARTILLERY REEL, 1909M1— STANDARD

Headquarters units of certain horse-drawn light field artillery organizations use the Artillery Reel, M1909M1, instead of the Battery Reel, M1917A2, for laying wire. The artillery reel consists of a frame, tool chest, drums, drum clutch, drum driving mechanism, drum brake, seat, wheels, drawbar or pole, doubletree, singletree and neck yoke. The two drums, mounted between the wheels, carry 4 miles of 11-strand insulated wire. They are driven from the wheel axle sprocket to the jackshaft sprocket and from the jackshaft sprocket to the drum sprocket, a chain drive being employed in each instance. The right drum is rotated from the drum sprocket through the clutch to the drum. It may be revolved singly or both drums may be revolved simultaneously by engaging the left drum to the right drum by means of a second clutch. A drum latch lever operates a latch for locking the right drum. Attached to the drum latch lever is a leather-faced brake shoe which comes against the flanged rim of the right drum end plate to act as a brake. A brake shoe which engages the left drum end plate is controlled by the foot lever near the operator's seat.

REFERENCE—TM 9–305.

BATTERY REEL, M1917A2— STANDARD

The Battery Reel, M1917A2, is used in 75 mm gun batteries of horse-drawn artillery to carry, lay and recover insulated wire for communication by field telephone or buzzer. It is also employed to transport certain other communication, fire control and topographical equipment. It consists essentially of a frame, drum, operating gear, front chest, rear chest, seat, wheels, pole, doubletree, singletree and neck yoke.

The drum is 1 foot in diameter and holds 1.7 miles of wire. A driving gear attached to the left wheel operates the drum through the medium of a driving clutch. The driving clutch is engaged and disengaged by a hand lever which simultaneously disengages or engages a brake clutch used for braking the drum when it is desired to stop it from rotating. As the wire pays out it is guided by a guide bar which runs the length of the drum.

REFERENCE—TM 9–305.

105 MM HOWITZER M2 AND M2A1 ON CARRIAGE M2, M2A1 AND M2A2 — STANDARD

CHARACTERISTICS

Weight of gun . . . . .1064lbs.
Weight of gun and carriage
in firing position 4475lbs. (M2A1; 4980lbs. (M2A2)
Length of gun . . . . .101.5ins.
Rifling:
    grooves 34
    twist . . . . Uniform, right-hand 1 turn in 20 calibers
Type of breech mechanism . . . . Horizontal sliding wedge, hand operated
Type of firing mechanism . . . . Percussion, continuous pull
Type of recoil mechanism . . . . Hydro-pneumatic, constant length
Recoil length . . . . 42 inches
Maximum elevation . . . . + 64 degrees 15 minutes
Maximum depression . . . . – 4 degrees 45 minutes
Traverse . . . . 45 degrees (22½ R to 22½ L)
Weight of HE shell . . . . .33lbs.
Weight of powder charge . . . . 3.66 pounds Dualgran FNH
Weight of complete round . . . . .42lbs.
Maximum range . . . . .12,200 yards
Muzzle velocity . . . . .1550 feet per second
Chamber pressure . . . . 28,000 pounds per square inch
Rate of fire . . . . 2–4 rounds per minute

The 105mm Howitzer M2 is the standard field artillery piece, forming the principal component of the divisional artillery and acting in direct support of the infantry. The howitzer is manually operated, single-loaded, air-cooled and uses semi-fixed ammunition. The firing mechanism is a continuous pull (self-cocking) type, actuated by pulling a lanyard. The recoil mechanism is of the hydro-pneumatic variety, using a floating piston to separate the oil from the nitrogen. The carriage is of the two-wheel, split-trail type and is provided with a shield for the protection of the crew. The M2 can deliver high angle plunging or direct fire and is provided with an anti-tank shell. It is normally towed by a 6 x 6 2½ ton truck.

The 105mm Howitzer M2 originated in a report by the Caliber Board in 1919 which made recommendations for future equipment as a result of experiences in France. Among other things the Board called for a weapon of about 105mm caliber, capable of 65 degrees of elevation and firing a shell weighing about 35 pounds. A maximum range of 12,000 yards was desirable, and the ammunition was to be semi-fixed. Development began in 1920 and the 105mm Howitzer M1 and Carriage M1 were standardized by OCM 6684 of 5 January 1928. No manufacture was undertaken, the design being prepared for production when circumstances required.

When mechanization of the army began, it became necessary to modernize all horse-drawn equipment, and in 1933 work on the 105mm Carriage M1 began, but was then shelved and not restarted until 1936 when OCM 13109 authorized the redesign. It was found easier to begin a completely fresh design instead of modifying the existing M1, and several different designs were built and tested before the Carriage M2 was standardized by OCM 15639 of 23 February 1940. The Carriage M2 is classified Limited Standard.

In early 1942 the use of electric brakes on towed equipments under 5000 pounds gross weight was discontinued, and the M2 carriage was modified by the removal of the Warner brakes, becoming the M2A1. The Carriage M2A1 is classified Limited Standard.

As a result of combat experience, in 1943 a new, larger shield was fitted, a larger buffer and an enclosed screw traverse mechanism. This became the Carriage M2A2, standardized in August 1943.

The Howitzer M1 had been modified in 1934 to permit loading the shrapnel round as a fixed round, and this was standardized as the 105mm Howitzer M2 by OCM 11395 of 5 April 1934. In January 1935 this modification was rescinded, since shrapnel was no longer considered the primary projectile. In spite of this the M2 remained the standard model but in the course of adapting it to the new Carriage M2 changes had to be made to the breech ring, resulting in the standardization of the Howitzer M2A1 in March 1940.

Ammunition

Ammunition for the Howitzer M2 is of the semi-fixed type; it is supplied as a complete round, and the shell can be removed from the cartridge case for adjustment of the charge zone, after which the shell is replaced in the mouth of the case and the round loaded as one unit. The standard projectile is the HE Shell M1, weighing 33 pounds and fuzed PD M51 or MT M67. The propelling charge weighs 3.66 pounds and divides into 7 zones. Chemical smoke, base ejection smoke, and HEAT anti-tank projectiles are also provided.

REFERENCES—OCM 6684, 13109, 11395, 15639; TM 9-325; TM 9-1325; SNL C-21

105 MM HOWITZER M3 ON CARRIAGE M3 ON M3A1 — STANDARD

CHARACTERISTICS

Weight of gun . . . . 955lbs.

Weight of gun and carriage
in firing position . . . . 2495lbs.

Length of gun . . . . 74.35ins.

Length of bore . . . . 68.2ins.

Rifling

    grooves 34

    twist . . . . Uniform, right-hand, 1 turn in 20 calibers

Type of breech mechanism . . . . Horizontal sliding wedge, hand operated

Type of firing mechanism . . . . Percussion, continuous pull

Type of recoil mechanism . . . . Hydro-pneumatic, constant length

Recoil length . . . . 29ins.

Maximum elevation . . . . + 65°

Maximum depression . . . . − 9°

Traverse . . . . 45 degrees (22½ R to 22½ L)

Weight of HE shell . . . . 33lbs.

Weight of complete round . . . . 40.6lbs.

Maximum range . . . . 8295 yards

Muzzle velocity . . . . 1550 feet per second

Rate of fire . . . . 15 rounds per minute

RECONSTRUCTED PAGE 1 June 1944

The 105mm Howitzer M3 is a lightweight version of the Howitzer M2 designed for use by airborne forces or for other tasks where light weight is an advantage. It fires the same ammunition as the Howitzer M2 except that the propelling charge is smaller in order to achieve the desired rapid combustion in the shorter barrel. In an emergency the standard ammunition for the M2 Howitzer may be used, but is restricted to firing with Zones 1 to 3 inclusive.

The barrel and breech mechanism are those of the M2 Howitzer, with the barrel reduced in length by 27 inches. The Carriage M3 is assembled from the 75mm Howitzer Carriage M3A1 and the 75mm Howitzer Carriage M8 recoil mechanism, both items being modified to suit the larger and more powerful 105mm howitzer tube. This design was standardized as the Howitzer M3 on Carriage M3 in February 1943. Trials of production equipments revealed weaknesses in the carriage, and a new design with stronger trail legs was standardized as the M3A1, the M3 being classified Substitute Standard. The carriage is also fitted with a combined firing base and traveling lock which is lowered to the ground to provide a base for the howitzer when firing.

The Carriage M3A2, which was fitted with shields, was produced in 1942 when the 105mm Howitzer M3 was issued to infantry cannon companies. These were used in North Africa, but the cannon companies were discontinued in 1943 and the Carriage M3A2 had the shields removed and reverted to being Carriage M2A1. Since that time the M3 Howitzer has been solely issued to airborne formations.

Ammunition

The Howitzer M3 uses the same type of semi-fixed ammunition as the Howitzer M2, except that the propelling charge is different. The standard HE shell weighs 33 pounds, is loaded with 4.8 pounds of TNT and is fitted with the Fuze PD M51 or MT M67. The propelling charge is of a smaller granulation to the M2 charge so as to ensure complete combustion of the propellant in the shorter barrel. It is divided into 5 zone bags, the total weight of the complete charge being 21.3 ounces. The same chemical smoke and base ejection smoke shells provided for the Howitzer M2 can be used with the Howitzer M3. Zone 5 is restricted to firing at angles of elevation of 45 degrees or less; Zones 1–4 inclusive may be fired at any elevation. The HEAT anti-tank round is a fixed round with a non-adjustable propelling charge of 1.2 pounds to give a muzzle velocity of 1250 feet per second and a maximum range of 8500 yards.

In emergency the Charge, Propelling, for Howitzer M2 may be used, but only Zones 1–3 inclusive may be fired.

REFERENCES—TM 9-326; SNL C-50

155 MM HOWITZER M1—CARRIAGE M1—STANDARD
155 MM HOWITZER M1918—CARRIAGE M1918A3—SUBSTITUTE STANDARD

PRINCIPAL CHARACTERISTICS OF 155 mm HOWITZER, M1, AND CARRIAGE, M1

HOWITZER, M1
Caliber..............................155 mm
Weight.............................3,825 lb.
Overall length......................150 ins.
Length of bore......................20 cals.
Muzzle velocity....680, 770, 880, 1,020, 1,220,
1,520, 1,850 f./s.
Volume of chamber.................725 cu. ins.
Travel of projectile in bore........120.675 ins.
Maximum powder pressure.....32,000 lb./sq. in.
Type of block mechanism.......Interrupted screw
Rate of fire........................2 rds./min.
Range (maximum)................16,000 yds.

RECOIL MECHANISM
Type....................Hydropneumatic, T2
Weight.............................1,570 lb.
Normal recoil variable
(supercharge, Zone VII).......58 ins. at 0° to
41 ins. at 65°
Maximum piston-
rod pull..........64,000 lb. at 65° elevation

CARRIAGE, M1
Total weight without howitzer..........8,141 lb.
Height of lunette (limbered position).....29 ins.
Width of carriage (overall)............95½ ins.
Tread width........................81½ ins.
Trail spread (included angle)...30° right; 30° left
Elevation (maximum) (on firing base)........65°
Depression.............................0°
Traverse (maximum, right) (on firing base).26°30'
Traverse (maximum, left) (on firing base).26°30'
Total weight with weapon
(without cover or accessories).......11,966 lb.

AMMUNITION
Weight of complete round,
H.E., M107.....................108.42 lb.
Weight of projectile...................95 lb.
Weight of projectile explosive charge..15.87 lb.
Weight of propelling charge.........13.42 lb.
Type of ammunition..........Separate loading

155 mm HOWITZER, M1918, AND CARRIAGE, M1918A3

HOWITZER, M1918
Weight............................2,740 lb.
Length of barrel....................91.81 ins.
Length of bore.....................13.64 cals.
Travel of projectile................69.88 ins.
Volume of chamber.................425 cu. ins.
Maximum pressure...........26,500 lb./sq. in.
Maximum range....................12,400 yds.

CARRIAGE, M1918A3
Weight of sleigh and recoil mechanism....863 lb.
Weight of howitzer and carriage in
firing position....................8,184 lb.
Total weight, matériel in traveling
position, complete.................9,518 lb.
Height above ground, highest point,
top of shield....................77.36 ins.
Range of elevation............0° to +42° 20'
Traverse to right or left................3°
Width of tread.....................75½ ins.
Tires, pneumatic...................13.00x24

155 mm HOWITZER, M1918, ON CARRIAGE, M1918A3

155 mm HOWITZER, M1, ON CARRIAGE, M1

The first 155 mm howitzers used by the U. S. Army were the M1917 and M1917A1, designed and manufactured in France by the Schneider Company during the last war. These were succeeded by the M1918, constructed in America, which was in turn superseded by the M1 as the standard 155 mm howitzer matériel.

155 mm HOWITZERS, M1917 AND M1917A1—These are short, heavy cannon with built-up barrels, interrupted-screw, carrier-supported breechblocks of the lever-pull type and continuous-pull, vertical-sliding firing mechanisms. These weapons are classified as Limited Standard.

155 mm HOWITZER, M1918—The M1918 howitzer is similar in build, weight, dimensions and ballistics to the M1917 and M1917A1. The firing mechanism is of the screw-type, provided with a block-latch assembly as a safety measure. This howitzer is classified as Substitute Standard.

155 mm HOWITZER, M1—The barrel of this howitzer is of monobloc construction. It is considerably longer and heavier than the barrels in previous models, and is equipped with an interrupted-thread, screw-type breechblock. The range is nearly 4,000 yards greater than that of the M1918. This howitzer was classified as Standard in O.C.M. 16724 dated 15 May 1941.

155 mm CARRIAGE, M1917—This is a French manufactured carriage with a box trail, steel-tired wood wheels and a curved shield. Recoil and counter recoil of the howitzer on its recoil are regulated by a hydropneumatic recoil system, housed in a sleigh to which the howitzer is connected. The trail flasks contain bearings in which the cradle trunnions are seated. This carriage is classified as Limited Standard.

155 mm CARRIAGE, M1917A1—This is the carriage, M1917, with a straight shield, a sight port, rubber-tired wheels and provision for Quadrant Sight, M1917A1, and Panoramic Sight, M1917. This carriage is classified as Limited Standard.

155 mm CARRIAGE, M1917A2—When the M1917A1 carriage is furnished with a cradle lock and drawbar for motor draft, it is designated Carriage, M1917A2. These modifications eliminate the need for a limber. This carriage is classified as Limited Standard.

155 mm CARRIAGE, M1917A3—This is the M1917 carriage with the addition of a high-speed axle, wheels with pneumatic tires, a drawbar and a cradle traveling lock. This carriage is classified as Limited Standard.

155 mm CARRIAGE, M1917A4—The addition of torque rods to Carriage, M1917A2, changes the model designation to M1917A4.

155 mm CARRIAGE, M1918—In its main constructional details this carriage is similar to the M1917. The wheels have rubber tires, and the shield consists of right and left shield plates suitably tied together. A panoramic-sight case is attached to the left shield plate. This carriage is classified as Limited Standard.

155 mm CARRIAGE, M1918A1—Experiments begun by the Ordnance Dept. in 1933 for the purpose of adapting 155 mm howitzer matériel to high-speed transport resulted in connecting the carriage to the prime mover by means of a drawbar and in new bearings designed to reduce friction. In 1934 the M1918E4 was produced with pneumatic-tired wheels possessing lubricant-retaining features in the bearings. Improvements in these modifications were incorporated in the M1918E5, standardized in 1936 as Carriage, M1918A1.

155 mm CARRIAGE, M1918A3—This is the Carriage, M1918A1, when equipped with torque rods. This carriage is classified as Substitute Standard.

155 mm CARRIAGE, M1—This carriage is interchangeable with the Carriage, M2, used for the 4.5" Gun, M1. The recoil mechanism is of the hydropneumatic type. Length of recoil varies automatically with the elevation and the zone of fire. Equilibrators of the spring type neutralize the unbalanced weight of the gun. The carriage has a split trail, pneumatic tires with self-sealing inner tubes and air brakes controlled by the driver of the prime mover. This carriage was classified as Standard by O.C.M. 16724 dated 15 May 1941.

REFERENCES—TM 9–2005, v.3; TM 9–330; TM 9–331; TM 9–1331.

Sighting and Fire Control Equipment

On Carriage Equipment

Panoramic Telescope, M12

Telescope Mount, M25

Off Carriage Equipment

Gunner's Quadrant, M1

Aiming Circle, M1

Bore Sight

1-meter-base Range Finder, M7 or M1916

Hand Fuze Setter, M1913A1

B. C. Telescope, M65 or M1915A1

Hand Fuze Setter, M21

Graphical Firing Table, M5 (with M1917 and M1918 matériel)

Graphical Firing Table, M12 (with M1 matériel)

155 mm HOWITZER, M1, IN TRAVELING POSITION

155 MM GUN M1918M1—CARRIAGE M3—SUBSTITUTE STANDARD

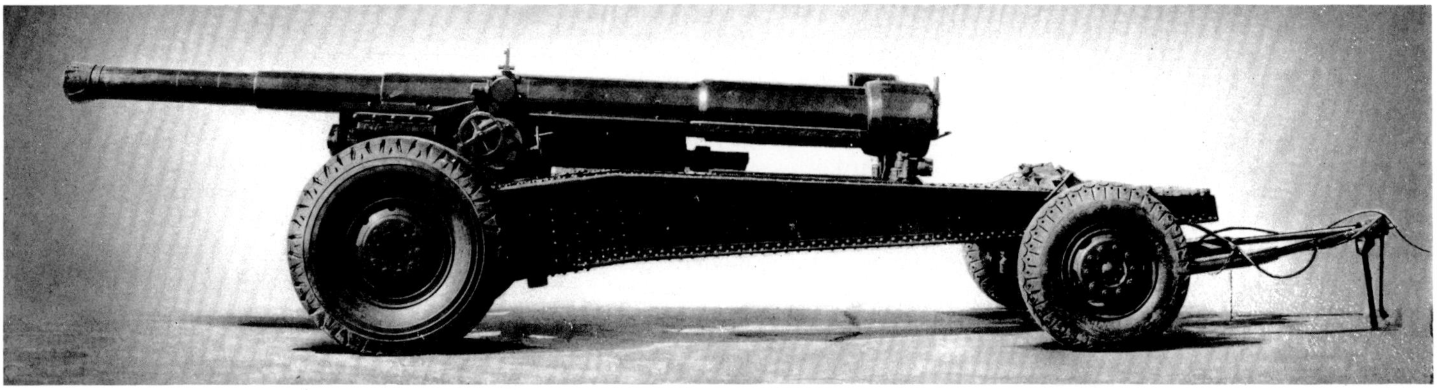

155 mm GUN, M1918M1, ON CARRIAGE, M3, IN TRAVELING POSITION WITH LIMBER, M3

The 155 mm Gun, M1918M1, is of French design, similar to the 155 mm Gun, M1917, G.P.F., manufactured in France and used by the American Expeditionary Force in 1917–18. Only slight variations exist between the basic G.P.F. and the gun as modified or constructed in the United States. In addition to their use as field pieces, all models of the G.P.F. are now mounted on the 155 mm Gun Motor Carriage, M12.

GUNS, M1917 AND M1918M1—The differences between these models are superficial, and the breech mechanisms are interchangeable. The M1917 is the French manufactured 155 mm G.P.F., numbers of which were purchased by the United States, while the M1918M1 is of American manufacture.

The built-up, alloy-steel barrel has a breech ring screwed on to the jacket. A cylindrical, interrupted-thread type breechblock contains a French screw-type firing mechanism. This gun is classified as Substitute Standard.

GUN, M1917A1—When an American manufactured breechblock is installed in the French 155 mm gun, the weapon takes the designation M1917A1. This gun is classified as Limited Standard.

CARRIAGES, M1917 AND M1918—These carriages are identical. They are of the split-trail type, with a cast-steel top carriage mounted and traversing on the chassis section of the bottom carriage assembly. The elevating and traversing mechanisms are affixed to the top carriage. A hydropneumatic, variable recoil, independent type recoil system with a floating piston is housed in a cradle supported by trunnions resting in bearings in the top carriage. The bottom carriage is a large steel casting which, when in traveling position, is suspended from the axle by a multiple leaf spring. These carriages are classified as Limited Standard.

CARRIAGE, M1917A1—This is the M1917 carriage equipped with anti-friction bearings, solid rubber tires, and driver-operated power brakes for high-speed transport. This carriage is classified as Limited Standard.

CARRIAGE, M1918A1—When the M1918 carriage is modified for high-speed transport in the same manner as the M1917A1, it takes the designation M1918A1. This carriage is classified as Limited Standard.

CARRIAGES, M2 AND M3—The addition of pneumatic tires and air brakes to the Carriage, M1917, changes its designation to M2. When similar modifications are made on the Carriage, M1918, it becomes the M3. These carriages are classified as Substitute Standard.

LIMBER, M3—This limber was specifically designed for high-speed transport. The axle is a steel forging. The axle body is I-sectional in form, terminating in right-angle bands with boss ends horizontally bored for spindles. Semi-elliptic leaf type springs are clamped to the axle by spring clips. Front and rear members are welded and riveted to the spring brackets and the fifth wheel base. A fifth-wheel assembly permits the limber to pivot under the front end of the trails to follow the movement of the drawbars.

Sighting and Fire Control Equipment

On Carriage Equipment
- Panoramic Telescope, M6
- Instrument Light, M9
- Quadrant Sight, M1918A1 or M1918

Off Carriage Equipment
- Aiming Post, M1
- Aiming Post Light, M14
- Gunner's Quadrant, M1 or M1918
- Graphical Firing Table, M6 (short range) and M15 (long range)
- B.C. Telescope, M65 or M1915A1
- Bore Sight

Ammunition

Ammunition is of the separate loading type. It consists of Projectile, A.P., M112 with Fuze, B.D., M60; Shell, gas, persistent, HS, M104, unfuzed, adapted for Fuze, P.D., M51, with Booster M21, or Fuze, P.D., M51A1, with Booster, M21A1; Shell, gas, persistent, H.S., Mk. VIIA1, unfuzed, adapted for Fuze, P.D., M51, with Booster M21, or Fuze, P.D., M51A1, with Booster, M21A1; Shell, H.E., M101, unfuzed, adapted for Fuze, P.D., M51, with Booster, M21 or M51A1, with Booster, M21A1, or Fuze, time, mechanical, M67, with Booster, M21A1; Shell, H.E., Mk. III, with Fuze, P.D., M46 or M47; Shell, H.E., Mk. IIIA1, with Fuze, M51A1, with Booster, M21A1, or Fuze, time, mechanical, M67, with Booster, M21A1; Shell, Smoke, FS, Mk. VIIA1, with Fuze, P.D., M51A1, with Booster, M21A1; Shell, Smoke, phosphorous, WP, M104, with Fuze, M51A1, with Booster, M21A1.

Trainer

The 37 mm Gun, M1916, on Subcaliber Mount, M1, is used for practice in laying and firing the 155 mm Guns, M1917, M1917A1, and M1918M1.

References—TM 9-2005, v.3; TM 9-345; TM 9-1345; FM 6-90.

PRINCIPAL CHARACTERISTICS

155 mm Gun, M1918M1

Weight, complete	8,715 lb.
Length	232.87 ins.
Chamber volume	1,329 cu. ins.
Travel of projectile in bore	185 ins.
Maximum pressure	31,500 p.s.i.
Muzzle velocity (projectile, A.P., M112)	2,360 f./s.
Maximum range (with supercharge shell, H.E., M101)	20,100 yds.
Rate of fire (with supercharge)	4 rds./min.

Carriage, M3

Recoil mechanism	hydropneumatic, variable recoil
Weight of recoil mechanism	3,114 lb.
Total weight (less gun and limber)	14,587 lb.
Weight of limber	2,630 lb.
Length overall, traveling position, gun, carriage and limber	31⅚ ft.
Width (outer walls of tires)	106 ins.
Height, extreme (traveling position)	74⅜ ins.
Diameter of turning circle	60¼ ft.
Road clearance	
Carriage	12½ ins.
Limber	9¼ ins.
Elevation	0° to 35°
Traverse (maximum right)	30°
Traverse (maximum left)	30°

155 MM GUN M1A1—CARRIAGE M1—STANDARD

155 mm GUN, M1A1, IN FIRING POSITION

The 155 mm Gun, M1A1, and Carriage, M1, are the results of an endeavor to secure a weapon for army artillery which would combine great firepower with a high degree of mobility. This gun is a development based on the French 155 mm Gun, M1917, G.P.F., used by the A.E.F. in 1917–18. With a muzzle velocity less than 400 feet per second greater than that of its predecessor, the M1A1 has a range of 25,395 yards instead of the 17,460 yards range of the M1917. The 155 mm Gun, M1A1, on Carriage, M1, is also utilized as a coast defense weapon.

GUN, M1—The M1 gun is basically an improved M1918M1 with a longer barrel; a larger powder chamber; an interrupted screw, carrier-supported, two-cycle type breech mechanism equipped with a spring-actuated counter-balance; a modernized type of firing mechanism, and a plastic type obturator with a mushroom head. This gun is classified as Substitute Standard.

GUN, M1A1—The only difference between this gun and the M1 is that the breech ring bushing has been eliminated in the former, the breech threads being cut directly in the breech ring. This gun was classified as Standard in OCM 16830 dated 12 June 1941.

PRINCIPAL CHARACTERISTICS

Gun, M1A1
Caliber	155 mm
Weight of gun complete	9,595 lb.
Length of bore	45 cals.
Length of gun	22.9 ft.
Muzzle velocity	2,800 f./s.
Weight of projectile	95 lb.
Weight of powder charge	30 lb.
Maximum rated pressure	38,000 lb./sq. in.
Number of grooves	48
Twist	Right-hand—uniform
Rate of fire	1 rd./min.
Range	25,395 yds.

Recoil Mechanism
Type	Hydropneumatic, variable recoil, M3
Weight	3,890 lb.

Normal recoil	54 ins. at 0°; 31½ ins. at 65°
Maximum recoil	57½ ins.
Maximum piston-rod pull at 65°	96,500 lb.

Carriage
Type	Split trail
Weight of carriage with gun	30,600 lb.
Maximum elevation	65°

Traverse (max., right)	30°
Traverse (max., left)	30°
Maximum spread of trails	60°
Overall height (traveling position)	102 ins.
Overall length (traveling position)	34.3 ft.
Overall width (traveling position)	99 ins.
Bogie	4 dual wheels
Brakes	Air, on each bogie wheel

Ammunition

	M101 H.E.	M112B1 A.P.
Weight of complete round	126.97 lb.	131.28 lb.
Weight of projectile	94.71 lb.	100 lb.
Weight of projectile explosive charge	15.13 lb.	14.4 lb.
Weight of propelling charge	32.26 lb.	31.75 lb.
Type of ammunition	Semi-fixed	Semi-fixed
Armor penetration, homogeneous plate, 20° from normal		3 ins. at 6,000 yds.

CARRIAGE, M1—This carriage is able to mount the 155 mm Gun, M1A1. It consists mainly of the bogie, bottom carriage, top carriage, cradle, recoil mechanism, equilibrators, and trails. The gun is supported in a cradle trunnioned in bearings in the top carriage. Two pneumatic type equilibrators, one on each side of the carriage, neutralize the unbalanced weight of the gun. The Recoil Mechanism, M3, is of the hydropneumatic, variable recoil type, assembled and attached to the cradle. The top carriage, which supports the tipping parts and mounts the elevating and traversing mechanisms, pivots about a vertical axis on the chassis section of the bottom carriage. When the bogie wheels are raised, the bottom carriage rests on the ground and, together with the spread trails, provides a three-point suspension. Air brakes, equalized on each of the four rear bogie wheels, are controlled from the driver's seat of the prime mover. Two handbrake levers are also provided to operate the brakes on the two front bogie wheels and for use when parking or in case of an emergency. All bogie wheels have pneumatic tires.

For travel, the gun is disconnected from the recoil mechanism by removing the piston-rod nuts, and retracted until the weight of the breech end is supported by the traveling lock. When it is desired to go into firing position, the gun is pulled into battery by the prime mover, the piston-rod nuts are replaced and the traveling lock is removed. The trails are then lowered to the ground by a screw mechanism on the limber and the limber is removed. Two jacks on the bogie lower the mount until the bottom carriage rests on the ground. Further rotation of the jacks raises the bogie clear of the ground.

This carriage is classified as Standard.

LIMBER, HEAVY CARRIAGE, M2—This limber is a two-wheeled, pneumatic-tired vehicle with a limber-lifting mechanism which holds the spade ends of the trails when the gun and carriage are in traveling position. The limber weighs 1,975 pounds, and its wheels are interchangeable with those on the bogie of the carriage. When the gun is truck drawn the limber is not needed.

Sighting and Fire Control Equipment

On Carriage Equipment
Telescope Mount, M18A1
Quadrant Mount, M1
Panoramic Telescope, M12

Off Carriage Equipment
Aiming Circle, M1
B.C., Telescope, M65 or M1915A1
Aiming Post, M1
Gunner's Quadrant, M1

Ammunition

Ammunition for the 155 mm Gun, M1A1, is of the separate-loading type, the propellant being ignited by a percussion primer. The standard projectiles for the gun are H.E. Shell, M101, with either point-detonating Fuze, M51A1, or mechanical time Fuze, M67; armor-piercing Shell, M112B1, with base-detonating Fuze, M60, and chemical Shell, M104, with point-detonating Fuze, M51A1.

Trainer

The 37 mm Gun, M1916, on Subcaliber Mount, M10, is used for practice in laying and firing the 155 mm Gun, M1A1.

REFERENCES—TM 9–2005, v.3; TM 9–345; TM 9–1345; TM 9–350; TM 9–1350; FM 6–90.

155 mm GUN, M1A1, ON CARRIAGE, M1, AND HEAVY LIMBER, M2, in Traveling Position with Gun Retracted and Supported by the Traveling Lock

8 INCH HOWITZER M1—CARRIAGE M1—STANDARD

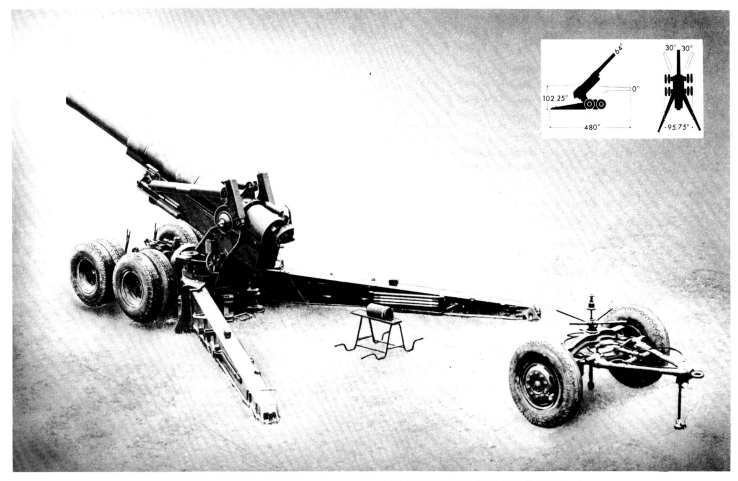

8 INCH HOWITZER, M1, IN FIRING POSITION, WITH LOADING TRAY AND HEAVY LIMBER, M2

PRINCIPAL CHARACTERISTICS

HOWITZER, M1
Caliber	8 ins.
Weight	10,240 lb.
Overall length	209.59 ins.
Length of bore	25 cals.
Muzzle velocity	820, 900, 1,000, 1,150, 1,380, 1,640, 1,950 f./s.
Volume of chamber	1,527 cu. ins.
Travel of projectile in bore	173.83 ins.
Maximum powder pressure	33,000 lb./sq. in.
Type of block mechanism	Interrupted-screw type
Rate of fire	1 rd. in 2 mins.
Range	18,510 yds.

RECOIL MECHANISM, M4
Type	Hydropneumatic
Weight	3,890 lb.
Normal recoil	63 ins. at 0° to 32 ins. at 64°
Maximum recoil	70 ins.
Maximum piston-rod pull at 65°	139,850 lb.

CARRIAGE, M1
Total weight of carriage and limber without howitzer	21,460 lb.
Height of lunette (limbered position)	27 ins.
Length of carriage (muzzle to lunette)	40 ft.
Width over hub caps	95¾ ins.
Width overall of bogie	98⅞ ins.
Tread width (c/—c/ of wheels) (limber)	83½ ins.
Height in traveling position	102¼ ins.
Trail spread (included angle)	60°
Elevation (maximum) (firing base)	64°
Depression (maximum) (firing base)	0°
Traverse (firing base) (right)	30°
Traverse (firing base) (left)	30°
Total weight of gun, mechanism and carriage	31,700 lb.

AMMUNITION
Weight of complete round	213.96 lb. 228.75 lb.
Weight of projectile shell, M106	200 lb.
Weight of projectile explosive charge	29.6 lb.
Weight of propelling charge	10.75 lb. (approx.)
Type of ammunition	Separate loading

The present 8″ howitzer used by the U. S. Army is the M1, a development from the Howitzers, Mk. VI, Mk. VII and Mk. VIII-½ issued to the A.E.F. during the first World War. These howitzers were manufactured in both England and the United States. While they differ in certain respects, they have the same types of breechblocks and firing mechanisms.

8 INCH HOWITZER, MK. VI — This howitzer is mounted on the Mk. VI carriage. The barrel is of built-up construction, consisting of a jacket shrunk on over a tube. A shrunk-on breech ring carries a lug for connecting the gun to the recoil mechanism. A breech bushing is provided for reception of a lever-operated breechblock of the interrupted-screw type having an asbestos obturator pad in the mushroom head. Two types of noninterchangeable firing mechanisms are utilized. In one a T-tube friction primer inserted in the breech is fired by means of a lanyard pulling a friction wire out of the tube. The other type is of the percussion variety, in which a percussion primer fitting into the breechblock is fired by a lanyard-operated hammer striking a firing pin. Front and rear guide rings support the howitzer in the cradle. This howitzer is classified as Limited Standard.

8 INCH HOWITZER, MK. VII — This howitzer, of wire-wound construction, was superseded by the Mk. VIII-½ because it was found necessary to thicken the powder chamber walls to prevent their cracking. It is classified as Limited Standard.

8 INCH HOWITZER, MK. VIII-½—This howitzer is also of the built-up type, but has an inner and an outer tube over which the jacket is shrunk. No guide rings are included, as the jacket supports the weight of the cannon. Other details are identical with those of the Mk. VI. This howitzer is mounted on the Mk. VII carriage, and is classified as Limited Standard.

8 INCH HOWITZER, M1—This weapon is of built-up construction. The tube screws into a breech ring fitted with lugs for support of the breechblock carrier and attachment of the recoil mechanism. The carrier-supported breechblock is of the two-cycle, interrupted-screw type. It is equipped with a spring-actuated counterbalance, a percussion type of firing mechanism and an obturator mechanism. With the exception of the spindle, pads and other parts of the obturator, the breech mechanisms of the 8" Howitzer, M1, and the 155 mm Gun, M1, are interchangeable. This howitzer is classified as Standard (O.C.M. 15938).

8 INCH HOWITZER PLATFORM, M1917 —When in firing position, the Mk. VII and Mk. VIII-½ howitzers rest on a demountable firing platform buried flush with the surface of the gound. For transport, the platform is loaded on a two-wheeled cart attached to the howitzer carriage. The cart and platform are each classified as Limited Standard.

CARRIAGES, MK. VI AND MK. VII (British)—These carriages differ mainly in the weight and clearance of the trails, those of the Mk. VII being raised and strengthened to accommodate the Mk. VIII-½ howitzer. The cradle rests in the trunnion bearings of a top carriage which is pivoted in the front transom of the trail to permit traverse. A hydropneumatic, long-recoil type recoil mechanism carried by the cradle contains both the recoil brake and the recuperator. The trail is of the box type cut away to allow clearance for recoil of the howitzer when it is fired at high angles of elevation. All-steel wheels, 66" in diameter, with tires 12" wide, are fitted with brakes acting independently on each wheel. These carriages are classified as Limited Standard.

CARRIAGE, M1—This carriage is identical in design and construction with the 155 mm Gun Carriage, M1. Since the howitzer is considerably heavier than the gun, it is necessary to increase the nitrogen pressure in the howitzer recoil mechanism, M4. The howitzer remains in the battery position during transport. This carriage is classified as Standard (O.C.M. 15938).

HEAVY CARRIAGE LIMBER, M2— This is the same limber used with the 155 mm Gun Carriage, M1.

Sighting and Fire Control Equipment

On Carriage Equipment

Quadrant Mount, M1
Panoramic Telescope, M12
Telescope Mount, M18A1

Off Carriage Equipment

Gunner's Quadrant, M1
Bore Sight
Aiming Post, M1
Aiming Circle, M1
B. C. Telescope, M65 or M1915A1
Hand Fuze Setter, M21
Graphical Firing Tables, M8 (short range) and M9 (long range)

Ammunition

The 8" Howitzer, M1, uses separate-loading, high-explosive ammunition with different weights of powder charges to give seven zones of fire. It consists of H.E. shell, M106, with P.D. fuze, M51A1, and M.T. fuze, M67.

Trainer

The 37 mm Gun, M1916, on Subcaliber Mount, M10, is used for practice in laying and firing the 8" Howitzer, M1.

REFERENCES—TM 9–2005, v.3; TM 9–335; TM 9–1335; FM 21–6.

8 INCH HOWITZER, M1, ON CARRIAGE, M1, IN TRAVELING POSITION

8 INCH GUN M1—CARRIAGE M2—STANDARD

8 INCH GUN, M1, CARRIAGE, M2, IN FIRING POSITION, AT 10° ELEVATION

The 8″ Gun, M1, on the Carriage, M2, was designed for use as a G.H.Q. reserve artillery weapon. The Caliber Board report of 5 May 1919, recommended the construction of an 8″ field gun, but all development work on this matériel was suspended by O.C.M. 4110, dated 8 September 1924. The project was formally resumed in 1939. O.C.M. 15791, dated 9 May 1940, approved the military characteristics of the 8″ Gun, T2, and the 8″ Gun Carriage, T2, and O.C.M. 17053, dated 31 July 1941, approved the design of the pilot matériel. O.C.M. 17241, dated 18 September 1941, approved the nomenclature of the 8″ gun matériel, when eventually standardized, as 8″ Gun, M1, 8″ Gun Carriage, M2, Recoil Mechanism, M7, Cannon Transport Wagon, M1, and Carriage Transport Wagon, M3.

8 INCH GUN, M1—The gun consists of a cold-worked tube with a shrunk-on jacket. The jacket contains a keyway to guide it in the recoil mechanism. The breech mechanism, with an interrupted step thread, rotating drop type breechblock, is interchangeable with that of the 240 mm Howitzer, M1.

CARRIAGE, M2—The carriage is similar to that for the 240 mm Howitzer, M1, with the exception that it has a minimum elevation of 10° and a maximum elevation of 50°, and such other modifications as are necessary to adapt it to the longer, heavier 8″ gun. The Recoil Mechanism, M7, is of the hydropneumatic type, the recoil and counter-recoil rod and the recoil control rod being longer than those

PRINCIPAL CHARACTERISTICS

GUN
Weight	29,800 lb.
Overall length	409.5 ins.
Length of bore	50 calibers
Muzzle velocity	2,950 f./s.
Volume of chamber	5,156 cu. ins.
Travel of projectile in bore	338.58 ins.
Maximum powder pressure	38,000 lb./sq. in.
Type of block mechanism	Rotating drop type breechblock
Rate of fire	1 rd./min.
Range—maximum (approx.)	35,000 yds.
Range—minimum (approx.)	22,000 yds.

RECOIL MECHANISM, M7
(Including Cradle)
Type	Hydropneumatic
Weight	7,021 lb.
Recoil	50 ins. at 50°
	47 ins. at 10°

CARRIAGE
Weight without gun	39,300 lb.
Trail spread (included angle)	45°
Elevation (maximum)	50°
Elevation (minimum)	10°
Traverse (maximum, right)	15°
Traverse (maximum, left)	15°
Total weight of gun, mechanism and carriage	69,300 lb.

CANNON TRANSPORT WAGON, M1
Weight (loaded)	49,200 lb.
Weight under front tires (loaded)	15,200 lb.

Weight under rear tires (loaded)	34,000 lb.
Overall length (loaded)	501 ins.
Overall height (loaded)	84 ins.
Overall width	111½ ins.
Wheel tread	92 ins.
Wheel base	192 ins.

CARRIAGE TRANSPORT WAGON, M3
Weight (loaded)	46,900 lb.
Weight under front tires (loaded)	14,360 lb.
Weight under rear tires (loaded)	32,540 lb.
Overall length (loaded)	429½ ins.
Overall height (loaded)	128¼ ins.
Overall width	111½ ins.
Wheel tread	92 ins.
Wheel base	264 ins.

TRUCK MOUNTED CRANE, M2
Gross weight	53,000 lb.
Wheel base	168½ ins.
Overall length (without boom)	298½ ins.
Overall height	130½ ins.
Overall width	108 ins.

AMMUNITION
Type of shell	H.E., M103
Weight of complete round	347.24 lb.
Weight of shell as fired	240.37 lb.
Weight of charge, propelling, NH powder	106.77 lb.
Weight of charge, bursting, TNT	20.90 lb.
Weight of primer, percussion, electric, Navy, Mk. XIM1	10 lb.

in the 240 mm howitzer recoil system. The gun is dismounted from the carriage for transport and loaded on the Cannon Transport Wagon, M1. The carriage is transported on the Carriage Transport Wagon, M3. Dismounting and assembling of the gun and carriage are accomplished

by the Truck Mounted Crane, M2, or by winches and cables on the tractors.

CANNON TRANSPORT WAGON, M1 —This is a 6 wheel wagon with a steel chassis, designed to transport the 8″ M1 gun and recoil mechanism. It is equipped

8 INCH GUN, M1, CARRIAGE, M2. GUN AND RECOIL MECHANISM SUPPORTED IN AIR BY CRANE, M2

with wheels having divided rims and combat tires and tubes. Air brakes are supplied for control of the vehicle.

CARRIAGE TRANSPORT WAGON, M3—This wagon is of the same general type as the Cannon Transport Wagon, M1, with such modifications as are required for securing and transporting the 8″ Carriage, M2.

TRUCK MOUNTED CRANE, M2—This vehicle comprises a steel boom, rigging, and crane-operating cab and machinery mounted on a 6 wheel motor truck.

Ammunition

Ammunition for the 8″ Gun, M1, is of the separate-loading type. It consists of H.E. shell, M103, weighing 240 lb., with P.D. fuze, M51A1.

Sighting and Fire Control Equipment

On Carriage Equipment
Panoramic Telescope, M12
Telescope Mount, M30
Elevation Quadrant, M1
Quadrant Adapter, M10

Off Carriage Equipment
B.C. Telescope, M1915A1, or M65
Aiming Circle, M1
Graphical Firing Table, M22

LORAIN TRUCK MOUNTED CRANE, M2

240 MM HOWITZER M1918M1A1—CARRIAGE M1918A2 LIMITED STANDARD

Removal of 240 mm Howitzer Carriage, M1918, Top Carriage to Top Carriage Transport Wagon, M1918, by Means of the Erecting Frame.

240 MM HOWITZER, M1918M1A1, ON CARRIAGE, M1918, IN FIRING POSITION

PRINCIPAL CHARACTERISTICS

Total weight of howitzer and carriage in firing position	41,296 lb.
Weight of howitzer	10,790 lb.
Weight of projectile	345 lb.
Weight of powder charge	36 lb.
Length of howitzer	199.6 ins.
Travel of projectile	164 ins.
Length of recoil, normal	44.83 ins.
Diameter of bore	9.45 ins.
Maximum elevation	60°
Maximum depression	1°
Loading angle	15°
Maximum traverse, left or right	10°
Number of grooves	84
Maximum range, approximate	16,400 yds.
Muzzle velocity	1,700 f./s.
Maximum pressure	33,000 lb./sq. in.
Maximum rate of fire	1 round in 2 minutes
Sustained rate of fire	1 round in 5 minutes

The 240 mm howitzer is a heavy weapon for army artillery. Although the A.E.F. did not possess such matériel, its desirability was apparent, resulting in the American manufacture of 330 of the French designed howitzers and carriages.

240 mm HOWITZER, M1918—A total of 182 of these weapons were fabricated at the Watervliet Arsenal. All 240 mm howitzers are of built-up construction. They consist of a tube, a jacket and a hoop with front and rear rollers for mounting. The breechblock is of the interrupted-screw type, hand operated by a lever which swings with the block and its carrier. As the howitzer uses separate-loading ammunition, a De Bange type obturator with a plastic gas-check pad is employed. The screw type firing mechanism is similar to that on the 155 mm Howitzer, M1918; the 155 mm Gun, M1918M1, and

the 8″ Howitzers, Mks. VI and VIII-½. The 240 mm Howitzer, M1918, is classified as Limited Standard.

240 mm HOWITZER, M1918A1—This howitzer is identical with the M1918 except for a change in the rifling. It is classified as Limited Standard.

240 mm HOWITZER, M1918M1—These howitzers, numbered 183 to 330 inclusive, were also built at Watervliet. They differ from the M1918 only in having a greater exterior diameter in the tapered portion of the barrel forward of the hoop. This necessitates the use of different front roller spindles and front roller fastening screws. The 240 mm Howitzer, M1918M1, is classified as Limited Standard.

240 mm HOWITZER, M1918M1A1—The M1918M1 takes the designation

M1918M1A1 when fitted with a new barrel liner which is rifled with increasing twist rifling; this commences with a twist of 1 turn in 40 calibers and increases to 1 turn in 20 calibers at the muzzle. The 240mm Howitzer M1918M1A1 is classified as Limited Standard.

CARRIAGE M1918

The Carriage M1918 is a siege type carriage, pintle mounted on a mobile platform. The platform and carriage are carried on the Carriage Transport Wagons. The Carriage M1918 is classified as Limited Standard.

CARRIAGE M1918A1

The Carriage M1918A1 is a modified version of the Carriage M1918 intended for mounting on a prepared concrete emplacement for coast artillery purposes. The Carriage M1918A1 is classified as Limited Standard.

CARRIAGE M1918A2

The Carriage M1918A2 is similar to the Carriage M1918 but with modifications to make assembly in the field easier. The Carriage M1918A2 is classified as Substitute Standard.

The Howitzer is carried on a Cannon Transport Wagon, and the equipment is accompanied by a wagon carrying aids to assembly (ramps and A-Frames). On arrival at the selected position a pit is dug. The platform is brought into position and lowered into the pit by use of the A-Frames. The ramps are then laid on the platform and the carriage transport wagon drawn across, the carriage removed, the wagon removed, and the carriage is lowered on to the platform. The cannon transport wagon is then brought into position and, using the ramps and winch, the cannon and recoil system are winched into place on the carriage and secured. The Carriage M1918A2 is transported attached to the platform and the two are emplaced in one unit, so saving time.

Ammunition

Ammunition for the 240mm Howitzer M1918 is in the form of separate-loading rounds. It consists of HE Shell Mk IIIA1 weighing 345 pounds and containing 49.79 pounds of TNT. It is fitted with PD Fuze M51A3 or MT Fuze M67A2. The powder charge provides ten zones with muzzle velocities from 615 to 1700 feet per second. The maximum range is 16,400 yards.

Development of the 240mm Howitzer M1 can be said to have begun in 1925 when extensive tests of the 240mm Howitzer M1918 revealed several shortcomings which only a complete redesign would rectify. The matter was given low priority but in 1934 a start was made with the design of a new carriage, suited to high-speed towing. In 1939 the project was reactivated and in April 1940 development of a completely new weapon was begun. The first model was the Howitzer T1, carried on a Cannon Transport Wagon, and with a carriage designed to be towed as a semi- trailer. This was replaced by a fresh design, using a conventional split-trail carriage which could be transported on a Carriage Transport Wagon and which could be winched or crane-lifted into position. The final designs covered the 240mm Howitzer M1, Carriage M1, Cannon Transport Wagon M2 and Carriage Transport Wagon M3, together with the Quadrant Adapter M10 and Elevation Quad

REFERENCES—OCM 20328; TM 9-341; SNL D-31

CHARACTERISTICS

Weight of gun	25,261lbs.
Weight of gun on transport wagon	47,720lbs.
Weight of carriage	32,800lbs.
Weight of carriage on transport wagon	51,100lbs.
Total weight of howitzer and carriage in firing position	64,700lbs.
Length of gun	27 ft 7in
Rifling	
grooves	68
twist	Uniform, right-hand 1 turn in 25 calibers
Type of breech mechanism	Interrupted step thread, drop block
Type of recoil mechanism	Hydro-pneumatic, constant length
Firing mechanism	Percussion Lock M1
Length of recoil	54.2 to 58.8Ins.
Maximum elevation	65°
Minimum elevation	15°
Loading angle	15°
Traverse	45 degrees (22½ R to 22½ L)
Maximum range	25,225 yards
Minimum range	8450 yards
Weight of projectile	360 lbs.
Weight of powder charge	78.5 lbs.
Muzzle velocity	2300 feet per second
Rate of fire:	
short bursts	⅔ round per minute
prolonged	1 round per 2 minutes

rant, M1, as standard sighting equipment for the weapon. This matériel was recommended for approval as required types, as adopted types, and as standard articles, by O.C.M. 20328, dated 3 May 1943.

240 mm HOWITZER, M1—The Howitzer, M1, consists of a built-up tube and a breech mechanism equipped with an interrupted step thread, rotating drop type breechblock. The recoil mechanism is below the howitzer, and the counter-recoil mechanism, of the hydropneumatic type, is housed in two cylinders mounted on the top of the cradle.

CARRIAGE, M1—The M1 carriage, together with the Transport Wagons, M2 and M3, designed and manufactured by the Bucyrus-Erie Company in collaboration with the Ordnance Department, can be used interchangeably with either the 240 mm Howitzer, M1, or the 8 inch Gun, M1. The carriage, which has split trails, consists of a cradle supporting the howitzer and recoil and recuperator cylinders; the top carriage, in which the cradle is trunnioned; the bottom carriage, and the trails. The elevating mechanism consists of spur gears that are locked by a large friction brake. The traversing mechanism is locked by a worm mechanism. Both mechanisms are hand operated. Each trail has "spades" near the center, and floats at the rear end, to stabilize the carriage during firing. It is necessary to excavate a pit to clear the recoiling parts at high angles. For transport the matériel

240 mm HOWITZER, M1, IN FIRING POSITION AT 64° ELEVATION

is divided into two loads, carried on transport wagons. One load consists of the howitzer and recoil mechanism assembly. The other load is composed of the remainder of the carriage and trails. Mounting and dismounting of the howitzer and carriage and the placing of the loads on the transport wagons is accomplished by means of the Truck Mounted Crane, M2, or by means of winches on the tractors.

CANNON TRANSPORT WAGON, M2—This wagon is a steel frame chassis with 6 divided rim wheels equipped with combat tires and tubes, and air brakes. The front is pivoted for steering. It can be towed at speeds up to 25 miles an hour when loaded. Manually operated parking brakes are also provided.

CARRIAGE TRANSPORT WAGON, M3—This wagon is of the same general type as the Transport Wagon, M2, with such structural modifications as are required for securing and transporting the 240 mm howitzer carriage and spades, floats, etc.

Both transport wagons were approved as required types, adopted types, substitute standard articles, by O.C.M. 20328, dated 6 May 1943.

Sighting and Fire Control Equipment

On Carriage Equipment
Panoramic Telescope, M12
Telescope Mount, M30
Elevation Quadrant, M1
Quadrant Adapter, M10

Off Carriage Equipment
B.C. Telescope, M1915A1, or M65
Aiming Circle, M1
Graphical Firing Tables, M9 (short range) and M19 (long range)
Hand-fuze Setter, M21

Ammunition

Ammunition for the 240 mm Howitzer, M1, is in the form of separate-loading rounds. It consists of H.E. Shell M114, weighing 360 pounds, with P.D. fuze, M51A3, or M.T. fuze, M67A2. The powder charges provide four zones, with muzzle velocities of 1,500, 1,740, 2,020 and 2,300 feet per second. The maximum range is 25,275 yards.

CARRIAGE TRANSPORT WAGON, M3, LOADED WITH 240 mm HOWITZER CARRIAGE, M1

Left View of 8 INCH GUN, MK. VI, M3A2, ON RAILWAY MOUNT, M1, with Gun at 0° Elevation and Outriggers in Place

PRINCIPAL CHARACTERISTICS

Depth of rifling..07 in.
Length of bore..45 calibers
Length of rifling.......................................288.79 ins.
Type of breechblock.............................Interrupted screw
Type of firing mechanism.............Electrical and percussion
Type of rifling..........Right hand, uniform twist, one turn in 25 calibers
Weight of gun with breech mechanism.....................42,000 lb.
Maximum range (260 lb. shell)..............32,000 yds. (approx.)
Maximum service powder pressure............38,000 lb./sq. in.
Muzzle energy (A.P., 260 lb. shell) ....15,300 ft.-tons
Muzzle velocity
  A.P., 260 lb., Mk. XX (Normal charge)................2,100 f./s.
                         (Super charge)...............2,750 f./s.
  H.E., 240 lb., M103 (Normal charge)................2,150 f./s.
                         (Super charge)...............2,840 f./s.
Weight of powder charge (Normal)................75 lb., 12 oz.
Weight of powder charge (Super).................108 lb., 8 oz.
Mount, 8 inch Gun, Railway, M1A1
  Brakes, type........................Mechanical, air operated
  Maximum elevation....................................45°
  Maximum firing elevation.............................45°
  Minimum elevation...................................−5°
  Minimum firing elevation ....0°
  Overall weight (carriage and gun)................230,000 lb.

RECOIL MECHANISM

Final air pressure in recuperator.............2,683 lb./sq. in.
Final liquid pressure in intensifier..........3,065 lb./sq. in.
Initial air pressure in recuperator...........1,600 lb./sq. in.
Initial liquid pressure in intensifier........1,828 lb./sq. in.
Normal recoil..27 ins.

TRAVELING DIMENSIONS

Height...13 ft., 10 ins.
Length overall....................................49 ft., 4 ins.
Width...10 ft., 3 ins.
Traverse....................................360° (continuous)

During the first World War, railway artillery played an increasingly important part in major operations. Mortars and guns removed from seacoast fortifications, together with certain naval guns, were mounted on improvised railway mounts for service in France. Most of these mounts were expedients lacking wide traverse, high elevation and ease of emplacement. Many of them were of the rolling or sliding types no longer utilized because of the time needed for emplacement and the return of the gun to battery after firing.

Efforts to improve the design of railway mounts continued after the war, culminating in the 8″ Railway Mount, M1A1, for the 8″ Gun, Mk. VI, Mod. 3A2. This combination comprises the most modern railway matériel possessed by the U. S. Army. It is intended for employment by either a field army or the coast defense forces.

8 INCH GUN, MK. VI, MOD. 3A2—The barrel is of built-up construction with a liner, tube, jacket and hoops of nickel steel. A nickel steel locking ring holds the liner in position. The breech mechanism is a modified Navy design, Mk. V, with an obturator; a breechblock of the tray-supported Welin stepped thread type; a breech operating crank and gears, and a firing lock using a combination electric and percussion primer. This gun is classified as Standard.

8 INCH RAILWAY MOUNT, M1A1—The mount consists of a top carriage rotating on a drop frame car body of cast and structural steel riding upon two six-wheeled standard gauge 70-ton trucks. It is equipped with air brakes and hand brakes and standard couplers. The base ring is an integral part of the car. The gun rests in a cradle which serves as a slide for the gun and carries the recoil and recuperator mechanisms. The cradle is supported in the side frames of the mount by its trunnions. A main platform of structural steel rotates with the top carriage, and a steel plate breech platform extends rearward from the breech end of the cradle. The traversing and elevating mechanisms are of the regular barbette type design, employing worm and spur gears operated by handwheels. The recoil mechanism is of the hydraulic type, while the recuperator is of the pneumatic variety.

A heavy counterweight at the breech end enables the gun to be mounted well toward the front, making the use of equilibrators unnecessary. Projectiles and powder are transferred from the ammunition car to the mount car by means of an overhead trolley and hoist. Two cranes at the rear corners of the main platform then lift the projectiles to a loading trough with an angle of –5° down which they are slid by hand into the breech of the gun.

Eight tubular steel outriggers with floats act as supports to prevent the mount from tipping or sliding when fired. Four lifting jacks in the corners of the base plate raise the mount for insertion of eight firing pedestals under the base plate. The weapon may be emplaced for all-round fire within a few hours of reaching its destination. The 8″ Gun Railway

Mount, M1A1, is classified as Standard.

The 8″ railway matériel is accompanied by a modified commercial steel box car for ammunition, a Fire Control Car, M2, and a Machine Shop Car, M1, equipped for making necessary repairs to the gun and mount in the field. These cars are all classified as Standard. When traveling a gondola or flat car is required at the front end of the mount.

Sighting and Fire Control Equipment

On Carriage Equipment
Telescope Mount, M20
Elevation Quadrant, M1
Panoramic Telescope, M8

Off Carriage Sighting Equipment
Clinometer, M1912A1
Gunner's Quadrant, M1
Bore Sight

Equipment in Fire Control Car
Fire Adjustment Board, M1
Range Correction Board, M1A1
Deflection Board, M1

Data Transmission System, M9, of which Azimuth Indicator, M5, and Elevation Indicator, M5, are on carriage. The other elements are in the Fire Control Car.
Plotting and Relocating Board, M1
Spotting Board, M3
Percentage Corrector, M1
Set-forward Rule, Type B
Prediction Scale, M1
Generating Unit, M1

Ammunition

Ammunition is in the form of separate loading rounds. The standard service projectiles are A.P. shell, 260 lb. (Navy), Mk. XX, with B.D. fuze, Mk. X, and H.E. shell, 240 lb., M103, with P.D. fuze, M51A1, Model 1, with booster, M21A1.

Subcaliber Gun

For practice in laying and firing the 8″ gun a 75 mm subcaliber gun is mounted in the bore of the larger gun.

REFERENCES—TM 9–2005, v.4; TM 9–463; TM 4–210.

8 INCH GUN, MK. VI, MOD. 3A2, ON RAILWAY MOUNT, M1, with Gun at 45° Elevation and Outriggers in Place

SEACOAST EMPLACEMENT FOR 155 MM MOBILE GUNS—PANAMA MOUNT

PANAMA MOUNT FOR SEACOAST EMPLACEMENT OF 155 mm MOBILE GUNS, WITH 155 mm GUN, M1918M1, ON GUN CARRIAGE, M1918

The 155 mm field guns are the only mobile weapons regularly used as seacoast artillery. Since the 60° traverse of the 155 mm gun is insufficient for harbor defense, the gun is mounted on a concrete emplacement designed by the Corps of Engineers. The emplacement, known as the "Panama Mount," consists of a centrally located, round base, raised above a semicircular rim. The gun carriage rests on the base, the altitude of which provides a recoil pit and allows the gun to be fired at a greater elevation than would be possible otherwise. The spade plates are removed from the ends of the trails and are replaced by plates which fit a curved rail embedded in the semicircular rim of the emplacement. This permits the carriage to be rotated 180°. The additional 60° traverse of the gun thus makes a 240° field of fire practicable.

Sighting and Fire Control Equipment

When the 155 mm gun is used as coast artillery matériel, the following sighting and fire control equipment is employed.

In Panama
Telescope Mount, M4
Panoramic Telescope, M3A1
Telescope, M1909A1

Outside Panama
Telescope Mount, M6
Panoramic Telescope, M4
Telescope, M1909A1

Future Installations
Telescope Mount, M6A1
Panoramic Telescope, M8

REFERENCES—TM 4–210; TM 9–2005, v.4.

PANAMA MOUNT WITHOUT RECOIL PIT OR ELEVATION PLATFORM

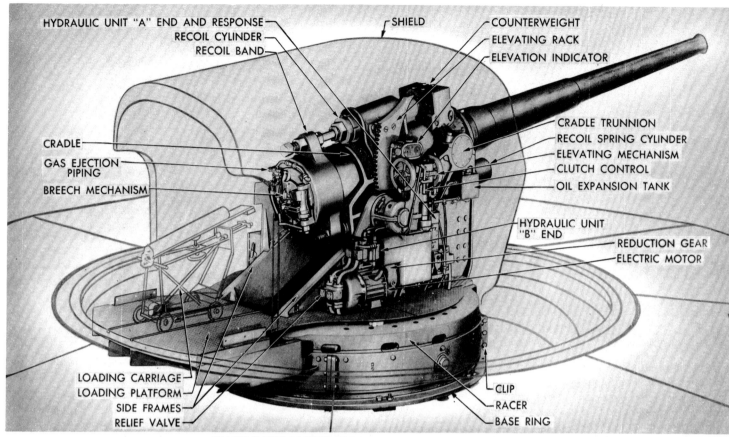

PHANTOM VIEW OF RIGHT SIDE OF 6 INCH BARBETTE CARRIAGE, M1

The 6″ Barbette Carriage, M1, is a modernization of earlier types of seacoast weapons. It was instituted for the purpose of supplying the United States with coast defense guns and carriages capable of protecting bases and harbors against cruisers and destroyers. Military characteristics of the carriage were approved in O.C.M. 15930, dated 5 July 1940, and standardization was approved in O.C.M. 17748 of 5 February 1942.

The Barbette Carriage, M1, was designed to utilize 6″ Guns, M1903 and M1905, on hand in considerable numbers. Since either gun can be fired at the rate of six rounds a minute, it has the speed of service possessed by a light gun in combination with a destructive power approaching that of the larger calibers. It may be used effectively against ships moving at 27 knots within 3,000 yards of the emplacement, or at a maximum range of 25,000 yards.

GUN, M1903—The gun is of built-up construction without a replaceable liner. When it is no longer accurate, a similar new gun of monobloc construction can be substituted for it. A breechblock of the interrupted thread variety is supplied with a firing mechanism for both percussion and electric primers.

GUN, M1905—The main difference between this gun and the M1903 is in the location of the center of gravity. This is compensated for by adjustable stops on the cradles.

BARBETTE CARRIAGE, M1—The carriage is designed for 360° traverse at a rate of not less than 1½° a second. A hydrospring recoil mechanism is employed. Elevation is accomplished by hydraulic power drive. In order to afford protection to the crew and carriage from bombing and shell fire, a deep shield of 6″ armor plate is placed overhead, in front and on both sides. The shield is open in the rear to permit service of the piece.

Sighting and Fire Control Equipment

Sighting equipment consisting of the Telescope, M31, and Mount, M35, is provided for Case II pointing. On carriage data receivers are provided for Case III pointing. Off carriage equipment varies with different gun batteries.

PRINCIPAL CHARACTERISTICS OF 6 INCH BARBETTE CARRIAGE, M1, WITH GUN, M1905

Weight of gun, carriage, shield, and base ring	176,000 lb.
Weight of gun	22,000 lb.
Length of bore	50 cals.
Number of grooves in barrel	76
Twist, one turn in	25 cals.
Weight of A. P. projectile	105 lb.
Muzzle velocity	2,800 f./s.
Maximum range	27,500 yds.
Maximum powder pressure	38,000 lb./sq. in.
Maximum elevation	47°
Minimum elevation	−5°
Traverse	360°
Normal recoil	19 ins.
Type of breechblock	interrupted screw
Type of recoil mechanism	hydrospring

Ammunition

Ammunition is in the form of separate loading rounds. It consists of A.P. Shell, Mk. XXXIII, and A.P. Shell, M1911, both furnished with B.D. fuze, M60; H.E. Shell, M1911, with B.D. fuze, M60, and H.E. Shell, Mk. II, with P.D. fuze, M47.

8 INCH GUN MK. VI, MOD. 3A2—BARBETTE CARRIAGE M1—STANDARD

The 8″ Gun, M1888, on Barbette Carriage, M1892, was the only 8″ matériel emplaced on fixed mounts until the adoption of the 8″ Gun, Mk. VI, Mod. 3A2, mounted on Barbette Carriage, M1. This latter combination of gun and carriage permits fire at a maximum range more than twice that of the earlier weapon.

8 INCH GUN, MK. VI, MOD. 3A2—This is the same gun used with the 8″ Railway Mount, M1A1.

8 INCH BARBETTE CARRIAGE, M1—The barbette carriage consists of a base ring bolted to a concrete emplacement, a traversing roller system, and a gun-supporting structure.

A tubular cradle containing the recoil and recuperator cylinders, the elevating rack, a liquid pump, air-pressure gage, air-charging and maneuvering valve and the breech platform is supported by trunnions in the side frames of the top carriage. The cradle serves to guide the gun in recoil and counter recoil.

The top carriage consists of the racer, the side frames, the front and rear transoms, the main platforms for securing the piece, dust guards and the racer clips.

The hydraulic recoil system is composed of a long and a short recoil cylinder. The recuperator system is pneumatically operated and consists of a cylinder and a plunger. An intensifier and air-charging mechanism is used to maintain pressure on the liquid seal in the stuffing box around the recuperator plunger and facilitates charging the recuperator.

The elevating mechanism is mounted on the right side frame of the top carriage. Emergency elevation and depression stops are provided.

The traversing mechanism is placed on the right side of the mount. An azimuth indicator drive mechanism pinion meshes with the data receiver drive rack on the base ring. An azimuth index plate graduated in tenths and fifteenths of a degree is mounted on the main platform.

A loading stand and trough facilitate loading of the gun and the ramming of projectiles.

The gun may be fired electrically by a firing pistol used in conjunction with a gun commander's push button. The gun cannot be fired until a complete circuit has been established. Current for the fir-

THREE-QUARTER REAR VIEW OF 8 INCH GUN, MK. VI, MOD. 3A2, ON BARBETTE CARRIAGE, M1

PRINCIPAL CHARACTERISTICS

Total weight of gun and carriage	103,000 lb.
Weight of gun and band	55,000 lb.
Weight of carriage	103,000 lb.
Overall length of gun	369 ins.
Length of barrel	45 cals.
Number of grooves in barrel	64
Rifling, uniform R.H., one turn in	25 cals.
Muzzle velocity (260 lb. shell)	2,750 f./s.
Total traverse	360°
Depression, maximum (loading angle)	−5°
Elevation, maximum	45°
Maximum range, A.P. 260 lb. projectile	32,980 yds.
Maximum range, H.E. 240 lb. projectile	35,635 yds.

Muzzle energy (A.P. 260 lb. shell)	15,300 ft.-tons
Rate of fire, approximate	2 rds./min.
Construction of gun	Built-up

RECOIL

Distance	27 ins.
Mechanism type	Hydraulic
Number of cylinders	2

COUNTER RECOIL

Mechanism type	Pneumatic
Number of cylinders	1

ing circuit is furnished by a storage battery.

Certain M1 carriages (Nos. 1 to 4 inclusive) are fitted with a counterweight on top of the cradle over the trunnions, carriages Nos. 5 and upward do not have this counterweight, the trunnions being placed lower on the cradle than is the case with the lower numbered carriages.

Carriages Nos. 1 to 4 inclusive have a simple elevation disk for showing elevation of the gun, and a similar azimuth disk. On carriage No. 5 and upward, the finished surface of a lug on the upper right side of the cradle is not level and is not intended as a seat for the gunner's quadrant.

Subcaliber Gun

For practice in laying and firing the 8″ gun a 75 mm gun is mounted in the bore of the larger gun.

Sighting and Fire Control Equipment

On Carriage Equipment

Telescope Mount, M35; Telescope, M31

Off Carriage Equipment

Off carriage fire control equipment is of the usual seacoast artillery type, the instruments for the individual position being determined by the local coast-defense commander according to the nature of the fire control system used in that area.

Ammunition

Ammunition is in the form of separate loading rounds. The standard service projectiles are A.P. shell, 260 lb. (Navy), Mk. XX, with B.D. fuze, Mk. X, and H.E. shell, 240 lb., M103, with P.D. fuze, M51A1, Model 1, with Booster, M21A1.

REFERENCES—TM 9-2005, v.4; TM 4-210.

12 INCH GUNS M1895A2, M1895A3, M1895M1A2, M1895M1A3
BARBETTE CARRIAGE M1917—SUBSTITUTE STANDARD

The 12″ Guns, M1895A2, M1895A3, M1895M1A2 and M1895M1A3, on Barbette Carriage, M1917, are classified as Substitute Standard. There is no Standard 12″ weapon in service, although a new model barbette carriage to meet modern requirements is under development. All older models are classified as Limited Standard.

12 INCH GUNS OF 1895 TYPE—These guns are of built-up construction, with variable rifling. The breechblock is of the Stockett, three-cycle, tray-supported type, consisting of a cylindrical, single-thread, slotted block operated by hand. A seacoast firing mechanism, M1903, is housed in a seat on the rear end of the obturator spindle, and is designed for firing primers electrically.

12 INCH BARBETTE CARRIAGE, M1917—The Barbette Carriage, M1917, was developed from 1917 to 1922 without parapets or shields. Casemates are now being built over all carriages. The mount is constructed in the usual manner for a barbette carriage. The gun is carried in a cradle which contains the recoil and counter-recoil system. The hydraulic recoil mechanism permits a 30 inch recoil. Counter recoil is accomplished by a 4 cylinder, spring-type recuperator assembly. Return of the gun to battery is eased by a plug-type counter-recoil buffer.

The elevating mechanism, of the screw type, is motor driven, but in case of power failure the gun can be elevated by hand. Traversing is by handpower only, the mechanism consisting of a spur gear meshing with a circular rack inside and concentric with the base ring. The top carriage is bolted to a racer which rides on rollers between it and the base ring and rotates with the racer when the traversing handwheel is turned to operate the spur gear.

An azimuth circle and index are employed in laying the piece for direction. The azimuth and elevation setters work below the ground level.

Ammunition is served to the gun on shot trucks and powder trays operating on the surface of the ground. Loading is by hand, but experiments are under way to develop a suitable electric rammer for this weapon.

Subcaliber Gun

Subcaliber equipment for these 12″ Guns comprises the 75 mm Gun, which is mounted in the bore of the larger weapon.

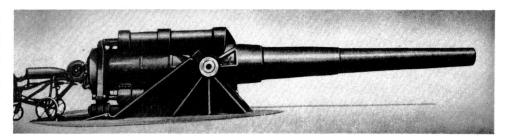

12 INCH GUN, M1895, ON BARBETTE CARRIAGE, M1917

PRINCIPAL CHARACTERISTICS

Total weight of gun and carriage....406,700 lb.
Weight of gun and band...........118,200 lb.
Overall length of barrel...............36.9 ft.
Length of barrel....................35 cals.
Rifling...................twist 1–50 to 1–25
Number of grooves......................72
Muzzle velocity (1,070 lb. proj.)....2,250 f./s.
Total traverse in casemate...............145°
Depression, maximum.....................0°
Elevation, maximum.....................35°
Maximum range, 1,070 lb. projectile. 27,600 yds.
Maximum range, 975 lb. projectile..30,100 yds.
Maximum range, 900 lb. projectile..29,200 yds.
Volume of powder chamber......12,403 cu. ins.
Maximum powder pressure....38,000 lb./sq. in.
Life (full charge)..................350 rounds
Rate of fire.....................1⅓ rds./min.
Construction of gun...................Built-up
Muzzle energy............36,754 ft. long tons

Breechblock
Type.........................Stockett
Single or step cut ....Single
Operating handles......................1
Operation....................Hand only
Firing mechanism..........Seacoast, M1903

Recoil
Distance..........................30 ins.
Mechanism type........Hydraulic (grooves)
Number of cylinders....................1

Counter recoil
Mechanism type....................Spring
Number of cylinders...................4
Buffer type.............Hydraulic plug type
Primers......Combination electric and friction

Sighting and Fire Control Equipment
On Carriage Equipment
Telescope Mount, M1912M1, 3″
Telescope, M1912, 3″

Six carriages have T11 Data receivers. Receivers for M10 Data Transmission System to be applied to other carriages.

Off Carriage Equipment
Off carriage fire control equipment is of the usual seacoast artillery type, the instruments for the individual position being determined by the local coast defense commander according to the nature of the fire control system used in that area.

REAR VIEW OF 12 INCH GUN, M1895, ON BARBETTE CARRIAGE, M1917

Ammunition

Service ammunition for the 12″ Gun, M1895M1, is in the form of separate loading rounds. It consists of A.P. Shell, Mk. VI, with B.D. Fuze, Mk. X, and H.E. Shell, Mk. X, with P.D. Fuzes, M46 and M47.

REFERENCES—TM 9–2005, v.4; TM 9–2400; FM 4–60.

16 INCH GUN MK. II, MOD. 1—BARBETTE CARRIAGE M5—STANDARD

16 INCH GUN, MK. II, MOD. 1, ON CARRIAGE, M5

The 16 inch gun is the largest and most powerful American coast defense weapon. The Mk. II, Mod. 1, gun with its recoil mechanism and cradle, is of Navy design. The Barbette Carriage, M4, was designed by the Army as a modification of the earlier 16 inch Barbette Carriage, M1919. The gun is mounted in a casemate type of emplacement.

16 INCH GUN, MK. II, MOD. 1—This gun is of built-up construction. It consists of a tube, liner, jacket, hoops, rings, recoil band and a breech mechanism with closing cylinders and gas-ejector systems. Rotation of the gun during recoil and counter recoil is prevented by a stake-in key. Automatic elevating stops confine elevation or depression within prescribed limits.

The breechblock is of interrupted-thread design, dropping on hydraulic buffers when opened. It is opened by hand, but is closed by a piston actuated by compressed air. The Firing Lock, Mk. I, resembles the firing lock on all Navy cannon employing separate-loading ammunition. It uses a combination electric-percussion primer which may be fired by electricity or by lanyard.

After each round, the bore of the gun is blown free of gases by a jet of compressed air.

BARBETTE CARRIAGE, M4—The main structure of the carriage consists of two side frames which support the tipping parts and provide trunnion bearings for the cradle; a front transom tying together the side frames; floor beams to support the floor of the mount and stiffen the racer; a cast-steel racer bolted to the side frames and riding on conical rollers rest-

PRINCIPAL CHARACTERISTICS

16 INCH GUN, MK. II, MODEL 1

Weight of gun with band	307,185 lb.
Weight of gun without band	287,050 lb.
Caliber	16 ins.
Length of bore	50 cals.
Length (muzzle to rear face of breech ring)	821 ins.
Weight of projectile { Mk. XII, A.P.	2,240 lb.
Mk. II, M2, A.P.	2,100 lb.
Weight of powder charge (for both Mk. XII and Mk. II, M2, full charge)	672 lb.
Chamber pressure	38,000 lb./sq. in.
Muzzle velocity { Mk. XII projectile	2,650 f./s.
Mk. II, M2 projectile	2,750 f./s.
Range (46° elevation) { Mk. XII projectile	45,100 yds.
Mk. II, M2 projectile	44,670 yds.
Travel of projectile in barrel	681.68 ins.
Capacity of powder chamber	30,000 cu. ins.
Rifling:	
Length	675.992 ins.
Number of grooves	96
Twist	Right-hand uniform, 1 turn in 32 cals.

16 INCH BARBETTE CARRIAGE, M4

Weight of carriage without shield, gun and band	665,315 lb.
Total dead load on emplacement including shield	1,172,500 lb.
Weight of recoiling parts including gun and band	316,853 lb.
Weight of tipping parts including gun and band	385,377 lb.
Weight of tipping parts not including gun and band	78,192 lb.
Weight of base ring and stationary parts	186,426 lb.
Weight of traversing parts including shield	986,074 lb.
Weight of air compressor	4,200 lb.
Traverse	145°
Maximum elevation	46°
Maximum depression	Depends on location
Normal recoil	48 ins.
Maximum recoil	49 ins.

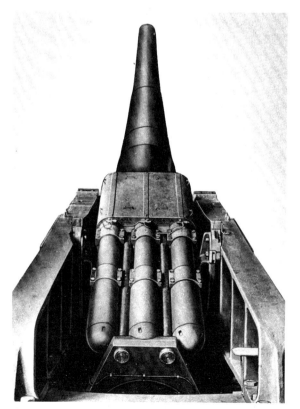

REAR VIEW OF 16 INCH GUN, MK. II, MOD. 1 WITH GUN ELEVATED, SHOWING RECUPERATOR CYLINDERS

ing on the upper surface of the base ring; a base ring of four sections bolted together and anchored in a concrete foundation, and a traversing rack bolted to the outside of the base ring.

The gun is supported in a cradle of gridiron design with trunnions so located in relation to the center of gravity of the tipping parts that there is a slight breech preponderance when the gun is loaded and a muzzle preponderance when it is unloaded. This feature, together with anti-friction bearings at the trunnions, permits the gun, after it is fired, to be dropped smoothly to loading position by a spin of the handwheel.

The recoil mechanism consists of a single recoil cylinder and three recuperator cylinders. The recoil cylinder is located on the under side of the cradle, while the recuperator cylinders are assembled at the top. Recoil is controlled hydraulically, but recuperation is accomplished by the hydropneumatic method. Buffer action for counter recoil is obtained by means of a buffer plunger functioning in a cavity in the recoil cylinder head.

The elevating mechanism comprises two spur-gear racks mounted on either side of the cradle, the anti-friction mechanism incorporated in the trunnion bearings, a Waterbury hydraulic speed gear, shafts, trains of gears leading to the handwheel and the elevating motor. A buffer in each side frame stops the gun at either extreme of elevation without serious jar-

ring. Friction handbrakes are included in the mechanism. Elevation is normally effected by electric motor through the speed gear, but there are handcranks for manual operation in case of power failure.

An elevation data receiver, part of the Data Transmission System, M5, gives the correct elevation for the gun and makes unnecessary the range disk used in earlier 16 inch barbette carriages.

The carriage can be traversed either by hand through a train of bevel and spur gears leading from the slow- and high-speed handwheels to the traversing rack on the base ring, or by an electric motor through a Waterbury speed gear.

An azimuth data indicator is located near the left traversing handwheel for tracking in azimuth with off carriage fire control equipment which transmits azimuths mechanically to one of the dials of the indicator.

The carriage is mounted in a circular pit so that all mechanism is below the ground level. Additional protection is afforded by an armored shield 4 inches thick with side walls 12 feet high.

Ammunition trucks are loaded at the magazines, pushed to the carriage by hand and unloaded onto parking tables in rear of the mount whence it is rolled onto the rammer. A power rammer operated by an electric motor through a hydraulic speed gear is utilized to increase rapidity of fire and to insure uniform seating of

the heavy projectile. In case of power failure, manual loading may be accomplished by two handcranks each manned by four men.

Electric power for operating the various mechanisms of the carriage is produced by a Diesel engine generator located in the emplacement. An overhead trolley is provided as an alternate means of transporting projectiles. The M4 Carriage is now Substitute Standard.

BARBETTE CARRIAGE, M5—The chief differences between Carriages, M4 and M5, are that in the M5 roller bearings replace the trunnion anti-friction device of the M4; the air compressor, compressor motor, and air tanks are removed from the carriage; a redesigned traversing mechanism with a motor of greater horsepower raises the traversing rate to 3.5° per second, and a new type of hydraulic speed gear is employed. Increased power of the rammer motor is also a factor in faster operating speed of the Carriage, M5.

Compressed air for scavenging and for closing the breechblock of the M5 is brought through piping from the power room to the carriage.

Sighting and Fire Control Equipment

On Carriage Equipment
Telescope Mount, M35
Telescope, M31

Off Carriage Equipment
This may vary depending upon the system of position finding and the type of plotting room equipment used.

Ammunition

Ammunition for the 16 inch gun, Mk. II, M1, is in the form of separate loading rounds. It consists of A. P. shell, Mk. XII, with B. D. fuze, Mk. X, and A. P. shell, Mk. II, M2, with B. D. fuze, Mk. X.

Subcaliber Gun

Subcaliber equipment for the 16 inch Gun, Mk. II, M1, consists of a 75 mm gun for mounting in the bore of the larger gun.

REFERENCES—TM 9-2005, v.4; TM 9-471.

16 INCH GUN, MK. II, MOD. 1, ON MOUNT, M4, MOUNTED IN A CASEMATE

37 MM GUN M6—STANDARD FOR TANKS

37 mm TANK GUN, M6. RIGHT-SIDE VIEW WITH
BREECH-OPERATING MECHANISM ASSEMBLED

The 37 mm tank guns were developed from the 37 mm Antitank Gun, M3, the first model being the 37 mm Tank Gun, M5. Addition of an automatically opened breechblock changed the designation to the M6, standardized by O.C.M. 16279 dated 14 Nov. 1940. The M5 barrel is shorter by about 5 inches than the barrels of the other guns.

The 37 mm Gun, M6, is standard for use on Light Tanks, M3A1, M3A3, M5 and M5A1; on Medium Tank, M3, and its variations, and on the 37 mm Light Armored Car, M8. The gun is carried on the M23, M24 or M44 Mount.

The barrel is a one-piece forging or casting with a rifled bore, threaded to screw into the breech ring. Two bearings support the barrel and align it in the yoke of the sleigh. Keys are employed to prevent rotation of the barrel.

The breech ring is broached to receive the drop-type breechblock. A breech-operating mechanism is bolted to the recoil cylinder. Recoil of the gun automatically opens the breechblock, extracts the empty cartridge case, locks the breech in an open position and cocks the gun. Rounds are inserted into the breech manually.

The recoil cylinder is assembled with the trunnion pins mounted in the trunnions of the yoke. It is provided with rails to guide the sleigh and contains a recoil mechanism of the hydrospring type, the counter-recoil spring, and a buffer mechanism.

In tanks with power traverse the gun is fired by a solenoid-firing device connected with the trigger. In other cases the hand-operated trigger actuator causes the firing process to start.

The gun may be elevated by a hand-wheel, but a throw-out lever permits free movement of the weapon.

Traverse of guns mounted in tanks with power-traversing mechanisms is obtained by power-drive rotation of the turret. In tanks equipped with manually operated turrets only, the gun can be traversed 10° right or left by means of a traversing knob. When greater traverse is necessary the turret must be rotated or the tank turned in direction.

A shield is attached to the yoke and recoil cylinder by bolts, or, in some tanks, direct to the turret.

PRINCIPAL CHARACTERISTICS

Weight of gun	190 lb.
Total weight of gun and mount	700 lb.
Length of barrel	78 ins.
Overall length of gun	82.5 ins.
Diameter of bore	1.457 ins.
Rifling, uniform R.H.	1 turn in 25 cals.
Weight of powder charge	8 oz. (approx.)
Volume of powder chamber	19.92 cu. ins.
Maximum powder pressure (Rated for A.P.C. Shot, M51B2)	50,000 lb./sq. in.
Maximum rate of fire	30 rds./min.
Maximum rate of fire, aimed	15–20 rds./min.
Muzzle vel., A.P.C. Shot, M51B2	2,900 f./s.
Muzzle vel., H.E. Shell, MK. II	2,750 f./s.
Muzzle vel., H.E. Shell, M63	2,600 f./s.
Maximum range (M51B2)	12,850 yds.
Weight of H.E. projectile	1.61 lb.
Weight of A.P.C. Shot, M51B2	1.92 lb.
Weight of recoil mechanism	77.5 lb.
Length of recoil	6–8 ins.
Maximum elevation	+20°
Minimum elevation	−10°
Maximum traverse (manually operated turret)	10° in each direction

ARMOR PENETRATION AT 20°	Homo. Plate		Face-Hard. Plate	
	500 yards	1,000 yards	500 yards	1,000 yards
A.P.C. Shot, M51B2, Supercharge	2.4 ins.	2.1 ins.	2.1 ins.	1.8 ins.

37 mm GUN, M6, MOUNTED IN COMBINATION MOUNT, M23, IN TURRET OF LIGHT TANK, M5

A traveling lock inside the turret is utilized to prevent undue wear on the elevating mechanism.

A spent-case deflector is bolted to the recoil cylinder and has suspended from it a bag to receive the ejected cartridge cases.

Ammunition

Ammunition is in the form of fixed rounds. It consists of a Canister, M2, H. E. Shell, M63, with B.D. Fuze, M58; H. E. Shell, Mk. II, with B. D. Fuze, M38A1, and A.P.C. Shot, M51B2, with tracer.

Sighting Equipment

Sighting equipment varies with the tank in which the gun is mounted. The following table designates the sighting equipment used with each tank.

Tank	Tele-scope	Peri-scope
Light Armored Car, M8	M70D	——
Light Tanks, M3A1, M3A2	M40A2	M4A1
Light Tanks, M3A3, M5A1	M70D, M40A2	M4A1
Light Tank, M5	M40A2	M4A1
Medium Tank, M3, and variations	M19A1	M2
Heavy Tanks, M6, M6A1*	M15, M39A2	M8A1

*O.C.M. 19199 specifies that all 37 mm guns shall be removed from heavy tanks.

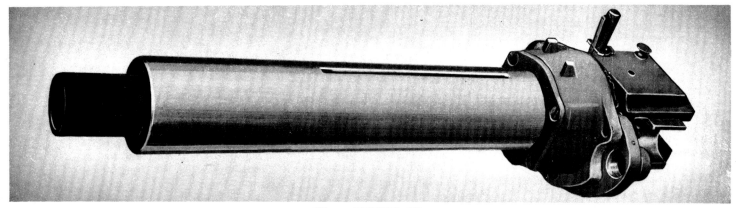

75 mm HOWITZER, M3

The decision to adapt the Pack Howitzer, M1 or M1A1, for use in the Howitzer Motor Carriage, M8, necessitated spot welding and keying a tube mounting support in place over the howitzer tube. This mounting support increased the outside diameter of the tube to fit the central bore of the cradle. Pack howitzer tubes modified in this manner were designated Howitzers, M2. They are now classified as Substitute Standard.

Since there were insufficient M2 tubes to supply the required number of howitzer motor carriages, new tubes were made with the howitzer mounting support integral with the tube. These tubes were given the designation of 75 mm Howitzer, M3, and classified as Standard.

Howitzers, M2 and M3, are manually loaded weapons fired electrically by means of a solenoid, or manually by a hand firing mechanism handle. The tube assembly differs from that of the M1 or M1A1 Howitzers only in the hoop at the rear end of the mounting support on the M2 and in the flash detector which is integral with the howitzer shield in both the M2 and M3 models.

The tube is screwed into a breech ring containing a breechblock of the horizontal sliding wedge type. A recoil tube retainer, which provides the means of attaching the two recoil cylinder assemblies to the tube assembly, is bolted to a breech yoke support on the tube.

The tube assembly is supported and alined in a cradle which is a part of the mount assembly. The tube mounting support, which is finish-ground, rides in liners inside the cradle.

The Firing Lock, M13, fits into an axial hole in the breechblock. It is of the continuous-pull, self-cocking type, and is retained in position by sector lugs on its exterior which engage with lugs in the breechblock.

The hydrospring recoil mechanism consists of two recoil cylinders, one on each side of the howitzer, which are held and located in the cradle. A counter-recoil buffer is attached to the front cover of each cylinder.

Howitzers, M2 and M3, are mounted in 75 mm Howitzer Mount, M7, which rests on trunnions in the turret of the Howitzer Motor Carriage, M8. The mount assembly is composed of a cradle with two recoil cylinders, a firing mechanism, and a recoil guard. The shield is attached to the forward end of the cradle and is elevated and depressed with it. Rotation of the howitzer is prevented by a key in the cradle which rides in a groove in the howitzer tube mounting support.

The firing mechanism is mounted on the rear end of the recoil guard. An electrical system is provided for primary use, with current supplied by the vehicle battery. The system operates electrically from a firing button, activating the electro-magnetic solenoid, and then through a mechanical series of linkages to a trigger chain hooked directly to the trigger. A hand firing system, which may be employed in case of failure of the elevation system, is operated by the hand firing mechanism handle and utilizes the mechanical linkage of the electrical firing system.

A recoil guard of tubular framework with right and left shields surrounds the breech. It is attached to the cradle and acts as a support for the electrical firing mechanism.

Elevation is accomplished by means of an elevating mechanism mounted on the right rear wall of the turret. A train of gears inside the elevating mechanism case connects with a pinion that meshes with the elevating quadrant rack on the howitzer cradle. The elevating mechanism is operated by a handwheel which may be engaged with or disengaged from the gear train by means of a shifter lever and a sliding gear.

Traverse is obtained by rotating the turret. A handwheel operates a gear train and a pinion meshed with the traversing rack bolted to the under side of the turret roof. A traversing lock is provided to lock the turret in traveling position.

Sighting and Fire Control Equipment

Telescope, M70C
Telescope Mount, M44, with Panoramic Telescope, M12A5
Gunner's Quadrant, M1

Ammunition

Ammunition is in the form of fuzed, fixed and semifixed complete rounds. It consists of Shell, fixed, H.E., A.T., M66, with Fuze, B.D., M62; Shell, fixed, H.E., A.T., M66, steel case, with Fuze, B.D., M62; Shell, semifixed, H.E., M41A1, with Fuze, P.D., M48, M48A1, or M48A2; Shell, semifixed, H.E., M41A1, with Fuze, P.D., M54; Shell, semifixed, H.E., M48, with Fuze, P.D., M48, M48A1, M48A2 or M54; Shell, semifixed, H.E., M48, steel case, with Fuze, P.D., M48, M48A1, M48A2, or M54; Shell, semifixed, gas, persistent, H, M64, with Fuze, P.D., M57; Shell, semifixed, gas, persistent, H, M64, steel case, with Fuze, P.D., M57; Shell, semifixed, smoke, FS, M64, with Fuze, P.D., M57; Shell, semifixed, smoke, phosphorous, WP, M64, with Fuze, P.D., M57; Shell, semifixed, smoke, phosphorous, WP, M64, Steel case, with Fuze, P.D., M57.

REFERENCES — OCM 21025; OCM 21293; TM 9–318.

CHARACTERISTICS

Weight of 75 mm Howitzer, M2.........318 lb.
Weight of 75 mm Howitzer, M3.........421 lb.
Length of bore.......................35.91 ins.
Length overall.......................54.18 ins.
Rifling
    Length...........................35.91 ins.
    Twist........Uniform, right; one turn in 20 cals.
    Number of grooves.....................28
    Depth of grooves...................0.03 in.
    Width of grooves................0.1866 in.
    Width of lands................0.14439 in.
Type of breechblock.........Horizontal sliding
Maximum powder pressure..........20,600 lb.
Muzzle velocity....700, 810, 950, 1,250 f./s.
Maximum range (Shell, H.E., M41)..9,760 yds.
Maximum elevation.....................40°
Maximum depression...................−20°
Traverse of turret (with howitzer)..........360°
Normal recoil.......................11.62 ins.
Type of recoil mechanism..........Hydrospring

75 MM GUN M3—STANDARD FOR TANKS

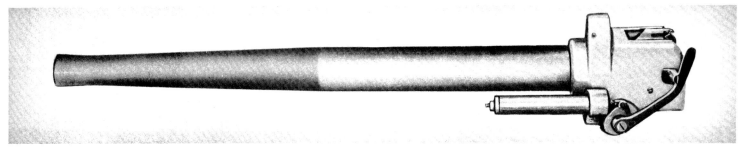

75 mm GUN, M3, SHOWING TUBE, BREECH RING, COCKING LEVER, CLOSING SPRING CYLINDER AND OPERATING HANDLE

The 75 mm Gun, M3, a development from the Tank Gun, M2, was standardized by O.C.M. 17018, dated 24 July 1941. The M2 gun is now designated as Limited Standard.

The M3 gun is a single-shot, flat-trajectory weapon differing from the M2 only in having the tube lengthened by 26.6″, with a higher muzzle velocity and greater range as a result. It is equipped with a drop-type breechblock automatically opened. This weapon is mounted in Medium Tanks, M4, M4A1, M4A2, M4A3, M4A4, and in Medium Tank, M7, using Mounts, M34, M34A1 and M47.

The alloy steel tube screws into the breech ring, where it is locked into position with a key. The breech ring contains the vertical sliding breechblock assembly and the principal operating parts of the gun. The breech mechanism is composed of the breechblock assembly, firing mechanism, extractors, spline shaft, breechblock crank, operating crank, closing mechanism and related parts. A hole bored through the center of the breechblock houses the percussion mechanism.

The breech may be opened by means of an operating handle secured to the spline shaft.

Manual loading of each round automatically closes the block. The gun can be fired either manually or by means of a solenoid. During counterrecoil after firing, the gun is cocked, the block is opened, the cartridge case is extracted and the breechblock is locked in an open position for insertion of the next round.

The gun recoils in the mount, which consists of a horizontal rotor upon which is mounted the elevating mechanism and traversing mechanism; the hydraulic recoil mechanism, supported by trunnions which rotate in the trunnion seats of the horizontal rotor; an elevating shield, bolted to the trunnions of the recoil mechanism and projecting through an opening in the rotor; two recoil cylinders, held by the cradle and trunnion assembly upon which are mounted the solenoid, firing lever link, and firing lever of the firing mechanism; and a shoulder guard, bolted to the cradle, covering the firing mechanism and extending beyond the rear face of the breech.

CHARACTERISTICS

Weight of gun, recoil mechanism and
 elevating shield at trunnion..........1,763 lb.
Weight of gun........................910 lb.
Length of gun......................118.38 ins.
Muzzle velocity, A.P. shell
 (weight 14.92 lb.)...............2,030 f./s.
Muzzle velocity, H.E. shell
 (weight 14.60 lb.)...............1,515 f./s.
Maximum powder pressure ....38,000 lb./sq. in.
Rate of fire........................20 rds./min.
Maximum range, A.P. shell........14,000 yds.
Maximum elevation...................19°12′
Maximum depression...................7°48′
Traverse, left............................14°
Traverse, right..........................14°

Sighting Equipment

Periscope, M10, or M4A1
Telescope, M38A1
Azimuth Indicator, M19

Ammunition

Ammunition is in the form of complete, fixed rounds. It consists of A.P.C. shell, M61, with tracer, and B.D. fuze, M66A1; H.E. shell, M48, normal charge, with P.D. fuze, M48.

References—FM 23–95; TM 9–307; TM 9–2005, v.5; Oldsmobile Training Manual, 75 mm, M3, Tank Gun.

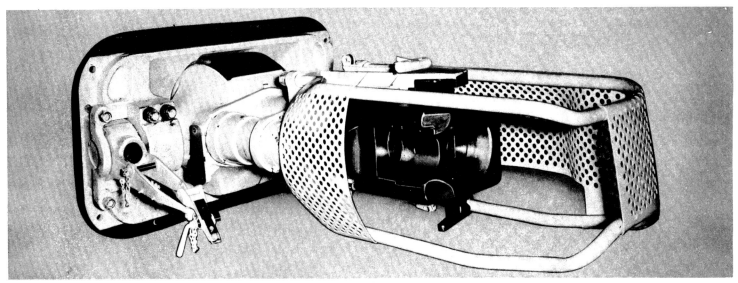

BREECH END OF 75 mm GUN, M3, WITH RECOIL MECHANISM AND SHOULDER GUARD

76 MM TANK GUN M1A2—STANDARD

76 MM TANK GUN, M1A1. THE M1A2 DIFFERS FROM THE M1A1 ONLY IN HAVING THE MUZZLE END THREADED FOR ATTACHMENT OF A MUZZLE BRAKE

The 76 mm Gun, M1A2, is a modification of the M1 Gun of the same caliber. The original 76 mm Gun, M1, was designed to provide tank weapons of greater power and armor penetration than were possible with 75 mm armament.

76 mm GUN, M1—This gun was designed to use the 3″ H.E. Shell or A.P.C. Projectile with a different cartridge case. The gun tube and extractors were constructed to accommodate the redesigned cartridge, but the breech ring and breech mechanism were similar to those used on the 75 mm Gun, M3. This 76 mm Gun, M1, is now Limited Standard.

76 mm GUN, M1A1—In order to better adapt the M1 Gun to use with various tanks and gun motor carriages, the contour of the tube was changed, and the recoil slide surface on the tube was lengthened 12 inches, thus permitting the trunnion position to be set farther forward to obtain better balance. The M1 gun with these modifications was designated 76 mm Gun, M1A1, and is classified as Limited Standard.

76 mm GUN, M1A2—In the 76 mm Gun, M1A2, the rifling twist is one turn in 32 calibers instead of one turn in 40 calibers as in the M1 and M1A1 Guns. All tubes are threaded at the muzzle to allow assembly of a muzzle brake, and a ring is provided to cover the threaded portion of the tube when the muzzle brake is not in place. This gun is classified as Standard.

Sighting Equipment

Telescope, M47A2
Periscope, M4A1

Ammunition

Ammunition is in the form of complete fixed rounds. It consists of Shell, H.E., 3 Inch, M42A1, with Fuze, P.D., M48A1; Projectile, 76 mm, A.P.C., M62, with Fuze, B.D., M66A1, and Shell, Smoke, M88.

CHARACTERISTICS

Diameter of bore.............76.2 mm (3 ins.)
Length of bore.....................52 cals.
Overall length of gun.............167.75 ins.
Weight of gun.....................1,204 lb.
Weight of tube.....................940 lb.
Capacity of chamber.............142.6 cu. ins.
Muzzle velocity (H.E. Shell, M42A1) 2,800 f./s.
Rated maximum powder pressure....43,000 p.s.i.
Maximum range (H.E. Shell,
 M42A1)......................14,780 yds.
Type of breechblock...........Semi-automatic, vertical drop

3 INCH TANK GUN M7—STANDARD

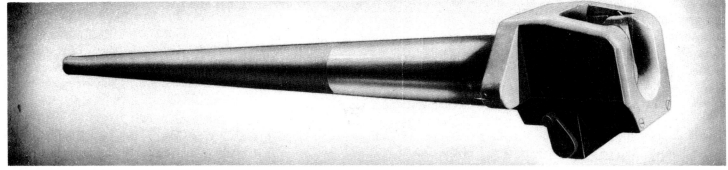

3 INCH TANK GUN, M7

The 3″ Gun, M7, was designed for use in Heavy Tanks, M6 and M6A1. It was also adopted as standard armament for the 3″ Gun Motor Carriage, M10. Ammunition for this weapon is the same as that for the 3″ antitank and antiaircraft guns.

O.C.M. 16200, dated 24 October 1940, initiated the development of a 3″ gun similar to 3″ Gun, T9, for the Heavy Tank, T1. It was designated 3″ Gun, T12, with interior dimensions and ballistics practically identical with those of the 3″ Antiaircraft Gun, M3, and the 3″ Antitank Gun, M5. After firing tests, the T12 was standardized as 3″ Gun, M7, by O.C.M. 18467, dated 9 July 1942.

The 3″ Gun, M7, is a high-velocity, manually loaded weapon employing a semi-automatic breech mechanism with a vertical drop-type breechblock. The general functioning of the gun is very similar to that of the 75 mm Gun, M3. A solenoid-actuated mechanism is used for firing the gun. The recoil mechanism and mount for this gun are supplied along with the vehicle.

Ammunition

Ammunition is in the form of complete fixed rounds. It consists of A.P.C. projectile, M62, with B.D. fuze, M66A1; A.P. shot, M79, and H.E. shell, M42A1, with M.T. fuze, M43.

CHARACTERISTICS

Diameter of bore.......................3 ins.
Length of bore.......................50 cals.
Overall length of gun...............158.1 ins.
Travel of projectile.................128.49 ins.
Weight of gun only..................1,990 lb.
Capacity of chamber (with A.P.C., M62)
 205.58 cu. ins.
Maximum powder pressure.....38,000 lb./sq. in.
Muzzle velocity (A.P.C., M62)......2,600 f./s.
 (H.E., M42A1).....2,800 f./s.
Maximum range (A.P.C., M62)....16,100 yds.
Breech mechanism.....semi-automatic drop block
Recoil mechanism.......................hydraulic

SIGHTING EQUIPMENT—Sighting equipment for the 3″ Gun, M7, varies according to the type of vehicle in which the gun is installed.

Tank or Armored Car	Telescope	Telescope Mount	Panoramic Telescope	Azimuth Indicator	Periscope
M10, M10A1	M70G	M30	M12A4	M18	M6
M6, M6A1	M39A1	——	——	——	M8A1

90 MM GUN M3—STANDARD

90 mm TANK GUN, M3

Battle experience in North Africa indicated the desirability of a weapon which would materially increase the firepower of tanks and gun motor carriages. The high velocity, range, and relatively flat trajectory of the 90 mm Gun, M1, were thought to make it particularly suitable for this use. Weight was also given to the availability of all types of ammunition for the M1 gun, including armorpiercing projectiles. A project was therefore initiated to investigate the feasibility of installing this gun in the 3 Inch Gun Motor Carriage, M10, in place of the 3 Inch Gun, M7. Experiments were conducted which indicated the necessity of modifying the gun before it could be successfully utilized for this purpose. Upon completion of the modifications required to adapt the M1 gun to the Mount, M7, of the 3 Inch Gun Motor Carriage, the weapon was standardized as 90 mm Gun, M3.

The 90 mm Gun, M3, has the same exterior and interior ballistics as the M1, and uses the same ammunition. A new breech ring was provided with a lug on each side for attaching the piston rods of the 3 inch recoil mechanism. In the M3, the breech-operating handle is mounted directly on the breech mechanism assembly. The breech mechanism is semi-automatic in operation and required changes in the breech-operating cam of the M1 gun. It also was essential to alter the trigger mechanism to enable the M3 gun to be fired when mounted in tanks or gun motor carriages.

A longitudinal key-way and a cylindrical recoil surface directly on the exterior of the M3 tube, added to permit the weapon to fit the 3 Inch Mount, M7, resulted in a decreased exterior diameter of the tube and thinner powder chamber walls than those of the Gun, M1.

In order to secure the desired throttling action for the Gun, M3, it was necessary to substitute new sleeves in the 3 inch recoil mechanism. The 90 mm Gun, M3, is now mounted on the 90 mm Gun Motor Carriage, T71, which is a modification of the 3 Inch Gun Motor Carriage, M10A1.

Ammunition

Ammunition is in the form of fuzed, complete, fixed rounds. It consists of Shell, H.E., M58, with Fuze, time, mechanical, M43; Shell, H.E. (Ammonal), M58, with Fuze, time, mechanical, M43; Shell, H.E., M71, with Fuze, time, mechanical, M43; Shell, H.E., M71, with Fuze, time, mechanical, M43; Shell, H.E., M71, with Fuze, P.D., M48; Shell, H.E., M71, with Fuze, P.D., M48A1; Projectile, A.P.C., M82, with Fuze, B.D., M68, and Tracer; Shot, A.P., M77, with Tracer; Ammunition, Blank, 90 mm Gun, M1, and Cartridge, drill, M12, with Fuze, dummy, M44A2.

PRINCIPAL CHARACTERISTICS

Caliber	90 mm
Weight, complete	2,260 lb.
Length overall	186.15 ins.
Length of bore	50 cals.
Length of rifling	152.4 ins.
Grooves, number	32
width	.1978 in.
depth	.04 in.
Width of lands	.15 in.
Twist, uniform, R.H.	1 turn in 32 cals.
Travel of projectile	156.4 ins.
Chamber capacity	300 cu. ins.
Maximum powder pressure	38,000 lb./sq. in.
Muzzle velocity	
H.E., M71 (23.4 lb.)	2,700 f./s.
A.P., M77 (23.4 lb.)	2,700 f./s.
A.P.C., M82 (24.06 lb.)	2,680 f./s.
Range at 20° elevation (computed)	
H.E., M71	13,000 yds.
A.P., M77	10,200 yds.
A.P.C. M82	14,800 yds.
Breech mechanism	Drop block, semi-auto.
Recoil	12⅜ ins.
Elevation	−10° to +20°
Traverse	360°

90 mm GUN, M3, MOUNTED ON 90 mm GUN MOTOR CARRIAGE, T71

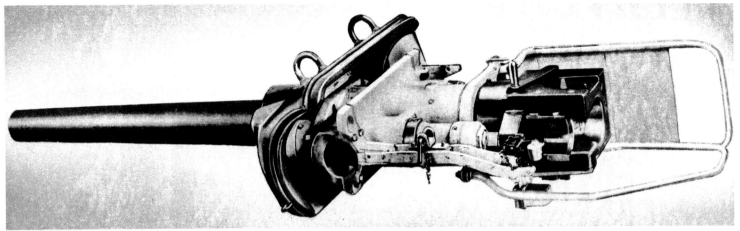

105 mm HOWITZER, M4, AND COMBINATION GUN MOUNT, M52

The 105 mm Howitzer, M4, was developed following reports from battle fronts which indicated that there was definite need for a 105 mm howitzer mounted in a medium tank. In the Medium Tanks, M4 and M4A3, the howitzer can now be carried in the most forward combat areas with less danger of being neutralized by small arms and light cannon fire than the lightly armored 105 mm Howitzer Motor Carriage, M7.

The M4 Howitzer consists of a tube screwed into a breech ring, where it is locked in place by a locking screw. Rotation of the tube in the mount is prevented by engagement of a key in the bottom of the breech ring with a groove in the cradle.

The breech mechanism is of the horizontal sliding wedge type, manually operated. A percussion firing mechanism in the breechblock is actuated either electrically or manually. A separate firing mechanism located on the under side of the cradle yoke provides a means of releasing the percussion mechanism that fires the howitzer. It is operated by a firing pedal connected to a solenoid with a plunger that pushes the firing trigger plunger and results in release of the percussion firing mechanism.

The M4 Howitzer is mounted in the Combination Gun Mount, M52. This mount is fastened to the turret of the tank by trunnions around which the howitzer and mount are elevated and depressed. The mount consists of a cradle, two recoil cylinders, an elevating mechanism, a firing mechanism, a co-axial machine-gun mount, and a shield.

The howitzer is supported in a central longitudinal hole in the cradle, with the two recoil cylinders in smaller holes on each side of the howitzer tube. Bronze liners in the howitzer hole provide a bearing surface for the tube. A yoke welded to the front end of the cradle extends rearward from the bottom of the cradle. A groove machined in the top surface of the yoke engages a key on the bottom of the breech ring and guides the howitzer during recoil and counterrecoil.

The recoil mechanism is of the hydrospring type. Counterrecoil is controlled by two large counterrecoil springs. A counterrecoil buffer is located in the front of each recoil cylinder.

Elevation is accomplished by means of an elevating mechanism located under the telescope mount on the right side of the turret and fastened directly to the right trunnion. The elevating rack is secured to the right side of the cradle beneath the trunnion. The elevating mechanism is operated by a handwheel connected to a system of gears which moves the elevating rack pinion up or down and transmits this movement to the cradle.

The coaxial machine-gun mount is fastened to the left trunnion cap. It is formed by two side rails separated and secured to a pintle support and pintle bearing. A freely revolving pintle to which the machine gun is fastened by a fastening pin enables the gun to be elevated or depressed around the pin and to traverse with the pintle. An elevation clamp is fastened between the mount sides on the rear end. Elevation and depression of the machine gun are caused by an elevation screw, and traverse is accomplished by means of a traversing screw and wedge.

The shield is a large rectangular steel piece curved to close the opening in the front of the turret. It is pierced for the howitzer, machine gun, and sighting telescope.

Sighting and Fire Control
ON CARRIAGE EQUIPMENT
Telescope, T92E2
Telescope Mount, M56, and headrest
Instrument Light, M33
Azimuth Indicator, M19
Elevation Quadrant, M9
Instrument Light, M30
Periscope, M6
Periscope, M8, with telescope

PRINCIPAL CHARACTERISTICS

Length of bore	22.5 cals.
Muzzle velocity	1,550 f./s.
Twist of rifling	1 turn in 20 cals.
Volume of chamber	153 cu. ins.
Weight of projectile	
H.E.	33 lb.
H.E., A.T.	29.22 lb.
Weight of charge	
H.E.	3.04 lb.
H.E., A.T.	1.60 lb.
Weight of complete round	
H.E.	42.07 lb.
H.E., A.T.	36.85 lb.
Travel of projectile in tube	81.67 ins.
Maximum powder pressure	28,000 lb./sq. in.
Muzzle energy	549.6 ft.-tons
Type of recoil mechanism	Hydrospring
Recoil length	12⅞ ins.
Maximum elevation	+35°
Maximum depression	−10°
Traverse	360° cont., hand or power operated

2 INCH MORTAR M3 (BRITISH BOMB THROWER, 2 INCH, MK. I)—STANDARD

2 INCH MORTAR, M3

The Mortar, 2 Inch, M3, is identical with the British Bomb Thrower, 2 Inch, Mk. I, and is used for projecting smoke bombs from tanks. By this means retreating tanks can form protective smoke screens concealing their movements. Mounted on the tank turret at a fixed elevation, the mortar can be traversed through 360° by rotation of the turret.

It is very effective in throwing smoke bombs at ranges of 35, 75 and 150 yards. The variation in range is obtained by the use of a gas regulator on the mortar which governs the escape of the propellant gases. The Smoke bomb, Mk. I/L, fired from the M3 Mortar, begins to produce smoke while in flight and ejects an effective screen in from five to eight seconds after it strikes the ground. This screen will last approximately 70 seconds in an eight mile per hour wind. As a result of its superiority over the Hand Grenade, Smoke, M15, and its ability to throw bombs without the necessity of

opening the tank hatch, the Mortar, 2 Inch, M3, was standardized 2 September 1943.

The chief components of the Mortar, 2 Inch, M3, are the barrel, barrel clamp, clamp carrier, breech tube, gas regulator and trigger housing. When the barrel clamp is unlocked, the mortar can be opened and pivoted on the locking pin, enabling the operator to load a bomb through the opening in the barrel clamp.

The bomb is chambered in the breech tube, which is locked to the trigger housing by a screw. This screw prevents vibrations from loosening the tube.

The gas regulator, which adjusts the range of the mortar by controlling the escape of propellant gases, may be mounted either on the left or right side of the breech tube. Similarly, the gas regulator nut can be attached either to the top or bottom end of the gas regulator body. This is determined by the type of installation.

The firing mechanism, of the continuous hull type, is contained in the trigger housing. The mechanism of the safety rod, safety crank and safety link, is so designed that the trigger will not operate when the mortar is open.

When the bomb is fired, the propellant gases tend to escape through the gas regulator body, which contains the valve. When most of these gases escape, the range will be very short. As the valve is rotated clockwise, and holes in the valve no longer are aligned with the escape hole, the rate of gas escape is reduced and consequently the range is increased.

CHARACTERISTICS

Weight of mortar	18 lb.
Weight of bomb	2.1 lb.

Controllable ranges
Short	35 yds. (approx.)
Medium	75 yds. (approx.)
Long	150 yds. (approx.)

37 MM ANTIAIRCRAFT GUN **M1A2**—CARRIAGE **M3A1**—SUBSTITUTE STANDARD

37 mm A.A. GUN, M1A2, ON CARRIAGE, M3A1, IN FIRING POSITION AT 45° ELEVATION

PRINCIPAL CHARACTERISTICS

Weight of gun and carriage, complete . . 6,124 lb.

Weight of carriage, w/o gun and tube . . 5,759 lb.

Weight of gun, complete . . . . 365 lb.

Weight of tube . . . . 119 lb.

Type of breechblock . . . . Vertical sliding

Recoil mechanism . . . . Hydrospring

Weight of complete round of H.E.
    ammunition, M54 . . . . 2.62 lb.

Weight of projectile, H.E. . . . . 1.34 lb.

Weight of powder charge . . . . 6.00 oz.

Overall length of vehicle in traveling
    position . . . . 241 ins.

Overall height of gun in traveling
    position . . . . 72 ins.

Overall width of vehicle in traveling
    position . . . . 69.5 ins.

Length of tube . . . . 78.2 ins.

Diameter of bore . . . . 1.457 ins.

Maximum length of recoil at
    elevation 0°-85° . . . . 10.75 ins.

Length of rifling, approximate . . . . 68.35 ins.

Number of grooves in barrel 12

Maximum elevation . . . . 90°

Minimum elevation . . . . −5°

Traverse . . . . 360°

Maximum vertical range (H.E. shell) . . 6,200 yds.

Maximum horizontal range (H.E.
    shell) . . . . 8,875 yds.

Muzzle velocity . . . . 2,600 f./s.

Rated maximum powder pressure . 30,000 lb./sq. in.

Volume of powder chamber for
    M54 shell . . . . 17.80 cu. ins.

Maximum rate of fire . . . . 120 rds./min.

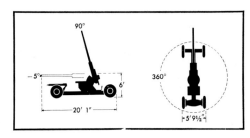

The 37 mm Antiaircraft Gun, M1A2, is a fully automatic, air-cooled weapon which may be employed against both airplanes and tanks. It fires high-explosive and armor-piercing shells at a cyclic rate of 120 rounds per minute. When mounted on the Carriage, M3A1, it can be towed at the speed of 50 miles an hour on good roads.

37 mm GUN, M1A2—The tube for this gun is one-piece forging or casting, threaded at its breech end to screw into the tube extension. The tube extension houses the breechblock with firing pin, cartridge extractor, carrier cam and front bracket supports for the driving spring tubes. It is fitted with bronze bearing strips which slide between the top and bottom sides of the gun casing. The recuperator piston rod is attached to the bottom side of the tube extension.

The gun casing is attached to the trunnion block which also supports the recuperator cylinder. The feed box is fastened to the top flange of the side plates at a point just to the rear of the breech end of the tube. Ammunition is fed to the gun from feeders or clips holding 10 rounds each. The recuperator mechanism is of the hydrospring type.

CARRIAGE, M3A1—The carriage is of the two-axle trailer type, with wheels mounted on spindles offset from the longitudinal axis of the axles. A leveling mechanism permits tilting of the carriage through a range of 10°.

The trunnion block, containing the gun and recuperator cylinder, slides in a cradle of frame construction with top, bottom and front removable covers. The cradle is supported in the top carriage by trunnions, the top carriage in turn rotating on a pintle, integral with the bottom carriage. Twin spring action counterpoise assemblies are contained in cylinders at either end of both axles to allow the carriage to be lowered to firing position without undue force and to enable it to be lifted to traveling position by one man at each wheel. Rotation of the axles lowers the chassis into firing position on the ground, the wheels being lifted from the ground at the same time.

A single spring equilibrator is utilized to counterbalance the muzzle preponderance of the gun. It is attached to the cradle by means of a rod and a chain.

Hand- and power-operated traversing and elevating mechanisms are attached to the carriage.

Two outriggers, pivoted about brackets, are attached to the side members of the chassis; when rotated to the ground they give stability to the carriage when it is in firing position. They are rotated to and secured in a vertical position for traveling.

Adjustment is provided for semi-automatic or automatic firing; firing is controlled by a lever and cable arrangement operated by two foot pedals.

Disk and lever type electric brakes operated from the prime mover are on all 4 wheels. Handbrakes are also installed on the rear wheels.

Sighting and Fire Control Equipment

On Carriage Equipment
Remote Control System, M9
Sighting System, M5
Telescope, M7 (azimuth), M64 (elevation)

Off Carriage Equipment
Cable System, M8
Director, M5
Generating Unit, M17
Gunner's Quadrant, M1

Ammunition

Ammunition is in the form of complete fixed rounds. It consists of A.P. Shot, M74, with tracer; A.P.C. Shot, M59, with tracer; H.E. Shell, M54, with SD tracer and P.D. Fuze, M56, and Practice Shell, M55A1, with tracer and Dummy Fuze, M50.

References—TM 9–2005, v.6; TM 9–235; TM 9–1235; FM 4–140.

37 mm A.A. GUN, M1A2, ON CARRIAGE, M3A1, IN TRAVELING POSITION

40 MM AUTOMATIC GUN M1 ON CARRIAGE M2 OR M2A1 — STANDARD

RA PD 45857

FIRING POSITION

The 40mm Automatic Gun M1 was originally developed by the Bofors Company of Sweden and is in wide use in European armies. American interest began with the U.S. Navy in 1938, and in December 1940 the U.S. Army were able to obtain a gun from Britain for trial. After testing, approval was given by OCM 16787 of 29 May 1941 for Standardization, and a license agreement with the Bofors Company was obtained to permit manufacture in the U.S.A.

THE 40MM AUTOMATIC GUN M1 is essentially the original Bofors design but with dimensions, clearances and threads to U.S. standards so as to facilitate manufacture. It is a recoil- operated automatic weapon using a vertical sliding wedge breech-block. Ammunition is supplied in four-round clips. A clip is placed in the clip guides and the first round is manually loaded into the breech. Upon firing, the gun recoils, the empty case is ejected down a chute to the front of the gun, and the next round is loaded during the run-out to battery, the breech closing automatically. If the foot-pedal is held down, then the gun will fire and the automatic action will repeat so long as the clip guide is kept supplied with ammunition.

THE CARRIAGE M1 was the original Bofors design and was not suited to American manufacturing processes. It used a cable-actuated braking system. It is now classified as Substitute Standard.

THE CARRIAGE M2 is the M1 redesigned to suit U.S. manufacturing processes and to simplify manufacture, by using a welded frame, simplified pintle, tubular axles and electric four-wheel brakes. It is classified as Standard.

THE CARRIAGE M2A1 is the M2 carriage but fitted with high-ratio gears in the elevating and traversing mechanisms so as to obtain faster rates of elevation and traverse. It is classified as Standard.

Ammunition

The gun fires a fixed round of ammunition carrying the HE Shell Mark 2 fitted with

Fuze PD Mk 27 (from Naval sources) or Fuze PD M71 (from Army sources) and the shell-destroying tracer M3. The projectile weighs 2.06 pounds and the complete round 4.82 pounds. Ammunition of British manufacture can be used interchangeably.

REFERENCES—OCM 16787; TM 9-252; SNL A-50

CHARACTERISTICS

Weight of gun . . . . .356lbs.
Length of bore . . . . .88.58ins.
Diameter of bore . . . . .40mm (1.575 inches)
Rifling:
    grooves 16
    twist . . . . Increasing right-hand from 1 turn in 45 calibers
    . . . . at the chamber to 1 turn in 30 calibers at the muzzle
Weight of gun and carriage . . . . 5549lbs.
Overall length in travel position . . . . 225.5ins.
Overall height . . . . 79.5ins.
Overall width . . . . 72ins.
Type of breech mechanism . . . . Vertical sliding wedge, automatic
Type of recoil mechanism . . . . Hydro-spring, constant length
Length of recoil . . . . 7.75ins.
Maximum elevation . . . . +90°
Maximum depression . . . . −11°
Traverse . . . . 360°
Weight of HE shell . . . . 2.06lbs.
Weight of complete round . . . . 4.82lbs.
Weight of powder charge . . . . 0.68 pound FNH
Muzzle velocity . . . . 2870 feet per second
Maximum vertical range . . . . 7625 yards
Maximum ground range . . . . 10,850 yards
Rate of fire . . . . 120 rounds per minute

40 MM GUN CARRIAGE M5 (AIRBORNE)—STANDARD

The need for an automatic antiaircraft gun and mount that could be transported by air for use as an antitank or antiaircraft battalion weapon within the Airborne Division resulted in the development of the 40 mm Gun Mount, M5.

A 40 mm Gun, M1, and the Carriage, M5, comprise a mobile unit designed for delivery to its destination by Transport Planes C46, C46A, C47 or C54. It can be unloaded from the plane and moved by manpower for short distances, or be towed by any prime mover. Care must be taken that speeds on rough roads do not exceed five miles per hour in order to avoid tire and wheel failures. Three men can emplace the carriage in approximately five minutes and raise it from firing position to traveling position in approximately eight minutes.

The top carriage of the Carriage, M5, is similar to that of the 40 mm Gun Carriage, M2A1, except for minor modifications to the platform and foot rests which reduce the width of the mount sufficiently to permit its passage through the doorway of the plane.

The chassis consists of a center base with one permanently attached outrigger and three removable outriggers which may be fastened to the mount by brackets and tapered wedges. Each outrigger has a leveling jack. In traveling position the side outriggers are removed and hung by steel straps to the rear outrigger or are carried separately. Individual right and left wheel assemblies for maneuvering the mount are attached to each side of the base in place of the outriggers.

The wheels are of the airplane type with 7.25 x 11.50 plain tread airplane tires inflated to 50 pounds pressure. No system of spring suspension is utilized. Airplane type mechanical brakes operated by a lever and cable are fitted to each wheel.

Before loading the carriage into a plane it is necessary to remove the gun barrel and the detachable outriggers. When the carriage is to be transported in C47 or C54 airplanes the automatic loader and the Computing Sight, M7, must also be taken off the mount.

Power operation of the carriage, identical to that of the 40 mm Gun Carriage, M2A1, is effected by means of the Remote Control System, M5, and Director, M5A1E1.

Sighting and Fire Control Equipment

Director, M5A1E1
Remote Control System, M5
Generating Unit, M5
Computing Sight, M7

REFERENCES—OCM 18883, 20 August 1942; OCM 21099, 20 June 1943; OCM 21280, 9 August 1943; OCM 21516, 9 September 1943.

40 mm GUN CARRIAGE, M5, IN FIRING POSITION

CHARACTERISTICS

Weight overall, maneuvering position	4,495 lb.
Weight overall, traveling position	3,480 lb.
(detachable outriggers and barrel removed)	
Weight overall, traveling position, tube installed	3,375 lb.
Overall length, maneuvering position	194½ ins.
Overall length, traveling position	117¾ ins.
Overall width, maneuvering position	68¾ ins.
Overall width, traveling position	56 ins.
Overall height, maneuvering position	75¾ ins.
Overall height, traveling position	75¾ ins.
Turning radius when towed by 1½-ton truck	202 ins.
Elevation	−5° to +90°
Traverse	360°

40 mm GUN CARRIAGE, M5, IN TRAVELING POSITION, WITH GUN AND OUTRIGGERS REMOVED FOR LOADING IN AN AIRPLANE OR TOWING WITH A LIGHT VEHICLE

3 INCH ANTIAIRCRAFT GUN M3—MOUNT M2A2—STANDARD

3 INCH ANTIAIRCRAFT GUN AND MOUNT, M1918

CHARACTERISTICS OF 3 INCH A.A. GUNS, M1, M3, AND MOUNTS, M1A1, M1A2, M2A1, M2A2

Weight of gun, M3, and mount, M2A2, total	16,800 lb.
Weight of gun, complete	2,302 lb.
Weight of liner	538 lb.
Weight of complete round of ammunition (M42A1, H.E.)	24.6 lb.
Weight of projectile (M42A1, H.E.)	12.8 lb.
Overall length of vehicle	300 ins.
Overall height of vehicle, with gun in traveling position	113 ins.
Overall width of vehicle	83 ins.
Overall length of gun, muzzle to rear face of breech ring	158.2 ins.
Caliber of bore	3 ins.
Length of bore	50 cals.
Maximum length of recoil at 85° elevation	32 ins.
Maximum length of recoil at 0° elevation	23.5 ins.
Length of rifling	125.83 ins.
Number of grooves in barrel	28
Rifling, uniform R.H., one turn in	40 cals.
Travel of projectile in bore of gun (M42A1, H.E.)	127.73 ins.
Maximum elevation	80°
Maximum depression	-1°
Traverse	360°
Maximum range, at 85° elevation	10,400 yds.
Maximum range, at 45° elevation (M42A1, H.E.)	14,780 yds.
Muzzle velocity (M42A1, H.E.)	2,800 f./s.
Maximum powder pressure (M42A1, H.E.)	36,000 lb./sq. in.
(M62, A.P.C.)	38,000 lb./sq. in.
Volume of powder chamber (M42A1, H.E.)	2,035 cu. ins.
Maximum rate of fire	25 to 30 rds./min.

The development of medium caliber mobile antiaircraft artillery for the U. S. Army was initiated when a 75 mm Gun, M1916, was placed on a Truck Mount, M1917, during the First World War. Shortly thereafter, the caliber of antiaircraft guns was fixed at 3 inches, the cartridge case then employed in the 3″ (15 pdr.) Gun, M1898, being adopted as standard for antiaircraft use.

The first mobile antiaircraft gun and mount of 3″ caliber to be designed and manufactured in the United States was the 3″ Gun, M1918, and the Mount, M1918. This mount was standard for issue until replaced by the Mount, M2. Postwar development continued in an endeavor to increase muzzle energy and rate of fire for antiaircraft guns, to improve road performance and stability of carriages and to produce more efficient fire control systems. A 3″ pilot mount, T1, was built and tested in 1927. Tests continued throughout 1928 and 1929 on the Mounts, M1 and M2, the latter being standardized to replace the Mount, M1918. Development of mounts progressed thereafter until the present 3″ Mount, M2A2, was standardized in O.C.M. 14339, dated 24 Feb. 1938. While this mount is still standard, further procurement will be made only upon specific authority of the Secretary of War.

A new 3″ Gun, M1, with removable liner and ballistic qualities superior to those of the M1918, was the first gun in a series that culminated in the 3″ Gun, M3, classified as Standard by O.C.M. 7186, dated 30 August 1928.

GUNS, M1918, M1918M1—The construction of these guns was similar to that of the M1917 series antiaircraft guns designed for use on fixed mounts for harbor defense. The only difference in these guns is in the greater length of the breech ring of the M1918M1 gun. The gun is built up of alloy steel, with the tube shrunk in place in the jacket. The breech end of the jacket is threaded to receive the breech ring which is screwed and shrunk·on the jacket and held by a lock screw. The breech mechanism is of the hand-operated drop block type. Originally, rifling for this weapon had an increasing twist, from 1 turn in 50 to 1 turn in 25 calibers.

GUNS, M1918A1, M1918M1A1—Guns with rifling having a uniform twist of 1 in 25 were designated as M1918A1 and M1918M1A1.

3 INCH ANTIAIRCRAFT GUN, M3, ON MOUNT, M2A2, IN TRAVELING POSITION

3 INCH ANTIAIRCRAFT GUN, M3, ON MOUNT, M2A2, IN FIRING POSITION

GUN, M3—This gun is similar to the M1 except that the diameter of the removable liner for the M3 is greater than that of the M1. The autofrettage method is used for the manufacture of the liner, the interior of the tube being taper bored for the removable liner. The exterior of the tube is threaded at the breech end for attachment of the breech ring. The rectangular breechblock, of the vertical sliding type, moves up and down in its recess in the breech ring. It may be operated either semi-automatically or manually. In semi-automatic operation the breechblock is opened, as the gun returns to battery, by means of a cam mounted on the cradle. Upon insertion of a round in the chamber the extractors are tripped by the rim of the cartridge case and the breechblock closes automatically. A breech-operating handle is used for manual opening of the breechblock and for closing it when firing is discontinued. A Firing Lock, M14, of the continuous pull type is housed in the breechblock. The gun is fired by means of a lanyard attached to the trigger shaft.

MOUNT, M2A2—This mount differs from the Mounts, M2A1, M1A2, M1A1, T1A2 and T1A1, primarily in the commercial brake system, the fabricated parts and method of carrying the spare tires. These models derive from the T1.

The Mount, M2A2, is of the trailer type, possessing a mobility that permits it to be drawn at high speeds over good roads and at medium speed over irregular terrain. It is of the variety familiarly known as a spider mount, with folding perforated platforms and four folding outriggers fastened to the undercarriage. These outriggers, when folded, form the chassis. For transport the chassis rests on the front and rear pneumatic-tired bogies, secured in place by clamp screws and equipped with four-wheel electric brakes operated from the prime mover. The gun is mounted in a cradle which is supported on its trunnions in antifriction bearings on the arms of the pivot yoke in the top carriage. The top carriage, which supports the cradle, elevating and traversing mechanisms and the recoil mechanism, is in turn mounted on the undercarriage. The top carriage is supported on a spherical bearing; at the lower end is the leveling mechanism mounted in the pedestal. The leveling mechanism permits adjustment of the axis of the top carriage to a vertical position when the ground on which the mount is placed is not level. Two level vials, set at right angles to each other, are attached to the top carriage for the guidance of the operator in leveling the mount.

Sighting and Fire Control Equipment for 3 Inch A.A. Gun, M3, on Mount, M2A2

On Carriage Equipment

Elbow Telescope, M24, M25
Telescope Mount, M26, M27
Bore Sight

Off Carriage Equipment

Height Finder, M1A1 or M2A1
Director, M7 (Standard), or M1, M1A1, M2, M3, M4A1B6, M4A1B2, M7A1, or M7A1B2
B.C. Observation Instrument (A.A.), M1
Data Transmission System, M4
Gunner's Quadrant, M1918
Generating Unit, M6 (Standard) or M4 (Limited Standard)
Slide Rule, M1
Fuze Setter, M8
Flank Spotting Instrument, M1

Ammunition

Ammunition is in the form of complete fixed rounds. It consists of A.P. Projectile, M79; H.E. Shell, Mk. IX, with M.T. Fuze, M43, and modifications; H.E. Shell, M42A1, with M.T. Fuze, M43, and modifications, or P.D. Fuze, M48, and modifications; and A.P.C., Projectile, M62, with B.D. Fuze, M66A1.

REFERENCES—TM 9–2005, v.6; TM 9–360; TM 9–1360; FM 4–125.

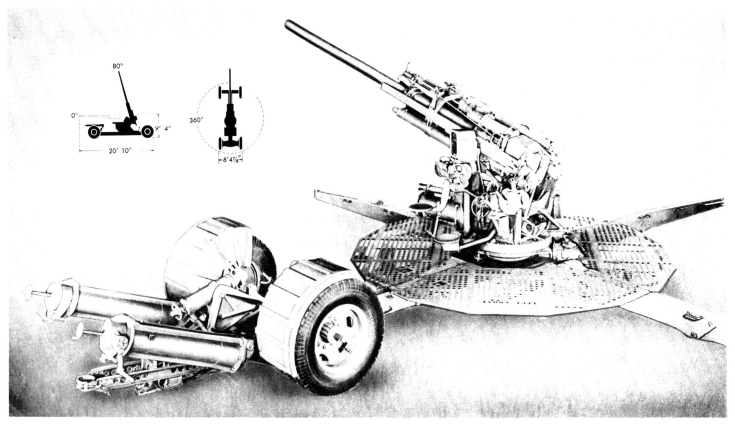

90 MM ANTIAIRCRAFT GUN, M1A1, ON MOUNT, M1A1, IN FIRING POSITION

Aviation progress, especially in the field of high-altitude bombing, demanded reconsideration of requirements for mobile antiaircraft artillery. In order to cope with rapidly maneuvering bombers flying at modern speeds at extreme heights, it was essential to have guns with longer range, greater muzzle velocity, and a larger effective shell-burst area than those previously considered satisfactory. The desired increase in firepower which could be obtained from guns of larger calibers than 3 inch dictated the adoption of a 90 mm antiaircraft weapon by the U. S. Army.

Development of 90 mm antiaircraft matériel was instituted by O.C.M. 14531, dated 9 June 1938, for the 90 mm Gun, T2, and O.C.M. 14633, dated 18 August 1938, for the 90 mm Mount, T1, approving military characteristics of the gun and mount.

O.C.M. 15688, dated 21 March 1940, recorded standardization of the T2 gun as 90 mm Gun, M1, the T1 mount as 90 mm Gun Mount, M1, and the recoil mechanism for the mount as 90 mm Recoil Mechanism, M1.

O.C.M. 16755, dated 22 May 1941, approved standardization of the 90 mm Gun Mount, M1A1, and reclassification of 90

PRINCIPAL CHARACTERISTICS

Gun, M1, M1A1

Total weight of gun and mount, M1A1	19,000 lb.
Weight of gun, complete	2,445 lb.
Weight of gun tube	1,465 lb.
Weight of recoil mechanism	1,740 lb.
Length of bore	50 cals.
Length (muzzle to rear face of breech ring)	186.51 ins.
Muzzle velocity (M71 H.E., M77 A.P.)	2,700 f./s.
Weight of complete round (M71 H.E., M77 A.P.)	42.04 lb.
Weight of projectile (M71 H.E., M77 A.P.)	23.4 lb.
Chamber capacity (cartridge case) (M71 H.E.)	298.04 cu. ins.
Maximum powder pressure	38,000 lb./sq. in.

Length overall in traveling position	250 ins.
Height overall in traveling position	112 ins.
Width overall in traveling position	100⅞ ins.
Weight of rammer	500 lb. (approx.)
Elevation	
Maximum	80°
Minimum (without depression stops)	0°
Minimum (with depression stops)	22½°
Traverse	360° cont.
Maximum slope on which mount can be leveled	4°
Diameter of circle of emplacement	35 ft.
Distance from center to center of outside wheel treads	87⅞ ins.
Tire size and type	10.00 x 22, combat or bus balloon
Type of brakes	Electric

mm Gun Mount, M1, as Limited Standard.

O.C.M. 19946, dated 15 January 1943, approved model designations of components of 90 mm A.A. Gun Mount, M1A1, as 90 mm Gun, M1A1, Recoil Mechanism, M1A1, Spring Rammer, M8, and Fuze Setter, M13.

GUN, M1—The tube for this gun is of monobloc construction and cold worked. The tube, which screws into the breech ring, is readily removed for replacement or repair. A locking key prevents rota-

tion of the tube in the breech ring. The tube and breech mechanism are supported and guided in recoil and counter-recoil by recoil slide rails fastened to the breech ring and front tube supports. A cam in the right side rail prevents opening the breech by hand when the gun is out of battery.

The breech mechanism employs a vertical sliding breechblock that may be opened either manually or automatically. It is closed automatically when a cartridge is rammed in the chamber. Extraction is automatic or by hand.

The firing mechanism is automatically cocked upon opening the breech.

GUN, M1A1—This is the 90 mm Gun, M1, modified by adding a hook on the front tube support and by changing the design of the cocking lever, in order to accommodate the Spring Rammer, M8, which is utilized to facilitate loading.

90 mm A.A. GUN MOUNT, M1A1— The mount, M1A1, is a self-contained mobile unit provided with a single-axle, dual-wheeled bogie and drawn by the trail. It is adapted for use with the Remote Control System, M2, as well as for manual operation.

The mount consists basically of bogie, trail, outriggers, pedestal, leveling mechanisms, top carriage, elevating and indicator drive mechanisms, equilibrator, cradle, recoil mechanism and rammer.

The top carriage rests on and pivots about the leveling socket which, together with the other components of the leveling mechanism, rests in turn on the pedestal. The trails and outriggers are hinged to the pedestal.

The cradle is suspended from the top carriage on its trunnions, which rest in trunnion bearings at the top rear of the top carriage. The cradle houses the three cylinders of the hydropneumatic recoil system. A spring type equilibrator provided for neutralizing the unbalanced weight of the gun and cradle is located on the lower left front of the top carriage.

The elevating and indicator drive mechanism is located on the right side of the top carriage and the traversing and indicator drive mechanism on the left side. Elevation and traverse are accomplished either mechanically by remote control or manually by handwheels.

The Rammer, M8, operates from the gun recoil, the springs in the rammer cylinder being compressed by the rearward movement of the barrel. After the round is placed in position, pulling back on the rammer trip lever frees the springs which then move the rammer plunger and rammer arm forward, the latter pushing the cartridge into the breech.

The bogie is equipped with disk and rim wheels, combat tires and tubes, and electric brakes operated from the prime mover. For parking, or when the electric brakes are not functioning, each brake can be operated independently by means of a hand lever.

When in firing position, the outriggers are spread, the bogie is removed, and the mount is lowered to the ground until it rests on the pedestal base. The mount is then leveled and the firing platform is unfolded and fastened to the outriggers and trails.

Sighting and Fire Control Equipment

On Carriage Equipment
Elbow Telescope, M24, M26
Telescope Mount, M28, M54
Remote Control System, M2

Off Carriage Equipment
Bore Sight
Director, M7A1B1, MTA1B2, M9A1
Height Finder, 13½-foot, M1A1, or M2A1
Antiaircraft B.C. Observation Instrument, M1
Gunner's Quadrant, M1, M1918
Slide Rule, M1
Fuze Setter, M13
Generating Unit, M18
Cable System, M1

Ammunition

Ammunition is in the form of fuzed complete fixed rounds. It consists of H.E. Shell, M58, with M.T. fuze, M43A4; H.E. Shell, M71, with M.T. fuze, M43A4; A.P. Shot, M77, with tracer, and A.P.C. Shot, M82, with B.D. fuze, M68.

REFERENCES—TM 9-2005, v.6; TM 9-370; TM 9-371; TM 9-1370A; TM 9-1370B; FM 4-126.

90 MM ANTIAIRCRAFT GUN, M1A1, ON MOUNT, M1A1, IN TRAVELING POSITION

90 MM GUN M1—MOUNT M3 (ANTI-MOTOR-TORPEDO-BOAT)—STANDARD

anchor bolts to a prepoured concrete base which incorporates an ammunition storage place below the ground level. A manhole gives accessibility to the stored ammunition.

90 mm GUN MOUNT, M3 (ANTI-MOTOR-TORPEDO-BOAT)

In 1941 it was decided to construct a fixed mount for the 90 mm, M1, Gun that would permit it to be used effectively as an anti-motor-torpedo-boat weapon.

The resultant Mount, M3, permits direct fire against water, land, and air targets. It may be controlled either manually or automatically through the medium of a remote control system. A gun depression of −8° allows fire against enemy boats, while the elevation of +80° makes it practicable for antiaircraft use.

The principal components of the 90 mm Gun Mount, M3, are the pedestal, base ring, top carriage, traversing mechanism, elevating mechanism, equilibrator, cradle, recoil mechanism, and shield and platform assembly.

The cradle, in which the gun is mounted, is composed of a body, yoke, two trunnions, and a hydropneumatic recoil mechanism consisting of a recoil cylinder, a floating piston cylinder, and a gas cylinder. The recoil piston rod screws into a threaded hole in the front under surface of the breech ring. A counterrecoil buffer on top of the cradle eases the gun back into battery during the last 7 inches of counterrecoil.

A spring type equilibrator is mounted on the left front of the top carriage and connected to the cradle equilibrator arm by a chain.

Gears which can be operated manually by handwheels or automatically by re-mote control comprise the elevating mechanism located on the right side of the top carriage. A transfer valve enables the operator to change from remote control to manual operation.

The traversing mechanism is also capable of operation by hand or by remote control. The traversing mechanism is located on the left side of the top carriage.

The top carriage supports the gun and all parts of the mount above the base ring, including the shield assembly and platform. The cradle trunnions are seated in bearings on the top of the top carriage side frames. The circular base of the top carriage traverses through 360° on the bearing surface of the base ring. The shield assembly encloses the gun except in the rear, where an opening permits entrance of the crew and the passing of ammunition. The shield is in two main sections, with an opening between them that enables the gun to be elevated and depressed. The shield provides full overhead protection and includes a sliding shield which moves on rollers as the gun is elevated or depressed.

The base ring is a steel casting with machined top and bottom surfaces. While the top surface supports the top carriage, the bottom surface rests on the top surface of the pedestal.

The cast steel pedestal, to which the base ring is secured, is fastened by

Sighting and Fire Control Equipment

On Carriage

Elbow Telescope, M6A1 } Case II Firing
Telescope Mount, M52C }

Elbow Telescope, M24A1 }
Telescope Mount, M47 } Direct Firing
Elbow Telescope, M26A1 }
Telescope Mount, M46 }

Remote Control System, M13

Off Carriage

Cable System, M10
Director, M7A1B1, M9, or M9A1
Height Finder, M1A1, or M2A1
Antiaircraft B.C. Observation Instrument, M1
Gunner's Quadrant, M1, M1918
Slide Rule, M1
Fuze Setter, M13

Ammunition

Ammunition is in the form of fuzed, complete, fixed rounds. It consists of Shell, H.E., M58, with Fuze, time, mechanical, M43; Shell, H.E. (Ammonal), M58, with Fuze, time, mechanical, M43; Shell, H.E., M71, with Fuze, time, mechanical, M43; Shell, H.E., M71, with Fuze, time, mechanical, M43; Shell, H.E., M71, with Fuze, P.D., M48; Shell, H.E., M71, with Fuze, P.D., M48A1; Projectile, A.P.C., M82, with Fuze, B.D., M68, and Tracer; Shot, A.P., M77, with Tracer; Ammunition, Blank, 90 mm Gun, M1, and Cartridge, drill, M12, with Fuze, dummy, M44A2.

PRINCIPAL CHARACTERISTICS

Caliber................................90 mm
Length of bore.........................50 cals.
Length of gun tube.................186.15 ins.
Weight.............................1,465 lb.
Maximum powder pressure.....38,000 lb./sq. in.
Muzzle velocity....................2,700 f./s.
Maximum range (vertical).........13,170 yds.
Maximum range (horizontal).......18,960 yds.
Recoil mechanism............Hydropneumatic
Elevation......................−8° to +80°
Traverse.............................360°
Weight of recoil mechanism and cradle.1,740 lb.
Weight of base ring..................1,109 lb.
Weight of pedestal...................1,250 lb.
Height (base of pedestal to top of shield). .103 ins.

REFERENCES — OCM 15688; OCM 17537; OCM 17609; OCM 18632; OCM 20674; OCM 21065; OCM 22029; TM 9-373.

90 mm ANTIAIRCRAFT GUN, M2, ON MOUNT, M2, EMPLACED FOR FIRING

In July, 1941, it was decided that all mobile antiaircraft guns should be dual-purpose weapons that could be fired against both aerial and ground targets when the mount was on wheels. This was impossible with the M1A1 mount, since it was necessary to remove the wheeled bogie and emplace the mount on its pedestal base with outriggers extended before opening fire. It was also desired that the 90 mm gun should be capable of use against motor torpedo boats and other small craft, a function that required a greater depression than the 0° which was the minimum of the Mount, M1A1.

In order to fill the need for a 90 mm dual-purpose gun, a project to design and manufacture such a weapon and its mount was initiated on 11 September 1941. On 13 May 1943 the gun was standardized as M2, the Mount as M2, the recoil mechanism as M17, and the combination fuze setter-rammer as M20.

GUN, M2—The gun assembly of the M2 consists of the gun tube, recoil slide rails, breech mechanism, and firing mechanism. The tube, manufactured by the autofrettage method, is in one piece. It is attached to the breech ring by interrupted threads. Rotation of the tube

in the breech ring is prevented by a locking key. A tube support fastened to the recoil slide rails supports the muzzle end of the tube.

The breech mechanism uses a vertical sliding block which opens and closes automatically when a round is fired and a cartridge is rammed home in the chamber of the gun. The breech must be opened manually for insertion of the initial round. Downward movement of the breechblock cocks the percussion firing mechanism through the medium of the automatic cocking lever. In case of a misfire, the percussion mechanism can be recocked with the breech closed by depressing the hand cocking lever handle.

COMBINATION FUZE SETTER-RAMMER, M20—The purpose of the combination fuze setter-rammer, which is operated automatically and is controlled by a director through remote control, is to shorten and hold constant the time interval between setting a time fuze and firing the round, and to facilitate loading cartridges into the gun. The fuze setter is normally used only with time-fuzed ammunition for antiaircraft fire. A selective control lever makes the fuze setter inoperative when armor-piercing, point-detonating, or base-detonating ammunition is employed against mechanized

targets. The power rammer is used in both instances.

In the event of power failure, malfunctioning of the fuze setter-rammer, or for emergency firing from the wheels of the mount, the gun can be loaded manually and fuzes set by means of the manual Fuze Setter, M13.

The nonrecoiling parts of the fuze setter-rammer are mounted on the recoil mechanism cradle, while the recoiling parts are attached to the gun breech ring. The complete unit consists of a 3 hp., 110-volt, 3-phase, 60-cycle induction motor for driving the fuze setter-rammer; a transmission which transmits power to the ramming and fuze setting mechanisms; a ramming mechanism which drives and opens and closes the rubber ramming rolls; a fuze setter mechanism which rotates the fuze setter jaws for setting the fuze and provides a means of opening and closing the jaws, and a fuze setter torque amplifier servo mechanism which receives the fuze setter time signal from the remote control director and converts it into power for setting the fuze setting mechanism.

In operating the fuze setter a round of ammunition is loaded into the slowly rotating ramming rolls which draw the round into the fuze setter jaws, where it is stopped and held stationary. The jaws

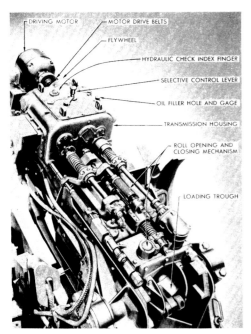

COMBINATION FUZE SETTER-RAMMER, M20

then rotate the fuze to the position signaled by the remotely located director, following which the jaws open and the round is rammed by the ramming rolls into the open breech. The breech closes and the round is fired. As the gun recoils, the fuze setter jaws and the ramming rolls open to allow ejection of the cartridge case, and the ramming roll rotational speed is changed from high to low. During counterrecoil the breech is opened automatically, the ramming rolls and fuze setter jaws are closed, and the fuze setter-rammer is ready for loading the next round.

When the fuze setter is inoperative the fuze setter jaws are open, the ramming rolls are driven at high speed, and the round is rammed without interruption.

RECOIL MECHANISM, M17—This recoil mechanism is of the hydropneumatic type, with variable recoil to compensate for change in weight transfer of the gun

when it is fired at different elevations. Shortening the recoil at higher elevations permits the use of a lower, more compact top carriage and prevents the possibility of the gun assembly striking the operator's platform. Longer recoil at near-horizontal elevations enables greater shock absorption to be employed. Movement of the gun assembly in recoil and counterrecoil is utilized to change operating speeds of the fuze setter-rammer and to open the breech after firing.

The recoil cylinder, containing a recoil piston connected to the breech ring, is between the floating piston cylinder on its left and the gas cylinder on its right. The three cylinders, mounted under the gun, are held in place by cylinder supports. The recoil and floating piston cylinders are screwed into the cradle yoke which contains the stuffing box for the recoil piston rod and valves for controlling the recoil of the gun. The floating piston cylinder contains both recoil oil and nitrogen under a normal operating pressure of 1,000 pounds. The gas and oil are separated by the floating piston. A gas bypass connection provides a passage for gas between the floating piston cylinder and the gas cylinder. In effect, the gas cylinder is an extension of the floating piston cylinder. It contains only gas under pressure.

The yoke not only provides support for the recoil cylinders, but also serves as a crosstie for the cradle side frames. It contains the oil filling valve, throttling valve, counterrecoil valve, and passages for recoil oil between the floating piston cylinder and recoil cylinder.

After firing, the gun is eased back into battery by the action of a hydraulic counterrecoil buffer located on the front end of the cradle. The buffer in recoil and counterrecoil also changes the operating speeds of the rammer rolls of the fuze setter-rammer.

MOUNT, M2—The mount is composed of the cradle; equilibrators; elevating, traversing, and leveling mechanism; top carriage; pedestal, and outriggers. It is supported in the traveling position by two unsprung two-wheeled bogies equipped with 14 x 24 inch balloon tires. In the theaters of operations combat balloon tires with bullet-resisting inner tubes are used.

The cradle, which is mounted on anti-friction bearings on the top carriage, contains all the tipping parts of the gun, the combination fuze setter-rammer, the recoil mechanism, and the counterrecoil buffer.

The top carriage carries all the traversing parts of the mount, the cradle, the equilibrator mechanism, the elevating, traversing, and leveling mechanisms, and the on-carriage elements of the remote control system. The elevating mechanism and elevation indicator-regulator and power unit of the remote control system are mounted on the right side of the gun, while the traversing mechanism, azimuth indicator, and the azimuth power unit are on the left side. The firing platform sections, held in the raised traveling position by swiveled rods, are also mounted on the top carriage. Chains attached to the side frames hold the platforms in the slightly raised position necessary when the gun is fired from the wheels. A signal light for manual firing indicates to the gunner that the gun is on the target. Folding shields, with sight openings and covers to provide access to the remote control power units, are secured to each side of the top carriage.

Two spring-type equilibrators are mounted horizontally between the side frames of the top carriage. Chains from the equilibrator spring piston rods pass over chain wheels at the front end of the top carriage and are attached to arms on the under side of the cradle.

PRINCIPAL CHARACTERISTICS

Caliber	90 mm
Length of bore	50 cals.
Length of tube	186.15 ins.
Weight of tube	1,465 lb.
Maximum powder pressure	38,000 lb./sq. in.
Muzzle velocity (H.E., M71)	2,700 f./s.
Maximum range (vertical) (H.E., M71)	13,170 yds.
Maximum range (horizontal) (H.E., M71)	19,500 yds.
Weight of projectile (H.E., M71)	23.40 lb.
Weight of fuze setter-rammer	975 lb.

Aver. firing cycle—max. fuze setting	2.6 secs.
Aver. firing cycle—min. fuze setting	2.1 secs.
Aver. firing cycle—selective control lever set	2.0 secs.
Recoil mechanism	Hydropneumatic
Recoil length	Variable
Normal recoil at 0° elevation	44 to 46 ins.
Normal recoil at 80° elevation	28 to 31 ins.
Traverse, continuous	360°
Elevation	−10° to +80°
Equilibrators	Spring, adjustable
Wheel base	164 ins.
Length (lunette to gun muzzle)	355.15 ins.
Max. height (traveling position)	121 ins.

Weight of complete gun and mount (approx.)	32,300 lb.
Weight of front bogie	3,250 lb.
Tread, front bogie	72 ins.
Tires, regular or combat	14 x 24 ins.
Turning angle	35°
Weight of rear bogie	3,200 lb.
Brakes, electric, compound	16 x 5 ins.
Length across side outriggers, gun emplaced	380 ins.
Rated capacity of hydraulic jacks	10 tons each
Prime mover	Medium Tractor, M4
Towing speed	Moderate speed on good roads; approx. 20 m.p.h. on sec. roads

The elevating mechanism may be operated either manually or by remote control. The traversing mechanism comprises upper and lower housing units, the remote control power unit, and the azimuth indicator. The carriage is rotated by a series of spur and bevel gears on vertical shafts which drives a pinion meshed with the traversing gear rack fixed to the stationary leveling socket.

A leveling mechanism, consisting of the leveling socket and bearing and four locking screws, enables the top carriage to be leveled when the gun is to be fired from the ground. Spirit level vials are mounted near each of the leveling screws.

The gun, cradle, top carriage and all mechanisms are supported on the pedestal. The pedestal forms the base of the mount and functions as a chassis for the bogies when the gun and mount are in traveling position. A front, rear, and two side outriggers attached to the pedestal are extended and rigidly locked by means of wedge keys when the gun is fired from the ground. The folders and locked outriggers are fastened to the side frames for traveling.

The pedestal lower base plate, prevented from slipping when in firing position by vertical spade plates welded to the bottom, forms the ground base of the mount. Two hydraulic jacks are used for raising and lowering the mount so that the bogies may be removed or placed in traveling position.

When traveling, the mount rests on front and rear bogies. The front bogie is connected by a draft spindle pin to a draft spindle at the front of the pedestal chassis, while the rear bogie is attached to a groove in the rear of the pedestal.

The front bogie is equipped with single wheels which, with the electric brakes mechanism, are mounted on the spindles of a box-section axle. The drawbar is a three-member pipe section hinged to the bogie when traveling and keyed to the bogie so that it may be used for maneuvering when detached from the pedestal. A standard M1 lunette is provided for coupling the bogie to the Medium Tractor, M4, which is used as a prime mover. The turning angle of the bogie is limited to 35°. A break-away switch sets the electric brakes in the event that the mount becomes accidentally separated from the prime mover.

The rear bogie is similar in construction to the front bogie. It has a box section axle to which a maneuvering bar is rigidly fixed for ease of handling when the bogie is detached from the mount. The electric brakes are energized from the prime mover, and a hand-operated parking brake is provided for each wheel.

REFERENCES — OCM 17213; OCM 20401; TM 9–372.

Sighting and Fire Control Equipment

On Carriage

Sighting System, M7
Torque Amplifier, M1 or T5
Cable System, M1
Bore Sight

Off Carriage

Director, M7A1B1, M9 or M9A1
Remote Control System, M12
Height Finder, M1A1 or M2A1
Generating Unit, M18
Fuze Setter, M13
Antiaircraft B.C. Observation Instrument, M1
Gunner's Quadrant, M1
Slide Rule, M1

Ammunition

Shell, fixed, H.E., M58, with Fuze, M.T., M43 (all modifications); Shell, fixed, H.E. (ammonal), M58, with Fuze, M.T., M43 (all modifications); Shell, fixed, H.E., M71, with Fuze, M.T., M43 (all modifications); Shell, fixed, H.E., M71, with Fuze, P.D., M48A1; Shell, fixed, M71, with Fuze, P.D., M48A1; Projectile, fixed, A.P.C., M82, with Fuze, B.D., M68, and Tracer; Shot, fixed, A.P., M77, with Tracer; Shell, fixed, Practice, inert loaded, M71, with Fuze, inert or dummy; Ammunition, Blank; Cartridge, Drill, M12, with Fuze, Dummy, M44A2.

90 mm GUN, M2, ON MOUNT, M2, IN TRAVELING POSITION

120 MM GUN, M1, ON ANTIAIRCRAFT MOUNT, M1, IN FIRING POSITION

PRINCIPAL CHARACTERISTICS

GUN, M1

Weight (complete)	10,675 lb.
Weight of projectile	50 lb.
Weight of powder charge	24 lb.
Dimensions	
Length of bore	60 cals.
Length (Muzzle to rear face of breech ring)	291 ins.
Caliber	4.7 ins.
Travel of projectile in barrel	248.35 ins.
Chamber capacity	1,046 cu. ins.
Muzzle velocity	3,100 f./s.
Maximum powder pressure	38,000 lb./sq. in.
Rate of firing	10 rds./min.
Type of breechblock	Vertical sliding
Type of recoil mechanism	Hydropneumatic with variable recoil

MOUNT, M1

Type	2 bogie, 8 wheel trailer, portable in one load
Weight (Gun and mount complete, traveling position)	61,500 lb.
Rear bogie	4,100 lb.
Front bogie	3,850 lb.
Mount in firing position	48,800 lb.

Dimensions of Mount, Traveling

Overall length lunette to rear muzzle	369 ins.
Maximum height	124 ins.
Maximum width	123.5 ins.
Wheelbase	186 ins.
Center road clearance under spade	15 ins.
Size of tires (duals)	13 x 24 ins.

Dimensions of Mount, Emplaced

Height of trunnions above ground	79 ins.
Height of platform above ground	36 ins.
Diagonal of spread outriggers	33 ft. (approx.)

Maneuvering Data

Maximum elevation	+80°
Maximum depression	−5°
Leveling adjustment (each way)	4°
Traverse	360°
Capacity of hydraulic jacks	15 tons each

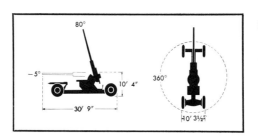

Development of 120 mm antiaircraft matériel for the U.S. Army began with the 120 mm Antiaircraft Gun, M1918, designed and built at the request of General Pershing for an antiaircraft weapon more powerful than those in service during the first World War. The pilot model, tested in October, 1918, was found unsatisfactory. Development work on this gun was under way until 1921, when the project was discontinued.

The fact that bombing altitudes had increased to over 30,000 feet, and the need for a heavy antiaircraft gun for the defense of large area targets, resulted in the approval of military characteristics and the development of a 120 mm antiaircraft gun and mount by O.C.M. 15059, dated 1 June 1939, and supplemented by O.C.M. 15126, dated 22 June 1939; O.C.M. 15725, dated 8 April 1940; and O.C.M. 16220, dated 10 Oct. 1940.

120 mm GUN, M1—This gun consists of a 1-piece cold-worked tube screwed into the rectangular breech ring. It is supported and aligned in the cradle by gun rails attached to the breech ring at the rear and the tube support in front. A locking key prevents rotation of the tube in the breech ring. The breech mechanism employs a vertical sliding type breechblock opened automatically during counterrecoil and closed automatically by insertion of the cartridge.

A percussion type firing mechanism is contained in the breechblock. The gun is fired by means of a firing lever located on the cradle.

MOUNT, M1—The mount is of the spider type, supported on two dual-wheel bogies when in the traveling position. It consists basically of the cradle supporting the gun, hydropneumatic recoil mechanism, and the power rammer; the top carriage, trunnioning the cradle and forming a structure for the attachment of the elevating and traversing mechanisms, remote-control power apparatus, equilibrator cylinders and pressure tank, working platforms and data receivers, and the pedestal, which serves as the base of the mount and functions as a chassis to which the bogies are connected when the mount is prepared for travel. Four outriggers are attached to the pedestal. The two side

outriggers house hydraulic jacks which are used when lowering and raising the mount for firing and traveling positions. Spade plates on the bottom of the pedestal dig into the ground and give additional stability to the emplaced matériel.

Elevation and traverse are accomplished either mechanically by means of hydraulic force supplied by electric motor driven pumps and controlled by the remote control system, or by manually operated handwheels.

The Power Rammer, M9, is a cam-driven, arm type rammer, bolted to the rammer mounting pads on the left side of the cradle. It is supplied with a tray hinged above and to the left of the breech which carries both projectile and cartridge case. An automatic fuze setter is geared to the rammer; both are operated by an electric motor.

The bogies have dual wheels equipped with standard 13 x 24 bus balloon tires, and are furnished with Warner-electric brakes operated from the prime mover. A handbrake lever for parking or emergency use is provided on each of the rear bogie brakes. The electric brakes are automatically applied in the event that

the mount becomes separated from the prime mover during transport.

Sighting and Fire Control Equipment

On Carriage Equipment
Remote Control System, M6

Off Carriage Equipment
Cable System, M3
Director, M10
Height Finder, M1A1 or M2A1
A.A. Battery Commander's Observation Instrument, M1
Gunner's Quadrant, M1
Generating Unit, M18
Slide Rule, M1
Graphical Firing Table, M2
Powder Temperature Indicators, M12, M3

Ammunition

The ammunition is of the separate-loading type and consists of a projectile and a brass cartridge case containing the propelling charge. A Palmatex plug serves as a cushion between the cartridge case and the projectile and as a seal to keep the charge in the case. The projectile is designated as H.E. Shell, M73, with M.T. Fuze, M61, and the cartridge case is designated as M24.

REFERENCES—TM 9–2005, v.6; TM 9–380.

120 MM ANTIAIRCRAFT GUN, M1, ON MOUNT, M1, IN TRAVELING POSITION

SUBCALIBER RIFLE, CAL. .22, M2A1—STANDARD

SUBCALIBER RIFLE, CAL. .22, M2A1

The Subcaliber Rifle, cal. .22, M2A1, is standard subcaliber equipment for mounting in the 37 mm Antitank Gun, M3A1. The interior mount used with the rifle is the Subcaliber Mount, cal. .22–.30, M6.

This rifle is the cal. .22 U. S. Rifle, M2, with the stock and the sights removed. A bronze bushing, designed to fit readily into the mount, is fitted on the front end of the barrel.

SUBCALIBER RIFLE, CAL. .22, M5—STANDARD

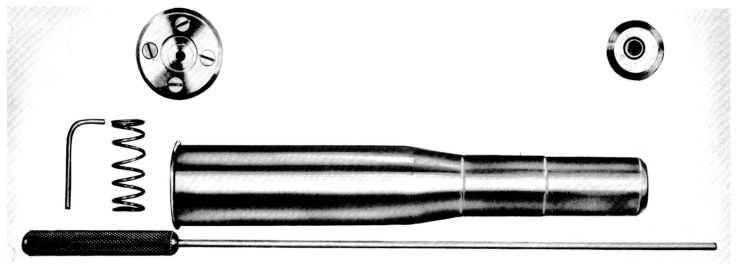

SUBCALIBER RIFLE, CAL. .22, M5

This weapon supersedes the cal. 22 Subcaliber Rifle, M2A1, the cal. .30 Subcaliber Rifle, M1903A2, and the subcaliber mount, cal. .22–.30, M6, for use in the 37 mm Tank Guns, M5 and M6. It was standardized by O.C.M. 18169, dated 5 May 1942.

The Subcaliber Rifle, M5, comprises a short commercial type, cal. .22, M2, rifle barrel mounted in a bronze casting similar in form to a 37 mm complete round in such a way that, when inserted in the chamber of the 37 mm gun, the center firing pin of the cannon can strike the rim of the cal. .22 cartridge. The casting has a steel flange which engages the extractors of the tank gun. The M5 rifle is loaded before insertion in the barrel of the 37 mm weapon. After firing, the breech mechanism of the larger gun is opened, extracting the subcaliber rifle. The empty cal. .22 cartridge is then removed by the use of a rod or a hand extractor.

SUBCALIBER RIFLE, CAL. .30, M1903A2—STANDARD

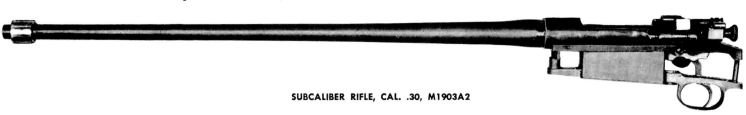

SUBCALIBER RIFLE, CAL. .30, M1903A2

This weapon is the cal. .30 U. S. Rifle, M1903, from which the stock and front sight have been removed. The front end of the rifle is fitted with a bronze bushing which has a diameter equal to the bore of the gun in which the subcaliber rifle is to be mounted. The rifle is 32 inches long and weighs $4\frac{7}{8}$ pounds. It may be used interchangeably with the Subcaliber Rifle, cal. .22, M2A1, in the Subcaliber Mount, cal. .22–.30, M6, which fits in the bore of the 37 mm Antitank Guns, M3 and M3A1. The standard cartridge, Tracer, cal. .30, M1, is used for training.

SUBCALIBER MOUNT, CAL. .22-.30, M6—STANDARD
SUBCALIBER MOUNT, CAL. .22-.30, M14—STANDARD

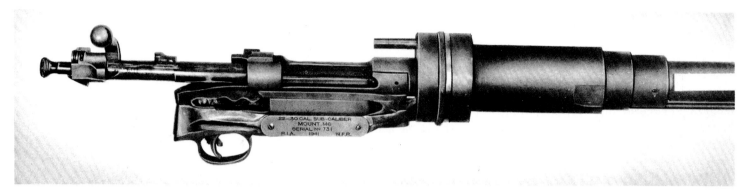

SUBCALIBER MOUNT, CAL. .22-.30, M6

The Mount, M6, consists of a rifle tube extending the length of the 37 mm gun tube, a firing-support assembly fastened to the rear end of the rifle for the support of the receiver and firing mechanism of the rifle, and a firing mechanism assembly fastened to the left side of the firing support and connected with the firing mechanism of the 37 mm gun. Cocking of the rifle must be done by hand. It is used with Subcaliber Rifle, cal. 22, M2A1, and Subcaliber Rifle, cal. .30, M1903A2.

The Mount, M14, is the Mount, M6, modified to fit the 57 mm Gun.

SUBCALIBER MOUNT, CAL. .30, M8—STANDARD

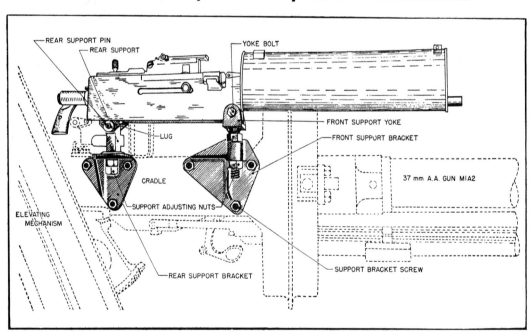

SUBCALIBER MOUNT, CAL. .30, M8

SUBCALIBER FIRING MECHANISM, MOUNT, M8

This Mount is for use with the Browning Subcaliber Machine Gun, cal. .30, M1917A1, on the 37 mm Gun, M1A2, on the Carriage, M3. It was standardized by O.C.M. 16696, dated 8 May 1941.

The mount, which is bolted to the right side of the 37 mm gun cradle, consists of front and rear supports. The front support is a triangular bracket holding the U-shaped yoke which surrounds a portion of the subcaliber gun. Adjusting nuts which secure the yoke to the bracket may be tightened or loosened to effect slight changes in elevation of the subcaliber weapon. The rear bracket holds the rear support consisting of a T-shaped rectangular block with its projection toward the center of the carriage. This bracket contains a slot in which the support slides horizontally for adjustments in azimuth. In making such adjustments the nut on the front support serves as a pivot. During adjustments in elevation, the rear end of the gun pivots vertically in the rear support pin.

REFERENCE—TM 9–235.

SUBCALIBER MOUNTS, CAL. .50, M9, M10, M12—STANDARD

CALIBER .50 SUBCALIBER MOUNT, M12, ON 3" GUN CARRIAGE, M1, WITH BROWNING MACHINE GUN, CAL. .50, HB, M2

Subcaliber Mounts, Cal. .50, M9, M10, and M12, were developed in order to provide subcaliber training equipment for tank destroyer guns where range facilities are not available for firing service ammunition. They are to be used in training gunners in firing at moving targets.

The mounts are designed to support the Browning Machine Gun, Cal. .50, HB (flex.), M2, and to fit all guns assigned to the Tank Destroyer Battalion. The mount and top bracket are universal, and the steel securing straps vary for each type of gun for which the mount is intended. These straps are so constructed that they are removable, permitting them to be stowed in the smallest possible space.

The proper firing solenoid is furnished for attachment to the Browning Machine Gun, Cal. .50, together with sufficient electric cable to connect the solenoid with the solenoid switch in the motor carriage. When it is desired to fire the cal. .50 machine gun as a single-shot weapon, using a lanyard, it is necessary to install a trigger motor on the machine gun casing, together with a rocker arm to reverse the direction of pull and a cable fastened to the firing mechanism of the major caliber weapon.

REFERENCES—OCM 21024; OCM 21244.

37 MM SUBCALIBER GUN M1916 STANDARD—SUBCALIBER MOUNTS M1, M4, M7, M8, M9, M10 STANDARD

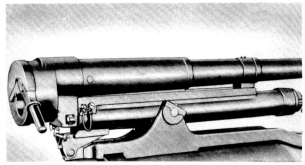

37 MM GUN, M1916—SUBCALIBER MOUNT, M1   37 MM GUN, M1916—SUBCALIBER MOUNT, M4   37 MM GUN, M1916—SUBCALIBER MOUNT, M7

The 37 mm Subcaliber Gun, M1916, is standard for subcaliber use with various mobile artillery weapons. It consists of the 37 mm Gun, M1916, and its cradle. In all cases it is mounted on the larger gun by means of a mount adopted as standard for that matériel.

CHARACTERISTICS

Weight of gun unit.....................104 lb.
Weight of gun.........................57 lb.
Length of barrel..........29.13 ins., 19.94 cals.
Diameter of bore....................1.457 ins.
Length of recoil......................7–10 ins.
Rifling, uniform L.H., one turn in.....43.582 ins.
Maximum effective range...........1,800 yds.
Maximum rate of fire, aimed.......25 rds./min.
Ammunition....Subcaliber ammunition consists of fixed round, designated as 37 mm Practice Shell, Mk. II, with Practice Fuze, M38.

The different subcaliber mounts used with the gun, M1916, are constructed on

the same general principles, differing only in details necessary for use with different weapons. Each mount consists of a mounting bracket which, when in position, lies between the barrels of the two guns and is parallel to them. Either forming a part of the bracket, or firmly attached to it, are the supports which hold the mount on the larger weapon to keep the subcaliber gun in place. The lower supports are firmly attached to the main gun, in some cases by a U-bolt which encircles a portion of the barrel. The upper supports are adjustable at the trunnion, and at the front end of the cradle, which permits adjustment of the 37 mm weapon to parallelism with the main weapon.

37 mm SUBCALIBER MOUNT, M1— This mount is used on the 155 mm Guns, M1917 and M1918M1.

37 mm SUBCALIBER MOUNT, M4—

This mount is used on the 155 mm Howitzers, M1917 and M1918.

37 mm SUBCALIBER MOUNT, M7— This mount is used on the 75 mm Guns, M1897, M1897A1, M1897A2, M1897A3 and M1897A4, on 75 mm Carriages, M1897M1 and M1897A4.

37 mm SUBCALIBER MOUNT, M8— This mount is used on the 75 mm Gun Carriages, M1897M1 and M1897A4.

37 mm SUBCALIBER MOUNT, M9— This mount is used on the 75 mm Gun Carriage, M1916A1.

37 mm SUBCALIBER MOUNT, M10— This mount is used on the 155 mm Gun Carriage, M1, and 8″ Howitzer Carriage, M1.

References—TM 9–2005, v.3; III, TM 9–320; TM 9–335; TM 9–345; TM 9–350.

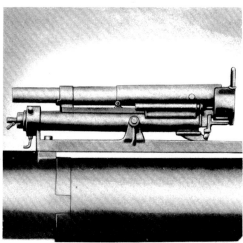

37 MM GUN, M1916—SUBCALIBER MOUNT, M8   37 MM GUN, M1916—SUBCALIBER MOUNT, M9   37 MM GUN, M1916—SUBCALIBER MOUNT, M10

37 MM SUBCALIBER GUN M1916A1—STANDARD

The 37 mm Subcaliber Gun, M1916A1, consists of the barrel of the 37 mm Gun, M1916, modified so that it can be installed in the chamber of the 75 mm Gun, M1917, rather than mounted on the barrel of the larger weapon. It was originally designed for use in the 75 mm Gun, M1916, as well, but it has been supplanted for that weapon by the 37 mm Gun, M1916, and the 37 mm Subcaliber Mount, M9, above the recoil mechanism.

37 MM SUBCALIBER GUN M12—STANDARD

The 37 mm Subcaliber Gun, M12, is of the "internal" type, designed for use in 75 mm Howitzers, M1A1, M2, and M3, and is suitable for use in training with the 75 mm Howitzer Motor Carriage, M8. It is capable of rapid installation in, and removal from, the major weapon.

37 mm Subcaliber Gun, M12, was developed to eliminate the long tubes of former subcaliber guns inserted in the bores of howitzers, since the longer tubes affected accuracy. The M12 also can be locked in the howitzer chamber when the breech is open.

Use of the M12 subcaliber gun is not injurious to howitzer tubes, which may be cleaned easily after subcaliber firing.

A special rammer for loading the 37 mm shells is not required with the manually operated breechblock.

References—OCM 22419; OCM 22618.

37 MM SUBCALIBER GUN M13—STANDARD

The 37 mm Subcaliber Gun, M13, is preferable to the 37 mm Subcaliber Mount, M16, for use with the 75 mm Howitzer Carriage, M2A1, and the 105 mm Howitzer Motor Carriage, M7, because it is fired with the normal howitzer breechblock and firing mechanism, may be accurately installed in an already bore-sighted 105 mm howitzer, and can be installed and removed with greater speed and accuracy.

Use of the M13 subcaliber gun is not injurious to howitzer tubes, which may be cleaned easily after subcaliber firing.

A special rammer for loading the 37 mm shells is not required with the manually operated breechblock.

References—OCM 22419; OCM 22618.

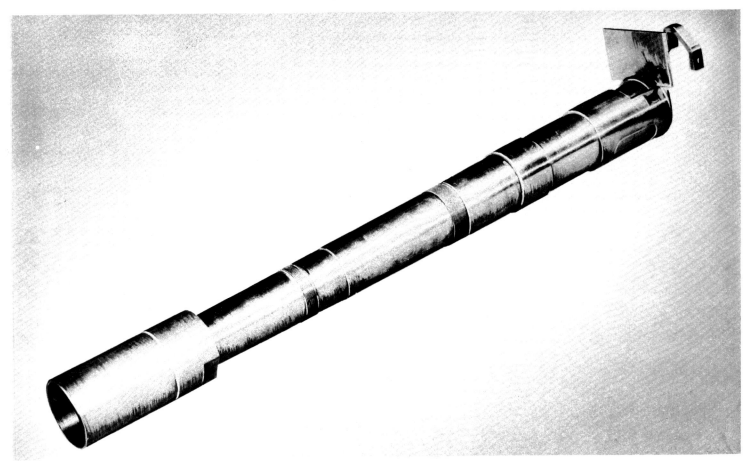

37 mm SUBCALIBER GUN (INTERNAL)—37 mm SUBCALIBER GUNS, M12 AND M13, ARE OF THIS TYPE

37 mm SUBCALIBER MOUNT, M13A1, ON 4.5 INCH GUN CARRIAGE, M1

The 37 mm Subcaliber Mount, M13A1, is used on the 4.5 Inch Gun Carriage, M1, and the 155 mm Howitzer Carriage, M1.

Due to accidents caused by premature bursts of the Mk. II projectile, the 37 mm gun and recoil system were relocated to place the muzzle of the subcaliber weapon 17½ inches farther forward on the 4.5 inch gun and 155 mm howitzer carriages, thus reducing the hazard to men serving the piece. Further protection from fragments of a premature burst at or within a few inches of the muzzle was provided by Flash Hider, TAC-4. The flash hider also tends to reduce blast effect on the gunner.

Tests indicated that Flash Hider, TAC-4, increased the average muzzle velocity of the practice round from 1,232 feet per second to 1,256 feet per second.

The Flash Hider, TAC-4, is locked securely to the barrel of the 37 mm gun by means of a clamping bolt that engages a notch near the muzzle of the weapon. It may be used on the 37 mm Gun, M1916, mounted on 37 mm Subcaliber Mounts, M1, M5, M10, M13A1, and M16.

CHARACTERISTICS OF FLASH HIDER, TAC-4

Length................................15 ins.
Diameter..............................2.5 ins.
Wall thickness..........................25 in.

SUBCALIBER MOUNT, M13A1, ON 155 mm HOWITZER CARRIAGE, M1

1-POUNDER SUBCALIBER GUN—STANDARD

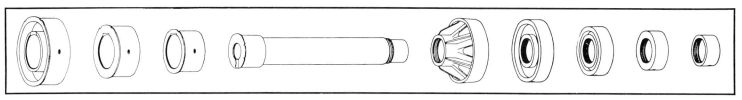

1-POUNDER (1.457 INCH) SUBCALIBER GUN, WITH FRONT AND REAR ADAPTERS FOR WEAPONS OF VARYING CALIBER

The 1-pounder subcaliber gun is used with the 6 inch guns, M1897M1, M1900, M1903, M1905, M1908, M1908M1, M1908M2; 8 inch guns, M1888 and modifications; 10 inch guns, M1888, M1895, M1900, and modifications, and with 14 inch guns, M1907, M1907M1, and M1909.

The 1-pounder subcaliber gun is inserted in the chamber of the larger cannon where it is held in place by means of adapters screwed over the muzzle and breech of the smaller weapon. When the subcaliber gun is inserted the adapters are expanded to hold it firmly in position. A center support screws on threads near the middle of the 1-pounder tube in order to insure rigidity of the gun.

The round is fired by the firing mechanism of the major weapon, and the supply cartridge case is removed by means of a hand extractor.

2.95 INCH SUBCALIBER GUN—STANDARD

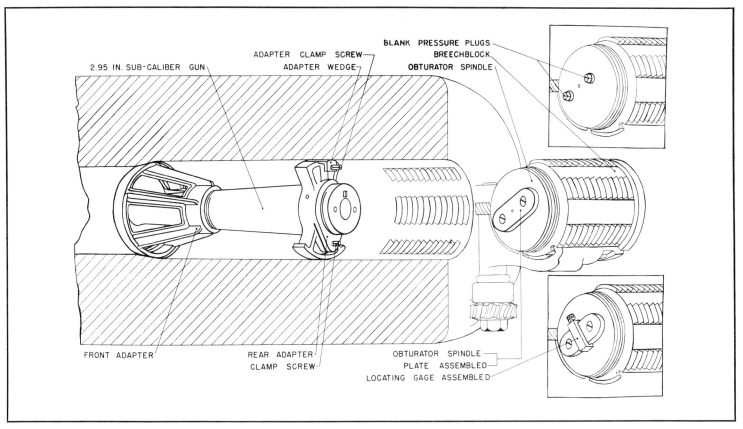

2.95 INCH SUBCALIBER GUN, WITH ADAPTERS

The 2.95″ subcaliber gun is used in conjunction with all models of 12″ seacoast mortars. The gun is supplied with rear and front adapters screwed over the subcaliber tube at the breech and muzzle. These adapters permit the subcaliber gun to be inserted in the bore of the mortar, where the rear adapter is expanded until it is wedged against the walls of the chamber. The round is fired by the mortar firing mechanism, and the empty cartridge case is extracted by means of a hand extractor.

Ammunition for the 2.95″ subcaliber gun is in the form of a complete fixed round with a solid steel or cast-iron projectile weighing 18 pounds. Three distinct rounds are furnished with a different propelling charge in each round to provide for zone 1, 2 and 3 firing. Muzzle velocity for zone 1 is 550 feet per second; for zone 2, 625 feet per second, and for zone 3, 700 feet per second.

REFERENCES—TM 9–456; TM 9–457; TM 9–458.

CHARACTERISTICS

Weight of subcaliber tube	224 lb.
Caliber	2.953 ins.
Length of bore, including chamber	31.6 ins.
Length of rifled portion of bore	24.33 ins.
Rifling, uniform R.H. twist	1 turn in 25 cals.
Rifling, number of grooves	30
Capacity of powder chamber	34.9 cu. ins.
Weight of projectile	18 lb.
Weight of cartridge case	1.45 lb.
Muzzle velocity— three zones	550, 625, 700 f./s.
Maximum chamber pressure	18,000 lb./sq. in.
Maximum range	4,142 yds.
Minimum range	1,975 yds.

SUBCALIBER KITS AND DRILL CARTRIDGES FOR 3 INCH (15 PDR.) GUNS M1902, M1903—STANDARD

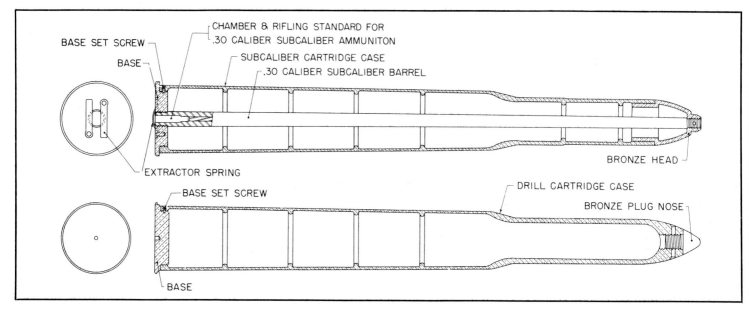

SUBCALIBER AND DRILL CARTRIDGES FOR 3 INCH (15 PDR.) GUNS, M1902, M1903

Subcaliber equipment for the 3 inch (15 pdr.) Guns, M1902 and M1903, is stored in a subcaliber and drill cartridge kit which contains: 1 cleaning brush, 3 drill cartridges, 1 subcaliber cartridge, 1 extension piece, 1 cleaning rod, 2 flathead special screws, 1 slotted tip, 1 extra base and 1 storage chest.

DRILL CARTRIDGE—This is a dummy cartridge for use in drilling cannoneers in the service and loading of the gun. It is a bronze casting of the shape and dimensions of the service round of fixed ammunition.

SUBCALIBER CARTRIDGE—The subcaliber cartridge consists of a cal. .30 rifle barrel mounted axially in a bronze subcaliber cartridge case, and is of the same weight and exterior dimensions as the cartridge case for the service ammunition. The breech end of the rifle screws into the base of the subcaliber cartridge, while the muzzle end is threaded to take the ogival-shaped bronze head, which accurately fits the bore of the 3 inch gun at the front end of the subcaliber case, and is capable of longitudinal motion to allow for expansion of the barrel when it becomes heated. Two extractor springs are provided for extracting the subcaliber ammunition from the cal. .30 barrel. They are secured to the base of the 3 inch subcaliber cartridge by two flathead special screws so that the springs catch the rim of the cal. .30 subcaliber cartridge as it is inserted into the cal. .30 barrel.

75 MM SUBCALIBER GUN M1916MIIA1—STANDARD

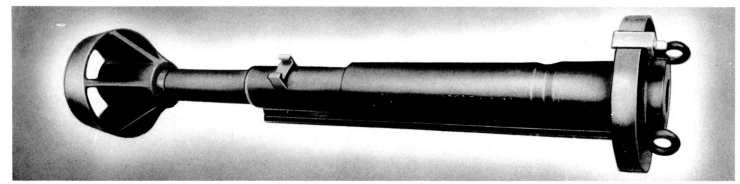

75 mm SUBCALIBER GUN, M1916MIIA1

The 75 mm Subcaliber Gun, M1916MIIA1, is used as subcaliber matériel with the 14 Inch Gun, M1910M1, on 14 Inch Disappearing Carriage, M1906M1. No mount is used with this gun, the tube being fitted with front and rear adapters which permit it to be inserted in the chamber of the 14 inch weapon.

206

75 MM GUN M1916—MOUNTS M1, M2, M3, M4—STANDARD

75 MM SUBCALIBER MOUNT, M3, ON 16 INCH HOWITZER CARRIAGE, M1920

The 75 mm Gun, M1916, is used as sub-caliber equipment with 75 mm Subcaliber Mount, M1, for the 12 inch Barbette Carriage, M1917; with Mount, M2, for 16 inch Barbette Carriage, M1919; with Mount, M3, for 16 inch Howitzer Carriage, M1920; and with Mount, M4, for 16 inch Barbette Carriage, M1919.

The 75 mm Gun, M1916, is a built-up weapon of alloy-steel forgings. It consists of a tube, jacket breech hoop and clip. The clip has two lugs on the under side to guide the gun in the carriage. The breech mechanism is of the semi-automatic drop-block type, closing automatically when a round is inserted in the chamber. Manual opening of the breechblock extracts the empty cartridge case. The firing mechanism is of the continuous pull type. The recoil mechanism is of the hydrospring design.

The Mounts, M1, M2, M3, and M4, vary only in minor details. They are attached to the cradle of the major caliber weapon and support the 75 mm Gun, M1916, together with its recoil mechanism.

CHARACTERISTICS

Total weight of gun.....................749 lb.
Overall length ....90.9 ins.
Length of bore.....................28.4 cals.
Muzzle velocity.....................1,780 f./s.
Maximum range (with H.E. Shell,
   Mk. I)...........................8,780 yds.
Type of breech mechanism.......semi-automatic
              vertical sliding wedge block
Firing mechanism...............continuous pull
Recoil mechanism....hydrospring, variable recoil

75 MM SUBCALIBER MOUNT, M2, ON 16 INCH BARBETTE CARRIAGE, M1919

HARBOR DEFENSE BY CONTROLLED MINES

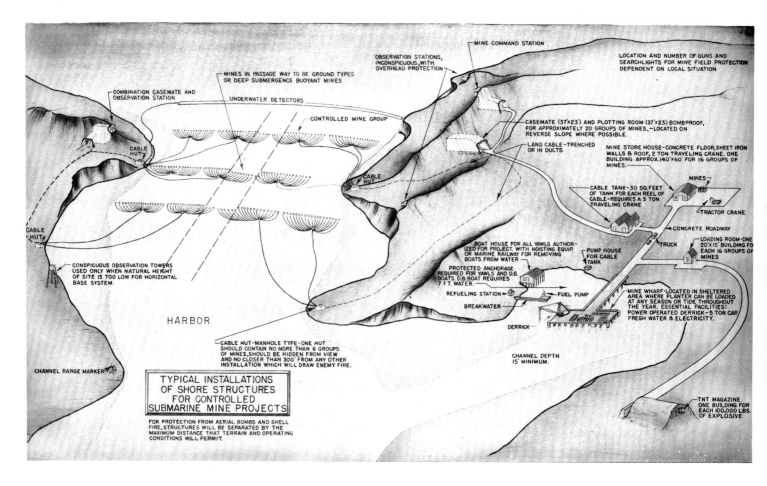

TYPICAL INSTALLATIONS
OF SHORE STRUCTURES
FOR CONTROLLED
SUBMARINE MINE PROJECTS

FOR PROTECTION FROM AERIAL BOMBS AND SHELL
FIRE, STRUCTURES WILL BE SEPARATED BY THE
MAXIMUM DISTANCE THAT TERRAIN AND OPERATING
CONDITIONS WILL PERMIT.

Controlled submarine mines are utilized in conjunction with other defense measures employed for the protection of important harbors. The tactical operation of all controlled submarine mine equipment is a function of the Coast Artillery Corps.

Controlled mine fields are planted to effect the destruction or damage of hostile vessels attempting to enter such portions of harbor entrances as lead to channels used by friendly shipping. The fields are normally limited to distances of 10,000 yards from shore and to water not over 300 feet deep.

A mine field consists of from two to four parallel lines of mines. Individual lines are composed of groups, each of which contains nineteen buoyant mines or thirteen ground mines. This arrange-ment insures the probability of a vessel passing over at least one mine and probably several other mines. Mines within a group are separated by 100 foot intervals in the case of buoyant mines and by 150 foot intervals in the case of ground mines.

The approach of a hostile vessel to the mine field may be detected by visual observation, by an audio reception system or by a signal light on the mine control panel which flashes on when a ship strikes a buoyant mine or comes within actuating distance of an influence-operated ground mine.

Observation and command stations are located in specially protected shore installations. Observers in the shore stations communicate to the casemate plotting room the azimuth, speed and course of an approaching enemy vessel which they can see. These data enable the plotting board operators to determine the mine which should be fired in order to destroy or put the hostile vessel out of action. Commands are communicated to the casemate electrician to fire the mine by closing the proper group firing switch.

The shore installations for controlled mine harbor defense consist of the mine casemate, housing the power and control equipment; a mine storehouse; a loading room; a cable tank for storage of cable; a mine wharf and derricks; trackage or roads to connect the various structures; a mine group commander's station; base end stations; a plotting room, and cable terminal huts. There are also boathouses and anchorages for the mine yawls and DB boats.

SUBMARINE MINE FLOTILLA

MINE YAWL, USED TO ASSIST MINE PLANTERS AND DB-BOATS, TO ACT AS A SAFETY BOAT, AND AS A UTILITY AND MESSAGE DELIVERY BOAT

U. S. ARMY MINE PLANTER *MAYBACK*, USED FOR LOCATING, PLANTING, REPAIRING AND CLEARING MINE FIELDS

DISTRIBUTION BOX BOAT, USED TO ASSIST THE OPERATIONS OF THE MINE PLANTER AND AS A PATROL BOAT

AUDIO RECEPTION SYSTEM M1—STANDARD

AUDIO RECEPTION SYSTEM, M1, SHOWING HYDROPHONES AND MOUNTS, MAIN AMPLIFIER, PREAMPLIFIER AND SOUND RECORDER

The Audio Reception System, M1, was developed as a result of a request from the Commanding Officer of Fort Mills, Corregidor, P.I., for some method of determining the difference between bomb or shell bursts and an approaching hostile vessel when mines in a defense field were armed. As designed, the system will distinguish between mines being armed by the explosion of depth bombs, aerial bombs, and shells, by wave action, and by the approach of a vessel.

The distinctive sounds of an approaching vessel are audible at distances of from 500 to 3,500 yards, depending on hydrographic conditions. The audible sounds are picked up and translated to a visual signal as the vessel comes closer to the hydrophones. Experienced operators can often identify the nature of a vessel as it passes over the line by the character of its signature and sound output.

The audio reception system is composed of underwater and shore equipment. The underwater components consist of two hydrophones connected together and to the shore equipment by single-conductor submarine mine cable. The shore equipment comprises a preamplifier installed in an M1 selector box buried in the beach where the cable comes ashore; a main amplifier, including a loud speaker, which is connected to the preamplifier; and a sound recorder which is a standard 5 milliampere, direct current, recording milliammeter. The sound recorder graphically translates sound reception in a series of lines varying in length and character according to the nature and volume of the originating sounds.

REFERENCE—Coast Artillery Training Bulletin, Vol. I, No. 14, "Audio Reception System, M–1."

ARMY CONTROLLED SUBMARINE MINES

SUBMARINE MINE SYSTEM, M4

SUBMARINE MINE SYSTEM, M3 (BUOYANT)

The Submarine Mine System, M3, is composed of underwater and shore units. The underwater equipment consists of loaded mines, distribution boxes containing selector boxes and selector assemblies, mine cables, mooring and raising ropes, anchors, and buoys. The shore equipment comprises electric power plants and control panels situated in the casemate for electrically controlling the mines, and land cables for electrically connecting the control panels to the groups of mines. Specifically, the land cables establish electrical connection between the casemate and the terminal huts near the water's edge.

CASEMATE CONTROL SYSTEM, M3—

This system is composed of a series of panels from which all planted mines are fired, cleared, or tested. Each group of underwater equipment is connected to the shore equipment by a single-conductor submarine cable which extends from the selector assembly to the shore cable. The shore control equipment requires a permanent casemate installation.

SELECTOR ASSEMBLY, M3—

The selector assembly in the planted distribution box provides a means for electrically selecting, testing, or firing any mine in the group which it controls.

SELECTOR BOXES, M4 AND M4A1—

The Selector Boxes, M4 and M4A1, provide watertight, shockproof containers for the selector assembly and a means for connecting the shore cable and mine cables to their corresponding leads in the selector assembly.

SELECTOR BOXES, M4 AND M4A1—CLOSED AND OPENED

DISTRIBUTION BOXES, M2B1 AND M2—CLOSED AND OPENED

DISTRIBUTION BOXES, M2 AND M2B1 —the Distribution Boxes, M2 and M2B1, provide a rigid clamp for holding the ends of the shore and the mine cables to give mechanical protection to the selector box.

MINE CABLE, M4—This cable has a 7-strand, soft-drawn, annealed copper conductor, covered by a $\frac{3}{32}$ inch layer of insulating compound containing 50% crude rubber or Buna S by weight. Number 12 galvanized steel armor wire provides a protective cover for the insulation.

BUOYANT MINE CASE, M2—The Mine Case, M2, has a cylindrical center section with flanged, curved end sections. It contains a firing device, M4A1, which is actuated by impact of a vessel. It is loaded with from 300 to 500 pounds of granulated TNT depending on hydrographic conditions. In the M3 system the mines may be fired by manual control from shore, in conjunction with observation fire, or automatically when the mine is struck by a vessel. The mine will not fire when struck unless the firing power switch is closed.

CAST-IRON MINE ANCHORS—Anchors of 1,000, 2,000, or 3,000 pounds are supplied, the size depending upon the weight necessary to hold the buoyant mine case at the proper submergence and in its proper location under all conditions of weather, tide, and firing of adjacent mines.

MINE BUOY, WOODEN BLOCK TYPE —These buoys are used to mark the positions of mines during planting operations.

STEEL MARKING BUOYS—These buoys are used to mark the position of the distribution box and the line of mines prior to and during planting.

SUBMARINE MINE SYSTEM, M4 (GROUND)

This system differs from the M3 in that the mine employed rests on the floor of the ocean and is influence operated. It is, therefore, spoken of as a ground mine. The magnetic field of an approaching

DISTRIBUTION BOX RELEASE BUOY

BUOYANT MINE CASE, M2, ATTACHED TO A CAST-IRON ANCHOR. THIS MINE CASE IS USED WITH SUBMARINE MINE SYSTEM, M3

vessel induces a minute current in the windings of a coil rod. This current then causes a series of relays to operate resulting in the mine control system selecting the mine. Ground mines may be set for fire automatically when influenced, or for manual firing upon receipt of a signal in the casemate. Observation firing may be employed from data transmitted from the shore stations to the plotting room. The ground mine will not fire unless the firing power switch is closed.

GROUND MINE CASES, M3 AND M3A1
—The Ground Mine Cases, M3 and M3A1, are similar except for the manner in which they are reinforced and a provision on the case, M3A1, for lead or iron loading to give additional weight where hydrographic conditions so necessitate. Both cases are welded steel containers designed to hold 3,000 pounds of granular TNT. The base of either case is flat to permit resting on the bottom of the sea. The firing device, M5, is located in the lower part of the case. The booster charge, electrically connected to the firing device, is approximately in the center of the mine, close to the bottom. The loaded case weighs approximately 5,800 pounds.

EMERGENCY MINE CONTROL, M4—
The Emergency Mine Control, M4, is a compact and readily portable unit for the control of 10 groups of buoyant or ground mines. It is designed for either independent or parallel operation with the standard Mine Control, M3. For carrying, it is broken down into three components: the operating panel—19″ high, 25½″ wide, and 20″ deep, weighing 75 pounds; a power pack—16″ high, 25½″ wide, and 19″ deep, weighing 104 pounds; and the power plant composed of a generator rated at 2½ KVA, 130 volts, 60 cycle AC, driven by a 6.5 hp. single cylinder, 4-cycle gasoline engine, Signal Corps type PE-75, weighing 324 pounds.

The M4 control may be installed and operated in submarine mine casemates, on L-boats, mine planters, or in any emergency shelter as required by the tactical situation.

Two power plants are provided for each 10-group control so that plants can be serviced without interruption of mine protection.

Any power source capable of supplying at least 2½ KVA of 110-volt, 60-cycle electric power may be used instead of the gasoline driven plant where installation does not require portability.

PORTABLE CABLE REELER, M1—The
portable cable reeler is a mechanical unit designed to reel and unreel submarine mine cable. The use of mechanical power to rotate the reels cuts to a minimum the time and manpower required. The cable reeler can be used for all types of cable reeling work such as re-reeling, repairing cable, unreeling for figure eights, and measuring cable lengths.

The crew required to reel cable from one reel to another after setting up the equipment is three men instead of the eight men needed formerly. 10,000 feet of cable can be rewound in 2½ hours' operation. Use of the M1 reeler also tends to eliminate hand injuries which are frequent when cables are reeled manually.

The variable speeds of the machine allow the operator to select the most practical speed to make smooth and uniform lays.

More cable will be reeled per hour with steady operation at medium speeds than with intermittent operation at high speeds.

The power unit of the portable cable reeler is a 6.5 hp. single cylinder, 4-cycle, air-cooled gasoline engine running at 2,700 r.p.m. This engine is identical with the engine used in Power Unit, PE-75-5, procured by the Signal Corps, U. S. Army. The power is taken off by a quadruple "V" belt driving an expanding type clutch.

The operation of the clutch is accomplished by remote control through the medium of a vacuum cylinder controlled by a solenoid that derives its power from a 6-volt battery. Functioning of the solenoid is effected by a foot pedal. Hand operation of the clutch is provided for in case of failure of the vacuum control system.

Selection of three forward speeds of 4, 8, and 15 r.p.m. and one reverse speed of 3 r.p.m. is by an automobile truck transmission.

Reduction of output of the transmission to three forward and one reverse speeds is by a 32 to 1 worm gear speed reducer.

The battery is kept in fully charged condition by a generator connected to the transmission drive shaft. Charging rate is controlled automatically by a voltage regulator.

Reels weighing not more than 6 tons can be used on this cable reeling machine by properly connecting the output end of the driving arm to the driven reel.

The cable reeler is built on a four leg platform and can be moved about by means of a Mechanical Lift Truck, Submarine Mine Depot, No. 5395.

REFERENCES — OCM 21657; OCM 22015.

PORTABLE CABLE REELER, M1

BROWNING MACHINE GUN, CAL. .30, **M2**, AIRCRAFT—STANDARD

BROWNING MACHINE GUN, CAL. .30, M2, AIRCRAFT, ON FLEXIBLE MOUNT

In World War I the .30 caliber machine gun was the predominant aircraft weapon; in World War II it has been reduced to a secondary role by guns of heavier caliber. Its tactical use now is as a supplementary weapon with a high cyclic rate for fire at close ranges.

The Browning Machine Gun, cal. .30, M2, Aircraft, is recoil-operated and air-cooled. It is fed by a metallic link, disintegrating belt in all firing. This gun is designed for both fixed and flexible use and, by replacing some of the component parts, it may be fed from either the left or the right side as desired. The fixed and flexible guns are identical except for the mounting parts.

FIXED GUN—This type is rigidly mounted in the fuselage in front of the gunner or it may be mounted in the wings for firing by remote control. In hand operation an operating slide retracts the breech mechanism for loading, un-loading, and clearance of stoppages. A cable may be attached to permit remote control. The fixed gun is normally assembled with a back plate having a horizontal buffer but without spade grips.

The fixed gun, when mounted adjacent to the airplane engine, is fired through the arc of propeller rotation by a synchronizing system which delivers semi-automatic fire timed with the revolutions of the propeller. Fire of wing-mounted guns is controlled by a solenoid and operated by a switch, usually mounted on the pilot's control stick.

FLEXIBLE GUN—This type is installed in the fuselage on a mount which permits free aiming. It has a retracting slide, on the right side of the gun, which connects with the bolt by means of the retracting slide bolt stud. The retracting slide permits retraction of the breech mechanism by hand for loading, unloading, and clearance of stoppages in firing. The flexible gun is provided with a back plate carrying a horizontal buffer, double spade grips, and a hand trigger. It delivers full automatic fire.

REFERENCES—TM 9–205; TM 9–1205; TM 9–2200.

CHARACTERISTICS

Weight of fixed gun	21.5 lb.
Weight of flexible gun	23 lb.
Length, overall	39.8 ins.
Weight of recoiling parts	6.56 lb.
Weight of barrel	3.81 lb.
Length of barrel	23.9 ins.
Length of rifling	70.9 cals.; 21.35 ins.
Rifling	
Number of grooves	4
Right-hand twist: 1 turn in	33.3 cals.; 10 ins.
Depth of grooves	0.0040 in.
Cross-sectional area of bore	0.0740 sq. in.
Rate of fire	1,000–1,350 rds./min.
Firing-pin release	
Pressure applied to sear: 12–17 lb.	
Pressure applied to sear holder: 25–35 lb.	
Ammunition, types	Ball; A.P.; tracer; incendiary

BROWNING MACHINE GUN, CAL. .50, **M2**, AIRCRAFT—STANDARD

There are three main types of Browning Machine Guns, cal. .50, M2—water-cooled, heavy barrel, and aircraft—and among these the aircraft type was given prime consideration in all phases of design. All these guns may be used in the same mount; and by changing barrels and barrel jackets, and by changing the position of certain minor components, any of the three types may be converted to either of the other two. This interchangeability of the important parts of the gun greatly facilitates mass production with the same tooling setup.

The Browning Machine Gun, cal. .50, M2, Aircraft, is a recoil-operated, belt-fed, air-cooled weapon. The barrel reciprocates in a steel outer jacket drilled to enhance cooling. By repositioning some of the component parts, the gun may be fed from either the right or left side. The disintegrating metallic link belt is used with all installations of the gun.

BASIC GUN—The Browning Machine Gun, cal. .50, M2, Aircraft, is now furnished as a basic gun which may be equipped with either an operating slide group assembly, a retracting slide group assembly, or a retracting slide group assembly and spade grip back plate. The various installations are classified as follows:

WING GUN—This is the basic gun on a fixed mount in the wing of the aircraft. The wing gun may be equipped with a retracting slide assembly, in which case a

BROWNING MACHINE GUN, CAL. .50, M2, AIRCRAFT, MOUNTED IN AN ATTACK BOMBER

charging cable is attached to the slide lever. With either this cable attachment or a hydraulic charger the gun is charged from the cockpit.

Wing-mounted guns are fired by a solenoid attached to the gun receiver and controlled from the cockpit. The solenoid and hydraulic charger are supplied by the Army Air Forces.

SYNCHRONIZED GUN—For synchronized firing, the basic gun is supplied with the operating slide assembly which is provided for retraction of the breech mechanism by hand. The synchronizing mechanism, consisting of an impulse generator attached to the airplane engine, a solenoid, and a trigger motor mounted on the receiver side plate of the gun, is supplied by the Army Air Forces.

FUSELAGE GUN — This type is mounted in the nose, waist, or tail of the plane on a flexible gun mount adapter supplied by the Army Air Forces. The gun mount adapter is equipped with spade grips, back plate trigger, and trigger safety, and is usually provided with a shock-dampening device. The fuselage gun is equipped with the retracting slide assembly, located on either the right-hand or left-hand side of the gun. In some flexible installations, the back plate assembly with spade grips is added. Nose-mounted guns are fired by a solenoid.

TURRET GUN—When installed on a fixed mount in an airplane turret, the

basic gun is equipped with a charger and is fired by a solenoid mounted on the back plate, top plate, or side plate. A shock-dampening adapter is usually mounted on the gun. In some turrets the gun is moved both horizontally and vertically by moving the turret as a whole; in others the gun and mount only are moved.

SIGHTS—Sighting equipment for the Browning aircraft machine guns is considered to be plane equipment and is furnished by the Army Air Forces.

ACCESSORIES—Parts added to the gun for firing by trigger motor or solenoid are supplied by the Army Air Forces.

Two devices for accelerating the rate of fire are supplied with the gun as accessories—these are the Flash Hider, cal. .50, M1, and the Aircraft Machine Gun Booster, cal. .50. Either device may be attached to the muzzle end of the barrel jacket and when assembled takes the place of the standard front barrel bearing. The flash hider is usually attached to flexibly installed guns and the booster is used mainly on wing guns or those of fixed installation where muzzle flash is unimportant and where added air resistance would be detrimental. The flash hider boosts the rate of fire approximately 50 rounds per minute and the booster raises it 100 rounds per minute.

RATE OF FIRE—During training a maximum burst of 75 rounds is permitted from a cool gun. One minute after firing

this first burst, firing may be resumed at the rate of one 20-round burst per minute. Combat firing is unrestricted but bursts longer than 75 rounds (5-second bursts) will overheat the barrel and if repeated without pause may cause stoppages or "cooked-off" rounds. Prolonged firing may lead to the scrapping of the barrel, since a new barrel may be ruined by a prolonged burst of about ½ minute duration. After long bursts from synchronized guns the mechanism of the gun must be locked to the rear for 2 minutes to avoid having "cooked-off" rounds strike the propeller blade.

REFERENCES—TM 9-225; TM 9-1225; TM 9-2200.

CHARACTERISTICS

Weight of basic gun . . . . 58.32 lb.
Weight of retracting slide group assembly . 3.00 lb.
Weight of operating slide group assembly . 1.62 lb.
Weight of back plate with horizontal
   buffer assembly . . . . 2.68 lb.
Weight of back plate with spade grips,
   trigger safety, trigger assembly . . . . 4.01 lb.
Weight of side plate trigger assembly . . . . 0.44 lb.
Weight of recoiling parts . . . . 19.2 lb.
Weight of barrel . . . . 9.8 lb.
Length of basic gun, overall . . . . 57 ins.
Length of barrel . . . . 36 ins.
Length of rifling . . . . 63.8 cals.; 31.91 ins.
Rifling
   Number of grooves 8
   Right-hand twist: 1 turn in . . . . . 30 cals.; 15 ins.
   Depth of grooves . . . . 0.0050 in.
Cross-sectional area of bore . . . . . . 0.2021 sq. in.
Rate of fire . . . . 750–850 rds./min.
Firing-pin
   release . . . . . Pressure applied to sear: 10–20 lb.
         Pressure applied to sear slide: 30–35 lb.
Ammunition, types. Ball; A.P.; tracer; incendiary

20 MM AUTOMATIC GUN AN-M2—STANDARD

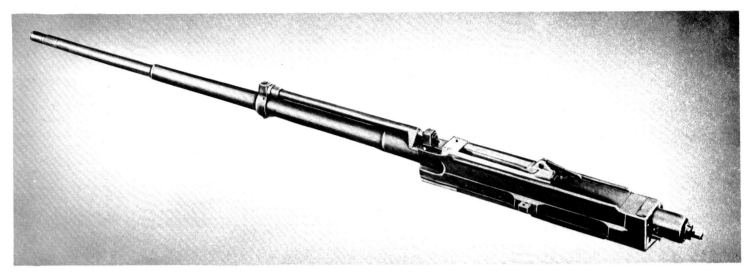

BASIC 20 mm AUTOMATIC GUN, AN-M2

The 20 mm Automatic Gun, AN–M2, is a fully automatic aircraft cannon with a muzzle velocity of 2,850 feet per second and a cyclic rate of from 600 to 700 rounds per minute. It is an air-cooled weapon of the gas-unlocking, semi-blowback type. Designed for fixed mounting in the wing or fuselage of an airplane, the gun may be mounted to fire through the hub of a propeller, and it may also be mounted as a flexible gun in a turret. The gun is seared electrically by remote control but it is not designed for synchronized fire between the blades of a propeller. The 20 mm Gun, AN–M2, was standardized in February, 1941. The 20 mm Automatic Gun, M1, classified as Substitute Standard, is identical with the AN–M2 gun in the tube and working parts, differing only in the dimensions of some of the receiver parts.

The principal components of the basic gun are the receiver, housing most of the working parts, and the tube. The breech end of the tube is screwed into the receiver and secured with a locking pin to prevent its vibrating loose during firing. Mounted on the tube is a gas cylinder and sleeve group, the function of which is to unlock the bolt. In firing, the only parts of the gun that do not recoil are the forward mount ring, the magazine slide assembly, and the magazine.

Changes in the 20 mm Automatic Guns, M1 and AN–M2, made early in February, 1943, included:

(a) The removal of $\frac{1}{16}$ inch from the back of the key slot of the standard firing pin (making it a floating firing pin).

(b) The adoption of a modified extractor spring (Wallace-Barnes strut type).

(c) The strength of the breechblock slide springs was increased.

(d) The chamber was shortened 1 mm.

There are seven gun type designations based on the kind of adapter, sear-actuating mechanism, and charger used with the basic M1 or AN–M2 gun, as follows:

Type A, used by the U. S. Army Air Forces, consists of the basic M1 or AN–M2 gun with AN–M1 adapter, AN–M1 electric trigger, and M2 manual charger.

Type B, used by the U. S. Army Air Forces, consists of the basic M1 or AN–M2 gun with M6 adapter, AN–M1 electric trigger, and M2 manual charger.

Type C, used by the U. S. Army Air Forces, consists of the basic M1 or AN–M2 gun with M7 adapter (with thread protector), AN–M1 electric trigger, and M2 manual charger.

Type D, used by the U. S. Army Air Forces, consists of the basic M1 or AN–M2 gun with M7 adapter (with M1 muzzle brake), AN–M1 electric trigger, and M2 manual charger.

Type E, used by the U. S. Navy, consists of the basic AN–M2 gun with the AN–M1 adapter, AN–M1 electric trigger, and M1 hydraulic charger.

Type F, used by the British, consists of the basic M1 gun with M7 adapter (with thread protector) and M1 sear mechanism.

Type G, used by the British, consists of the basic AN–M2 gun with M7 adapter (with thread protector) and M1 sear mechanism.

ADAPTERS—The AN–M1 adapter is a self-contained tubular unit consisting of a ring spring in series with a coil spring. Fitted over the tube of the gun, it serves as a front mounting and also controls the recoil of the gun within definite limits (0.875 inch to 1.25 inches) sufficient to operate the feed mechanisms which derive their operating power from the recoil movement of the gun.

CHARACTERISTICS

Weight of basic gun, AN-M2 or M1....102 lb.
Length of basic gun overall.............94 ins.
Weight of 20 mm Adapter, AN-M1....11.3 lb.
Weight of 20 mm Adapter, M6.........14 lb.
Weight of 20 mm Adapter, M7 (with
   thread protector)....................7.5 lb.
Weight of 20 mm Adapter, M7 (with
   muzzle brake)......................10.7 lb.
Weight of Muzzle Brake, M1...........4.6 lb.
Weight of Electric Trigger, AN-M1........5 lb.
Weight of Sear Mechanism, M1........1.3 lb.
Weight of Manual Charger, M2........1.5 lb.
Weight of Hydraulic Charger, M1......2.6 lb.
Weight of 20 mm Feed Mechanism,
   AN-M1A1.......................18½ lb.
Weight of 20 mm 60-round Magazine,
   M1A1 (empty)....................22 lb.
Weight of projectiles
   H.E.I., Mk. I....................0.286 lb.
   A.P., M75.......................0.363 lb.
   Ball............................0.276 lb.
Muzzle velocity
   H.E.I., Mk. I.................2,800 ft./sec.
   A.P., M75...................2,615 ft./sec.
   Ball.........................2,850 ft./sec.
Maximum powder pressure.....48,000 lb./sq. in.
Rate of fire.................600-700 rds./min.

Adapter, M6, consists of an AN–M1 adapter with a rear extension body added to increase the overall length of the adapter by $8\frac{1}{16}$ inches in order to meet special Air Force mounting requirements.

Adapter, M7, consists of a dashpot piston, a recoil spring with a recoil spring filler sleeve, a recoil spring sleeve, and a muzzle brake lock. It reduces the force of recoil on the airplane structure by the resistance of the spring which is compressed against the shoulder in the mounting when the gun recoils. Muzzle Brake, M1, is screwed on the barrel of the gun when the M7 adapter is used in conjunction with the 60-round Magazine, M1-A1, to reduce recoil distance. When the AN–M1A1 feed mechanism and M7 adap-

CUTAWAY VIEW OF 20 mm AN-M1 ADAPTER

20 mm ADAPTER, M6

20 mm ADAPTER, M7, WITH MUZZLE BRAKE, M1

ter are used together, the muzzle brake must be replaced by a thread protector.

SEAR-ACTUATING MECHANISMS—Electric Trigger, AN–M1, is designed to fire the 20 mm guns in airplanes that are equipped with 24-volt electrical systems. It consists essentially of a mounting plate assembly and solenoid body and is attached to the receiver plate of the gun. The solenoid plunger and attached sear shaft are moved magnetically against spring tension by a force of approximately 75 pounds to depress the sear and fire the gun.

Sear Mechanism, M1, uses a bowden cable to move a sear spring plunger against the sear. A groove in the bowden connection shaft accommodates a safety trigger pin operated by a safety lever which is held in two positions, "Safe" and "Fire."

CHARGERS—Hydraulic Charger, M1, is used with Naval installations of the 20 mm AN–M2 gun where it is required that the gun be charged or "safetied" by remote control.

Manual Charger, M2, was previously designated as the B6 charger by the U.S.A.A.F. It consists essentially of a flanged charger slide for engaging and retracting the bolt assembly.

FEED MECHANISMS—The 20 mm Feed Mechanism, AN–M1A1, utilizes the recoil energy of the gun to draw a belt up to the gun, separate the rounds from the disintegrating links, and feed the rounds, one at a time, into the breech of the gun. This feed mechanism is made for both right-hand and left-hand feeding.

In the cylindrical metal case of the AN–M1A1 feed mechanism four sprockets, with hubs keyed on a rotatable central shaft, form an assembly which rotates as a whole. A link-ejector bracket is mounted on the hub of the front sprocket, a front feed lever carrying a last round retainer is mounted on the hub of the center sprocket, and a rear feed lever is mounted on the hub of the rear sprocket. The fourth sprocket was added in the AN–M1A1 mechanism at the forward position of the shaft to aid in supporting the projectile. Riveted to the front sprocket is a driving spring case within which is a spiral driving spring.

The mechanism is operated by the tension of the initially wound driving spring, this tension being maintained by the recoil of the gun which actuates a charging cam assembly. A recoil of approximately $\frac{13}{16}$ inch is required to operate the feed properly. As each round leaves the mouth, the driving spring acts in the driving spring case to rotate the shaft and the feed sprockets, thus feeding another round into the mouth.

Changes distinguishing the AN–M1A1 feed mechanism from the AN–M1 included an increase in the torsional pull of the spring from 180 pounds to 210 pounds, welding of the clutch into one piece, and hardening of the lips of the feed mouth to reduce wear.

The cartridges and disintegrating links can be assembled into a belt by hand or by means of the 20 mm Ammunition Linking Machine, M4.

The 20 mm 60-round Magazine, M1A1, is operated by spring tension alone. Initial tension is applied during assembly and further tension is applied progressively in loading. The tensioned spring acts through the tensioning tube, feed arm axis tube, and feed arm to maintain the platform or follower in contact with the last round. Thus a round is always in position in the magazine mouth. The M1A1 magazine differs from its predecessor, the M1, in that the spring was changed to that used with the Oerlikon magazine, the spring case cover was changed from a forging to a stamping, and an improved method of fastening the spring to the case was adopted. A muzzle brake must be used with this magazine as it does not perform the function of the Feed Mechanism, AN–M1A1, in absorbing a portion of energy from the recoil.

FIRING CYCLE—When the sear is depressed, releasing the bolt assembly, the driving spring forces this bolt assembly forward, picking up the round from the mouth of the feed mechanism and forcing it into the chamber. When the round is chambered and the bolt assembly is in the forward position, the bolt lock drops into position and releases the breechblock slide assembly which allows the driving spring and breechblock slides to carry the firing pin forward to strike the primer. As the projectile passes the gas port a pressure is exerted against the gas piston which actuates the bolt-unlocking mechanism. The bolt is then forced backward by the then-existing pressures in the chamber and the force of the piston rods, compressing the driving and buffer springs. Extraction is accomplished by an extractor on the face of the bolt and ejection of the round is done by an ejector attached to the magazine slide upon which the feed mechanism is mounted. For automatic firing the sear is held in a depressed position, allowing the gun to fire continuously until the sear is released to engage the bolt assembly at the rear of the receiver.

AMMUNITION—This is issued in the form of fuzed complete rounds of fixed ammunition, classified as high-explosive-incendiary, armor-piercing, or ball. The M1, AN–M2, and British Hispano-Suiza guns fire the same ammunition. Service ammunition includes cartridge, H.E.I., Mk. I, with fuze, percussion, D.A., no. 253, Mk. III/A/; cartridge, A.P.-T., M75; and cartridge, projectile, ball.

REFERENCES—*Guns, M1 and M2:* O.C.M. 16429, 16530; *Gun, AN–M2:* O.C.M. 18019, 19654; *Adapter, AN–M1:* O.C.M. 17820, 18109; *Adapter, M6:* O.C.M. 20968; *Adapter, M7:* O.C.M. 20853; *Manual Charger, M2:* O.C.M. 21192; *Feed Mechanism, AN–M1A1:* O.C.M. 20746, TM 9–227.

37 MM AUTOMATIC GUN M4—STANDARD

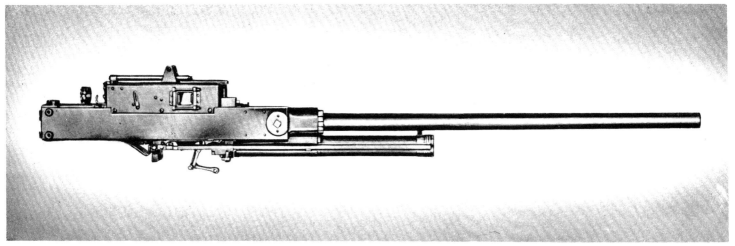

37 MM AUTOMATIC GUN, M4

The 37 mm Automatic Gun, M4, is a plane-to-plane and plane-to-ground weapon with a muzzle velocity of 2,000 feet per second and a cyclic rate of 150 rounds per minute. The armor-piercing projectile, M80, fired from this gun will penetrate 1 inch of homogeneous armor plate at 500 yards. The gun is constructed to fire in any position, all of its parts functioning independently of gravity. It is magazine fed and may be fired manually or by remote control through a solenoid mounted at the rear of the gun. The 37 mm Gun, M4, was standardized from Limited Procurement type, T9, in December, 1939.

Recoil and counter-recoil are controlled hydraulically by means of a piston and spring combination connected to the recoiling parts and operating in an oil-filled recuperator cylinder mounted on the stationary trunnion block assembly. The recoiling parts of the gun include the tube and tube extension, the recuperator piston and piston rod, the lock frame assembly, the driving spring assemblies, and the breechblock assembly. The nonrecoiling parts include the trunnion block group, the feed box and feeding mechanism, the recuperator cylinder and bushing, the back plate group, and the manual charger assembly.

MOUNTS—The gun may be mounted in either a flexible or fixed mount, as provided by the Air Force.

FEEDING MECHANISM—As the gun was originally designed, ammunition could be fed by a 5-round clip, a 15-round link belt, or a nondisintegrating 30-round endless belt (horsecollar) magazine. The 30-round endless belt Magazine, M6, is now used exclusively with this gun. The M4 gun feeds only from left to right. Mounted on the trunnion block assembly is the feed box containing the feed mechanism which draws the belted ammunition from the magazine and feeds it into the gun automatically. The 30-round endless belt Magazine, M6, is an oval-shaped framework providing a track for the endless belt. The articulated link belt contains 33 clips, although only 30 rounds are ordinarily loaded into the magazine. Modified M6 magazines are provided with a loading index, the purpose of which is to provide a lock for the belt when the feed slide is half-way across the full travel and thus reduce double feeding, particularly when the magazine is half empty.

FIRING CYCLE—Initial loading and cocking of the gun are accomplished manually. A safety feature incorporated in the design of the trigger mechanism prevents firing the round until the breechblock assembly is in the battery position.

The breech is locked and unlocked by recoil action which brings the operating lever guide pins against cams to raise and lower the breechblock. The function of the breechblock is to assist in the final chambering of the round, close the breech, and actuate the trigger trip. It also provides a mounting for the firing pin.

The lock frame, during automatic firing, is retracted by recoil action and is forced forward by the driving springs. The major function of the lock frame assembly is to force the cartridge into the chamber, actuate the breechblock, fire the round by means of the hammer striking the fir-

ing pin, extract the cartridge case from the chamber, and operate the ejector.

The back plate assembly, by absorbing the energy of the lock frame, reduces the shock against the carrier pin as the lock frame is latched to the rear.

The driving spring assemblies hold the lock frame against the carrier dog until the carrier is released by the carrier catch which is pivoted by the incoming round. The springs then drive the lock frame assembly forward, to operate the ejector, chamber the round, and raise the breechblock.

Initial extraction occurs during recoil. Extraction, ejection, feeding, and loading are accomplished during counter-recoil. If the trigger is held in the firing position, the gun will continue to fire automatically until the magazine is empty.

AMMUNITION—Ammunition is issued in the form of fixed rounds, consisting of H.E. shell, M54, with P.D. fuze, M56; practice shell, M55A1, with dummy fuze, M50; and A.P. shot, M80.

REFERENCES—O.C.M. 15542, 15619; TM 9-240.

CHARACTERISTICS

Weight of gun	213 lb.
Weight of 30-round Magazine, M6 (empty)	35.5 lb.
Length of gun overall	89.5 ins.
Weight of projectiles	
H.E., M54	1.34 lb.
Practice, M55A1	1.34 lb.
A.P., M80	1.66 lb.
Muzzle velocity	
H.E., M54	2,000 ft./sec.
Practice, M55A1	2,000 ft./sec.
A.P., M80	1,825 ft./sec.
Maximum powder pressure	23,200 lb./sq. in.
Length of recoil	9⅝ ins.
Rate of fire	150 rds./min.

37 MM AUTOMATIC GUN M9—STANDARD

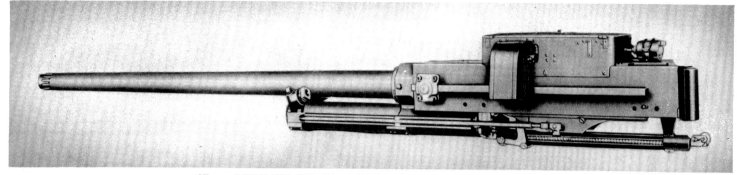

37 mm AUTOMATIC GUN, M9—RIGHT-HAND FEED GUN—LEFT SIDE VIEW

The 37 mm Gun, M9, is a fully automatic aircraft weapon firing high-explosive and armor-piercing projectiles at a rate of 140 rounds per minute. The muzzle velocity of this gun firing the 1.66-pound A.P. round, M80, is 3,050 feet per second and this shot will penetrate 3.1 inches of homogeneous armor plate at 500 yards. It is therefore an effective plane-to-plane and plane-to-ground weapon. Basically a modification of the 37 mm Antiaircraft Gun, M1A2, the M9 gun was standardized in January, 1943.

The 37 mm Gun, M9, may be mounted in the propeller shaft or in the wings, for which right- and left-hand disintegrating link belt feed mechanisms are provided. It is fired electrically by remote control but it is not designed for synchronized firing between the propeller blades.

The major components of the gun are the trunnion block group, the tube and tube extension, the recuperator group, the lock frame assembly, the breechblock assembly, the back plate group, the driving spring assemblies, and the feeding mechanism. The trunnion block group may be considered as housing the gun, as it provides for mounting the weapon and supports all the operating mechanism. The breech end of the one-piece tube screws into the tube extension, the tube extension in turn being connected to the hydraulic recuperator mechanism by means of the piston rod and nuts. The breechblock is of the vertical drop type, automatically operated.

The gun consists of two distinct groups,

recoiling and nonrecoiling. The nonrecoiling unit contains the trunnion block group, the feed box and feed mechanism, the recuperator, the recuperator bushing, the expansion chamber, and the back plate group. The recoiling portion of the gun consists of the tube and tube extension, the recuperator piston and piston rod, the lock frame assembly, the driving spring assemblies, and the breechblock assembly.

MOUNTS—The gun may be mounted on either a fixed or flexible mount as provided by the Air Force.

OPERATION—Initial loading and cocking of the gun are accomplished manually. After the first round has been fired the gun will continue to function automatically while the trigger is held in firing position. Explosion of the propellant forces the recoiling parts of the gun rearward, the breechblock being lowered in the process. Recuperator springs return the tube and tube extension to battery while the lock frame assembly, which moves independently of the tube extension, is carried forward by action of the driving springs and the compressed buffer springs.

When the lock frame assembly separates from the tube extension during recoil an extractor lip engages the rim of the empty cartridge case and partially withdraws it from the chamber. Extraction is completed during the forward movement of the tube extension in counter-recoil, the case being deflected downward out of the gun.

CHARACTERISTICS

Weight of gun	398 lb.
Length of gun overall	104 ins.
Weight of projectiles	
H.E., M54	1.34 lb.
A.P.C., M59	1.91 lb.
A.P., M80	1.66 lb.
Practice, M55A1	1.34 lb.
Muzzle velocity	
H.E., M54	2,600 ft./sec.
A.P.C., M59	2,800 ft./sec.
A.P., M80	3,050 ft./sec.
Practice, M55A1	2,600 ft./sec.
Maximum powder pressure	46,000 lb./sq. in.
Length of recoil	10¾ ins.
Rate of fire	140 rds./min.

Forward movement of the lock frame causes the charger to drive the round into the cartridge chamber, while coincident rotation of the operating lever lifts the breechblock into the closed position, the taper on the upper front side of the block completing the chambering of the round as the breechblock slides past the base of the cartridge. As it moves upward the breechblock raises the front end of the trigger trip, releasing the hammer if the trigger is held in firing position.

AMMUNITION—Ammunition is issued in the form of fuzed complete rounds of fixed ammunition. It consists of shell, H.E., M54, with fuze, P.D., M56; shot, A.P.C., M59; shot, A.P., M80; and shell, practice, M55A1, with fuze, dummy, M50.

REFERENCES—O. C. M. 19378; TM 9–241.

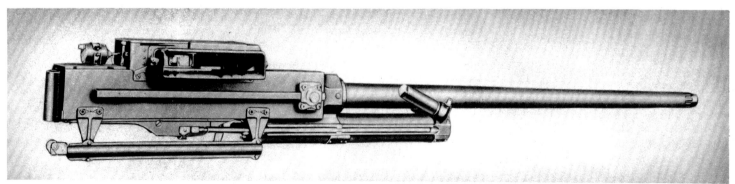

RIGHT SIDE VIEW

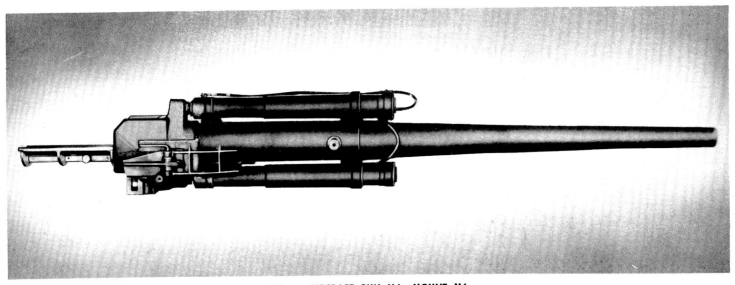

75 mm AIRCRAFT GUN, M4—MOUNT, M6

The 75 mm Aircraft Gun, M4, is a modification of the 75 mm Tank Gun, M3, designed for aircraft installation for tactical plane-to-ground use against sea and land targets. The M4 gun is mounted in the airplane on Mount, M6, a development of the Mount, T3E1. Military characteristics for this gun were approved in January, 1937, and Mount, M6, was approved for development in April, 1942. The 75 mm Aircraft Gun, M4, and the Mount, M6, were standardized in October, 1942.

The 75 mm Aircraft Gun, M4, is a single-shot, hand-loaded weapon with a vertical sliding, automatically operated breechlock. A removable, manually operated crank is provided to open the breech in the event of a misfire and for initial loading. A loading tray used with a loading ram is situated in back of the breech.

MOUNT, M6—The cradle of Mount, M6, consists of three tubular sections, mounted one above the other. The center section contains the barrel assembly and provides a mounting for the trunnions; the upper and lower sections carry the two cylinders of the hydrospring recoil mechanism. An electrical firing circuit is mounted on the left rear side of the center section. A cam ejector mechanism is mounted on the right rear side of the center section.

RECOIL MECHANISM—When the gun is fired the breeching, tube, recoil cylinder piston rods, and pistons move rearward as a unit. As each piston moves rearward, the recoil oil behind the piston is forced past the piston through the throttling grooves in the sleeve. Throttling the oil through the orifices thus formed absorbs a part of the recoil energy (part of the recoil energy is stored in the counter-recoil springs). The grooves in the recoil sleeve are tapered toward the rear so that the gun is gradually slowed down and finally stopped when the piston reaches the end of the grooves (21 inches of recoil). When the recoil action ceases, the counterrecoil inner and outer springs force the recoil cylinder pistons, piston rods, breech ring, and tube forward. When the gun is six inches out of battery, a tapered buffer enters a cylindrical buffer chamber in the center of the recoil piston and piston rod. The oil trapped inside this chamber is forced out through an orifice in the center of the buffer, through a spring loaded valve, as well as between the chamber wall and the buffer. When the pressure inside the chamber becomes large enough, it moves the valve which further restricts the oil through the valve and increases the buffing action until the gun comes to rest. By adjusting the compression of the buffer valve spring, the amount of buffing is adjusted.

FIRING MECHANISM—The breech is opened manually. A round is placed in the loading tray and shoved into the breech. The flange on the rear of the case will engage the extractors and pull them forward, thereby releasing the breechblock which is moved upward by the tension of the closing spring to close the breech. The gun is fired electrically by means of a firing solenoid which becomes energized when the firing switch is closed, causing the solenoid plunger to move rearward. The solenoid plunger actuates the firing mechanism which presses the firing plunger, thereby releasing the sear and firing the gun.

EJECTOR MECHANISM—The ejector mechanism functions in conjunction with the semi-automatic operation of the breechblock. During recoil the spring-actuated ejector cam is operated by a boss on the crank, the spring then returning the cam to its original position. As the gun slides forward in counter-recoil the boss strikes the end of the cam, rotating the operating shaft of the breech mechanism, dropping the breechblock and ejecting the empty cartridge case. The boss on the crank then passes under the ejector cam. Insertion of the shell causes the breechblock to return to the closed position.

MUZZLE COVER—An automatically functioning aluminum muzzle cover was formerly provided which opened when the breech was closed and closed when the breech was opened. It consisted of a rear tube surrounding the barrel and secured to the cradle, a collar secured to the gun tube, a retractor in the rear, and a retriever with moveable petals on the front end.

AMMUNITION—This is issued in the form of fuzed complete rounds of fixed ammunition. The rounds include the shell, H.E., M48, with fuze, P.D., M57, and the projectile, A.P.C., M61A1, with fuze, B.D., M66A1. A steel cartridge case is not used for the shell, H.E., M48, in the M4 aircraft gun because of the possibility of poor extraction which would jam the gun.

REFERENCES—O. C. M. 18699; TM 9-311.

CHARACTERISTICS

Weight of gun........................893 lb.
Weight of gun and mount...........1,200 lb.
Length of tube overall............110.575 ins.
Weight of projectiles
  H.E., M48.....................14.6 lb.
  A.P.C., M61...................14.96 lb.
Muzzle velocity
  H.E., M48...................1,974 f../sec.
  A.P.C., M61.................2,024 ft./sec.
Maximum powder pressure.....38,000 lb./sq. in.

3
SMALL ARMS

Machine Guns, 221

Submachine Guns, 230

Rifles, 231

Shotguns, 236

Projectors and Dischargers, 239

Grenade and Rocket Launchers, 242

Machine Gun Mounts, 245

Small Arms Ammunition, 251

Helmets, 255

Body Armor, 256

Bayonets, Knives and Sabers, 257

Miscellaneous Items, 258

BROWNING MACHINE GUN, AIRCRAFT FIXED & FLEXIBLE CAL. .30, M2—STANDARD

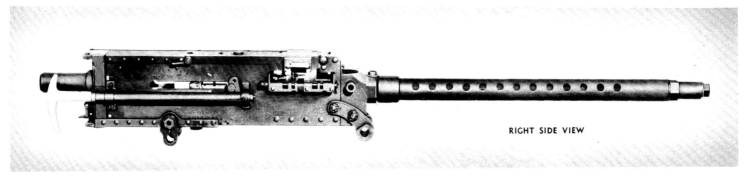

RIGHT SIDE VIEW

BROWNING MACHINE GUN, AIRCRAFT, CAL. .30, M2, FIXED

This air-cooled weapon is a Standard item for installation in all types of aircraft in either fixed or flexible mounts, but since the trend in aircraft armament has been steadily toward greater fire-power from weapons of larger caliber, this gun has been supplanted almost entirely by the caliber .50 weapon.

The caliber .30 gun operates on the short-recoil principle which characterizes all Browning machine guns. The barrel reciprocates in a steel outer jacket drilled to facilitate cooling. The fixed and flexible guns are basically identical and guns of either type may be assembled to use either right-hand or left-hand feeds.

FEED—Feed is from a disintegrating metallic-link belt loaded in increments of 250 rounds. Two or more increments may be assembled in larger units of any desired capacity.

MOUNTING—Mounts for the gun are supplied by the Air Corps or are built into the plane at time of manufacture. Synchronized guns may be installed either singly or in pairs. The mounts are rigidly attached to the structure of the plane and fire is approximately parallel to the line of flight. Flexible mounts are installed so as to permit wide-angle fire in both azimuth and elevation. Guns so mounted are fired by a hand trigger.

FIXED GUNS—Fixed guns of this caliber are now mounted within the wings and fire through ports in the leading edge. The practice of mounting fixed guns within the fuselage, firing through the arc of propeller rotation, is rapidly becoming obsolescent in U. S. Army aircraft. Guns so mounted are controlled by a synchronizing device which times the fire in relation to the moving blades. The device permits only semi-automatic fire and reduces greatly the fire-power available and the combat efficiency of the plane.

The fire of wing-mounted guns is fully automatic and is controlled by a solenoid operated by a switch which is customarily mounted on the control stick of the plane.

All solenoids and other firing devices are Air Corps equipment and are supplied by that service.

FLEXIBLE GUNS—The back plates of guns in flexible mounts are equipped with spade grips and manually operated triggers. They are fired by a gunner from a cockpit, "blister," or turret. The retracting slide is operated by hand and remains forward while the gun is firing, a feature which eliminates external moving parts and which is shared by all Browning machine guns. Fire of flexible guns may be full- or semi-automatic as the operator

may select. The usual fire is in short bursts, full-automatic.

SIGHTS—All sights and sighting equipment required for any installation of the Aircraft Machine Gun, caliber .30, M2, are supplied by the Air Corps. Sights for fixed guns are usually attached to the structure of the plane, those for flexible guns are mounted on the barrel jacket.

CHARACTERISTICS

Weight, total	Fixed, 21.5 lb.
	Flexible, 23.0 lb.
Weight of recoiling parts	6.56 lb.
Weight of barrel	3.81 lb.
Length, overall	39.8 ins.
Length of barrel	23.9 ins.
Rifling, length	21.35 ins., 70.9 cals.
No. of grooves	4
Twist	Right-hand, 1 turn in 10 ins. or 33.3 cals.
Depth of grooves	0.004 in.
Cross-sectional area of bore	0.074 sq. in.
Operation	Short-recoil
Feed	Link belt
Cooling	Air
Rate of fire	1000–1350 rds. min.
Firing pin release	Pressure applied to sear, 12–17 lb.
	Pressure applied to sear, holder, 25–35 lb.
Normal breech pressure	50,000 lb./sq. in. (copper)

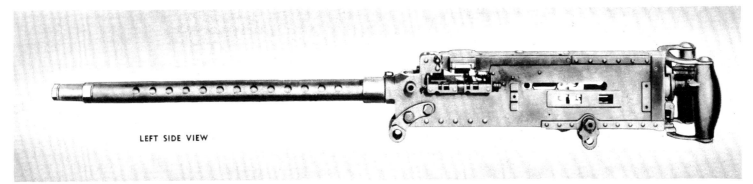

LEFT SIDE VIEW

BROWNING MACHINE GUN, AIRCRAFT, CAL. .30, M2, FLEXIBLE—LEFT HAND FEED

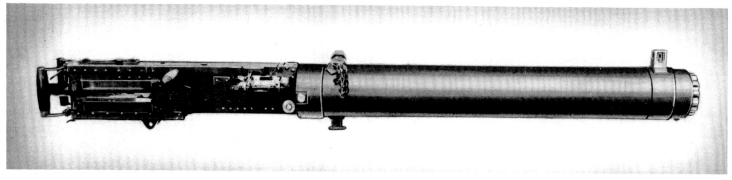

BROWNING MACHINE GUN, CAL. .50, M2, WATER-COOLED, FLEXIBLE

This gun is a recoil-operated, belt-fed, water-cooled weapon used principally as an antiaircraft weapon or against ground or floating targets from both movable and fixed mounts on docks and other shore installations and on shipboard. The water-cooling permits long bursts of fire without excessive overheating of the barrel. It is used on the antiaircraft machine gun tripod mount, cal. .50, M3; on the cal. .50 mount, M43, Substitute Standard; and on the twin antiaircraft machine gun mount, cal. .50, M46, Substitute Standard. It may also be used on the older antiaircraft machine-gun tripod and pedestal mounts, M2 and M2A1, which are still in use but classified as Limited Standard.

The retracting slide is on the right side of the receiver. The back plate is of the flexible type, with or without spade grips. Removal of the spade grip assembly permits installation in positions where clearance is limited.

FEED—The caliber .50 cartridges are fed to the gun from either a fabric belt or a metallic-link belt of the disintegrating type loaded in increments of 110 rounds each. The gun is normally assembled for left-hand feed and when the gun is mounted on the Tripod Mount, M3, this feed must be used. Should installation requirements demand, the weapon may

be changed to right-hand feed by reversing the position of the bolt switch, belt feed slide, belt feed pawl arm and lever plunger, cartridge stops and link stripper, and the belt holding pawl.

As with all Browning machine guns, the retracting slide is connected with the bolt by a stud. The slide handle remains stationary in the forward position which the gun is firing.

COOLING—The gun barrel is surrounded with a water-jacket of ten quarts capacity connected by hose to a water chest which holds approximately 10 quarts. Water is circulated between chest and jacket by a hand-operated rotary pump.

A steam tube, sliding in front and rear supports, is in the top of the jacket. Movement of the tube covers and uncovers holes in the supports, the hole in the front support being covered when the muzzle is depressed, the rear hole being covered when the muzzle is elevated. Steam generated by the heat of prolonged firing passes through the uncovered hole and escapes through the steam tube into the circulating system where it is condensed.

Sights mounted on the gun are of the conventional machine gun type, a blade front sight, protected by a cover, and a folding-leaf rear with adjustments for

windage and elevation. The necessity of protecting the gunner by armor plate shields makes necessary the use of other sights when the gun is placed on the mounts on which it is used. The rear sight is a monocular peep sight, with rubber eyepiece and a sun-ray filter. It may be equipped with a rotatable disk providing peepholes of $\frac{5}{16}$, $\frac{1}{4}$, $\frac{3}{16}$, and $\frac{1}{8}$ inch diameter. The front sight is of the ring or "cartwheel" type and may be mounted so as to permit automatic adjustment in elevation and traverse by off-carriage control.

CHARACTERISTICS

Weight, total...100 lb., less water (water, 21 lbs.)
Weight of recoiling parts..............24.5 lb.
Weight of barrel.....................15.2 lb.
Length, overall........................66 ins.
Length of barrel.......................45 ins.
Rifling, length...........40.11 ins., 81.8 cals.
   No. of grooves..........................8
   Twist...Right-hand, 1 turn in 15 ins., 30 cals.
   Depth of grooves.................. 0.005 in.
Cross-sectional area of bore.......0.2021 sq. in.
Operation........................Short-recoil
Feed.....Metallic link belt, 110 round capacity
Cooling......................Water, 10 qts.
Rate of fire................500–650 rds./min.

Firing pin release..........{ Pressure at sear, 10–20 lb. / Pressure at sear slide, 30–35 lb.

Normal breech pressure. 48,000 lb./sq. in. (copper)

BROWNING MACHINE GUN, AIRCRAFT FIXED & FLEXIBLE CAL. .50, M2—STANDARD

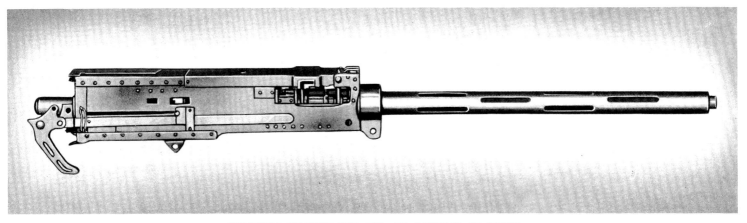

BROWNING MACHINE GUN, CAL. .50, AIRCRAFT, M2 (FIXED)

This gun is standard equipment for all U. S. airplanes carrying weapons of this caliber. It may be installed as a fixed gun in mounts that are a part of the aircraft or used in flexible form from turret or blister mounts.

FIXED TYPE—Customary installation of the fixed gun is in batteries of varying numbers of guns in the wings of the aircraft. When so mounted, the gun is fired by means of a solenoid attached to the receiver and controlled by a switch in the pilot's cockpit. Guns are now rarely installed so as to fire through the path of propeller rotation. Fixed guns are aimed by movements of the plane and sights are mounted on the aircraft. Sighting equipment for aircraft armament is supplied by the Air Corps.

FLEXIBLE TYPE—Flexible guns are installed as nose, tail, top, side, and belly guns as required by the particular aircraft. They are fired by hand and are equipped with spade grips. Flexible mount-ing permits a wide field of fire in both azimuth and elevation. Sight bases are mounted on the receiver of the gun for such aircraft sights as may be used.

RATE OF FIRE—The rate of fire of the caliber .50 aircraft machine gun is controlled by adjustment of the oil buffer. A maximum burst of 75 rounds may be fired from the standard 36-inch barrel. After one minute firing may be resumed at the rate of one 20-round burst per minute.

The gun should be cooled for at least fifteen minutes before another long burst is attempted. If long bursts are not fired, the gun may be fired at a rate of 25 rounds per minute over a long period.

FEED—The gun is fed from a disintegrating metallic-link belt loaded in increments of 110 rounds. Any number of increments may be linked one to another to supply additional firepower. The caliber .50 aircraft machine gun, like all Browning machine guns, may be converted from left-hand to right-hand feed.

CHARACTERISTICS

Weight, total...............	{ Fixed, 64 lb. { Flexible, 65.1 lb.
Weight of recoiling parts.............	19.2 lb.
Weight of barrel......................	9.8 lb.
Length, overall.......................	57 ins.
Length of barrel......................	36 ins.
Rifling, length............	31.91 ins.; 63.8 cals.
No. of grooves...........................	8
Twist....Right-hand, 1 turn in 15 ins., 30 cals.	
Depth of grooves..................	0.005 in.
Cross-sectional area of bore.......	0.2021 sq. in.
Operation......................	Short-recoil
Feed............Metallic-link belt, 110 round	
Cooling................................	Air
Rate of fire................	750–850 rds./min.
Firing pin release......	{ Pressure at sear, 10–20 lb. { Pressure at sear slide, 30–35 lb.
Normal breech pressure. 48,000 lb./sq. in. (copper)	

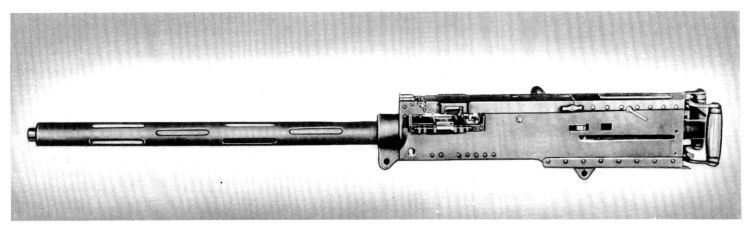

BROWNING MACHINE GUN, CAL. .50, AIRCRAFT, M2 (FLEXIBLE)

BROWNING MACHINE GUN, HEAVY BARREL, CAL. .50, M2, HB—STANDARD (FIXED, FLEXIBLE AND TURRET TYPES)

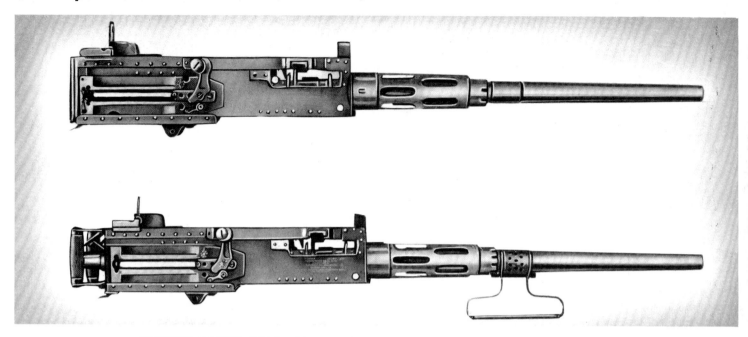

BROWNING MACHINE GUN, HEAVY BARREL, CAL. .50, M2, HB, FIXED (UPPER) AND FLEXIBLE (LOWER)

Assembly of a heavy barrel (27 pounds) in the receiver of the caliber .50 Browning machine gun permits continued firing over a longer period, or firing of longer bursts, with less danger of damage to the weapon by overheating. The heavy barrel is quickly and easily dismounted to form a separate load for carriage by pack or for limited movement by hand. Any type of caliber .50 barrel, light or heavy, air- or water-cooled, may be fitted to any caliber .50 receiver. By changing the back plate assembly any air-cooled gun may be adapted for either fixed or flexible use.

FEED—All types of caliber .50 ammunition may be used. Feed is from a disintegrating metallic-link belt loaded in increments of 110 rounds. The gun is normally assembled for left-hand feed, which may be changed to right-hand feed by reversal of certain parts.

FIXED TYPE—The fixed type of caliber .50, heavy barrel, machine gun is used only in Heavy Tanks, M6 and M6A1. Two of these guns are rigidly mounted in Twin Mount, T52, in the bow of the tank below the 3 inch and 37 mm guns which are the principal weapons. While the guns are fixed, the mount may be moved by hand in limited traverse and elevation. Fixed guns are identical with those of flexible type except that the spade grip assembly has been removed from the horizontal buffer back plate and filler plates added.

FLEXIBLE TYPE—The Browning machine gun, heavy barrel, caliber .50, M2, in flexible and turret types, is the most widely used of any U. S. machine gun. It is used by infantry and special weapon units from the Tripod Mount, M3, as an anti-tank weapon. The limited elevation of the mount restricts its use in antiaircraft fire.

It is installed in both medium and heavy tanks both as a turret gun and in ring mounts and is standard armament in truck trailer, tank recovery, M7, in the 75 mm, 76 mm, 3 inch, and 105 mm gun motor carriages; in the Multiple Gun Motor Carriages, M13, M15, and M16; in the Armored Utility Car, M20; in half-track cars, scout cars, medium and heavy tractors, and tracked landing vehicles. In many of these the gun is installed in ring mounts permitting maximum elevation as an antiaircraft weapon.

TURRET TYPE—The standard caliber .50, heavy barrel, machine gun is slightly modified for installation in tank turrets. The conventional blade and folding-leaf sights are replaced by antiaircraft sights and an Edgewater ring spring adapter is placed on the barrel. The distinguishing designation "Turret Type" is used for manufacturing, supply, and administration identification.

SIGHTS—Usual sight equipment is the conventional blade and folding-leaf sights. A mount is provided for either the T3, M1, or M1918A2 telescopic sights.

RATE OF FIRE—The timed cyclic rate of the caliber .50, heavy barrel, gun is from 450 to 575 rounds per minute. Normal fire is in short bursts or single shots in swift succession. A single burst of from 100 to 150 rounds may be fired from a cool gun. At the rate of 40 rounds per minute, 500 rounds may be fired without overheating.

CHARACTERISTICS

Weight, total	Fixed, 82 lb.
	Flexible, 84 lb.
	Turret, 81 lb.
Weight of recoiling parts	38.8 lb.
Weight of barrel	27 lb.
Length, overall	65 ins.
Length of barrel	45 ins.
Rifling, length	40.91 ins., 81 cals.
No. of grooves	8
Twist	1 turn in 15 ins., 30 cals.
Depth of grooves	0.005 in.
Cross-sectional area of bore	0.2021 sq. in.
Operation	Short-recoil
Feed	Metallic-link belt, increments of 110 rds.
Cooling	Air
Rate of fire	450–575 rds./min.
Firing pin release	Pressure at sear, 10–20 lb.
	Pressure at sear bar, 30–35 lb.
Normal breech pressure	48,000 lb./sq. in. (copper)

BROWNING MACHINE GUNS, CAL..30, M1919A4, M1919A5—STANDARD AND M1919A6—SUBSTITUTE STANDARD

BROWNING MACHINE GUN, CAL. .30, M1919A4, ON TRIPOD MOUNT, M2

The Browning Machine Guns, cal. .30, M1919A4, M1919A5, and M1919A6, represent modifications and improvements upon the older M1919A2 which evolved from the M1919, originally designed as armament for the M1917 and Mk. VIII tanks, now obsolete.

They are air-cooled, fabric-belt-fed weapons operating on the short-recoil principle common to all Browning machine guns. All have heavy barrels reciprocating within a steel sleeve, perforated to facilitate cooling. Mechanically they are identical with the Browning water-cooled machine gun, M1917, and working parts are interchangeable.

M1919A4—STANDARD—This gun is issued in two types, fixed and flexible. The fixed gun is used only for tank installation and is mounted as a unit with 37 mm or 75 mm guns. The two move together within the limited elevation and traverse of the tank mounts and the machine gun so installed cannot be aimed individually. It has a vertical buffer tube and is without pistol grip.

The flexible gun is for more general use. It is used as armament for combat vehicles, armored and unarmored, or may be fired as a ground weapon from the machine gun tripod mount, M2. It is equipped with a pistol grip and is fired from the back plate trigger.

As used by motorized and mechanized units the gun is installed on mounts of various types, depending upon the type of vehicle and the position of the gun thereon. It is customary to carry a tripod mount, M2, for each gun to adapt the weapon for ground use.

Barrels of the M1919A4, A5, and A6 guns are 24 inches long, 5.37 inches longer than the barrel fitted to the M1919A2. The barrel sleeve has been correspondingly lengthened from 13.7 inches to 19.08 inches. Separate front barrel bearing plugs are provided to permit the use of either M1 or M2 ammunition.

The M1919A2 gun was also modified by the addition of a belt feed lever group assembly which permits assembly and disassembly of the lever from above.

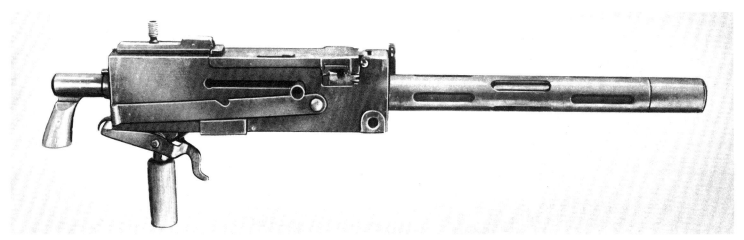

BROWNING MACHINE GUN, CAL. .30, M1919A5

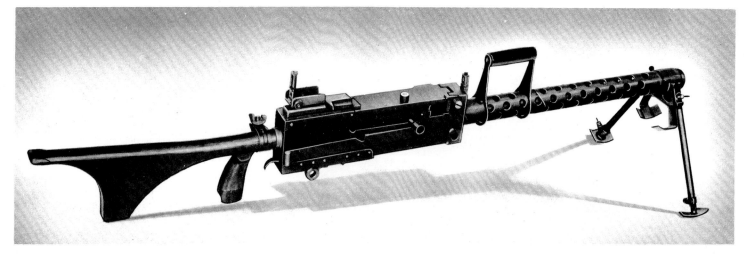

BROWNING MACHINE GUN, CAL. .30, M1919A6

The trunnion block was equipped with a bunter plug to resist wear by the points of the bullets.

Further modifications have been made since the weapon was designated M1919-A4. These include substitution of a buffer plug, buffer ring, and buffer disks for the older tapered form of plug with ring and filler. The change eliminates the "freezing" of ring and plug which retarded buffer spring action.

The bottom plate has been redesigned so that plate, stirrup, and elevating bracket are now a unit. The bottom plate is riveted to the receiver and a recess in the plate serves to locate the gun in the pack hanger.

SIGHTS—Sights are of the conventional machine gun type with the front sight mounted on the gun's trunnion block. The rear sight base is mounted on a bracket on the left side plate of the receiver. The folding leaf bears a mil elevation scale graduated for the sight radius of 13.94 inches. Each division on the elevation scale represents 100 yards

and the scale is graduated up to 2,400 yards.

M1919A5—STANDARD—In mounting the Browning machine gun, cal. .30, M1919A4, in the Light Tank, M3, it was found necessary to provide a special bolt-retracting slide and a different cover detent. To identify the weapon and to facilitate field supply and maintenance, the gun so modified was designated M1919A5 and classified as Standard.

M1919A6—SUBSTITUTE STANDARD— The designation of M1919A6 is given the Browning Machine Gun, cal. .30, M1919-A4, as modified for infantry use. The principal modifications, shown in the illustration herewith, include a shoulder stock, a carrying handle, and a bipod mount fixed to the barrel sleeve. A new front barrel bearing was provided and the cover latch changed to permit easier opening of the cover. Changes were made in the barrel plunger and driving spring to assure proper functioning without the muzzle plug.

CHARACTERISTICS OF BROWNING MACHINE GUNS, M1919A4, M1919A5

Weight, total	Fixed, 30.5 lb. / Flexible, 31 lb.
Weight of recoiling parts	11.7 lb.
Weight of barrel	7.35 lb.
Length, overall	M1919A5, fixed, 40.8 lb. / M1919A4, fixed, 37.94 lb. / M1919A4, flexible, 41.11 lb.
Length of barrel	24 ins.
Rifling, length	21.38 ins., 71 cals.
No. of grooves	4
Twist	Right-hand, 1 turn in 10 ins., 33.3 cals.
Depth of grooves	0.004 in.
Cross-sectional area of bore	0.074 sq. in.
Operation	Short-recoil
Feed	Fabric belt, 250 rds.
Cooling	Air
Rate of fire	400–550 rds./min.
Sear release	9 lb.
Trigger pull	7–12 lb.
Normal breech pressure	50,000 lb./sq. in. (copper)

CHARACTERISTICS OF BROWNING MACHINE GUN, M1919A6

Weight, total	32.5 lb.
Weight of recoiling parts	7.5 lb.
Weight of barrel	4.65 lb.
Length, overall	53 ins.
Length of barrel	24 ins.
Rifling, length	21.38 ins., 71 cals.
No. of grooves	4
Twist	1 turn in 10 ins., 33.3 cals.
Depth of grooves	0.004 in.
Cross-sectional area of bore	0.074 sq. in.
Operation	Short-recoil
Feed	Fabric belt, 250 rds.
Cooling	Air
Rate of fire	400–450 rds./min.
Trigger pull	8½ lb.
Normal breech pressure	50,000 lb./sq. in. (copper)

BROWNING MACHINE GUN, CAL. .30, M1919A4, IN A. A. BRACKET MOUNT ON LIGHT TANK, M5

BROWNING MACHINE GUN, CAL. .30, **M1917A1**—STANDARD

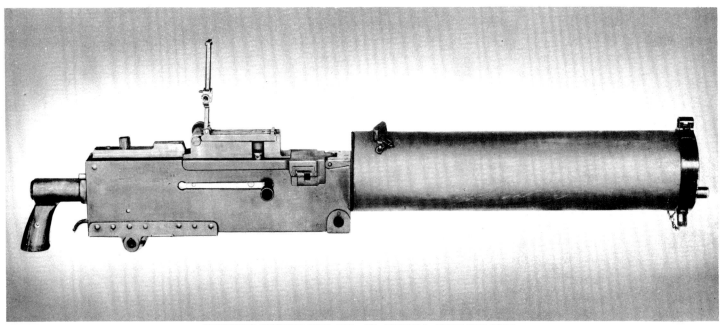

BROWNING MACHINE GUN, CAL. .30, M1917A1, RIGHT SIDE VIEW

This water-cooled machine gun, standard for ground use, is a development of the M1917 which proved its worth in World War I. Modifications upon the older weapon are designed to permit the gun to be used, from the ground, against aerial targets. The tripod mount, M1917A1, on which the gun is placed, is a modification of the M1917 tripod to permit fire in a wider angle of elevation. Water-cooling of the barrel of the M1917A1 gun permits sustained fire over comparatively long periods.

Modifications of the M1917 gun include a new assembly which eliminates the separate stirrup, bottom plate, and elevating bracket by making those components integral; an improved steam tube assembly (see cut) of the type used in the caliber .50, M2, gun; and a cylindrical bunter plate of the type used in the caliber .30 gun, M1919A4. The belt feed lever and mounting of the M1919A4 gun has also been added to the M1917A1. This stronger mechanism is necessary to lift a loaded belt from an ammunition chest placed on the ground instead of being hung on the mount. Steel end caps and trunnion blocks replace the bronze parts used in the M1917 gun.

SIGHTS—Sights are of the conventional machine gun type. The front sight is mounted at the outer end of the water jacket. Vibration of the rear sight is dampened by a tension spring. The slide is graduated to permit use of either M1 or M2 ammunition.

FEED—Feed is from a woven fabric belt with a capacity of 250 rounds of caliber .30 ammunition. The only metal used in the belt is a brass tab at either end to facilitate entering the belt in the gun.

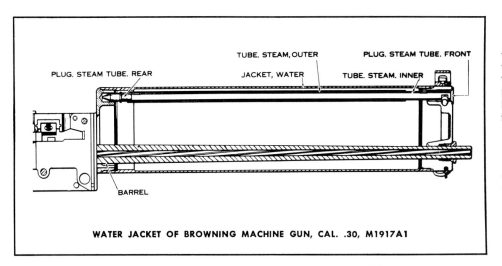

WATER JACKET OF BROWNING MACHINE GUN, CAL. .30, M1917A1

CHARACTERISTICS

Weight, total	32.6 lb., less water
Weight of recoiling parts	7.35 lb.
Weight of barrel	.3 lb.
Length, overall	38.64 ins.
Length of barrel	23.9 ins.
Rifling, length	21.28 ins., 71 cals.
No. of grooves	4
Twist	Right-hand, 1 turn in 10 ins. or 33.3 cals.
Depth of grooves	0.004 in.
Cross-sectional area of bore	0.074 sq. in.
Operation	Short-recoil
Feed	Fabric belt, 250 rds.
Cooling	Water, 8 pts.
Rate of fire	450–600 rds./min.
Trigger pull	9 lb.
Normal breech pressure	48,000 lb. (copper)

TRAINER, MACHINE-GUN, CAL. .22, M3, ASSEMBLED TO MACHINE-GUN, CAL. .30, BROWNING, M1917A1

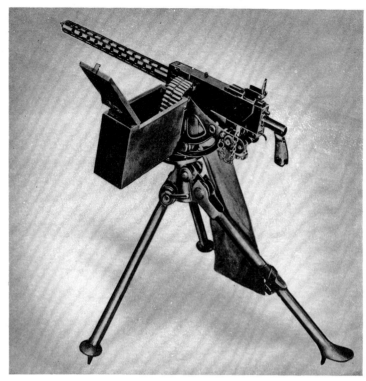

TRAINER, MACHINE-GUN, CAL. .22, M4, ASSEMBLED TO MACHINE-GUN, CAL. .30, BROWNING, M1919A4

These trainers consist of the Browning Machine Guns, caliber .30, M1917A1, water-cooled, and M1919A4, air-cooled, with such conversion parts as are necessary to adapt them to handle caliber .22 long rifle rimfire ammunition. Use of the small caliber cartridges permits the economical training of personnel in the handling of machine guns and the tactical uses of those weapons.

Either gun may be restored quickly and easily to caliber .30 should occasion require. This was not true of the original caliber .22 Machine-Gun Trainer, M1, now obsolete.

Requisite power for the operation of the guns is obtained by use of the Williams floating chamber. With this device the cartridge to be fired is seated in a loosely fitting chamber which "floats" within the receiver. Closing of the breech thrusts the chamber closely against the rear of the barrel and the bullet enters the rifling in the normal manner. The loose fit of the chamber permits it to move a short distance to the rear under the force of recoil and a portion of the gases of explosion escape between the chamber and the receiver walls, adding their pressure to that of the normal recoil of the cartridge.

This additional power is sufficient to operate the recoiling parts of the gun, extracting and ejecting the fired case and feeding a new round into the chamber. The loud report of service ammunition is also approximated, a feature to be desired in training personnel.

In addition to the caliber .22 barrel, the standard caliber .30 machine guns parts are replaced by a modified bolt, firing pin, driving spring and spring rod, cartridge

CHARACTERISTICS OF TRAINER, M3

Weight. . . .Less water, 32 lb.; with water, 39 lb.
Weight of conversion parts. M3, 6.5 lb.; M4, 7lb.
Weight of barrel......................3.01 lb.
Length overall........................38.6 ins.
Length of barrel....................22.75 ins.
Length of rifling.........22.25 ins., 101 cals.
Number of grooves.........................4
Twist....Right-hand, 1 turn in 16 ins., or 73.4 cals.
Depth of grooves...................0.0025 in.
Area of bore...................0.0383 sq. in.

Operation.........Short-recoil, floating chamber
Feed.....................Fabric belt, 250 rds.
Cooling.........................Water, 7 pts.
Cyclic rate of fire...........550–650 rds./min.
Sear release (trigger pull).................9 lb.

(The characteristics of the Machine-Gun Trainer, M4, are identical with those of the M3 except that it is air-cooled and the overall length is 41.1 ins. The weight is the same as that of the M3 less water.)

stop, barrel bearing, and barrel locking nuts.

The standard fabric belt for caliber .30 ammunition is used with the caliber .22 machine gun trainers, the smaller cartridges being held in adapters inserted in the pockets of the standard belt. Clips link the adapters in pairs and secure them in the belt.

MACHINE-GUN TRAINER, M9

Illustration and description of the electrically operated Machine-Gun Trainer, M9, will be found in the Fire Control section of this catalogue.

BROWNING AUTOMATIC RIFLE, CAL. .30, M1918A2—STANDARD

BROWNING AUTOMATIC RIFLE, CAL. .30, M1918A2

This gas-operated, air-cooled shoulder weapon represents successive modifications of the M1918A1 and the M1918, developed during World War I to meet infantry requirements for an easily transported weapon with a high fire-potential.

Commonly known in the service as the "BAR," the M1918A2 is now in active use on all fighting fronts.

The differences between BAR, M1918A2, and its predecessor models are summarized below:

BIPOD—A bipod with spiked feet was clamped to the gas cylinder of the M1918A1. This has been replaced by a bipod with skid type shoes, mounted on a bearing integral with the flash hider.

The legs may be folded to the rear or extended in the tubes in which they slide and locked in the extended position.

RECOIL SPRING—A metal shield has been set in the wooden forearm of the M1918A2 to protect the recoil spring from heat generated during sustained fire.

CYCLIC RATE—The M1918A2 differs from both prior models in that it is equipped with a selector mechanism, housed in the butt, which permits either a high-speed automatic fire of 500–600 rounds per minute or a retarded fire of 300–350 rounds per minute. The gun cannot be operated as a single-shot or semi-automatic weapon.

BUTT PLATE—A hinge lug welded to the butt plate permits the mounting of an outer plate which may be swung parallel with the top line of the stock to serve as an additional support for the gun against the operator's shoulder. When not in use the outer plate folds against the inner and is retained by a spring-ball latch.

GUIDE—A right-and-left guide fastened to the trigger guard facilitates insertion of the magazine.

SIGHT—A new rear sight provides adjustments for both elevation and windage by large mounts equipped with click mechanism for minutes of angle.

CHARACTERISTICS

Weight, complete	19.4 lb.
Weight, less bipod	17 lb.
Weight of barrel	3.65 lb.
Length overall	47.8 ins.
Length of barrel	24.07 ins.
Rifling, length	21.41 ins.; 71.1 cals.
No. of grooves	4
Twist	Right-hand, 1 turn in 10 ins., 71.1 cals.
Depth of grooves	0.004 in.
Cross-sectional area of bore	0.074 sq. in.
Operation	Gas
Feed	20-round box magazine
Cooling	Air
Rate of fire	High-speed, 500–600 rds./min. Retarded, 300–350 rds./min.
Trigger pull	10 lb. max., 6 lb. min.

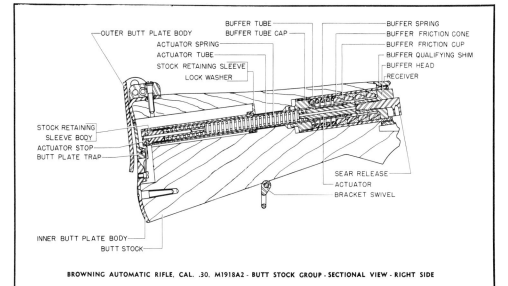

BROWNING AUTOMATIC RIFLE, CAL. .30, M1918A2 - BUTT STOCK GROUP - SECTIONAL VIEW - RIGHT SIDE

SUBMACHINE GUN, CAL. .45, M3—STANDARD

SUBMACHINE GUN, CAL. .45, M3

This weapon has been designed and put in quantity production since the outbreak of World War II to fill the requirements for a light, portable arm with a high fire-potential.

Although the submachine gun (or "machine pistol," as it is known in Europe) has been a standard weapon of the U. S. Armed Forces for nearly 15 years, the cal. .45, M3, is an entirely new weapon, the result of study and experimentation and the testing of more than twenty foreign and domestic weapons of this type.

The Submachine Gun, M3, is now in use in all theaters of operation. It is the primary weapon for such shock units as commando raiders and paratroopers and is carried as an auxiliary arm in tanks and other vehicles.

It is a straight blowback operated weapon weighing 8.9 pounds complete with magazine, oiler, and sling. It is chambered for the cal. .45, M1911, cartridge but may be converted to 9 mm by substitution of a barrel of that caliber, a replacement bolt, a 9 mm magazine and a magazine adapter. Conversion to 9 mm permits use of the Parabellum cartridge, standard in the British Armed Forces, as well as use of certain types of captured enemy ammunition.

The overall length is 29.8 inches which is shortened to 22.8 inches when the extension stock, which may be used in emergency as a cleaning rod, is closed.

The fixed firing pin in the heavy bolt fires the cartridge at the completion of the forward stroke and the major portion of the energy of the explosion is absorbed by the inertia of the bolt. When this is overcome the remaining energy is sufficient to drive the bolt to the rear against the compression of the operating springs. The fired case is ejected on the retracting stroke and the fully compressed dual spring returns the bolt to firing position, picking up and chambering another round on the forward movement.

Use of a heavy bolt holds the cyclic rate of fire to 350–450 rounds per minute. This low rate of fire and the design which places the stock in almost a straight line with the axis of the bore combine to reduce recoil, virtually to eliminate muzzle-climb, and to produce exceptional accuracy whether the weapon be used from the shoulder or as a "two-hand" pistol.

Stampings are used wherever possible in the manufacture of the M3, only the barrel and bolt require machine operations, no critical metals are employed, and the gun may be produced at a minimum cost for one of this type.

The gun may be taken down without tools and folded into a space 12⅝ inches long, 7⅜ inches high, and 3⅛ inches deep, or about 291 cubic inches. This permits convenient stowing in a soldier's pack for shipment or for packing in a standard container to be dropped by parachute.

Exhaustive tests conducted on the M3 have proved that it functions excellently under conditions of excessive dust or mud. Excessive moisture, such as would be encountered in tropical operations, has no effect whatever upon the weapon's functioning. The following sentence from the final report made upon the test program is significant: "Although it would be dangerous to state that further improvements and developments are unlikely, the ultimate has been reached in this type of weapon for the time being."

CHARACTERISTICS

Weight, complete	8.9 lb.
Weight, less magazine, oiler, and sling	8.1 lb.
Weight of recoiling parts	2.0 lb.
Weight of barrel	0.62 lb.
Weight of barrel assembly	1.43 lb.
Length, overall, stock extended	29.8 ins.
Length, stock closed	22.8 ins.
Length of barrel	8.0 ins.
Rifling, length	7.2 ins.
Number of grooves	4
Twist { Right-hand, 1 turn in 16 ins., 35.5 cals.	
Alternate: 1 turn in 15 ins., 33.3 cals.	
Depth of grooves	0.0035 in.
Cross-sectional area of bore	0.1581 sq. in.
Operation	Straight blowback
Feed	30-round magazine
Cooling	Air
Cyclic rate of fire	350–450 rds./min., full-automatic only
Sights	Fixed peep rear, A-blade front (zeroed at 100 yds.)
Sight radius	10.8 ins.
Trigger pull	5–7 lb.
Pull to retract bolt	18–23 lb.

U. S. RIFLE, CAL. .30, M1—STANDARD

U. S. RIFLE, CAL. .30, M1, RIGHT SIDE

The "Garand" rifle, designated as U. S. Rifle, cal. .30, M1, is a self-loading, semi-automatic shoulder weapon produced according to the design of Mr. John C. Garand, an employee at the Springfield Armory of the Ordnance Department. The rifle is gas-operated, clip-fed and air-cooled. It weighs 9½ pounds without the bayonet of approximately 1 pound weight.

Ammunition is loaded in clips of eight rounds carried in a bandoleer with six pockets holding a total of 48 rounds. Bandoleers weigh 3¼ pounds each.

The advantages of this rifle are inherent in the fact that it reloads itself after each shot. This prevents disturbance of aim or increase in fatigue due to manual operation of a bolt handle. It enables the soldier to deliver a volume of fire limited only by his proficiency as a marksman and his dexterity in inserting clips into the magazine. Troops equipped with this rifle possess greatly increased firepower with which to combat enemy ground forces, rapidly moving armored vehicles and low-flying planes.

The rifle consists of three main groups: a barrel and receiver group, a trigger-housing group, and the stock. The principal components of the barrel and receiver group are the barrel, gas cylinder lock, gas cylinder, operating rod, bolt assembly and hand guard. The trigger housing supports the hammer, safety, trigger and trigger guard.

When the rifle is loaded and the bolt closed the hammer is held in the cocked position. Pressure on the trigger releases the hammer to strike the firing pin which transmits the blow to the primer of the cartridge.

As the bullet passes the gas port some of the gas enters the gas cylinder, where it drives the operating rod back, compresses the operating rod spring and carries the bolt to the rear. The empty cartridge case is extracted and ejected to the right front. The rearward movement of the bolt cocks the hammer and uncovers the magazine. The operating rod spring then forces the cartridges upward in the clip and the forward movement of the bolt slides the top cartridge into the chamber. The bolt is then locked by being rotated clockwise to engage the locking lugs in the receiver. The rifle is then ready to be fired again.

The entire clip is placed in the gun without removing the cartridges from the clip. It is necessary to squeeze the trigger to fire each cartridge. When the last round in the clip has been fired the clip is automatically ejected to the right from the top of the receiver and the bolt remains open. The rifle is now ready for the insertion of another clip.

A receiver sight is used for greater ease of aiming and to obtain a longer sight radius. It is adjustable for range and windage. The elevation knob on the left side has numbered graduations for ranges of 100, 300, 500, 700 and 1100 yards. The windage knob is on the right side and each windage graduation represents an angular adjustment of 4 minutes. Both elevation and windage knobs are provided with clicks which represent approximately one minute of windage or one inch elevation at the target for each 100 yards of range.

CHARACTERISTICS

Weight . 9.5 lb. (with Bayonet, M1905: 10.5 lb.)
Length (over-all). .43.6 ins.
Length of barrel. . . . . .24 ins.
Length of rifling . . . . .21.30 ins.; 70.8 cal.
Rifling
    Number of grooves. . . . . .2 or 4
    R.H. twist; 1 turn in. . . . . .33.3 cal.; 10 ins.
    Depth of grooves. . . . . .0.0040 in.
Cross-sectional area of bore. . . . . . .0.0740 sq. in.
Type of mechanism . Gas-operated, semi-automatic
Feeding device. . . . . .Clip
Capacity of feeding device. . . . . .8 rounds
Rate of fire. . . . . .Semi-automatic
Cooling. . . . . .Air
Sight radius. . . . . .27.9 ins. at 100 yd. range
Trigger pull. . . . . .7.5 lb. max.; 4.5 lb. min.
Normal pressure. . . . . . .50,000 lb./sq. in. (copper)
Ammunition types. . . . . .Ball, A.P., trace

U. S. RIFLE, CAL. .30, M1, LEFT SIDE

U. S. CARBINE, CAL. .30, M1 AND M1A3—STANDARD

PHANTOM VIEW OF U. S. CARBINE, CAL. .30, M1, from Which U. S. Carbine, M1A2, Differs Only in Employing an
Aperture Type Rear Sight Instead of an L-Type Rear Sight

This compact, light-weight, semi-automatic weapon is now standard for those groups and units formerly equipped with the caliber .45 pistol, M1911A1. It is the regulation arm for all officers up to the rank of major.

The caliber .45 pistol is essentially a defensive weapon. The development of the caliber .30 carbine has placed in the hands of our troops not only a high-speed, accurate defensive arm but an offensive weapon as well. The carbine is capable of delivering effective fire at ranges as great as 300 yards—at least four times the effective range of the pistol which it has replaced.

The carbine is gas-operated, a portion of the gases of the explosion being admitted to a gas cylinder through a port in the barrel. Travel of the piston under pressure of the gases drives the bolt to the rear against the compression of the operating spring and extracts and ejects the fired case. The spring closes the bolt which picks up and chambers a new round on its forward travel. Operation, functioning, and general design of the carbine are similar in many respects to those characteristics of the caliber .30 Rifle, M1.

Like the Rifle, M1, the carbine is a semi-automatic arm and the trigger must be pulled for each shot. In case of failure of the gas-operated mechanism, the gun may be used as a hand-operated repeating arm, the slide being retracted and returned to position by hand.

The weapon is fed from a box magazine with a capacity of fifteen rounds of ammunition designated Cartridge, Carbine, Cal. .30, M1. The bullet weighs 110 grains and is propelled by a 14-grain charge of military smokeless powder.

SIGHTS—The original models of the carbine were equipped with an "L" type of rear sight with no adjustments for windage and with elevation adjustments of only 150 and 300 yards. This has been replaced by a ramp type of rear sight with click adjustments permitting three points of either right or left windage. The peep eyepiece slides upon the ramp which is graduated for elevation from 100 to 300 yards in 50-yard increments.

The front sight is an "A" blade protected by wings.

M1A3—The designation M1A3 is given the carbine when equipped with a pantograph stock which when folded reduces the overall length of the weapon to 25.5

inches. The pantograph stock has proved itself more rigid and generally more satisfactory than the folding stock previously used.

The M1A3 is issued to paratroopers and such other units as require a weapon which may be carried or stored within a limited space.

Both the M1 and M1A3 carbines may be fitted with a sling if necessary.

CHARACTERISTICS OF CARBINE, M1

Weight, total . . . . 5.2 lbs.
Length, overall . . . . 35.6 ins.
Length of barrel . . . . 18 ins.
Rifling, length . . . . 16.77 ins., 55.7 cals.
   No. of grooves 4
   Twist . . . Right-hand, 1 turn in 20 ins., 66.6 cals.
   Depth of grooves . . . . 0.004 in.
Cross-sectional area bore . . . . 0.074 sq. in.
Operation . . . . Gas, semi-automatic
Feed . . . . 15-rd. magazine
Cooling . . . . Air
Trigger pull . . . . 4–6 lb.

(Carbine, M1A3, differs only slightly from the M1. The pantograph stock adds approximately 0.3 lb. to the weight. The length with stock extended is virtually the same. With stock folded the length is reduced to 25.5 inches.)

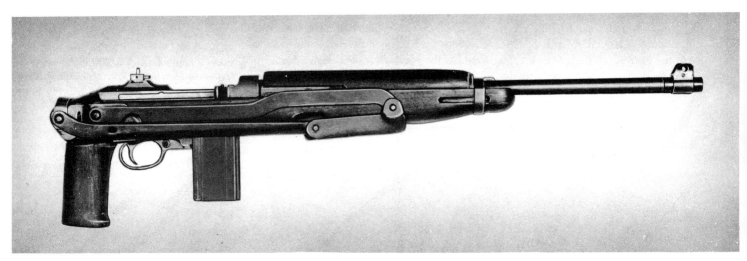

U. S. CARBINE, CAL. .30, M1A3, WITH FOLDING PANTOGRAPH STOCK

U.S. RIFLE, CAL .30, M1903 — STANDARD

PRINCIPAL CHARACTERISTICS

	M1903	M1903A1	M1903A3	M1903A4
Weight	8.69lbs	8.69lbs	8.0lbs	9.38lbs
Length	43.2in	43.2in	43.5in	43.5in
Length of barrel	24in	24in	24in	24in
Length of rifling				
Number of grooves	4	4	2 or 4	4
RH Twist, 1 turn in	10in	10in	10in	10in
Depth of grooves	.004in	.004in	.004in	.004in
Cross-sectional area of bore	0.074 sq.in.			
Type of mechanism	Manual turn bolt			
Feeding device	Clip			
Capacity of feeding device	5 rounds			
Sight radius	22.14in	22.14in		
Trigger pull	3 to 4.5 pounds			
Normal pressure	50,000 lbs per sq in (copper)			
Ammunition types	Ball, AP, Tracer			

RECONSTRUCTED PAGE 1 March 1944

The 'Springfield' rifle, designated as U.S. Rifle M1903, is a bolt-action shoulder weapon, developed at Springfield Arsenal. The rifle is magazine fed, loading from a five-round clip, and weighs 8³/₄ pounds without the bayonet which is approximately 1 pound weight.

The rifle was developed as a result of experience in the Spanish-American War and replaced the U.S. Rifle and U.S. Carbine, Cal .30, M1898 (Krag). During the development of the M1903 design it was decided to utilize one rifle for all arms of the service, instead of having a rifle and a carbine, and the barrel length was set at 24 inches to produce an intermediate size of weapon suitable for both infantry and cavalry use. Opportunity was also taken to adopt a rimless .30 cartridge with 220 grain round-nose bullet. The rifle and cartridge were issued for troop trials in 1905, after which the cartridge was redesigned with a pointed 150 grain bullet, and the rifles altered to conform. The cartridge became the Cartridge, Ball, .30 Model

1906, the rifle the U.S. Rifle M1903. The current standard cartridge for use with this rifle is the Cartridge, Ball, Cal .30 M2.

Ammunition is loaded from clips of five rounds supplied in a bandoleer with six pockets, each holding two clips, totaling 60 rounds. The contents of the clip are loaded into the rifle by opening the bolt, placing the clip above the magazine, and pressing the cartridges out of the clip and into the magazine. The clip is then discarded. A magazine cutoff on the left side of the rifle may be turned down to reveal the word 'Off'. In this position the bolt is prevented from moving far enough to the rear to allow a cartridge to feed up, and the rifle can then be loaded with individual cartridge, retaining the contents of the magazine. When turned up to show the word 'On', the bolt may be drawn all the way back and cartridges will then be loaded from the magazine each time the bolt is operated.

U.S. RIFLE, CAL .30, M1903.

This is the basic model and is now classified as Limited Standard. It has a straight stock and has the tangent leaf rear sight mounted above the barrel, in front of the chamber, giving a sight base of 22.14 inches.

U.S. RIFLE, CAL .30, M1903A1.

Standardized in 1929, this model has a pistol grip stock without finger grip grooves in the fore-end. The butt plate is checkered in order to give better support on the shoulder and a serrated trigger is fitted.

U.S. RIFLE, CAL .30, M1903A2.

This is not a shoulder rifle, but consists of a receiver and barrel fitted with special mounts to enable it to be located in the breech of certain artillery pieces for sub-caliber practice.

U.S. RIFLE, CAL .30, M1903A3.

Standardized on 21 May 1942, this is essentially the same as the M1903 pattern rifle but with modifications which permit faster production at less cost but without affecting the accuracy or reliability of the rifle. The rear sight is a receiver-type sight mounted on the rear of the receiver bridge. It has a dovetail base and a windage yoke with range scale graduated in 100 yard divisions with 50 yard adjustment. A windage knob moves the yoke to either side in clicks, each click representing a movement of one minute of angle, giving a shift in the point of impact of one inch for each 100 yards of range. The stock may be straight or of the pistol grip type, and a longer barrel guard now extends back to cover the area occupied by the leaf sight on earlier models. Various components are now stamped metal, and the trigger guard and magazine units are staked and welded. Rifling may have five or two grooves.

U.S. RIFLE, CAL .30, M1903A4.

Standardized on 14 January 1943, this is intended for use by snipers. It is the same as the M1903A3 except there are no metallic sights on the rifle. Sighting is performed by using the Telescope M72B1 (Weaver 330C) sight which is mounted to the receiver by means of a bridge-type mount which attaches to the receiver. The bolt handle is altered in shape so as to provide clearance for the telescope when the bolt is operated. Because the telescope blocks the clip guides in the receiver bridge, this rifle can only be loaded with single rounds. No bayonet mount is provided.

U. S. RIFLE, CAL. .22, M2—STANDARD

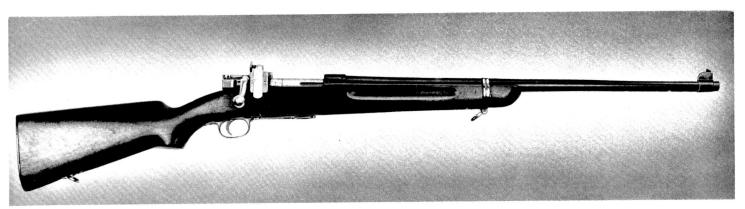

U. S. RIFLE, CAL. .22, M2, RIGHT VIEW

This rifle was designed for indoor or short-range target practice and the economical training of personnel.

It was originally developed by the Ordnance Department with the collaboration of the National Rifle Association to provide a highly accurate small-bore weapon for civilian rifle clubs and the rifle teams of high schools and colleges. It was subsequently adopted for small-bore marksmanship courses in the Army, Navy, Marine Corps, and Coast Guard.

As initially produced, this gun was designated M1922 and was essentially a small-bore reproduction of the M1903

service rifle. Subsequent refinement and modification changed the designation to M1922M1 and the current M2. In its present form the rifle is equipped with the Lyman 48C receiver sight with click adjustments for both elevation and windage.

Firing-pin travel has been reduced to one-half that of the previous models and the trigger formerly used has been replaced by one of the speed-action type. Ammunition used is the commercial cal. .22 long rifle fed from detachable box magazines of either 5-round or 10-round capacity.

CHARACTERISTICS

Weight, with sling	9.3 lb.
Length, overall	43.7 ins.
Length of barrel	24 ins.
Rifling, length	23.35 ins., 107 cals.
No. of grooves	4
Twist	Right, 1 turn in 16 ins., 73.4 cals.
Depth of grooves	0.0025 in.
Cross-sectional area of bore	0.0383 sq. in.
Operation	Manual
Feed	Magazine, 5- or 10-round
Cooling	Air
Trigger pull	3.5–5 lb.

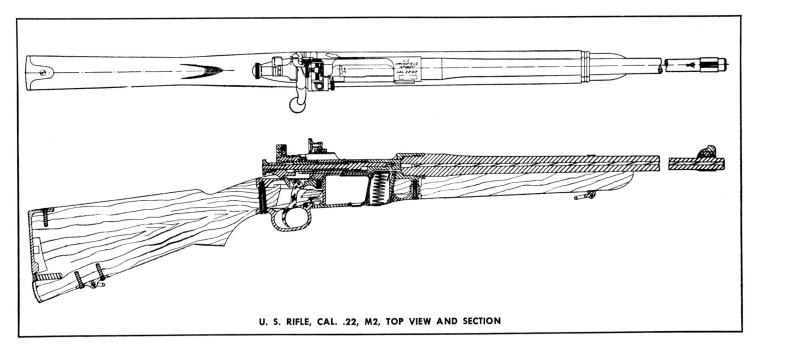

U. S. RIFLE, CAL. .22, M2, TOP VIEW AND SECTION

SHOTGUNS

Shotguns as produced by commercial manufacturers are procured by the Ordnance Department and issued for training personnel in firing on moving targets, for hunting purposes, and as riot guns for guard duty in congested areas or where firing will be at limited ranges.

Listed as Standard are the Winchester, M12; Remington, M31; Ithaca, M37; and Stevens, M620A. All are 12-gage, hammerless, repeating arms of that type of action known variously as slide, pump, or trombone in which a manually operated sliding fore-end serves to extract and eject the fired case and to feed a new round from a tubular magazine beneath the barrel.

Emergency requirements, however, frequently make necessary the purchase of such shotguns as may be obtainable and various other shotguns are in use today. These include: Winchester, M97; Stevens, M520 and M620A; Remington, M10, M11, and Sportsman; and Savage, M720.

All are 12-gage—a classification determined by the fact that twelve round lead balls exactly fitting the bore of the gun would weigh one pound. If measured in hundredths of inches, the 12-gage ball would be equivalent to caliber .729. The Winchester, M97, is a slide-action, 5-shot weapon originally introduced by the Winchester Repeating Arms Co. in 1897. It is a "hammer" gun, the hammer being exposed and in a position where it may be cocked or lowered by hand. In the so-called "hammerless" actions of later models, the hammer is completely enclosed by the receiver housing. The Stevens, M620A, is a model of more recent design than the M620 and the Stevens, M520, is the designation applied to the short-barreled riot gun produced by that manufacturer. The Stevens guns are all hammerless, slide action, repeaters differing one from another only in minor construction details. The Remington, M10, many of which are in use, is also a hammerless, slide action. It loads and ejects from the bottom; the Remington, M31, is bottom-loading and side-ejection.

The Savage, M720, and Remington, M11 and Sportsman, represent an entirely different type of action. These are semi-automatic weapons operating on the long-recoil principle as distinguished from the short-recoil system of other automatic and semi-automatic weapons. Barrel, barrel extension, and breechblock, locked together, are moved to the rear by the expansion of the explosion gases and are not unlocked until the end of that rearward travel is reached. At that point the barrel is returned to position by the pull of the recoil spring.

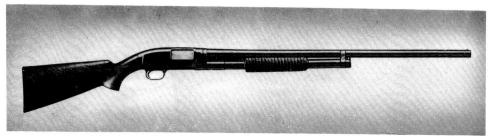

WINCHESTER SHOTGUN, 12 GAGE, M12, RIGHT SIDE VIEW

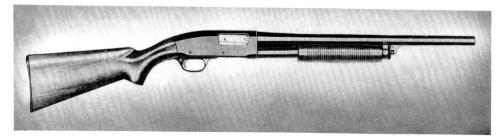

REMINGTON SHOTGUN, 12 GAGE, M31, RIOT TYPE, RIGHT SIDE

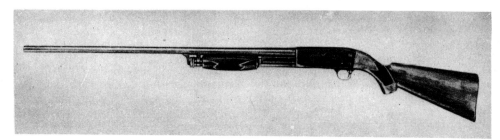

ITHACA SHOTGUN, M37, TRAP TYPE

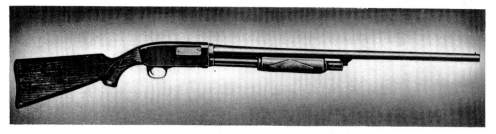

STEVENS SHOTGUN, 12 GAGE, M620A, TRAP TYPE

The bolt is unlocked from the barrel and is held momentarily by engagement with the operating slide of a dog on the rear of the carrier.

As the assembly moves to the rear a new round is released from the magazine and enters the receiver where it is held by the shell stop until released by the forward motion of the barrel as it returns. The shell then springs to the rear, strikes and depresses the rear end of the carrier latch, and frees the carrier to be rotated upward. As the forward end of the carrier rises, the dog is released from engagement with the operating slide. This in turn frees the breechblock which completes its forward travel.

Both Remington and Savage guns of this type are manufactured under Brown-ing patents and are virtually identical in action and operation.

The designations given shotguns in Ordnance Department classification are, in all cases, the model numbers assigned the gun by the manufacturer.

All shotguns, regardless of make or model, are furnished in three types—riot guns, skeet guns, and trap guns—with various barrel lengths and type of boring.

Riot guns are for use in suppressing disorders or for guard purposes where ranges are short and where the use of rifles and ball ammunition would be dangerous. Guns of this type are furnished with 20-inch barrels bored to a true cylinder. They are frequently equipped with a stud which permits mounting a

SHOTGUNS (Continued)

STEVENS SHOTGUN, M520, RIOT TYPE

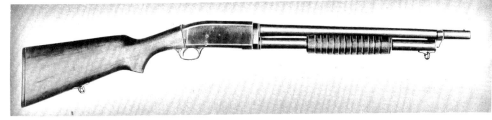

REMINGTON SHOTGUN, M10, RIOT TYPE

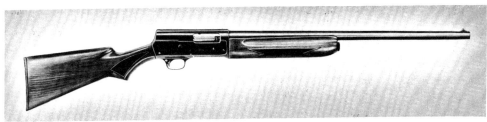

REMINGTON SHOTGUN, M11, SPORTSMAN

SAVAGE SHOTGUN, M720, RIOT TYPE

WINCHESTER SHOTGUN, M97, TRAP TYPE

bayonet. The shot charge used with riot guns consists of nine pellets of size 00 shot, generally known as "buckshot."

Skeet Guns are supplied with 26-inch barrels with "improved" cylinder boring. This boring concentrates approximately 40 percent of the shot pellets of the charge within a 30-inch circle at a distance of 40 yards. The "true cylinder" bore of the 20-inch barrel on the riot gun places only $33\frac{1}{3}$ percent of the pellets in such a circle.

Skeet shooting is an adaptation of the older sport of trap shooting at inanimate targets—saucer-shaped disks made of pressed clay and known variously as clay pigeons or Bluerocks. In skeet shooting the gunners move from one station to another and the gun is kept at waist level until the target is released. A round of skeet includes firing at targets released at unknown angles, at incoming targets, at targets from overhead traps, and at doubles. The game closely approximates conditions to be expected in actual field shooting and tests to the utmost the gunner's skill and co-ordination.

Skeet guns may be fitted with tubular sleeves known as compensators which serve to convert the open-bored improved cylinder to any desired degree of choke.

Trap guns have 30-inch barrels with full-choke boring which permits the closest possible concentration of the shot charge. From 65 to 70 percent of the pellets are evenly distributed over a 30-inch circle at a range of 40 yards. Guns of this type are used for trap shotting from fixed stations at inanimate targets which may be released at both known or unknown angles but from known ranges.

A load of $1\frac{1}{8}$ oz. of No. 8 shot is used for both trap and skeet shooting. Shells loaded with No. 6 shot are procured by the Ordnance Department and supplied as a hunting load.

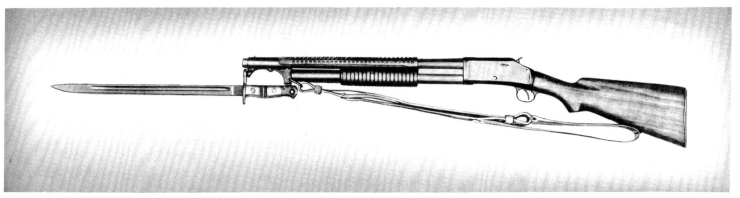

WINCHESTER SHOTGUN, M97, RIOT TYPE, WITH SLING AND M1917 BAYONET

CHARACTERISTICS

Gun		Remington, M31	Remington, M10	Remington, M11 and Sportsman	Winchester, M12	Winchester, M97	Ithaca, M37	Stevens, M520, M620, M620A§	Savage, M720
Weight	Riot	6⅞ lb.	7½ lb.	7¾ lb.	6½ lb.	8 lb.	6 lb.	7 lb.	7⅝ lb.
	Skeet	7⅝ lb.	†	8½ lb.	7 lb.	7⅝ lb.	6¼ lb.	7⅝ lb.	8 lb.
	Trap	7¾ lb.	7¾ lb.	8½ lb.	7⅜ lb.	7¾ lb.	6⅝ lb.	7¾ lb.	8¼ lb.
Length, overall	Riot	40 ins.	39½ ins.	40 ins.	40 ins.	39 ins.	40 ins.	40 ins.	39½ ins.
	Skeet	46 ins.	†	46 ins.	46 ins.	45 ins.	46 ins.	46 ins.	45½ ins.
	Trap	50 ins.	49½ ins.	50 ins.	50 ins.	49 ins.	50 ins.	50 ins.	49½ ins.
Length, barrel	Riot	20 ins.	20 ins.	20 ins.	20 ins.	20 ins.	20 ins.	20 ins.	20 ins.
	Skeet	26 ins.	†	26 ins.	26 ins.	26 ins.	26 ins.	26 ins.	26 ins.
	Trap	30 ins.	30 ins.	30 ins.	30 ins.	30 ins.	30 ins.	30 ins.	30 ins.
Boring	Riot	cylinder	cylinder	cylinder	cylinder	cylinder	cylinder	cylinder	cylinder
	Skeet	imp. cyl.	†	imp. cyl.	imp. cyl.	imp. cyl.	imp. cyl.	imp. cyl.	imp. cyl.
	Trap	full choke	full choke	full choke	full choke	full choke	full choke	full choke	full choke
Gage		12	12	12	12	12	12	12	12
Cross-sectional area of bore		0.4174 sq. in.	0.4174 sq. in.	0.4174 sq. in.	0.4174 sq. in.	0.4174 sq. in.	0.4174 sq. in.	0.4174 sq. in.	0.4174 sq. in.
Operation		Manual Slide action	Manual Slide action	Semi-automatic Long recoil	Manual Slide action	Manual Slide action	Manual Slide action	Manual Slide action	Semi-automatic Long recoil
Feed		Tubular magazine 3–4 rounds*	Tubular magazine 5 rounds	Tubular magazine 4–2 rounds‡	Tubular magazine 5 rounds	Tubular magazine 5 rounds	Tubular magazine 4 rounds	Tubular magazine 5 rounds	Tubular magazine 4 rounds
Pressure (copper)		Approximately 11,000 lb./sq. in.	Approximately 11,000 lb./sq. in.	Approximately 11,000 lb./sq. in.	Approximately 11,000 lb./sq. in.	Approximately 11,000 lb./sq. in.	Approximately 11,000 lb./sq. in.	Approximately 11,000 lb./sq. in.	Approximately 11,000 lb./sq. in.

*Remington, M31, is furnished with magazine capacity of both 3 and 4 rounds.

†Remington, M10, is not regularly supplied as a skeet gun.

‡The manufacturer's designation of "Sportsman" is given to those models of the Remington, M11, with magazine capacity of two rounds.

§The Stevens, M620A, is the maker's designation of an improved model of the M620; the designation M520 is given to the same gun in the "riot" type.

This is a double-action, hammerless, single-shot pistol firing all types of aircraft signals, rimmed and rimless. The rimmed signals must be loaded into the weapon from the breech but rimless signals may be inserted from either breech or muzzle.

The barrel is of seamless steel tubing, 4.12 inches long, with a bore of 1.58 inches. Pressure on the knurled undersurface of the breech lock—the lower of the two curved levers projecting from the top of the pistol—opens the breech for loading.

There is no external hammer nor any provision for single-action operation. A spring-actuated safety lever within the frame turns with the breech lock and prevents the internal hammer from rising unless the breech is fully closed and locked.

The Mount, M1, permits the projection of signals from the cabin or pilot's compartment of aircraft. The mount is permanently positioned in the airplane wall and secured by screws passing through an external flange. A spring-retained cover closes the interior opening when the mount is not in use.

Four lugs machined on the pistol barrel engage corresponding keyways within the sleeve of the mount. The pistol is then rotated one quarter-turn and locked in position by a latch on top of the barrel which snaps into a slot in the sleeve. The latch is disengaged by pressure on the upper of the curved levers shown in the illustration.

The sleeve is supported by four coil springs which absorb recoil when the pistol is fired. A cushioning gasket at the outer end of the sleeve takes up any counter-recoil.

CHARACTERISTICS

Length of pistol	8.2 in.
Length of pistol and mount	9.9 in.
Weight of pistol	2.1 lb.
Weight of mount	1.1 lb.
Height of pistol	8.4 in.
Length of barrel	4.12 in.
Diameter of bore	1.58 in.
Trigger pull	5 to 8 lb.

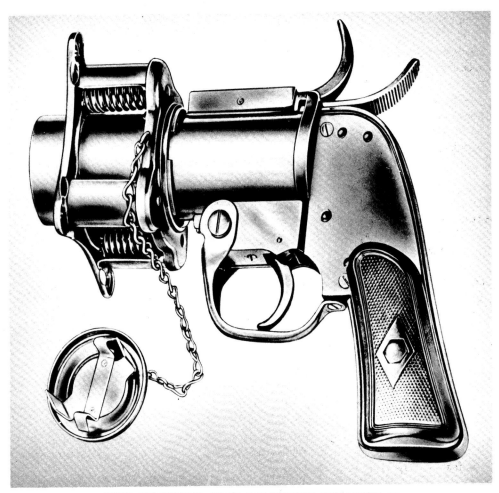

PISTOL, PYROTECHNIC, AN-M8, LEFT SIDE VIEW, WITH MOUNT, M1

PYROTECHNIC PISTOL MOUNT, M1

239

DISCHARGER, PYROTECHNIC, AN-M5—STANDARD

The Pyrotechnic Discharger, AN–M5, was designed to permit signals to be fired from aircraft in flight without the necessity of reloading the projecting device for each shot. It is rigidly mounted in any suitable position in the airplane, the muzzle projecting through the metal covering, and is fired by a cable from a remote control unit.

The action and operation of the discharger is similar in every way to that of the ordinary revolver. Six smoothbored sections of seamless steel tubing are rigidly bound about a central tube or bushing which, in turn, rotates on a fixed spindle exactly as the six-chambered cylinder of a revolver rotates to aline the chambers successively with the firing pin and the barrel.

In the pyrotechnic discharger, that rotation is controlled by an index plate and index flange. The chambers in which the signals are placed are alined with the short muzzle which protrudes through the outer skin of the airplane and is secured by a mounting plate to which the barrel and body groups of the discharger are fastened by tie rods.

A pull upon the cable rotates the pulley and index shaft and cams the double-action hammer backward. A cylinder is lined up in firing position as the cam action ceases and the hammer spring drives the hammer forward until its pin strikes the primer of the signal and discharges it. The cases of the fired signals remain in the barrels and are removed singly by hand.

The signals are loaded into the barrels through a pivoted loading gate, or trap, which may be seen in the left foreground of the illustration covering the lowest of the three barrels visible. The operating cable, also shown, must be pulled a full stroke and released in order to rotate the barrel group ⅙ revolution and bring another barrel into loading position.

Accidental discharge of a signal during the loading operation is prevented by a safety spindle lever which is raised by the opening of the loading trap and while raised blocks the hammer in the half-cocked position and prevents its fall. A sliding catch locks the loading trap in the

DISCHARGER, PYROTECHNIC, AN-M5

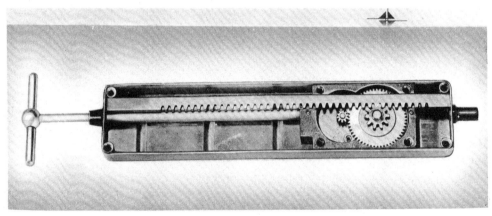

REMOTE CONTROLLER, M2

closed position and must be pushed down in its slot before the trap can be opened.

Once loaded, the entire operation of the discharger is by means of the Remote Controller, M2, here illustrated with cover removed to show the rack and pinion mechanism. The controller is mounted at any convenient point in the airplane or at the station of that crew member designated to operate the discharger. Each pull on and release of the handle of the controller rotates the body

group of the discharger ⅙ revolution and fires a signal.

CHARACTERISTICS

Weight of discharger	8.6 lb.
Weight of controller (9.9 in.)	0.9 oz.
Length of discharger	9 ins.
Length of controller	9.9 to 15 ins.
Length of barrels	4.5 ins.
Bore	1.58 ins.
Signals used	AN-M37 through AN-M45

PROJECTOR, PYROTECHNIC, HAND, M9—STANDARD

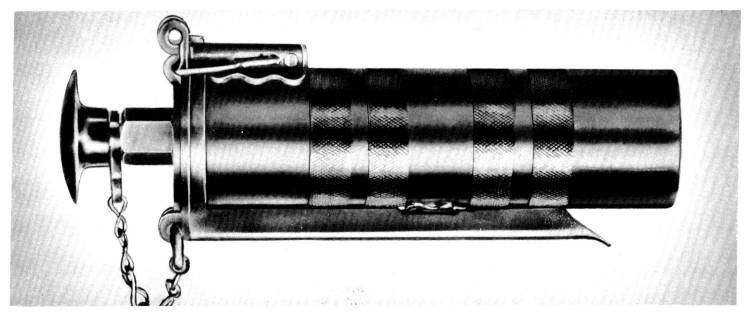

PROJECTOR, PYROTECHNIC, HAND, M9, WITH SAFETY SET

This simple device consists of a short smooth-bored barrel with a hinged breechplate in which a firing-pin and cocking-piece are mounted. There is no trigger and the arm may be fired by striking the rounded base of the cocking-piece with the hand or against the ground. A spring clip attached by a short chain to the hinge pin of the breech latch is used to hold the hand knob and pin in the retracted position and prevent accidental discharge.

The ejector is linked to the breech plate and opening of the breech extracts the round.

Projector, M9, is used in firing the double-star Aircraft Signals, AN-M37 through AN-M42; the single-star Aircraft Signals, AN-M43 through AN-M45; and the rimless signals AN-M28 through AN-M36, no longer standard.

The projector weighs 14 ounces, measures 7.6 inches overall, and has a bore diameter of 1.58 inches.

PROJECTOR, SIGNAL, GROUND, M4—STANDARD

The manually operated Ground Signal Projector, M4, is used in firing the single-star parachute Signals, M17A1B2, M19A1B2, and the Cluster Signals, M18A1B2, M20A1B2, M22A1B2. The high-burst ranging Ground Signal (smoke), M27, may also be launched from this projector.

The projector is a smooth-bored tube, one end of which is closed by a threaded cap which holds in place a base assembly on which is mounted a fixed firing pin and four retaining springs. The signal is inserted from the muzzle and pushed into the projector until gripped by the retaining springs which prevent premature discharge by holding the primer end of the signal away from contact with the firing pin.

The operator lies prone and fires the signal by striking the cap of the projector smartly against the ground. The signal is projected fin first but reverses at approximately 100 feet and continues to rise to 600 feet.

The Projector, M4, measures 11.9 inches overall and weighs 2.63 lb. The barrel is 1.66 inches in diameter and 11.6 inches long.

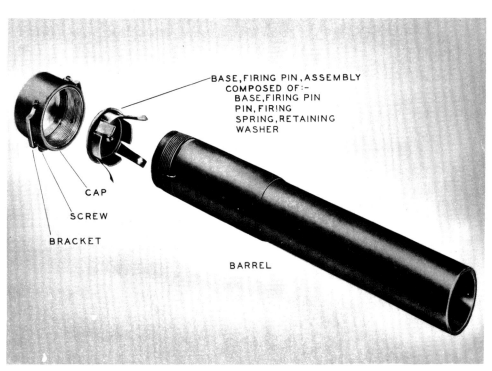

PROJECTOR, SIGNAL, GROUND, M4, DISASSEMBLED

LAUNCHERS, GRENADE, M1, M2, M7, M8—STANDARD

Grenade launchers are tubular devices attached to the muzzles of U. S. rifles and carbines to permit launching or firing of the various standard rifle grenades, explosive or practice, and the parachute and cluster Ground Signals, M17A1 to M22A1, inclusive. The Mark II fragmentation hand grenade may be converted to a rifle grenade by means of the Grenade Projection Adapter, M1, and may then be fired from the standard grenade launchers.

The M1 launcher is for use with caliber .30 rifles of the M1903 (Springfield) series, and the virtually identical M2 launcher (not illustrated) for use with the M1917 (Enfield) rifle. The gas-operated, semi-automatic M1 rifle and M1 carbine employ the M7 and M8 grenade launchers respectively.

All launchers are of the same outside diameter, 0.86 inch, a dimension determined by the interior diameter of the stabilizer tube of the rifle grenades and ground signals. The tubular body of the launcher fits snugly within the stabilizer tube and the depth to which the launcher is inserted in the tube determines the

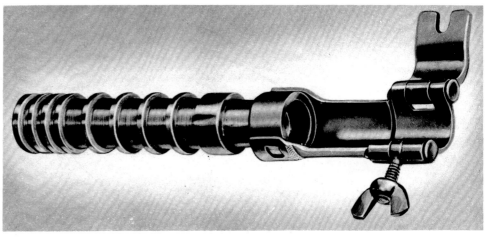

GRENADE LAUNCHER, M1

range attained by the fired grenade.

Reference to the illustrations will show that the exterior surface of each launcher is marked in a series of rings. These rings are numbered consecutively from the rear to the muzzle on the M7 and M8 launchers. By counting the rings exposed, the firer can adjust for range. The rings are raised so that they may be counted and the range determined in night firing.

As an example, when the M17 fragmentation rifle grenade is fired from the M7 launcher on the M1 rifle, five rings visible indicates that the grenade will attain a range of approximately 55 yards; four rings, 80 yards; three rings, 105 yards; two rings, 130 yards; and one ring, approximately 165 yards.

In all cases the actual launching is accomplished by means of a special

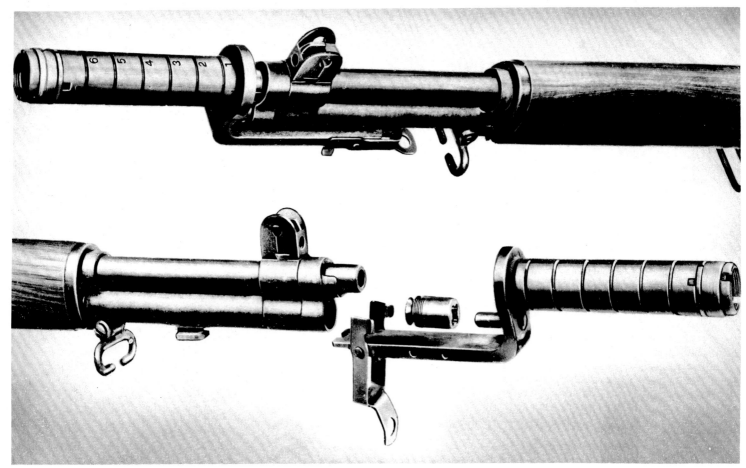

GRENADE LAUNCHER, M7, MOUNTED ON U. S. RIFLE, CAL. .30, M1, AND (BELOW) LAUNCHER DETACHED SHOWING VALVE SCREW TO REPLACE GAS-CYLINDER LOCK SCREW

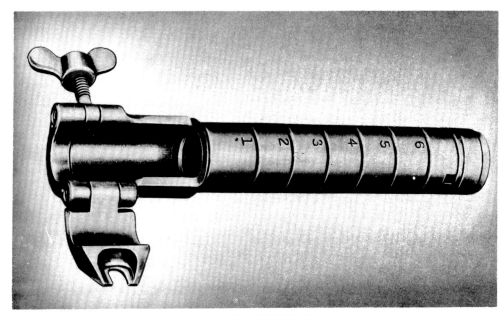

GRENADE LAUNCHER, M8

blank cartridge, caliber .30, fired in the usual way in the rifle or carbine. The grenade cartridge may be distinguished from the ordinary blank cartridge by a rose crimp in the mouth of the case. These cartridges are illustrated and described in the small arms ammunition section of this Catalogue.

Modern warfare has emphasized the need for grenades to be fired at longer ranges and at higher velocities than were possible with the standard blank grenade cartridges. This has been accomplished by the so-called "vitamin pill," recommended for standardization on 15 January 1944 as Cartridge, Grenade, Auxiliary, Cal. .30, M7.

The designation as caliber .30 is somewhat misleading but refers to the rifle with which the auxiliary cartridge is used. The cartridge itself is a tube of drawn brass 0.45 inch in diameter and open at both ends. The open ends are sealed with paper wads after the tube is loaded with 20 grains of powder.

One end of the auxiliary cartridge is finished with a beveled rim which serves to keep it in place when it is inserted into the muzzle end of the launcher. The body of the launcher is then inserted in the stabilizer tube of the grenade as in normal firing. The effect is that of a booster, the flame of the grenade cartridge igniting the charge of the auxiliary cartridge and the power of the two combining to project the grenade from the launcher. Tests have determined that from 100 to 150 yards greater range is obtained when the auxiliary cartridge is used.

The auxiliary cartridge case is ejected from the launcher simultaneously with the launching of the grenade.

Since a maximum range is desired, the grenade is set as far back as possible on the launcher when the auxiliary is used. The auxiliary also increases the grenade's velocity, however, so that it may be used at shorter ranges where a reduced time of flight is desired.

LAUNCHER, GRENADE, M7—This launcher represents an improvement, without change in designation, upon the original model designed for use with the U. S. Rifle, M1. A launcher of simple clamp-on design could not be used with this gas-operated weapon because of the creation of excess pressures which caused premature opening of the breech and drove operating rod and bolt back with sufficient force to break the receiver.

The problem was solved by the development of a valve screw to be inserted in the gas cylinder of the rifle in place of the regular gas-cylinder lock screw. The valve within the screw opens to permit the escape of excessive pressures. Service ammunition may be fired from the M1 rifle with the grenade launcher in place. Since the valve is fully open, operating pressures are not developed within the cylinder and the rifle can be used only as a single-shot weapon.

The M7 launcher as first designed fastened to the muzzle of the M1 rifle by means of a two-armed, hinged clamp. Service tests demonstrated that three distinct motions were necessary to attach or remove the device. Technicians at Springfield Armory developed a superior fastening in the form of a simple clip which locked behind the bayonet stud on the gas cylinder. Manufacturing was facilitated by using larger parts and reducing the total number of parts of the launcher from ten to five.

LAUNCHER, GRENADE, M8—Development of a grenade launcher for the Carbine, M1, was deferred until after a satisfactory launcher had been developed for the M1 rifle. Both weapons are gas-operated, semi-automatic arms and it was felt that the many difficulties encountered in designing a launcher for the rifle would be greatly augmented with the lighter gun.

The problem proved much simpler than had been expected. It was found that immobilization of the semi-automatic feature of the carbine was not necessary and that a simple clamp-on launcher similar to the M1 and M2 could be used. The carbine may be operated semi-automatically with the launcher attached and there is little loss of accuracy.

SIGHT:—By action of the Ordnance Committee 10 February 1944 (OCM 22847) a new and more accurate sight, adaptable to all U. S. rifles and carbines, was standardized as Sight, Rifle Grenade Launcher, M15. It consists of a five-inch sighting bar which may be quickly attached to or removed from a plate permanently mounted on the left side of the rifle stock. The bar carries a leveling bubble, a front sight, and an aperture rear sight with click adjustments for elevation.

CHARACTERISTICS

Launcher	Weight	Length	Outside Diameter	Diameter of Bracket	Diameter of Bore
M1	0.53 lb.	7.1 in.	0.86 in.	0.68 in.	0.50 in.
M2	0.50 lb.	6.7 in.	0.86 in.	0.62 in.	0.47 in.
M7	0.75 lb.	7.5 in.	0.86 in.		0.50 in.
M8	0.75 lb.	6.0 in.	0.86 in.		0.40 in.

LAUNCHER, ROCKET, ANTITANK, 2.36 INCH, M9—STANDARD

ROCKET LAUNCHER, A.T., M9, LEFT SIDE

The rocket launcher, popularly known and widely publicized as the "Bazooka," represents the adaptation to modern warfare of one of the oldest forms of military pyrotechnics, the rocket. It represents, too, the first practical development of a rocket gun or rocket launcher as a shoulder weapon for infantry use against tanks and other armored targets.

The launcher is an open tube approximately 54 inches long and 2.365 inches in internal diameter equipped with a shoulder stock, a pistol grip, electrical firing mechanism, and sights. The Rocket, M6A3, is 19.4 inches long and weighs 3.38 pounds. It carries a shaped charge of TNT capable of penetrating heavy armor at angles of impact up to 30°. The optimum range is approximately 200 yards although the rocket may be em-

ployed at ranges as great as 600 yards. The Rocket, 2.36 inch, M6A3, is illustrated and described in the ammunition section of this catalogue.

In its original form the rocket launcher was supplied with a wooden shoulder stock midway of its length and was not reinforced for additional bore-safety. A two-cell dry battery supplied the spark for ignition of the rocket's propelling charge, pressure on the trigger completing the circuit.

The first models of the launcher were equipped with a hinged rear sight and fixed front sights. These were followed by a peep rear sight and a front sight in the form of a rectangular frame at the muzzle of the launcher. The vertical sides of the frame carried graduations for ranges of 100, 200, and 300 yards.

The rocket launcher was introduced as a combat weapon during the North African campaign of 1942–43. Use in battle indicated the need for various improvements and for a model which could be broken down into two approximately equal loads for use by parachute troops. The present launcher, M9, represents the development of those tactical requirements.

Since a higher safety factor was required, the tube of the launcher is now wrapped with wire around all that portion adjacent to the operator's face. The skeleton stock is of metal and is shaped so as to permit two shoulder positions for ease of sighting at high and low elevations and for prone shooting. Midway of the tube is a flange with bayonet joints which breaks the launcher into sections which may be carried by paratroopers or packed into containers for aerial delivery. Reassembly can be effected in a few seconds without tools and the joint locked rigidly.

The dry cells which supplied the ignition spark in the earlier models have been replaced by a self-contained magneto operated by pressure on the "squeezer" type trigger. A one-way safety switch incorporated in the trigger mechanism cuts out the magneto and prevents generation of an electrical impulse as the trigger returns to position.

The sight is an optical ring hinged to fold against the tube when not in use and protected by a cover. An adjustable range scale provides graduations from 50 to 700 yards in 50-yard increments.

Assembled and ready for firing, the rocket launcher measures 55 inches overall and weighs approximately 14½ pounds.

ROCKET LAUNCHER, M9, BROKEN DOWN

MACHINE GUN MOUNTS

Machine gun mounts designed for installation on trucks and other vehicles are illustrated and described in the Tank and Automotive volume of this Catalogue. Included in the category of Vehicular Mounts are: Truck Pedestal Mounts, M24, M24A1, M24A2, and M31; Dash Mount, M48; Ring Mounts, M49 and M49C; and Truck Mounts, M32, M36, M37, M37A1, M37A2, M37A3, M50, M56, M57, M58, M59, M60, and M61.

MOUNT, TRIPOD, MACHINE GUN, CAL. .30, M1917A1 — STANDARD

This mount, which accommodates any caliber .30 Browning machine gun, air- or water-cooled, is the older mount, M1917, modified to permit elevation through a wider arc in operation against hostile aircraft. As now issued, the gun may be elevated to +65° and depressed to −28° from the horizontal.

The central member of the mount is a socket in which the three legs are mounted and in which the cradle pintle fits and rotates as a pivot. A clamp prevents the pintle from being pulled from its socket and serves as a brake against too free rotation.

The traversing dial is mounted on top of the socket. Two types of dials are now in use. The older type is graduated clockwise in azimuth from 0 to 6,400 mils; the later dials are graduated to 3,200 mils clockwise and counter-clockwise from 0. Both type dials are subdivided to permit readings in 20-mil units. A clamp secures the traversing dial in any desired position.

Elevation is through the arc shown in the side of the cradle as illustrated. Rapid and free adjustments in elevation may be obtained by release of the cradle clamp. The upper side of the elevation arc carries a mil-graduated scale reading from 500 to 0 to 400, subdivided in 20-mil units.

Both elevating and traversing mechanism are housed in the rear of the cradle frame. Screws controlled by handwheels permit mechanical manipulation in single mil units.

The legs of the tripod mount, M1917A1, may be adjusted independently to obtain firm footing on uneven ground. Stability has been improved by mounting the gun so that the center of the tripod absorbs the major portion of the recoil.

MOUNT, TRIPOD, MACHINE GUN, CAL. .30, M1917A1

CHARACTERISTICS

Weight	53.2 lb.
Length, extended	42 ins.
folded for transportation	36 ins.
Spread of front legs, extended	39 ins.
Command	23 ins.
Traversing range, free	6,400 mils (360°)
mechanical	50 mils
least increment	1 mil
Elevating limits, free	+1,156 mils (65°)
	−498 mils (28°)
mechanical	50 mils
least increment	1 mil
Elevating arc graduated	Every 25 mils for 900 mils

MOUNT, TRIPOD, MACHINE GUN, CAL. .30, M2—STANDARD

This tripod mount was developed for the air-cooled caliber .30 Browning machine gun, M1919A2. It is the standard mount for that gun as modified to the current designation of M1919A4. It is carried as auxiliary equipment in combat vehicles and is used by cavalry as a pack mount. The tripod mount, M2, is for use against ground targets only, its limited range of elevation precluding its employment in antiaircraft fire.

The mount consists of three telescoping tubular steel legs in a tripod head. The two rear legs are joined by and obtain additional support from a graduated traversing bar which also carries the elevating mechanism and supports the rear of the gun.

The dial with which the bar was originally equipped has been replaced by a more easily read scale graduated in 100-mil increments and 5-mil subdivisions.

The scale has a range of 444.5 mils to right and left from 0.

With the rear of the gun supported by the bar, elevation of +19° and depression of −21° may be obtained by use of the elevating mechanism. Free elevation, with the gun supported only at the trunnion, is through an arc of 21°. Free depression may be obtained up to −45°.

The tapered steel pintle on the receiver of the gun mates with a bronze bushing in the tripod head and is held securely by a latch which engages in an annular groove on the pintle.

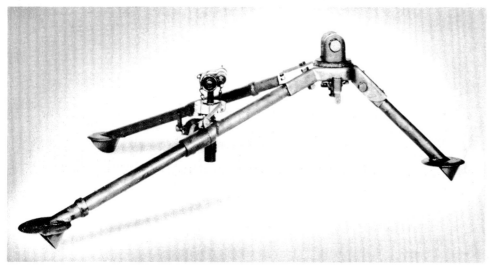

MOUNT, TRIPOD, MACHINE GUN, CAL. .30, M2

CHARACTERISTICS

Weight	14 lb.
Length, extended	32.5 ins.
folded for transportation	27 ins.
Spread of rear legs	30 ins.
Command	11 ins.
Traversing range, free	6,400 mils (360°)
mechanical (without release)	50°
Traversing bar graduated	800 mils
Elevating range, free	+21°, −45°
mechanical	+19°, −21°
least increment	1 mil
Elevating handwheel graduated	every mil

MOUNT, MACHINE GUN, CAL. .50, ANTIAIRCRAFT, TRIPOD AND PEDESTAL M2A1—STANDARD

MOUNT, MACHINE GUN, CAL. .50, A.A., M2A1, ON TRIPOD

This mount was designed to accommodate the caliber .50 water-cooled Browning machine gun, M2, in semipermanent and permanent positions as a defensive weapon against hostile aircraft. The cradle in which the gun rests is supported by a tubular column, or pedestal, which may be placed upon a tripod for semi-permanent mounting or upon a pedestal base in permanent positions. When used with the tripod legs, the mount occupies a circle 104 inches in diameter.

When the gun is installed on this mount the back plate and spade grips are replaced by a flexible back plate assembly. Firing is from the side plate trigger and the gunner is supported by a body rest and protected by two shields of ¼ inch armor 32 inches wide.

The design of the cradle and the mounting of the gun are similar in all major respects to the caliber .30 mount,

M1917A1, although the cradle is of heavier construction throughout to adapt it to the caliber .50 gun.

The gun may be traversed throughout the full range of 360° and has an elevation range of +60° and −15° from the horizontal.

The unarmored gun is illustrated as equipped with the Sight, cal. .50, Antiaircraft, M1. Use of this sight with the armored gun is optional.

CHARACTERISTICS

Weight, complete, without armor	{ tripod, 375 lb.
	{ pedestal, 315 lb.
Weight of upper shield, armor	72 lb.
Weight of lower shield, armor	46 lb.
Weight of bracket, armor	8.5 lb.
Weight of sight, A.A., cal. .50, M1	10 lb.
Weight of legs, tripod mount	112 lb.
Weight of pedestal base	52 lb.
Weight of back rest	17 lb.
Weight of cradle	119 lb.
Command	48.8 ins.
Height of sights above ground	74.2 ins.
Traverse	360°
Elevating limits, tripod mount	+60°, −15°
pedestal mount	+69°, −15°

MOUNT, MACHINE GUN, CAL. .50, A.A., M2A1, ON PEDESTAL BASE

MOUNT, MACHINE GUN, CAL. .50, A.A., M3—STANDARD (NAVY DESIGNATION, Mk. 30)

Experience with the caliber .50 mounts, M2 and M2A1, developed the need for a mount of greater stability which would permit more accurate fire and meet the "close-in" defensive conditions under which antiaircraft machine guns must operate against low-flying, high-speed targets at ranges of less than 1,000 yards.

The caliber .50 antiaircraft mount, M3, embodies those improvements. It is built to accommodate the water-cooled, flexible, caliber .50 Browning machine gun, M2, but may be adapted to take any Browning machine gun in that caliber. Like its predecessors, this mount may be assembled as a tripod mount for ground use in semi-permanent positions or may be set on a pedestal base in fixed positions.

In general, the operation of the M3 mount is similar to that of the M2 and M2A1. Traverse through the full arc of 360° is possible and elevation range has been increased to 90°. The gun on the M3 mount may be depressed through an arc of 15°.

The trigger control mechanism is

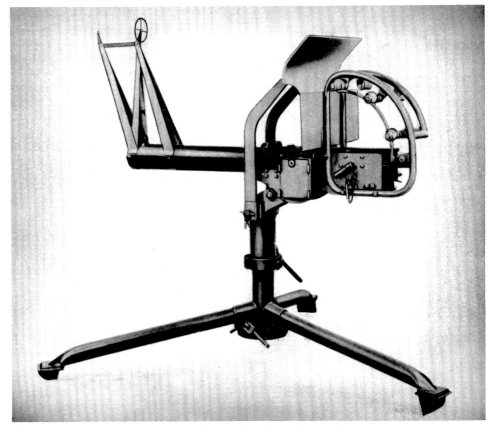

MOUNT, MACHINE GUN, CAL. .50, A.A., M3

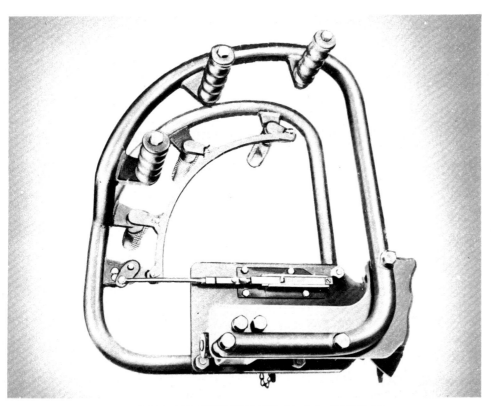

TRIGGER CONTROL MECHANISM, CAL. .50, A.A., MOUNT, M3

entirely different from that of the M2 and M2A1 mounts. It consists of a curved frame of steel tubing (shown in the illustration) fastened to the rear of the cradle side plates. Six trigger control grips are assembled in pairs, one above the other, three grips on the right member of the frame, three on the left. The grips are pivoted to a radial segment which connects by a bracket and rods with the trigger.

Rotation of any one of the grips moves the radial segment and fires the gun. The design permits the gunner to remain upright instead of reclining in the back-rest as was necessary with the M2 and M2A1 mounts.

CHARACTERISTICS

Weight, complete with armor plate	380 lb.
Weight of cradle and carriage, less shield	120 lb.
Weight of pedestal assembly	112 lb.
Weight of legs, tripod mount	81 lb.
Radius of legs	49 ins.
Command	37.1 ins.
Space required, axially	73.6 ins.
Space required, transversely	84.8 ins.
Traverse	360°
Elevating limits	+90°, −15°

MOUNT, TRIPOD, MACHINE GUN, CAL. .50, M3—STANDARD

This mount is similar in all essentials to the .30 caliber tripod mount, M2, but is of more rugged construction throughout to accommodate the heavier caliber .50 weapon. It is designed for ground fire with the caliber .50, heavy barrel, flexible Browning gun.

Each leg consists of two telescoping sections of seamless steel tubing. A shoe with spade extension is welded to the end of each lower section. Normal mounting of the tripod is with the front leg at an angle of 60° and with all extensions closed. In this position the gun trunnion is 10 inches above the ground. Minor adjustments in command height may be obtained by changing the angle of the front leg or by extending the telescoping sections of all three legs. A clamping ring on the sleeve section of each leg permits locking the extension at any desired length.

A bronze bushing in the tripod head mates with the pintle of the gun which is locked in position by a pintle-latch. A free traverse of 360° is possible. As with the mount for the caliber .30 gun, a traversing bar joins the two rear legs, supports the rear of the gun, and carries the elevating and traversing mechanism. The traversing scale is graduated in 5-mil subdivisions to 400 mils right and left from zero. The traversing dial formerly furnished with this caliber .50 mount has been eliminated.

The lower end of the elevating mechanism attaches to the traversing bar through the traversing slide; the upper end is attached to the gun by a pin. The mechanism is a double screw assembly and affords an elevating range from +100 mils to −250 mils in increments of 50 mils or in 1-mil subdivisions.

CHARACTERISTICS

Weight	44 lb.
Length, folded for transportation	41 ins.
legs fully extended	71 ins.
Height of trunnion, legs retracted	10 ins.
legs extended	13 ins.
Range of traverse	6,400 mils (360°)
Range of elevation	+100, −250 mils
Elevating handwheel graduated	every mil

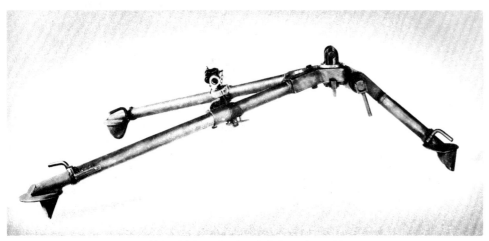

MOUNT, TRIPOD, MACHINE GUN, CAL. .50, M3

MOUNTS, PEDESTAL, MACHINE GUN, A.A., CAL. .50, M39, M43, M46—SUBSTITUTE STANDARD

MOUNT, PEDESTAL, MACHINE GUN, CAL. .50, M39
(NAVY DESIGNATION, Mk. 21)

MOUNT, PEDESTAL, MACHINE GUN, CAL. .50, M43
(NAVY DESIGNATION, Mk. 21)

These mounts were designed to provide rigid mounting of caliber .50 Browning machine guns, air- and water-cooled, in permanent positions for defense against hostile aircraft. They may be installed on ships, on docks, or in defense positions on bridges, rooftops, or elevated platforms erected especially to accommodate them.

Mounts, M39 and M43, are single gun mounts. The M39 is built for the air-cooled model of the Browning caliber .50 machine gun, Aircraft, M2; the M43 is for the water-cooled model of the same gun. The M46 is a twin mount, accommodating two water-cooled guns, with heavier equilibration springs, two heavy barrel, M2, or aircraft, M2, guns.

In both the single and twin mounts the aggregate weight of the carriage and mounted parts—gun, armor, ammunition, and ammunition chest — is counterbalanced by a helical spring within the pedestal tube. No counterweight is used, since the equilibrator spring cushions the fall of gun and carriage in moving from an elevated toward a horizontal position and serves the purpose of a counterweight in reducing the effort required to elevate the weapon for high-angle fire. This spring counterbalancing permits easy handling of the gun without the use of auxiliary power.

Both single and twin mounts may be trained by hand through the full 360° of traverse and may be elevated from −10° to +80°. All mounts may be quickly locked in any position for oper-

ation against stationary targets. All are designed to accommodate the ammunition chest, M2, with a capacity of 200 rounds of caliber .50 ammunition.

PEDESTALS—The pedestals for both single and twin mounts are identical. The circular base is of ½-inch mild steel plate 30 inches in diameter. The tube and its supporting flanges are made of ⅛-inch plate. The upper end of the tube is machined to take the ball thrust bearing on which the cradle moves in traverse.

CARRIAGE—In both single and twin mounts the carriage for cradle and gun is a one-piece casting, the base of which forms the upper half of the race housing of the ball thrust bearing. A single lever on the right side locks the carriage to

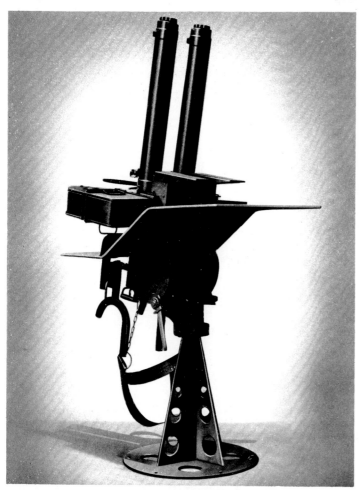

MOUNT, CAL. .50, M46 (NAVY DESIGNATION, Mk. 22)

the pedestal in traverse and to the side plate of the cradle in elevation. Pulling the lever to the rear and upward locks the carriage in both planes. The handle is held in its unlocked position by a stop and spring clip.

CRADLE AND SHIELD—The shields of both single and twin mounts are bolted to angle-pieces welded to the side plates of the cradle, and the two are considered a single assembly. The single mount cradle has no recoil-absorbing device and the inner plates, on which the gun is mounted, are fixed to the outside plates. The twin mount cradle is equipped with a dual-action recoil absorber. The inner plates and guns slide back and forth within the outer plates in recoil. Springs in the forward end of the cradle dampen this movement.

The M39 and M43 mounts use a shield of ½-inch armor plate; the shield of the M46 mounts is of ⅜-inch plate. Both shields are resistant to cal. .30 and cal. .303 bullets at test range.

CHARACTERISTICS

	M39, M43	M46
Weight complete except for gun and ammunition	725 lb.	825 lb.
Working space, maximum radius of	40 ins.	40 ins.
Command	48.5 ins.	48.5 ins.
Height of sights above ground	64.1 ins.	64.1 ins.
Traverse	360°	360°
Elevation	+80°	+80°
	−10°	−10°

ELEVATOR-CRADLE, A.A., CAL. .50, M1—STANDARD

This elevator and cradle assembly consists of an adapter, with tripod legs for additional stability, for the Standard tripod machine gun mount, cal. .50, M3. It is for the use of ground troops and enables those troops to convert their ground mounts to antiaircraft fire and to adapt low ground mounts for enfilade fire over high banks, out of trenches or ditches, or from the concealment of high grass or brush. It also permits a machine gun mount to be installed in any vehicle for protection against hostile aircraft or for use as a mobile fire platform.

The assembly consists of a cylindrical pedestal which fits in the Standard tripod mount and which carries a cradle for installation of the caliber .50 Browning machine gun, heavy barrel, M2. The cradle permits unlimited traverse in azimuth, elevation to 90°, and depression to −45° or more, depending upon the position in which the basic mount is installed and the nature of the terrain in front of the gun.

The complete assembly of elevator, cradle, and tripod stabilizing legs weighs 95 lb.

ELEVATOR-CRADLE, A.A., CAL. .50, M1, WITH GUN IN POSITION

SMALL ARMS AMMUNITION—STANDARD

CALIBER .30 CARTRIDGES

The caliber .30 cartridge, standard for all rifles and machine guns manufactured in that caliber, is issued in the following forms: Ball, M2; Tracer, M1; Incendiary, M1; Armor-Piercing, M2.

The caliber .30 cartridge is also issued in the following special-purpose forms: Rifle Grenade, M3; Dummy, M2; Blank, M1909; Guard, M1; and High-Pressure Test, M13.

BALL, CAL. .30, M2—The cartridge so loaded is for use against enemy personnel and those matériel targets which do not require the employment of armor-piercing or other special-purpose rounds. The complete round includes primer, case, propelling charge of approximately 50 grains of IMR 4895 powder, and 150-grain bullet. The case is of drawn brass. Production of the steel case is being discontinued. The bullet consists of a gilding metal jacket on an alloy core of 90% lead, 10% antimony. As an alternate, a core of 97.5% lead, 2.5% antimony may be used. The bullet is not boattailed. The neck of the case is crimped into a cannelure in the bullet and yields to a minimum pull of 45 pounds.

Tested for accuracy, the M2 ball groups within a 13-inch circle at 500 yards and within a 15-inch circle at 600 yards.

The following range table gives the external ballistics of the M2 150-grain service bullet. Those of the armor-piercing, incendiary, and tracer bullets vary slightly therefrom due to minor differences in bullet weights and velocities. Use of the IMR 4895 powder, which replaced the older IMR 4876, has shown a decrease in flight time of from one to two seconds at the ranges listed.

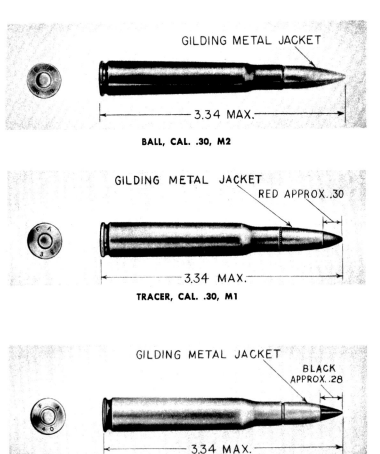

BALL, CAL. .30, M2

TRACER, CAL. .30, M1

ARMOR-PIERCING, CAL. .30, M2

RANGE TABLE

Range (Yards)	Angle of Elevation (Mils)	Time of Flight (Seconds)	Maximum Ordinate (Inches)	Angle of Fall (Mils)
100	0.7	0.12	0	1
200	1.5	0.25	3.6	2
300	2.4	0.38	7.2	3
400	3.4	0.53	14.4	4
500	4.6	0.70	21.6	6
600	6.0	0.89	36.0	9
700	7.7	1.11	61.2	12
800	9.6	1.35	86.4	17
900	11.9	1.62	159.6	22
1,000	14.6	1.91	183.6	28

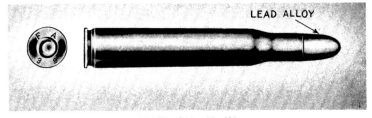

GUARD, CAL. .30, M1

TRACER, CAL. .30, M1, is used in machine guns and rifles to indicate the path of the bullet in flight as an aid in fire against moving targets. The round is identified by a red point, approximately .30 inch long, on the bullet. A 17-grain tracer compound is ignited by the propelling charge and burns with a brilliant red flame. The length of the trace is approximately 1,000 yards. Tracer bullets have an incendiary effect upon targets struck before the trace has burned out, but this action is not so pronounced nor so reliable as with rounds loaded for incendiary purposes.

The trajectory of the Tracer, M1, bullet crosses that of the Ball, M2, and Armor-Piercing, M2, at approximately 600 yards.

ARMOR-PIERCING, CAL. .30, M2, is designed for fire against enemy aircraft, lightly armored vehicles, and similar targets. The round is identified by a black tip on the bullet. The core is of hardened steel instead of the lead alloy used in the ball cartridge.

INCENDIARY, CAL. .30, M1—This round, used for the purpose indicated by its designation, has not been manufactured since November, 1943. Existing stocks are issued for use in caliber .30 rifles and machine guns. The round is identified by the light-blue tip, approximately .30 inch in length, on the bullet. The bullet is not boattailed and contains a chemical incendiary compound which ignites upon contact.

GUARD, CAL. .30, M1—This round was formerly designated Gallery Practice, cal. .30, M1919, and was used as a reduced load for indoor and short-range outdoor practice. It is now standard for guard purposes where long-range, high-velocity loads are neither necessary nor desirable. It may be identified by its shorter length (2.95 inches overall) and the short, round-nose, lead bullet.

RIFLE GRENADE, CAL. .30, M3—This specialized cartridge is used in caliber .30 rifles of all types for firing rifle grenades from the Grenade Launchers, M1, M2, and M7. It is not used in machine guns. It may be identified by the five-petal rose crimp of the nose of the case.

The case is base-loaded with 5 grains of FFFG black powder for rapid ignition, then with 45 grains of a progressive-burning IMR powder.

BLANK, CAL. .30, M1909—This round is a standard item of issue for use in all caliber .30 rifles during maneuvers, for signaling, and for firing salutes. By means of a blank-firing adapter it may be used for training purposes in machine guns and automatic rifles. The round may be identified by the absence of a bullet and a cannelure in the neck of the case against which the cardboard wad is seated and sealed with a drop of shellac. Blank rounds may be distinguished from rifle grenade cartridges by a roll crimp at the neck of the case. The rifle grenade cartridge case is closed with a rose crimp.

The complete assembly of the blank round weighs approximately 207 grains. Second-grade cases may be used in the assembly of blank ammunition.

DUMMY, CAL. .30, M2—This dummy cartridge was standardized by Ordnance Committee action 23 March 1944 (OCM 23258). It replaces the Cartridge, Dummy, Cal. .30, M1906,

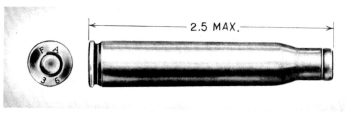

RIFLE GRENADE, CAL. .30, M3

2.5 MAX.

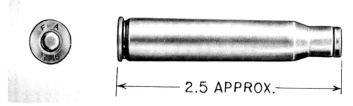

BLANK, CAL. .30, M1909

2.5 APPROX.

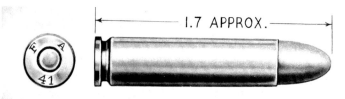

CARBINE, BALL, CAL. .30, M1

1.7 APPROX.

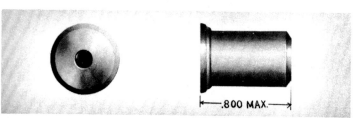

GRENADE, AUXILIARY, M7

.800 MAX.

for use in training personnel in loading weapons and in simulated fire. The longitudinal corrugations which identified the M1906 cartridge prevented proper fit in belts and magazines and caused failures to feed. Manufacture of cases with longitudinal corrugations was discontinued and the new dummy round, Cal. .30, M2, is identified by two holes drilled through the case, which may be of either steel or brass. Cartridge, Dummy, Cal. .30, M1906, was reclassified as Limited Standard.

HIGH-PRESSURE TEST, M1—This cartridge is used for proof-firing rifles, automatic rifles, and machine guns and is loaded with a powder charge sufficient to develop breech pressure of approximately 68,000 pounds. Due to the danger involved in such pressures, weapons under test are fired from a fixed rest under a hood and the trigger is released mechanically. Only authorized personnel are permitted to fire this cartridge and great care is taken with its issue to prevent it becoming mixed with service ammunition. The cartons in which the cartridges are packed are labeled with a description of the round and the word "Dangerous." Individual cartridges are identified by the tinned brass case, the color of which is different from that of any service round.

SUBCALIBER, CAL. .30, M1925—This is a Limited Standard item and is issued only for firing from the subcaliber tube in the 3-inch (15 pounder) Guns, M1902 and M1903. It differs from all other caliber .30 cartridges in that it uses a rimmed case. The complete round weighs 385.5 grains.

CARBINE, BALL, CAL. .30, M1—This is the standard cartridge for use in the U. S. Carbines, Cal. .30, M1 and M1A3. It can be fired in no other caliber .30 weapon and is immediately identified by its small size (1.68 inches overall) and the straight case. It is manufactured as Ball, M1; Tracer, M16; Grenade Cartridge, M6, for firing rifle grenades from Launcher, M8; as a Dummy, M13; and as a high-pressure test load developing a breech pressure of approximately 50,000 pounds. There is no blank cartridge for the Carbine, M1, nor are cartridges made with armor-piercing or incendiary bullets. The grenade cartridge is identified by the absence of a bullet and the rose crimp which closes the mouth of the case; dummy cartridges are identified by the usual holes in the case.

RANGE TABLE

Range (Yards)	Angle of Elevation (Mils)	Time of Flight (Seconds)	Angle of Fall (Mils)
100	1.5	0.17	1.7
200	3.5	0.38	4.8
300	6.2	0.64	9.4
400	9.7	0.94	15.6
500	14.0	1.28	23.5

GRENADE, AUXILIARY, M7—This special-purpose round was developed as a booster to obtain increased ranges and higher velocities with rifle grenades and ground signals fired from grenade launchers mounted on U. S. rifles and carbines. The name "vitamin pill" was given the cartridge during its development and has clung to it since it has been made an item of standard issue.

Actually, the cartridge is a tube of drawn brass 0.45 inch in diameter and resembling in every way a caliber .45 blank cartridge, rimmed. There is a no primer but a hole is drilled through the center of the base. Both that hole and the mouth of the case are sealed by paper wads against the escape of the 20 grains of powder with which the cartridge is loaded.

The cartridge is inserted in the muzzle of the grenade launcher and retained there by the rimmed base. The flame of the regular grenade cartridge fired in the chamber of the rifle burns through the paper wad sealing the mouth of the case and ignites the auxiliary charge. The effect is that of a booster and the grenade is launched at greater speed and attains a range of from 100 to 150 yards above that to be expected when the grenade cartridge is used alone. The fired auxiliary cartridge is expelled from the launcher with the grenade.

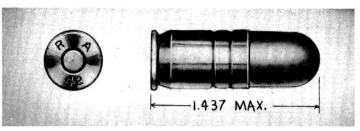

SHOT, CAL. .45, M12

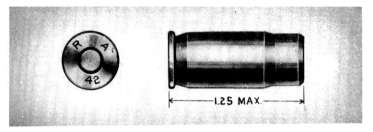

SHOT, CAL. .45, M15

CALIBER .45 CARTRIDGES

BALL, CAL. .45, M1911—This cartridge is standard for the Pistol, M1911A1, the Colt and Smith & Wesson Revolvers, M1917 (Limited Standard), and the Submachine Gun, Cal. .45, M3. Substitute and Limited Standard submachine guns are also chambered for this cartridge. When fired in the M1917 revolvers the cartridges must first be loaded in lunate clips holding three rounds.

The round is made as a Dummy, M1921, for training personnel in loading pistols and submachine guns. The dummy cartridge uses a steel case and may be distinguished by the absence of a primer and by three ⅛-inch holes drilled equidistantly about the case.

Cartridge, Blank, Cal. .45, M1, is issued only for use in training cavalry horses and for saluting purposes in the M1917 revolvers. It is made with a rimmed case to permit its use without clips in the revolvers. There is no bullet and the mouth of the case is taper-crimped for 5⁄16 inch. The rim prevents the use of the caliber .45 blank cartridge in either pistols or submachine guns. A rimless caliber .45 blank cartridge which may be used in those weapons was standardized 11 November 1943. It is designated Cartridge, Blank, Cal. .45, M9 (Rimless).

RANGE TABLE

Range (Yards)	Time of Flight (Seconds)	Drop (Inches)
10	0.037	0.3
20	0.075	1.1
30	0.113	2.4
40	0.151	4.4
60	0.229	9.9
80	0.308	18.0
100	0.388	28.0

HIGH-PRESSURE TEST, CAL. .45, M1—This special cartridge is loaded for testing caliber .45 weapons at arsenals or at their places of manufacture. Its excessive powder charge develops a breech pressure of approximately 20,000 pounds, 4,000 pounds above normal pressure. The high-pressure test cartridge is fired by mechanical means with the weapon in a fixed rest and shielded. Only authorized personnel are permitted to conduct such tests. The high-pressure test cartridge may be identified by the tinned case.

SHOT, CAL. .45, M12, M15—This round was developed as an article of issue to Air Corps personnel and others who might be compelled to land upon uninhabited islands or in jungle areas where survival might depend upon small birds and animals shot "for the pot." The bullet is replaced by a capsule of wax-impregnated paper, red in color, which contains approximately 118 pellets of size 7½ shot. Reports from using arms indicated that difficulty had been experienced with swelling of the paper-capsule M12 cartridge in excessively humid areas and that the shot patterns produced by that cartridge were not

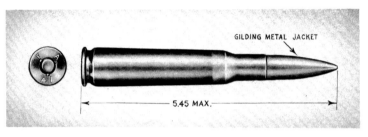

BALL, CAL. .50, M2

consistent. Cartridge, Shot, Cal. .45, M15, was developed to overcome those difficulties. It is a straight brass case, closed by a top wad, and containing both the powder charge and the shot. It is similar in construction and appearance to a brass shotgun shell. The M15 cartridge was standardized 30 December 1943.

CALIBER .50 CARTRIDGES

BALL, CAL. .50, M2—The standard service cartridge for all types of the caliber .50 machine gun, used in all theaters of operation by land, sea, and air forces. The round is also issued as Tracer, M1 (red-tipped bullet); as Armor-piercing, M2 (black tip); and as Incendiary, M1, identified by a light-blue tip on the bullet. A bullet combining the armor-piercing and incendiary characteristics is in process of development.

The mouth of the case of the caliber .50 round is crimped into a cannelure machined on the bullet. A minimum pull of 100 pounds is required to remove the bullet from the case.

The Tracer Bullet, M1, is not boattailed, the base of the projectile being open to permit ignition of the tracer compound. The trace, bright red in color, begins at a point not more than 250 feet from the muzzle and continues for approximately 1,600 yards.

DUMMY, CAL. .50, M2, is used for training personnel in loading and unloading machine guns and ammunition belts. The round may also be used for testing extraction and ejection and other mechanical features of the gun. It is identified by the absence of a primer and by three holes drilled equidistantly about the case at its midpoint. Both brass and steel cases are used in assembling dummy rounds.

SMALL ARMS AMMUNITION (Continued)

HIGH-PRESSURE TEST, CAL. .50, M1—This cartridge is overloaded with a charge of IMR powder sufficient to develop a breech pressure of 62,500 pounds for any ten consecutive shots. Guns under test are fired mechanically from a fixed rest and from under a hood.

The high-pressure round, caliber .50, is identified by the tinned case.

RANGE TABLE

Range (Yards)	Angle of Elevation (Mils)	Time of Flight (Seconds)	Maximum Ordinate (Inches)	Angle of Fall (Mils)
200	1.2	0.22	3.6	1.4
400	2.7	0.46	10.8	3.3
600	4.3	0.72	25.2	5.2
800	6.1	1.00	50.4	7.4
1,000	8.2	1.32	86.4	10.5
1,200	10.7	1.69	131.4	15.4
1,400	13.7	2.10	216.0	22.0
1,600	17.3	2.56	311.4	30.5
1,800	21.5	3.07	457.2	40.6
2,000	26.3	3.61	630.0	52.3

CALIBER .22 CARTRIDGES

BALL, CAL. .22, LONG RIFLE—This cartridge superseded the caliber .30 Gallery Practice Cartridge, M1919. It is used in the caliber .22 U. S. Rifles, M1922, M1922A1, and M2; in caliber .22 Machine Gun Trainers, M3 and M4, and in pistols and revolvers for gallery practice and training purposes. It is not manufactured by the Ordnance Department but is purchased from commercial makers.

This cartridge is the only rimfire round used by the armed forces. The cartridge case is of steel, brass, copper, or gilding metal and the ignition charge is spun into a circular recess inside the rim instead of being seated in the head of the case as a separate component. A blow from the firing pin on any point of the rim explodes the priming composition and ignites the propelling charge. Caliber .22 long rifle ammunition as purchased is manufactured with a noncorrosive, nonmercuric primer compound.

Characteristics of various makes of caliber .22 ammunition vary slightly. The powder charge is approximately 1.7 grains and the weight of the lead bullet is approximately 40 grains. Caliber .22 rifles and ammunition are notoriously "temperamental" and the rifle which gives only a fair performance with ammunition of one make may produce excellent targets when fired with cartridges of another manufacturer or even of another lot.

Containers of caliber .22 ammunition are marked by the manufacturer with the lot number and such trade names as "Kleanbore," "Lubaloy," "Tackhole," etc. This practice provides a means of identifying and reporting any ammunition which may become defective.

Caliber .22 long rifle cartridges of different manufacturers show slight variations in velocity and pressure. The average muzzle velocity is 1,100 feet per second and the chamber pressure averages 16,000 pounds. The maximum range is approximately 1,500 yards with the muzzle elevated at an angle of 30°.

Neither dummy nor high-pressure test cartridges are purchased or manufactured by the Ordnance Department in caliber .22 long rifle. A blank cartridge, designated Cartridge, Field Artillery Trainer, M2, is issued to field artillery units as the propellant for a 1-inch diameter steel ball, hardened, ground, and polished, which serves as the projectile in the Field Artillery Trainer, M2 and M2A1. The ball weighs 1,024 grains and is propelled at an estimated velocity of 100 feet per second.

SHOTGUN SHELLS

SHELL, SHOTGUN, 12 GAGE—Shotgun shells are purchased by the Ordnance Department from commercial manufacturers for use in sporting and riot type shotguns, issued for guard and combat use and for hunting and trap or skeet shooting. The purpose for which the shell is intended may be determined by inspection of the top wad which is marked with the size shot loaded in the shell. Shells for guard or combat use are loaded with 26 grains of a dense smokeless powder and 1¼ ounces of No. 00 shot—"buckshot." Shells for trap shooting or sporting use have a lighter load of 3 drams of bulk smokeless powder and 1¼ ounces No. 8 chilled shot. Shells loaded with No. 6 shot are issued as a hunting load.

The cases of shotgun shells are customarily of wax-impregnated paper. Brass shells may be issued for use in the excessive moisture of the tropics.

Primer, make of powder used in the charge, and other characteristics of shotgun shells are as supplied by the manufacturer.

CHARACTERISTICS

(External ballistics, as here shown, are approximate figures only. Muzzle velocity of the cal. .30, Ball, M2, when fired from a rifle will differ from that obtained from the same cartridge fired from a machine gun. The performance of the cal. .45 ball cartridge fired in the Pistol, M1911A1, is not identical with that of the cartridge fired in the Submachine Gun, M3.)

	Weight, Round (Grs.)	Weight, Bullet (Grs.)	Weight, Powder (Grs. approx.)	Length, Round (Inches)	Length, Bullet (Inches)	Muzzle Velocity (Ft. per sec.)	Muzzle Energy (Ft.-lb.)	Pressure (Lb.) (Copper)	Maximum Range (Yds.)
.30 Ball, M2	396	152	50	3.34	1.125	2,805	2,429	50,000	3,500
.30 A-P, M2	414	162	51	3.34	1.39	2,775	2,780	50,000	3,500
.30 Tracer, M1	396	152.5	50	3.34	1.45	2,750	2,775	50,000	3,450
.30 Incend., M1	386	140	54	3.32	1.41	3,050	2,700	52,000	5,500
.30 Guard, M1	346	142	10.5	2.95	0.82	1,200	376	15,000	2,500
.30 Carbine, M1	193	110	14	1.68	0.69	1,975	775	41,000	2,000
.45 Ball, M1911	327	234	6	1.28	0.68	825	383	14,000	1,700
.50 Ball, M2	1,830	711.5	250	5.45	2.29	2,935	10,765	52,000	7,200
.50 Tracer, M1	1,789	681	220	5.45	2.40	2,865	10,400	52,000	6,000
.50 A.P., M1	1,837	718	250	5.45	2.31	2,985	10,700	52,000	7,200
.22 l.r., ball	53	40	1.7	.984	0.46	1,100	102	16,000	1,500

HELMETS M1, M3, M4—STANDARD

HELMET, M1

HELMET, M1, is a standard article of issue for the use of ground troops in all branches of the service. It was designed as an improvement on the M1917A1 helmet, now Limited Standard. Changes in design were to provide maximum protection with no increase in weight or interference with vision or hearing. The M1 helmet is shaped to stay on the head while the wearer is running, and the narrower brim does not interfere with aiming or firing.

Two linings are provided; one to protect the wearer from heat in tropical operations, the other as a protection against extreme cold.

All U. S. helmets are non-magnetic, an important feature when worn by men whose duties require the use of compasses or other instruments which might be affected by magnetism.

HELMET, M3—The M3 helmet was designed for use in air operations and is satisfactory equipment for the majority of crew members of combat aircraft. It is made on the same draw dies used in the manufacture of the M1 helmet but is equipped with hinged earflaps to permit its use with the earphones of aircraft intercommunication systems.

Since it fits directly over the leather flying helmet, the M3 is not provided with a liner.

HELMET, M4, is a series of laminated steel plates shaped to fit the head and covered by leather and fabric. The original design was battle-tested by members of the Eighth Air Force and was submitted by that organization. It is for the use of turret gunners and other crew members who operate in quarters so cramped that use of the M3 helmet would be impracticable if not impossible. The M4 helmet has no liner and fits snugly over the leather flying helmet.

HELMET, M3

HELMET, M4

BODY ARMOR—STANDARD

VESTS, FLYER'S, M1 AND M2—APRONS, FLYER'S, M3 AND M4—ARMOR, GROIN, M5—STANDARD

FLYER'S VEST, M1

FLYER'S VEST, M2

An urgent request for body armor for pilots and crews of aircraft was received 6 July 1943. Within thirty days 3,960 armored vests and 3,320 armored aprons had been delivered for overseas shipment. More than 20,000 additional units were shipped within the five weeks following.

The five items listed are basically similar, being composed of overlapping steel plates, flat or curved, in pockets of elastic webbing which are covered with a backing of nylon duck. Tests proved this material superior in shock-resistant qualities to rayon, linen, or cotton duck. Corduroy and a light cotton duck are used for the back and front facings.

Since any additional weight greatly increases the shock of landing from a parachute jump, all armor is designed so that it may be thrown aside without loss of time in case a parachute escape from a disabled plane should be necessary.

ARMOR, FLYER'S VEST, M1—Both front and back of this garment are fully armored and afford a maximum of protection to the wearer's chest and upper dorsal region. Front and back are joined together by snap fasteners over the shoulders and by a belt about the waist. Greater flexibility is obtained by the use of an elastic shock cord securing the lower edge of the armored back.

ARMOR, FLYER'S VEST, M2—This garment is similar to the M1 vest but is shorter and is designed to protect only the upper chest. The back is unarmored. The M2 vest is intended for wear by pilots and others whose station is in a seat which in itself gives protection to the back.

ARMOR, FLYER'S APRONS, M3 AND M4—These aprons are attached to the M1 and M2 vests as a protection to the wearer's abdomen. The M4 tapered apron protects a somewhat smaller area than the rectangular M3 apron and is worn where greater freedom of movement is required. Both aprons are of curved plates of manganese steel in a backing of nylon duck.

ARMOR, GROIN, M5—This item consists of three units, hinged one to another, and each composed of overlapping plates shaped so as to afford maximum protection to the wearer's abdomen, inguinal areas, and thighs. It attaches to the vests and replaces the aprons.

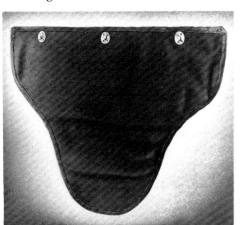

FLYER'S APRON, M4

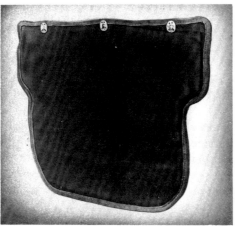

FLYER'S APRON, M3

ARMOR AS WORN

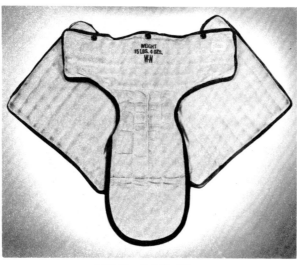

ARMOR, GROIN, M5

BAYONET M1—SCABBARD, BAYONET, M7—STANDARD

This offensive and defensive weapon has replaced the M1905 bayonet on all U. S. Army rifles and incorporates various improvements which experience with the older model had shown to be desirable. The new bayonet is shorter, better balanced, and may be used if necessary as a trench knife in hand-to-hand combat. It measures 14.4 inches long overall, has a ten-inch blade, and weighs 13.5 ounces.

A bayonet is now being developed for the Carbine, M1.

SCABBARD, BAYONET, M7, has replaced the M3 scabbard issued with the M1905 bayonet. It is made of plastic, is 11.2 inches long, and weighs 5 ounces.

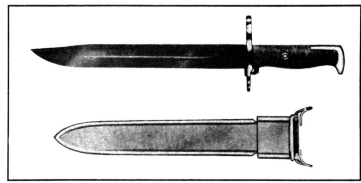

BAYONET, M1, AND SCABBARD, BAYONET, M7

KNIFE, TRENCH, M3—SCABBARD, TRENCH KNIFE, M8—STANDARD

The Trench Knife, M3, has been developed to fill the need in modern warfare for an efficient weapon for hand-to-hand fighting. While designated for issue to soldiers not armed with the bayonet, it was especially designed for such shock units as parachute troops and rangers.

The shaped and corrugated handle is of leather washers under compression. One cutting edge runs the full length of the blade; the other edge of the blade is ground to a cutting edge for 2¾ inches from the point, then tapers to a thicker section for rigidity and strength.

The knife weighs 9 ounces and measures 11.7 inches overall. The blade is 6.7 inches long.

Experiments are being conducted with modifications of the trench knife which would permit its use as a bayonet for the Carbine, M1.

SCABBARD, TRENCH KNIFE, M8, is made of plastic and replaces the leather scabbard, M6, formerly issued as a sheath for this weapon. The plastic is reinforced with metal about the

TRENCH KNIFE, M3, AND SCABBARD, M8

tip of the blade to protect the wearer from injury in event of a fall or other accident. The scabbard weighs approximately 4 ounces and is 14 inches long overall.

SABER, OFFICER'S, M1907—SCABBARD, SABER, OFFICER'S, M1907—STANDARD

The saber and its scabbard are maintained as standard items of officer's equipment but their use and issue have been discontinued for the period of the war. The saber is procured and stored by the Ordnance Department but is issued by the Quartermaster Corps.

The M1907 saber is furnished in three blade-lengths, 30, 32, and 34 inches; the overall lengths being 35½, 37½ and 39½ inches. The grip is of hard rubber and is 5½ inches long. The weight of the saber with 30 inch blade is 1.3 pounds.

The Scabbard, M1907, is issued in three lengths corresponding to those of the saber. It is of metal construction throughout and weighs 12 ounces in 30-inch length.

SABER, OFFICER'S, M1907

SCABBARD, SABER, OFFICER'S, M1907

HOLSTERS, PISTOL, CAL. .45, M1916, M7—STANDARD

HOLSTER, PISTOL, CAL. .45, M1916—
This item is the standard belt holster for the caliber .45 pistol, M1911A1. It is made of heavy grain leather and fitted with metal hooks for mounting on standard web belts. Slots in the leather below the metal hook permit the insertion of a belt not fitted with eyelets.

The holster is closed by a flap which buttons over a bronze stud. An eyelet in the bottom permits the insertion of a thong for tying the lower end of the holster to the leg.

HOLSTER, PISTOL, CAL. .45, M7—
Under many conditions a pistol can be carried more advantageously in a holster slung from the shoulder than in the more conventional belt holster. Mounted men, drivers and crews of motor-driven vehicles, airplane crew members who carry the pistol as a defense weapon in the event of a forced landing, infantrymen who are called upon to ford streams, paratroops and ranger units—all these find a shoulder holster superior to one worn on the belt.

The present shoulder holster, M7, embodies certain modifications and im-

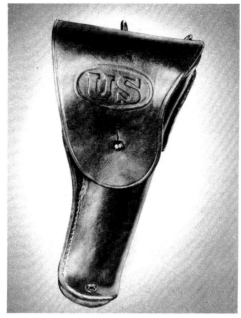

HOLSTER, PISTOL, CAL. .45, M1916

SHOULDER HOLSTER, CAL. .45, M7

provements upon the M3 holster. The shoulder strap fastens with a ring and snap and may be removed more quickly than the buckle fastening used on the M3 holster. Supplementary adjustments in the strap are made by a thong hitch instead of a buckle, a method which insures a smooth surface between the wearer and the back of a chair or seat. If desired, the shoulder straps may be removed and the holster worn upon a waist belt.

The M7 holster was standardized by O.C.M. 21938, 28 Oct. 1943.

AMMUNITION BOXES—CAL. .30, M1, AND CAL. .50, M2—STANDARD

These sheet-steel containers have completely replaced the wooden boxes formerly used for small arms ammunition. They are fire-resistant, virtually moisture-proof, and since no wood is used in their construction will never be attacked by termites—a constant menace to wooden boxes in storage. Low manufacturing cost permits their being classified as expendable items yet if transportation to supply centers is available they may be refilled over and over again.

The hinged lids seal tightly but may be completely removed if necessary; hasps permit either box to be hung on the brackets of .30 caliber and .50 caliber machine gun mounts; the carrying handles fold into recesses flush with the lids and the boxes may be packed solidly one on top of another.

Illustrated herewith is Box, Ammunition, Cal. .30, M1. It weighs empty 3.5 lb.—one-half the weight of a wooden container of the same size—and is $10\frac{3}{16}$ ins. long, $3\frac{3}{4}$ ins. wide, and $7\frac{7}{32}$ ins. high. It will contain one M1917 ammunition belt loaded with 250 rounds of cal. .30 ammunition.

The caliber .50 box, M2, is similar in shape but of heavier construction. It weighs 4.4 lb. empty, is $12\frac{1}{4}$ ins. long, $6\frac{1}{4}$ ins. wide, and $7\frac{1}{2}$ ins. high. Its capacity is one 110-round fabric belt, M7, or 105 rounds of linked cal. .50 ammunition.

AMMUNITION BOX, CAL. .30, M1

HAND CARTS M3A4, M4A1, M5A1—STANDARD

HAND CART, M3A4, WITHOUT FITTINGS

HAND CART, M4A1, WITH CAL. .30
MACHINE GUN ON MOUNT

All three of these carts are built upon the same basic design with superstructure varied to suit different purposes. Cart, M3A4, has a plain crate-type body. Cart, M4A1, has three clamp-type brackets to receive the legs of a tripod mount. Cart, M4A1, is adapted for transportation of a Browning Machine Gun, cal. .30, M1917, on Mount, Tripod, M1917A1, the mount being fastened to the cart by means of the brackets. Straps are provided to hold ammunition chests in place.

Cart, M5A1, has brackets to secure the Browning machine gun, cal. .50, M2, HB, flexible, and the machine gun tripod mount, cal. .50, M3, during transit. The brackets are equipped with quick-release clamps to facilitate speedy unloading of the hand carts. With the exception of the tires, all parts of these carts are of aluminum alloy, instead of the steel formerly used in the construction of these vehicles. Tires are of the pneumatic type, 4.00 x 12, 2 ply, high-speed balloon, and are operated at 24 pounds pressure. The overall length of cart and handle is 69.5 inches; width overall, 39.1 inches; height, 19.8 inches; wheel tread, center to center, 32.5 inches; road clearance, 12 inches.

Cart, M3A4, stripped, weighs 74 pounds. The canvas cover of the cart weighs 6 pounds. With brackets for receiving the machine gun mount, Cart, M4A1, weighs 87.5 pounds. The cal. .30, M1917A1, mount, weighs 30 pounds, and the machine gun, cal. .30, M1917, 32.5 pounds. The gun cradle and pintle weigh 21 pounds.

The remainder of the load comprises five ammunition chests, a water chest, and a spare parts chest. Weight of cover for this assembly is 7.5 pounds.

These carts can be drawn by hand-power and, in addition, are equipped with a lunette for limbering to a motorized or animal-drawn vehicle. When pulled by manpower, a drawbar is secured to the lunette with the hand cart drawbar retaining pin. When not in use, the drawbar is carried on the drawbar bracket which is riveted to the front of the body. Provision is made for attaching two ropes on the cart body when additional manpower is required to pull the load. The pneumatic tires enable the device to be towed at high speeds behind trucks or other motor vehicles. The carts are so designed that two loaded carts can be transported on trucks, placed between the seats provided for personnel.

HAND CART, M4A1, WITH BRACKETS FOR RECEIVING MOUNT

4
AMMUNITION

20mm Ammunition, 261
37mm Ammunition, 263
40mm Ammunition, 269
57mm Ammunition, 271
60mm Ammunition, 273
75mm Ammunition, 275
3 inch Ammunition, 281
81mm Ammunition, 289
90mm Ammunition, 291
105mm Ammunition, 293
4.5 inch Ammunition, 298
120mm Ammunition, 299
6 inch Ammunition, 300
155mm Ammunition, 302
8 inch Ammunition, 315
240mm Ammunition, 320
12 inch Ammunition, 322
16 inch Ammunition, 324
Hand and Rifle Grenades, 326
Mines, 330
Sub Caliber and Practice Ammunition, 336
Artillery Fuzes. 338
Bomb Fuzes, 354
Rockets, 370
Rocket Launchers, 379

SHELL, HIGH-EXPLOSIVE INCENDIARY, 20 MM, MK. I—STANDARD

ROUND FOR GUNS M1, AN-M2, AND BRITISH HISPANO-SUIZA /A/

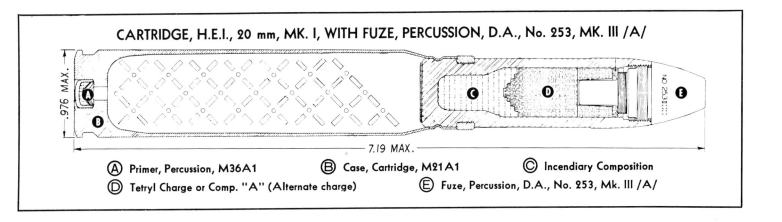

CARTRIDGE, H.E.I., 20 mm, MK. I, WITH FUZE, PERCUSSION, D.A., No. 253, MK. III /A/

.976 MAX.

7.19 MAX.

(A) Primer, Percussion, M36A1 (B) Case, Cartridge, M21A1 (C) Incendiary Composition

(D) Tetryl Charge or Comp. "A" (Alternate charge) (E) Fuze, Percussion, D.A., No. 253, Mk. III /A/

SHELL, HIGH-EXPLOSIVE INCENDI-ARY, 20 mm, Mk. I—STANDARD—This shell for the 20 mm automatic guns, M1, AN-M2, and British Hispano-Suiza /A/, was adopted from the British early in 1941 and standardized in August of that year. There have been few changes except in the redesign of the cartridge case and primer.

The fuzed projectile remains essentially the same, as may be recognized from the adopted British nomenclature, Fuze, Percussion, D.A., No. 253, Mk. III /A/, which signifies that the shell is used for aircraft and has a delay action percussion fuze. The shell is designed for fire from aircraft guns against enemy aircraft, but it may be used against ground targets.

The complete round weighs 0.566 pound and consists of a cartridge case, M21A1, weighing 0.205 pound, and measuring 4.34 inches in length; a percussion primer, M36A1, weighing 0.003 pound, a propelling charge of Improved Military Rifle Powder weighing 0.072 pound, and the loaded and fuzed shell. The cartridge case is crimped to the fuzed and loaded projectile. A substitute standard for the cartridge case, M21A1, is the steel cartridge case, M21A1B1.

The projectile is of the high-explosive incendiary type. As fired, it weighs 0.286 pound and measures 3.23 inches in length by 0.784 inch in diameter. The bursting charge weighs 174.25 grains; 107.75 grains are tetryl and the remaining 66.5 grains

are incendiary composition. The alternate bursting charge consists of 100.3 grains of composition A and 66.5 grains of incendiary composition.

The propelling charge is an IMR powder formula of single-perforation grains with a web of 0.021 inch.

The standard muzzle velocity with this propelling charge is 2,800 feet per second.

A cover is fixed to the base of the shell by a continuous resistance weld, and serves as a seal to prevent gas or flasl from the propelling charge from entering the shell and prematurely detonating the bursting charge. This may happen as the shell is not forged or cast, but is turned from steel bar stock which may have fissures in its center.

CHARACTERISTICS

Caliber. . . . . 20 mm	Propelling Charge and Weight. . . . . .IMR powder, 0.072 lb.
Model of Gun. . . . . ‡	Complete Round Weight. . . . . .0.566 lb.
Proj. Weight. . . . . .0.286 lb.	Muzzle Velocity. . . . . .2,800 f/s
Proj. Charge and Weight. . . . . .174.25 gr.*	Maximum Range. . . . . .5,100 yards
Fuze. . . . . .Percussion, D.A., No. 253, Mk. III /A/	Chamber Capacity. . . . . .2.22 cu. ins.
Primer. M36A1	Rated Max. Pressure p.s.i.. 48,000
Cartridge Case. .M21A1†	

*107.75 grains of tetryl, 66.5 grains of incendiary composition. (Alternate loading: 100.3 grains of Composition "A" and 66.5 grains of incendiary composition.)
†The steel cartridge case, M21A1B1, is substitute standard.
‡M1, AN-M2 and British Hispano-Suiza /A/.

SHOT, ARMOR-PIERCING, 20 MM, *M75*—STANDARD
PROJECTILE, BALL (PRACTICE), 20 MM—STANDARD

ROUNDS FOR GUNS, M1, AN-M2, AND BRITISH HISPANO-SUIZA /A/

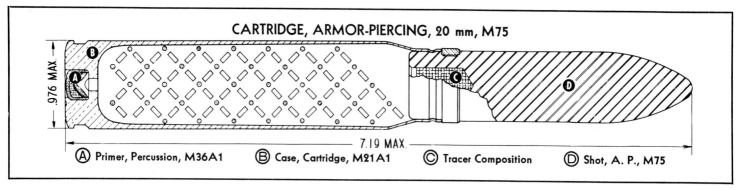

CARTRIDGE, ARMOR-PIERCING, 20 mm, M75

.976 MAX.   7.19 MAX.

Ⓐ Primer, Percussion, M36A1   Ⓑ Case, Cartridge, M21A1   Ⓒ Tracer Composition   Ⓓ Shot, A. P., M75

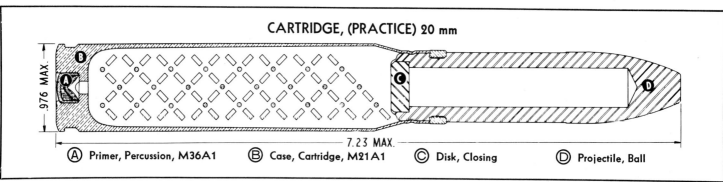

CARTRIDGE, (PRACTICE) 20 mm

.976 MAX.   7.23 MAX.

Ⓐ Primer, Percussion, M36A1   Ⓑ Case, Cartridge, M21A1   Ⓒ Disk, Closing   Ⓓ Projectile, Ball

The armor-piercing, shot, M75, and ball projectile (practice) are standard ammunition and are turned out of steel bar stock instead of being forged or cast. The propelling charges used with these cartridges are made from IMR powder of single-perforated grains with a 0.021 inch web.

SHOT, ARMOR-PIERCING, 20 mm, M75—STANDARD—The complete round weighs 0.64 pound and measures 7.19 inches in length and consists of the M21A1

cartridge case, a 480 grain IMR powder propelling charge, and the armor-piercing shot, M75. The steel cartridge case, M21A1B1, is substitute standard for the brass cartridge case, M21A1.

The M36A1 percussion primer weighs 0.003 pound and the cartridge case into which it is inserted weighs 0.205 pound. The M75 shot has no fuze or bursting charge, but contains a tracer composition which is ignited by the propelling charge and burns for 4 seconds. The body

of this shot weighs 0.363 pound and is of monobloc construction.

PROJECTILE, BALL (PRACTICE), 20 mm,—STANDARD—This ball projectile has the same percussion primer, M36A1, and the same cartridge case, M21A1, as the A. P. Shot, M75. The steel cartridge case, M21A1B1, is substitute standard. Weight of the complete round is 0.556 pound. The ball projectile weighs 0.276 pound and is propelled by 507 grains of IMR powder. The projectile is hollow and is sealed at the base by a closing disk.

CHARACTERISTICS

	Shot, A.P., M75	Proj. Ball (Prac.)		Shot, A.P., M75	Proj. Ball (Prac.)
Caliber	20 mm	20 mm	Maximum Range	6,300 yards	5,300 yards
Model	British Hispano-Suiza /A/	British Hispano-Suiza /A/	Chamber Capacity	2.22 cu. ins.	2.20 cu. ins.
Proj. Weight	0.363 lb.	0.276 lb.	Rated Max. Pressure, p.s.i.	48,000	48,000
Primer	M36A1	M36A1	Armor Penetration at 20°		
Cartridge Case	M21A1*	M21A1*	Homogeneous Plate		
Propelling Charge and Weight	IMR powder, 480 grs.	IMR powder, 507 grs.	500 yards	0.7 ins.	——
Complete Round Weight	0.64 lb.	0.556 lb.	1,000 yards	0.5 ins.	——
Muzzle Velocity	2,550 f/s	2,850 f/s	Face-Hard. Plate		
			500 yards	0.65 ins.	——
			1,000 yards	0.4 ins.	——

*The steel cartridge case, M21A1B1, is substitute standard.

SHELL, HIGH-EXPLOSIVE, 37 MM, M54—STANDARD
SHOT, ARMOR-PIERCING, 37 MM, M80—STANDARD
SHELL, PRACTICE, 37 MM, M55A1—STANDARD
ROUNDS FOR 37 mm AUTOMATIC GUN, M4 (AIRCRAFT)

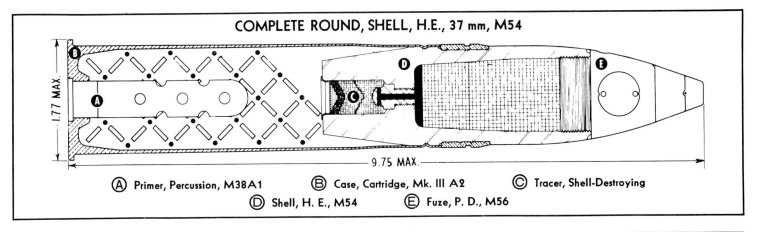

COMPLETE ROUND, SHELL, H.E., 37 mm, M54

1.77 MAX.   9.75 MAX.

(A) Primer, Percussion, M38A1   (B) Case, Cartridge, Mk. III A2   (C) Tracer, Shell-Destroying
(D) Shell, H. E., M54   (E) Fuze, P. D., M56

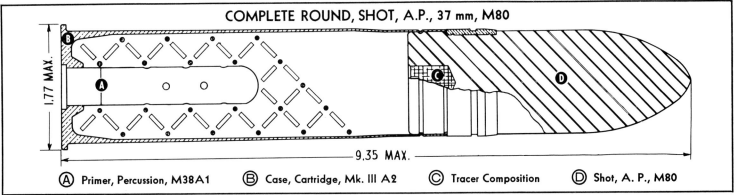

COMPLETE ROUND, SHOT, A.P., 37 mm, M80

1.77 MAX.   9.35 MAX.

(A) Primer, Percussion, M38A1   (B) Case, Cartridge, Mk. III A2   (C) Tracer Composition   (D) Shot, A. P., M80

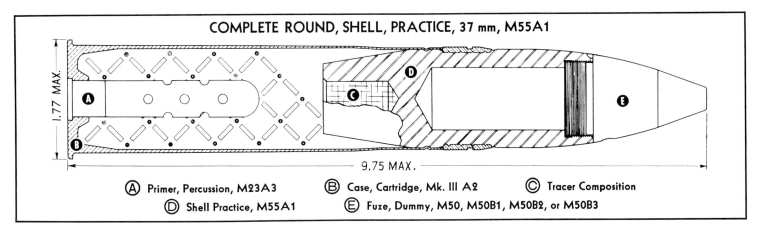

COMPLETE ROUND, SHELL, PRACTICE, 37 mm, M55A1

1.77 MAX.   9.75 MAX.

(A) Primer, Percussion, M23A3   (B) Case, Cartridge, Mk. III A2   (C) Tracer Composition
(D) Shell Practice, M55A1   (E) Fuze, Dummy, M50, M50B1, M50B2, or M50B3

The rapid strides in aircraft protection made it necessary to develop an aircraft weapon that would fire projectiles with greater explosive and armor-piercing qualities than smaller caliber weapons. As a result, the 37 mm automatic gun, M4, was developed and standardized for aircraft use.

The 37 mm automatic gun, M4, uses the same high-explosive (M54) and practice (M55A1) projectiles as the 37 mm antiaircraft gun, M1A2, but different cartridge cases are necessary due to the larger chamber of the M4 gun.

However, the over-all length of the armor-piercing projectiles, M51 and M74, which are used in the M3A1, M5A1, and M6 tank and antitank guns, was too great to permit their use in the M4 gun and the 37 mm armor-piercing shot, M80, was developed and standardized.

SHELL, H.E., 37 mm, M54—STANDARD

—This shell uses the point detonating fuze, M56. The complete round weighs 1.99 pounds; as fired, the projectile weighs 1.34 pounds. The 0.16 pound charge of M2 powder is a Hercules NG formula of single perforated grains with 0.030 inch web and gives the projectile the prescribed muzzle velocity of 2,000 feet per second.

The M54 features the shell-destroying tracer in addition to the point-detonating

(Continued on next page)

SHELL, HIGH-EXPLOSIVE, 37 MM, M54
SHOT, ARMOR-PIERCING, 37 MM, M80
SHELL, PRACTICE, 37 MM, M55A1
(Continued)

fuze. The tracer, which has a burning time of three seconds, sets off an igniting relay charge of 1.68 grains of Grade A-5 Army Black Powder which ignites a relay pellet to detonate the charge and destroy the shell before ground impact.

The bursting charge of tetryl weighs 0.10 pound, and the alternate Composition "A" charge 0.105 pound. The tetryl loading consists of a 200 grain tetryl pellet pressed into the shell cavity under 9,000 to 10,000 p.s.i. pressure and the remainder of the charge of two equal increments pressed under approximately 9,000 p.s.i. pressure. The Composition "A" bursting charge is loaded in the same manner as the tetryl charge, except that the relay pellet

with the Composition "A" weighs 36 grains as against 23 grains for the pellet used with the tetryl load.

SHOT, A.P., 37 mm, M80—STANDARD —The weight of the complete round is 2.31 pounds; the weight of the A.P. shot is 1.66 pounds. The propelling charge is 0.15 pound of M2 powder of a Hercules NG formula with a single-perforated grain and a 0.030 inch web. The shot is a monobloc projectile with a tracer element of three seconds burning time and has no fuze or bursting charge.

SHELL, PRACTICE, 37 mm, M55A1— STANDARD—This shell is the high-explosive shell, M54, modified slightly for prac-

tice purposes. It contains a red tracer and a dummy fuze, M50, M50B1, M50B2, or M50B3. The M50 dummy fuze is made from a plastic composition and the M50B1, M50B2, and M50B3 fuzes are made from low carbon steel machined to give the same contour and weight as the point-detonating fuze, M56, used with the M54 projectile.

As used in the automatic gun, M4, the complete round weighs 1.99 pounds, and as fired the shell weighs 1.34 pounds. The 0.16 pound charge of M2 powder is Hercules NG formula of single-perforated grains with a 0.030 inch web and gives the prescribed muzzle velocity of 2,000 feet per second.

CHARACTERISTICS

	Shell, H.E., M54	Shot, A.P., M80	Shell, Prac., M55A1
Caliber	37 mm	37 mm	37 mm
Model of Gun	M4	M4	M4
Proj. Weight	1.34 lb.	1.66 lb.	1.34 lb.
Proj. Charge and Weight	Tetryl, 0.10 lb.†	—	Empty
Fuze	P.D., M56	—	Dummy, M50, M50B1, M50B2, or M50B3
Primer	M38A1††	M38A1††	M38A1**
Cartridge Case	Mk. III A2	Mk. III A2	Mk. III A2
Propelling Charge and Weight	FNH powder, 0.16 lb.	FNH powder, 0.15 lb.	FNH powder, 0.16 lb.
Complete Round Weight	1.99 lb.*	2.31 lb.	1.99 lb.
Muzzle Velocity	2,000 f/s	1,825 f/s	2,000 f/s
Chamber Capacity	6.90 cu. ins.	8.34 cu. ins.	6.90 cu. ins.
Rated Max. Pressure, p.s.i.	27,000	27,000	27,000
Armor Penetration at 20°			
Homogeneous Plate			
500 yards	—	1.0 in.	—
1,000 yards	—	0.6 in.	—
Face-Hard. Plate			
500 yards	—	0.8 in.	—
1,000 yards	—	0.4 in.	—

†Composition "A" 0.105 lb.
††Or M38B2, substitute standard.
*1.985 lb. with Comp. "A" bursting charge.
**The M23A3 percussion primer is authorized for assembly to this round until present stocks are exhausted.

SHOT, ARMOR-PIERCING CAPPED, 37 MM, M51B1, M51B2—STANDARD

ROUND FOR ANTITANK GUN, M3A1; TANK GUNS, M5A1 AND M6

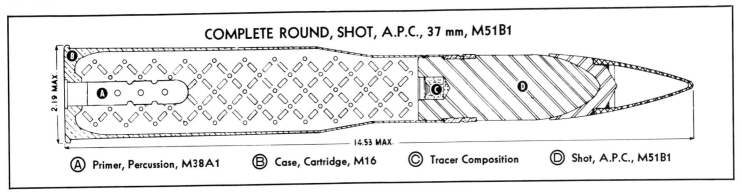

COMPLETE ROUND, SHOT, A.P.C., 37 mm, M51B1

Ⓐ Primer, Percussion, M38A1   Ⓑ Case, Cartridge, M16   Ⓒ Tracer Composition   Ⓓ Shot, A.P.C., M51B1

14.53 MAX.   2.19 MAX.

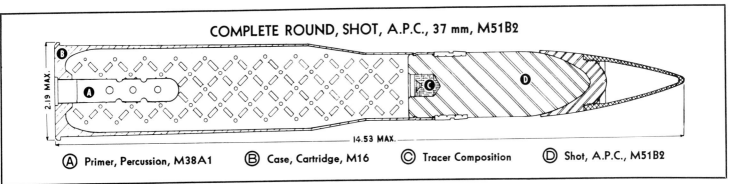

COMPLETE ROUND, SHOT, A.P.C., 37 mm, M51B2

Ⓐ Primer, Percussion, M38A1   Ⓑ Case, Cartridge, M16   Ⓒ Tracer Composition   Ⓓ Shot, A.P.C., M51B2

14.53 MAX.   2.19 MAX.

During World War I, slow-moving, lightly armored vehicles were extremely vulnerable to guns of 37 mm and 75 mm calibers. With increased mobility, speed, and armor protection of tanks and combat vehicles, these weapons became limited in use.

The mobile antitank guns were developed to meet the new conditions. The standardization of the mobile 37 mm antitank gun, M3A1, together with the tank guns, M5A1 and M6, with their higher muzzle velocities, compensated for the added protection which the increased mobility and thicker armor plate gave tanks and combat vehicles.

SHOT, ARMOR-PIERCING CAP, 37mm,

M51B1 and M51B2—STANDARD—The shots, A.P.C., M51B1 and M51B2, consist of three components: body, cap, and windshield. The windshield improves the ballistics of the shell and the cap gives better penetration against face-hardened armor plate. The sole difference between the two shots lies in the armor-piercing cap. The cap on the M51B1 shot comes to a point; the cap on the M51B2 shot has a rounded point. The shot includes neither fuze nor bursting charge, but contains a tracer element with a burning time of three seconds. The regular wind shield is a thin steel ogive 360° crimped onto the cap; an alternate is the aluminous windshield.

The complete round, weighing 3.48

pounds, consists of the M16 brass cartridge case, or the M16B1 substitute standard steel case; the M38A1 primer; either the M51B1 or the M51B2 A.P.C. projectile; and a propelling charge of 0.53 pound of M2 powder or 0.57 pound of M5 powder.

The M2 and M5 FNH powders are an Hercules NG formula with 7-perforation grains having a web of 0.04 inch. The standard muzzle velocity with this charge is 2900 feet per second in the M3A1 and M6 guns. In the shorter M5A1 gun the velocity is 2855 feet per second.

(Note: Target practice shot, M51A2, is listed in the Table of Characteristics below.)

CHARACTERISTICS

	Shot, A.P.C., M51B1 Shot, A.P.C., M51B2	Shot, T.P., M51A2		Shot, A.P.C., M51B1 Shot, A.P.C., M51B2	Shot, T.P., M51A2
Caliber	37 mm	37 mm	Maximum Range	12,850 yards‡	—
Model of Gun	M3A1, M5A1, and M6	M3A1, M5A1, and M6	Chamber Capacity	19.35 cu. ins.	19.35 cu. ins.
Proj. Weight	1.92 lb.	1.92 lb.	Rated Max. Pressure, p.s.i.	50,000	45,000
Primer	M38A1*	M38A1†††	Armor Penetration at 20°		
Cartridge Case	M16**	M16**	Homogeneous Plate		
Propelling Charge and Weight	FNH powder, 0.53 lb.***	FNH powder, 0.47 lb.	500 yards	2.4 ins.	—
			1,000 yards	2.1 ins.	—
			Face-Hard. Plate		
Complete Round Weight	3.48 lb.†	3.42 lb.	500 yards	2.1 ins.	—
Muzzle Velocity	2,900 f/s††	2,600 f/s	1,000 yards	1.8 ins.	—

*Or M38B2 Substitute Standard.
**The steel cartridge case, M16B1, is substitute standard for use in the M3A1, M5A1, and M6 guns.
***0.53 lb. of M2 powder, 0.57 lb. of M5 powder.
†3.52 lb. with M5 powder.
††2,855 f/s in M5A1 gun.
‡12,725 yds. in M5A1 gun.
†††The M23A3 percussion primer is authorized for assembly in this round until present stocks are exhausted.

SHELL, HIGH-EXPLOSIVE, 37 MM, M63— STANDARD
CANISTER, 37 MM, M2—STANDARD

ROUNDS FOR ANTITANK GUN, M3A1; TANK GUNS, M5A1 AND M6

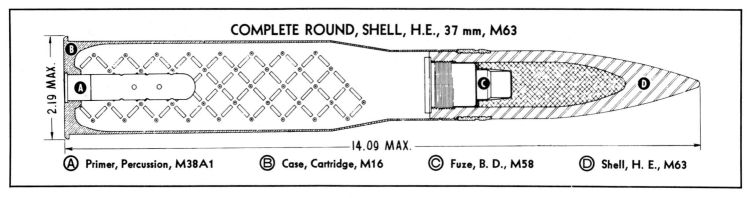

COMPLETE ROUND, SHELL, H.E., 37 mm, M63

2.19 MAX. — 14.09 MAX.

Ⓐ Primer, Percussion, M38A1   Ⓑ Case, Cartridge, M16   Ⓒ Fuze, B. D., M58   Ⓓ Shell, H. E., M63

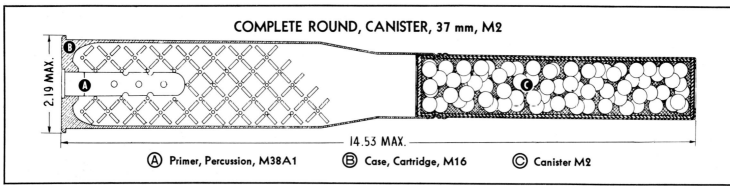

COMPLETE ROUND, CANISTER, 37 mm, M2

2.19 MAX. — 14.53 MAX.

Ⓐ Primer, Percussion, M38A1   Ⓑ Case, Cartridge, M16   Ⓒ Canister M2

HIGH-EXPLOSIVE, 37 mm, M63—STANDARD—This shell has superseded the Mk. II high-explosive shell, now used only as subcaliber ammunition. The bursting charge is 0.085 pound of TNT, functioned by the base detonating fuze, M58. Weights of the cartridge case, M16, and propelling charge of FHN powder are 0.93 pound and 0.49 pound, respectively. The steel cartridge case, M16B1, is substitute standard for use in the M3A1, M5A1 and M6 guns.

The complete round uses the M38A1 percussion primer and a propelling charge of M1 powder with single perforation grains and 0.027 inch web.

CANISTER, 37 mm, M2—STANDARD —Canister, M2, as the designation implies, is little more than a can filled with approximately 122 lead balls which are imbedded in a resin matrix.

The canister is used primarily as tank armament against personnel. The shock of discharge ruptures the case and the canister leaves the gun with a muzzle velocity of 2,500 feet per second. The case bursts within 100 feet after discharge.

The weight of the complete round is 3.49 pounds of which 1.94 pounds is the canister load. Weight of the propelling charge of FNH powder is 0.52 pound.

The propelling charge is an M1 class powder having an 85–10–5 formula, seven perforations per grain with a web of 0.019 inch.

CHARACTERISTICS

	Shell, H.E., M63	Canister, M2		Shell, H.E., M63	Canister, M2
Caliber	37 mm	37 mm	Propelling Charge and Weight	FNH powder, 0.49 lb.	FNH powder, 0.52 lb.
Model of Gun	M3A1, M5A1, and M6	M3A1, M5A1, and M6	Complete Round Weight	3.13 lb.	3.49 lb.
Proj. Weight	1.61 lb.	1.94 lb.	Muzzle Velocity	2,600 f/s**	2,500 f/s
Proj. Charge and Weight	TNT, 0.085 lb.	122 balls	Maximum Range	9,500 yards***	—
Fuze	B.D., M58	—	Chamber Capacity	19.19 cu. ins.	19.35 cu. ins.
Primer	M38A1†	M38A1†	Rated Max. Pressure, p.s.i.	40,000	—
Cartridge Case	M16*	M16*			

†Or M38B2 substitute standard.
*The steel cartridge case, M16B1, is substitute standard for use in the M3A1, M5A1 and M6 guns for training only.

**2,565 f/s in M5A1 gun.
***9,425 yds. in M5A1 gun.

SHELL, HIGH-EXPLOSIVE, 37 MM, M54—STANDARD
SHOT, ARMOR-PIERCING CAPPED, 37 MM, M59—STANDARD
SHELL, PRACTICE, 37 MM, M55AI—STANDARD
ROUNDS FOR AUTOMATIC GUNS, M1A2 (ANTIAIRCRAFT) AND M9 (AIRCRAFT)

SHOT, ARMOR-PIERCING, 37 MM, M80—SUBSTITUTE STANDARD
ROUND FOR 37 mm AUTOMATIC GUN, M9 (AIRCRAFT)

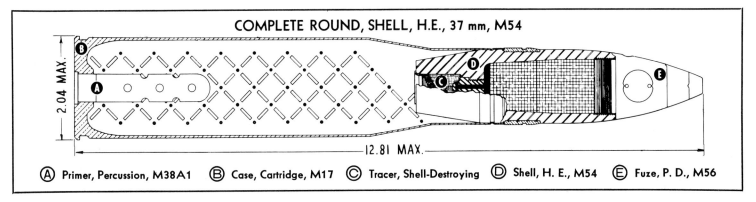

COMPLETE ROUND, SHELL, H.E., 37 mm, M54

2.04 MAX.

12.81 MAX.

Ⓐ Primer, Percussion, M38A1 Ⓑ Case, Cartridge, M17 Ⓒ Tracer, Shell-Destroying Ⓓ Shell, H. E., M54 Ⓔ Fuze, P. D., M56

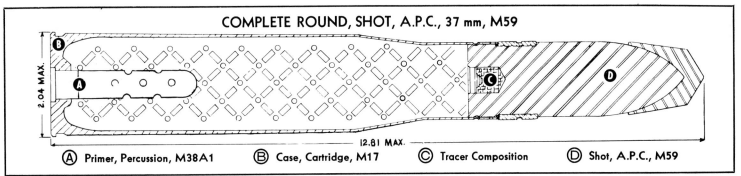

COMPLETE ROUND, SHOT, A.P.C., 37 mm, M59

2.04 MAX.

12.81 MAX.

Ⓐ Primer, Percussion, M38A1 Ⓑ Case, Cartridge, M17 Ⓒ Tracer Composition Ⓓ Shot, A.P.C., M59

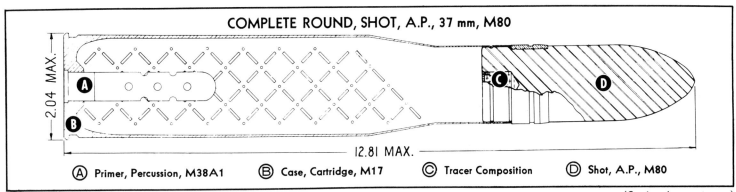

COMPLETE ROUND, SHELL, PRACTICE, 37 mm, M55A1

2.04 MAX.

12.81 MAX

Ⓐ Primer, Percussion, M38A1 Ⓑ Case, Cartridge, M17 Ⓒ Tracer Composition Ⓓ Shell, Practice, M55A1 Ⓔ Fuze, Dummy, M50

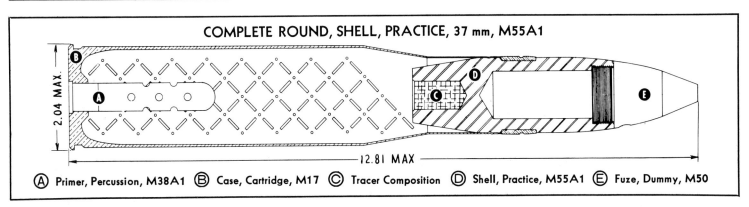

COMPLETE ROUND, SHOT, A.P., 37 mm, M80

2.04 MAX.

12.81 MAX.

Ⓐ Primer, Percussion, M38A1 Ⓑ Case, Cartridge, M17 Ⓒ Tracer Composition Ⓓ Shot, A.P., M80

(Continued on next page)

SHELL, HIGH-EXPLOSIVE, 37 MM, M54
SHOT, ARMOR-PIERCING CAPPED, 37 MM, M59
SHELL, PRACTICE, 37 MM, M55AI
SHOT, ARMOR-PIERCING, 37 MM, M80

(Continued)

To combat low-flying, strafing or dive bombing planes, the 37 mm gun, M1A2, was developed and standardized by the Ordnance Department to meet that requirement.

Ammunition for this gun is of the fixed type, fired automatically from ten-round clips, at a rate of approximately 120 rounds per minute.

Cartridge case, M17, standard for all 37 mm ammunition fired from the automatic gun, M1A2, and the aircraft gun, M9, is a bottlenecked, tapered case weighing 0.85 pound. The steel cartridge case, M17B1, is substitute standard for the M1A2 gun, and is used exclusively for training purposes within the continental United States.

Rounds for both guns use the percussion primer, M38A1, or as an alternate the M38B2.

The Shot, A.P.C., M59, is fired from both the M1A2 and M9 guns. For better armor penetration the muzzle velocity was elevated to 2,800 feet per second by increasing the propelling charge. As the A.P., M74, Shot could not give a high enough velocity without developing excessive pressure, the A.P., M80, was made substitute standard for the M9 aircraft gun. The A.P., M80, the A.P.C., M59, the H.E., M54, and the Practice Shell, M55A1, are standard for this gun; the latter two at the same muzzle velocity and maximum rated pressure as when used in the M1A2 gun.

SHELL, HIGH-EXPLOSIVE, 37 mm, M54 — STANDARD — A direct hit must be scored on the objective for this high explosive shell to function.

Both the M1A2 and M9 guns use 0.39 pound of FNH powder, M2 class, propelling charge. In the M9 gun, the round also can be loaded with 0.29 pound of an M5 class propelling charge. The weight of the complete round is 2.68 pounds using M1 powder and 2.58 pounds using M2 or M5 powders.

The M1 powder has an 85–10–5 formula and uses single-perforation grains with a 0.022 inch web.

The M2 powder is an Hercules NG formula with single-perforation grains and a web of 0.034 inch.

The M5 powder also is an Hercules NG formula but uses seven-perforation grains and a 0.039 inch web.

SHOT, ARMOR-PIERCING, CAPPED, 37 MM, M59A1 — STANDARD — The A.P.C., M59A1 is a modified A.P.C., M59 Shot. The armor-piercing cap on the former was secured to the shot body by soldering, while on the latter it is attached by a 360 degree crimp. The body of the shot and the cap are manufactured from forgings or bar stock. The built-in tracer has a three seconds burning time.

When fired from the M1A2 gun, a propelling charge of 0.33 pound is used while 0.53 pound is used in the M9 gun.

The weight of the complete round in the M1A2 gun is 3.19 pounds, and 3.39 pounds in the M9 gun. The shot itself weighs 1.91 pounds.

Both the M1 class powder, used in the M1A2 gun, and the M5 class powder, used in the M9 gun, are FNH powders. The M1 powder has an 85–10–5 formula, single-perforation grains and a web of 0.023 inch. The M5 powder has an Hercules NG formula, seven-perforation grains and a 0.039 inch web.

SHELL, PRACTICE, 37-MM, M55A1 — STANDARD — This shell is similar to the High-Explosive Shell, M54, but it does not contain the shell-destroying tracer, the bursting charge or the Fuze, P.D., M56. Instead, it contains a tracer which burns for approximately 8 seconds and the Fuze, Dummy, M50 or modifications.

The propelling charges for both guns are the same as those used with the M54 Shell as fired from the M1A2 and M9 guns.

SHOT, ARMOR-PIERCING, 37 mm, M80 — SUBSTITUTE STANDARD — The A.P., M80 Shot is manufactured from forgings or bar stock and has a 3-second tracer. As fired the shot weighs 1.66 pounds and the complete round 3.28 pounds.

The 0.54 pound propelling charge of FNH powder gives the shot a muzzle velocity of 3,050 feet per second in the M9 gun. This round is not fired in the M1A2 gun.

The M5 class powder of the propelling charge has an Hercules NG formula, seven-perforation grains and a web of 0.039 inch.

CHARACTERISTICS

	Shell, H.E., M54	Shot, A.P.C., M59	Shot, A.P.C., M59	Shell, Practice, M55A1	Shot, A.P., M80
Caliber	37 mm	37 mm	37 mm	37 mm	37 mm
Model of Guns	M1A2 & M9	M1A2	M9	M1A2 & M9	M9
Proj. Weight	1.34 lb.	1.91 lb.	1.91 lb.	1.34 lb.	1.66 lb.
Proj. Charge and Weight	Tetryl, .10 lb.¶	——	——		——
Fuze	P.D., M56			Dummy M50*	
Primer	M38A1	M38A1	M38A1	M38A1††	M38A1
Cartridge Case	M17**	M17**	M17	M17**	M17
Propelling Charge and Weight	FNH powder, 0.39 lb.†	FNH powder, 0.33 lb.†	FNH powder, 0.53 lb.	FNH powder, 0.39 lb.†	FNH powder, 0.54 lb.
Complete Round Weight	2.68 lb.§	3.19 lb.	3.39 lb.	2.68 lb.§	3.15 lb.
Muzzle Velocity	2,600 f/s	2,050 f/s	2,800 f/s	2,600 f/s	3,050 f/s
Max. Horiz. Range	8,875 yds.‡	5,790 yds.		8,875 yds.‡	
Chamber Capacity	17.91 cu. ins.	19.35 c.i.	19.35 c.i.	17.91 c.i.	19.35 c.i.
Rated Max. Pressure, p.s.i.	30,000	30,000	46,000	30,000	46,000
Armor Penetration at 20°					
Homogeneous Plate					
500 yards	——	1.0 ins.	2.2 ins.***	——	3.1 ins.****
1,000 yards	——	0.6 ins.	1.3 ins.***	——	2.2 ins.****
Face-Hard. Plate					
500 yards	——	1.9 ins.	1.9 ins.***	——	2.6 ins.****
1,000 yards	——	0.6 ins.	1.2 ins.***	——	2.0 ins.****

¶Alternate, Comp. "A" 0.105 lb.
*Alternates M50B1, M50B2, and M50B3.
**The steel cartridge case, M17B1, is Substitute Standard for use in the M1A2 gun. Steel cartridge case is not used with M9 aircraft gun.
***For 2,800 f/s M. V. plus 350 m.p.h. airspeed.

****For 3,050 f/s M. V. plus 350 m.p.h. airspeed.
†M1 powder indicated.
‡6,200 yds. vertical range.
§With M2 or M5 powder 2.58 lb., M1 powder indicated.
††M23a3 percussion primer may be used until present stocks are exhausted.

SHELL, H.E.—T (S.D., M3), 40 MM, MK. II—STANDARD
SHELL, H.E.—T (S.D., NO. 12), 40 MM, MK. II—LIMITED STANDARD
SHOT, ARMOR-PIERCING, 40 MM, M81A1—STANDARD
ROUNDS FOR 40 mm BOFORS GUN, M1 (ANTIAIRCRAFT)

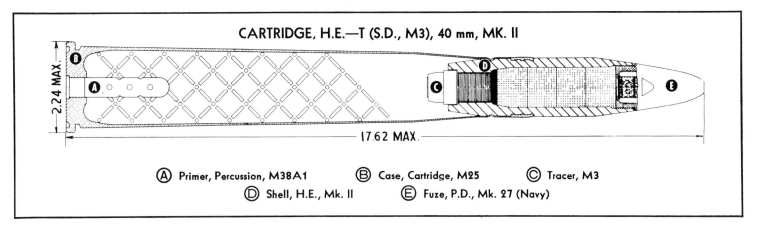

CARTRIDGE, H.E.—T (S.D., M3), 40 mm, MK. II

2.24 MAX. — 17.62 MAX.

Ⓐ Primer, Percussion, M38A1   Ⓑ Case, Cartridge, M25   Ⓒ Tracer, M3
Ⓓ Shell, H.E., Mk. II   Ⓔ Fuze, P.D., Mk. 27 (Navy)

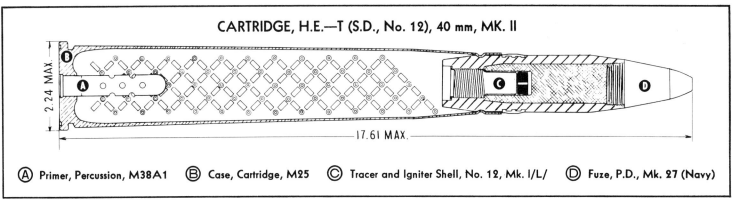

CARTRIDGE, H.E.—T (S.D., No. 12), 40 mm, MK. II

2.24 MAX. — 17.61 MAX.

Ⓐ Primer, Percussion, M38A1   Ⓑ Case, Cartridge, M25   Ⓒ Tracer and Igniter Shell, No. 12, Mk. I/L/   Ⓓ Fuze, P.D., Mk. 27 (Navy)

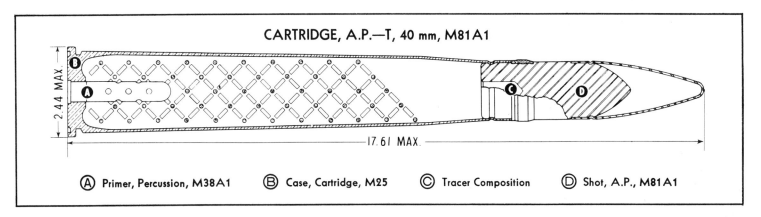

CARTRIDGE, A.P.—T, 40 mm, M81A1

2.44 MAX. — 17.61 MAX.

Ⓐ Primer, Percussion, M38A1   Ⓑ Case, Cartridge, M25   Ⓒ Tracer Composition   Ⓓ Shot, A.P., M81A1

SHELL, H.E.—T (S.D., M3), 40 mm, Mk. II—STANDARD—This shell was developed and standardized as an improvement on the Mk. II, H.E. Shell. The only difference between the two lies in the shell-destroying tracer. The newer shell uses the recently developed tracer, M3, which does not depend on set-back to ignite the tracer composition, but is ignited directly by the burning propelling gases. Due to the difference in tracer construction, the shell contains a heavier bursting charge than the limited standard H.E. Mk. II shell. The complete round components are: cartridge case M25 or M25B1, which is the substitute standard steel case; percussion primer, M38A1, Navy primer Mk. 22, or the substitute standard primer, M38B2; an FNH propelling charge; and the loaded and fuzed shell, Mk. II, H.E.—T (SD, M3). Either the Navy P.D. fuze, Mk. 27 or the P.D. fuze, M71, is used with the round.

SHELL, H.E.—T (S.D., No. 12), Mk. II—LIMITED STANDARD—These quick-firing, high-explosive shells are used in the 40 mm Bofors antiaircraft gun, M1.

The P.D. fuze, M71, and the Navy fuze, Mk. 27, are standard with these (Continued on next page)

SHELL, H.E.—T (S.D., M3), 40 MM, MK. II
SHELL, H.E.—T (S.D., NO. 12), 40 MM, MK. II
SHOT, ARMOR-PIERCING, 40 MM, M81A1

(Continued)

shells. The P. D. fuze, M64A1, and D.A. No. 251, Mk. I/L/, have been reclassified as limited standard.

The complete round includes the D. A. No. 251, Mk. I/L/ fuze, the tracer and igniter shell No. 12, the M22 cartridge case, and the percussion primer, Q.F. cartridge No. 12, Mk. I/L/. It is an adaptation of the British complete round for the 40 mm Bofors gun. This round, however, is an "issue only" item.

The same round equipped with the M22A1 cartridge case and the percussion primer, M38A1, is an "issue only" item.

The round fuzed with the P.D. M71 fuze or the Navy Mk. 27 fuze and using the M25 cartridge case and the percussion primer, M38A1, is also an "issue only" item, and is also a limited standard round. The steel cartridge case, M25B1, is substitute standard for the M25 cartridge case.

Differences between the booster cavities for the several fuzes causes the TNT bursting charges to vary. For the shell with the D.A. No. 251, Mk. I/L/ fuze, the TNT charge is 0.150 pound; the P.D. M64A1 fuze, 0.140 pound; and for the Navy Mk. 27 fuze, 0.168 pound. All three shells use also a black-powder pellet weighing 0.005 pound as a booster.

These shells use the tracer and igniter, No. 12, which destroys the projectile if the target is missed. The self-destroying feature functions in the same manner as that used with the 37 mm H.E. Shell, M54, except that the set-back energy of the shell forces a primer against a firing pin and ignites the tracer.

SHOT, ARMOR-PIERCING, 40 mm, M81A1—STANDARD—The M81A1 shot has a monobloc type body to which a windshield is attached by a 360° crimp. The tracer composition used has a burning time of approximately twelve seconds.

The weight of the M81A1 complete round is 4.58 pounds; the shot weighs 1.96 pounds.

CHARACTERISTICS

	Shell, Mk. II, H.E.—T (S.D., M3)	Shell, Mk. II, Q.F., H.E.	Shell, Mk. II, H.E.—T (S.D. No. 12)	Shot, M81A1, A.P.
Caliber	40 mm	40 mm	40 mm	40 mm
Model of Gun	Bofors (A.A.), M1	Bofors (A.A.), M1	Bofors (A.A.), M1	Bofors (A.A.), M1
Proj. Weight	2.061 lb.	1.93 lb.	1.95 lb.	1.96 lb.
Proj. Charge and Weight	Tetryl, 0.05 lb. B.P.P., .008 lb.	TNT, 0.15 lb.	TNT, 0.130 lb. B.P.P., 0.005 lb.	—
Fuze	P.D., Mk. 27††	Mk. I/L/*	P.D., M71†	—
Primer	M38A1‡	M38A1	M38A1	M38A1
Cartridge Case	M25	M22	M25	M25
Propelling Charge and Weight	FNH powder, 0.72 lb.	FNH powder, 0.65 lb.	FNH powder, 0.65 lb.	FNH powder, 0.65 lb.
Complete Round Weight	4.823 lb.	4.69 lb.	4.71 lb.	4.72 lb.
Muzzle Velocity	2,870 f/s	2,870 f/s	2,870 f/s	2,870 f/s
Maximum Range	—	H. 10,850 yards V. 7,625 yards	H. 10,850 yards V. 7,625 yards	9,475 yards
Chamber Capacity	—	28.97 cu. ins.	29.54 cu. ins.	30.73 cu. ins.
Rated Max. Pressure, p.s.i.	40,000	40,000	40,000	40,000
Armor Penetration at 20°				
Homogeneous Plate				
500 yards	—	—	—	2.05 ins.
1,000 yards	—	—	—	1.65 ins.
Face-Hard. Plate				
500 yards	—	—	—	1.75 ins.
1,000 yards	—	—	—	1.40 ins.

*Percussion fuze, D.A., No. 251, Mk. I/L/.
†Fuze, P.D., M71, or Navy Mk. 27 fuze.
††Alternate P.D., M71.
‡Alternate Navy Mk. 22 or M38B2.

SHOT, ARMOR-PIERCING, 57 MM, M70—SUBSTITUTE STANDARD
PROJECTILE, A. P. C., 57 MM, M86—STANDARD
ROUNDS FOR GUN, 57 mm, M1 (ANTITANK)

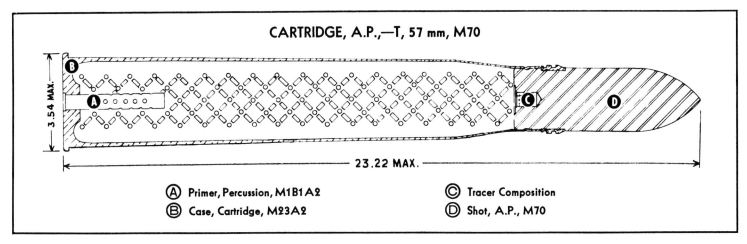

CARTRIDGE, A.P.,—T, 57 mm, M70

23.22 MAX.

Ⓐ Primer, Percussion, M1B1A2   Ⓒ Tracer Composition
Ⓑ Case, Cartridge, M23A2   Ⓓ Shot, A.P., M70

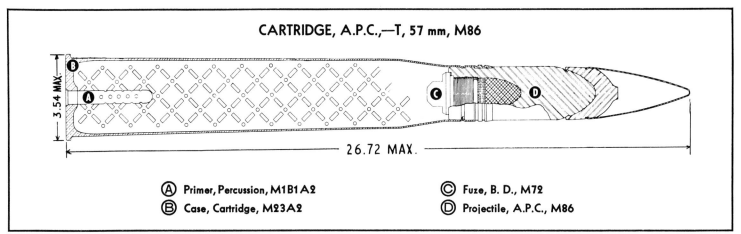

CARTRIDGE, A.P.C.,—T, 57 mm, M86

26.72 MAX.

Ⓐ Primer, Percussion, M1B1A2   Ⓒ Fuze, B. D., M72
Ⓑ Case, Cartridge, M23A2   Ⓓ Projectile, A.P.C., M86

SHOT, ARMOR-PIERCING, 57 mm, M70—SUBSTITUTE STANDARD—The ammunition for the 57 mm gun is issued in complete rounds of the fixed type. The round consists of a cartridge case, containing a primer and propelling charge, firmly attached by crimping to a solid projectile which has a built-in tracer.

The shot, M70, is particularly suited for firing against targets protected by homogeneous armor plate, especially in view of the muzzle velocity of 2,950 feet per second.

The complete round weighs 12.82 pounds and is 23.22 inches long. The cartridge

(Continued on next page)

CHARACTERISTICS

	Shot, A.P., M70	Projectile, A.P.C., M86		Shot, A.P., M70	Projectile, A.P.C., M86
Caliber	57 mm	57 mm	Muzzle Velocity	2,950 f/s	2,700 f/s
Model of Gun	M1 (Antitank)	M1 (Antitank)	Maximum Range	9,275 yards	13,555 yards
Proj. Weight	6.28 lb.	7.27 lb.	Chamber Capacity	100.05 cu. ins.	98.87 cu. ins.
Proj. Charge and Weight	—	Explosive "D," 0.076 lb., Tetryl, 0.018 lb.	Pressure, p.s.i.	44,000	44,000
			Armor Penetration at 20°		
Fuze	—	B.D., M72	Homogeneous Plate		
Primer	M1B1A2	M1B1A2	500 yards	3.9 ins.	3.3 ins.
Cartridge Case	M23A2*	M23A2*	1,000 yards	2.9 ins.	2.9 ins.
Propelling Charge and			Face-Hard. Plate		
Weight	FNH powder, 2.61 lb.	FNH powder, 2.58 lb.	500 yards	3.2 ins.	3.4 ins.
Complete Round Weight	12.82 lb.	13.88 lb.	1,000 yards	2.4 ins.	3.1 ins.

*Steel cartridge case, M23A2B1, is substitute standard.
‡At 15° elevation.

case, M23A2, is standard for all rounds of 57 mm ammunition. This case is 17.40 inches long, and weighs 3.9 pounds. The base is reamed to receive the M1B1A2 primer.

The cartridge case M23A2B1, is substitute standard for the same rounds. This case is made of steel with the same exterior dimensions as the brass case. However, the base of the steel case is thinner and weighs only 0.3 pound less than the brass case.

To give the shot the required muzzle velocity of approximately 2,950 feet per second, a charge of 2.61 pounds of FNH smokeless powder is packed loosely into the cartridge case. The propelling charge is an M1 class powder having an 87-10-3 formula, seven-perforation grains and a web of 0.037 inch. The 2.58 pounds of FNH powder give the projectile a muzzle velocity of 2,700 feet per second.

The shot, A.P., M70, consists of a solid shot of hardened steel with a tracer cavity in the base. The shot itself is 6.81 inches long and weighs 6.28 pounds. The tracer cavity is 0.5 inch in diameter. The tracer charge consists of approximately 73 grains of red tracer composition in three solid pellets, set off by a 20-grain igniter pellet. Both tracer and igniter charges are inclosed in a cup of clear celluloid. The entire tracer assembly weighs approximately 0.1 pound and is designed to burn for approximately 4.5 seconds.

PROJECTILE, ARMOR-PIERCING CAPPED, 57 mm, M86—STANDARD

The A.P.C. projectile, M86, and base detonating fuze, M72, were developed to meet the demands for an A.P.C. round containing a high-explosive charge similar to 75 mm, M61, and 3", M62.

The projectile is similar in appearance to the 75 mm and 3" A.P.C. projectiles in that it has a blunt nose and a cavity to contain a bursting charge. The base end of the cavity is threaded for the base detonating fuze, M72. The cap differs from the 75 mm and 3" projectile caps in that instead of having a rounded nose, it has an approximate ½ inch width "wart" on the nose.

The windshield is held to the cap and the cap to the body of the projectile by 360° crimps.

The base detonating fuze, M72, operates on the inertia principle which permits the projectile completely to penetrate the armor plate before detonating the bursting charge.

Measuring 26.72 inches in length, the complete round weighs 13.88 pounds; the projectile itself weighs 7.27 pounds.

As with the A.P. 57 mm M70 round, the M1B1A2 primer and the M23A2 brass cartridge case or the M23A2B1 steel cartridge case are used.

A tracer with a burning time of approximately 4.5 seconds is built into the body of the fuze.

The 0.094 pound of bursting charge consists of 0.018 pound of tetryl to facilitate the detonation of 0.076 pound of Explosive "D."

SHELL, HIGH-EXPLOSIVE, 60 MM, M49A2—STANDARD
SHELL, ILLUMINATING, 60 MM, M83—STANDARD
SHELL, PRACTICE, 60 MM, M50A2—STANDARD
PROJECTILE, DRILL, 60 MM, M69—STANDARD

ROUNDS FOR MORTAR M2

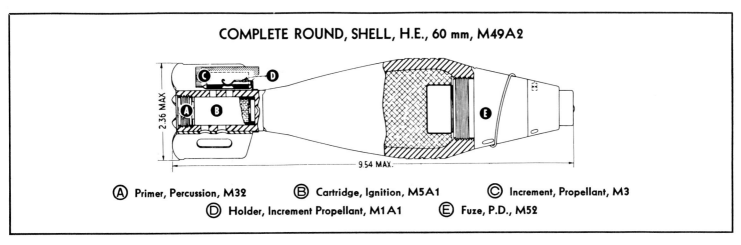

COMPLETE ROUND, SHELL, H.E., 60 mm, M49A2

Ⓐ Primer, Percussion, M32　　Ⓑ Cartridge, Ignition, M5A1　　Ⓒ Increment, Propellant, M3
Ⓓ Holder, Increment Propellant, M1A1　　Ⓔ Fuze, P.D., M52

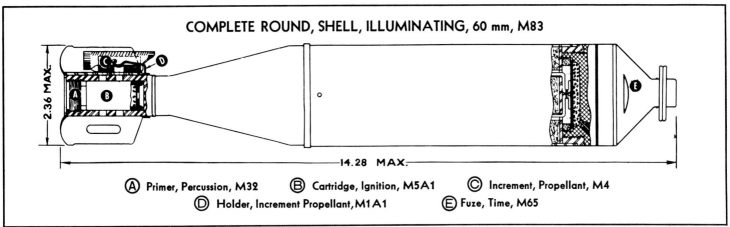

COMPLETE ROUND, SHELL, ILLUMINATING, 60 mm, M83

Ⓐ Primer, Percussion, M32　　Ⓑ Cartridge, Ignition, M5A1　　Ⓒ Increment, Propellant, M4
Ⓓ Holder, Increment Propellant, M1A1　　Ⓔ Fuze, Time, M65

CHARACTERISTICS

	Shell, H.E., M49A2	Shell, Ill., M83	Shell, Prac., M50A2	Projectile, Drill, M69
Caliber	60 mm	60 mm	60 mm	60 mm
Model of Mortar	M2	M2	M2	M2
Proj. Weight	2.90 lb.	3.70 lb.	2.90 lb.	2.90 lb.
Proj. Charge and Weight	TNT, 0.34 lb.	Expelling Charge, 0.06 lb., black powder.	Inert, 0.29 lb., B.P.P. 0.05 lb.	——
Fuze	P.D., M52*	Time, M65	P.D., M52*	——
Primer	M32	M32	M32	——
Cartridge (Ignition)	M5A1	M5A1	M5A1	——
Propelling Charge and Weight	(Wt. of 4), 0.024 lb.	(Wt. of 4), 0.018 lb.	(Wt. of 4), 0.024 lb.	——
Complete Round Weight	2.94 lb.	3.72 lb.	2.94 lb.	2.94 lb.
Muzzle Velocity	518 f/s†	390 f/s	518 f/s†	——
Maximum Range	45° 0'—1,985 yds.‡ 85° 30'—300 yds.	——	45° 0'—1,985 yds.‡ 85° 30'—300 yds.	——
Rated Max. Pressure, p.s.i.	6,000	6,000	6,000	——

*Alternate, Fuze, P.D., M52B1.
†535 f/s with M52B1 fuze.
‡Ranges with M52B1 fuze, firing in 5th zone:
　　45° 0'—2,017 yds.
　　85° 40'—300 yds.

(Continued on next page)

SHELL, HIGH-EXPLOSIVE, 60 MM, M49A2
SHELL, ILLUMINATING, 60 MM, M83
SHELL, PRACTICE, 60 MM, M50A2
PROJECTILE, DRILL, 60 MM, M69
(Continued)

The Mortar, M2, fires projectiles weighing approximately three to four pounds and is accurate up to 1,985 yards at 45° elevation.

A round consists of projectile, fuze, propellant charges for zone ranging, primer, and a cartridge loaded with ballistite explosive.

The primer strikes a firing pin (or anvil) at the base of the mortar tube. This action ignites the primer, setting off the charge in the ignition cartridge and firing the propellant charges attached to the fin assembly.

SHELL, H.E., 60 mm, M49A2—STANDARD—The complete round, weighing 2.94 pounds, consists of the fuzed and finned Shell, H.E., M49A2, the M32 percussion primer, the M5A1 ignition cartridge, and the M3 propellant increment.

The shell body is manufactured from either a steel casting or forging. A bursting charge of 0.34 pound of flake TNT is loaded into the shell body in two 0.17 pound increments. The first increment is consolidated at 2,000 p.s.i. pressure, and the second under 5,000 p.s.i. pressure.

The propelling charge consists of a Hercules NG formula powder in sheet form having a single perforation. Several sheets are sewn together and assembled in a cellophane bag, the purpose of the cellophane being to keep the powder dry and to facilitate attaching the increments to the shell. The number of increments depends on the range desired. Four of the M3 increments weigh 0.024 pound. Each M3 increment weighs approximately 35 grains.

The increment propellant holder, M1, is used to attach the increments between the fins. The holder is a ring fitted with metal clips each of which has a loop on the end. The loop is pushed through the hole in the increment, thereby holding it in place between the fins.

SHELL, ILLUMINATING, 60 mm, M83—STANDARD—This shell has been designed for use in illuminating a target. Upon functioning of the time fuze, M65, an expelling charge is ignited which starts the flare burning, shears a number of pins holding the tail of the shell to the body and then expels the flare and parachute assembly from the shell body. The expelling charge is 0.06 pound of black powder.

The M83 shell is 4.74 inches longer than the high-explosive, M49A2, and the complete round weighs 3.72 pounds. The propelling charge is a Hercules NG formula of several perforated sheets sewn together. The charge is assembled in a cellophane bag which is attached between the fins by the increment propellant holder, M1A1. The maximum pressure is obtained with 130 grains of this powder.

The range at the maximum setting (14 seconds) of the time fuze, M65, is 1,040 yards at 50° elevation.

SHELL, PRACTICE, M50A2—STANDARD—Loaded and fuzed, the projectile weighs 2.90 pounds, of which 0.34 pound is the weight of the charge which includes 0.29 pound of inert loading and 0.05 pound of black-powder pellet. Practice shells are filled with sand to make their weight approximately the same as high-explosive shells in order to obtain identical ballistic properties. The propelling charge for this shell is a Hercules NG formula, in sheet form, perforated and with several sheets sewn together. There is one hole in the middle of each sheet. The increments are attached to the shell by the M1A1 increment propellant holder after being assembled in a cellophane bag. The maximum pressure is obtained with 168 grains of this powder.

PROJECTILE, DRILL, 60 mm, M69—STANDARD—(See Table of Characteristics.)

PROJECTILE, ARMOR-PIERCING CAPPED, 75 MM, M61—STANDARD
ROUND FOR GUNS, M1897A4, M1916, M1917, M2, M3 (TANK), M4 (AIRCRAFT)

SHELL, SMOKE (BASE EMISSION), 75 MM, M89—SUBSTITUTE STANDARD
ROUND FOR GUNS, M2 AND M3 (TANK)

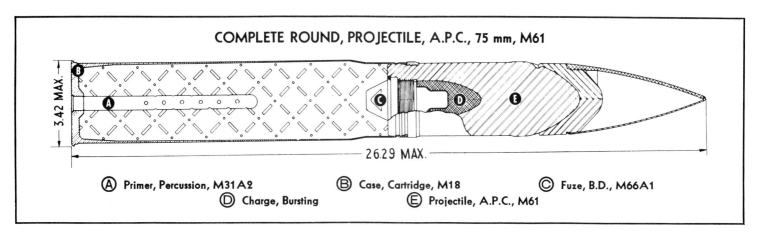

COMPLETE ROUND, PROJECTILE, A.P.C., 75 mm, M61

3.42 MAX. — 26.29 MAX.

Ⓐ Primer, Percussion, M31A2　　Ⓑ Case, Cartridge, M18　　Ⓒ Fuze, B.D., M66A1
Ⓓ Charge, Bursting　　Ⓔ Projectile, A.P.C., M61

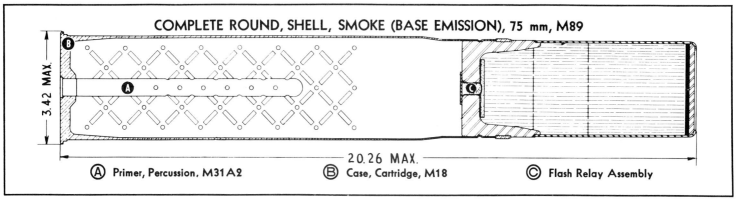

COMPLETE ROUND, SHELL, SMOKE (BASE EMISSION), 75 mm, M89

3.42 MAX. — 20.26 MAX.

Ⓐ Primer, Percussion, M31A2　　Ⓑ Case, Cartridge, M18　　Ⓒ Flash Relay Assembly

CHARACTERISTICS

	Proj. A.P.C., M61	Proj. A.P.C., M61	Proj. A.P.C., M61	Shell, Smoke M89
Caliber	75 mm	75 mm	75 mm	75 mm
Model of Guns	M1897A4	M3, M4	M2, M1916, M1917	M2, M3
Proj. Weight	14.96 lb.	14.96 lb.	14.96 lb.	6.61 lb.
Proj. Charge and Weight	Expl. "D" 0.144 lb.	Expl. "D" 0.144 lb.	Expl. "D" 0.144 lb.	H.E., 1.68 lb.
Fuze	B.D., M66A1	B.D., M66A1	B.D., M66A1	——
Primer	M31A2	M31A2	M31A2	M31A2
Cartridge Case	M18*	M18*	M18*	M18*
Propelling Charge and Weight	FNH powder, 2.16 lb.	FNH powder, 2.16 lb.	FNH powder, 2.16 lb.	FNH powder, 0.16 lb.
Complete Round Weight	20.02 lb.	20.02 lb.	20.02 lb.	9.83 lb.
Muzzle Velocity	2,000 f/s	2,024 f/s	1,926 f/s	850 f/s**
Maximum Range	13,870 yds.	14,000 yds.	13,600 yds.	——
Chamber Capacity	88.05 cu. ins.	88.05 cu. ins.	88.05 cu. ins.	——
Rated Max. Pressure, p.s.i.	38,000	38,000	38,000	8,000
Armor Penetration at 20° Homogeneous Plate				
500 yards	2.8 ins.	2.9 ins.	2.6 ins.	——
1,000 yards	2.5 ins.	2.6 ins.	2.3 ins.	——
Face-Hard. Plate				
500 yards	3.4 ins.	3.4 ins.	3.1 ins.	——
1,000 yards	3.0 ins.	3.1 ins.	2.7 ins.	——

*Steel cartridge case, M18B1 is substitute standard for M1897A4, M2, M3, guns.
Not used with M4 gun.
**In M3 gun; 820 f/s in M2 gun.

(Continued on next page)

PROJECTILE, ARMOR-PIERCING CAPPED, 75mm, M61—STANDARD—The projectile contains the Fuze, B.D., M66A1, which detonates a 0.144 pound bursting charge of explosive "D." Cartridge case, M18, contains the percussion primer, M31A2, and a propelling charge of 2.16 pounds of FNH powder. The steel cartridge case, M18B1, is substitute standard for use in the M1897, M1916, M1917, M2, M3, and M4 guns. The percussion primer, M31B1A2, can be used as an alternate for the M31A2. Weight of the complete round is 20.02 pounds. The projectile weighs 14.96 pounds.

The 2.16 pounds of M1 class propelling charge is an 85–10–5 formula, has a web size of 0.025 inch, and seven perforations per grain.

To the nose of the projectile is soldered a steel armor-piercing cap on which is screwed a ballistic cap or windshield giving the projectile an over-all length of 14.47 inches.

This method of attaching the windshield is one of four which may be used. The steel windshield may be brazed to a steel adapter and the whole assembly screwed onto the cap and staked to it. A third method uses a windshield adapter that is forced onto the cap after the windshield is brazed to it. The fourth method is to crimp the windshield directly to the cap.

The B.D. fuze, M66A1, used with this projectile is an inertia type fuze and has a built-in tracer which burns for approximately three seconds.

SHELL, SMOKE (BASE EMISSION), 75 mm, M89—SUBSTITUTE STANDARD—This shell, which has been made substitute standard for the tank guns M2 and M3, functions in the same manner as the M88 round described under the 76 mm gun, M1.

The propelling charge uses an M2 powder, Hercules NG formula, with a single perforation and a web size of 0.015 inch.

SHELL, HIGH-EXPLOSIVE, 75 MM, M48—STANDARD

ROUND FOR GUNS, M1897A4, M1916, M1917, M2 M3, (TANK) AND FOR GUN, M4 (AIRCRAFT)

SHELL, CHEMICAL (W.P.), 75 MM, M64, WITH FUZE, P.D., M57—STANDARD

ROUND FOR 75 MM GUNS, M1897, M2, M3

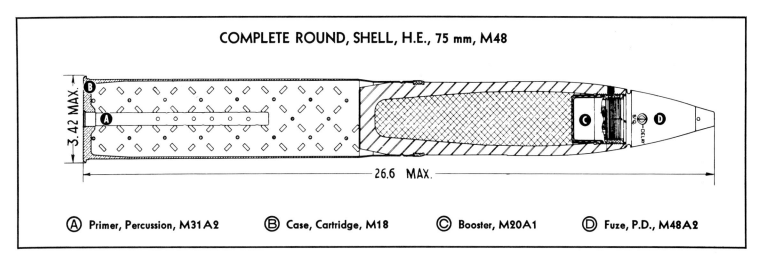

COMPLETE ROUND, SHELL, H.E., 75 mm, M48

Ⓐ Primer, Percussion, M31A2   Ⓑ Case, Cartridge, M18   Ⓒ Booster, M20A1   Ⓓ Fuze, P.D., M48A2

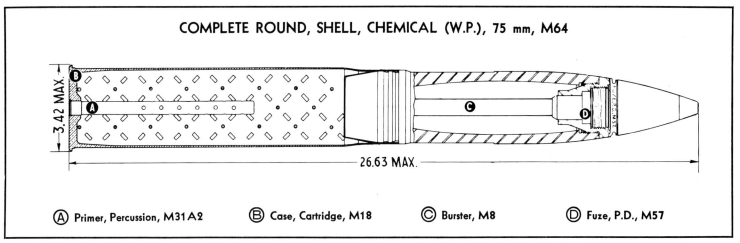

COMPLETE ROUND, SHELL, CHEMICAL (W.P.), 75 mm, M64

Ⓐ Primer, Percussion, M31A2   Ⓑ Case, Cartridge, M18   Ⓒ Burster, M8   Ⓓ Fuze, P.D., M57

TABLE A

(SHELL, H. E., M48)

GUN	PROPELLING CHARGE	MUZZLE VELOCITY	MAXIMUM RANGE	FUZE	PRIMER
M1897A4	Super, 1.93 lb.	1,950 f/s	13,953 yds.	P.D., M48A2 (.05 sec.) & T & SQ., M54	M31A2
	Normal, 1.05 lb.	1,500 f/s	11,195 yds.	P.D., M48A2 (.15 sec.) & T & SQ., M54	M22A3
	Reduced, 0.38 lb.	950 f/s	6,960 yds.	P.D., M48A2 (.15 sec.) & T & SQ., M54	M22A3
M1916, M1917, & M2	Super, 1.93 lb.	1,889 f/s	13,305 yds.	P.D., M48A2 (.05 sec.)	M31A2
	Normal, 1.05 lb.	1,468 fs	10,995 yds.	P.D., M48A2 (.15 sec.)	M22A3
	Reduced, 0.38 lb.	923 f/s	6,735 yds.	P.D., M48A2 (.15 sec.)	M22A3
M3	Super, 1.93 lb.	1,974 f/s	14,000 yds.	P.D., M48A2 (.05 sec.)	M31A2
	Normal, 1.05 lb.	1,518 f/s	11,400 yds.	P.D., M48A2 (.15 sec.)	M22A3
	Reduced, 0.38 lb.	960 f/s	7,200 yds.	P.D., M48A2 (.15 sec.)	M22A3
M4	Super, 1.93 lb.	1,974 f/s	14,000 yds.	P.D., M57	M31A2

SHELL, HIGH-EXPLOSIVE, 75 mm, M48—STANDARD—The components of a complete round consist of: the loaded and fuzed shell, the M18 cartridge case, containing either the M22A3 or M31A2 percussion primer and a propelling charge of FNH powder. A steel cartridge case M18B1 is substitute standard for the M18 case, however, the steel case is not to be used in the M4 aircraft gun.

The shell contains 1.47 pounds of TNT bursting charge or as an alternate, 1.36 pounds of 50–50 Amatol with 0.11 pound of Cast TNT surrounding the booster. The fuze is screwed into the Booster,

M20A1, which is assembled and staked into the shell after loading operations are concluded. The base of the shell is protected by a base cover, which either is spot or circumferentially welded to the shell.

Various fuzes and primers are authorized for this round, depending upon the gun from which the shell is fired and the propelling charge that is being employed. Table A gives the proper fuzes and primers to be used:

The 1.93 pounds supercharge is an M1 class powder of an 85–10–5 formula, the grains having seven perforations and a web of 0.025 inch.

The normal charge, weighing 1.05 pounds, also is an M1 class powder having the same formula as the supercharge, however, the grains have a single perforation and a web of 0.014 inch.

The 0.38 pound reduced charge is an M2 class powder of an Hercules NG formula, with single-perforation grains having a web of 0.015 inch.

SHELL, CHEMICAL (W.P.), 75 mm, M64 —STANDARD—In view of the Ordnance Department's requirements for a W.P. Smoke Shell for use in 75 mm Guns, the Shell, Chemical, (W.P.), 75 MM, M64, with Fuze, P.D., M57, was tested and found to be more efficient than the Shell, Chemical, Mk. II.

The exterior ballistic characteristics of the M64 Shell are superior to those of the Mk. II Shell. However, due to the difference in the cavity shape the M64 shell contains a slightly smaller amount of W.P. than the Mk. II shell.

The stability factor of the M64 is equivalent to the M48 Shell, from which it was patterned. Both shells have the same shape and the same firing table may be used. The weight variation is approximately ½ pound. The difference in weight is corrected by the usual firing table values.

The Shell, M64, may be used without altering existing tank reticles.

A complete round consists of the loaded and fuzed M64 Chemical shell cartridge case, M18, containing the M31A2 percussion primer and the FNH propelling charge. Supercharge is the only charge authorized for this round. Using this charge, 1.93 pounds of M1 class powder, the muzzle velocity is 1950 f/s in the M1897A4 gun.

CHARACTERISTICS

	Shell, H.E., M48	Shell, Chem. (W.P.), M64
Caliber	75 MM	75 MM
Model of guns	M1897A4, M2, M1916, M1917, M3 & M4	M1897A4, M2, M3
Proj. Weight	14.70 lbs.	15.25 lbs.
Fuze	See Table A	P.D., M57
Primer	See Table A	M31A2
Complete round weight	19.59 lbs.*	20.04 lbs.
Propelling charge	See Table A	FNH powder, 1.93 lb.
Muzzle Velocity	See Table A	1950 f/s****
Max. Range	See Table A	13,730 yds.†
Cartridge case	M18**	M18**
Chamber Capacity	80.57 cu. ins.	80.57 cu. ins.
Rated Max. pressure, p.s.i.	36,000***	36,000***

*Supercharge indicated; normal charge, 18.66 lbs.; reduced charge, 17.99 lbs.

**Steel cartridge case, M18B1, is substitute standard for use in all guns except the M4 gun.

***Supercharge indicated.

****In M1897A4 gun, 1889 f/s in M2 gun and 1974 f/s in M3 gun.

†In M1897A4 gun, 13,420 yds. in M2 gun and 14,130 yds. in M3 gun.

SHELL, HIGH-EXPLOSIVE, 75 MM, M48—STANDARD
SHELL, CHEMICAL, 75 MM, M64—STANDARD
WITH SMOKE (F.S.), SMOKE (W.P.) OR GAS, PERSISTENT (H.) FILLERS
SHELL, HIGH-EXPLOSIVE, ANTITANK, 75 MM, M66—STANDARD
ROUNDS FOR HOWITZERS, 75 mm, M1, M1A1, M2 AND M3

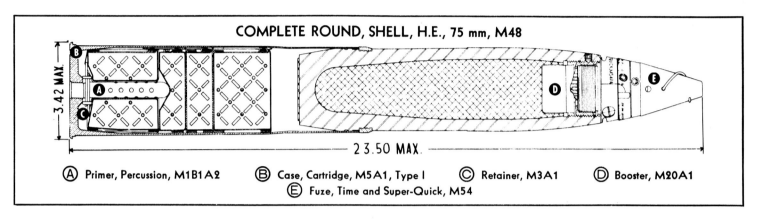

COMPLETE ROUND, SHELL, H.E., 75 mm, M48

3.42 MAX. 23.50 MAX.

Ⓐ Primer, Percussion, M1B1A2   Ⓑ Case, Cartridge, M5A1, Type I   Ⓒ Retainer, M3A1   Ⓓ Booster, M20A1
Ⓔ Fuze, Time and Super-Quick, M54

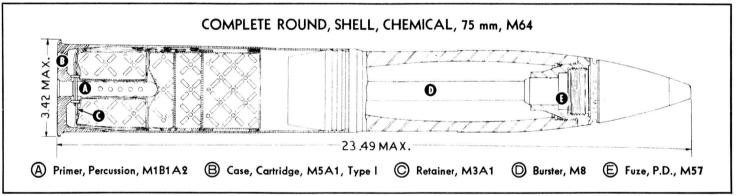

COMPLETE ROUND, SHELL, CHEMICAL, 75 mm, M64

3.42 MAX. 23.49 MAX.

Ⓐ Primer, Percussion, M1B1A2   Ⓑ Case, Cartridge, M5A1, Type I   Ⓒ Retainer, M3A1   Ⓓ Burster, M8   Ⓔ Fuze, P.D., M57

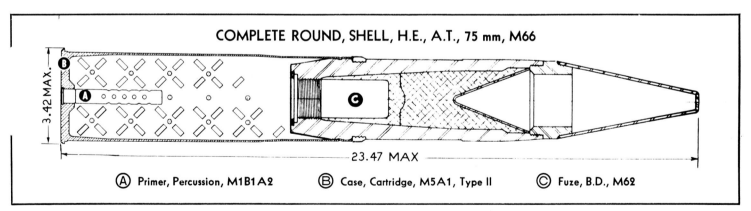

COMPLETE ROUND, SHELL, H.E., A.T., 75 mm, M66

3.42 MAX. 23.47 MAX

Ⓐ Primer, Percussion, M1B1A2   Ⓑ Case, Cartridge, M5A1, Type II   Ⓒ Fuze, B.D., M62

The propelling charge for the M48 and M64 rounds is contained in four-section powder bags. In the M66 round the propelling charge is in loose form. The powder bags are held in place in the cartridge case by the M3A1 retainer. The retainer is forced over the primer, and then is tied to the base charge of the four-section powder bag.

SHELL, HIGH-EXPLOSIVE, 75 mm, M48 —STANDARD—The standard components of the complete round consist of the following: the M48 projectile, the M20A1 booster, the M54 time and super-quick fuze or the M48A2 (.15 Sec.) point-detonating fuze, and the M5A1 type I cartridge case containing the M1B1A2 percussion primer. The steel cartridge case, M5A1B1, Type I, is a substitute standard.

The M5A1 cartridge case is loosely fitted to the projectile to permit ready access to the four-zone powder bags. Three increments are connected to the base charge by a cord. Any or all of the increments may be removed as required to obtain a given range. (See Table A.)

(Continued on next page)

SHELL, HIGH-EXPLOSIVE, 75 MM, M48
SHELL, CHEMICAL, 75 MM, M64
SHELL, HIGH-EXPLOSIVE, ANTITANK, 75 MM, M66

(Continued)

The projectile weighs 14.70 pounds. The propelling charge of FNH powder weighs 0.92 pound, and the bursting charge of TNT weighs 1.47 pounds.

The propelling charge is an M1 class powder. The formula is 85–10–5 and the grains have a single perforation and a web of 0.019 inch.

SHELL, CHEMICAL, 75 mm, M64— STANDARD—The complete round for this four-zone charge chemical shell consists of the following: point-detonating fuze, M57; M8 burster; the M5A1, Type I, cartridge case containing the M1B1A2 percussion primer and the FNH powder propelling charge of 0.92 pound. The burster contains 0.11 pound of tetryl. The steel cartridge case, M5A1B1, Type I, is substitute standard. The formula of the M1 class propelling charge is 85–10–5 and the grains have a single perforation and a web of 0.019 inch.

The following table gives the weights of the complete round, the shell as fired, and the chemical charge for each type of shell:

	(W.P.) Smoke	(H.) Gas, Pers.	(F.S.) Smoke
COMPLETE ROUND	18.77 lb.	18.46 lb.	18.93 lb.
SHELL, AS FIRED	15.25 lb.	14.94 lb.	15.41 lb.
CHARGE, CHEMICAL	1.35 lb.	1.04 lb.	1.51 lb.

SHELL, HIGH-EXPLOSIVE, ANTI-TANK, 75 mm, M66—STANDARD—This projectile embodies the "hollow charge," or "Munroe," principle. It is a remarkable armor-piercing round and will penetrate approximately 3½ inches of armor. A bursting charge of 0.81 pound of 50/50 Pentolite and 0.19 pound of 10/90 Pentolite is used.

The complete round consists of the M66 projectile; the base-detonating fuze, M62; the cartridge case, M5A1, Type II, which contains the percussion primer, M1B1A2. The steel cartridge case, M5A1B1, Type II, is substitute standard.

The 0.41 pound of M2 class Hercules NG formula propelling charge has a web of 0.015 inch and a single-perforated grain.

TABLE A
FOUR-ZONE CHARGE ANALYSIS

Charge	Powder Weight	Muzzle Velocity	Maximum Range	Elevation
ZONE 1—Base 1	0.37 lb.	700 f/s	4,190 yds.	43° 40'
ZONE 2—Base 1, Incr. 2	0.48 lb.	810 f/s	5,360 yds.	43° 40'
ZONE 3—Base 1, Incr. 2, 3	0.62 lb.	950 f/s	6,930 yds.	43° 0'
ZONE 4—Base 1, Incr. 2, 3, 4	0.92 lb.	1,250 f/s	9,610 yds.	43° 30'

CHARACTERISTICS

	Shell, H.E., M48	Shell, Chem., M64 (FS)	Shell, H.E., A.T., M66
Caliber	75 mm	75 mm	75 mm
Model of Howitzers	M1, M1A1, M2, and M3	M1, M1A1, M2, and M3	M1, M1A1, M2, and M3
Proj. Weight	14.70 lb.	15.41 lb.	13.27 lb.
Proj. Charge and Weight	TNT, 1.47 lb.	1.51 lb.	1.00 lb.‡
Booster or Burster	M20A1	M8	—
Fuze	T. and S.Q., M54*	P.D., M57	B.D., M62
Primer	M1B1A2	M1B1A2	M1B1A2
Cartridge Case	M5A1, Type I†	M5A1, Type I†	M5A1, Type II††
Propelling Charge and Weight	FNH powder, 0.92 lb.	FNH powder, 0.92 lb.	FNH powder, 0.41 lb.
Complete Round Weight	18.22 lb.	18.93 lb.	16.30 lb.
Muzzle Velocity	1,250 f/s	1,250 f/s	1,000 f/s
Maximum Range	9,610 yds.	9,630 yds.**	7,900 yds.
Chamber Capacity	59.08 cu. ins.	59.08 cu. ins.	59.08 cu. ins.
Rated Max. Pressure, p.s.i.	29,000	29,000	26,000

‡Consists of 0.81 lb. of 50/50 Pentolite, 0.19 lb. of 10/90 Pentolite.
*Or, Fuze, P.D., M48A2. (.15 sec.)
†Steel cartridge case, M5A1B1, Type I, is substitute standard.
**For W. P. and F. S. loaded shell; 9620 yards for H. loaded shell.
††Steel cartridge case, M5A1B1, Type II, is substitute standard.

SHELL, HIGH-EXPLOSIVE, 3 INCH, M42A1—STANDARD

ROUND FOR GUN, 3 INCH (ANTIAIRCRAFT), M1917, M1917MII, M1925M1, M2 AND M4

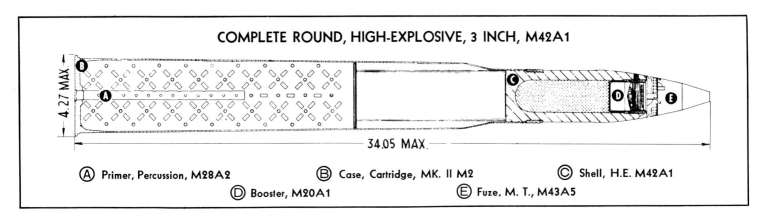

COMPLETE ROUND, HIGH-EXPLOSIVE, 3 INCH, M42A1

4.27 MAX · 34.05 MAX

Ⓐ Primer, Percussion, M28A2   Ⓑ Case, Cartridge, MK. II M2   Ⓒ Shell, H.E. M42A1
Ⓓ Booster, M20A1   Ⓔ Fuze, M. T., M43A5

There are two general types of 3-inch antiaircraft guns: the M1918, M1 and M3, provided with mobile mounts; and the M1917, M1925M1, M2 and M4, designed for fixed mounts.

As the fixed type of gun has a larger powder chamber than the gun of the mobile type, a larger cartridge case is required in the complete round. The cartridge case, Mk. I M2, has a volume of 293 cubic inches, and the cartridge case Mk. II M2, used in the mobile type gun, has a volume of 212 cubic inches. Because of this difference, the rounds are not interchangeable between the two types of guns even though the same projectiles are fired. The steel cartridge case, Mk. II M2B1, is a substitute standard.

The complete round of ammunition used in antiaircraft guns consists of the loaded and fuzed projectile, the cartridge case containing a primer, propelling charge and distance wad. In general, two types of service ammunition are provided for 3-inch antiaircraft guns: high-explosive and shrapnel. The M3, M1 and M1918 antiaircraft guns use also the M62, A.P.C., and the M79, A.P., rounds for anti-tank use.

Shrapnel now on hand is "Limited Standard" but is available as substitute for high-explosive shells until the supply is exhausted. It is used primarily for target practice.

SHELL, H.E., 3 INCH, M42A1—STANDARD—The 3 inch, M42A1, was designed to take the mechanical time fuze, M43A5, without using an adapter as was neces-

sary with the Mk. IX shell. The base of the M42A1 was also strengthened for additional bore safety. The use of the M43A5 fuze without an adapter gives a better ballistic outline to the M42A1 shell.

The interior of the booster body is threaded to take the mechanical time fuze, M43A5.

The complete round weighs 26.76 pounds and the weight of the projectile is 12.87 pounds. The shell contains a TNT bursting charge of 0.86 pound. The weight of the NH propelling charge is 4.56 pounds. The 21-second time fuze, Mk. IIIA2, is the approved substitute standard for the M.T., M43A5 fuze.

The propelling charge is an M1 class powder of an 87–10–3 formula. The grains have seven perforations and a web of 0.032 inch.

CHARACTERISTICS

	Shell, H.E., M42A1	Shell, H.E., M42A1		Shell, H.E., M42A1	Shell, H.E., M42A1
Caliber	3 inch	3 inch			
Model of Guns	*	*			
Proj. Weight	12.65 lb.	12.87 lb.			
Proj. Charge and Weight	TNT, 0.86 lb.§	TNT, 0.86 lb.§	Propelling Charge and Weight	NH powder, 4.56 lb.	NH powder, 4.56 lb.
Booster	M20A1	M20A1			
Fuze	21 sec., Mk. III A2	M.T., M43A5	Complete Round Weight	26.34 lb.	26.39 lb.
Primer	M28A2	M28A2	Muzzle Velocity	2,800 f/s	2,800 f/s
Cartridge Case	†	†	Maximum Range	H.—12,100 yds. V.— 8,000 yds.	H.—14,600 yds. V.—10,500 yds.
			Chamber Capacity	284.50 cu. ins.	284.50 cu. ins.
			Rated Max. Pressure, p.s.i.	36,000	36,000

*Guns, M1917, M1917A1, M1917A2, M1917A3, M1917M1, M1917M1A1, M1917M1A2, M1917M1A3, M1917MII, M1917MIIA3, M1925M1, M1925M1A1, M2 and M4.
†Cartridge case, Mk. I M2, is used for fixed type of guns: M1917, M1925M1, M2, M4. Steel Cartridge case, Mk. I M2B1, is substitute standard. Cartridge case, Mk. II M2, is used for mobile mounts: M1918, M1 and M3. Steel cartridge case, Mk. II M2B1, is a substitute standard.
§Or 50/50 Amatol, 0.77 lb.; cast TNT, 0.08 lb.

SHELL, HIGH-EXPLOSIVE, 3 INCH, M42A1—STANDARD

ROUND FOR 3 INCH SEACOAST GUNS, M1902 AND M1903

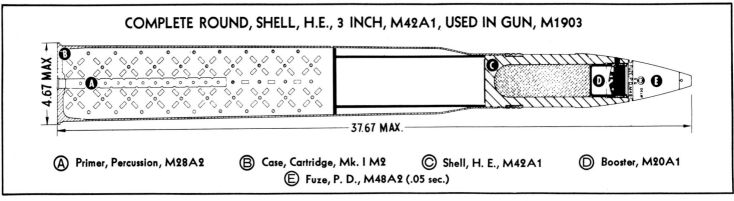

COMPLETE ROUND, SHELL, H.E., 3 INCH, M42A1, USED IN GUN, M1903

4.67 MAX · 37.67 MAX.

Ⓐ Primer, Percussion, M28A2   Ⓑ Case, Cartridge, Mk. I M2   Ⓒ Shell, H. E., M42A1   Ⓓ Booster, M20A1
Ⓔ Fuze, P. D., M48A2 (.05 sec.)

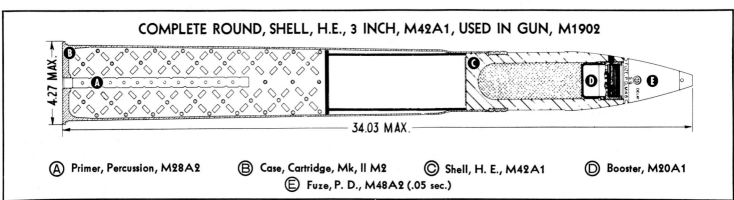

COMPLETE ROUND, SHELL, H.E., 3 INCH, M42A1, USED IN GUN, M1902

4.27 MAX · 34.03 MAX.

Ⓐ Primer, Percussion, M28A2   Ⓑ Case, Cartridge, Mk. II M2   Ⓒ Shell, H. E., M42A1   Ⓓ Booster, M20A1
Ⓔ Fuze, P. D., M48A2 (.05 sec.)

Ammunition for the two models of 3 inch seacoast guns, M1902 and M1903, is still known as 3 inch "15 pounder" ammunition although the older model projectiles of that weight are no longer standard. Two types of ammunition were formerly provided for the 3 inch seacoast guns, but the high-explosive shell, M42A1, is the only standard item for issue and manufacture since the armor-piercing and high-explosive shells, M1915 and Mk. I, became obsolete.

The cartridge case, Mk. I M2, is required for use with the M1903 gun due to its larger powder chamber. The chamber volume is 284.50 cubic inches as compared with 203.50 cubic inches for the M1902 gun's chamber. The M1902 takes the smaller cartridge case, Mk. II M2. The steel cartridge case, Mk. II M2B1, is substitute standard. The shells for these two guns are issued as fixed rounds, and the ammunition is not interchangeable due to the different cartridge cases used.

SHELL, H.E., 3 INCH, M42A1—STANDARD—This is the same projectile that is used with mechanical time fuze, M43A5, for 3 inch antiaircraft guns. The complete round consists of the following: fuze, P.D., M48A2 (.05 sec.); booster, M20A1; the Mk. II M2 or Mk. II M2B1 steel cartridge case with M1902 gun, or Mk. I M2 or Mk. II M2B1 steel cartridge case containing the percussion primer, M28A2,

and the NH powder propelling charge of 4.62 pounds in M1902 gun and 4.87 pounds in M1903 gun. The bursting charge of TNT weighs 0.86 pound, or, with the alternate bursting charge of 50/50 Amatol and cast TNT booster surround, 0.85 pound. Loaded and fuzed, the projectile weighs 12.87 pounds as fired.

The NH propelling charge has an 87–10–3 formula and is an M1 class powder. The grains have seven perforations and a web size of 0.043 inch.

A distance wad is used to hold the propelling charge firmly about the 300-grain primer and to keep the charge at a uniform density. The wad is made of cardboard, in cylindrical form with a disk at each end, held in place by cord.

CHARACTERISTICS

	Shell, H.E., M42A1	Shell, H.E., M42A1		Shell, H.E., M42A1	Shell, H.E., M42A1
Caliber	3 inch	3 inch	Cartridge Case	Mk. II M2*	Mk. I M2†
Model of Guns	M1902	M1903	Propelling Charge and Weight	NH powder, 4.62 lb.	NH powder, 4.87 lb.
Proj. Weight	12.87 lb.	12.87 lb.	Complete Round Weight	24.42 lb.	26.39 lb.
Proj. Charge and Weight	TNT, 0.86 lb.‡	TNT, 0.86 lb.‡	Muzzle Velocity	2,800 f/s	2,800 f/s
Booster	M20A1	M20A1	Maximum Range	12,100 yds.**	12,100 yds.**
Fuze	P.D., M48A2 (.05 sec.)	P.D., M48A2 (.05 sec.)	Chamber Capacity	203.50 cu. ins.	284.50 cu. ins.
Primer	M28A2	M28A2	Rated Max. Pressure, p.s.i.	36,000	36,000

‡Or 50/50 Amatol, 0.77 lb.; cast TNT, 0.08 lb.
*Steel cartridge case, Mk. II M2B1, is substitute standard.
†Steel cartridge case, Mk. I M2B1, is substitute standard.
**At 20°20′ Elevation.

SHELL, HIGH-EXPLOSIVE, 3 INCH, **M42A1**—STANDARD

ROUND FOR GUNS, 3 INCH, M1918; M1 and M3 (ANTIAIRCRAFT); M5 and M7 (ANTITANK); AND M6 (TANK)

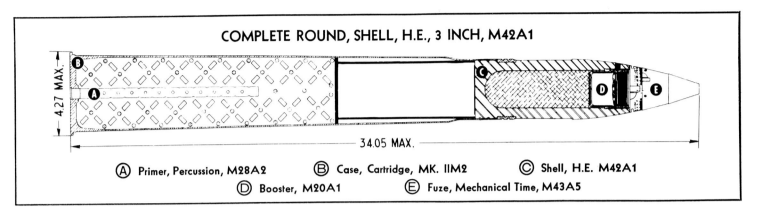

COMPLETE ROUND, SHELL, H.E., 3 INCH, M42A1

4.27 MAX.

34.05 MAX.

(A) Primer, Percussion, M28A2   (B) Case, Cartridge, MK. IIM2   (C) Shell, H.E. M42A1
(D) Booster, M20A1   (E) Fuze, Mechanical Time, M43A5

SHELL, H.E., 3 INCH, M42A1—STANDARD—The high-explosive ammunition fired in the above antiaircraft guns consists of the M42A1 round which varies from its predecessor round, the Mk. IX high-explosive shell (now limited standard), in the following respect: the M42A1 shell's one-piece construction, with inside threading of the nose, eliminates the necessity for an adapter which the Mk. IX shell requires.

The round consists of the cartridge case, Mk. IIM2; the M28A2 percussion primer; a propelling charge of 4.56 pounds of NH powder; a distance wad; and the loaded and fuzed projectile.

As fired, the shell weighs 12.87 pounds, of which 0.86 pound is a TNT bursting charge, or an 0.85 pound bursting charge consisting of 0.77 pound 50/50 Amatol and 0.08 pound Cast TNT booster surround. The complete round weighs 24.36 pounds.

The propelling charge uses an M1 class powder of an 87–10–3 formula. The grains have seven perforations and a web of 0.043 inch.

The mechanical time fuze, M43A5, is used in the M1918, M1 and M3 guns. The point-detonating fuze, M48A2 (.05 sec.), is used in the M1, M3, M5, M6 and M7 guns, and the P. D. fuze M48A2 (.05 sec.) in the M1918 gun.

The mechanical time fuze, M43A5, used in this shell is driven by a pair of weights which are acted upon by the centrifugal force set up by the rotation of the shell in flight. The time ring is graduated for 30 seconds maximum setting.

The steel cartridge case, Mk. II M2B1, is a substitute standard for use in the M1918, M1, M3, M5, M6 and M7 guns.

CHARACTERISTICS

	Shell, H.E., M42A1	Shell, H.E., M42A1	Shell, H.E., M42A1
Caliber	3 inch	3 inch	3 inch
Model of Guns	M1, M3	M1, M3, M5, M6, M7	M1918
Proj. Weight	12.87 lb.	12.87 lb.	12.87 lb.
Proj. Charge and Weight	TNT, 0.86 lb.†	TNT, 0.86 lb.†	TNT, 0.86 lb.†
Booster	M20A1	M20A1	M20A1
Fuze	P.D., M48A2 (.05 sec.)	M.T., M43A5	M.T., M43A5 or P.D., M48A2 (.15 sec.)
Primer	M28A2	M28A2	M28A2
Cartridge Case	Mk. II M2*	Mk. II M2*	Mk. II M2*
Propelling Charge and Weight	NH powder, 4.56 lb.	NH powder, 4.56 lb.	NH powder, 4.56 lb.
Complete Round Weight	24.36 lb.	24.36 lb.	24.36 lb.
Muzzle Velocity	2,800 f/s	2,800 f/s	2,600 f/s
Maximum Range	Horiz., 14,780 yds. Vert., 10,100 yds.	Horiz., 14,780 yds.	Horiz., 13,500 yds. Vert., 9,420 yds.
Chamber Capacity	203.50 cu. ins.	203.50 cu. ins.	203.50 cu. ins.
Rated Max. Pressure, p.s.i.	36,000	36,000	36,000

†Or 50/50 Amatol 0.77 lb.; Cast TNT 0.08 lb.
*Steel cartridge case, Mk. II M2B1, is substitute standard for use in M1918, M1, M3, M5, M6 and M7 guns.

PROJECTILE, ARMOR-PIERCING CAPPED, 3 INCH, M62A1—STANDARD
SHOT, ARMOR-PIERCING, 3 INCH, M79—SUBSTITUTE STANDARD

ROUNDS FOR GUNS, M1918, M3 (ANTIAIRCRAFT); M5 (ANTITANK); M6 AND M7 (TANK)

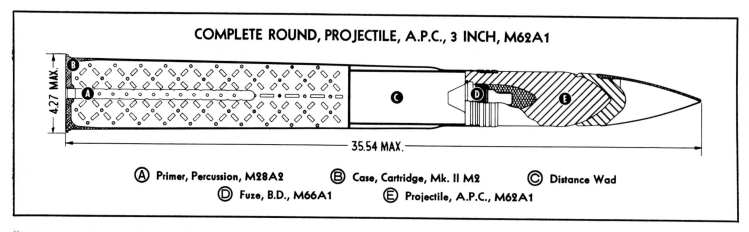

COMPLETE ROUND, PROJECTILE, A.P.C., 3 INCH, M62A1

4.27 MAX. — 35.54 MAX.

(A) Primer, Percussion, M28A2 (B) Case, Cartridge, Mk. II M2 (C) Distance Wad
(D) Fuze, B.D., M66A1 (E) Projectile, A.P.C., M62A1

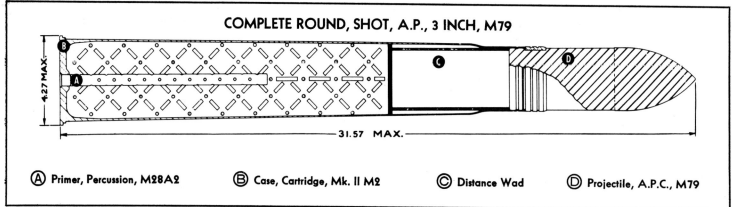

COMPLETE ROUND, SHOT, A.P., 3 INCH, M79

4.27 MAX. — 31.57 MAX.

(A) Primer, Percussion, M28A2 (B) Case, Cartridge, Mk. II M2 (C) Distance Wad (D) Projectile, A.P.C., M79

Due to the additional manufacturing steps necessary in the production of the three-piece M62A1 projectile, the easily made 3 inch monobloc projectile, M79, was classified as substitute standard for use in the 3 inch antitank guns, M3 and M5, and the 3 inch tank gun, M7. As the M62A1 now is in full production, the M79 shot will be manufactured and issued until the original procurement has been completed.

Both rounds use a propelling charge of

CHARACTERISTICS

	Projectile, A.P.C., M62A1	Projectile, A.P.C., M62A1	Shot, A.P., M79	Shot, A.P., M79	Projectile, Drill, M10
Caliber	3 inch	3 inch	3 inch	3 inch	3 inch
Model of Guns	M3, M5, M6, M7	M1918	M3, M5, M6, M7	M1918	All guns
Projectile Weight	15.43 lb.	15.43 lb.	15.0 lb.	15.0 lb.	24.50 lb.
Proj. Charge and Weight	Expl. "D," 0.144 lb.	Expl. "D," 0.144 lb.	——	——	
Fuze	B.D., M66A1	B.D., M66A1	——	——	Dummy, M42A1
Primer	M28A2	M28A2	M28A2	M28A2	
Cartridge Case	Mk. II M2*	Mk. II M2*	Mk. II M2*	Mk. II M2*	
Propelling Charge and Weight	NH powder, 4.62 lb.	NH powder, 4.62 lb.	NH powder, 4.62 lb.	NH powder, 4.62 lb.	
Complete Round Weight	27.23 lb.	27.23 lb.	26.80 lb.	26.80 lb.	24.50 lb.
Muzzle Velocity	2,600 f/s	2,400 f/s	2,600 f/s	2,400 f/s	
Maximum Range	16,100 yds.	15,300 yds.	12,770 yds.	11,000 yds.	
Chamber Capacity	205.585 cu. ins.	205.585 cu. ins.	203.50 cu. ins.	203.50 cu. ins.	
Rated Max. Pressure, p.s.i.	38,000	36,000	38,000	36,000	
Armor Penetration at 20°					
Homogeneous Plate					
500 yards	4.3 ins.	3.8 ins.	4.7 ins.	4.1 ins.	
1,000 yards	3.9 ins.	3.4 ins.	3.9 ins.	3.5 ins.	
Face-Hard. Plate					
500 yards	4.5 ins.	4.0 ins.	3.2 ins.	2.8 ins.	
1,000 yards	4.0 ins.	3.6 ins.	2.8 ins.	2.4 ins.	

*Steel cartridge case, Mk. II M2B1, is substitute standard.

(Continued on next page)

PROJECTILE, ARMOR-PIERCING CAPPED, 3 INCH, M62A1
SHOT, ARMOR-PIERCING, 3 INCH, M79
(Continued)

the same type and weight—4.62 pounds of NH powder. The M1 class powder used in the propelling charge has an 87–10–3 formula. The grains have seven perforations and a web of 0.043 inch. For powder-burning uniformity a distance wad insures that the propelling charge is confined around the primer.

PROJECTILE, ARMOR-PIERCING CAPPED, 3 INCH, M62A1—STANDARD

—This projectile is standard for issue to using forces with the 3 inch, M3, antiaircraft and M5 antitank guns, and the tank gun, M7. It also is used in the M1918, M1 and M6 guns.

The projectile measures 14.47 inches overall and consists of the projectile body to which the armor-piercing cap is soldered or crimped. The windshield nose is threaded to the cap. Alternate windshield-attachment methods are discussed under Projectile, A.P.C., 75 mm, M61, as both projectiles use the same methods.

The complete round consists of the projectile which weighs 15.43 pounds as fired and contains a bursting charge of 0.144 pound of explosive "D," the base-detonating fuze, M66A1; the Mk. II M2 cartridge case, with a 212 cubic inch volume, which contains the M28A2 percussion primer to detonate 4.62 pounds of NH powder. The steel cartridge case, Mk. II M2B1, is substitute standard for use in the M1918, M1, M3, M5 and M7 guns.

SHOT, ARMOR-PIERCING, 3 INCH, M79—SUBSTITUTE STANDARD

—The complete round for this shot is composed of the A.P. Shot and the Mk. II M2 cartridge case containing the M28A2 percussion primer and a propelling charge of NH powder. The Mk. II M2B1 steel cartridge case is substitute standard.

The shot is manufactured from WD-4150 steel bar stock and is given a special heat treatment to improve its armor-penetration properties. Red tracer composition is pressed into a cavity in the base of the shot. The burning time of the tracer is 3 seconds.

A complete round of this shot measures 31.57 inches in length and weighs 26.8 pounds. The shot itself measures 9.22 inches in length and weighs 15 pounds.

PROJECTILE, DRILL, M10—STANDARD

—(See Table of Characteristics.)

SHELL, HIGH-EXPLOSIVE, 3 INCH, **M42A1**—STANDARD
PROJECTILE, ARMOR-PIERCING CAPPED, 3 INCH, **M62A1**—STANDARD
SHELL, SMOKE, 3 INCH, **M88**—STANDARD
SHOT, ARMOR-PIERCING, 3 INCH, **M79**—SUBSTITUTE STANDARD
ROUNDS FOR GUNS, 76 mm, M1, M1A1, AND M1A2

COMPLETE ROUND, SHELL, H.E., 76 mm, M42A1

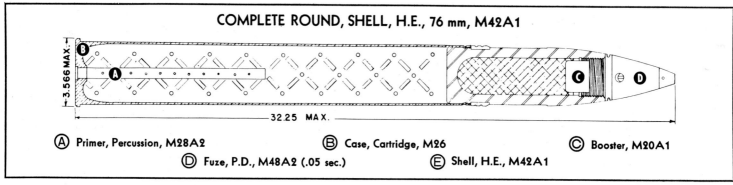

Ⓐ Primer, Percussion, M28A2   Ⓑ Case, Cartridge, M26   Ⓒ Booster, M20A1
Ⓓ Fuze, P.D., M48A2 (.05 sec.)   Ⓔ Shell, H.E., M42A1

COMPLETE ROUND, PROJECTILE, A.P.C., 76 mm, M62A1

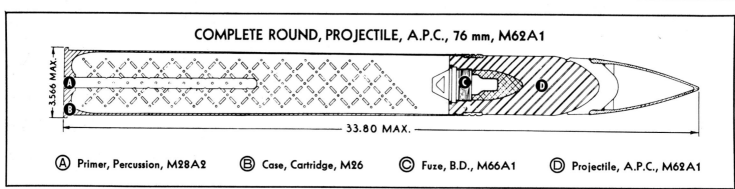

Ⓐ Primer, Percussion, M28A2   Ⓑ Case, Cartridge, M26   Ⓒ Fuze, B.D., M66A1   Ⓓ Projectile, A.P.C., M62A1

COMPLETE ROUND, SHELL, SMOKE, 76 mm, M88

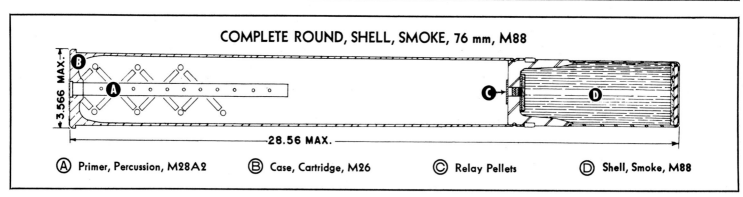

Ⓐ Primer, Percussion, M28A2   Ⓑ Case, Cartridge, M26   Ⓒ Relay Pellets   Ⓓ Shell, Smoke, M88

COMPLETE ROUND, SHOT, A.P., 76 mm, M79

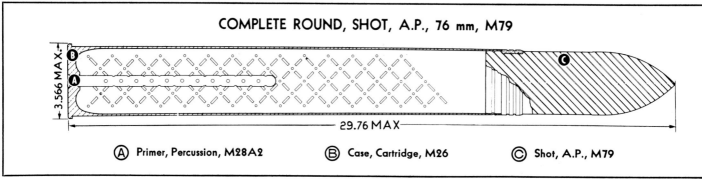

Ⓐ Primer, Percussion, M28A2   Ⓑ Case, Cartridge, M26   Ⓒ Shot, A.P., M79

(Continued on next page)

SHELL, HIGH-EXPLOSIVE, 3 INCH, **M42A1**
PROJECTILE, ARMOR-PIERCING CAPPED, 3 INCH, **M62A1**
SHELL, SMOKE, 3 INCH, **M88**
SHOT, ARMOR-PIERCING, 3 INCH, **M79**

(Continued)

The three projectiles above are classified as standard for use in the guns, 76 mm, M1, M1A1, and M1A2. Three-inch shells may be used since the gun is actually 76.2 mm, or 3 inches, in caliber. The principal difference between the 3 inch and the 76 mm complete rounds is in the capacity of the cartridge case. Due to this, the rounds are not interchangeable between the 3 inch and 76 mm guns.

SHELL, H.E., 3 INCH, M42A1—STANDARD—This round uses the M26 cartridge case with a chamber capacity of 140.50 cubic inches. A complete round of this ammunition for the 76 mm gun consists of the high-explosive shell, M42A1, fuzed with the P.D. fuze, M48A2 (.05 sec.); the M26 cartridge case containing the percussion primer, M28A2; and the FNH propelling charge.

With a propelling charge of 3.62 pounds of FNH powder in the 76 mm gun the shell attains a muzzle velocity of 2,700 feet per second; in the 3 inch gun the shell, propelled by 4.56 pounds of NH powder, attains a muzzle velocity of 2,800 feet per second. Maximum range of the 76 mm gun is 14,650 yards; that of the 3 inch gun is 14,780 yards at 42° 45′ elevation when firing the M42A1 shell.

The 3.62 pounds of M1 powder for the 76 mm gun has an 87–10–3 formula. The powder grains have seven perforations and a 0.0395 inch web.

Weight of the bursting charge is 0.86 pound of TNT, or an alternate charge of 0.85 pound, consisting of 0.77 pound 50/50 Amatol and 0.08 pound cast TNT booster surround. The shell as fired weighs 12.87 pounds. Complete round weights are 22.11 pounds for the 76 mm round, and 24.61 pounds for the 3 inch round.

PROJECTILE, ARMOR-PIERCING, CAPPED, 3 INCH, M62A1 — STANDARD —This round uses the M26 cartridge case with a chamber capacity of 142.6 cubic inches compared with the 203.5 cubic inch chamber capacity of the Mk. II M2 cartridge case used with the 3 inch round. The 76 mm round develops a muzzle velocity of 2,600 feet per second and a maximum range of 16,100 yards at 45° elevation. The 3 inch round develops the same muzzle velocity and maximum range.

The weight of the armor-piercing cap round is 15.43 pounds. The shot uses the base-detonating fuze, M66A1, to ignite 0.144 pound of explosive "D" bursting charge. Complete round weights are 24.55 pounds for the 76 mm round, and 27.23 pounds for the 3 inch round.

The 3.62 pounds of M1 powder has an 87–10–3 formula. The grains have seven perforations and a web of 0.0395 inch.

For description of projectile, see 3 inch gun rounds.

Comparative data on armor penetration at 20° for the 76 mm, 75 mm, and 3 inch armor-piercing cap rounds follow:

At 500 yds.	Homo. Plate	Face-Hard. Plate
76 mm, M62 Projectile*	4.3 ins.	4.5 ins.
75 mm, M61 Projectile	2.9 ins.	3.5 ins.
3 inch, M62 Projectile*	4.3 ins.	4.5 ins.

At 1,000 yds.	Homo. Plate	Face-Hard. Plate
76 mm, M62 Projectile*	3.8 ins.	4.0 ins.
75 mm, M61 Projectile	2.6 ins.	3.1 ins.
3 inch, M62 Projectile*	3.8 ins.	4.0 ins.

CHARACTERISTICS

	Shell, H.E., M42A1	Proj. A.P.C., M62A1	Shell, Smoke, M88	Shot, A.P., M79
Caliber	76 mm	76 mm	76 mm	76 mm
Model of Guns	M1, M1A1, M1A2	M1, M1A1, M1A2	M1, M1A1, M1A2	M1, M1A1, M1A2
Proj. Weight	12.87 lb.	15.43 lb.	7.60 lb.	15.00 lb.
Proj. Charge and Weight	TNT, 0.86 lb.**	Expl. "D," 0.144 lb.	H.C., 3.13 lb.	——
Booster	M20A1	——	——	——
Fuze	P.D., M48A2	B.D., M66A1	——	——
Primer	M28A2	M28A2	M28A2	M28A2
Cartridge Case	M26†	M26†	M26†	M26†
Propelling Charge and Weight	FNH powder, 3.62 lb.	FNH powder, 3.62 lb.	FNH powder, 0.219 lb.	FNH powder, 3.62 lb.
Complete Round Weight	22.11 lb.	24.55 lb.	13.43 lb.	24.24 lb.
Muzzle Velocity	2,700 f/s	2,600 f/s	900 f/s	2,600 f/s
Maximum Range	14,650 yds.	16,100 yds.	2,000 yds.***	12,770 yds.
Chamber Capacity	140.50 cu. ins.	142.6 cu. ins.	143.6 cu. ins.	143.66 cu. ins.
Rated Max. Pressure, p.s.i.	43,000	43,000	4,000	43,000
Armor Penetration at 20°				
Homogeneous Plate				
500 yards	——	4.3 ins.	——	4.6 ins.
1,000 yards	——	3.8 ins.	——	4.0 ins.
Face-Hard. Plate				
500 yards	——	4.5 ins.	——	3.2 ins.
1,000 yards	——	4.0 ins.	——	2.8 ins.

*Same Projectile.
**Or 50/50 Amatol 0.77 lb. plus Cast TNT 0.08 lb.
***At 15° Elevation.
†The M26B1 steel cartridge case is substitute standard.

(Continued on next page)

SHELL, HIGH-EXPLOSIVE, 3 INCH, M42A1
PROJECTILE, ARMOR-PIERCING CAPPED, 3 INCH, M62A1
SHELL, SMOKE, 3 INCH, M88
SHOT, ARMOR-PIERCING, 3 INCH, M79

(Continued)

SHOT, ARMOR-PIERCING, 3 INCH, M79 — SUBSTITUTE STANDARD — The M79 Shot is authorized as a substitute standard for the M62A1 Projectile. It is a solid monobloc construction shot containing a built-in tracer, which has a burning time of 3 seconds. For a more complete description of shot see 3 inch gun rounds.

A complete round consists of the M79 A.P. Shot, the M26 or M26B1 cartridge case, containing the M28A2 percussion primer and a propelling charge of FNH powder.

The shot weighs 15.0 pounds and when assembled to form a complete round the weight is 24.24 pounds. As fired the round measures 29.76 inches in length.

The same charge and type of propellant as used with the Projectile, A.P.C., M62A1 is used.

SHELL, SMOKE, 3 INCH, M88 — STANDARD — This unfuzed, base-emission round differs completely from other standard rounds fired in this gun. In appearance the shell resembles a canister. It was adapted from the British base-emission type shell and has the advantage of emitting smoke from the base of the projectile toward the end of the shell's trajectory.

This effect is obtained by use of a set of special composition pellets which are ignited when the shell is fired. They burn for a specific length of time, enough to insure that the H. C. smoke filler is ignited, and allowed to escape through the hole in the base of the shell, toward the end of its trajectory.

The advantage of this round is that it uses no burster in the shell but disperses the smoke cloud gradually, forming a more concentrated "curtain" than the fuzed smoke shells which produce the "puff" type cloud.

The 0.219 pound of M2 powder is a Hercules NG formula. The web size is 0.015 inch and the grain has a single perforation.

SHELL, HIGH-EXPLOSIVE, 81 MM, M43A1—STANDARD
SHELL, HIGH-EXPLOSIVE, 81 MM, M56—STANDARD
SHELL, CHEMICAL, 81 MM, M57—STANDARD
ROUNDS FOR MORTAR, 81 mm, M1, AND MORTAR, 3 INCH, MK. IA2

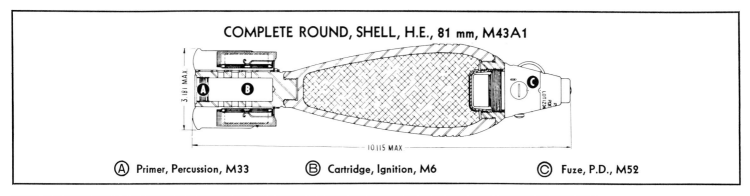

COMPLETE ROUND, SHELL, H.E., 81 mm, M43A1

Ⓐ Primer, Percussion, M33 Ⓑ Cartridge, Ignition, M6 Ⓒ Fuze, P.D., M52

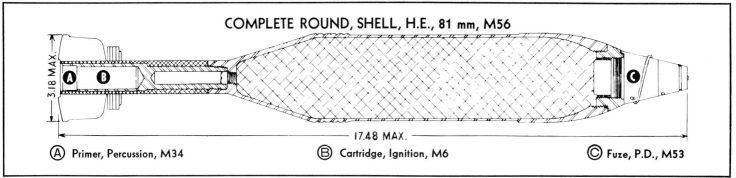

COMPLETE ROUND, SHELL, H.E., 81 mm, M56

Ⓐ Primer, Percussion, M34 Ⓑ Cartridge, Ignition, M6 Ⓒ Fuze, P.D., M53

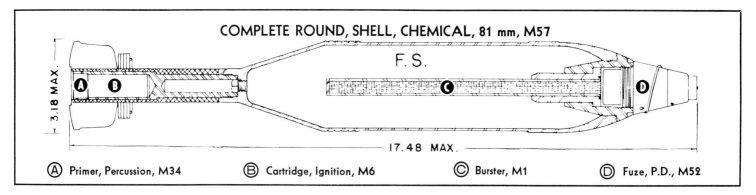

COMPLETE ROUND, SHELL, CHEMICAL, 81 mm, M57

Ⓐ Primer, Percussion, M34 Ⓑ Cartridge, Ignition, M6 Ⓒ Burster, M1 Ⓓ Fuze, P.D., M52

Since the last war, vast changes in design have been made in the old "Stokes" mortar projectiles to improve their ballistics and functioning.

All the existing 3 inch and 81 mm mortar shells have a fin assembly to give greater stability to the shell in flight. Due to the improved stability, the present standard projectiles use a point-detonating fuze, the M52 or M53, in place of the "all ways" fuze that was necessary in World War I shells.

The interior of the fin assembly is machined to take the ignition cartridge and is perforated by a number of holes to permit the flame from the ignition cartridge to flash through to the propelling increments which are clipped between the fins by the M2A1 propellant increment holder in the M43A1 high-explosive round. On the M56 and M57 rounds the increments are placed around the cartridge holder tube. The shells are loaded through the muzzle of the mortar and ignition occurs when the primer strikes the fixed firing pin in the base of the barrel.

Both the 81 mm and 3 inch mortars are smoothbored. The 81 mm mortar, M1, is the present standard for manufacture and issue, and it has superseded the 3 inch mortar, Mk. IA2. The ammunition is the same for both although a larger propelling charge can be used in the 81 mm mortar.

SHELL, HIGH-EXPLOSIVE, M43A1— STANDARD—This high-explosive shell is intended primarily for use against enemy personnel. As fired, the shell with fuze, P.D., M52, weighs 6.92 pounds. Of this the TNT bursting charge weighs 1.22 pounds; an alternate charge consists of 0.98 pound of 50/50 Amatol and 0.19 pound Cast TNT booster surround. Another loading consists of 1.28 pounds of trimonite. The weight of six M1 increments of sheet powder propellant is 0.097 pound. The sheet powder used has a Hercules NG formula. Several of the sheets are sewn together, each sheet having five perforations, one in the middle and one in each corner, the web size being 0.008 inch. Each increment is contained in a Cellophane bag which protects the charge and insures dry powder. The complete round weighs 7.05 pounds.

(Continued on next page)

SHELL, HIGH-EXPLOSIVE, 81 MM, M43A1
SHELL, HIGH-EXPLOSIVE, 81 MM, M56
SHELL, CHEMICAL, 81 MM, M57

(Continued)

An alternate method of manufacture is a one piece shell body which does away with the adapter needed with the M43A1 round. This is the M43A1B1 shell. The shell body is produced by any of the following methods: forging, cupping of specially rolled plates, welded longitudinally, or casting. Firing data are given in Table A.

SHELL, HIGH-EXPLOSIVE, M56—STANDARD—The M56 projectile embodies a relatively large charge, 4.30 pounds of TNT, in relation to the total weight, 10.62 pounds, of the shell as fired with the fuze, P.D., M53. It is designed primarily for use against light emplacements. Alternate bursting charges are: 3.89 pounds of 50/50 Amatol and 0.20 pound of Cast TNT booster surround, or 4.46 pounds of trimonite. The maximum range is less than the M43A1. Ranges are listed in Table B. The M2 increment powder used in this round comes in sheets and is a Hercules NG formula. Several sheets are sewn together and each sheet has one perforation and a web of 0.008 inch.

SHELL, CHEMICAL, M57—STANDARD—The chemical shell, M57, with WP or FS filler, is used to make a smoke screen. When the shell is detonated, the burster charge fragments the shell body, scattering the filler to form the smoke cloud. The round uses the same increment powder as the M56, HE, shell.

As fired, the shell weighs 11.86 pounds when FS filled, and 11.33 pounds when WP filled. The weights of the chemical charge are 4.59 pounds with FS, and 4.06 pounds with WP filler. The weight of the tetryl burster charge is 0.08 pound. Complete round weights are as follows: 12 pounds when FS filled, and 11.47 pounds when WP filled. Firing table data for these shells are given in Tables C and D.

SHELL, TARGET PRACTICE, M44—STANDARD—Loaded and fuzed, the cast-iron shell of this round weighs 6.92 pounds, the same as the high-explosive shell, M43A1. The charge used is 0.2 pound of black powder. Fuze, P.D., M52, is used. A propelling charge consists of

sheet powder in 6 increments of approximately 172 grains each. Only four increments are used in the 3 inch trench mortar, due to the lower pressures allowed in this mortar.

The sheet powder used has a Hercules NG formula. Several of the sheets are sewn together, each sheet having five perforations, one in the center and one in each corner, the web size being 0.008 inch. The round is assembled with percussion primer, M33.

SHELL, PRACTICE, M43A1—STANDARD—O.C.M. 12734 approved this round as an alternative to the M44 practice round. The M43A1 practice shell uses a black powder charge of 0.16 pound in place of the 1.22 lb. TNT charge used in the high-explosive round, M43A1. In all other respects the M43A1 practice shell is identical with the high-explosive shell, M43A1. The round is assembled with percussion primer, M33.

PROJECTILE, DRILL, M68—STANDARD—(See Table of Characteristics.)

(TABLE A) SHELL, HIGH-EXPLOSIVE, M43A1 WITH FUZE, P.D., M52

Charge		Muzzle Velocity	Maximum Range	Elevation
Zone 0........	Cartridge	235 F/S	541 yds.	45°
Zone 1.......	Cartridge + 1 Incr.	332 F/S	1,020 yds.	45°
Zone 2.......	Cartridge + 2 Incr.	419 F/S	1,500 yds.	45°
Zone 3.......	Cartridge + 3 Incr.	499 F/S	2,042 yds.	45°
Zone 4.......	Cartridge + 4 Incr.	572 F/S	2,517 yds.	45°
Zone 5*.......	Cartridge + 5 Incr.	638 F/S	2,963 yds.	45°
Zone 6*.......	Cartridge + 6 Incr.	700 F/S	3,288 yds.	45°

*Not to be used in 3 inch mortar, Mk. IA2.

(TABLE B) SHELL, HIGH-EXPLOSIVE, M56

Charge		Muzzle Velocity	Maximum Range	Elevation
Zone 1........	Cartridge + 1 Incr.	306 F/S	875 yds.	45° 00'
Zone 2.......	Cartridge + 2 Incr.	412 F/S	1,474 yds.	45° 00'
Zone 3.......	Cartridge + 3 Incr.	502 F/S	2,046 yds.	45° 00'
Zone 4*.......	Cartridge + 4 Incr.	583 F/S	2,558 yds.	45° 00'

*Not to be used in 3 inch mortar, Mk. IA2.

(TABLE C) SHELL, CHEMICAL, M57 (FS)

Charge		Muzzle Velocity	Maximum Range	Elevation
Zone 1........	Cartridge + 1 Incr.	291 F/S	808 yds.	45° 00'
Zone 2.......	Cartridge + 2 Incr.	390 F/S	1,374 yds.	45° 00'
Zone 3.......	Cartridge + 3 Incr.	472 F/S	1,916 yds.	45° 00'
Zone 4*.......	Cartridge + 4 Incr.	544 F/S	2,431 yds.	45° 00'

*Not to be used in 3 inch mortar, Mk. IA2

(TABLE D) SHELL, CHEMICAL, M57 (WP)

Charge		Muzzle Velocity	Maximum Range	Elevation
Zone 1........	Cartridge + 1 Incr.	297 F/S	833 yds.	45° 00'
Zone 2.......	Cartridge + 2 Incr.	399 F/S	409 yds.	45° 00'
Zone 3.......	Cartridge + 3 Incr.	484 F/S	1,952 yds.	45° 00'
Zone 4*.......	Cartridge + 4 Incr.	560 F/S	2,466 yds.	45° 00'

*Not to be used in 3 inch mortar, Mk. IA2

CHARACTERISTICS

	Shell, H.E., M43A1†	Shell, H.E., M56	Shell, Chem., M57	Shell, T.P., M44	Shell, Training, M68
Caliber....................	81 mm and 3 in.	81 mm and 3 in.	81 mm and 3 in.	81 mm and 3 in.	81 mm and 3 in.
Model of Mortars.....................	M1, Mk. IA2**	M1, Mk. IA2**	M1, Mk. IA2**	M1, Mk. IA2**	M1, Mk. IA2**
Proj. Weight.....................	6.92 lb.‡	10.62 lb.††	11.33 lb.¶¶	6.92 lb.	—
Proj. Charge and Weight...............	TNT, 1.22 lb.§	TNT, 4.30 lb.‡‡	Chem. (FS) 4.59 lb. Chem. (WP) 4.06 lb. M1	BP, 0.2 lb.	—
Burster.....................	—	—		—	
Fuze.....................	P.D., M52¶	P.D., M53	P.D., M52¶	P.D., M52¶	—
Primer.....................	M33	M34	M34	M33	M34
Ignition Cartridge..................	M6	M6	M3	M6	M6
Propelling Charge and Weight..........	Sheet pwdr., 0.097 lb.	Flake prop. pwdr. 0.116 lb.	Flake prop. pwdr. 0.116 lb.	Sheet pwdr., 0.097 lb.	NG pwdr., 120 grs.
Complete Round Weight............	7.05 lb.***	10.77 lb.§§	11.59 lb.¶¶	7.05 lb.	—
Muzzle Velocity............	700 f/s	583 f/s	560 f/s	700 f/s	172.8 f/s
Maximum range............	3,288 yds.	2,558 yds.	2,466 yds.¶¶	3,288 yds.	310 yds.
Rated Max. Pressure, p.s.i............	6,000	6,000	6,000	6,000	

**81 mm Mortar, M1, 3 inch Mortar, Mk. IA2.
†The Shell, Practice, M43A1, not listed in above table, differs only in the amount of charge: 0.16 lb. of black powder as against 1.22 lb. of TNT.
‡6.86 lb. with Amatol and TNT loading and 7.02 lb. with trimonite loading.
§1.17 lb. consisting of 0.98 lb. 50/50 Amatol and 0.19 lb. Cast TNT or 1.28 lb. trimonite.
¶P.D., M52B1, alternate fuze.

***6.99 lb. with Amatol and TNT loading and 7.11 lb. with trimonite loading.
††10.41 lb. with Amatol and TNT loading and 10.79 lb. with trimonite loading.
§§10.56 lb. with Amatol and TNT loading and 10.94 lb. with trimonite loading.
‡‡Alternate bursting charges: 3.89 lb., 50/50 Amatol and 0.20 lb. Cast TNT booster surround, 4.46 lb. of trimonite.
¶¶For W. P. Chemical Shell.

SHELL, HIGH-EXPLOSIVE, 90 MM, **M71**—STANDARD

PROJECTILE, ARMOR-PIERCING CAPPED, 90 MM, **M82**—STANDARD

SHOT, ARMOR-PIERCING, 90 MM, **M77**—SUBSTITUTE STANDARD

ROUNDS FOR GUNS, 90 mm, M1, M1A1, M2 AND M3 (ANTIAIRCRAFT)

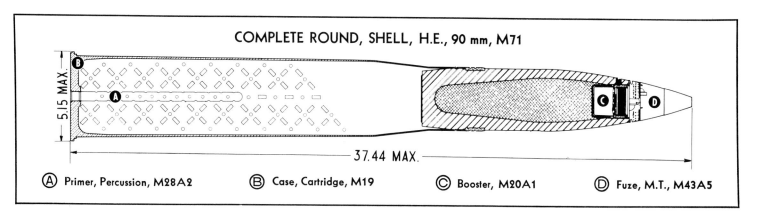

COMPLETE ROUND, SHELL, H.E., 90 mm, M71

5.15 MAX. 37.44 MAX.

Ⓐ Primer, Percussion, M28A2 Ⓑ Case, Cartridge, M19 Ⓒ Booster, M20A1 Ⓓ Fuze, M.T., M43A5

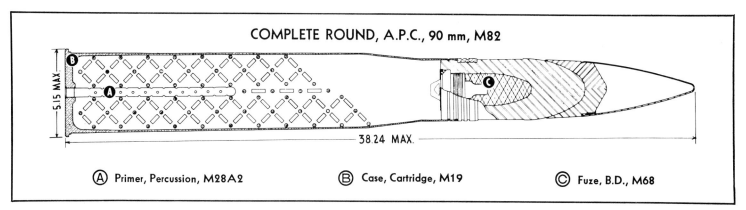

COMPLETE ROUND, A.P.C., 90 mm, M82

5.15 MAX. 38.24 MAX.

Ⓐ Primer, Percussion, M28A2 Ⓑ Case, Cartridge, M19 Ⓒ Fuze, B.D., M68

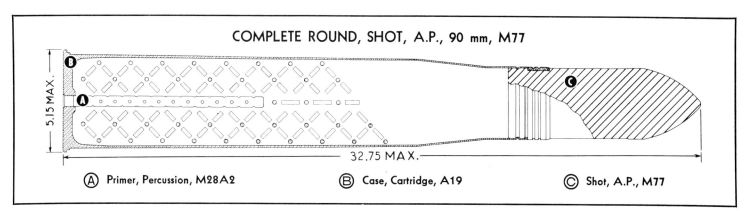

COMPLETE ROUND, SHOT, A.P., 90 mm, M77

5.15 MAX. 32.75 MAX.

Ⓐ Primer, Percussion, M28A2 Ⓑ Case, Cartridge, A19 Ⓒ Shot, A.P., M77

These rounds use an NH propelling charge of M1 class powder with a formula of 87–10–3. The grains of this powder have seven perforations and a web of 0.049 inch.

SHELL, HIGH-EXPLOSIVE, 90 mm, M71 —STANDARD—The 90 mm high-explosive shell, M71, was designed and standardized to replace the now obsolete 90 mm, M58, when it was discovered that the latter when manufactured from high - sulfur, high - manganese, free - machining steel without a final heat treatment would not stand up under the strain of firing.

The shell, M71, is of the streamlined type with a tapered or boat-tailed base. This streamlining is completed by a con- tinuation of the projectile's radius of ogive over the exterior surface of the fuze, M.T., M43A5.

When used for antitank purposes, the M71 shell is also furnished with the P.D. fuze, M48A2 (.05 sec.). The Fuze, P.D. M48A2 (.15 sec.) is used against motor torpedo boats.

The bursting charge consists of 2.04

pounds of TNT in the shell which weighs 23.40 pounds as fired, and has an over-all length of 16.34 inches. Alternate loadings consist of 1.81 lbs. of 50/50 Amatol and 0.15 lb. of TNT booster surround, or 2.13 lbs. of Composition "B."

A propelling charge of 7.31 pounds of NH powder is used in the M19 cartridge case. (See † under "Characteristics.") The complete round weighs 42.04 pounds.

The booster, M20A1, in combination with the mechanical time fuze, M43A5, or with the P.D. fuze, M48A2, provides a bore-safe combination, since the rotor of the booster holds the detonator out of line with the flash hole until the shell has cleared the muzzle of the weapon.

The M28A2 percussion primer contains 300 grains of black powder and extends well up into the cartridge case to insure uniform ignition of the propelling charge.

PROJECTILE, ARMOR-PIERCING, CAPPED, 90 mm, M82—STANDARD—This projectile has been standardized as the companion projectile to the M71. The components of the complete round consist of the M82 projectile, loaded and fuzed with the B.D. fuze, M68; the M19 cartridge case containing the M28A2 percussion primer; and a propelling charge of 7.31 pounds.

Soldered to the nose of the body is a mild steel armor-piercing cap to which a windshield assembly is screwed. The assembly consists of a windshield adapter made from cold drawn seamless steel tubing, and attached to it by brazing a cold rolled steel windshield ogive. An alternate manufacture of windshield permits direct 360° crimping to the cap. The over-all length of the shot is 15.49 inches and as fired weighs 24.06 pounds. The complete round weighs 42.75 pounds.

SHOT, ARMOR-PIERCING, 90 mm, M77 — SUBSTITUTE STANDARD — The M77 shot is substitute standard for the M84 projectile. It is a solid monobloc shot and does not contain a bursting charge or armor-piercing cap. It has a tracer plug which is screwed into the body of the shot. The tracer consists of 49 grains of red tracer composition and 20 grains of igniter composition. A celluloid closing cup seals the tracer into the plug. The tracer has a 3 second burning time. A complete round consists of the Shot, A.P., M77, it measures 32.75 inches in length and weighs 42.04 pounds. The shot measures 10 inches and weighs 23.4 pounds.

PROJECTILE, DRILL, 90 mm, M12 — STANDARD—(See Table of Characteristics.)

CHARACTERISTICS

	Shell, H.E., M71	Proj., A.P.C., M82	Proj., Drill, M12	SHOT, A.P., M77
Caliber	90 mm	90 mm	90 mm	90 mm
Model of Gun	M1, M1A1, M2, and M3	M1, M1A1, M2, and M3	M1, M1A1, M2, and M3	M1, M1A1, M2, and M3
Proj. Weight	23.40 lb.‡	24.06 lb.	——	23.40 lb.
Proj. Charge and Weight	TNT, 2.04 lb.§	Expl. "D", 0.31 lb.	——	——
Booster	M20A1			
Fuze	M.T., M43A5*	B.D., M68	M44A2, Dummy	——
Primer	M28A2	M28A2	——	M28A2
Cartridge Case	M19†	M19†	——	M19†
Propelling Charge and Weight	NH powder, 7.31 lb.	NH powder, 7.31 lb.	——	NH powder, 7.31 lb.
Complete Round Weight	42.04 lb.¶	42.75 lb.	39.15 lb.	42.04 lb.
Muzzle Velocity	2,700 f/s	2,670 f/s	——	2700 f/s
Maximum Range	H-18,960 yds., V-13,170 yds.	13,540 yds.	——	12,790 yds.
Chamber Capacity	298.04 cu. ins.	312.185 cu. ins.	——	312.185 cu. ins.
Rated Max. Pressure, p.s.i.	38,000	38,000	——	38,000
Armor Penetration at 20°				
Homogeneous Plate				
500 yards	——	5.12 ins.	——	5.6 ins.
1,000 yards	——	4.8 ins.	——	4.8 ins.
Face-Hard. Plate				
500 yards	——	5.5 ins.	——	4.8 ins.
1,000 yards	——	5.1 ins.	——	4.0 ins.

*Or P.D., Fuze, M48A2 (.05 sec.) for antitank use; for anti-motor torpedo boat use P.D. Fuze, M48A2 (.15 sec.)
†The steel cartridge case, M19B1, is substitute standard.
‡23.32 lb. with Amatol and TNT loading and 23.49 lb. with Composition "B" loading.
§Or 2.13 lb. of Composition "B" or 1.96 lb. consisting of 1.81 lb. 50/50 Amatol and 0.15 lb. TNT.
¶41.96 lb. with Amatol and TNT loading and 42.13 lb. with Composition "B" loading.

SHELL, HIGH-EXPLOSIVE, 105 MM, M38A1—STANDARD

ROUND FOR GUN, 105 mm, M3 (ANTIAIRCRAFT)

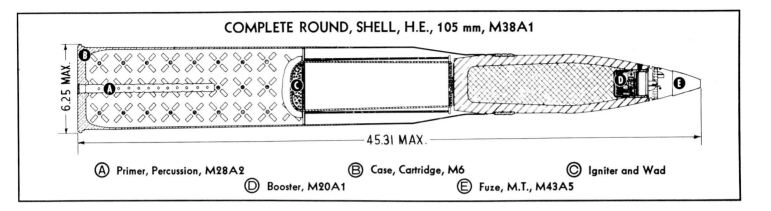

COMPLETE ROUND, SHELL, H.E., 105 mm, M38A1

6.25 MAX.

45.31 MAX.

Ⓐ Primer, Percussion, M28A2   Ⓑ Case, Cartridge, M6   Ⓒ Igniter and Wad

Ⓓ Booster, M20A1   Ⓔ Fuze, M.T., M43A5

The ammunition used in the 105 mm antiaircraft gun is issued to the using arms in complete rounds of the fixed type. The round consists of a cartridge case, containing a primer and propelling charge, and a fuzed and loaded high-explosive shell.

Owing to the availability at the time of the M2 mechanical time fuze, approximately 18,000 of the M38 high-explosive shells were issued as complete rounds with this fuze. When these shells were exhausted, the M38 was modified and standardized as the M38A1 with the fuze, M.T., M43. The modification consisted of increasing the ogive length of the shell to take the M20A1 booster into which the M43 mechanical time fuze was screwed. In other respects the present M38A1 is identical with the M38.

SHELL, H.E., 105 mm, M38A1—STAND-ARD—The M38A1 is of the streamlined type with a tapered base and long ogive. The radius of ogive is approximately 8.3 calibers. An inch below the rotating band, the shell body tapers at a 6.75° angle for approximately two inches to the base. The cone-shaped fuze, M.T.-M43A5, completes the projectile's streamlining. Thus, the sharp nose and tapered base reduce the air resistance and add greatly to the ballistic efficiency of the shell in flight.

The M6 cartridge case as provided for the 105 mm anti-aircraft gun has a volume of 638 cubic inches. The 300-grain percussion primer, M28A2, is standard. As fired the shell weighs 32.77 pounds and is propelled by 10.56 pounds of FNH powder. The bursting charge of TNT weighs 3.59 pounds. An alternate charge consists of 3.37 lb. of 50/50 Amatol and 0.15 lb. of Cast TNT booster surround. Still another bursting charge is 3.68 lb. of trimonite. The weight of the complete round is 63.29 pounds.

The M1 class propelling charge has an 85–10–5 formula and has seven perforations per grain, the web size being 0.039 inch.

SHELL, PRACTICE, M38A1—STAND-ARD—This shell is identical with the live ammunition of the same designation except that it contains a practice loading of 0.80 pound of black powder in a bag. This charge is exploded by action of the Fuze, M.T., M43A5, and the booster, M20A1, and is sufficient to rupture the forward portion of the shell and produce a cloud of white smoke. The practice shell is inert loaded to give it a weight comparable to that of the live shell.

The M1 class propelling charge has an 85–10–5 formula and has seven perforations per grain, the web size being 0.039 inch.

DRILL PROJECTILES—STANDARD —(See Table of Characteristics.)

CHARACTERISTICS

	Shell, H.E., M38A1	Shell, Prac., M38A1	Proj. Drill, M11	Proj. Drill, M8
Caliber	105 mm	105 mm	105 mm	105 mm
Model of Gun	M3 (AA)	M3 (AA)	M3 (AA)	M3 (AA)
Proj. Weight	32.77 lb.*	32.85 lb.	—	—
Proj. Charge and Weight	TNT, 3.59 lb.†	BP, 0.80 lb.	—	—
Booster	M20A1	M20A1	—	—
Fuze	M.T., M43A5	M.T., M43A5	M.T., M44A2, Dummy	T23, Dummy
Primer	M28A2	M28A2	—	—
Cartridge Case	M6	M6	—	—
Propelling Charge and Weight	FNH powder, 10.56 lb.	FNH powder, 10.56 lb.	—	—
Complete Round Weight	63.29 lb.‡	63.37 lb.	63.55 lb.	63.55 lb.
Muzzle Velocity	2,800 f/s	2,800 f/s	—	—
Maximum Range	H-20,000 yds. V-14,000 yds.	H-20,000 yds. V-14,000 yds.	—	—
Chamber Capacity	600.22 cu. ins.	600.22 cu. ins.	—	—
Rated Max. Pressure, p.s.i.	36,000	36,000	—	—

*32.70 lb. with 50/50 Amatol loading and 32.86 lb. with trimonite loading.

†Alternate bursting charges: 3.37 lb. of 50/50 Amatol with 0.15 lb. of Cast TNT booster surround, or 3.68 lb. of trimonite.

‡63.22 lb. with Amatol bursting charge or 63.38 lb. with trimonite charge.

SHELL, HIGH-EXPLOSIVE, 105 MM, *M1*—STANDARD
SHELL, HIGH-EXPLOSIVE, ANTITANK, 105 MM, *M67*—STANDARD

ROUNDS FOR HOWITZERS, 105 mm, M2, M2A1, M3 AND M4

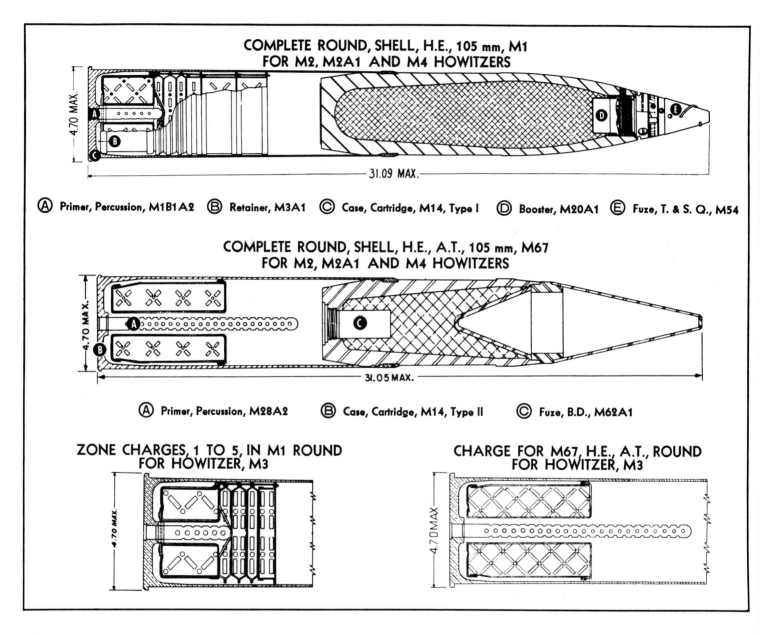

COMPLETE ROUND, SHELL, H.E., 105 mm, M1 FOR M2, M2A1 AND M4 HOWITZERS

31.09 MAX. — 4.70 MAX.

Ⓐ Primer, Percussion, M1B1A2   Ⓑ Retainer, M3A1   Ⓒ Case, Cartridge, M14, Type I   Ⓓ Booster, M20A1   Ⓔ Fuze, T. & S. Q., M54

COMPLETE ROUND, SHELL, H.E., A.T., 105 mm, M67 FOR M2, M2A1 AND M4 HOWITZERS

31.05 MAX. — 4.70 MAX.

Ⓐ Primer, Percussion, M28A2   Ⓑ Case, Cartridge, M14, Type II   Ⓒ Fuze, B.D., M62A1

ZONE CHARGES, 1 TO 5, IN M1 ROUND FOR HOWITZER, M3

4.70 MAX.

CHARGE FOR M67, H.E., A.T., ROUND FOR HOWITZER, M3

4.70 MAX

The M2 and M2A1 howitzers were developed to take the place of the 75 mm pack howitzers of World War I. To provide an airborne weapon heavier and more powerful than existing airborne matériel the M3 howitzer was standardized. As the M2 and M2A1 howitzers proved so successful on the howitzer motor carriage a tank mount with the 105 mm howitzer was developed. The M4 howitzer was standardized for use in the Medium Tanks, M4 and M4A3. The M2, M2A1 and M4 howitzers fire the same complete rounds of ammunition,

while the M3 howitzer uses different complete rounds due to its shortened barrel.

The ammunition used in the 105 mm howitzers, M2, M2A1 and M4, is issued in complete rounds of the semi-fixed type. The M1 shell round includes a cartridge case containing a primer and propelling charge, consisting of a base charge and six increments. The projectile may be easily removed from the cartridge case in order to adjust the propelling charge for the desired range.

The propelling charge for the 105 mm howitzer rounds are in powder bags.

Instead of the old method of tying the zone charges to screw eyes in the base of the cartridge case, the bags are held in the retainer, M3A1, which is pushed down over the percussion primer, M1B1A2, to prevent the bags from slipping forward.

In the case of the H.E., A.T., M67, round, a long primer, the M28A2, is used. The retainer is eliminated as this primer is long enough to prevent the propelling charge bag from shifting within the case.

The cartridge cases for the 105 mm howitzers are M14, Type I and Type II,

(Continued on next page)

SHELL, HIGH-EXPLOSIVE, 105 MM, M1
SHELL, HIGH-EXPLOSIVE, ANTITANK, 105 MM, M67
(Continued)

which differ only in the diametral taper of the wall of the case.

In addition, the chemical and smoke shells described separately, the high-explosive shell, M1, and the high-explosive antitank shell, M67, are authorized at the present time for use in the 105 mm howitzers, M2, M2A1 and M4.

SHELL, H.E., 105 mm, M1—STANDARD —The H.E., 105 mm, M1, round for the new howitzer, M3, is identical to the round as fired in the howitzers, M2, M2A1 and M4, except that the zone charges used are only 1 to 5 instead of 1 to 7.

The 105 mm H.E. shell, M1, is of stream-lined design with a long pointed nose and tapered base. Either the point-detonating fuze, M48A2 (.15 sec.), or the time and superquick fuze, M54, is authorized for use with this shell. Both fuzes are assembled with the M20A1 booster and are considered bore-safe.

The shell as fired weighs 33 pounds and contains a TNT bursting charge of 4.80 pounds. The complete round weighs 42.07 pounds. The M14, Type I, cartridge case is used and contains a 100-grain percussion type primer, M1B1A2. The steel cartridge case, M14B1, is substitute standard. The fuze, P.D., M48A2 (.15 sec.), is a selective point-detonating fuze which may be set for superquick action or for a short delay action. The fuze, T. & S. Q., M54, is a point-detonating combination superquick and 25-second delay powder time-train fuze.

The propelling charge for the M2, M2A1 and M4 howitzers is the M1 class powder, having an 85–10–5 formula with seven perforations per grain and a web of 0.025 inch.

In the M3 howitzer the charge is the M1 class powder, having an 85–10–5 formula with single-perforation grains and a web of 0.014 inch.

The propelling charge consists of a base charge and six increments, the zone ranges of which are tabulated below.

SHELL, H.E., A.T., 105 mm, M67— STANDARD—This howitzer shell is identical in design with the 75 mm high-explosive, antitank howitzer shell, M66.

The complete round consists of the cartridge case, M14, Type II, containing the M28A2 primer, a propelling charge of 1.50 pounds of FNH powder and the loaded and fuzed projectile. The steel cartridge case, M14B1, is substitute standard. The complete round weighs 36.95 pounds, of which the shell accounts for 29.22 pounds.

The explosive charge is detonated on impact by the fuze, base-detonating, M62A1. The charge consists of 2.93 pounds of Pentolite. Good penetration of armor plate is obtained with this shell due to the shaped-charge or "Monroe" principle used. The shell will penetrate about 4½ inches of homogeneous armor plate at any range.

In the M2, M2A1 and M4 howitzers the propelling charge is an M1 class powder with a formula of 85–10–5 and has seven perforations per grain and a web of 0.025 inch.

The charge for the M3 howitzer has an 85–10–5 formula and is an M1 class powder with single-perforated grains having a web of 0.014 inch.

PROJECTILE, DRILL, M14—STANDARD—(See Table of Characteristics.)

Charge	Powder Charge	M2, M2A1 & M4 Howitzers			M3 Howitzer	
		MV. (F/S)	Range (yds.)	Elevation	Range (yds.)	Elevation
1	Base Sec. No. 1	650	3,825	43.5°	3,825	43.5°
2	Base & Incr. No. 2	710	4,475	43.6°	4,475	43.5°
3	Base & Incr. No. 2, 3	780	5,280	43.4°	5,280	43.2°
4	Base & Incr. No. 2, 3, 4	875	6,430	43.4°	6,430	43.2°
5	Base & Incr. No. 2, 3, 4, 5	1,020	8,295	43.2°	8,295	43.0°
6	Base & Incr. No. 2, 3, 4, 5, 6	1,235	10,150	43.3°	—	—
7	Base & Incr. No. 2, 3, 4, 5, 6, 7	1,550	12,205	43.7°	—	—

CHARACTERISTICS

	Shell, H.E., M1	Shell, H.E., A.T., M67	Shell, H.E., M1	Shell, H.E., A.T., M67	Proj. Drill, M14
Caliber........................	105 mm	105 mm	105 mm	105 mm	105 mm
Models of Howitzers....................	M2, M2A1, M4	M2, M2A1, M4	M3	M3	M2, M2A1, M4
Proj. Weight........................	33.0 lb.	29.22 lb.	33.0 lb.	29.22 lb.	—
Proj. Charge and Weight..............	TNT, 4.8 lb.	Pentolite, 2.93 lb.	TNT, 4.8 lb.	Pentolite, 2.93 lb.	—
Booster........................	M20A1		M20A1		—
Fuze..........................	P.D., M48A2* (.15 sec.)	B.D., M62A1	P.D., M48A2* (.15 sec.)	B.D., M62A1	Dummy, M59
Primer........................	M1B1A2	M28A2	M1B1A2	M28A2	†
Cartridge Case................	M14, Type I‡	M14, Type II‡‡	M14, Type I‡	M14, Type II‡‡	—
Propelling Charge and Weight........	FNH pwdr., 2.94 lb.	FNH pwdr., 1.50 lb.	FNH pwdr., 1.32 lb.	FNH pwdr., 1.20 lb.	—
Complete Round Weight..............	42.07 lb.	36.95 lb.	40.36 lb.	36.65 lb.	41.35 lb.
Muzzle Velocity..................	1,550 f/s	1,250 f/s	1,020 f/s	1,020 f/s	—
Maximum Range..................	12,205 yds.	8,590 yds.	8,295 yds.	8,490 yds.	—
Chamber Capacity................	153.80 cu. ins.	153.80 cu. ins	153.80 cu. ins.	153.80 cu. ins.	—
Rated Max. Pressure, p.s.i.	30,000	26,000	25,000	20,000	—

*Or Combination T. & S.Q., M54.
†Either the inert 100-grain primers, M1B1A1 or M1A1, may be used.
‡Steel cartridge case, M14B1, Type I, is substitute standard.
‡‡Steel cartridge case, M14B1, Type II is substitute standard.

SHELL, CHEMICAL, 105 MM, (H.S.), **M60**—STANDARD

SHELL, CHEMICAL, 105 MM, (F.S.), **M60**—SUBSTITUTE STANDARD
ROUNDS FOR HOWITZERS, 105 MM, M2, M2A1, M3 AND M4

SHELL, CHEMICAL, 105 MM, (W.P.), **M60**—SUBSTITUTE STANDARD
ROUND FOR HOWITZERS, 105 MM, M2, M2A1, M3 AND M4

SHELL, SMOKE, 105 MM, (B.E.), **M84** AND **M84B1**—STANDARD
ROUND FOR HOWITZERS, 105 MM, M2, M2A1, M3 AND M4

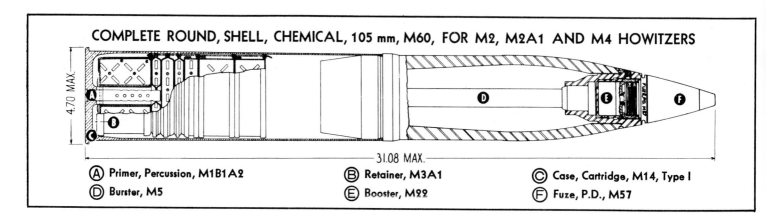

COMPLETE ROUND, SHELL, CHEMICAL, 105 mm, M60, FOR M2, M2A1 AND M4 HOWITZERS

4.70 MAX. — 31.08 MAX.

Ⓐ Primer, Percussion, M1B1A2 Ⓑ Retainer, M3A1 Ⓒ Case, Cartridge, M14, Type I
Ⓓ Burster, M5 Ⓔ Booster, M22 Ⓕ Fuze, P.D., M57

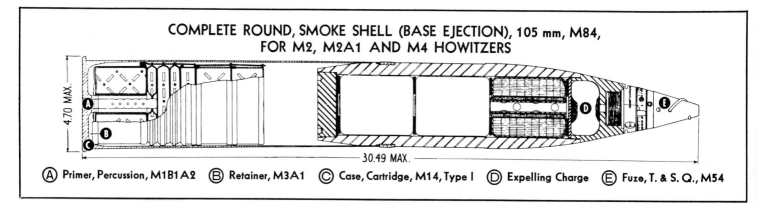

COMPLETE ROUND, SMOKE SHELL (BASE EJECTION), 105 mm, M84, FOR M2, M2A1 AND M4 HOWITZERS

4.70 MAX. — 30.49 MAX.

Ⓐ Primer, Percussion, M1B1A2 Ⓑ Retainer, M3A1 Ⓒ Case, Cartridge, M14, Type I Ⓓ Expelling Charge Ⓔ Fuze, T. & S. Q., M54

SHELL, CHEMICAL, 105 mm, (W.P.), M60 —SUBSTITUTE STANDARD—This shell is authorized for use in the 105 mm howitzer and may be loaded with any of the three following chemical fillers: F.S. (Smoke), W.P. (Smoke) or H.S. (Persistent Gas). The F.S. (Smoke) chemical shell is substitute standard for the M2, M2A1 and M4 howitzers, the W.P. (Smoke) loaded shell is substitute standard for the M2, M2A1, M3 and M4 howitzers while the H.S. (Persistent Gas) is standard for the M2, M2A1 and M4 howitzers.

The weights of the loaded and fuzed projectiles vary with the chemical fillers used, as the following table indicates:

Chemical Filler	Weight of Chem. Filler	Proj. Weight Loaded and Fuzed
F.S.	4.61 lb.	34.86 lb.
W.P.	4.10 lb.	34.35 lb.
H.S.	3.17 lb.	33.42 lb.

After loading, the M5 burster well tube is pressed into place. This tube forms a gas-tight seal at the shell's nose. It has a cavity through the center of the shell into which the tetryl burster charge is placed after the burster well tube has been seated. The P.D. fuze, M57, with booster, M22, is used. The M57 fuze is similar to the P.D. fuze, M48A2, except that it contains no delay element and provides superquick action only.

The propelling charges for the M2, M2A1 and M4 howitzers are contained in seven-section powder bags which are held in the cartridge case by the M31A1 retainer.

The propelling charge is an M1 class powder having an 85–10–5 formula with seven perforations per grain and a web of 0.025 inch. The round as fired in the M3 howitzer is identical except that a five-section propelling charge is used instead of seven. Consequently the muzzle velocity and powder pressures in the M3 howitzer are not so great as in the M2, M2A1 and M4. The M1 powder used with the M3 howitzer round has an 85–10–5 formula. The grains are single perforated and have a web of 0.014 inch. The maximum ranges for the shell are indicated in Tables A and B.

(Continued on next page)

SHELL, CHEMICAL, 105 MM, (H.S.), M60
SHELL, CHEMICAL, 105 MM, (F.S.), M60
SHELL, CHEMICAL, 105 MM, (W.P.), M60
SHELL, SMOKE, 105 MM, (B.E.), M84 AND M84B1

(Continued)

CHARACTERISTICS

	Shell, Chem., Smoke (F.S.), M60	Shell, Chem., Smoke (W.P.), M60	Shell, Chem., Gas (H.S.), M60	Shell, Chem., Smoke (B.E.), M84 and M84B1
Caliber	105 mm	105 mm	105 mm	105 mm
Models of Howitzers	M2, M2A1, M3 and M4	M2, M2A1, M3 and M4	M2, M2A1 and M4	M2, M2A1, M3 and M4
Proj. Weight	34.86 lb.	34.34 lb.	33.42 lb.	32.87 lb.
Proj. Charge and Weight	Smoke (F.S.), 4.61 lb.	Smoke (W.P.), 4.10 lb.	Gas (H.S.), 3.17 lb.	(Smoke, 7.50 lb.) (TNT, 0.14 lb.)
Booster	M22	M22	M22	
Fuze	P.D., M57	P.D., M57	P.D., M57	T. and S. Q., M54
Primer	M1B1A2	M1B1A2	M1B1A2	M1B1A2
Cartridge Case	M14, Type I†	M14, Type I†	M14, Type I†	M14, Type I†
Propelling Charge and Weight	FNH pwdr., 2.94 lb.*	FNH pwdr., 2.94 lb.	FNH pwdr., 2.94 lb.	FNH pwdr., 3.04 lb.*
Complete Round Weight	43.85 lb.	43.35 lb.‡	42.41 lb.	41.84 lb.¶
Muzzle Velocity	1,550 f/s	1,550 f/s**	1,550 f/s	1,550 f/s**
Maximum Range	12,319 yds.	12,281 yds.††	12,243 yds.	12,243 yds.‡‡
Chamber Capacity	153.80 cu. ins.	153.80 cu. ins.	153.80 cu. ins.	153.80 cu. ins.
Rated Max. Pressure, p.s.i.	30,000	30,000§	30,000	30,000§

*1.33 lb. for M3 howitzer.
†Steel cartridge case, M14B1, Type I, is substitute standard.
‡41.71 lb. in M3 howitzer.
§25,000 p.s.i. in M3 howitzer.
¶40.22 lbs. in M3 howitzer.
**1,020 f/s in M3 howitzer.
††8,197 yds. in M3 howitzer.
‡‡8,246 yds. in M3 howitzer.

SMOKE SHELL (BASE EJECTION), 105 mm, M84 AND M84B1—STANDARD— This shell contains three chemical charges with an aggregate weight of 7.50 pounds. It is propelled by 3.04 pounds of FNH powder—slightly more than is used in the M60 chemical shell.

The point-detonating combination superquick and 25-second delay powder time-train fuze, M54, detonates the expelling charge of 0.14 pound of TNT. This amount of expelling charge is sufficient to blow out the closing disk at the base of the shell and to eject the three smoke canisters.

The propelling charges for the M2, M2A1 and M4 howitzers are contained in seven-section powder bags which are held in the cartridge case by the M3A1 retainer.

The propelling charge is an M1 class powder of 85–10–5 formula. The grains have seven perforations and a web of 0.025 inch.

As fired, the M84 shell weighs 32.87 pounds. The complete round weight is 41.84 pounds. The round fired in the M3 howitzer is identical except for a five-section propelling charge. The M1 powder has the same characteristics as that used with the M60 smoke shell in the M3 howitzer.

The M84 shell body is manufactured from steel tubing and consequently an adapter is needed to receive the fuze. An alternate method of manufacture is to make the shell body from a forging. In this case the ogive is continued so that the fuze may be assembled to the shell without the use of an adapter.

TABLE A: (SHELL, CHEMICAL, 105 mm, (H.S.), M60) / (SHELL, CHEMICAL, 105 mm, (F.S.), M60)

		M2, M2A1 and M4 Howitzers			M2, M2A1 and M4 Howitzers	
Charge	Powder Charge	M.V. (f/s)	Range (yds.)	Elevation	Range (yds.)	Elevation
1	Base Sect. No. 1	650	3,789	43.5°	3,717	43.5°
2	Base and Incr. No. 2	710	4,433	43.6°	4,349	43.6°
3	Base and Incr. No. 2, 3	780	5,232	43.4°	5,136	43.4°
4	Base and Incr. No. 2, 3, 4	875	6,387	43.4°	6,301	43.4°
5	Base and Incr. No. 2, 3, 4, 5	1,020	8,246	43.2°	8,148	43.2°
6	Base and Incr. No. 2, 3, 4, 5, 6	1,235	10,138	43.3°	10,114	43.3°
7	Base and Incr. No. 2, 3, 4, 5, 6, 7	1,550	12,243	43.7°	12,319	43.7°

TABLE B: (SHELL, CHEMICAL, 105 mm, (W.P.), M60)

		M2, M2A1 and M4 Howitzers			M3 Howitzer	
Charge	Powder	M.V. f/s	Range (yds.)	Elevation	Range (yds.)	Elevation
1	Base Sect. No. 1	650	3,753	43.5°	3,753	43.5°
2	Base and Incr. No. 2	710	4,391	43.6°	4,391	43.5°
3	Base and Incr. No. 2, 3	780	5,184	43.4°	5,184	43.2°
4	Base and Incr. No. 2, 3, 4	875	6,344	43.4°	6,344	43.2°
5	Base and Incr. No. 2, 3, 4, 5	1,020	8,197	43.2°	8,197	43.0°
6	Base and Incr. No. 2, 3, 4, 5, 6	1,235	10,126	43.3°	——	——
7	Base and Incr. No. 2, 3, 4, 5, 6, 7	1,550	12,281	43.7°	——	——

SHELL, HIGH-EXPLOSIVE, 4.5 INCH, **M65, M65B1** AND **M65B2**—STANDARD

ROUND FOR FIELD GUN, 4.5 INCH, M1

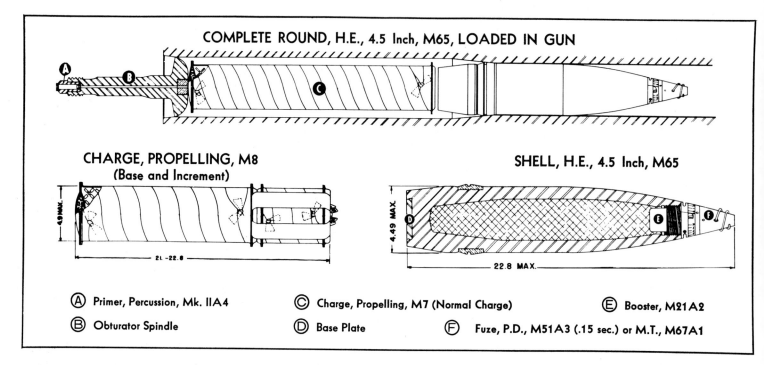

COMPLETE ROUND, H.E., 4.5 Inch, M65, LOADED IN GUN

CHARGE, PROPELLING, M8
(Base and Increment)

SHELL, H.E., 4.5 Inch, M65

Ⓐ Primer, Percussion, Mk. IIA4   Ⓒ Charge, Propelling, M7 (Normal Charge)   Ⓔ Booster, M21A2

Ⓑ Obturator Spindle   Ⓓ Base Plate   Ⓕ Fuze, P.D., M51A3 (.15 sec.) or M.T., M67A1

SHELL, HIGH-EXPLOSIVE, 4.5 INCH, M65, M65B1 and M65B2—STANDARD —These shells are classified as standard ammunition for the 4.5 inch field gun, M1. The separate loaded complete round consists of the loaded and fuzed shell, M65, M65B1 or M65B2, with either the normal base-propelling charge, M7, or the supercharge, M8, and the percussion primer MK. II A4.

The percussion primer, 17 grains, Mk. IIA4, is seated in the base of the obturator spindle and the propelling charge fits against the face of the percussion primer MK. II A4 spindle. The propelling charge, M7, measures 22.8 inches in length and 3.9 inches in diameter. The M8 propelling charge base section measures 16.1 inches in length and 4.9 inches in diameter and the increment measures 6.7 inches in length. The base and increment together measure 22.8 inches in length. The shell is 22.8 inches in length and 4.49 inches in diameter.

As fired the shell weighs 54.90 pounds

and contains a bursting charge of 4.49 pounds of TNT. Assembled in the gun, the complete round weighs 65.99 pounds with the M8 base and increment charge. The M8 is the supercharge and consists of a base section and increment. The total weight of the charge is 11.06 pounds. The M7 charge is the normal charge and weighs 7.44 pounds. The base section of the M8 charge weighs 8.328 pounds. The M8 powder has an 85–10–5 formula with a web of .054 and seven perforations. The M7 powder has an 87–10–3 formula with a web of .025 and seven perforations. The M7 charge and the M8 charge base section give a muzzle velocity of 1,820 feet per second, and at 45° elevation, a maximum range of 16,650 yards. The M8 supercharge gives a muzzle velocity of 2,275 feet per second and a range at 45° elevation, of 21,125 yards.

The M7 normal charge will give more accurate fire than the M8 (base charge alone) although each has the same range

and muzzle velocity. However, a higher muzzle velocity was unobtainable with the M7 powder as it would exceed the rated maximum pressure. Hence, the M8 powder was necessary and was made up in base charge and increment so that it could be used in place of the M7 if the M7 were not available.

The M65, M65B1 and M65B2 shell are identical in appearance, weight and contour. However, the M65 is made from a steel casting and has a steel base plate. The M65B1 also has a steel base plate but the shell is made from a steel forging. The M65B2 is made from a steel forging, but no base plate is used. It does have a base cover. The base plate and cover both serve the same purpose, preventing gas leakage into the shell. The English method is used with the M65 and M65B1 and shells made with the base plate are manufactured in Canada. The base cover type, M65B2, is American.

CHARACTERISTICS

	Shell, H.E., M65, M65B1, M65B2	Shell, H.E., M65, M65B1, M65B2	Shell, H.E., M65, M65B1, M65B2			Shell, H.E., M65, M65B1, M65B2	Shell, H.E., M65, M65B1, M65B2	Shell, H.E., M65, M65B1, M65B2
Caliber	4.5 inch	4.5 inch	4.5 inch	Propelling Charge				
Model of Gun	M1	M1	M1	and Weight		M7, FNH pwdr., 7.44 lb.	M8, Base Sec., FNH pwdr., 8.328 lb.	M8, Base and Incr., FNH pwdr., 11.06 lb.
Proj. Weight	54.90 lb.	54.90 lb.	54.90 lb.					
Proj. Charge and Weight	TNT, 4.49 lb.	TNT, 4.49 lb.	TNT, 4.49 lb.	Complete Round Weight		61.36 lb.	63.258 lb.	65.96 lb.
Booster	M21A2	M21A2	M21A2	Muzzle Velocity		1,820 f/s	1,820 f/s	2,275 f/s
Fuze	M.T.M67A1*	M.T.M67A1*	M.T.M67A1*	Maximum Range		16,650 yds.	16,650 yds.	21,125 yds.
Primer	Mk. IIA4	Mk. IIA4	Mk. IIA4	Chamber Capacity		531.00 cu. ins.	531.00 cu. ins.	531.00 cu. ins.
				Rated Max. Pressure, p.s.i.		40,000	24,000	40,000

* Or P. D. Fuze, M51A3 (.15 sec.)

SHELL, HIGH-EXPLOSIVE, 120 MM, **M73**—STANDARD

ROUND FOR GUN, 120 MM, M1 (ANTIAIRCRAFT)

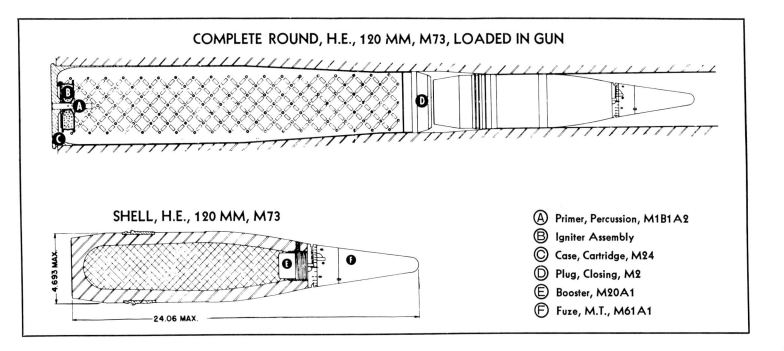

COMPLETE ROUND, H.E., 120 MM, M73, LOADED IN GUN

SHELL, H.E., 120 MM, M73

4.693 MAX.

24.06 MAX.

- (A) Primer, Percussion, M1B1A2
- (B) Igniter Assembly
- (C) Case, Cartridge, M24
- (D) Plug, Closing, M2
- (E) Booster, M20A1
- (F) Fuze, M.T., M61A1

SHELL, HIGH-EXPLOSIVE, 120 MM, M73—STANDARD—This shell is standard ammunition for the 120 MM antiaircraft gun, M1.

The round consists of a loaded and fuzed projectile and a cartridge case containing the propelling charge and a primer. The standard closing plug, M2, which replaces the cork plug, M1, is made of palmatex. This plug serves as a cushion between the cartridge case and the shell and prevents the loss of powder.

The round is separate-loaded, but the propelling charge is in the cartridge case instead of in a bag. This was adopted because a cartridge case and fixed powder charge are desirable for rapid-fire antiaircraft use, but a fixed type round weighing 100 pounds was considered too unwieldy.

In firing, the projectile and the cartridge case are loaded into the chamber and rammed home by the power rammer.

The shell as fired weighs 49.74 pounds and employs the M61A1 mechanical time fuze and M20A1 booster. The shell contains a bursting charge of 5.26 pounds of TNT. Cartridge Case, M24, is used with the M1B1A2 percussion primer, an igniter assembly and a propelling charge of 23.62 pounds of NH powder. The complete round weighs 98.54 pounds. Alternate bursting charges are 4.80 lb. of 50/50 amatol with 0.19 lb. of cast TNT booster surround or 5.42 lb. of trimonite. With the trimonite loading a booster cavity cup is used.

As the M1B1A2 primer does not insure complete burning of the propelling charge, an igniter is attached to the primer. The igniter contains 0.54 pound of black powder.

The propelling charge is M1 powder of an 87–10–3 formula with seven perforations per grain and a web of 0.068 inch.

The shell develops a muzzle velocity of 3,100 feet per second and has a maximum horizontal range of 27,160 yards and a maximum vertical range of 19,150 yards.

CHARACTERISTICS

	Shell, H.E., M73
Caliber	120 MM
Model of Gun	M1
Proj. Weight	49.74 lb.
Proj. Charge and Weight	TNT, 5.26 lb.*
Booster	M20A1
Fuze	M. T., M61A1
Primer	M1B1A2

	Shell, H.E., M73
Cartridge Case	M24
Propelling Charge and Weight	NH powder, 23.62 lb.
Complete Round Weight	98.41 lb.
Muzzle Velocity	3,100 f/s
Maximum Range	Horiz.—27,160 yds.
	Vert. —19,150 yds.
Chamber Capacity	1,048 cu. ins.
Rated Max. Pressure, p.s.i.	38,000

*Alternate loadings 4.80 lb. 50/50 Amatol with 0.19 lb. Cast TNT booster surround or 5.42 lb. of trimonite.

PROJECTILE, ARMOR-PIERCING, 6 INCH, MK. XXXIII—STANDARD
SHELL, HIGH-EXPLOSIVE, 6 INCH, MK. IIA2—LIMITED STANDARD
ROUND FOR 6 INCH SEACOAST GUNS, M1900A2, M1903A2, M1905A2

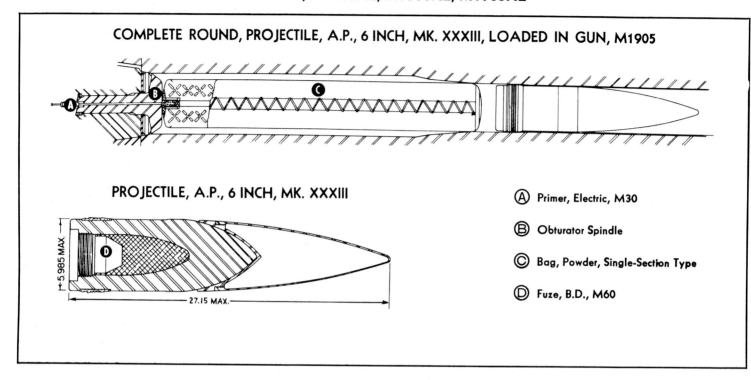

COMPLETE ROUND, PROJECTILE, A.P., 6 INCH, MK. XXXIII, LOADED IN GUN, M1905

PROJECTILE, A.P., 6 INCH, MK. XXXIII

5.985 MAX.

27.15 MAX.

Ⓐ Primer, Electric, M30

Ⓑ Obturator Spindle

Ⓒ Bag, Powder, Single-Section Type

Ⓓ Fuze, B.D., M60

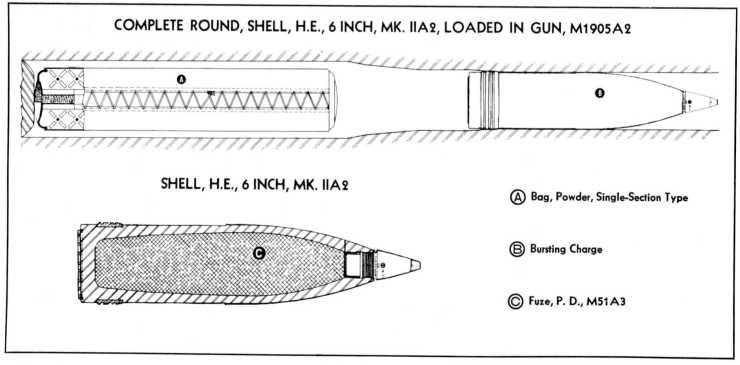

COMPLETE ROUND, SHELL, H.E., 6 INCH, MK. IIA2, LOADED IN GUN, M1905A2

SHELL, H.E., 6 INCH, MK. IIA2

Ⓐ Bag, Powder, Single-Section Type

Ⓑ Bursting Charge

Ⓒ Fuze, P. D., M51A3

PROJECTILE, ARMOR - PIERCING, 6 INCH, MK. XXXIII—STANDARD—This, the only standard combat ammunition for the 6 inch seacoast guns, is a Navy design projectile. The projectile is identical in design with the Projectile, A.P.C., 155 mm, M112.

A bursting charge of 2.17 pounds of explosive "D" is detonated by the M60 base-detonating fuze. To improve the flight characteristics a ballistic windshield is attached to the projectile body. This windshield is screwed onto an adapter which is soldered and crimped in five places to the projectile body.

A single-section type powder bag contains the propelling charge—37 pounds of NH powder. This charge gives the 105 pound projectile a muzzle velocity of 2,800 f/s. The propellant is an M1 class powder, 87–10–3 formula. The web size

PROJECTILE, ARMOR-PIERCING, 6 INCH, **MK. XXXIII**

SHELL, HIGH-EXPLOSIVE, 6 INCH, **MK. IIA2** (Continued)

is 0.068 inch and the grains have seven perforations. The electric primer, M30, is used to ignite the propelling charge.

The projectile measures 27 inches in length and the powder bag a maximum of 42⅜ inches by 6½ inches in diameter.

SHELL, HIGH-EXPLOSIVE, 6 INCH, MK. IIA2—LIMITED STANDARD—This shell was developed by the redesign of the MK. II high-explosive shell. The Mk. II shell was manufactured so that an adapter was required to assemble the Fuze, P.D., M47, to the shell, resulting in a shell contour that was unsatisfactory ballistically. To rectify this the shell was modified and was designated the Shell, H.E., MK. IIA1. The modification consisted of lengthening the ogive so that the P.D., fuze, M51A3, could be assembled directly to the shell without using an adapter. With the new shell and fuze contour the ballistic characteristics were improved. A further modification, this time to the rotating band, resulted in the MK. IIA2 shell.

The shell is manufactured from steel forging, and to insure that no gases leak into the bursting charge the base of the shell is protected by a steel base cover.

Two different bursting charges are permitted, 13.98 pounds of Grade I, Cast TNT or 13.11 pounds of 50–50 Amatol with 0.20 pound of Grade I, Cast TNT surrounding the booster. Both type loadings require fuze well cups to prevent broken pieces of the charge interfering with the assembly of the Fuze, P.D., M51A3. The shell is shipped with an eye-bolt closing plug and the fuze assembled prior to firing.

The 89.53 pound shell is propelled by 32.5 pounds of NH powder. The propelling charge, contained in a single-section type powder bag, is ignited by the M30 electric primer. The propellant is an M1 class powder, 87–10–3 formula. The grains have seven perforations and a web of 0.055 inch.

Fuze, P.D., M51A3 is a selective superquick or delay (0.15 sec.) fuze.

The fuzed shell measures 25.22 inches in length and the powder bag a maximum of 42⅜ inches by 6½ inches in diameter.

PROJECTILE, TARGET PRACTICE, 6 INCH, M911—STANDARD—This projectile is used as a target practice shell to simulate the 108 pound, M1911, A.P.

Shell and A.P. Shot. It weighs 108 pounds, measures approximately the same in length as the A.P. shell and shot and has the same body contour. As a result the T.P. projectile has the same exterior ballistic characteristics as the simulated projectiles.

The projectile is manufactured from cast iron and is hollow to give the desired weight. The same propelling charge that is used with the MK. IIA2 shell also is used with this projectile.

PROJECTILE, TARGET PRACTICE, 6 INCH, MK. XXIX—STANDARD—The projectile is used, in target practice, to simulate the MK. XXXIII projectile. It is the same weight and has the same exterior ballistic characteristics as the MK. XXXIII.

PROJECTILES, DUMMY, 6 INCH, MK. IA1 and MK. IIA1—STANDARD—These dummy projectiles are used to teach the gun crew handling and loading techniques. The projectile has a built-up body. Bronze is used for those portions of the projectile body that might come in contact with the bore of the gun. This protects the gun tube from rough loading.

CHARACTERISTICS

	Proj., A.P., Mk. XXXIII	Shell, H.E., Mk. IIA2	Proj., T.P., M1911	Proj., Drill Mk. 1A1	Proj., Drill Mk. IIA1	Proj., T.P. Mk. XXIX
Caliber	6 inch	6 inch	6 inch	6 inch	6 inch	6 inch
Model of Guns	M1900A2, M1903A2, M1905A2	M1900A2, M1903A2, M1905A2	M1900A2, M1903A2, M1905A2	M1900A2, M1903A2, M1905A2	M1900A2, M1903A2, M1905A2	M1900A2, M1903A2, M1905A2
Proj. Weight	105 lb.	89.53	108 lb.	85 lb.	102 lb.	105 lb.
Proj. Charge and Weight	Expl. "D," 2.17 lb.	TNT, 13.98 lb.	—			—
Fuze	B.D., M60	M51A3				—
Primer	M30, Elec.	M30, Elec.	M30, Elec.	M30, Elec.	M30, Elec.	M30, Elec.
Propelling Charge and Weight	Single-sec., NH pwdr., 37.00 lb.	Single-sec., NH pwdr., 32.50 lb.	Single-sec., NH pwdr., 32.50 lb.	—	Dummy, Mod. 1917, 29.00 lb.	Single-sec., NH pwdr., 37.00 lb.
Complete Round Weight	142.00 lb.	122.06 lb.	140.50 lb.	85.00 lb.	131.00 lb.	142.00 lb.
Muzzle Velocity	2,800 f/s	2,770 f/s	2,600 f/s	—	—	2,800 f/s
Maximum Range	27,150 yds.	20,995 yds.	17,000 yds.	—	—	27,150 yds.
Chamber Capacity	2,082 cu. ins.*	2,082 cu. ins.*	2,077 cu. ins.†	—	—	2,082 cu. ins.*
Rated Max. Pressure, p.s.i.	38,000	38,000	38,000	—	—	38,000

*2,144 cu. ins. in M1905 gun.
†2,122 cu. ins. in M1905 gun.

301

SHELL, HIGH-EXPLOSIVE, 155 MM, M101—STANDARD
ROUND FOR GUNS, M1917, M1918M1, M1 AND M1A1

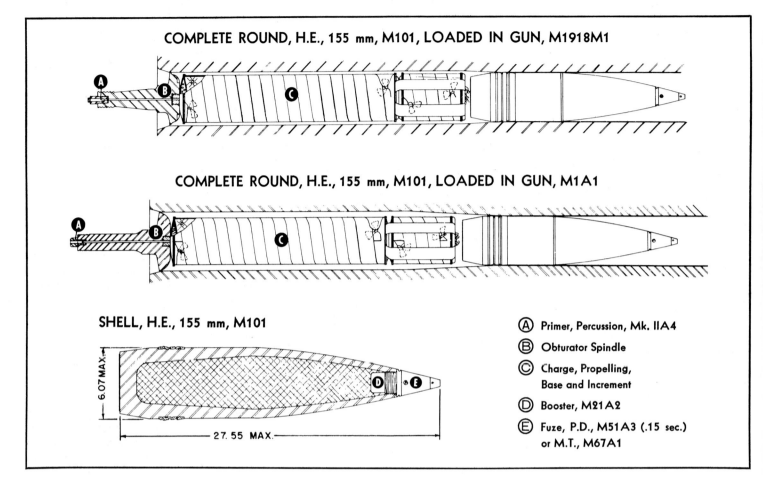

COMPLETE ROUND, H.E., 155 mm, M101, LOADED IN GUN, M1918M1

COMPLETE ROUND, H.E., 155 mm, M101, LOADED IN GUN, M1A1

SHELL, H.E., 155 mm, M101

6.07 MAX.

27.55 MAX.

(A) Primer, Percussion, Mk. IIA4

(B) Obturator Spindle

(C) Charge, Propelling, Base and Increment

(D) Booster, M21A2

(E) Fuze, P.D., M51A3 (.15 sec.) or M.T., M67A1

The 155 mm guns, M1917, M1918M1, M1 and M1A1, take the same separate-loading projectiles. Loading is accomplished in three operations: (1) inserting the projectile in the gun, (2) inserting the propelling charge and (3) inserting the primer in the breech mechanism of the gun. Five general types of ammunition are provided: (1) high-explosive shell, (2) armor-piercing shot, (3) chemical shell, (4) target-practice projectile and (5) drill projectile.

The high-explosive and chemical rounds are issued unfuzed; the armor-piercing round is issued fuzed. An eye-bolt lifting plug or an adapter plug is shipped assembled in the fuze seat with unfuzed rounds. This type of projectile is also issued unboxed, and shipped with the rotating band protected by a rope grommet.

Propelling charges are shipped com-
(Continued on next page)

CHARACTERISTICS

	Shell, H.E., M101	Shell, H.E., M101	Shell, H.E., M101	Shell, H.E., M101	Proj., Target, Mk. III
Caliber	155 mm	155 mm	155 mm	155 mm	155 mm
Models of Guns	M1917, M1918M1	M1917, M1918M1	M1, M1A1	M1, M1A1	All
Proj. Weight	94.70 lb.	94.70 lb.	94.70 lb.	94.70 lb.	95.33 lb.
Proj. Charge and Weight	TNT, 15.13 lb.	TNT, 15.13 lb.	TNT, 15.13 lb.	TNT, 15.13 lb.	Inert, 15.13 lb.
Booster	M21A2	M21A2	M21A2	M21A2	MIII AM2
Fuze	P.D., M51A3 (.15 sec.) or M.T., M67A1	P.D., M51A3 (.15 sec.) or M.T., M67A1	P.D., M51A3 (.15 sec.) or M.T., M67A1	P.D., M51A3 (.15 sec.) or M.T., M67A1	P.D., M46 or M47 inert
Primer	Mk. IIA4, 17 grs.	Mk. IIA4, 17 grs.	Mk. IIA4, 17 grs.	Mk. IIA4, 17 grs.	Mk. IIA4, 17 grs.
Propelling Charge and Weight	(Base) NH pwdr., 18.66 lb.	(Base & Incr.) NH pwdr., 24.45 lb.	(Base) NH pwdr., 20.35 lb.	(Base & Incr.) NH pwdr., 30.74 lb.	(Base & Incr.) NH pwdr., 24.75 lb.
Complete Round Weight	113.80 lb.	119.48 lb.	115.17 lb.	125.48 lb.	121.53 lb.
Muzzle Velocity	1,955 f/s	2,410 f/s	2,100 f/s	2,800 f/s	2,410 f/s
Maximum Range	16,100 yds. at 35° 30′ elev.	20,100 yds. at 35° 24′ elev.	18,605 yds. at 45° elev.	25,715 yds. at 46° 49′ elev.	17,900 yds. at 35° 15′ elev.
Chamber Capacity	1,330 cu. ins.	1,330 cu. ins.	1,640 cu. ins.	1,640 cu. ins.	——
Rated Max. Pressure, p.s.i.	31,500	31,500	40,000	40,000	——

plete with igniting charges in waterproof fiber containers, one complete charge being packed in each cartridge storage case.

Before discussing the present standard item, Shell, H.E., M101, a comparative tabulation of the shell's antecedents will clarify the major points of difference and modifications which developed into the present M101 shell as shown in Table A.

The high-explosive shell, Mk. III, was adapted from a French design and had a sharp nose and tapered base to add to its efficiency in flight. The explosive charge was about 15.2 pounds of TNT. Some rounds were loaded with 50/50 or 80/20 amatol.

The Mk. IIIA1 high-explosive shell is a modification of the Mk. III shell. The modification consists of changing the ogival length to take the M51A1 point-detonating fuze and the M21A2 booster. This modification makes it possible to use the bore-safe fuze, M51A1, instead of the M46 or M47 point-detonating fuze. The modification of the ogive and the use of a better ballistic shape fuze improve the ballistic characteristics of the shell, as can be seen in Table A.

SHELL, HIGH-EXPLOSIVE, 155 mm, M101—STANDARD

—This standard issue and manufacture round was developed from the Mk. III high-explosive round (now classified as limited standard) and from the Mk. IIIA1 high-explosive round (now classified as substitute standard).

The M101 shell may be fired in either the M1918M1 guns or the new M1 and M1A1 guns. The shell is similar in appearance and construction to the Mk. IIIA1 high-explosive shell. The M51A3 point-detonating fuze or M67A1 mechanical time fuze is used with the M21A2 booster. The shell weighs 94.70 pounds as fired. The weight of the TNT bursting charge is 15.13 pounds. This projectile is shipped and issued unfuzed; the fuzes, with booster attached, are shipped separately in fiber containers.

When fired in the M1918M1 gun, with the normal base-propelling charge, the complete round weighs 113.80 pounds. The weight of the NH powder base-section

charge is 18.66 pounds, giving a muzzle velocity of 1,955 feet per second and a maximum range of 16,100 yards at 35° 30' elevation. When fired with the base and increment charge, the weight of the NH powder charge is 24.45 pounds, giving a muzzle velocity of 2,410 feet per second and a maximum range of 20,100 yards at 35° 24' elevation. The weight of the complete round then becomes 119.48 pounds.

When fired in the M1A1 gun, with the normal base-section charge, the complete round weighs 115.17 pounds. The weight of the NH powder base-section is 20.35 pounds, giving a muzzle velocity of 2,100 feet per second and a maximum range of 18,605 yards at 45° elevation. When fired with the base-increment charge, the weight of the NH powder charge is 31.25 pounds, giving a muzzle velocity of 2,800 feet per second and a maximum range of 25,715 yards at 46° 49' elevation. The weight of the complete round then becomes 126.37 pounds.

The propelling charge for the 155 mm gun, M1918M1, is nonhygroscopic smokeless powder. The cartridge bags containing the propelling charge are the "base and increment type" consisting of a base section and one increment section, permitting two zones of fire. The base section has an 8 ounce black powder igniter pad attached. Both base section and increment section are wrapped spirally with strips of cartridge-bag cloth to make the bags firm and compact for handling.

The propelling charge for use in the new 155 mm guns, M1 and M1A1, is similar to the M1918M1 propelling charge. The base section of the charge used in the M1 and M1A1 guns is 25.25 inches in length and weighs approximately 20.35 pounds. The increment section is 11.75 inches in length and weighs approximately 10.90 pounds. The total length of the charge is approximately 37 inches and the total weight is 31.25 pounds. In addition to being slightly longer and heavier than the M1918M1 propelling charge, the charges for the M1 and M1A1 guns are larger in diameter and can be used only in those guns.

The base and increment charges are made from class M1 powder with an 87–10–3 formula. Grains of this powder have a web of 0.057 inch and seven perforations.

The projectile measures 23.62 inches in length.

PROJECTILE (SPECIAL TARGET), MK. III—STANDARD

—This shell consists of an empty high-explosive Mk. III shell body, an inert adapter-booster, and an inert fuze. The shell is shipped empty and must be sand loaded to the proper weight of 95.33 pounds before it is issued to using troops. The complete round weighs 121.53 pounds.

PROJECTILE, DUMMY (DRILL), MK. I—STANDARD

—(See Table of Characteristics.)

TABLE A

	Mk. III (Limited Standard)	Mk. IIIA1 (Substitute Standard)
Model of guns	M1917, M1918M1	M1917, M1918M1
Weight of complete round	120.11 lb.	120.93 lb.
Weight of shell, as fired	95.33 lb.	96.15 lb.
Weight of bursting charge (TNT)	15.17 lb.	15.21 lb.
Weight of normal charge (NH powder, base section)	21.00 lb.	21.00 lb.
Muzzle velocity, normal charge	1,955 f/s	1,955 f/s
Maximum range, normal charge	14,900 yds. (35° elev.)	15,500 yds. (35° 38' elev.)
Weight of supercharge (NH powder, base and increment)	24.75 lb.	24.75 lb.
Muzzle velocity, supercharge	2,410 f/s	2,410 f/s
Maximum range, supercharge	17,900 yds. (35° 15' elev.)	19,100 yds. (35° 22' elev.)
Adapter and booster	Mk. IIIAM2	M21A1
Fuze	P.D., M46 or M47	P.D., M51A1, or M.T., M67
Primer	Mk. IIA4, 17 grs.	Mk. IIA4, 17 grs.

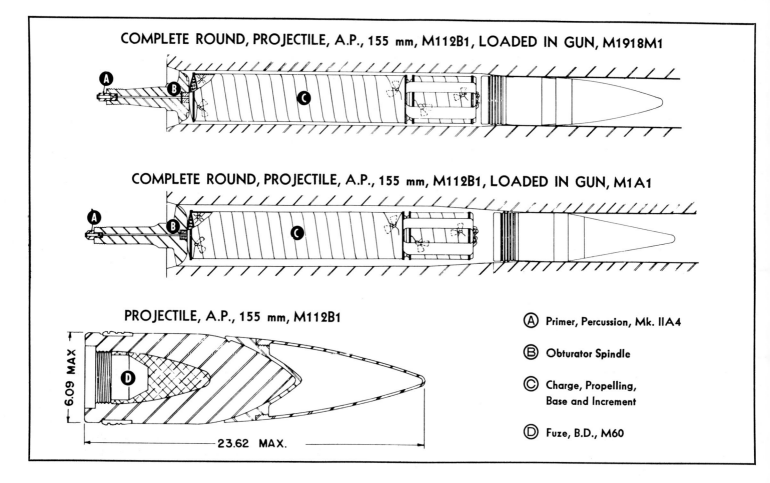

COMPLETE ROUND, PROJECTILE, A.P., 155 mm, M112B1, LOADED IN GUN, M1918M1

COMPLETE ROUND, PROJECTILE, A.P., 155 mm, M112B1, LOADED IN GUN, M1A1

PROJECTILE, A.P., 155 mm, M112B1

6.09 MAX

23.62 MAX.

- (A) Primer, Percussion, Mk. IIA4
- (B) Obturator Spindle
- (C) Charge, Propelling, Base and Increment
- (D) Fuze, B.D., M60

PROJECTILE, ARMOR-PIERCING, 155 mm, M112B1—STANDARD—The projectile measures 23.62 inches in length over-all, and as fired weighs 100 pounds. It contains 1.44 pounds of explosive "D" bursting charge which is detonated by fuze, B.D., M60. In the M1918M1 gun, the projectile is propelled by a base and increment charge of 24.75 pounds of NH powder. This provides a muzzle velocity of 2,360 feet per second and a maximum range of 19,200 yards at 35° 24' elevation. The complete round weighs 124.75 pounds.

When used in the M1 and M1A1 guns, the larger base and increment charge of 31.25 pounds of NH powder is used to propel the projectile. The complete round then weighs 131.25 pounds.

The larger base and increment charge provides a muzzle velocity of 2,745 feet per second and a maximum range of 24,075 yards.

The base and increment charge for the M1917 and 1918 guns measures 37 inches in length and 5.8 inches in diameter, while the base and increment charge for the M1 and M1A1 guns is 37.4 inches in length and 6.5 inches in diameter.

The base and increment charges are made from class M1 powder with an 87–10–3 formula. Grains of this powder have a web of 0.057 inch and seven perforations.

CHARACTERISTICS

	Proj., A.P., M112B1	Proj., A.P., M112B1		Proj., A.P., M112B1	Proj., A.P., M112B1
Caliber	155 mm	155 mm	Muzzle Velocity	2,360 f/s	2,745 f/s
Models of Guns	M1917, M1918M1	M1, M1A1	Maximum Range	19,200 yds.	24,075 yds.
Proj. Weight	100 lb.	100 lb.	Chamber Capacity	1,394 cu. ins.	1,691 cu. ins.
Proj. Charge and Weight	Expl. "D," 1.44 lb.	Expl. "D," 1.44 lb.	Rated Max. Pressure, p.s.i.	31,500	40,000
Fuze	B.D., M60	B.D., M60	Armor Penetration at 20° Obliquely		
Primer	Mk. IIA4, 17 grs.	Mk. IIA4, 17 grs.	Homogeneous Plate		
Propelling Charge and			500 yards	5.4 ins.	6.8 ins.
Weight	(Superchg., Base and	(Superchg., Base and	1,000 yards	5.1 ins.	6.5 ins.
	Incr.) NH powder,	Incr.) NH powder,	Face-Hard. Plate		
	24.75 lb.	31.25 lb.	500 yards	4.7 ins.	5.8 ins.
Complete Round Weight	124.75 lb.	131.25 lb.	1,000 yards	4.4 ins.	5.6 ins.

SHELL, CHEMICAL, 155 MM, **M104**—STANDARD

ROUND FOR GUN, 155 mm, M1917, M1918M1, M1 AND M1A1

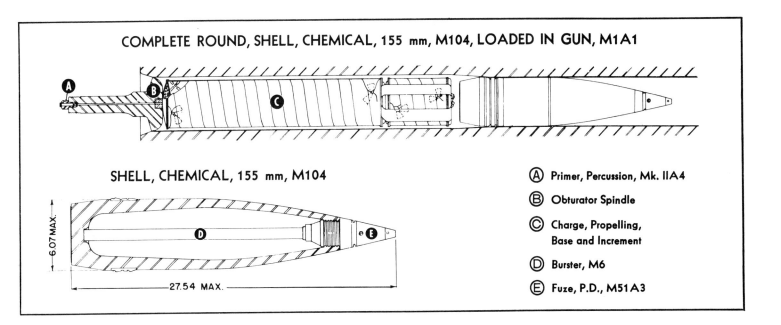

COMPLETE ROUND, SHELL, CHEMICAL, 155 mm, M104, LOADED IN GUN, M1A1

SHELL, CHEMICAL, 155 mm, M104

6.07 MAX.

27.54 MAX.

Ⓐ Primer, Percussion, Mk. IIA4

Ⓑ Obturator Spindle

Ⓒ Charge, Propelling, Base and Increment

Ⓓ Burster, M6

Ⓔ Fuze, P.D., M51A3

SHELL, CHEMICAL, 155 mm, M104—STANDARD—This is a standard issue and manufacture round for use in the M1 and M1A1 guns and consists of the chemical shell, M104, with burster, M6, booster, M22, and fuze, P.D., M51A3. The shell measures 27.54 inches in length.

The 17 grain, percussion primer, Mk. IIA4, is used to fire the normal or supercharge propelling charge of NH powder.

In the M1 and M1A1 guns, the normal base charge weighs 20.00 pounds and develops a muzzle velocity of 2,100 feet per second with maximum range of 18,605 yards at 45° elevation when the HS

(Continued on next page)

CHARACTERISTICS

	Shell, (FS) M104	Shell, (WP) M104	Shell, (HS) M104	Shell, (FS) M104	Shell, (WP) M104	Shell, (HS) M104
Caliber	155 mm	155 mm	155 mm	155 mm	155 mm	155 mm
Models of Guns	M1917 M1918M1	M1917 M1918M1	M1917 M1918M1	M1, M1A1	M1, M1A1	M1, M1A1
Proj. Weight	99.73 lb.	98.18 lb.	94.53 lb.	99.73 lb.	98.18 lb.	94.53 lb.
Proj. Charge & Weight	16.90 lb. Chem., 0.59 lb. TNT	15.68 lb. Chem., 0.36 lb. Tetryl	11.70 lb. Chem., 0.36 lb. Tetryl	16.90 lb. Chem., 0.36 lb. Tetryl	15.60 lb. Chem., 0.36 lb. Tetryl	11.70 lb. Chem., 0.36 lb. Tetryl
Booster	M22	M22	M22	M22	M22	M22
Fuze	P.D., M51A3	P.D., M51A3	P.D., M51A3	P.D., M51A3	P.D., M51A3	P.D., M51A3
Burster	M6	M6	M6	M6	M6	M6
Primer	Mk. IIA4, 17 grs.	Mk. IIA4, 17 grs.	Mk. IIA4, 17 grs.	Mk. IIA4, 17 grs.	Mk. IIA4, 17 grs.	Mk. IIA4, 17 grs.
Propelling Charge & Weight	*	*	*	§	§	§
Complete Round Weight	124.51 lb.	122.96 lb.	119.31 lb.	130.51 lb.	128.96 lb.	125.31 lb.
Muzzle Velocity	**	††	†	¶¶	§§	‡
Maximum Range	**	††	†	¶¶	§§	‡
Chamber Capacity	1,330 cu. ins.	1,330 cu. ins.	1,330 cu. ins.	1,640 cu. ins.	1,640 cu. ins.	1,640 cu. ins.
Rated Max. Pressure, p.s.i.	31,500	31,500	31,500	40,000	40,000	40,000

*Normal charge, base section, NH powder, 21.00 lb. Supercharge, base and increment, NH powder, 24.75 lb.

†With normal charge: M.V., 1,955 f/s; max. range, 16,100 yds. With supercharge: M.V., 2,410 f/s; max. range, 20,100 yds.

‡With normal charge: M.V., 2,100 f/s; max. range, 18,605 yds. With supercharge: M.V., 2,800 f/s; max. range, 25,715 yds.

§Normal charge, base section, NH powder, 20.35 lb. Supercharge, base and increment, NH powder, 31.25 lb.

**With normal charge, M.V., 1955 f/s; max. range, 16,260 yds. With supercharge: M.V., 2,410 f/s; max. range, 20,296 yds.

††With normal charge: M.V., 1955 f/s; max. range, 16,220 yds. With supercharge: M.V., 2,410 f/s; max. range, 20,247 yds.

§§With normal charge: M.V., 2,100 f/s; max. range, 18,701 yds. With supercharge: M.V., 2,800 f/s; max. range, 25,940 yds.

¶¶With normal charge: M.V., 2,100 f/s; max. range, 18,733 yds. With supercharge: M.V., 2,800 f/s; max. range, 26,015 yds.

loaded shell is used. Using the same shell the base and increment supercharge weighs 31.25 pounds and develops a muzzle velocity of 2,800 feet per second with a maximum range of 25,715 yards at 47° elevation.

In the M1918M1 gun, the normal base charge of 21 pounds develops a muzzle velocity of 1,955 feet per second and a maximum range, with the HS loaded shell, of 16,100 yards at 35° 30' elevation. The supercharge weighs 24.75 pounds and develops a muzzle velocity of 2,410 feet per second and a maximum range of 20,100 yards at 35° 14' elevation.

The base and increment charge for the M1917 and M1918M1 guns is 37 inches in length and 5.8 inches in diameter. The charge for the M1 and M1A1 guns measures 37.4 inches in length and 6.5 inches in diameter. The base and increment charges are made from class M1 powder with an 87–10–3 formula. Grains of this powder have a web of 0.057 inch and seven perforations.

The shell may be loaded with either WP (Smoke), FS (Smoke), or HS (Persistent Gas) filler. The chemical filler is loaded into the shell and the burster well tube is pressed into place, forming a gas-tight seal. At the time of loading the chemical filler and assembling the burster well tube into the shell, no explosive charge is present. The explosive charge of the burster is contained in a cardboard or thin aluminum casing and is loaded into the shell either at the depot or in the field at the time of fuzing.

After the shell has been loaded and the burster well tube assembled in place, a bakelite cup is placed over the empty burster cavity to prevent the entrance of foreign matter and an eyelet lifting plug screwed into the nose of the shell. The tetryl bursting charge weighs 0.36 pound.

The weights of the shell, as fired in the M1917, M1918M1, M1 and M1A1 guns, with the various loadings, are as follows:

Kind	Filler Weight	Weight of Shell Loaded and Fuzed
WP	15.68 lb.	98.18 lb.
FS	16.90 lb.	99.73 lb.
HS	11.70 lb.	94.53 lb.

Complete round weights with base section charge and base and increment charge follow:

Filler	Gun	Weight with Base Section Charge	Weight with Base & Incr. Chg.
WP	M1917, M1918M1	119.05 lb.	122.96 lb.
FS	M1917, M1918M1	120.27 lb.	124.51 lb.
HS	M1917, M1918M1	115.07 lb.	119.31 lb.
WP	M1 and M1A1	118.40 lb.	128.96 lb.
FS	M1 and M1A1	119.62 lb.	130.51 lb.
HS	M1 and M1A1	114.42 lb.	125.31 lb.

The following data for the limited standard, Mk. VIIA1, may be compared with those for the M104 standard round in the M1917 and 1918M1 guns (the Mk. VIIA1 shell being the antecedent of the M104 shell).

	HS	FS	WP
Weight of complete round	119.63 lb.	124.46 lb.	123.03 lb.
Weight of shell, as fired	94.88 lb.	99.71 lb.	98.28 lb.
Weight of charge, chemical	11.40 lb.	16.23 lb.	14.84 lb.
Weight of normal charge (NH powder, base section)	21.00 lb.	21.00 lb.	21.00 lb.
Muzzle velocity, normal charge	1,955 F/S	1,955 F/S	1,955 F/S
Maximum range, normal charge	15,500 yds.	15,500 yds.	15,500 yds.
Weight of supercharge (NH powder, base and increment)	24.75 lb.	24.75 lb.	24.75 lb.
Muzzle velocity, supercharge	2,410 F/S	2,410 F/S	2,410 F/S
Maximum range, supercharge	20,100 yds.	20,296 yds.	20,247 yds.

SHELL, HIGH-EXPLOSIVE, 155 MM, M107 – STANDARD
ROUND FOR HOWITZER, 155 mm, M1

SHELL, HIGH-EXPLOSIVE, 155 MM, M102 – STANDARD
ROUND FOR HOWITZER, 155 mm, M1917, M1917A1, M1918

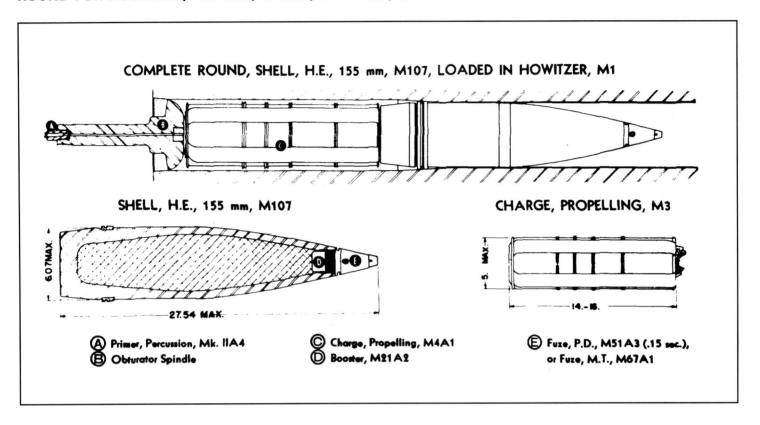

COMPLETE ROUND, SHELL, H.E., 155 mm, M107, LOADED IN HOWITZER, M1

SHELL, H.E., 155 mm, M107

CHARGE, PROPELLING, M3

Ⓐ Primer, Percussion, Mk. IIA4
Ⓑ Obturator Spindle
Ⓒ Charge, Propelling, M4A1
Ⓓ Booster, M21A2
Ⓔ Fuze, P.D., M51A3 (.15 sec.), or Fuze, M.T., M67A1

Standard ammunition for the howitzers M1, M1917, M1917A1 and M1918 is issued with high explosive or chemical fillings and with an inert filling for drill purposes.

The 155mm gun shells should not be fired in the 155mm howitzer as these projectiles would seat differently in the howitzer – thus reducing the chamber space for the propelling charge and giving different interior and exterior ballistics.

The high explosive round M102 was developed from the Mk 1 high explosive shell which is now classified as limited standard. The Mk I became the Mk IIA1, which is also now classified as limited standard. Both these projectiles used an adapter in the nose to accept the Fuze PD M46 (Superquick) or Fuze PD M47 (Delay). Upon the standardization of the M48 series fuzes which have a larger thread diameter the MkIIA1 shell was re-designed by removing the adapter and threading the shell nose to accept the Booster M21 and Fuze PD M48 and other appropriate fuzes of the same thread size.

Only the M102 high explosive shell is to be used in the M1917, M1917A1 and M1918 howitzers. No other high explosive shells from any other 155mm gun or howitzer may be used in these weapons.

The M1A1 and M2A1 propelling charges are used in the M1917, M1917A1 and M1918 howitzers. The weight of the M1A1 charge is 3.06 pounds of FNH powder; the weight of the M2A1 charge is 8.09 pounds of FNH powder. The propelling charge M1A1 measures 11 inches in length and 5 inches in diameter. The M2A1 propelling charge is also 11 inches in length but measures 6 inches in diameter.

The M1A1 propelling charge uses an M1 class powder, the grains of which have a web of 0.016 inch and are single perforated. The formula for this powder and that for the M2A1 charge is 85-10-5. The M2A1 charge also used M1 class powder with seven perforations per grain and a web size of 0.033 inch.

The high explosive round M107 was developed from the MkIIA1 high explosive shell by removing the adapter and threading the shell nose to accept the Booster M21 and Fuze PD M48 and other appropriate fuzes of the same thread size, and by the fitting of a new design of wide rotating band suited to the different interior ballistics of the M1 howitzer. In an emergency the high explosive round M102 can be fired from the howitzer M1 but this is not to be considered a normal procedure and the ballistic performance will differ from that obtained with the M107 round. The 155mm gun shell M101 must not be used in any 155mm howitzers.

The M3 and M4A1 propelling charges are used in the M1 howitzer. The weight of the M3 charge is 5.31 pounds of FNH powder; the weight of the M4A1 charge is

13.26 pounds of FNH powder. The M3 propelling charge has a length of 16 inches and a diameter of 5 inches, and the M4A1 charge is 21 inches in length and 5.8 inches in diameter.

The M3 propelling charge uses an M1 class powder, the grains of which have a web of 0.015 inch and are single perforated. The formula for this powder and that for the M4A1 charge is 85-10-5. The M4A1 charge also uses an M1 class powder with seven perforations per grain and a web size of 0.034 inch.

COMPLETE ROUND, SHELL, H.E., 155 mm, M102, LOADED IN HOWITZER, M1918

CHARGE, PROPELLING, M1A1

Ⓐ Primer, Percussion, Mk. IIA4

Ⓑ Obturator Spindle

Ⓒ Charge, Propelling, M2A1

Ⓓ Booster, M21A2

Ⓔ Fuze, P.D., M51A3 (.15 sec.), and Fuze, T. & S.Q., M55A1

PRINCIPAL CHARACTERISTICS

	Shell HE M102	Shell HE M107
Caliber	155mm	155mm
Model of howitzer	M1917, 1917A1, 1918	M1
Proj. weight	95.3 lb	95.01 lb
Proj. charge and weight	TNT, 15.13 lb	TNT, 15.13 lb
Booster	M21A2	M21A2
Primer	MkIIA4, 18 grs	MkIIA4, 18 grs
Fuze	PD M51A3 (.15 sec)	PD M51A3 (.15 sec)
	or MT M67A1	or MT M67A1
Propelling charge and weight	M1A1: 3.06 lb, FNH	M3: 5.31 lb, FNH
	M2A1: 8.09 lb, FNH	M4A1: 13.26 lb, FNH
Complete round weight	101.39lb	108.27 lb
Muzzle velocity	M1A1: 1082 ft/sec	M3: 1,220 ft/sec
	M2A1: 1475 ft/sec	M4A1: 1,850 ft/sec
Maximum range	M1A1: 9415 yards	M3: 10,780 yards
	M2A1: 12,400 yards	M4A1: 16,355 yards
Chamber capacity	355 cu. ins	795 cu. ins
Rated max pressure p.s.i.	30,000	32,000

RECONSTRUCTED PAGE 1 March 1944

SHELL, CHEMICAL, 155 MM, M110—STANDARD

ROUND FOR HOWITZER, M1

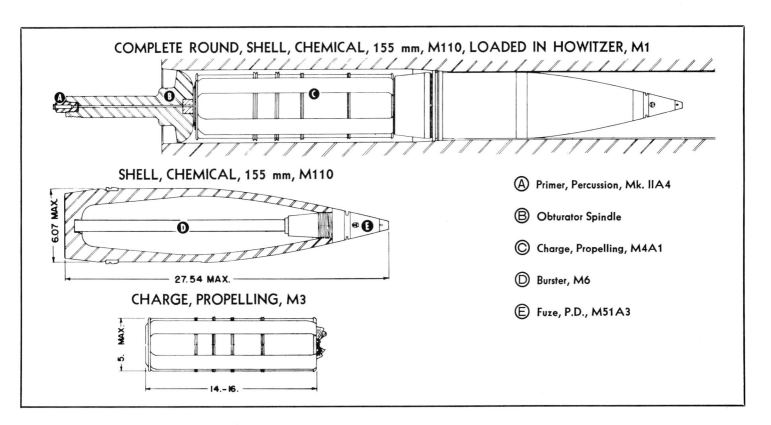

COMPLETE ROUND, SHELL, CHEMICAL, 155 mm, M110, LOADED IN HOWITZER, M1

SHELL, CHEMICAL, 155 mm, M110

6.07 MAX.

27.54 MAX.

CHARGE, PROPELLING, M3

5. MAX.

14.-16.

- (A) Primer, Percussion, Mk. IIA4
- (B) Obturator Spindle
- (C) Charge, Propelling, M4A1
- (D) Burster, M6
- (E) Fuze, P.D., M51A3

SHELL, CHEMICAL, 155 mm, M110—STANDARD—The M110 chemical shell uses the M6 burster and the fuze, P.D., M51A3 with the M21A2 booster.

The shell is loaded with HS (Persistent Gas) filler. The chemical filler is loaded into the shell and the burster well tube pressed into place, forming a gas-tight seal. At the time of loading the chemical filler and assembling the burster well tube into the shell, there is no explosive charge present.

The explosive charge of the burster is contained in a cardboard or thin aluminum casing and is loaded into the shell at the depot or in the field at the time of fuzing. After the shell has been loaded and the burster well tube assembled in place, a bakelite cup is placed over the empty burster cavity to prevent the entrance of foreign matter, and an eyebolt lifting plug assembled in the nose of the shell. The weight of the tetryl bursting charge is 0.36

pound; the weight of the loaded HS shell is 11.70 pounds.

Two propelling charges—M3 and M4A1 —are used in the M1 howitzer. The weight of the M3 charge is 5.31 pounds of FNH powder; the weight of the M4A1 charge is 13.26 pounds of FNH powder.

The shell measures 27.54 inches in length. The M3 propelling charge has a length of 16 inches and a diameter of 5

(Continued on next page)

CHARACTERISTICS

	Shell, Chem., M110 (HS)		Shell, Chem., M110 (HS)
Caliber	155 mm	Propelling Charge & Weight	†
Model of Howitzer	M1	Complete Round Weight	107.34 lb.‡
Proj. Weight	94.21 lb.	Muzzle Velocity	§
Proj. Charge & Weight*	HS, 11.70 lb.	Maximum Range	§
Booster	M21A2	Chamber Capacity	795 cu. ins.
Primer	Mk. IIA4, 18 grs.	Rated Max. Pressure, p.s.i.	32,000
Fuze	P.D., M51A3		

*Does not include 0.36 lb. of tetryl bursting charge.
†M3, FNH powder, propelling charge, weighs 5.31 lb.; M4A1, FNH powder, propelling charge, weighs 13.26 lb.

‡With M4A1 propelling charge.
§Charge, M3: muzzle velocity, 1,220 f/s; maximum range, 10,812 yds. at 43° 41' elevation.
Charge M4A1: muzzle velocity, 1,850 f/s; maximum range, 16,374 yds. at 45° 17' elevation.

inches, and the M4A1 charge is 21 inches in length and 5.8 inches in diameter.

The M3 propelling charge uses an M1 class powder, the grains of which have a web of 0.015 inch and are single perforated. The formula for this powder and that for the M4 charge is 85–10–5. The M4A1 charge also uses M1 class powder with seven perforations per grain and a web size of 0.034 inch.

The zone ranges for the M3 and M4A1 propelling charges are as follows:

Charge Zone	Charge	Section	Weight	M.V.	Max. Range	Elev.
1	M3	Base 1	2.19 lb.	680 f/s	4,327 yds.	43° 51′
2	M3	Base 1 plus Incr. 2	2.71 lb.	770 f/s	5,423 yds.	43° 41′
3	M3	Base 1 plus Incr. 2 and 3	3.39 lb.	880 f/s	6,829 yds.	43° 33′
4	M3	Base 1 plus Incr. 2, 3, and 4	4.35 lb.	1,020 f/s	8,666 yds.	43° 41′
5	M3	Base 1 plus Incr. 2, 3, 4 and 5	5.31 lb.	1,220 f/s	10,812 yds.	43° 41′
3	M4A1	Base 3	4.12 lb.	880 f/s	6,817 yds.	43° 33′
4	M4A1	Base 3 Incr. 4	5.30 lb.	1,020 f/s	8,654 yds.	43° 41′
5	M4A1	Base 3 Incr. 4 & 5	7.06 lb.	1,220 f/s	10,800 yds.	44° 16′
6	M4A1	Base 3 Incr. 4, 5, & 6	9.88 lb.	1,520 f/s	13,435 yds.	44° 44′
7	M4A1	Base 3 Incr. 4, 5, 6, & 7	13.26 lb.	1,850 f/s	16,374 yds.	45° 17′

SHELL, CHEMICAL, 155 MM, (F.S.), M105—LIMITED STANDARD
SHELL, CHEMICAL, 155 MM, (H.S.), M105—STANDARD
SHELL, CHEMICAL, 155 MM, (W.P.), M105—LIMITED STANDARD
ROUND FOR HOWITZER, M1917, M1917A1 AND M1918

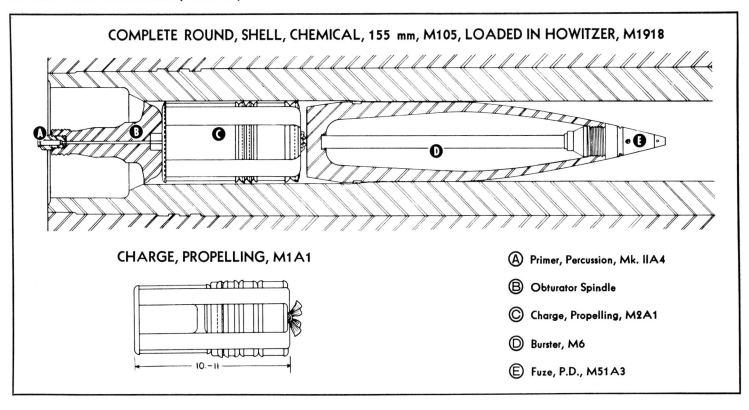

COMPLETE ROUND, SHELL, CHEMICAL, 155 mm, M105, LOADED IN HOWITZER, M1918

CHARGE, PROPELLING, M1A1

10. - 11

(A) Primer, Percussion, Mk. IIA4

(B) Obturator Spindle

(C) Charge, Propelling, M2A1

(D) Burster, M6

(E) Fuze, P.D., M51A3

The present standard chemical shell, M105, was developed from the Mk. IIA1 limited standard chemical round now an issue only item.

SHELL, CHEMICAL, 155 mm, (F.S.), M105 — LIMITED STANDARD; (H.S.), M105 — STANDARD; (W.P.), M105 — LIMITED STANDARD — This standard round is used in the M1917, M1917A1 and M1918 howitzers. It takes the M6 burster and the fuze, P.D., M51A3, with the M21A2 booster.

The shell is loaded with either WP (Smoke), FS (Smoke) or HS (Persistent Gas) fillers. As with the M110 shell, the chemical filler is loaded into the shell and the burster well tube is pressed into place, forming a gastight seal. The weight of the tetryl bursting charge is 0.36 pound; the weights of the various chemical charges are: WP, 15.60 pounds; FS, 16.90 pounds; HS, 11.70 pounds.

The M1A1 and the M2A1 propelling charges are used in the M1918 howitzer. The weight of the M1A1 charge is 3.06 pounds of FNH powder; the weight of the M2A1 charge is 8.09 pounds of FNH powder.

The shell measures 27.56 inches in length and the propelling charge, M1A1, measures 11 inches in length and 5 inches in diameter. The M2A1 propelling charge is also 11 inches in length, but measures 6 inches in diameter.

The M1A1 propelling charge uses an M1 class powder, the grains of which have a web of 0.016 inch and are single perforated. The formula for this powder and that for the M2A1 charge is 85–10–5. The M2A1 charge also uses M1 class powder with seven perforations per grain and a web size of 0.033 inch.

The zone ranges for the M1A1 and M2A1 propelling charges are shown in the table on the following page.

CHARACTERISTICS

	Shell, Chem., M105 (W.P.)	Shell, Chem., M105 (F.S.)	Shell, Chem., M105 (H.S.)		Shell, Chem., M105 (W.P.)	Shell, Chem., M105 (F.S.)	Shell, Chem., M105 (H.S.)
Caliber	155 mm	155 mm	155 mm	Fuze	P.D., M51A3	P.D., M51A3	P.D., M51A3
Models of Howitzers	M1917, M1917A1, M1918	M1917, M1917A1, M1918	M1917, M1917A1, M1918	Propelling Charge and Weight	†	†	†
Proj. Weight	97.68 lb.	99.23 lb.	93.78 lb.	Complete Round Weight	105.77 lb.‡	107.51 lb.‡	101.87 lb.‡
Proj. Charge and Weight*	WP, 15.60 lb.	FS, 16.90 lb.	HS, 11.70 lb.	Muzzle Velocity	§	§	§
Booster	M21A2	M21A2	M21A2	Maximum Range	§	§	§
Primer	Mk. IIA4, 17 grs.	Mk. IIA4, 17 grs.	Mk. IIA4, 17 grs.	Chamber Capacity	355 cu. ins.	355 cu. ins.	355 cu. ins.
				Rated Max. Pressure, p.s.i.	30,000	30,000	30,000

*Does not include 0.36 lb. of tetryl bursting charge.
†M1A1, FNH powder, propelling charge, weighs 3.06 lb.; M2A1, FNH powder, propelling charge, weighs 8.09 lb.
‡With M2A1 propelling charge.

§Charge M1A1: muzzle velocity, 1,082 f/s; maximum range: (W.P.) 9,321 yds.; (F.S.) 9,227 yds.; (H.S.) 9,462 yds.
Charge M2A1: muzzle velocity, 1,476 f/s; maximum range: (W.P.) 12,783 yds.; (F.S.) 12,791 yds.; (H.S.) 12,773 yds.

SHELL, CHEMICAL, 155 MM, (F.S.), M105

Charge Zone	Charge	Section	Weight	M.V.	Max. Range	Elev.
1	M1A1	Base 1	1.78 lb.	679 f/s	4,157 yds.	45° 5'
2	M1A1	Base 1 Incr. 2	2.05 lb.	741 f/s	4,859 yds.	45° 0'
3	M1A1	Base 1 Incrs. 2 & 3	2.52 lb.	831 f/s	5,955 yds.	43° 30'
4	M1A1	Base 1 Incrs. 2, 3 & 4	3.06 lb.	938 f/s	7,330 yds.	43° 30'
5	M1A1	Base 1 Incrs. 2, 3, 4 & 5	4.00 lb.	1,082 f/s	9,227 yds.	43° 30'
3	M2A1	Base 3	3.63 lb.	831 f/s	6,023 yds.	43° 30'
4	M2A1	Base 3 Incr. 4	4.37 lb.	938 f/s	7,402 yds.	43° 30'
5	M2A1	Base 3 Incrs. 4 & 5	5.37 lb.	1,082 f/s	9,335 yds.	43° 30'
6	M2A1	Base 3 Incrs. 4, 5 & 6	7.27 lb.	1,357 f/s	11,739 yds.	43° 45'
7	M2A1	Base 3 Incrs. 4, 5, 6 & 7	8.09 lb.	1,476 f/s	12,791 yds.	44° 15'

SHELL, CHEMICAL, 155 MM, (H.S.), M105

Charge Zone	Charge	Section	Weight	M.V.	Max. Range	Elev.
1	M1A1	Base 1	1.78 lb.	679 f/s	4,342 yds.	45° 5'
2	M1A1	Base 1 Incr. 2	2.05 lb.	741 f/s	5,079 yds.	45° 0'
3	M1A1	Base 1 Incrs. 2 & 3	2.52 lb.	831 f/s	6,205 yds.	43° 30'
4	M1A1	Base 1 Incrs. 2, 3 & 4	3.06 lb.	938 f/s	7,610 yds.	43° 30'
5	M1A1	Base 1 Incrs. 2, 3, 4 & 5	4.00 lb.	1,082 f/s	9,462 yds.	43° 30'
3	M2A1	Base 3	3.63 lb.	831 f/s	6,188 yds.	43° 30'
4	M2A1	Base 3 Incr. 4	4.37 lb.	938 f/s	7,593 yds.	43° 30'
5	M2A1	Base 3 Incrs. 4 & 5	5.37 lb.	1,082 f/s	9,435 yds.	43° 30'
6	M2A1	Base 3 Incrs. 4, 5 & 6	7.27 lb.	1,357 f/s	11,734 yds.	43° 45'
7	M2A1	Base 3 Incrs. 4, 5, 6 & 7	8.09 lb.	1,476 f/s	12,773 yds.	44° 15'

SHELL, CHEMICAL, 155 MM, (W.P.), M105

Charge Zone	Charge	Section	Weight	M.V.	Max. Range	Elev.
1	M1A1	Base 1	1.78 lb.	679 f/s	4,231 yds.	45° 5'
2	M1A1	Base 1 Incr. 2	2.05 lb.	741 f/s	4,947 yds.	45° 0'
3	M1A1	Base 1 Incrs. 2 & 3	2.52 lb.	831 f/s	6,055 yds.	43° 30'
4	M1A1	Base 1 Incrs. 2, 3 & 4	3.06 lb.	938 f/s	7,445 yds.	43° 30'
5	M1A1	Base 1 Incrs. 2, 3, 4 & 5	4.00 lb.	1,082 f/s	9,321 yds.	43° 30'
3	M2A1	Base 3	3.63 lb.	831 f/s	6,089 yds.	43° 30'
4	M2A1	Base 3 Incr. 4	4.37 lb.	938 f/s	7,479 yds.	43° 30'
5	M2A1	Base 3 Incrs. 4 & 5	5.37 lb.	1,082 f/s	9,375 yds.	43° 30'
6	M2A1	Base 3 Incrs. 4, 5 & 6	7.27 lb.	1,357 f/s	11,737 yds.	43° 45'
7	M2A1	Base 3 Incrs. 4, 5, 6 & 7	8.09 lb.	1,476 f/s	12,783 yds.	44° 15'

SHELL, SMOKE (BASE-EJECTION), 155 MM, **M115 & M115B1**—STANDARD
ROUNDS FOR HOWITZERS, M1917, M1917A1 AND M1918

SHELL, SMOKE (BASE-EJECTION), 155 MM, **M116 & M116B1**—STANDARD
ROUNDS FOR HOWITZER, M1

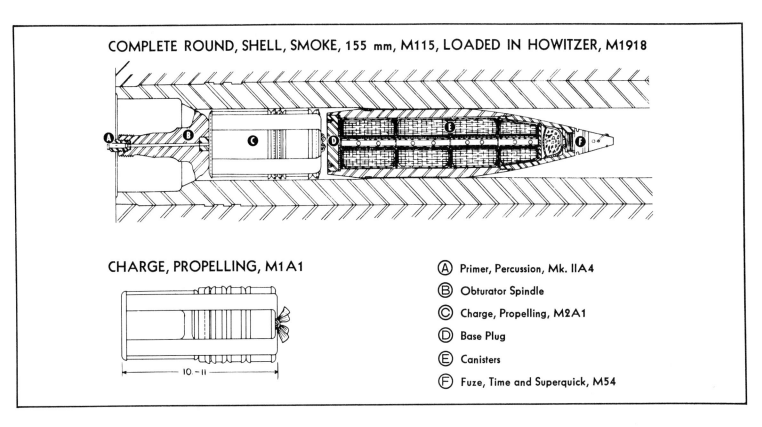

COMPLETE ROUND, SHELL, SMOKE, 155 mm, M115, LOADED IN HOWITZER, M1918

CHARGE, PROPELLING, M1A1

10.–11.

Ⓐ Primer, Percussion, Mk. IIA4

Ⓑ Obturator Spindle

Ⓒ Charge, Propelling, M2A1

Ⓓ Base Plug

Ⓔ Canisters

Ⓕ Fuze, Time and Superquick, M54

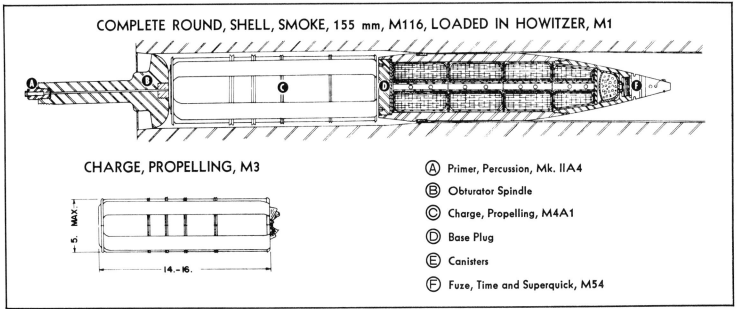

COMPLETE ROUND, SHELL, SMOKE, 155 mm, M116, LOADED IN HOWITZER, M1

CHARGE, PROPELLING, M3

5. MAX.

14.–16.

Ⓐ Primer, Percussion, Mk. IIA4

Ⓑ Obturator Spindle

Ⓒ Charge, Propelling, M4A1

Ⓓ Base Plug

Ⓔ Canisters

Ⓕ Fuze, Time and Superquick, M54

SHELL, SMOKE (BASE-EJECTION), 155 mm, M115 AND M115B1—STANDARD —These standard rounds are used in the M1917, M1917A1 and M1918 howitzers. As fired, the M115 shell weighs 94.88 pounds, and the M115B1 shell weighs 94.14 pounds.

Upon functioning of the time and superquick fuze, M54, the black powder charge is ignited, creating sufficient pressure to shear the threads holding the base plug and eject the three M1 canisters and M2 canister containing the smoke filler. The burning of the powder gives sufficient heat to ignite the smoke canisters before

(Continued on next page)

ejection. They follow the trajectory of the shell, usually falling so that the individual smoke clouds merge as one large cloud. The combined weight of the three smoke canisters comprising the M1 charge is 22.05 pounds. The weight of the M2 smoke canister, a single unit, is 3.79 pounds.

The M115 and M115B1 shells differ only in the construction of the ogive section of the body. This section of the M115 is an adapter which is screwed into the shell body. The M115B1 shell is of one piece construction.

The M115 complete round weighs 103.08 pounds with the M2A1 charge and is fired with either the M2A1 propelling charge (base charge 3 plus increments 4, 5, 6, and 7) weighing 8.25 pounds, or the M1A1 propelling charge (base 1 plus increments 2, 3, 4 and 5) weighing 3.06 pounds.

The M2A1 propelling charge uses an M1 class powder with an 85–10–5 formula. The grains have seven perforations and a web of 0.033 inch. The propelling charge, M1A1, uses a powder which has single-perforated grains with a web of 0.016 inch. The powder is an M1 class with a formula of 85–10–5.

The projectile as fired is 27.19 inches in length. The M2A1 propelling charge measures 11 inches, maximum length, and 6 inches in diameter. The M1A1 charge is 11 inches in length and 5 inches in diameter.

SHELL, SMOKE (BASE-EJECTION), 155 mm, M116 AND M116B1—STANDARD
—This round is standard for use in the M1 howitzer. It is the same as the M115 round except for the rotating band. The weight of the M116 shell as fired is 95.1

pounds; that of the M116B1 shell is 94.36 pounds. The complete round weighs 108.36 pounds with the M4A1 charge and is fired by either the M4A1 propelling charge, weighing 13.26 pounds, or the M3 propelling charge, weighing 5.31 pounds.

The M3 propelling charge uses an M1 class powder, the grains of which have a web of 0.015 inch and are single perforated. The formula for this powder and that for the M4A1 charge is 85–10–5. The M4A1 charge also uses M1 class powder with seven perforations per grain and a web size of 0.034 inch.

The projectile as fired is 27.19 inches in length. The M4A1 propelling charge measures 21 inches, maximum length, and 5.8 inches in diameter. The M3 charge is 16 inches in length and 5 inches in diameter.

CHARACTERISTICS

	Shell, Smoke, M115	Shell, Smoke, M116	Shell, Smoke, M115B1	Shell, Smoke, M116B1
Caliber	155 mm	155 mm	155 mm	155 mm
Models of Howitzers	M1917, M1917A1, M1918	M1 ——	M1917, M1917A1, M1918	M1 ——
Proj. Weight	94.88 lb.	95.10 lb.	94.14 lb.	94.36 lb.
Proj. Charge & Weight	TNT, 0.28 lb.*	TNT, 0.28 lb.*	TNT, 0.28 lb.*	TNT, 0.28 lb.*
Fuze	T. & S.Q., M54	T. & S.Q., M54	T. & S.Q., M54	T. & S.Q., M54
Primer	Mk. IIA4, 17 grs.	Mk. IIA4, 17 grs.	Mk. IIA4, 17 grs.	Mk. IIA4, 17 grs.
Propelling Charge & Weight	NH pwdr., 8.09 lb.†	NH pwdr., 13.26 lb.‡	NH pwdr., 8.09 lb.†	NH pwdr., 13.26 lb.‡
Complete Round Weight	103.08 lb.§	108.23 lb.¶	102.23 lb.§§	107.62 lb.¶¶
Muzzle Velocity	1,476 f/s**	1,850 f/s††	1,476 f/s**	1,850 f/s††
Maximum Range	12,405 yds.	16,355 yds.	12,405 yds.	16,355 yds.
Chamber Capacity	360 cu. ins.	795 cu. ins.	360 cu. ins.	795 cu. ins.
Rated Max. Pressure, p.s.i.	30,000	32,000	30,000	32,000

*H. C. Chemical filler, 25.84 lb.
†M1A1 propelling charge, 3.06 lb.
‡M3 propelling charge, 5.31 lb.
§97.89 lb. with M1A1 charge.
¶100.41 lb. with M3 charge.

**1,082 f/s with M1A1 charge.
††1,220 f/s with M3 charge.
§§97.20 with M1A1 charge.
¶¶99.67 with M3 charge.

SHELL, HIGH-EXPLOSIVE, 8 INCH, MK. IA1—STANDARD
SHELL, HIGH-EXPLOSIVE, 8 INCH, M106—STANDARD
ROUNDS FOR HOWITZER, 8 INCH, M1

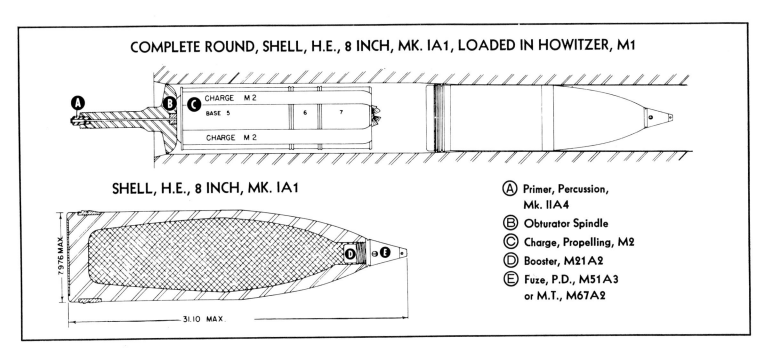

COMPLETE ROUND, SHELL, H.E., 8 INCH, MK. IA1, LOADED IN HOWITZER, M1

SHELL, H.E., 8 INCH, MK. IA1

Ⓐ Primer, Percussion, Mk. IIA4
Ⓑ Obturator Spindle
Ⓒ Charge, Propelling, M2
Ⓓ Booster, M21A2
Ⓔ Fuze, P.D., M51A3 or M.T., M67A2

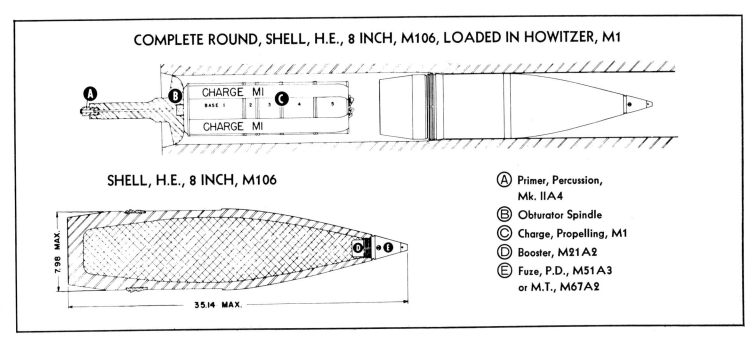

COMPLETE ROUND, SHELL, H.E., 8 INCH, M106, LOADED IN HOWITZER, M1

SHELL, H.E., 8 INCH, M106

Ⓐ Primer, Percussion, Mk. IIA4
Ⓑ Obturator Spindle
Ⓒ Charge, Propelling, M1
Ⓓ Booster, M21A2
Ⓔ Fuze, P.D., M51A3 or M.T., M67A2

The Mk. I high-explosive shell used in the 8 inch guns was modified to take either the point-detonating fuze, M51A3, or the mechanical time fuze, M67A2. This modification was designated high-explosive shell, Mk. IA1, and is used in the M1 howitzer.

The M1 propelling charge (base and increment type) measures 21 inches in length and 6.5 inches in diameter and the M2 charge is 24 inches in length and 7.5 inches in diameter. The M1 or the M2 propelling charges are used with all rounds in the M1 howitzer. The M1 charge contains an M1 class powder weighing 13.19 pounds. The formula of this powder is 85–10–5 and the grains have a web of 0.015 inch and are single perforated. The M2 charge weighs 28.19 pounds and has the same class powder and formula as the M1 charge. The grains have seven perforations and a web of 0.043 inch.

(Continued on next page)

SHELL, HIGH-EXPLOSIVE, 8 INCH, MK. IA1 AND M106 (Continued)

The shell weighs 200 pounds as fired and contains a bursting charge of 30.08 pounds of TNT. The complete round, with M1 charge, weighs 213.19 pounds and with the M2 charge, 228.19 pounds.

The zone ranges for the various weight propelling charges are as indicated in Table A.

SHELL, H.E., 8 INCH, M106—STANDARD—The separate-loading high-explosive round is standard for use in the 8 inch howitzer, M1. The shell weighs 200 pounds as fired and contains a bursting charge of 36.98 pounds of TNT.

The complete round weight, with M1 propelling charge, is 213.19 pounds, and with the M2 charge, 228.19 pounds.

Either the fuze, P.D., M51A3, or the M.T., M67A2, is used with the M21A2 booster. As with the Mk. IA1 round, the Mk. IIA4 17 grain percussion primer is seated in the base of the obturator spindle.

The zone ranges are as indicated in Table B.

PROJECTILE, DUMMY (DRILL), MK. I—STANDARD—(See Table of Characteristics.)

TABLE A—SHELL, H.E., 8 INCH, MK. IA1

Charge Zone	Charge	Section	Weight	M.V.	Max. Range	Elev.
1	M1	Base 1	4.41 lb.	795 f/s	5,475 yds.	42° 55'
2	M1	Base 1, Incr. 1	5.77 lb.	873 f/s	6,415 yds.	42° 55'
3	M1	Base 1, Incr. 2 & 3	7.68 lb.	970 f/s	7,630 yds.	42° 48'
4	M1	Base 1, Incr. 2, 3, 4	10.24 lb.	1,115 f/s	9,260 yds.	43° 0'
5	M1	Base 1, Incr. 2, 3, 4, 5	13.19 lb.	1,339 f/s	11,170 yds.	43° 36'
5	M2*	Base 5	16.50 lb.	——	——	——
6	M2*	Base 5, Incr. 6	21.72 lb.	——	——	——
7	M2*	Base 5, Incr. 6, 7	28.19 lb.	——	——	——

*At the present time range firings have not been conducted.

TABLE B—SHELL, H.E., 8 INCH, MK. IA1

Charge Zone	Charge	Section	Weight	M.V.	Max. Range	Elev.
1	M1	Base 1	4.41 lb.	820 f/s	6,230 yds.	44°
2	M1	Base 1, Incr. 2	5.77 lb.	900 f/s	7,385 yds.	44°
3	M1	Base 1, Incr. 2	7.68 lb.	1,000 f/s	8,850 yds.	44°
4	M1	Base 1, Incr. 2, 3, 4	10.24 lb.	1,150 f/s	10,705 yds.	44° 10'
5	M1	Base 1, Incr. 2, 3, 4, 5	13.19 lb.	1,380 f/s	12,975 yds.	44° 30'
5	M2	Base 5	16.50 lb.	1,380 f/s	12,975 yds.	44° 30'
6	M2	Base 5, Incr. 6	21.72 lb.	1,640 f/s	15,390 yds.	44° 50'
7	M2	Base 5, Incr. 6, 7	28.19 lb.	1,950 f/s	18,510 yds.	44° 50'

CHARACTERISTICS

	Shell, H.E., Mk. IA1	Shell, H.E., M106	Proj. Drill, Mk. I
Caliber	8 inch	8 inch	8 inch
Model of Howitzer	M1	M1	M1
Proj. Weight	200 lb.	200 lb.	200 lb.
Proj. Charge & Weight	TNT, 30.08 lb.	TNT, 36.98 lb.	——
Booster	M21A2	M21A2	——
Fuze	P.D., M51A3, or M.T., M67A2	P.D., M51A3, or M.T., M67A2	——
Primer	Mk. IIA4, 17 grs.	Mk. IIA4, 17 grs.	Mk. IIA4, 18 grs.
Propelling Charge and Weight	M1 Chg., FNH pwdr., 13.19 lb. M2 Chg., FNH pwdr., 28.19 lb.	M1 Chg., FNH pwdr., 13.19 lb. M2 Chg., FNH pwdr., 28.19 lb.	Mk. I, Dummy, 11.00 lb.
Complete Round Weight	213.19 lb. (with M1 Chg.) 228.19 lb. (with M2 Chg.)	213.19 lb. (with M1 Chg.) 228.19 lb. (with M2 Chg.)	211.00 lb.
Muzzle Velocity	1,339 f/s (with M1 Chg.) ——	1,380 f/s (with M1 Chg.) 1,950 f/s (with M2 Chg.)	——
Maximum Range	11,170 yds. (with M1 Chg.) ——	12,975 yds. (with M1 Chg.) 18,510 yds. (with M2 Chg.)	——
Chamber Capacity	1,757 cu. ins.	1,527 cu. ins.	——
Rated Max. Pressure, p.s.i.	33,000	33,000	——

SHELL, H.E., 8 INCH, M103—STANDARD
ROUND FOR 8 INCH GUNS, MK. VI, MOD. 3A2, AND 8 INCH GUNS, M1

PROJECTILE, ARMOR-PIERCING, 8 INCH, MK. XX, MOD. 1—STANDARD
ROUND FOR 8 INCH GUNS, MK. VI, MOD. 3A2, M1888, M1888MI AND M1888MII

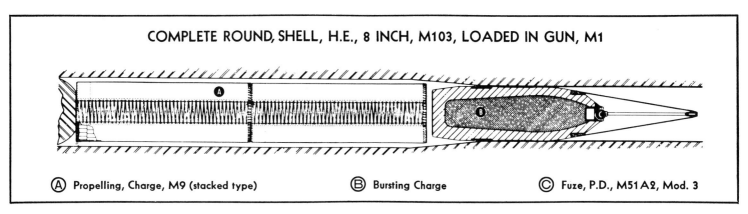

COMPLETE ROUND, SHELL, H.E., 8 INCH, M103, LOADED IN GUN, M1

Ⓐ Propelling, Charge, M9 (stacked type)　　　Ⓑ Bursting Charge　　　Ⓒ Fuze, P.D., M51A2, Mod. 3

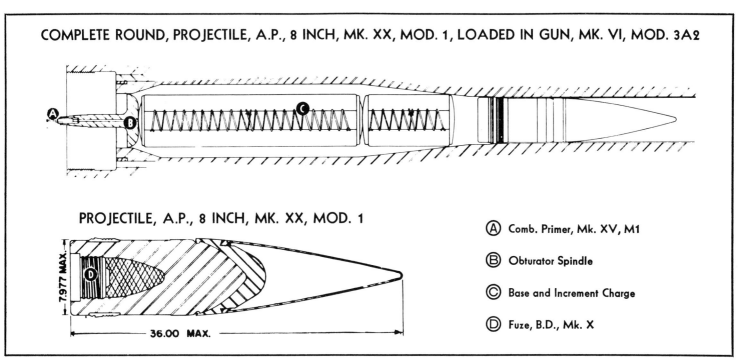

COMPLETE ROUND, PROJECTILE, A.P., 8 INCH, MK. XX, MOD. 1, LOADED IN GUN, MK. VI, MOD. 3A2

PROJECTILE, A.P., 8 INCH, MK. XX, MOD. 1

7.977 MAX.　　36.00 MAX.

Ⓐ Comb. Primer, Mk. XV, M1

Ⓑ Obturator Spindle

Ⓒ Base and Increment Charge

Ⓓ Fuze, B.D., Mk. X

SHELL, H.E., 8 INCH, M103—STANDARD —The Shell, H.E., M103, is standard for 8 inch Guns, Mk. VI, Mod. 3A2, and M1. As fired the shell weighs 240 pounds and contains a bursting charge of 20.9 pounds of cast TNT which is detonated by a Fuze, P.D., M51A2, Mod. 3, or Fuze, Mechanical, Time, M67A1. The shell is shipped fuzed with a Fuze, P.D., M51A2, Mod. 3. When the Mechanical Time Fuze, M67A1, is used, it is necessary that the false ogive be removed and replaced after the shell has been refuzed with the mechanical time fuze.

For the 8 inch Gun, M1, two types of charges are provided for use with the Shell, H.E., M103. One is identified as the M9 (green bag) and the other as M10 (white bag). Both types are of the base and increment type.

The powder in the M9 charge is in the M1 class with an 87–10–3 formula. The grains have seven perforations and a web of .0695 inch. The complete charge weighs 76 pounds.

The powder in the M10 charge is also in the M1 class with an 87–10–3 formula.

The grains have seven perforations and a web of .1000 inch. The complete charge weighs 106 pounds.

PROJECTILE, A. P., 8 INCH, MK. XX, MOD. 1—STANDARD—This projectile was standardized to replace the M1911 armor-piercing round when the latter was made Limited Standard and an issue only item.

Separate-loading ammunition, the Mk. XX projectile, is used in the 8 inch, M1888, the M1888MI, M1888MII and Mk. VI, Mod. 3A2, guns. As fired, the projectile weighs 261.8 pounds and contains a bursting charge of 3.4 pounds of explosive "D" which is detonated by the fuze, B.D., Mk. X.

The supercharge (base and increment) of 108 pounds of NH powder is fired by the M30 electric primer. The normal base section weighs 74.251 pounds. The complete round, including supercharge, weighs 369.8 pounds as fired in the Mk. VI, Mod. M3A2, gun.

The base and increment charge used with this projectile in the Mk. VI, Mod. 3A2, gun is 57 inches in length, and 9.25 inches in diameter. The powder in this charge is in the M1 class with an 87–10–3 formula. The grains have seven perforations and a web of 0.1 inch.

The stacked type, two-section propelling charge of NH powder used with this projectile in the M1888 series guns weighs 85.62 pounds. This charge measures 48.5 inches in length, and 8.75 inches in diameter.

The M1 class powder used in these charges has an 87–10–3 formula. The grains have seven perforations and a web size of 0.092 inch.

PROJECTILE, TARGET, 8 INCH, M109—STANDARD—See description of shell, high-explosive, 8 inch, Mk. I, round for M1888 guns.

CHARACTERISTICS

	Proj., A.P., Mk. XX	Proj., A.P., Mk. XX	Proj., A.P., Mk. XX	Proj., Target, M109	Shell, H.E., M103	Shell, H.E., M103
Caliber	8 inch	8 inch	8 inch	8 inch	8 inch	8 inch
Models of Guns	Mk. VI, Mod. 3A2	Mk. VI, Mod. 3A2	M1888, M1888M1, M1888M11	Mk. VI, Mod. 3A2	M1	Mk. VI, Mod. 3A2
Proj. Weight	261.8 lb.	261.8 lb.	261.8 lb.	260.0 lb.	240 lb.	240 lb.
Proj. Charge and Weight	Expl. "D," 3.4 lb.	Expl. "D," 3.4 lb.	Expl. "D," 3.4 lb.	——	TNT, 20.9 lb.	TNT, 20.9 lb.
Fuze	B.D., Mk. X	B.D., Mk. X	B.D., Mk. X	——	P.D., M51A2, Mod. 3, or M.T., M67A1	P.D., M51A2, Mod. 3, or M.T., M67A1
Primer	M30, Elec.	M30, Elec.	M30, Elec.	Comb. Mk. XV, M1	Mk. IIA4	Comb. Mk. XV, MI
Propelling Charge and Weight	Normal Chg., NH pwdr., 74.251 lb.	Superchg., NH pwdr., 108.0 lb.	Two-Sec., NH pwdr., 85.6 lb.	Base & Incr., NH pwdr., 107.0 lb.	M9 Base Sec., 54.896 lb.* M10 Base Sec., 93.1 lb.†	Base Sec., 74.251 lb.§
Complete Round Weight	336.05 lb.	369.8 lb.	345.80 lb.	367.00 lb.	315 lb. (M9 Chg.) 346 lb. (M10 Chg.)	314.24 lb. (with Base Sec.) 348.00 lb. (with Base Sec. & 2 Incr.)
Muzzle Velocity	2,100 f/s	2,750 f/s	2,450 f/s	2,750 f/s	2,100 f/s (M9 Base Sec.)‡ 2,100 f/s (M10 Base Sec.)**	2,150 f/s (Base Sec.) 2,840 f/s (Base Sec. & Incr.)
Maximum Range	22,180 yds. at 45° 5' Elev.	32,980 yds. at 47° 55' Elev.	23,917 yds.	32,980 yds. at 47° 55' Elev.	22,775 yds. (M9 Base Sec.)†† 30,315 yds. (M10 Base Sec.)§§	23,200 yds. (Base Sec.) 35,630 yds. (Base & Incr.)
Chamber Capacity	5,362.94 cu. ins.	5,362.94 cu. ins.	3,627.00 cu. ins.	5,362.94 cu. ins.	5,156 cu. ins.	5,188 cu. ins.
Rated Max. Pressure, p.s.i.	38,000	38,000	38,000	38,000	38,000	38,000

*76.013 lb. with M9 Base Sec. & increment.
†106.1 lb. with M10 Base Sec. & increment.
§108.000 lb. with Base and 1 increment.
‡2,600 f/s with M9 Base Sec. & increment.
**2,850 f/s with M10 Base Sec. & increment.
††30,315 yds. with M9 Base Sec. & increment.
§§35,630 yds. with M10 Base Sec. & increment.

SHELL, HIGH-EXPLOSIVE, 8 INCH, MK. I—STANDARD
ROUND FOR 8-INCH GUNS, M1888, M1888MI, M1888MII

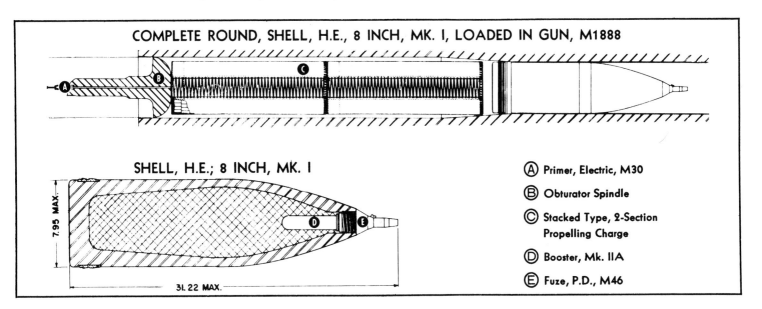

COMPLETE ROUND, SHELL, H.E., 8 INCH, MK. I, LOADED IN GUN, M1888

SHELL, H.E.; 8 INCH, MK. I

7.95 MAX.

31.22 MAX.

(A) Primer, Electric, M30

(B) Obturator Spindle

(C) Stacked Type, 2-Section Propelling Charge

(D) Booster, Mk. IIA

(E) Fuze, P.D., M46

SHELL, HIGH-EXPLOSIVE, 8 INCH, MK. I—STANDARD—The Mk. I round is used in the M1888, M1888MI and M1888MII guns. As fired, the shell weighs 200 pounds and contains a bursting charge of 29.6 pounds of TNT which is detonated by the fuze, P.D., M46, or P.D., M47, with the Mk. IIA booster.

The two section, stacked propelling charge of 85.6 pounds of smokeless nitrocellulose powder is fired by the M30 electric primer. (Guns in emplacements fitted with electrical equipment are provided with friction primer for emergency use.) The complete round, including two section propelling charge, weighs 285.6 pounds.

The propelling charge uses an M1 class powder the grains of which have a web of 0.076 inch and seven perforations. The formula is 87–10–3.

The propelling charge measures 49 inches in length and 8.25 inches in diameter.

PROJECTILE, TARGET, 8 INCH, M1911—STANDARD—This shot is standardized for target-practice use, although the M1911 armor-piercing rounds are now Limited Standard for issue only. The 8 inch, H.E. Shell, Mk. I, may also be used for a target projectile when specially authorized and in such cases it is sand loaded and assembled with an inert fuze.

The M1911 separate-loading projectile is used in the M1888, M1888MI and M1888MII guns. As fired the shot weighs

323 pounds and contains a bursting charge of 5.1 pounds of explosive "D," detonated by the fuze, B.D., Mk. V.

The projectile is 33 inches in length. The armor-piercing cap is soldered to the nose of the shot and the windshield is threaded to the armor-piercing cap.

The propelling charge is a single-section type powder bag containing 82.38 pounds of smokeless powder and is fired by the M30 electric primer. The complete round weighs 405.43 pounds.

The charge develops a muzzle velocity of 2,200 feet per second and a maximum range of 17,000 yards at 19° 34' elevation.

PROJECTILE, TARGET, 8 INCH, M109 —STANDARD—This target projectile is

standardized for use in the following 8 inch guns: M1888, M1888MI, M1888MII and Mk. VI, Mod. 3A2. It is made of cast iron and weighs 260 pounds. Propelling charges and primers are of two types and the weights of the charges vary as follows: 85.6 pounds of smokeless powder in a two-section bag, fired by the M30 electric primer when used with the M1888, M1888MI and M1888MII guns; 107 pounds of smokeless powder in a base and increment charge, fired by the Mk. XVMI Navy electric primer, when used with the Mk. VI, Mod. 3A2, gun.

PROJECTILE, DUMMY, DRILL, MK. I—STANDARD—(See Table of Characteristics.)

CHARACTERISTICS

	Shell, H.E., Mk. I	Proj., Target, M1911	Proj., Target, M109	Proj., Drill, Mk. I
Caliber	8 inch	8 inch	8 inch	8 inch
Models of Guns	M1888 M1888MI M1888MII	M1888 M1888MI M1888MII	M1888 M1888MI M1888MII	M1888 M1888MI M1888MII
Proj. Weight	200 lb.	323 lb.	260 lb.	200 lb.
Proj. Charge and Weigh	TNT, 29.6 lb.	Expl. "D," 5.1 lb.	——	——
Fuze	P.D., M46 or M47	B.D., Mk. V	——	——
Primer	M30, Elec.	M30, Elec.	M30, Elec.	——
Propelling Charge and Weight	Two-Sec., Smokeless, 85.6 lb.	Single-Sec., Smokeless, 82.38 lb.	Two-Sec., Smokeless, 85.6 lb.	Single-Sec., Dummy, 80.0 lb.
Complete Round Weight	285.6 lb.	405.43 lb.	345.6 lb.	280.0 lb.
Muzzle Velocity	2,600 F/S	2,200 F/S	2,450 F/S	——
Maximum Range	21,300 yds.	17,000 yds.	25,146 yds.	——
Chamber Capacity	3,543 cu. ins.	3,571.7 cu. ins.	3,627 cu. ins.	——
Rated Maximum Pressure, p.s.i.	38,000	38,000	38,000	——

SHELL, HIGH-EXPLOSIVE, 240 MM, MK. IIIA1—STANDARD

ROUND FOR HOWITZER, 240 mm, M1918M1

SHELL, HIGH-EXPLOSIVE, 240 MM, M114—STANDARD

ROUND FOR HOWITZER, 240 MM, M1

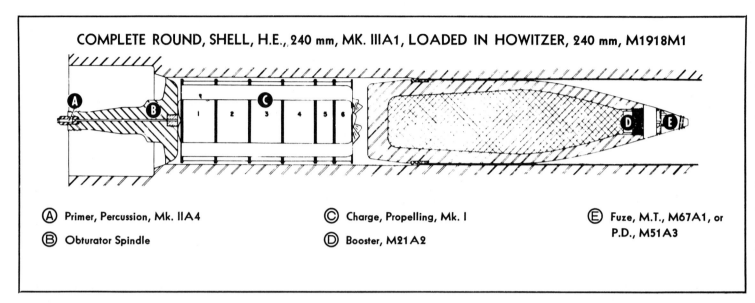

COMPLETE ROUND, SHELL, H.E., 240 mm, MK. IIIA1, LOADED IN HOWITZER, 240 mm, M1918M1

- Ⓐ Primer, Percussion, Mk. IIA4
- Ⓑ Obturator Spindle
- Ⓒ Charge, Propelling, Mk. I
- Ⓓ Booster, M21A2
- Ⓔ Fuze, M.T., M67A1, or P.D., M51A3

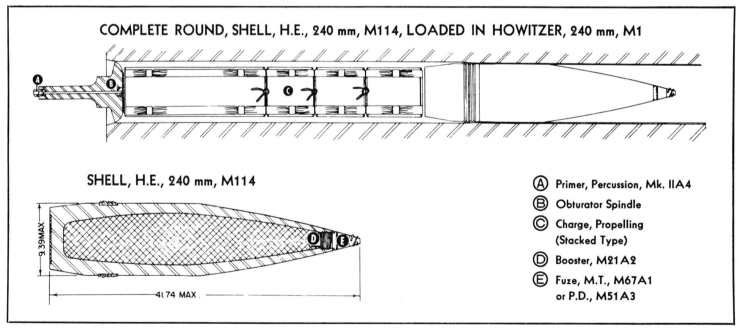

COMPLETE ROUND, SHELL, H.E., 240 mm, M114, LOADED IN HOWITZER, 240 mm, M1

SHELL, H.E., 240 mm, M114

9.39 MAX.

41.74 MAX.

- Ⓐ Primer, Percussion, Mk. IIA4
- Ⓑ Obturator Spindle
- Ⓒ Charge, Propelling (Stacked Type)
- Ⓓ Booster, M21A2
- Ⓔ Fuze, M.T., M67A1 or P.D., M51A3

The projectiles provided for use in the 240 mm howitzers, M1918M1 and M1 are of three types: high-explosive—for use against personnel and structures; target-practice—sand loaded; and dummy —for drill purposes.

The high-explosive and practice projectiles are issued unfuzed, an eyebolt lifting plug or an adapter plug being assembled in the fuze seat. To prepare the high-explosive shell for firing, it is necessary to remove the rope grommet which protects the rotating band and the plug in the nose of the shell, before inserting a fuze. In the case of the practice shell, the inert adapter-booster must be removed and the shell loaded to weight with sand.

The Mk. IIIA1 is a modification of the Mk. III to permit assembly of either the point-detonating fuze, M51A3, or the mechanical time fuze, M67A1, instead of the point-detonating fuzes, M46 or M47. The use of these bore-safe fuzes of better ballistic shape increased the range and safety in firing.

SHELL, H.E., 240 mm, MK. IIIA1— STANDARD—This high-explosive shell has a fairly sharp nose, the radius of the ogive being approximately 4½ calibers.

(Continued on next page)

The shell has a boat-tail base, tapered at an angle of 7°. The combination of sharp nose and tapered base adds to the efficiency of the shell in flight. The explosive charge is 49.79 pounds of TNT.

As fired the shell weighs 345 pounds and measures 37.9 inches in length. The complete round weighs 380.81 pounds.

The propelling charge is NH powder. A base-pad igniter pad is used, containing 5 ounces of black powder and placed to the rear of the charge.

The charges used are of the multi-section, aliquot part type (illustrated) and contain 35.81 pounds of powder. They are composed of four 1/5 equal weight sections, and two 1/10 equal weight sections.

The Mk. I propelling charge is 20.75 inches in length and 9.025 inches in diameter. The M1 class powder for this charge has an 87–10–3 formula and grains that have seven perforations. The web size of the grains is 0.051 inch.

The complete round weights vary from 352.41 pounds to 380.81 pounds, depending upon the zone charges used. (Note: the Table of Characteristics lists only the maximum zone charge with pertinent data.) See Table A for zone ranges.

SHELL, H.E., 240 mm, M114—STANDARD—This high-explosive round is used in the M1 howitzer. As fired the shell weighs 360 pounds and with the maximum propelling charge, 78.25 pounds of NH powder (4 sections), the complete round weighs 438.78 pounds.

Either the fuze, P.D., M51A3, or the fuze, M.T., M67A1, is used to detonate the TNT bursting charge of 54.06 pounds.

The M1 class of powder used in this charge has an 87–10–3 formula and grains with seven perforations.

The projectile as fired measures 41.74 inches in length.

The Table of Characteristics lists only the maximum zone charge with pertinent data. The table of zone ranges which follows gives data for the four sections of propelling charge:

Muzzle Velocity	Range
1,500 f/s	15,175 yds.
1,740 f/s	17,995 yds.
2,020 f/s	21,560 yds.
2,300 f/s	25,255 yds.

PROJECTILE, TARGET, PRACTICE, MK. III—STANDARD—When specially authorized, the Mk. III shell, sand loaded, may be used. The projectile is made up by using the empty body of the shell, Mk. III, which, although listed as standard, is now an issue only item and no longer manufactured. The shell is shipped empty and later sand loaded to the proper weight prior to issue to the using troops. All components of this projectile are inert.

PROJECTILE, DUMMY, DRILL, MK. I—STANDARD—(See Table of Characteristics.)

TABLE A

Zone	Powder Charge	Wt.	Powder Type	M.V.	Max. Range	Elev.	Time of Flight
2	.2	7.16 lb.	FNH-NH	615 f/s	3,594 yds.	43° 39'	25.9 sec.
3	.3	10.74 lb.	FNH-NH	770 f/s	5,464 yds.	43° 15'	32.2 sec.
4	.4	14.31 lb.	FNH-NH	910 f/s	7,368 yds.	43° 24'	38.2 sec.
5	.5	17.90 lb.	FNH-NH	1,045 f/s	9,316 yds.	43° 45'	42.6 sec.
6	.6	21.48 lb.	FNH-NH	1,180 f/s	11,300 yds.	44° 20'	47.6 sec.
7	.7	25.06 lb.	FNH-NH	1,310 f/s	12,657 yds.	44° 49'	51.1 sec.
8	.8	28.64 lb.	FNH-NH	1,435 f/s	13,905 yds.	45° 5'	54.3 sec.
9	.9	32.22 lb.	FNH-NH	1,570 f/s	15,168 yds.	45° 15'	57.4 sec.
10	1.00	35.81 lb.	FNH-NH	1,700 f/s	16,390 yds.	45° 10'	60.0 sec.

CHARACTERISTICS

	Shell, H.E., Mk. IIIA1	Shell, H.E., M114	Proj., T.P., Mk. III	Proj., Drill, Dummy, Mk. I
Caliber	240 mm	240 mm	240 mm	240 mm
Models of Howitzers	M1918M1	M1	All How.	All How.
Proj. Weight	345 lb.	360 lb.	345 lb.	356 lb.
Proj. Charge & Weight	TNT, 49.79 lb.	TNT, 54.06 lb.	Inert	——
Booster	M21A2	M21A2	——	——
Fuze	P.D., M51A3 or M.T., M67A1	P.D., M51A3 or M.T., M67A1	Dummy	——
Primer	Mk. IIA4 17 grs.	Mk. IIA4 17 grs.	Mk. IIA4 17 grs.	——
Propelling Charge & Weight	FNH–NH, 35.81 lb. (Zone 10)	FNH–NH, 78.75 lb. (4 sections)	FNH–NH, 35.81 lb. (Zone 10)	Dummy, 36.00 lb.
Complete Round Weight	380.81 lb.	438.78 lb.	380.81 lb.	392.00 lb.
Muzzle Velocity	1,700 f/s	2,300 f/s	1,700 f/s	——
Maximum Range	16,390 yds.	25,255 yds.	16,390 yds.	——
Chamber Capacity	1,790.0 cu. ins.	4,430.0 cu. ins.	1,790.0 cu. ins.	——
Rated Max. Pressure, p.s.i.	32,000	36,000	32,000	——

SHELL, HIGH-EXPLOSIVE, 12 INCH, MK. X—STANDARD
ROUND FOR SEACOAST GUNS, 12 INCH, M1895, M1895M1

PROJECTILE, ARMOR-PIERCING, 12 INCH, MK. XVI—STANDARD
ROUND FOR SEACOAST GUNS, 12 INCH, M1888, M1888MI, M1888MII, M1895, M1895M1, AND M1900

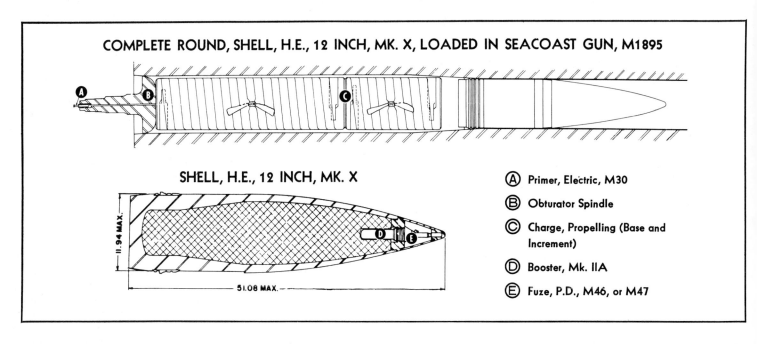

COMPLETE ROUND, SHELL, H.E., 12 INCH, MK. X, LOADED IN SEACOAST GUN, M1895

SHELL, H.E., 12 INCH, MK. X

11.94 MAX.

51.08 MAX.

(A) Primer, Electric, M30

(B) Obturator Spindle

(C) Charge, Propelling (Base and Increment)

(D) Booster, Mk. IIA

(E) Fuze, P.D., M46, or M47

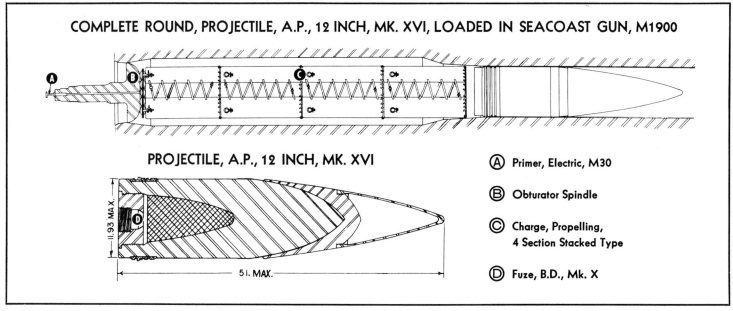

COMPLETE ROUND, PROJECTILE, A.P., 12 INCH, MK. XVI, LOADED IN SEACOAST GUN, M1900

PROJECTILE, A.P., 12 INCH, MK. XVI

11.93 MAX.

51. MAX.

(A) Primer, Electric, M30

(B) Obturator Spindle

(C) Charge, Propelling, 4 Section Stacked Type

(D) Fuze, B.D., Mk. X

The 12 inch separate loading ammunition is used in the 12 inch seacoast guns M1888, M1888MI, M1888MII, M1895, M1895MI and M1900.

Four types of projectiles have been standardized for use in those guns: high-explosive, armor-piercing shot, target-practice projectile and dummy drill projectile.

SHELL, HIGH-EXPLOSIVE, 12 INCH, MK. X—STANDARD—This round is used in the M1895, M1895MI guns and represents the only issue and manufacture high-explosive round which is standard today for use in guns on railway mounts for firing against land targets.

The Mk. X shell is a modification of the now limited standard Mk. VI for use in seacoast guns of the M1895 series. It is 12 pounds heavier than its predecessor and there are 31.88 pounds more of bursting charge. The Mk. X shell has a hollow windshield over the point-detonating M46 or M47 fuzes to improve ballistic qualities. The shape of this shell and increased weight improves its ballistic characteristics. This gives the Mk. X shell an ad-

(Continued on next page)

vantage in range of 2,300 yards over the Mk. VI at maximum range.

The electric primer, M30, is seated in the base of the obturator spindle and the propelling charge fits against the face of the spindle.

The base and increment propelling charge measures 71.5 inches in length, and 12.625 inches in diameter. Powder used in this charge is in the M1 class with an 87–10–3 formula. The grains have 7 perforations.

The shell as fired is 51.08 inches in length and weighs 712 pounds. It contains a bursting charge of 118.28 pounds of TNT. The maximum propelling charge consists of a base and increment charge of NC powder which weighs 300 pounds. This gives a muzzle velocity of 2,600 feet per second and a maximum range of 30,000 yards at 37° 57' elevation. The minimum base charge of NC powder weighs 225 pounds. As illustrated, the complete round weighs 1,012 pounds.

PROJECTILE, ARMOR-PIERCING, 12 INCH, MK. XVI—STANDARD—This round is used in the M1888, M1888MI, M1888MII, M1895, M1895MI and the M1900 seacoast guns.

The Mk. I armor-piercing shell, now classified as limited standard and used in the M1888 and M1895 series of seacoast guns, is the predecessor projectile from which the Mk. XVI armor-piercing projectile was developed. The Mk. XVI projectile is 75 pounds heavier than the Mk. I armor-piercing shell and the projectile contains 21.14 pounds less of explosive "D" bursting charge.

Data on the types of propelling charge and their weights follow:

	M1888, '88MI, '88MII, '95, '95MI	M1900
Type	NH powder	NH powder
Sections	Stacked, 4	Stacked, 4
Weight	268 lb.	334 lb.

The four-section propelling charge used with the M1888 series guns and the M1895 series guns uses an M1 class powder with a formula of 87–10–3. The grains of this powder have seven perforations and a web of 0.138 inch. The propelling charge used with the M1900 gun has the same powder characteristics as above except that the web size is 0.170 inch.

The projectile is 51 inches in length.

PROJECTILES, TARGET, PRACTICE, M1911, MK. XV, MK. XXI—STANDARD —There are three standard issue and manufacture rounds for target practice use.

The M1911 cast-iron projectile, weighing 1,070 pounds, is used in the M1888 series of guns, in the M1895 series and in the M1900 gun. The Mk. XV cast-iron projectile, weighing 900 pounds, is used in the M1895 gun. The Mk. XXI cast-iron projectile, weighing 975 pounds, is used in the M1888 and M1895 guns.

All target-practice rounds are fired by four-section NH powder charges weighing 270 pounds. The exception is when the M1911 projectile is fired in the M1900 gun, in which case the four-section charge weighs 334 pounds.

When specially authorized, a sand-filled common steel shell (the Mk. VI or the Mk. X) may be used for target practice with railway mount if suitable cast-iron projectiles are not provided.

All target-practice projectiles are shipped empty and later sand loaded to the proper weight prior to issue to the using troops. All components (loading, fuzes) of these projectiles are inert. Advantages of using the inert-loaded practice rounds are in the saving of the high-explosive filler normally used, and in the safety of the gun crew during training.

PROJECTILE, DUMMY, DRILL, M6—STANDARD—(See Table of Characteristics.)

CHARACTERISTICS

	Shell, H.E., Mk. X	Proj., A.P., Mk. XVI	Proj., A.P., Mk. XVI	Proj., T.P., M1911	Proj., T.P., Mk. XV	Proj., T.P., Mk. XXI	Proj., Drill, M6
Caliber	12 inch	12 inch	12 inch	12 inch	12 inch	12 inch	12 inch
Model of Guns	M1895 M1895M1	M1888 M1888M1 M1888MII M1895 M1895M1	M1900	All guns	M1895 M1895M1	M1888 M1888M1 M1888MII M1895	All guns
Proj. Weight	712 lb.	975 lb.	975 lb.	1,070 lb.	900 lb.	975 lb.	975 lb.
Proj. Charge and Weight	TNT, 118.28 lb.	Expl. "D," 22.2 lb.	Expl. "D," 22.2 lb.	—	—	—	—
Booster	Mk. IIA	—	—	—	—	—	—
Fuze	P.D., M46 or M47	B.D., Mk. X	B.D., Mk. X	—	—	—	—
Primer	M30, Elec.	M30, Elec.	M30, Elec.	M30, Elec.	M30, Elec.	M30, Elec.	M30, Elec.
Propelling Charge and Weight	NC pwdr., 300 lb.	NH pwdr., 268 lb.	NH pwdr., 334 lb.	NH pwdr., 270 lb.	NH pwdr., 268 lb.	NH pwdr., 268 lb.	—
Complete Round Weight	1,012 lb.	1,243 lb.	1,309 lb.	1,338 lb.†	1,168 lb.	1,243 lb.	—
Muzzle Velocity	2,600 F/S	2,260 F/S‡	2,275 F/S	2,250 F/S‡‡	2,325 F/S	2,260 F/S§	—
Maximum Range	30,000 yds.	30,100 yds.	30,100 yds.	27,000 yds.	29,200 yds.	30,100 yds.	—
Chamber Capacity	11,810 cu. ins.	11,840 cu. ins.**	16,300 cu. ins.	11,840 cu. ins.††	11,728 cu. ins.	11,840 cu. ins.**	—
Rated Maximum Pressure, p.s.i.	38,000	38,000	38,000	38,000	38,000	38,000	—

*334 lb. NH powder in M1900 gun.
†1,404 lb. in M1900 gun.
‡2,275 f/s in M1895 and M1895M1 guns.
§2,275 f/s in M1895 and M1895M1 guns.
**11,900 cu. ins. in M1895 and M1895M1 guns.
††11,900 in M1888 series, 16,300 in M1900.
‡‡2,235 f/s in M1888 series.

PROJECTILE, ARMOR-PIERCING, 16 INCH, MK. XII, MOD. 1—STANDARD

PROJECTILE, TARGET PRACTICE, 16 INCH, M108—STANDARD
ROUNDS FOR 16 INCH SEACOAST GUN, MK. IIM1 (NAVY)

PROJECTILE, TARGET PRACTICE, 16 INCH, M100—STANDARD
ROUND FOR 16 INCH SEACOAST GUNS, M1919 AND MK. IIM1 (NAVY)

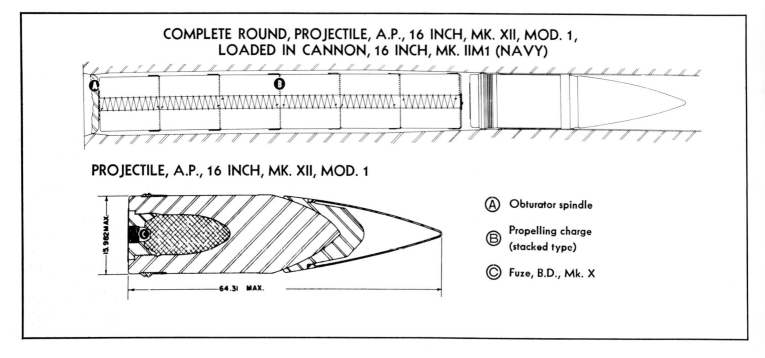

COMPLETE ROUND, PROJECTILE, A.P., 16 INCH, MK. XII, MOD. 1, LOADED IN CANNON, 16 INCH, MK. IIM1 (NAVY)

PROJECTILE, A.P., 16 INCH, MK. XII, MOD. 1

15.982 MAX.
64.31 MAX.

(A) Obturator spindle

(B) Propelling charge (stacked type)

(C) Fuze, B.D., Mk. X

Of the projectiles that have been made for 16 inch cannon only one is now standard for issue and manufacture—the 16 inch, Mk. XII, Mod. 1. The Mk. V, the Mk. II, Mod. 2, and the Mk. IX, 16 inch, projectiles are limited standard and are only for issue until present stocks are exhausted.

The Mk. XII, Mod. 1 projectile is used in the 16 inch cannon, Mk. II, Mod. 1 (Navy), and is of Navy design.

PROJECTILE, A.P., 16 INCH, MK. XII, MOD. 1—STANDARD—The projectile has an armor-piercing cap that is crimped and soldered to the body. A windshield is welded to the cap to improve ballistic shape.

An explosive "D" bursting charge of 34.18 pounds is detonated by the Mk. X base-detonating fuze. The volume of the bursting charge cavity with plug and fuze in place is 644.27 cu. ins.

To insure against the propelling charge

(Continued on next page)

CHARACTERISTICS

	Proj., A.P., Mk. XII, Mod. I	Proj., T.P., M108	Proj., T.P., M100	Proj., T.P., M100	Proj., Drill, M5
Caliber	16 inch	16 inch	16 inch	16 inch	16 inch
Models of Guns	Mk. IIM1 (Navy)	Mk. IIM1 (Navy)	Mk. IIM1 (Navy)	M1919	Mk. IIM1 (Navy)
Proj. Weight	2,240 lb.	2,240 lb.	2,100 lb.	2,100 lb.	2,240 lb.
Charge and Weight	Expl. "D," 34.18 lb.	Inert	Inert	Inert	——
Fuze	B.D., Mk. X	——	——	——	——
Primer	Mk. XV, Mod. I Comb.	Mk. XV, Mod. I Comb.	Mk. XV, Mod. I Comb.	Mk. XV, Mod. I Comb.	Mk. XV, Mod. I Comb.
Propelling Charge and Weight	6-sec., NH pwdr., 675 lb.	6-sec., NH pwdr., 675 lb.	6-sec., NH pwdr., 709 lb.	4-sec., NH pwdr., 870 lb.	6-sec., Dummy, 720 lb.
Complete Round Weight	2,915 lb.	2,915 lb.	2,809 lb.	2,970 lb.	2,960 lb.
Muzzle Velocity	2,650 f/s*	2,650 f/s*	2,750 f/s	2,750 f/s	——
Range	45,155 yds. at 47° 20' elev.*	45,155 yds. at 47° 20' elev.*	44,680 yds. at 50° 56' elev.	44,680 yds. at 50° 56' elev.	——
Chamber Capacity	29,525 cu. ins.	29,525 cu. ins.	30,000 cu. ins.	40,900 cu. ins.	——
Rated Maximum Pressure, p.s.i.	38,000	38,000	38,000	38,000	——

*1,900 f/s and 24,910 yds. at 47° 28' elevation with ⅔ powder charge.

PROJECTILE, ARMOR-PIERCING, 16 INCH, MK. XII, MOD. 1

PROJECTILE, TARGET PRACTICE, 16 INCH, M108

PROJECTILE, TARGET PRACTICE, 16 INCH, M100

(Continued)

flame entering the cavity and prematurely igniting the bursting charge, the plug is screwed down against a rubber gasket. As a further protection a lead disc is placed over the base of the assembled projectile and held in place by a copper base plate.

As fired the projectile measures 64.31 inches in length.

The Mk. XV, Mod. 1 combination percussion and electric primer is used to ignite the six-section powder bag. The M1 class powder used in this charge has an 87–10–3 formula. The grains have seven perforations and a web of 0.195 inch. The six-section stacked type powder bag is 109.5 inches long, 16 inches in diameter, and weighs 675 pounds. The complete round as fired weighs 2,915 pounds.

PROJECTILE, T.P., 16 INCH, M108—STANDARD—This target-practice projectile is fired in the 16 inch cannon, Mk. II, Mod. 1, and is an issue and manufacture item. The projectile is made from cast iron and is the same length and weight as the Mk. XII, Mod. 1. The projectile has a cavity but the only purpose it serves is to insure the same weight as the Mk. XII, Mod. 1 projectile. The cavity is closed by a base plug.

The same propelling charge used with the Mk. XII, Mod. 1, projectile is used with this target practice projectile.

PROJECTILE, T.P., 16 INCH, M100—STANDARD—Made of cast iron and weighing 2,100 pounds, this target practice projectile is used with both the Mk. II, Mod. 1 and the M1919, 16 inch cannon.

This projectile, like the M108, is inert, the only purpose of the cavity being to govern weight. The projectile is 57.04 inches long.

When used in the Mk. II, Mod. 1 cannon, a six-section stacked type propelling charge weighing 709 pounds is used. The NH powder used in this charge is M1 class powder with an 87–10–3 formula. The grains have seven perforations and a web of 0.195 inch. The powder bags are 109.5 inches long and 16 inches in diameter.

In the M1919 cannon a four-section stacked type propelling charge is used. The charge weighs 870 pounds and is 123.5 inches long and 16.25 inches in diameter. The M1 class powder used in this charge has an 87–10–3 formula. The grains have seven perforations and a web of 0.206 inch.

The Mk. XV, Mod. 1 combination percussion and electric primer is used to ignite the propelling charges in both cannon.

The complete round as fired weighs 2,809 pounds in the Mk. II, Mod. 1 cannon and 2,970 pounds in the M1919 cannon.

PROJECTILE, DUMMY, DRILL, M5—STANDARD—(See Table of Characteristics.)

HAND GRENADES

TYPES

1. FRAGMENTATION HAND GRENADES containing a high-explosive charge in a metallic body which is shattered by the explosion of the charge.

2. OFFENSIVE HAND GRENADES containing a high-explosive charge in a paper body, designed for demolition or lethal shock effect.

3. CHEMICAL HAND GRENADES containing a chemical agent which produces a toxic or irritant effect, a screening smoke, incendiary action or any combination of these actions.

4. PRACTICE HAND GRENADES containing a reduced charge; simulate fragmentation grenades.

5. TRAINING HAND GRENADES used in training troops; do not contain explosives or chemicals.

The filler in a grenade may be a powerful explosive, a gas, a smoke-producing or an incendiary agent. The filler in fragmentation grenades is either TNT (trinitrotoluene) or EC Blank Fire Smokeless Powder. The latter is used in loading blank ammunition for small arms weapons.

CHARACTERISTICS OF FILLERS

EC powder is less powerful than TNT and usually is exploded by an igniting rather than a detonating agent. Grenades loaded with EC powder are issued fuzed and ready for use. They are not susceptible to mass detonation.

The standard filler for offensive grenades is pressed TNT.

Fillers in chemical grenades consist of various chemical mixtures and solutions. The manufacturing, storage and issue of Chemical Grenades is a function of the Chemical Warfare Service.

Practice Grenades contain a small amount of black powder and are designed to give an indicating puff of smoke when the igniting type fuze functions.

TIME AND AUTOMATIC FUZES

The fuze is the device which causes the grenade to function. All standard hand grenade fuzes (including most of the chemical hand grenade fuzes) are Time and Automatic types. A "time" fuze fires the grenade after a lapse of time and not upon percussion or impact. Grenades which contain an "automatic" fuze function automatically as soon as the grenade leaves the hand, provided the safety pin has been removed and the safety lever held close to the body of the grenade prior to throwing. This lever provides a safety feature by eliminating the necessity of manually starting the fuze action before the grenade is thrown toward the target.

FUZE CLASSIFICATION

Hand grenade fuzes are either detonating or igniting types.

A detonating fuze is used when shock is necessary to initiate the action of the explosive filler.

Igniting fuzes are used when the filler is one which requires heat initiation. This type of fuze will ignite the filler as though it had been lighted by a match.

All detonating and igniting hand grenade fuzes have the same general form and appearance. The fuze assembly consists primarily of a fuze body, having a threaded portion to permit insertion into the grenade body, a safety lever which restrains a striker, a safety pin to hold the lever in place, and a deep cup which is crimped to the lower portion of the fuze body and extends inside the grenade body when the fuze is assembled. The compound in the cup determines whether the final action of the fuze will be one of detonation or ignition.

OPERATION

The safety device is a cotter pin with a ring attached which enables it to be withdrawn easily. One end of the safety lever covers the top of the fuze body, sealing it against foreign bodies, and hooks over a lip in the fuze body. The other end of the safety lever extends downward and follows the contour of the grenade.

A grenade should be held with the safety lever pressed close to the grenade body by the palm of the hand. The thrower must take every precaution after withdrawing the safety pin, not to release his grip on the safety lever.

When the grenade is thrown, the safety lever is detached by the release of the striker spring and the impact of the striker. When no longer restrained by the lever, the striker rotates about a hinge pin and strikes a primer in the upper part of the fuze body.

The primer is a center-fire type similar to a shotgun shell primer. The flame from the primer charge ignites a delay charge which in the M6A3 and M10A3 fuzes consists of a powder column compressed in a lead tube. The burning time varies from 4.0 to 5.0 seconds.

The delay charge ignites a black powder igniting charge in the M10A3 fuze and a tetryl detonator in the M6A3 fuze. The igniter or detonator initiates the filler charge. The total burning time of the assembly is the same as the fuze, namely from 4.0 to 5.0 sec.

GRENADES: HAND, FRAGMENTATION, MK. IIA1—STANDARD

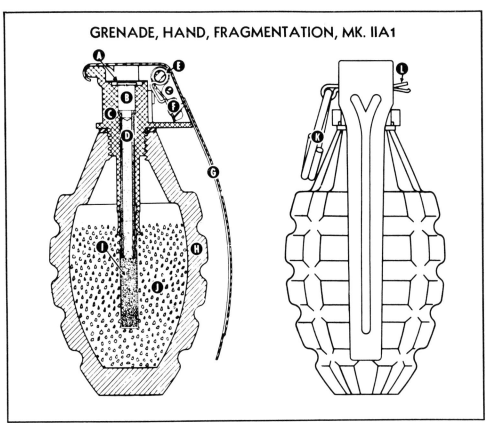

GRENADE, HAND, FRAGMENTATION, MK. IIA1

GRENADE, HAND, FRAGMENTATION, MK. IIA1 — STANDARD — The body of this grenade is made of cast-iron and is about the size of a large lemon. The outside surface is deeply serrated horizontally and vertically to assist in producing uniform fragments when the grenade explodes. The bursting charge is 0.74 ounce of EC Blank Fire Powder initiated by the M10A3 igniting fuze.

Ⓐ	Tin-foil disk	Ⓖ	Safety lever
Ⓑ	Primer	Ⓗ	Cast-iron body
Ⓒ	Fuze body	Ⓘ	Metal powder cap or detonator
Ⓓ	Powder train	Ⓙ	Charge
Ⓔ	Striker spring	Ⓚ	Pull ring
Ⓕ	Striker	Ⓛ	Safety pin

HAND, OFFENSIVE, MK. IIIA1—LIMITED STANDARD

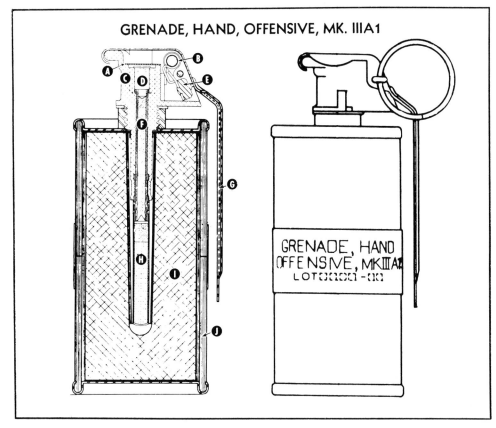

GRENADE, HAND, OFFENSIVE, MK. IIIA1

GRENADE, HAND
OFFENSIVE, MK IIIA1
LOT □□□□-□□

GRENADE, HAND, OFFENSIVE, MK. IIIA1—LIMITED STANDARD—This grenade consists of a sheet-metal top, threaded to receive the detonating fuze, M6A3, and a body of laminated cartridge paper which contains the high-explosive TNT charge. This grenade is for demolition. It may be used in the open more safely than the fragmentation grenade because there is no marked fragmentation. The grenade bodies and fuzes are shipped separately. The loaded and fuzed Mk. IIIA1 grenade weighs 14 ounces, 6.83 ounces of which is the TNT charge.

Ⓐ	Moisture cap	Ⓕ	Powder train
Ⓑ	Striker spring	Ⓖ	Safety lever
Ⓒ	Fuze body	Ⓗ	Detonator
Ⓓ	Primer	Ⓘ	Pressed TNT filler
Ⓔ	Striker	Ⓙ	Paper body

HAND, PRACTICE, MK. II—STANDARD

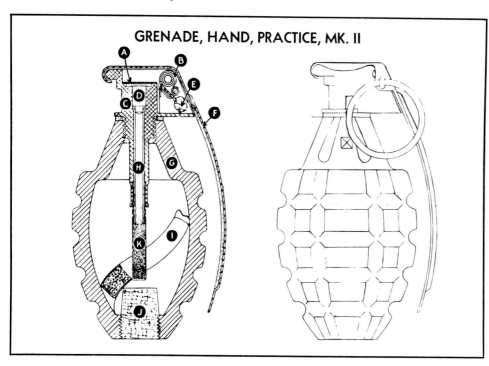

GRENADE, HAND, PRACTICE, MK. II

GRENADE, HAND, PRACTICE, MK. II—STANDARD—This is a standard practice grenade and is equipped with the igniting fuze, M10A3. The grenade is loaded with a small charge of black powder in a cloth bag.

Ⓐ Tin-foil disk

Ⓑ Striker spring

Ⓒ Fuze body

Ⓓ Primer

Ⓔ Striker

Ⓕ Safety lever

Ⓖ Cast-iron body

Ⓗ Powder train

Ⓘ Black powder charge in paper tube

Ⓙ Filling hole plug

Ⓚ Metal powder cap or detonator

HAND, TRAINING, MK. IA1—STANDARD

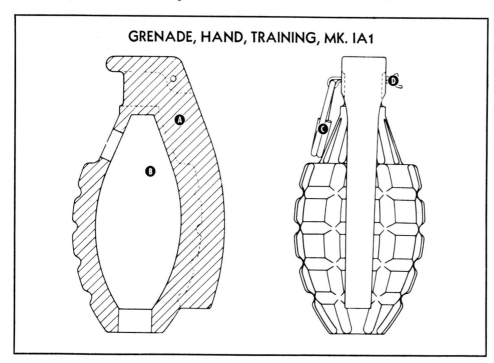

GRENADE, HAND, TRAINING, MK. IA1

GRENADE, HAND, TRAINING, MK. IA1—STANDARD—This grenade is the current standard for practice and training. It consists of a one piece cast-iron body in the shape of a Mk. II fuzed fragmentation grenade and a removable safety pin and ring. It is inert. The grenade weighs 22 ounces, 1 ounce more than the Mk. II.

Ⓐ One piece cast-iron body

Ⓑ Inert load

Ⓒ Pull ring

Ⓓ Safety pin

CHARACTERISTICS

	Mk. IIA1	Mk. IIIA1	MK. II	MK. IA1
Type and Use	Frag.; casualty	Offensive; casualty	Practice	Dummy, training
Fuze	M10A3, igniting	M6A3, detonating	M10A3, igniting	—
Weight Loaded and Fuzed	21.0 oz.	14.0 oz.	20.5 oz.	22.0 oz.
Charge and Weight	EC smokeless pwdr., 0.74 oz.	TNT, 6.83 oz.	Black pwdr.	—
Bursting Radius	30 yds.			—
Delay Time	4-5 sec.	4-5 sec.	4-5 sec.	—

RIFLE GRENADES
GRENADE, ANTITANK, M9A1; GRENADE, ANTITANK, PRACTICE, M11A2; ADAPTER, GRENADE-PROJECTION, M1; GRENADE, RIFLE, FRAGMENTATION, IMPACT, M17—STANDARD

Rifle grenades are designed to be fired from the U. S. rifle and carbine by a launcher which the soldier attaches to the muzzle. A special blank cartridge, issued with the grenade, must be used.

The Mk. IIA1 fragmentation hand grenade, with 5 seconds delay fuze, can be fired from the rifle or carbine by the M1 grenade-projection adapter.

Rifle grenades are divided into two general classes: (1) high-explosive grenades, containing an explosive charge, and (2) practice grenades, designed for training or practice.

GRENADE, ANTITANK, M9A1—STANDARD—The antitank grenade, M9A1, has a sheet steel body and tail assembly and weighs 1.23 pounds. The body is filled with 4 ounces of Pentolite using the "hollow charge" principle. The tail contains the impact fuze and the stabilizing fin is spot welded on a stabilizer tube screwed to the head. The impact fuze consists of a firing pin held by a spring in flight. When shipped, the firing pin is retained by a safety pin. When the grenade strikes a target the pin moves forward to activate the detonator and explode the charge. The hollow or shaped charge of this grenade has remarkable armor-penetrating qualities. The M9A1 anti-tank rifle grenade supersedes the grenade, A.T., M9.

GRENADE, ANTITANK, PRACTICE, M11A2—STANDARD—This is an inert-loaded dummy grenade similar in shape and weight to the antitank grenade, M9A1. This practice grenade superseded the M11 and M11A1 practice grenades. The M11A2 differs from the M9A1 in that the fin is replaceable. Extra fins are shipped with each grenade in the event the original one is bent or wears out.

GRENADE, RIFLE, FRAGMENTATION, IMPACT—M17—This grenade consists of a fin stabilizer assembly with impact type fuze similar to that used for Grenade, AT, M9A1. The head consists of a Mk. IIA1 hand grenade fuze body which is screwed in the fuze adapter on the stabilizer assembly. The M17 grenade is used in a manner identical with that of the Adapter, Grenade-Projection, M1, however, it offers a unit ready for firing without assembly in the field as is required for the M1 adapter.

ADAPTER, GRENADE-PROJECTION, M1—STANDARD—The grenade-projection adapter, M1, was designed to permit the projection of the Mk. IIA1 fragmentation grenade from the rifle. It has a fin assembly similar to that of the M9A1 grenade. The head of the fin assembly has four claws which clip around and hold the body of the Mk. IIA1 fragmentation grenade with the 5-second time fuze. One of the claws has an arming clip which holds the safety lever of the Mk. IIA1 grenade. Upon setback the arming clip releases the safety lever of the Mk. IIA1 fragmentation grenade and the fuze explodes the grenade after 5 seconds. The adapter with Mk. IIA1 fragmentation grenade is fired from the same launcher used to launch the M9A1 and other rifle grenades.

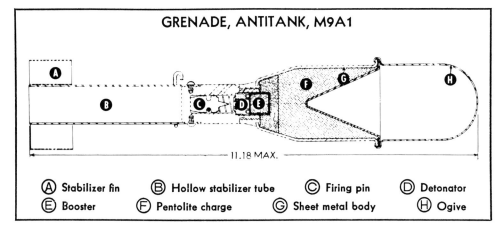

GRENADE, ANTITANK, M9A1

11.18 MAX.

(A) Stabilizer fin   (B) Hollow stabilizer tube   (C) Firing pin   (D) Detonator
(E) Booster   (F) Pentolite charge   (G) Sheet metal body   (H) Ogive

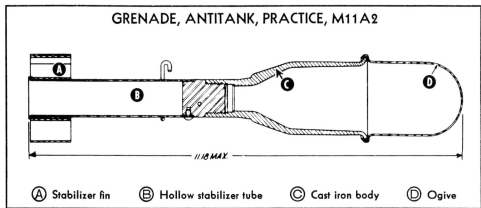

GRENADE, ANTITANK, PRACTICE, M11A2

11.18 MAX.

(A) Stabilizer fin   (B) Hollow stabilizer tube   (C) Cast iron body   (D) Ogive

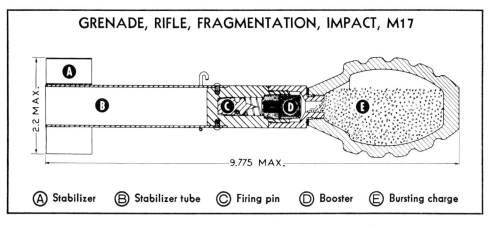

GRENADE, RIFLE, FRAGMENTATION, IMPACT, M17

2.2 MAX.

9.775 MAX.

(A) Stabilizer   (B) Stabilizer tube   (C) Firing pin   (D) Booster   (E) Bursting charge

MINES

LAND MINES—All combat types of land mines consist of a charge of high explosive and a device for detonating this charge under proper conditions.

In general, land mines are of the trap type, relying on unsuspected action of the enemy for initiation. Most types are simple and consist only of a container of high explosive and a firing mechanism to detonate the charge. Others are of complicated design such as the bounding mine, which projects a shell approximately five feet above ground where it explodes. Land mines are intended for antitank or anti-personnel use. Anti-tank mines are classified as high-explosive, practice, or dummy types. Anti-personnel mines are classified as high-explosive or practice types.

METALLIC ANTITANK MINES—An antitank mine contains a relatively large charge of explosive and is concealed or placed where it may be driven over and exploded by a vehicle. The metallic antitank mines consist of the mine body filled with explosive (with a booster charge inserted in the M1A1 and M4 mines), the spider, and the fuze.

The mine body is a squat cylindrical container of thin steel, filled with TNT or other high explosive. The bottom is plain and attached to the sides of the mine body is a carrying handle which may be folded back when not in use.

The top extends beyond the side and the edge is bent to form a grooved flange to which the spider is attached. The spider hooks fit into two slots cut in the flange. In the top is a capped filling hole, and in the center is an opening for the fuze cup. When shipped the spider is nested in the bottom of the mine body and when assembled its hub rests on the striker head of the fuze.

MINE, ANTITANK, HIGH-EXPLOSIVE, M1A1—STANDARD

MINE, ANTITANK, HIGH-EXPLOSIVE, M1A1—STANDARD—The M1A1 mine is the present standard high-explosive antitank mine. As originally designed, it was the M1 high-explosive antitank mine which, due to its fuze construction, was found to be dangerous when shipped or stored.

The original design of the M1 mine called for shipping the fuze, with the booster as an integral part, and the mine body in the same box. This method proved dangerous as blows on shipping crates could detonate the fuze, booster and explosive charge of the mine.

As a solution, the fuze was modified so that the firing mechanism was separate from the booster and the only explosive element remaining in the fuze was the detonator. The booster now is assembled in the fuze well cavity in the mine body. The detonator fits into the hole in the booster charge when the fuze is assembled to the mine. The modified fuze was designated as Fuze, Mine, Antitank, M1A1. It has since been replaced by the M1A2 fuze.

The same method of packing is retained with the fuze separated from the mine. If the modified fuze is set off accidentally, the explosion of the detonator is not sufficient to ignite the explosive charge of the mine.

The M1A2 fuze employs a more powerful detonator than the M1A1 fuze, but is identical in all other respects. The fuze consists of a striker assembly and a body which contains the detonator. To insure safety in shipping and handling, a safety fork with a cord attached to aid in its removal, is fitted over the collar between the striker head and the top of the fuze body. This safety fork is removed only when it is desired to arm the fuze. The firing mechanism contained within the striker assembly is restrained from firing by a thin aluminum collar placed immediately below the striker head, and by two shear pins, when in the armed condition. On the outer head of the striking assembly is a 2-inch head which protrudes approximately ⅜ inch beyond the body of the fuze.

The M1A2 fuze firing pin normally is held away from the detonator by two steel balls. When pressure is applied to the fuze head, it moves downward, shearing the pins and aligning grooves into which the two steel balls move. The firing mechanism spring then is free to throw the firing pin forward, striking the primer of the detonator which sets off the explosive charge. A pressure of approximately 500 pounds on the striker head will function the firing mechanism. However, when the fuze is inserted and the spider attached, a pressure of 250 pounds, at any point, on the spider is sufficient to activate the fuze, as a result of the lever action afforded by the spider.

The assembled mine is 8.2 inches in diameter and 4.25 inches high.

The weights of the components are:
Mine, complete assembly (Cast TNT)....10.67 lb.
Bursting charge (Cast TNT)............ 5.83 lb.
Fuze, Mine, Antitank, M1A2............ 1.11 lb.

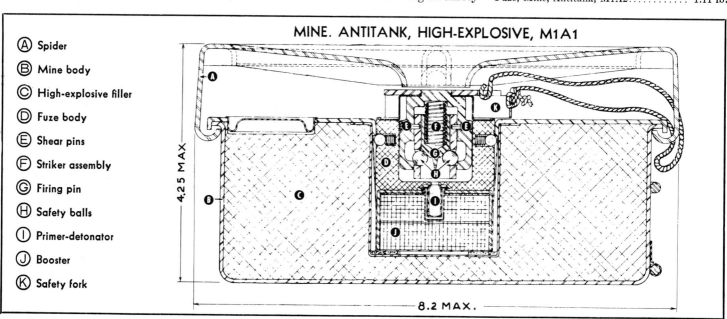

Ⓐ Spider
Ⓑ Mine body
Ⓒ High-explosive filler
Ⓓ Fuze body
Ⓔ Shear pins
Ⓕ Striker assembly
Ⓖ Firing pin
Ⓗ Safety balls
Ⓘ Primer-detonator
Ⓙ Booster
Ⓚ Safety fork

MINE. ANTITANK, HIGH-EXPLOSIVE, M1A1

4.25 MAX.

8.2 MAX.

MINE, ANTITANK, HIGH-EXPLOSIVE, **M4**—SUBSTITUTE STANDARD
MINE, ANTITANK, PRACTICE, **M1**—STANDARD
MINE, ANTITANK, PRACTICE, **M1B1**—STANDARD

MINE, ANTITANK, HIGH-EXPLO-SIVE, M4, SUBSTITUTE STANDARD—This substitute standard mine is similar in appearance to the M1A1 mine. The detonator, however, is incorporated within the fuze body and no cavity is required in the booster. The shear pins and cocked firing pin of the M1A2 fuze are eliminated in the M4 mine by the use of a cricket or Belleville-type spring. This spring merely

supports the firing pin when the fuze is not under pressure and exerts no force on it. The spider rests on the striker washer at the top of the fuze and any loads on the washer are transmitted harmlessly to the fuze body by the safety fork which is removed when the mine is armed.

The spider of the armed mine moves downward under pressure of a tank or other load and the striker washer crushes

the thin aluminum cover of the fuze. The striker is prevented from moving laterally by the striker guide so it moves straight downward, centering and depressing the firing pin guide cup.

The spherical portion of the striker is so designed that off-center loads on the washer do not result in binding the striker in its guide or in deflecting the firing pin. When the cricket spring reaches the point of snap it drives the firing pin into the detonator. The force of detonation ruptures the bottom of the fuze body. The detonator blast is directed into the booster, ignition of which explodes the bursting charge of the mine.

The mine is shipped with the booster assembled in the body and held in place by fingers on the outer booster cup, in the same manner as the M1A2 booster is held into the M1A1 Mine.

MINE, ANTITANK, PRACTICE, M1, STANDARD—This mine is identical in appearance to the M1A1 and M4 mines with the exception of five one-inch holes equally spaced around the body. The fuze also is the same as the M1 antitank fuze except that a smoke-puff charge is used instead of a booster. The charge produces smoke which escapes from the mine through the holes. It consists of 60 grains of Army black powder which ignites 100 grains of red phosphorous.

A steel filler ring is inserted in the mine body so that the M1 will equal the weight of the M1A1 and M4 mines. Holes are drilled in this ring to match the holes in the mine body.

The complete assembly weighs 10.67 pounds and is 8.2 inches in diameter, 4.25 inches high.

Components of the complete round weigh as follows:

Mine, complete assembly . . . . 10.67 lb.
Fuze, Mine, Antitank, M1, Practice . . . . . . 0.75 lb.
Metal parts assembly . . . . 9.92 lb.

MINE, ANTITANK, PRACTICE, M1B1, STANDARD—The five smoke holes are cut into the top of the M1B1 practice mine, instead of on the side as in the M1 mine, permitting the smoke to escape more readily. Both mines use the same fuze and the same smoke charge. However, instead of a steel filler ring inserted when the mine is manufactured, and shipped with it, the M1B1 mine is sand loaded in the field to save shipping weight.

The complete round components weigh as follows:

Mine, complete assembly . . . . 10.67 lb.
Fuze, Mine, Antitank, Practice, M1 . . . . . . 0.75 lb.
Metal parts assembly . . . . 4.26 lb.
Sand loading . . . . 5.66 lb.

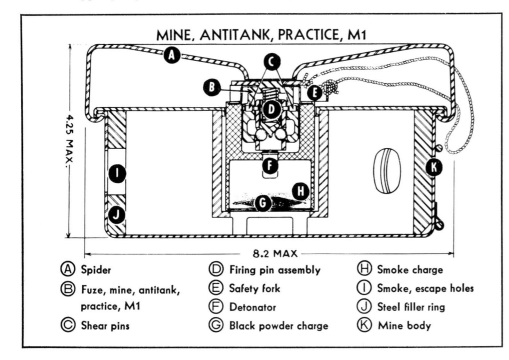

MINE, ANTITANK, PRACTICE, M1

4.25 MAX.

8.2 MAX

Ⓐ Spider
Ⓑ Fuze, mine, antitank, practice, M1
Ⓒ Shear pins
Ⓓ Firing pin assembly
Ⓔ Safety fork
Ⓕ Detonator
Ⓖ Black powder charge
Ⓗ Smoke charge
Ⓘ Smoke, escape holes
Ⓙ Steel filler ring
Ⓚ Mine body

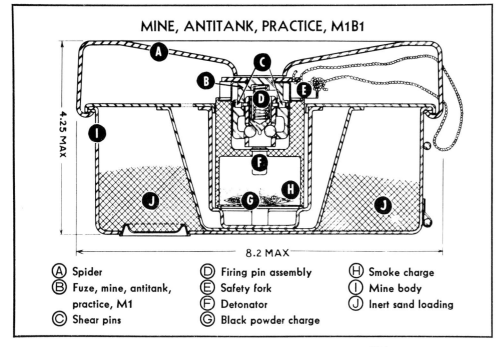

MINE, ANTITANK, PRACTICE, M1B1

4.25 MAX

8.2 MAX

Ⓐ Spider
Ⓑ Fuze, mine, antitank, practice, M1
Ⓒ Shear pins
Ⓓ Firing pin assembly
Ⓔ Safety fork
Ⓕ Detonator
Ⓖ Black powder charge
Ⓗ Smoke charge
Ⓘ Mine body
Ⓙ Inert sand loading

MINE, ANTITANK, NON-METALLIC, HIGH-EXPLOSIVE, M5

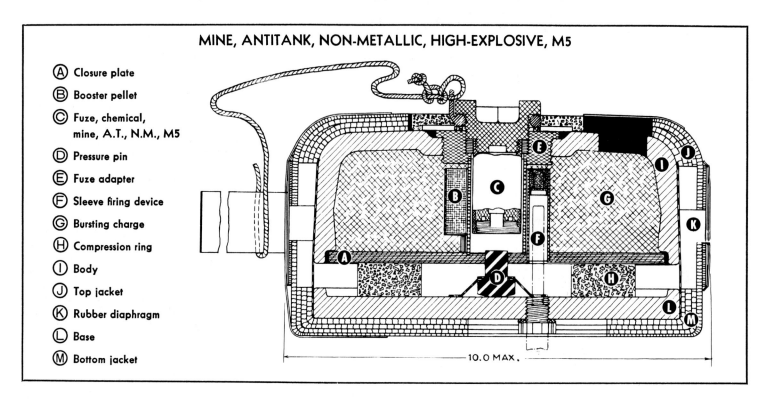

- (A) Closure plate
- (B) Booster pellet
- (C) Fuze, chemical, mine, A.T., N.M., M5
- (D) Pressure pin
- (E) Fuze adapter
- (F) Sleeve firing device
- (G) Bursting charge
- (H) Compression ring
- (I) Body
- (J) Top jacket
- (K) Rubber diaphragm
- (L) Base
- (M) Bottom jacket

10.0 MAX.

MINE, ANTITANK, NON-METALLIC, HIGH-EXPLOSIVE, M5—STANDARD— This mine is manufactured without materials which would betray its presence to an enemy using an electro-magnetic mine detector.

The mine body consists of a china or glass bowl (I) containing 5.4 pounds of TNT, or an alternate filling of 5.7 pounds of Tetrytol, and a china or glass plate (L).

These components are separated by a cushion of rubber (H) or similar material. There is a threaded opening in the top of the mine for the fuze (C) and in the bottom a bakelite plug which may be removed for the attachment of a device to prevent removal of the emplaced mine by enemy personnel. The engineer firing devices, in conjunction with the U. S. Army special blasting cap Type "A," may be attached to the bottom of these mines to prevent their removal. However these devices are made of magnetic materials and their use defeats the purpose of this non-magnetic mine.

The M5 mine may be buried without fear of stones or dirt jamming the firing mechanism. It is waterproof and may be installed under water or in swampy ground.

The high-explosive antitank fuze, M5, also is constructed without metal parts. The fuze consists of a cylindrical plastic body (Q) attached to a threaded plug (N). In addition to the safety cap (V), there is a safety ring around the fuze body (against the flange of the plug) which

FUZE, CHEMICAL, MINE, A.T., N.M., M5

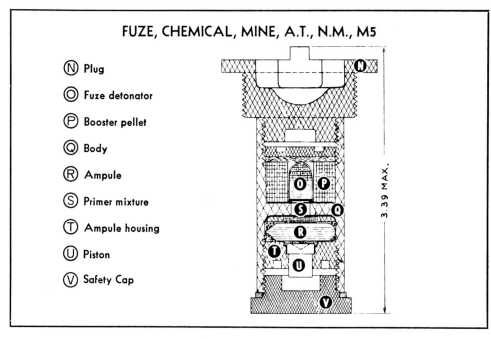

- (N) Plug
- (O) Fuze detonator
- (P) Booster pellet
- (Q) Body
- (R) Ampule
- (S) Primer mixture
- (T) Ampule housing
- (U) Piston
- (V) Safety Cap

3.39 MAX.

prevents the fuze from being screwed into functioning position in the mine.

When the mine is laid, the safety cap (V) is removed from the fuze and the fuze is inserted in the mine. Pressure on top of the mine forces the fuze onto a plastic pressure pin (D), which in turn forces a piston (U) into a glass ampule. This ampule contains a solution of concentrated sulfuric acid and an antifreeze.

Breaking the ampule releases the acid and permits it to react with a surrounding primer mixture (S), which fires and

explodes the detonator (O) and a booster (P). An auxiliary booster of tetryl (B) sealed in the mine body with the cast TNT, transmits the detonation to the mine filler.

The mine is 10 inches in diameter, 5.2 inches high, and when assembled, weighs 15 pounds. Components of this mine weigh as follows:

Mine, assembled (Cast TNT loaded)......15.0 lb.
Mine, assembled (Tetrytol loaded)........15.3 lb.
TNT bursting charge....................5.4 lb.
Tetrytol bursting charge................5.7 lb.
Fuze, Chemical, Mine, A.T., N.M., M5.... 0.2 lb.

MINE, ANTI-PERSONNEL, M2A1B1—LIMITED STANDARD
MINE, ANTI-PERSONNEL, M3—STANDARD

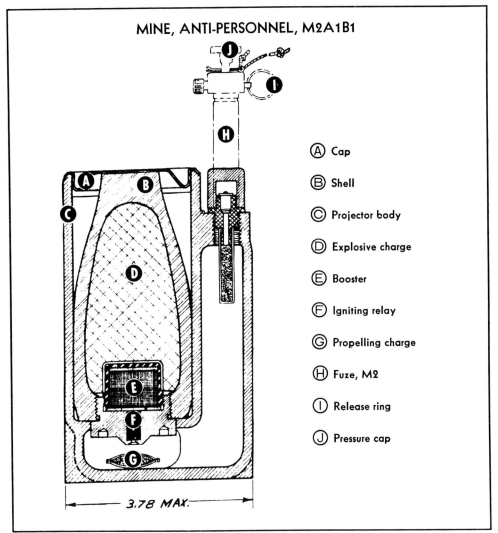

MINE, ANTI-PERSONNEL, M2A1B1

- (A) Cap
- (B) Shell
- (C) Projector body
- (D) Explosive charge
- (E) Booster
- (F) Igniting relay
- (G) Propelling charge
- (H) Fuze, M2
- (I) Release ring
- (J) Pressure cap

3.78 MAX.

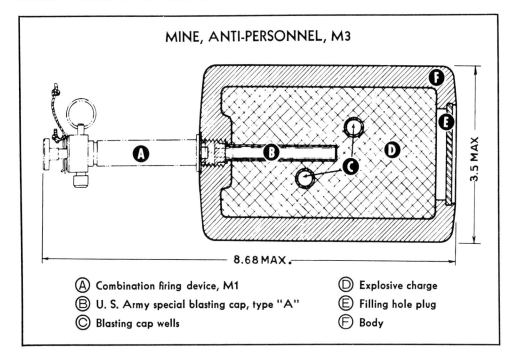

MINE, ANTI-PERSONNEL, M3

8.68 MAX.

3.5 MAX

- (A) Combination firing device, M1
- (B) U. S. Army special blasting cap, type "A"
- (C) Blasting cap wells
- (D) Explosive charge
- (E) Filling hole plug
- (F) Body

ANTI-PERSONNEL MINES—All anti-personnel mines depend upon some enemy action for initiation. As enemy personnel in the open will have unrestricted vision, it is important that full advantage be taken of every opportunity to conceal mines of this type.

MINE, ANTI-PERSONNEL, M2A1B1—LIMITED STANDARD—The action of this mine is similar to the M2A3 anti-personnel mine and the same shell and fuze are used in both mines. However the M2A1B1 has a one-piece projector body in place of the M2A1 mine body.

The body of the M2A1B1 is made entirely of cast-iron instead of the stamped steel base plate, steel pipe and steel tube body of the M2A1. This design simplifies mass production. The assembled round measures approximately $8\frac{5}{8}$ inches in height and $3\frac{25}{32}$ inches across the base. The complete round assembly components weigh:

Mine, Anti-Personnel, M2A1B1,
  complete assembly....................7.16 lb.
Shell, loaded and fuzed..................2.84 lb.
TNT bursting charge....................0.34 lb.
Projector body........................3.60 lb.
Fuze, M2, assembly....................0.25 lb.

MINE, ANTI-PERSONNEL, M3—STANDARD—This is a fragmentation trap-type land mine, intended for use against personnel. The complete round consists of the mine, a hollow cast-iron block containing TNT and mine fuze, M3. It has an effective radius of 10 yards when exploded on the ground, an even greater radius when used several feet above ground and slightly less when buried. Fragments may be thrown more than 100 yards and suitable protection should be provided for friendly troops within that radius.

The fuzed mine is 8.68 inches long and 3.5 inches square. The cast-iron casing (F) is filled with 0.9 pound of flaked TNT (D). Cap wells (C) closed by plastic plugs are located under holes in two opposite sides and one end of the casing. The fuze may be inserted in any one of these holes. The filling hole is closed with a metal disk (E).

The Fuze, Mine, Anti-Personnel, M3, consists of a special U. S. Army blasting cap, Type "A," crimped to the combination firing device, M1. The firing device contains a spring-loaded firing pin and a primer. As with the M2 mine, the M3 may be fired by cord or wire connected to the release pin or by pressure applied to the pressure cap. Wire is furnished to connect the pull ring to the tripping device. The pressures needed to fire the mine are the same as required by the M2 mine; 20 to 40 pounds pressure on the cap, or three to six pounds tension on the release plug.

MINE, ANTI-PERSONNEL, M2A3—STANDARD

ANTI-PERSONNEL, M2A3—STAND-ARD—This mine is similar to a small mortar. It projects a shell about six feet into the air, blasting fragments among many of the personnel in the vicinity. Its effective radius is about thirty feet. The projectile is the 60 mm mortar shell, M49A2. It weighs approximately three pounds, of which twelve per cent is the high explosive bursting charge of TNT. The shell igniting relay is set off by a delay element of pressed black powder which is ignited by the propelling charge. Detonation of the shell is delayed until it has attained an effective height which varies between two feet and seven feet. The mine is fired by a pull wire or pressure device. Firing of the primer ignites a 20 grain charge of black powder which propels the shell into the air and at the same time ignites the fuze delay element.

The fuze consists of a simple firing mechanism containing a spring-activated firing-pin. It may be fired by a trip wire connected to the release pin, or by pressure applied to the pressure cap. A pressure of from 20 to 40 pounds on the cap, or tension of from three to six pounds on the release pin will cause release of the firing pin and detonation of the mine. Lengths of wire are packed with the mine in order to connect it to the pull ring and to produce tripping devices. For effective camouflage, some of the wire is lustreless olive drab; the remainder is sand-colored.

The mine is shipped with the fuze, M2, disassembled. When assembled, the mine measures 8.25 inches in height and 4.04 inches across the base plate.

Weights of the components are as follows:

Mine, Anti-Personnel, M2A3, complete
  assembly............................5.01 lb.
Shell, loaded.........................2.12 lb.
TNT bursting charge...................0.34 lb.
Propelling charge.....................0.003 lb.
Fuze, M2, assembly ....0.25 lb.

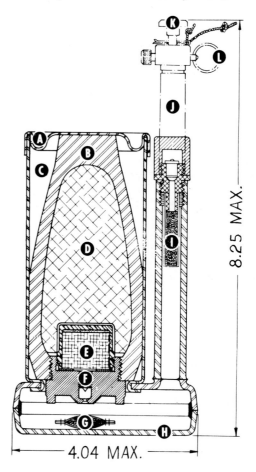

MINE, ANTI-PERSONNEL, M2A3

8.25 MAX.

4.04 MAX.

Ⓐ Cap
Ⓑ Shell
Ⓒ Tube
Ⓓ Explosive charge
Ⓔ Booster
Ⓕ Igniting relay
Ⓖ Propelling charge
Ⓗ Base plate
Ⓘ Igniter
Ⓙ Firing device
Ⓚ Pressure cap
Ⓛ Release ring

TORPEDO, BANGALORE, M1A1—STANDARD

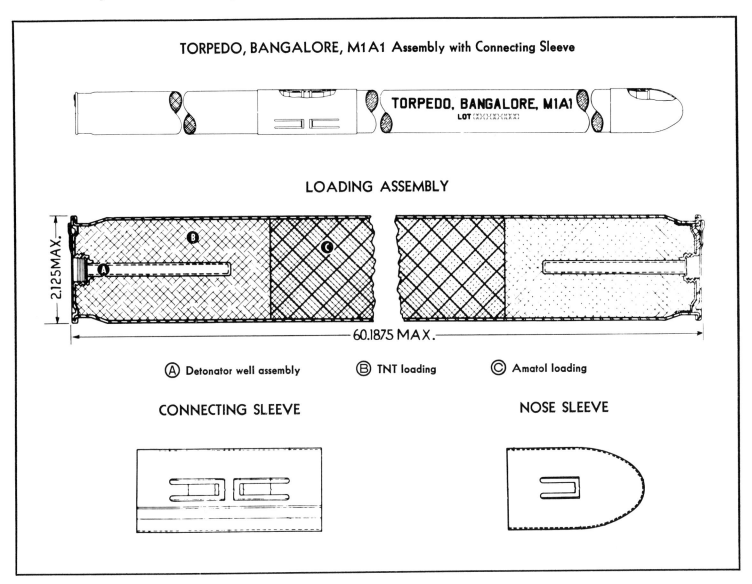

TORPEDO, BANGALORE, M1A1 Assembly with Connecting Sleeve

TORPEDO, BANGALORE, M1A1
LOT ☐☐-☐☐-☐☐☐☐

LOADING ASSEMBLY

2.125 MAX.

60.1875 MAX.

Ⓐ Detonator well assembly   Ⓑ TNT loading   Ⓒ Amatol loading

CONNECTING SLEEVE

NOSE SLEEVE

TORPEDO, BANGALORE, M1A1—STANDARD—The Bangalore torpedo is a tube filled with high explosive and used primarily for blasting an opening through wire entanglements and for clearing mine fields. The M1A1 Bangalore torpedo consists of a steel tube, 5 feet long and $2\frac{1}{8}$ inches in diameter, flanged and capped at each end.

The torpedo is loaded with four inches of TNT at both ends of the tube and the mid-section is filled with 80–20 amatol. The complete charge weighs about 9 pounds. Each end of the tube contains a threaded recess to accommodate a blasting cap. A nose sleeve fits on the end of the torpedo and connecting sleeves are provided for assembling torpedoes in multiple lengths. This torpedo also may be used as an anti-personnel mine or as a demolition charge.

Standard Corps of Engineers special blasting caps, either electric or fuzed, may be used to detonate the torpedo. The nose sleeve is held in place by a single clip. It aids while moving the torpedo through or around obstacles. The connecting sleeve is a short tube which has six spring clamps. When assembling two torpedo tubes with a sleeve, each tube is held by three spring clamps.

SUBCALIBER AMMUNITION FOR FIELD ARTILLERY, SEACOAST GUNS, AND MORTARS

Subcaliber ammunition is fixed ammunition, with special projectiles, used in a subcaliber tube for training in elevating, traversing, sighting the piece to which the tube is attached and in the use of firing tables.

The object of subcaliber firing is to train personnel and to check the orientation and adjustment of fire control and sighting equipment.

The advantages of subcaliber ammunition are it is economical and may be used in the vicinity of populated areas.

The tabulation in Table A lists the use of subcaliber projectiles in subcaliber guns:

TABLE A

Cannon, Subcalibered	Caliber of Subcaliber Gun	Projectile	Cannon, Subcalibered	Caliber of Subcaliber Gun	Projectile
3 inch (15 pdr.), M1902 and M1903	Cal. .30 rifle	Cartridge, sub-cal., cal. .30, M1925	6 inch, M1897, M1897M1, M1908, M1908M1, M1908M11 6 inch, M1900, M1903 8 inch, M1888 10 inch, M1888, M1895, M1900 12 inch, M1888, M1895, M1900 14 inch, M1907, M1907M1, M1909	1.457 inch gun	Shell, Practice, M94
2.95 Inch, V. M.* 75 mm How., M1*, M2** and M3** 75 mm, M1897,* M1897A1,* M1916, M1917 105 mm How., M2A1,† M3† and M4† 155 mm How.*, M1917, M1918, M1 155 mm gun*, M1917, M1918, M1A1 8 inch How., M1*	37 mm**†	Practice shell, M63, Mod. 1, and M92	12 inch mortar, M1890, M1890M1, M1908, M1912	2.95 inch gun	Fixed shot
			12 inch, M1895A2*, M1895M1A2* 14 inch, M1910*, M1910M1* 14 inch, M1920, M1920M11* 16 inch, M1919, M1919M11 and M1919M111* 16 inch Howitzer, M1920*	75 mm gun	Shell, H.E., M48 (inert loaded)

*Exterior mount.
**Uses 37 mm subcaliber mount M12.
†Uses 37 mm subcaliber mount M13.
(Note: Where not otherwise stated, the subcaliber guns are in-bore mounted.)

CARTRIDGE, BALL, CAL. .22, LONG RIFLE

This cartridge, standard in the cal. .22 U. S. rifles and the machine gun trainers, M3 and M4, also is used in the subcaliber tube of the 75 mm gun, M1897.

These cartridges are regular commercial products and measure 0.984 inch overall. The complete round weighs approximately 53 grains and consists of a cartridge case, priming composition, propelling charge and bullet.

The cartridge case is of the rim-fire type, i.e., the priming composition is spun into a circular recess inside the rim instead of being seated in the head as a separate component. A blow from the firing pin at any position on the rim will ignite the powder charge. The charge weighs 1.7 grains.

The lead bullet weighs 40 grains. The maximum range is approximately 1,500 yards at 30° elevation. The average muzzle velocity is 1,100 feet per second and chamber pressure averages 16,000 p.s.i.

This cartridge is fired from a subcaliber tube inserted in the bore of the 3 inch seacoast (15 pounder) guns, M1902 and M1903.

There are two types of cal. .30 subcaliber cartridges: the cartridge, subcaliber, cal. .30, M1925, and the cartridge, subcaliber, cal. .30, old stock. Both types are limited standard and the old stock on hand is given priority of issue. The cartridge is rimmed and must be used in "Krag"-type chambers.

CARTRIDGE, SUBCALIBER, CAL. .30, M1925

The M1925 subcaliber round consists of a cartridge case, primer, propelling charge and bullet. The primer is assembled in a monel metal primer cup so that it may function on the light blow of a rifle firing pin as well as the heavy blow of the gun's firing pin.

The propelling charge consists of approximately 35 grains of pyro D.G. powder. The bullet of the M1925 is boat-tailed and pointed, and consists of a gliding metal jacket surrounding a hardened lead filler. The bullet weighs 174 grains and the complete cartridge weighs 385.5 grains.

The ammunition is loaded in a cal. .30 barrel which is mounted axially in a 3 inch bronze subcaliber cartridge case which resembles, in weight and exterior

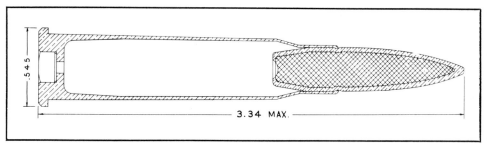

dimensions, the ammunition regularly used with the gun. To the base of the subcaliber cartridge case are fitted two flat steel extractor springs, secured by one screw each, which serve to eject the subcaliber ammunition.

The 3 inch subcaliber cartridge case (with the rifle barrel inserted) is set and

pushed home in the gun. The subcaliber ammunition, cal. .30, then is inserted in the chamber of the subcaliber barrel until its rim comes in contact with the extractor springs. Finally the breech of the gun is closed, the face of the breechblock meeting the subcaliber round, and shoving it into its seat.

SHELL, PRACTICE, M92 WITH FUZE, P.D., M74, AND SHELL, PRACTICE, M63, MOD. 1, WITH FUZE, BASE, PRACTICE, M58

Subcaliber equipment for larger guns includes the 37 mm guns, M1916, M12, M13, and M14. These are used as subcaliber equipment for 75 mm and 155 mm guns and howitzers and 105 mm howitzers.

The fixed complete round standard for issue and manufacture with this gun is Shell, Practice, M92. Shell, Practice, M63, Model 1, is substitute standard for issue.

When loaded and fuzed the M92 shell weighs 1.21 pounds and is propelled by .07 pound of FNH powder which is ignited by the 20 grain, M23A2, percussion primer. The M63 Model 1 prac-

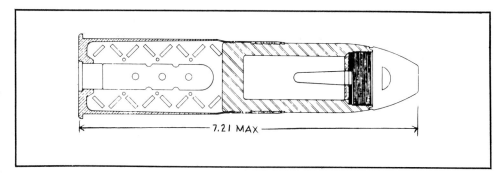

7.21 MAX

tice shell when loaded and fuzed weighs 1.63 pounds and is propelled by .056 pound of FNH powder which is ignited by an M23A2 percussion primer.

The standard cartridge case used is the Mk. 1A2, which is 3.64 inches in length.

SHELL, PRACTICE, 37 MM, M94

This fixed complete round, standard for issue and manufacture for the 1.457 inch subcaliber gun, is used with seacoast guns of 6 inch caliber or higher. The shell weighs 1.057 pounds, including the base plug.

The round requires the Mk. IIIA2 cartridge case which is 5.69 inches in length. The overall length of the round is 9.26 inches. The shell is propelled by 1,110 grains of FNH powder, fired by the M25A1, 20 grain, igniting primer.

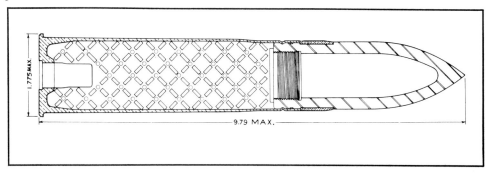

1.775 MAX

9.79 MAX.

SHOT, FIXED, SOLID, SUBCALIBER FOR THE 2.95 INCH SUBCALIBER GUN

This fixed complete round, standard for issue and manufacture for the 2.95 inch subcaliber gun, consists of the fixed shot weighing 18 pounds and the cartridge case containing the 100 grain igniting primer, M24A2. The complete round weighs 20 pounds of which from 0.27 to 0.38 pound constitutes the propelling charge.

The rounds are fixed, in that separate complete rounds are needed for each of the three zones, as each round is loaded for a certain zone and then the shot is crimped into the cartridge case.

The over-all length of the complete round is 16.57 inches when the shot is made from steel. When made from cast

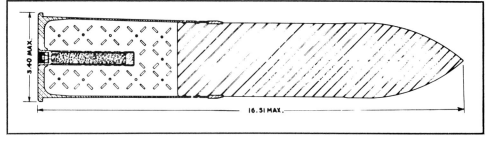

3.40 MAX

16.51 MAX.

iron the complete round measures 17.39 inches in length.

Three different zones are provided to simulate the three zones of fire of the 12 inch mortars in subcaliber practice. This is accomplished by varying the powder

charge to give different muzzle velocities as follows:

Zone 1 . . . .550 f/s—4.5 oz., FNH powder
Zone 2 . . . .625 f/s—5.0 oz., FNH powder
Zone 3 . . . .700 f/s—6.0 oz., FNH powder

SHELL, HIGH-EXPLOSIVE, 75 MM, SUBCALIBER, M48

This standard fixed complete round, for issue and manufacture for the 75 mm subcaliber gun, is now the inert-loaded shell, high-explosive, 75 mm M48. It has superseded the sand-loaded, Mk. I, high-explosive shell.

The complete round weighs 19.04 pounds. The shell weighs 14.70 pounds, inert loaded. Components of the complete round of the M48 shell consist of the projectile with dummy fuze, the M18 cartridge case containing the normal charge of 1.35 pounds of FNH powder ignited by the M22A3 percussion primer.

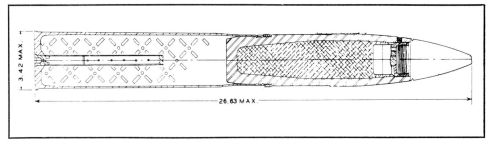

3.42 MAX.

26.63 MAX.

The normal charge gives a muzzle velocity of 1,470 f/s and a pressure of 26,000 p.s.i.

The M18 cartridge case is 13.82 inches in length. The shell is 15 inches and the complete round 26.6 inches in length.

ARTILLERY FUZES

A fuze may be defined as a mechanical device used with a projectile to detonate it at the time or under the circumstances desired.

Artillery fuzes are classified here as base-detonating (B.D.), point-detonating (P.D.), powder-train time (T.), or mechanical time (M.T.). They may be given additional classification as supersensitive, superquick (S.Q.), delay or nondelay, the various designations depending on the speed with which the fuze functions after impact.

Supersensitive fuzes are designed to function instantly on impact with such light and unsubstantial targets as airplane fabric. Superquick fuzes detonate immediately on impact with the ground or a solid target. Delay fuzes are designed to function after impact and when penetration into the target has reached the point desired, the delay period being determined mechanically or by an explosive train. Nondelay fuzes incorporate mechanical or explosive elements calculated to insure detonation just as penetration into the target begins.

Fuzes representing combinations of the above types are also used, such as time and superquick (T-SQ). The designation AN indicates fuzes which have been adopted as standard for use by both the Army and the Navy.

FUZE, BASE, PRACTICE, M38—LIMITED STANDARD

The M38 fuze is a nondelay, base-detonating fuze which contains no booster and requires but few parts for its functioning. The plunger assembly contains the firing-pin and a resistance ring which fits over the shoulder of the firing-pin in the unarmed position.

Upon firing of the propelling charge, setback moves the plunger to the rear and forces the resistance ring over the shoulders of the firing-pin until it seats in a groove in the pin. This action locks plunger and pin together. The plunger unit is now armed but held away from the detonating charge by a spring.

When the projectile strikes, the weight of the plunger and firing-pin unit compresses the spring. The pin strikes the detonator which ignites the bursting charge in the shell.

ROUND
Shell, Practice, Subcaliber, Mk. IIA1

CHARACTERISTICS
Length overall........................1.5 ins.
Weight............................0.125 lb.
Thread size.....................0.72–18NS–1

FUZE, B.D., M58—STANDARD

This fuze is identical mechanically with the base practice fuze, M38, but includes an integral booster pellet.

It is larger than the M38 fuze because of the larger projectile cavity of the 37 mm H.E. shell, M63, with which it is used.

ROUND
Shell, H.E., 37 mm, M63

CHARACTERISTICS
Length overall........................2.02 ins.
Weight............................0.30 lb.
Thread size...............1.02–18NS–3 L.H.

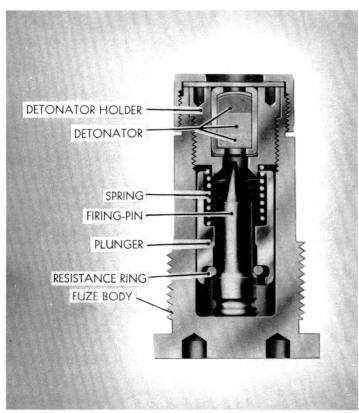

FUZE, BASE, PRACTICE, M38

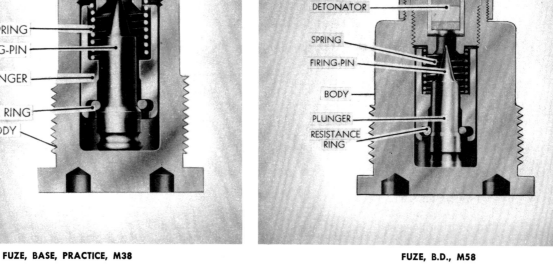

FUZE, B.D., M58

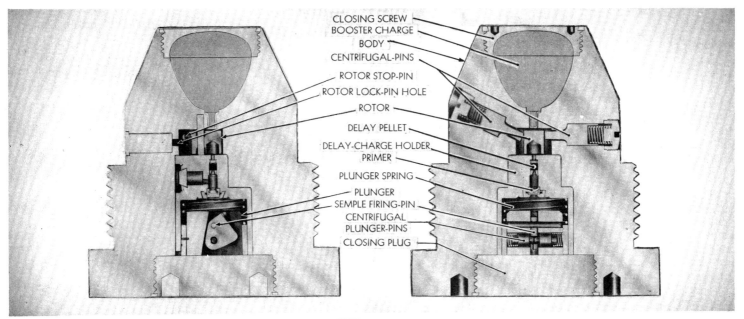

Labels on diagram:
CLOSING SCREW
BOOSTER CHARGE
BODY
CENTRIFUGAL-PINS
ROTOR STOP-PIN
ROTOR LOCK-PIN HOLE
ROTOR
DELAY PELLET
DELAY-CHARGE HOLDER
PRIMER
PLUNGER SPRING
PLUNGER
SEMPLE FIRING-PIN
CENTRIFUGAL
PLUNGER-PINS
CLOSING PLUG

FUZE, B.D., M60

FUZE, B.D., **M60**—STANDARD

This base-detonating fuze is standard for use in projectiles fired from 155 mm and 6 inch seacoast guns. It is of somewhat unusual construction in that it uses two rotors: one to hold the Semple firing-pin in the safe or unarmed position, the other holding the detonator out of line with the explosive train. Both rotors are released and move to their armed positions when the projectile's rotation reaches 1,450 r.p.m.

When the shell strikes its target the centrifugal plunger moves forward against the compression of its restraining spring and the firing-pin strikes the primer. The flash is communicated to a black-powder delay pellet and thence to the detonator which, in turn, ignites the booster charge of the fuze to function the main explosive charge of the projectile.

ROUNDS

Projectile, A.P., 155 mm, M112
Projectile, A.P., 155 mm, M112B1
Projectile, A.P., 6 inch, M1911
Projectile, A.P., 6 inch, Mk. XXXIII
Shell, H.E., 6 inch, M1911

CHARACTERISTICS

Length overall........................4.28 ins.
Weight.............................9.22 lb.
Thread size.................3.6–6NS–2 L.H.

FUZES, B.D., **M62**, LIMITED STANDARD—**M62A1**, STANDARD

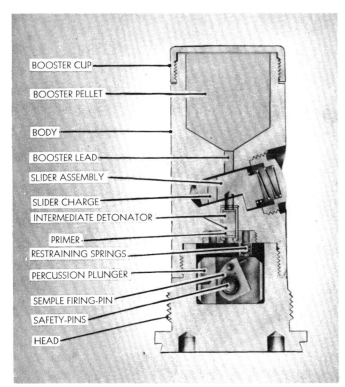

Labels on diagram:
BOOSTER CUP
BOOSTER PELLET
BODY
BOOSTER LEAD
SLIDER ASSEMBLY
SLIDER CHARGE
INTERMEDIATE DETONATOR
PRIMER
RESTRAINING SPRINGS
PERCUSSION PLUNGER
SEMPLE FIRING-PIN
SAFETY-PINS
HEAD

FUZE, B.D., M62

This fuze incorporates a plunger assembly of the Semple centrifugal plunger type. The firing-pin is mounted in the percussion plunger on a rotor which is held in the unarmed position by two safety-pins which compress their springs and move out of the rotor when the shell attains sufficient rotating speed. The rotor is then free to turn and the pin snaps into the armed position, where it is held away from the primer by two restraining springs.

Upon impact the plunger compresses the restraining springs and the firing-pin strikes the primer and fires successively the intermediate detonator charges.

The next element in the explosive train is the slider charge. This is contained in an interrupter assembly which is moved to the outer wall of the fuze by the rotation of the shell. When the slider is in the latter position the explosive element is alined with the detonator and is fired by it. This ignites the booster lead charge and the booster which explode the bursting charge of the projectile.

A new model of the M62 fuze incorporating a heavier plunger and a single large restraining spring has been designated as the M62A1 (Drawing 73–2–160, revision of 8 January 1944).

ROUND

M62	M62A1
Shell, H.E., A.T., 75 mm, M66	Shell, H.E., A.T., 105 mm, M67

CHARACTERISTICS

M62 and M62A1

Length overall...3.54 ins.
Weight...1.28 lb.
Thread size...1.5–12NS–1 L.H.

FUZE, B.D., M66A1— STANDARD

The mechanism of the M66A1 fuze consists only of a plunger firing-pin which is held safe in transportation, firing, and flight by a metal washer. Upon impact the force of inertia causes the firing-pin assembly to crash through the washer and strike the primer cup below.

The resulting flash is carried to a delay pellet of black powder which ignites the detonator, the booster charge, and the bursting charge.

A tracer composition is incorporated in the base of this fuze. This tracer is completely independent of the fuze and is ignited by the flame of the propelling charge.

ROUNDS

Projectile, A.P.C., 75 mm, M61A1
Projectile, A.P.C., 76 mm, M62A1
Projectile, A.P.C., 3 inch, M62A1

FUZE, B.D., M68—STANDARD

The M68 is identical in mechanism and operation with the M66A1, but is made with a larger body so as to seat in the larger cavity of the 90 mm projectile.

The diameter of the M68 is 2.00 inches across the threaded portion of the body—that of the M66A1 is 1.65 inches.

A tracer composition in the base of this fuze is ignited by the propelling charge.

ROUND

Projectile, A.P.C., 90 mm, M82

CHARACTERISTICS

Length overall......................3.463 ins.
Weight.............................1.56 lb.
Thread size...............2.00–10NS–1 L.H.

FUZE, B.D., M72—STANDARD

The M72 is similar in mechanism and the operation of its explosive train to the M66A1 and M68 but does not contain an integral booster. The diameter of the threaded part of the body is 1.375 inches —less than the diameter of the other fuzes mentioned.

This fuze has a tracer composition in the base which is ignited by the propellant.

ROUND

Projectile, A.P.C., 57 mm, M86

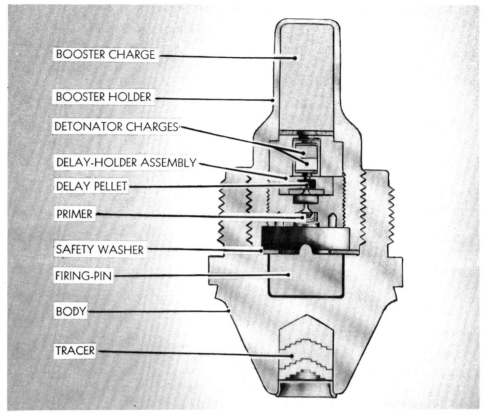

BOOSTER CHARGE
BOOSTER HOLDER
DETONATOR CHARGES
DELAY-HOLDER ASSEMBLY
DELAY PELLET
PRIMER
SAFETY WASHER
FIRING-PIN
BODY
TRACER

FUZE, B.D., M66A1

CHARACTERISTICS—M66A1

Length overall......................3.463 ins.
Weight.............................1 lb.
Thread size..............1.65–10NS–1 L.H.

CHARACTERISTICS—M72

Length overall......................2.167 ins.
Weight.............................0.86 lb.
Thread size.............1.375–10NS–2 L.H.

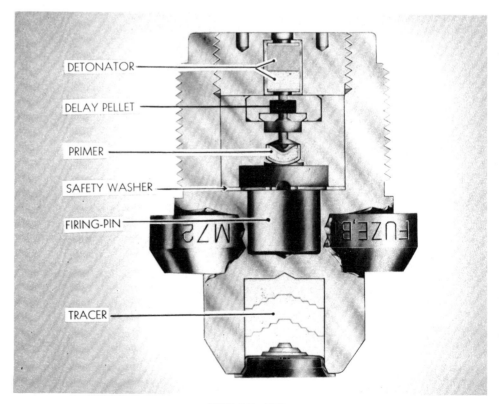

DETONATOR
DELAY PELLET
PRIMER
SAFETY WASHER
FIRING-PIN
TRACER

FUZE, B.D., M72

FUZE, B.D., Mk. V—
LIMITED STANDARD

This is a nondelay action fuze made in 2-inch thread diameter for use in heavy mortars and major caliber guns, and in a thread diameter of 1.5 inches for use in guns of medium caliber. The letter "M" stamped in the exact center of the base of the larger size fuzes designates them for use in mortar shells. All other fuzes, of both sizes, are stamped with "G," indicating use in guns of major and medium calibers.

Fuzes for use in mortar shells remain bore safe and unarmed until the shell's rotation is greater than 1,150 r.p.m. The firing-pin has snapped into position and the fuze is fully armed when a rotation of 1,450 r.p.m. has been attained.

When used in cannon shells, the Mk. V fuze of either size is designed to remain safe so long as the shell's rotation is less than 1,700 r.p.m. It is fully armed at a speed of 2,300 r.p.m.

The firing-pin is mounted in a rotor of conventional design within the percussion plunger and is locked in the safe position by safety-pins. A spring holds the percussion plunger and firing-pin away from the primer while the projectile is in flight. On impact with the target the plunger is driven forward against the resistance of the restraining spring and explodes the primer which fires, successively, two black-powder delay pellets, the detonator, the interrupter charges, the booster lead, and booster charges.

To provide bore safety an interrupter of two L-shaped blocks is incorporated between the detonator and the booster charges. This interrupter prevents transmission of the detonation from detonator to booster if the former should be ignited before the projectile gains the speed of rotation required for arming. When that speed is reached, the upper block of the interrupter compresses the spring and moves outward to aline the interrupter charges.

A steel ball locks the interrupter in the armed position.

ROUNDS

Projectile, A.P., 8 inch, M1911
Projectile, Target, 8 inch, M1911
Shell, H.E., 8 inch, M1911
Shell, A.P., 10 inch, Mk. III
Projectile, H.E., 14 inch, Mk. XI M2A1

CHARACTERISTICS

Length overall . . . . .6.67 ins. (major cal.)
5.77 ins. (medium cal.)
Weight . . . . .3.01 lb. (major cal.)
2.21 lb. (medium cal.)
Thread size . . . . .2.–10NS–1 L.H. (major cal.)
1.5–10NS–1 L.H. (medium cal.)

FUZE, B.D., Mk. X—
STANDARD

This fuze is mechanically identical with the M60. The body, however, is smaller in diameter to fit the fuze-wells of the 16 inch Navy and the 8 inch, 10 inch, and 12 inch seacoast gun projectiles with which it is used.

ROUNDS

Projectile, A.P., 8 inch, Mk. XX Mod. 1
Projectile, A.P., 8 inch, Mk. XX
Shell, A.P., 8 inch, Mk. VI
Shell, A.P., 8 inch, Mk. VII Mod. 6
Projectile, A.P., 12 inch, Mk. XVI
Shell, A.P., 12 inch, Mk. I
Shell, A.P., 12 inch, M1912A
Shell, A.P., 12 inch, Mk. VI
Shell, Deck-Piercing, 12 inch, M1898
Shot, A.P., 12 inch, M1913
Projectile, Deck-Piercing, 12 inch, M1911A
Projectile, H.E., 12 inch, Mk. XI
Projectile, Deck-Piercing, 12 inch, Mk. XXVIII
Projectile, A.P., 14 inch, Mk. VI
Projectile, A.P., 14 inch, Mk. VIII M9A1
Projectile, A.P., 14 inch, M1909
Projectile, A.P., 16 inch, Mk. II M2
Projectile, A.P., 16 inch, Mk. II Mod. 2
Projectile, A.P., 16 inch, Mk. V
Projectile, A.P., 16 inch, Mk. IX
Projectile, A.P., 16 inch, Mk. XII

CHARACTERISTICS

Length overall . . . . .4.27 ins.
Weight . . . . .7.5 lb.
Thread size . . . . .3.3 ins., 7 pitch, U. S. Std., L.H.

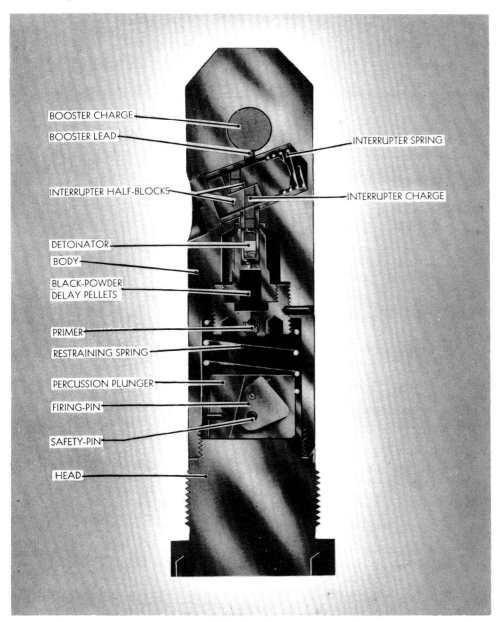

BOOSTER CHARGE
BOOSTER LEAD
INTERRUPTER SPRING
INTERRUPTER HALF-BLOCKS
INTERRUPTER CHARGE
DETONATOR
BODY
BLACK-POWDER DELAY PELLETS
PRIMER
RESTRAINING SPRING
PERCUSSION PLUNGER
FIRING-PIN
SAFETY-PIN
HEAD

FUZE, B.D., Mk. V

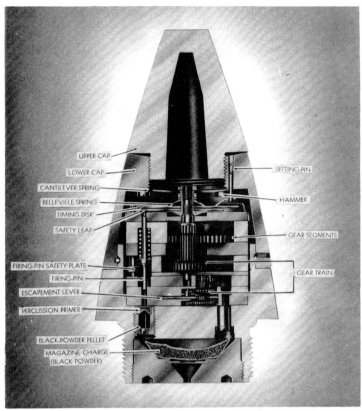

FUZE, M.T., M43A4

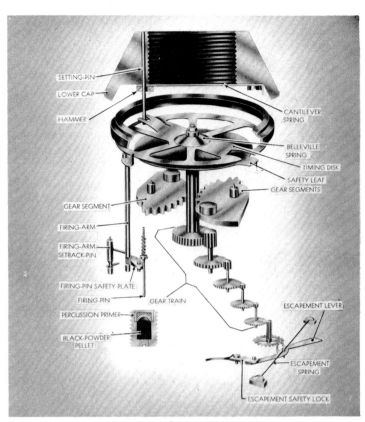

FUZE, M.T., M43A4—MECHANISM

FUZES, MECHANICAL TIME,

M43A5, STANDARD—M43, M43A1, M43A2, M43A3, M43A4, LIMITED STANDARD

All fuzes of the M43 series are mechanical time fuzes which contain no provision for detonation upon impact. The time mechanism may be set to ignite the explosive train at any period from 0.8 second to 30.0 seconds in increments of 0.2 second. This time period is determined by the position of an indicator (set line) on the movable ogive in relation to a graduated scale on the fixed base. The fuze is shipped with the indicator against the "S" (for "Safe") on the graduated scale. All elements are then effectively locked and the mechanism cannot be set in motion accidentally.

In assembling the fuze, the upper cap is staked to the lower and the two turn as a unit in the setting operation. A setting-pin in the lower cap engages the timing disk and serves to rotate the disk until the indicator stands at the desired time setting on the graduated scale.

The timing disk is mounted on the top of the vertical main pinion by a nut and washer screwed down on a Belleville spring. This assembly permits the timing disk to be slipped during the setting operation but holds it tightly to the main pinion when released from the setting-pin. In later models of the M43 fuzes a safety leaf has been added below

the timing disk to prevent functioning at dangerously short time-settings.

The time mechanism of the fuze is a gear train resembling that of a watch. Instead of a mainspring like that of a watch, however, there are two weighted gear segments which engage the main pinion and are actuated in flight by the centrifugal force of the projectile's rotation.

The complete gear train is illustrated in an exploded view. As assembled, it is placed as closely as possible about the axis of rotation. The escapement at the end of the train has a beat much more rapid than that of a watch escapement movement and is actuated by a flat spring instead of the more conventional spiral type.

The firing mechanism includes a firing-arm with setback-pin, a firing-pin safety plate, and a firing-pin and spring.

When the projectile is fired, setback force drives a hammer on a transverse cantilever spring against a raised lug on the timing disk and releases the disk from the setting-pin. Setback also frees the pin holding the firing-arm, leaving the arm free to rotate when the finger on its upper end is tripped by the notch in the firing disk.

After the shell has left the muzzle, centrifugal force turns the escapement safety lock and releases the escapement. The same force moves the weighted gear segments in their arcs to drive the time mechanism. The pinion and the timing disk rotate together and as the notch in the disk trips the finger on the firing-arm, the arm rotates and the safety plate turns from under the shoulder of the firing-pin. This releases the firing-pin spring to drive the pin into the percussion primer, igniting the black-powder pellet and magazine charge.

Illustrated herewith is the M43A4. The latest model is the M43A5 with malleable iron body and stamped steel cap.

ROUNDS
M43A5

Shell, H.E., 3 inch, M42A1
Shell, H.E., 3 inch, Mk. IX
Shell, H.E., 90 mm, M71
Shell, H.E., 105 mm, M38A1

CHARACTERISTICS

	M43A5
Length overall	4.55 ins.
Weight	1.41 lb.
Thread size	1.7–14NS–1

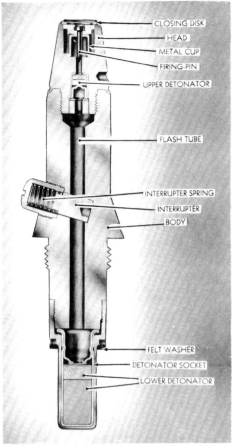

FUZE, P.D., M46

FUZE, P.D., M46—LIMITED STANDARD

The M46 is a superquick, point-detonating fuze.

A cavity in the forward end contains a firing-pin supported by a metal cup. The cup is sufficiently strong to resist the setback force produced by acceleration in the gun, but is crushed when the firing-pin is driven into the primer on impact.

The flash tube of this fuze is equipped with an interrupter of conventional type as a bore-safety measure. Setback holds the interrupter in place while the shell is in the bore, but after the projectile leaves the muzzle and its rotation reaches 1,800 r.p.m., centrifugal force causes the interrupter plunger to compress its retaining spring and move outward. This movement clears the flash tube and the fuze is armed.

When the firing-pin strikes the upper detonator the flash passes through the tube to the lower detonator and to the bursting charge in the projectile.

ROUNDS
Shell, Chemical, 75 mm, Mk. II
Shell, H.E., 75 mm, Mk. I
Shell, H.E., 155 mm, Mk. III
Shell, H.E., 8 inch, Mk. I
Shell, H.E., 12 inch, Mk. X

CHARACTERISTICS
Length overall.......................5.66 ins.
Weight.............................0.72 lb.
Thread size...........12.7 per in., Löwenherz

FUZE, P.D., M47—LIMITED STANDARD

This fuze is similar in appearance and in ballistic characteristics to the P.D. Fuze, M46, but is used when a slight delay element (0.05 second) is required. Mechanism and functioning of the two fuzes are alike except for the introduction in the M47 fuze of a delay element which is set off by the flash from the upper detonator. This delay element consists of a black-powder pellet which burns for the desired delay period before igniting the lower detonator.

Bore safety is obtained by use of an interrupter spring sufficiently strong to hold the interrupter in the safe, or unarmed, position, so long as the projectile's rotation is less than 1,300 r.p.m. Compression of the spring and arming of the fuze is positive when rotation reaches 1,800 r.p.m.

ROUNDS
Shell, H.E., 75 mm, Mk. I
Shell, H.E., 6 inch, Mk. II
Shell, H.E., 155 mm, Mk. III
Shell, H.E., 8 Inch, Mk. I
Projectile, H.E., 12 inch, Mk. X

CHARACTERISTICS
Length overall.......................5.66 ins.
Weight.............................0.74 lb.
Thread size...........12.7 per in., Löwenherz

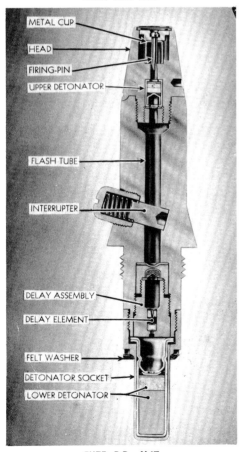

FUZE, P.D., M47

FUZES, P.D.,
M48, M48A1, LIMITED STANDARD—M48A2, STANDARD

These are selective superquick or delay point-detonating fuzes which may be set to function immediately on impact or with a delay of 0.15 second for the M48A1 and 0.05 second for the M48. Delays of 0.05 second and 0.15 second are used in the M48A2. They have a standard weight of 1.41 pounds, standard streamlined contour, and standard location of the center of gravity.

The mechanisms of the three fuzes are similar except for the addition of a centrifugal plunger-pin lock (noted below) to the M48A1 and M48A2. The M48A2 differs from the M48A1 in that the delay action is redesigned to provide additional insurance against premature detonation. The M48A2 has a modified plunger assembly, a weakened plunger-restraining spring, and uses the M29 primer.

Bore safety is obtained with all these fuzes when used in conjunction with the M20 booster.

The fuze is set for superquick action by adjusting a setting sleeve which permits the interrupter to move to its armed position when the shell has left the muzzle and is acted upon by centrifugal force. When set for delay action the off-center interrupter is prevented from moving to the armed position by the setting sleeve, hence upon impact the superquick action is checked by the solid mass of the interrupter.

SUPERQUICK ACTION—With the setting sleeve adjusted to the superquick position, the firing-pin in the nose of the fuze is supported by a metal cup sufficiently strong to withstand the force of setback while the projectile is in the bore.

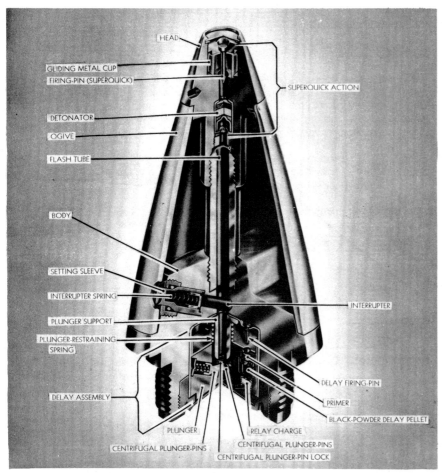

FUZE, P.D., M48A2

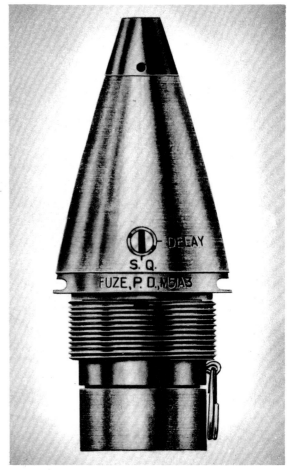

FUZE, P.D., M51A3

Upon impact this cup is smashed and the firing-pin driven into the detonator.

During the flight of the projectile the interrupter moves to the armed position, clearing the flash tube for the flash to pass from the detonator to the booster. The delay action is also set off upon impact but is negated by the prior action of the superquick element.

DELAY ACTION—When the setting sleeve is adjusted to the delay position, the firing of the detonator by the firing-pin in the nose of the fuze transmits no flash to the booster because of blocking by the unarmed interrupter. The delay element in the base of the fuze is actuated by the impact of the projectile.

The delay assembly consists of a fixed delay firing-pin, a plunger support, a plunger, a plunger-restraining spring, two centrifugal plunger-pins and springs, and a centrifugal plunger-pin lock. The delay explosive train is incorporated in the plunger body below the delay firing-pin.

During the period of setback the delay firing-pin in the M48 and M48A1 is restrained from striking the explosive train by the contact of the plunger support with the centrifugal plunger-pins. The firing-pin in the M48A2 fuze

is rigidly mounted and upon setback the plunger body naturally assumes the safe position.

When the projectile leaves the muzzle, centrifugal force moves the centrifugal plunger-pins to their outermost position. These pins are held by the lock which rotates and prevents them from returning to the unarmed position. The plunger head is held away from the delay firing-pin by the plunger-restraining spring.

Upon impact the plunger compresses the restraining spring and strikes the delay firing-pin, igniting the primer, and firing the delay pellet which burns for either 0.15 second or 0.05 second before igniting the relay pellet which transmits the explosion to the booster.

ROUNDS
M48A2
Shell, H.E., 75 mm, M41A1
Shell, H.E., 75 mm, M48
Shell, H.E., 3 inch, Mk. IX
Shell, H.E., 3 inch, M42A1
Shell, H.E., 105 mm, M1

CHARACTERISTICS

	M48A2
Length overall	4.55 ins.
Weight	1.41 lb.
Thread size	1.7–14NS–1

FUZES, P.D., **M51, M51A1, M51A2**—LIMITED STANDARD **M51A3, M51A3 MOD. 3**—STANDARD

All fuzes of the M51 series are mechanically similar to those bearing the M48 designation, but are always used with boosters which are assembled to the base of the fuze instead of being incorporated in the nose of the shell. The M48 fuzes are used without boosters or with the M20 booster assembled in the shell. The M51 series of fuzes use boosters, M21, M21A1, and M21A2. Fuzes and boosters are attached. All fuzes of this series may be set for either superquick or for delay action.

Fuze, M51, has a 0.05 second delay action and is assembled with the M21 booster.

Fuze, M51A1, has a 0.05 second delay action and is assembled with the M21A1 booster.

344

Fuze, M51A2, was originally designed for use with the M21A1 booster but before the fuze reached production the M21A2 booster was assigned to it and the designation was changed to M51A3. The delay period of this fuze was increased from 0.05 second to 0.15 second, effective with the M51A2 fuze.

The "Mod. 3" suffix applied to M51 fuzes identifies it as modified for use in the M103 8 inch H.E. shell fired from the M1 howitzer (Army) and the Mk. IX Mod. 2 (Navy) guns of the same caliber. Assembly of the fuze within the windshield of this shell requires a longer flash tube.

Since this fuze cannot be set by the setting screw when assembled in the M103 shell, two types of fuze heads are supplied. The fuze is shipped with a dummy head in place and a live head is shipped packed in the packing container. When superquick action is required the live head is substituted.

The M51 Mod. 1 and the M51A1 Mod. 1 fuzes incorporate a time delay of 0.05 second, the M51A3 Mod. 3 fuze has a 0.15 second time delay.

CHARACTERISTICS

	M51A3	M51A3 MOD. 3
Length overall	5.93 ins.	
Weight	2.15 lb.	2.47 lb.
Thread size	1.7–14NS–1 (fuze)	1.7–14NS–1
	2–12NS–1 (booster)	

ROUNDS
M51A3

Shell, H.E., 4.5 inch, M65
Shell, H.E., 4.5 inch, M65 B1
Shell, H.E., 4.5 inch, M65 B2
Shell, H.E., 6 inch, Mk. IIA1
Shell, H.E., 6 inch, Mk. IIA2
Shell, H.E., 155 mm, Mk. IA1
Shell, Chem., 155 mm, Mk. IIA1
Shell, H.E., 155 mm, Mk. IIIA1
Shell, Chem., 155 mm, Mk. VIIA1
Shell, H.E., 155 mm, M101
Shell, Chem., 155 mm, M104
Shell, H.E., 155 mm, M107
Shell, H.E., 155 mm, M102
Shell, Chem., 155 mm, M110
Shell, Chem., 155 mm, M105
Shell, H.E., 8 inch, M106
Shell, H.E., 8 inch, Mk. IA1
Shell, H.E., 240 mm, Mk. IIIA1
Shell, H.E., 240 mm, M114

M51A3 MOD. 3

Shell, H.E., 8 inch, M103

FUZES, P.D., M52, STANDARD—M52B1, M52B2, ALTERNATES

These three fuzes may be used interchangeably and differ only in the materials used in their construction. Fuze, M52, has an aluminum head and body; Fuze, M52B1, has a plastic head, body, and booster cup; and Fuze, M52B2, has a plastic head and aluminum body. All are superquick in action.

The firing assembly is in the nose of the fuze and consists of a striker and firing-pin held in position by a spring and pin.

The detonator cup in fuzes of this series is mounted in a slider assembly which secures it in the unarmed position until after the shell has left the muzzle of the gun.

Functioning of the slider to arm the fuze is shown in the illustrations herewith. These show (A) a section of the M52 fuze through the slider, and (B) a section through the safety-pin. When the safety wire is removed from the fuze before loading, the safety-pin is held within the fuze body only by the setback-pin. When the shell is fired, setback force withdraws the setback-pin and frees the safety-pin which is thrown clear of the fuze when the projectile leaves the muzzle. This releases the slider to move into its armed position where it is locked by the lock-pin which engages the notch shown in the slider body. The firing-pin is then alined with the detonator cup which contains a top closing disk, upper and intermediate detonating charges, a detonator pellet, and a base closing disk.

On impact with the target, the striker head collapses and the firing-pin is driven into the detonator cup, exploding all its charges. The flame passes to the booster lead and booster pellet, also shown in the illustrations, and is transmitted to the high-explosive charge of the projectile.

ROUNDS

Shell, H.E., 60 mm, M49A2
Shell, Practice, 60 mm, M50A2
Shell, Practice, 81 mm, M43A1
Shell, Chem., 81 mm, M57
Shell, H.E., 81 mm, M43A1B1

CHARACTERISTICS

Length overall	3.47 ins.
Weight	M52, 0.45 lb.; M52B1, 0.29 lb.
Thread size	1.5–12NS–1

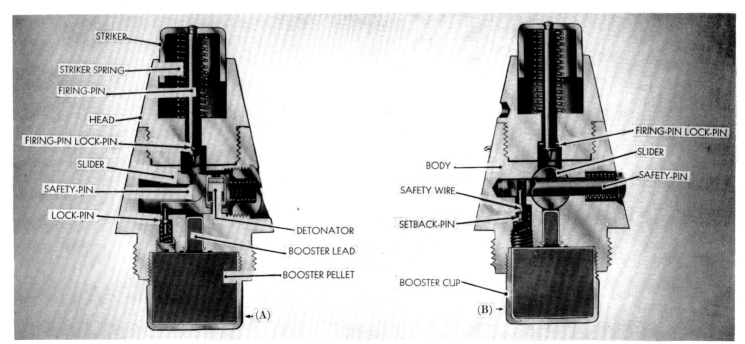

STRIKER
STRIKER SPRING
FIRING-PIN
HEAD
FIRING-PIN LOCK-PIN
SLIDER
SAFETY-PIN
LOCK-PIN
DETONATOR
BOOSTER LEAD
BOOSTER PELLET
(A)

FIRING-PIN LOCK-PIN
SLIDER
SAFETY-PIN
BODY
SAFETY WIRE
SETBACK-PIN
BOOSTER CUP
(B)

FUZE, P.D., M52

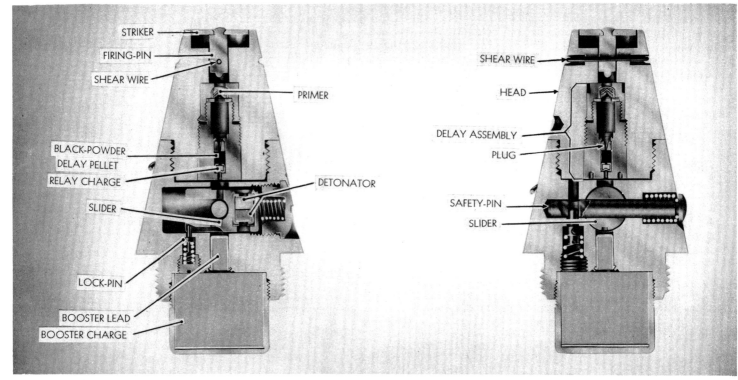

FUZE, P.D., M53

FUZE, P.D., M53—STANDARD

This fuze resembles the M52 super-quick fuze in that the detonator cup is mounted in a slider which holds it in the unarmed position until the projectile has left the muzzle of the gun. It differs from the M53 in that a delay element is installed between the firing-pin and the detonator assembly.

A striker and short firing-pin are held in position in the nose of the fuze by a shear wire which passes through the fuze body and the pin and is secured by bend-ing its end into a circumferential groove in the nose.

The delay element consists of a primer, an expansion chamber, a plug, a delay pellet of black powder, and the relay charge. The tapered hole in the plug forms a constriction for the release of burning gases from the delay pellet and thus controls the burning time of the pellet to 0.1 second.

The shear wire restraining the firing-pin is cut on impact with the target. The firing-pin is driven into the delay primer and the flash—after a delay of 0.1 sec-ond—passes to the detonator which moved into its armed position when the projec-tile left the muzzle.

The flash from the detonator is trans-mitted to the booster and main explosive charges as in the M52 fuze.

ROUND
Shell, H.E., 81 mm, M56

CHARACTERISTICS
Length overall........................3.47 ins.
Weight..............................0.54 lb.
Thread size.....................1.5–12NF–1

FUZES, P.D.,
M54, M55A2, STANDARD—M55, M55A1, LIMITED STANDARD

These are combination superquick and 25-second powder-train time fuzes which may be set to function either upon impact or after a predetermined period. So far as the fuze and its mechanism is con-cerned, the four are identical; the type numbers being assigned to designate the fuze as used with different boosters.

As M54, the fuze is used in conjunction with booster, M20, or booster, M20A1; as M55, with booster, M21; as M55A1, with booster, M21A1; and as M55A2, with booster, M21A2. These boosters are metal cases carrying a charge of tetryl. Exterior threads on the booster body permit its being screwed into the shell; interior threads in the nose of the body, above the charge, receive the fuze.

A booster supplies an intermediate detonating charge between the fuze and the high-explosive charge with which the shell is loaded. It amplifies the flash of the smaller detonating elements of the fuze and assures the explosion of the main charge. A booster cannot exert its in-fluence over an extensive area of the charge, but it initiates a maximum high-order detonation in that portion of the charge with which it is in contact. For this reason, a comparatively small booster charge at the end of the fuze detonator train produces better results than a larger

charge placed to surround the detonator. A booster which will function successfully in a 75 mm high-explosive shell will per-form equally well in a shell of 155 mm caliber or larger.

In a chemical shell the function of such a charge is to break the case of the shell into large fragments and permit the dispersion of the chemical filler without flash. It is therefore called a "burster" and is loaded with a "burster charge" larger than the booster charge used with high-explosive shell.

Boosters include their own detonator primers, loaded in a rotor which is held in the safe position until armed by set-

346

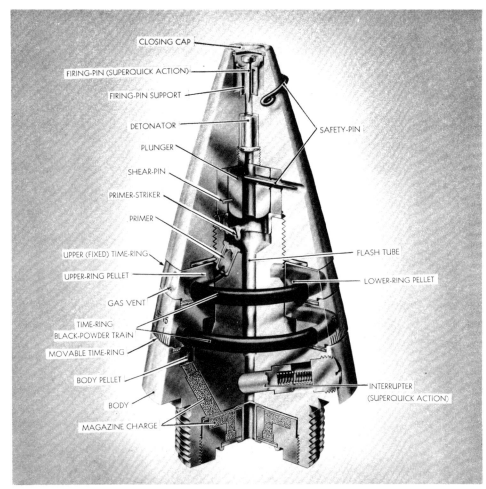

CLOSING CAP
FIRING-PIN (SUPERQUICK ACTION)
FIRING-PIN SUPPORT
DETONATOR
PLUNGER
SHEAR-PIN
PRIMER-STRIKER
PRIMER
UPPER (FIXED) TIME-RING
UPPER-RING PELLET
GAS VENT
TIME-RING BLACK-POWDER TRAIN
MOVABLE TIME-RING
BODY PELLET
BODY
MAGAZINE CHARGE
SAFETY-PIN
FLASH TUBE
LOWER-RING PELLET
INTERRUPTER (SUPERQUICK ACTION)

FUZE, P.D., M54

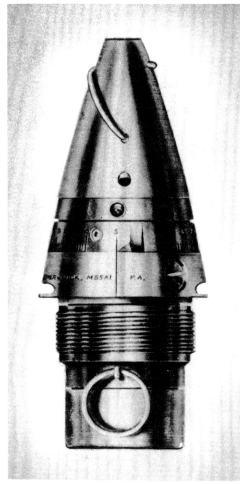

FUZE, P.D., M55A1

back plus centrifugal force when the projectile is fired. This additional factor of safety permits fuzes to be shipped with boosters attached or shells to be transported with both fuze and booster assembly in place, ready for loading.

The superquick action of the M54 differs slightly from that of the M48 fuze. There is no means of locking the interrupter of the M54 fuze as is done in setting the M48 fuze for delay action, and the flash tube is always clear for superquick action on impact with the target in the event that the shell is fired with the time element set on "Safe," or if the time of flight is less than that for which the time element was adjusted before firing.

The time element assembly includes a plunger, a primer-striker and primer, two brass time-train rings, upper- and lower-ring pellets, body pellet and body charge, and magazine charge.

When the gun is fired the plunger, acted on by the force of setback, cuts through the shear-pins and rams the striker against the primer. This ignites the upper-ring pellet, setting off the upper time-train ring which burns uniformly until the lower-ring pellet is ignited. This pellet transmits the flame to the movable time-train ring which may be set for burning time from 1 second to 25 seconds in increments of 0.2 second. This train fires the body pellet and body charge which ignite the magazine charge.

In addition to the firing-pin support and the interrupter, the following safety measures are provided.

Before placing the round in the gun, a member of the crew must remove a safety-pin which passes through both the fuze body and the plunger and holds the plunger safe in transport. When the fuze is set at "Safe" the ends of the time trains of both upper and lower rings are covered by metal and in the event of accidental ignition the rings can burn completely without communicating their flame to the base charge of the fuze. When the time element is set at less than 0.4 second a safety disk at the ignition end of the movable time train covers the body pellet and prevents its ignition from the movable ring.

To prevent premature ignition of either time train by chamber gases a foil cover is placed over the gas vent of each time-train ring. The foil is ruptured by pressure created by combustion of the powder in the ring and the gases escape through the vent.

ROUNDS
M54
Shell, H.E., 75 mm, M48
Shell, H.E., 105 mm, M1
Shell, Smoke, 105 mm, (B.E.), M84
Shell, Smoke, 105 mm, (BE.), M84B1
Shell, Smoke, 155 mm, M115
Shell, Smoke, 155 mm, M116

M55A1 and M55A2
Shell, H.E., 155 mm, M102
Shell, Chem., 155 mm, M105
Shell, H.E., 155 mm, Mk. IA1
Shell, Chem., 155 mm, Mk. IIA1

CHARACTERISTICS

	M54	M55A1 and M55A2
Length overall	4.57 ins.	5.95 ins.
Weight	1.42 lb.	2.16 lb.
Thread size	1.7–14NS–1	1.7–14NS–1

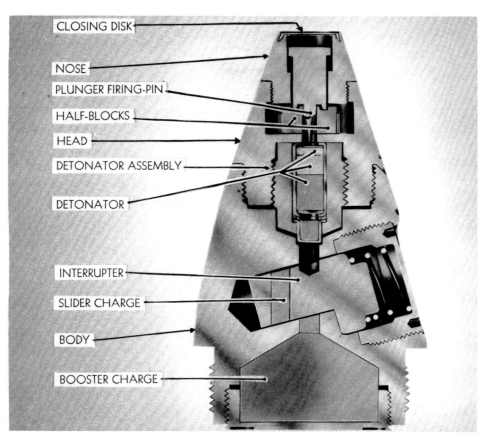

CLOSING DISK

NOSE

PLUNGER FIRING-PIN

HALF-BLOCKS

HEAD

DETONATOR ASSEMBLY

DETONATOR

INTERRUPTER

SLIDER CHARGE

BODY

BOOSTER CHARGE

FUZE, P.D., M56

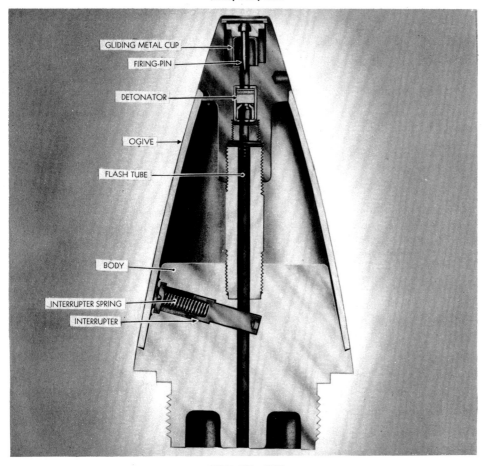

GLIDING METAL CUP

FIRING-PIN

DETONATOR

OGIVE

FLASH TUBE

BODY

INTERRUPTER SPRING

INTERRUPTER

FUZE, P.D., M57

FUZE, P.D., M56—STANDARD

This is a supersensitive, point-detonating fuze which will function on impact against two thicknesses of airplane fabric. A series of internal safety features renders this fuze relatively boresafe.

When the projectile is fired the fuze is completely unarmed and remains so until the force of setback is overcome. Centrifugal force causes two half-blocks supporting the plunger firing-pin to move apart. The inner edges of these half-blocks have an angular cut which serves to prevent motion of the half-blocks during setback and to lift the plunger firing-pin toward the closing disk as the blocks separate. As the blocks move farther apart an opening is provided for the firing-pin to descend against the detonator. "Creep" holds the firing-pin against the closing disk until it is driven backward by the force of impact. After the shell leaves the muzzle, centrifugal force compresses the interrupter-spring and moves the interrupter toward the nose of the fuze and outward against the outer wall, alining the slider charge with the detonator assembly and booster.

The detonator assembly is the initial explosive element and contains a primer-detonator, intermediate detonator, and a lead cup charge of tetryl.

The nose of the projectile is crushed on impact with the target and the firing-pin is driven into the primer to detonate the explosive train.

ROUND
Shell, H.E., 37 mm, M54

CHARACTERISTICS

Length overall.......................2.21 ins.
Weight............................0.17 lb.
Thread size...................1.125–20NS–1

FUZE, P.D., M57—STANDARD

The M57 is a superquick, point-detonating fuze with no delay element. Essentially it is the M48 fuze with the delay assembly omitted and with no setting sleeve on the centrifugal interrupter. This design adapts the fuze for use in chemical shells where it is essential that the shell burst before entering the ground.

The action is identical with that of the M48 when set for superquick functioning.

ROUNDS
Shell, H.E., 75 mm, M48
Shell, Chem., 75 mm, M64
Shell, Chem., 105 mm, M60

CHARACTERISTICS

Length overall.................4.55 ins., max.
Weight............................1.41 lb.
Thread size.....................1.7–14NS–1

FUZE, M.T., **M61A1**— STANDARD

The M61A1 Fuze is identical in mechanism and functioning with the M43A4 (illustrated on page 655) but differs from it in shape and weight. These variations have been made in order to adapt it for use with the 120 mm shell, M73.

ROUND
Shell, H.E., 120 mm, M73

CHARACTERISTICS

Length overall......................7.677 ins.
Weight..........................1.62 lb.
Thread size......................1.7–14NS–1

FUZE, T., **M65**—STANDARD

The M65 is a simple time-train fuze used in the 60 mm illuminating shell, M83A1.

During transportation and before loading the fuze striker is held in the safe position by a safety-pin and shear wire. Upon firing, the shear wire is immediately severed and the striker ignites the primer charge.

The flash from the primer passes through an orifice and a flash opening cut

at a right angle thereto and ignites a ¼ inch length of quickmatch. The time-train groove charge is ignited by the quickmatch and burns about the ring for $14 \pm ¾$ seconds before passing the flame on to the body pellet and the expelling charge in the base of the fuze. The flame from the expelling charge passes to the rear through apertures in the retainer disk.

The fixed burning time of this fuze permits the round, fired with full increment charge, to be at its optimum range and height when the fuze has completed its operation.

To permit powder gases to escape, a vent hole is drilled from the outer wall of the fuze to the time-train ring at the junction of the quickmatch hole. The vent hole is sealed by a lead closing disk and a washer. The disk melts on the ignition of the ring powder charge and permits the combustion gases to escape.

ROUND
Shell, Illum., 60 mm, M83A1

CHARACTERISTICS

Length overall.................2.53 ins., max.
Weight..........................0.80 lb.
Thread size......................2–20NS–1

FUZES, M.T., **M67, M67A1** —LIMITED STANDARD **M67A2**—STANDARD

These are mechanical time fuzes with selective time settings up to 75 seconds. The mechanism is the same as that of the M43 series of mechanical time fuzes. However, the escapement and gears are set to give functioning times up to 75 seconds.

The M67A1 is identical with the M67 in mechanism but has a minimum time-setting of 0.8 second instead of 0.2 second. The M67A2 model includes the M21A2 booster.

ROUNDS
M67A2
Shell, H.E., 155 mm, M101
Shell, H.E., 155 mm, M107
Shell, H.E., 155 mm, Mk. IIIA1
Shell, H.E., 8 inch, M103
Shell, H.E., 8 inch, M106
Shell, H.E., 8 inch, Mk. IA1
Shell, H.E., 240 mm, M114
Shell, H.E., 240 mm, Mk. IIIA1

CHARACTERISTICS
M67A2

Length overall ....5.93 ins. (incl. booster)
Weight.................2.14 lb. (incl. booster)
Thread size.........................2.12NS–1

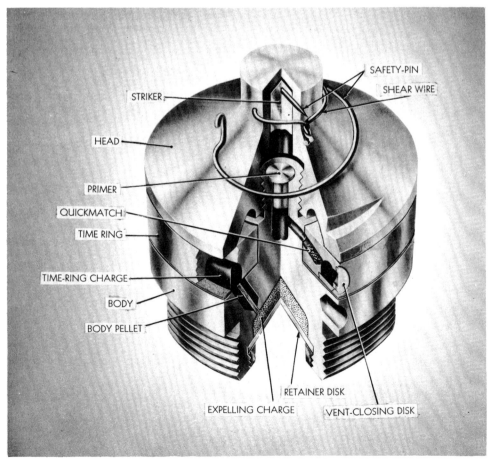

FUZE, T., M65

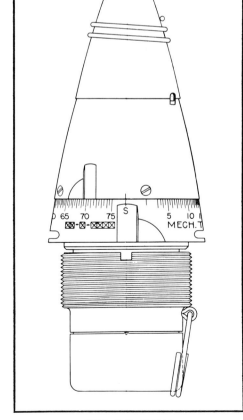

FUZE, M.T., M67A2

FUZE, P.D., M71—STANDARD

This is a point-detonating fuze incorporating the Semple-design rotor mechanism.

The fuze body is that of the Mk. 27 fuze. The mechanism is the same as that used in the M74 fuze.

ROUNDS
Shell, H.E.–T, (S.D. M3), 40 mm, Mk. II
Shell, H.E.–T, (S.D. No. 12), 40 mm, Mk. II

CHARACTERISTICS
Length overall.........................2.45 ins.
Weight..............................0.22 lb.
Thread size.....................1.18–14NS–2

FUZE, P.D., M74—STANDARD

Since this fuze is used in a practice shell it contains no booster charge.

The firing-pin "floats" in the forward end of the fuze.

A cylindrical rotor, set at right angles to the fuze axis, contains the detonator charge and setback-pin. The detonator is held diagonally across the fuze axis. The force of setback moves the setback-pin into the rotor and the rotor turns to the armed position when rotation of the shell is sufficiently high. The fuze is then fully armed.

Upon impact the firing-pin strikes the detonator and sends the flash into the black-powder spotting charge of the shell.

ROUND
Shell, Practice, 37 mm, M92

CHARACTERISTICS
Length overall.......................1.43 ins.
Weight..............................0.21 lb.
Thread size...................1.125–20NS–1

FUZE, P.D., M75—LIMITED PROCUREMENT

This fuze is similar in operation to the No. 253, Mk. III. The M75 has been adopted for limited procurement.

It consists of a brass body and a detonator assembly. The hollow head forms an air chamber at the base of which is a detonator of mercury fulminate and a magazine charge of tetryl pellets.

Upon impact the nose is crushed and compression of the air in the chamber ignites the detonator and pellets. The flame is then passed on to the high-explosive charge in the shell.

ROUND
Shell, H.E.I., 20 mm, M97

CHARACTERISTICS
Length overall.................1.20 ins., max.
Weight..............................0.5 lb.
Thread size....................0.56–32NS–1

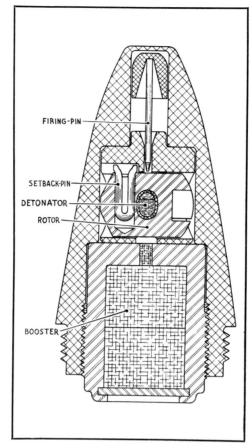

FUZE, P.D., M71

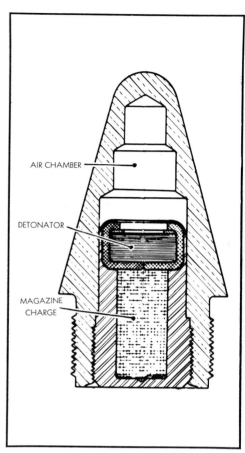

FUZE, P.D., M75

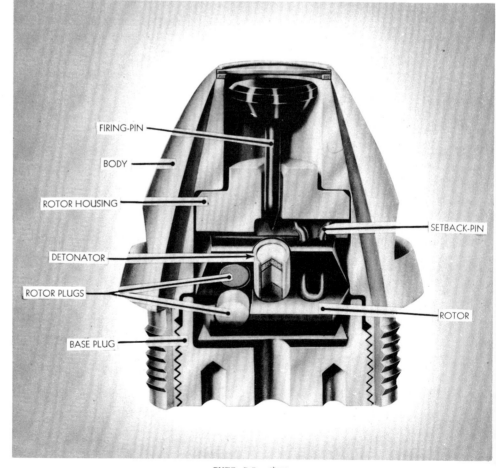

FUZE, P.D., M74

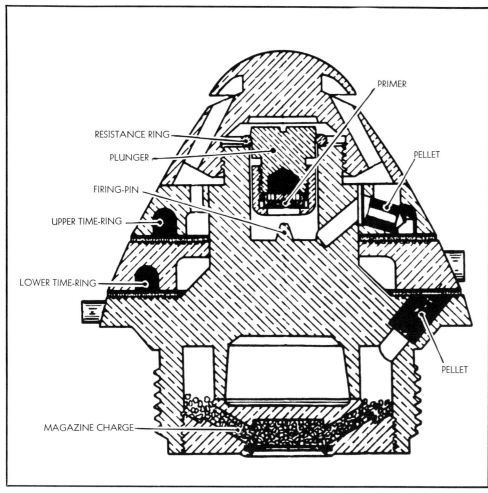

RESISTANCE RING
PLUNGER
FIRING-PIN
UPPER TIME-RING
LOWER TIME-RING
PRIMER
PELLET
PELLET
MAGAZINE CHARGE

FUZE, TIME, 21-sec., Mk. IIIA2

FUZE, TIME, 21-sec., Mk. IIIA2—SUBSTITUTE STANDARD

This modification of the Mk. IIIA1 time fuze contains a black-powder charge weighing 20 grains, sufficient to actuate the Mk. X and M20 boosters.

The delay principle used in this fuze is similar to the time and superquick, M54, in that there are two time-train rings separated by pellets. The Mk. IIIA2 may be set from 0 to 21.2 seconds in increments of approximately 0.2 second.

The ignition of the explosive train varies from the M54 in having the primer attached to the bottom of the concussion plunger. The concussion primer is held in its slot and kept safe by a resistance ring fitted around its head. Upon firing, setback forces the plunger through the resistance ring and into contact with a fixed firing-pin. This action fires the primer and communicates the flame to the first powder pellet and thence to the time train, which eventually sets off the magazine charge and the base charge of the projectile.

Provisions for safety in the time-train rings are similar to those in the M54. When set on "Safe," solid metal sections stand between the pellet of the lower time train and the magazine charge. Vents are provided in the rings to allow chamber gases to escape and prevent premature ignition of the powder trains.

Since this unit is susceptible to moisture a waterproof cover protects each fuze issued.

ROUND
Shell, H.E., 3 inch, M42A1

CHARACTERISTICS

Length overall	2.75 ins.
Weight	1.25 lb.
Thread size	1.7–14NS–1

FUZE, P.D., Mk. 27 (NAVY)—STANDARD

This Navy fuze has been standardized for Army use because of its excellent performance and the ease with which it may be procured. It is superquick in its action.

Striker and firing-pin are held in the nose of the fuze by two safety-pins under the shoulder of the firing-pin.

A rotor located below the firing-pin contains a primer-detonator held out of

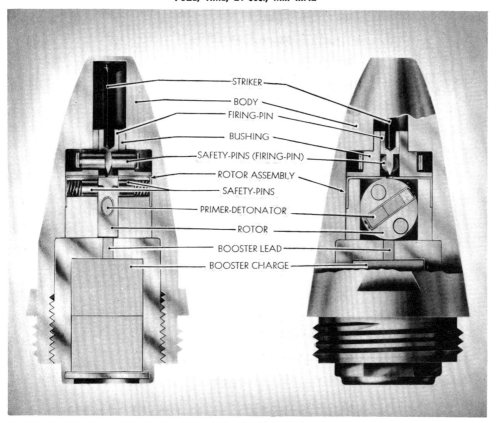

STRIKER
BODY
FIRING-PIN
BUSHING
SAFETY-PINS (FIRING-PIN)
ROTOR ASSEMBLY
SAFETY-PINS
PRIMER-DETONATOR
ROTOR
BOOSTER LEAD
BOOSTER CHARGE

FUZE, P.D., Mk. 27 (NAVY)

line with the firing-pin and booster lead charge by two safety-pins.

After the shell has left the muzzle and attained sufficient speed of rotation, the safety-pins move out from under the shoulder of the firing-pin. The firing-pin is restrained in the forward end of the fuze by creep force.

Centrifugal force also withdraws the safety-pin holding the rotor, permitting it to turn and bring the primer into line with the firing-pin.

Upon impact the striker and firing-pin hit the primer and ignite the detonator, booster lead, and booster charge.

ROUNDS

Shell, H.E.–T. (S.D. M3), 40 mm, Mk. II
Shell, H.E.–T. (S.D. No. 12), 40 mm, Mk. II

CHARACTERISTICS

Length overall........................2.45 ins.
Weight.............................0.22 lb.
Thread size....................1.18–14NS–2

FUZE, P.D., No. 251, Mk. I—LIMITED STANDARD

This superquick fuze was originally standardized when the Bofors gun and British 40 mm ammunition were adopted. The fuze was extremely complicated and gave way eventually to the now standard Mk. 27 (Navy) fuze. The No. 251, Mk. I is now classified as Limited Standard for 40 mm ammunition.

In the forward end of the fuze is a striker resting upon a firing-pin held safe by steel balls beneath its shoulder. These steel balls are retained by the arming sleeve. Surrounding the arming sleeve is a compressed spring which is locked by the ferrule and the stirrup spring.

The explosive train is interrupted by a pair of shutters and held by a ferrule and stirrup spring.

Upon setback the ferrule and stirrup spring in the head move rearward and release the arming sleeve. The compressed spring forces the arming sleeve toward the nose, unmasking the steel balls, and when sufficient centrifugal force has developed these fly from under the shoulders of the firing-pin, leaving it armed for functioning upon impact.

Setback also releases the ferrule and stirrup spring holding the shutters and under centrifugal force they fly outward. The detonator holder is then forced to the rear by its compressed spring and brings the detonator into direct communication with the relay charges.

Upon impact the striker and firing-pin hit the primer and ignite in turn the detonator, relay charges, and booster charge.

ROUND

Shell, quick-firing, H.E., 40 mm, Mk. II T/L/

CHARACTERISTICS

Length overall........................2.76 ins.
Weight.............................0.219 lb.
Thread size....................1.18–14NS–2

FUZES, P.D., No. 253, Mk. I, Mk. II, LIMITED STANDARD—No. 253, Mk. III, STANDARD

These superquick, point-detonating fuzes were developed for use with 20 mm high-explosive incendiary rounds. They differ only in minor construction details. The noses of the Mk. I and Mk. II fuzes are closed by their brass disks; the nose of the Mk. III is solid. The detonators in the Mk. II and Mk. III fuzes are covered by a pierced brass disk. A solid brass disk is used in this position in the Mk. I fuze.

The principle of functioning of the Mk. II and Mk. III fuzes is as simple as it is radical. There is no firing mechanism whatever, firing of the explosive train being initiated by heat generated by compression of the air in the hollow nose as the fuze head is crushed by impact. The Mk. I fuze, however, functions due to retardation which causes the lead-foil disk on top of the detonator charge to move forward through the washer, carrying with it a portion of the fulminate charge. This movement causes the fulminate to ignite.

The complete explosive train consists of a mercury fulminate detonator and booster cap, and a tetryl booster charge.

ROUND

No. 253, Mk. III
Shell, H.E.I., 20 mm, Mk. I

CHARACTERISTICS

	No. 253, Mk. III
Length overall	1.41 ins.
Weight	0.058 lb.
Thread size	0.625–36NS–2

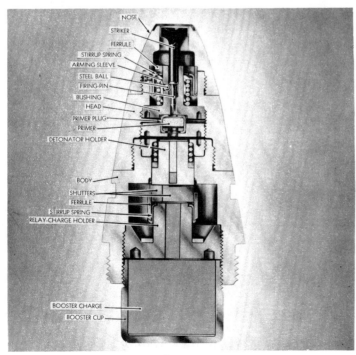

FUZE, P.D., No. 251, Mk. I

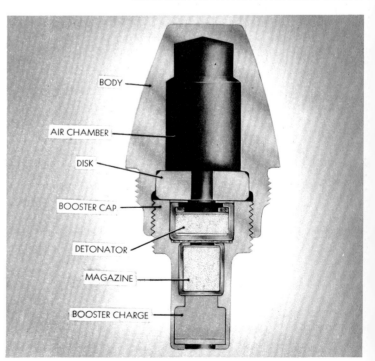

FUZE, P.D., No. 253, Mk. III

DUMMY FUZES

These fuzes for practice firing are designed to simulate actual models and have the same contour, size, weight, and ballistic qualities as the fuzes they simulate. Setting screws are incorporated where necessary.

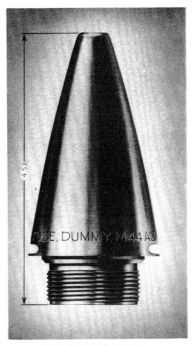

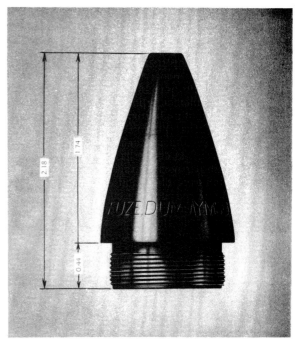

FUZE, DUMMY, 21-SEC., M42A1—
LIMITED STANDARD

FUZE, DUMMY, M44A2—
STANDARD

FUZES, DUMMY, M50, STANDARD—
M50B1, M50B2, ALTERNATES

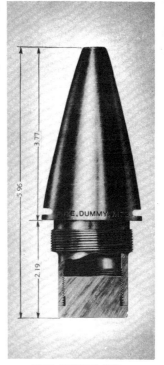

FUZE, DUMMY, M59—
STANDARD

FUZES, DUMMY, M69, STANDARD—
M69B1, ALTERNATE

FUZE, DUMMY, M73—
STANDARD

FUZE, DUMMY, T23—
EXPERIMENTAL

BOMB FUZES

Fuzes used in detonating bombs are classified as nose or tail (indicating their location in the bomb) or as hydrostatic fuzes. These last are placed in depth bombs and are operated by hydrostatic pressure. Bomb fuzes may be further classified according to the method by which the arming process is initiated—arming-pin or arming-vane. In fuzes classified as arming-pin type the arming process is begun by removal of an arming-pin from the fuze when the bomb is released. Arming-vane fuzes are armed by rotation of vanes in the airstream after the bomb is released. Arming may be accomplished immediately upon removal of the pin or may be delayed mechanically or by the timed burning of a powder train. The actual functioning of the firing elements of bomb fuzes may be time, superquick, delay, nondelay, or by combinations of these methods.

Hydrostatic fuzes depend upon water pressure for the functioning of their firing mechanisms. They may be set to detonate at required depths. In some designs the arming of the fuze is also accomplished by hydrostatic pressure.

FUZE, BOMB, NOSE, AN-M103—STANDARD

The AN-M103 is a nose fuze which functions on impact. It can be set for instantaneous functioning or 0.1 second delay action by means of an external setting-pin.

As supplied, the fuze is set for delay action (0.1 second) but instantaneous action may be obtained by removing the external setting-pin from its deep slot position, rotating it a quarter turn and inserting it in the shallow slot. As the vane cup moves away from the striker the safety blocks are exposed and ejected, leaving the striker held in the safe position by only a soft metal shear wire and the inner end of the setting-pin, which also acts as a shear wire. Under the action of its spring the arming stem travels with the head of the fuze as the latter moves forward in the arming operation. This forward movement of the arming stem releases the detonator slider assembly.

The detonator slider assembly contains the detonator charge which is held out of line with either the delay firing-pin or the instantaneous firing-pin by the blocking action of the arming stem. As the lower end of the stem reaches the upper edge of the detonator slider in its forward movement, the slider is pushed across by its springs until the upper step of the detonator slider again meets the arming stem. This position of the detonator slider places the detonator charge in direct contact with the delay explosive train and one of the two booster lead charges. Should the setting-pin be adjusted for delay action the inner end of the setting-pin engages the collar on the arming stem and prevents further advance of the arming stem. The stem reaches this point after approximately 180 turns of the arming vanes.

Should the setting-pin be adjusted for instantaneous action its inner end is entirely withdrawn from the arming-stem slot and the stem is free to continue its

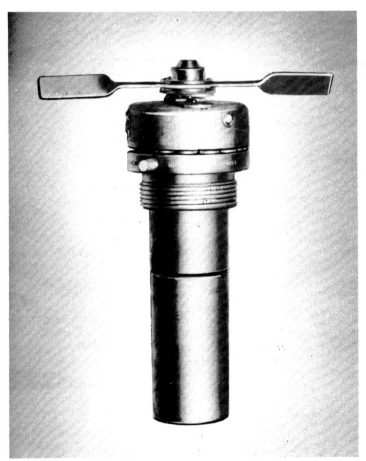

FUZE, BOMB, NOSE, AN-M103

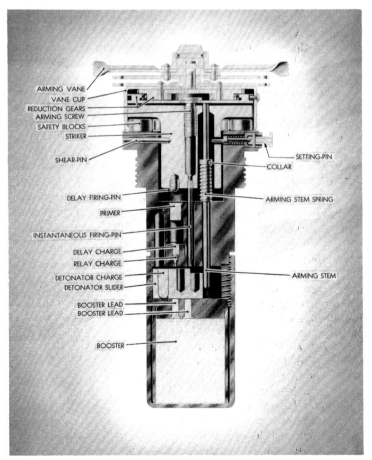

FUZE, BOMB, NOSE, AN-M103—UNARMED

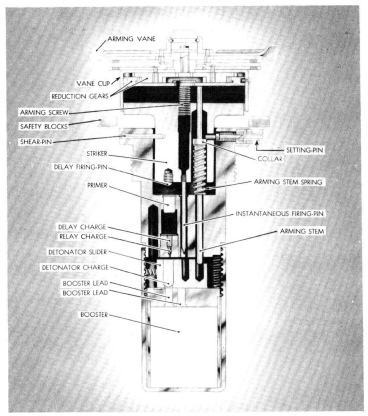

FUZE, BOMB, NOSE, AN-M103—ARMED FOR DELAY ACTION

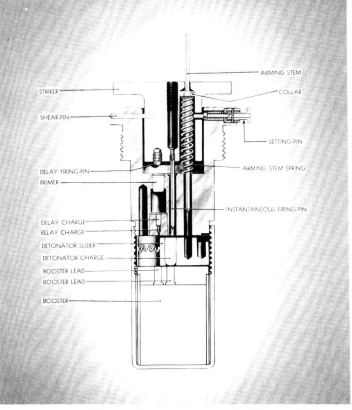

FUZE, BOMB, NOSE, AN-M103—ARMED FOR SUPERQUICK ACTION

forward movement. After some 300 revolutions of the arming vane the stem clears the end of the detonator slider and the slider is again pushed by its springs until the detonator is directly in line with the instantaneous firing-pin and the second booster lead charge. The detonator slider is locked in the armed position for either delay action or instantaneous action by a pin which moves from the fuze wall into a stepped-back surface on the slider.

At this point the fuze is fully armed and further rotation of the arming vane merely unscrews the delay-arming mechanism. The delay-arming mechanism will fall away from the fuze when air speed is less than approximately 150 miles per hour. At higher speeds air pressure may hold the mechanism on the nose but this does not affect the functioning of the fuze.

DELAY ACTION—Upon impact, after arming, the striker shears the shear pins and plunges the delay firing-pin into a primer which passes the flame to the delay and relay charges, the booster lead, the booster, and to the main bursting charge in the bomb. In delay action the instantaneous firing-pin is driven into a recess in the detonator slider and is inactive.

INSTANTANEOUS ACTION — When the bomb is set for instantaneous action upon impact, after arming the shear pins are sheared as above and the instantaneous firing-pin is driven directly into the detonator charge. The flash is passed to the second booster lead charge, the booster, and the bursting charge.

BOMBS

Bomb, General Purpose, 100 lb., AN-M30
Bomb, General Purpose, 100 lb., AN-M30A1
Bomb, General Purpose, 250 lb., AN-M57
Bomb, General Purpose, 250 lb., AN-M57A1
Bomb, Fragmentation, 260 lb., AN-M81
Bomb, General Purpose, 500 lb., AN-M64
Bomb, General Purpose, 500 lb., AN-M64A1
Bomb, Chemical, 500 lb., M78
Bomb, Incendiary, 500 lb., AN-M76
Bomb, General Purpose, 500 lb., AN-M43
Bomb, General Purpose, 1,000 lb., AN-M44
Bomb, General Purpose, 1,000 lb., AN-M65
Bomb, General Purpose, 1,000 lb., AN-M65A1
Bomb, Chemical, 1,000 lb., AN-M79
Mine, Aircraft, 1,000 lb., AN-Mk. 13 Mod. 1
Bomb, General Purpose, 2,000 lb., AN-M66
Bomb, General Purpose, 2,000 lb., AN-M66A1
Bomb, General Purpose, 2,000 lb., AN-M34
Bomb, Light Case, 4,000 lb., AN-M56
Bomb, Light Case, 4,000 lb., AN-M56A1

CHARACTERISTICS

Length overall........................7.08 ins.
Weight..............................3.7 lb.
Diameter...........................2.48 ins.

FUZE, BOMB, NOSE, AN-M104— SUBSTITUTE STANDARD

The AN-M104 is an arming-pin type of fuze with powder-train time delay arming. The firing-pin is held in direct contact with the striker assembly by a spring which also restrains the firing-pin from striking the primer until impact.

Primer and detonator are located below the firing-pin in a slider held in the unarmed position by a pin extending through the fuze. This pin also prevents the cocked delay firing-pin from striking the primer of the time train.

As the bomb parachute is pulled from its case the arming wire attached to the case is drawn from the arming-pin, which flies clear of the fuze under the impulse of the compressed spring at its other end. This allows the slider to move into contact with the delay-arming plunger and frees the cocked delay firing-pin to strike the primer of the time train and ignite the black powder train. The time train ring extends around 326° of the circumference

BOMB FUZES (Continued)

of the fuze and has a burning time of approximately 2.5 seconds.

After burning around the time-train ring the flame passes to a pellet charge and a black-powder delay-arming charge which blows out a delay-arming plug. The detonator slider, impelled by its compressed spring, ejects the delay-arming plunger through the opening thus created and moves into the armed position.

On impact with the target the striker drives the firing-pin into the primer which fires the intermediate detonator, the detonator pellet, and the integral booster.

BOMBS

Bomb, Practice (Parachute), 17 lb., M37
Bomb, Fragmentation, 23 lb., AN-M40
Bomb, Fragmentation, 23 lb., AN-M40A1
Bomb, Fragmentation, 23 lb., M72
Bomb, Fragmentation, 23 lb., M72A1

CHARACTERISTICS

Length overall.........................4.4 ins.
Weight.............................1.15 lb.
Diameter.............................2.25 ins.

FUZE, BOMB, NOSE, M108 —LIMITED STANDARD

This is an impact fuze of the arming-pin type which arms immediately on withdrawal of the arming wire. The body of the fuze is held in the bomb by two spring-actuated balls which latch in a groove in the fuze seat.

During fuzing of the bomb, the cotter-pin is replaced by the arming wire. When the bomb is dropped by the airplane the arming wire is withdrawn, releasing the arming-pin, safety plate, and safety block, which are ejected from the fuze by action of their compressed springs. The striker firing-pin is now armed but held safe by a thin shear wire.

Upon impact the striker firing-pin shears the shear wire and strikes the primer-detonator

BOMBS

Bomb, Chemical, 100 lb., Mk. 28
Bomb, Gas, Persistent (HS), 100 lb., M47A1
Bomb, Incendiary Liquid, 100 lb., M47A1
Bomb, Smoke (WP), 100 lb., M47A2
Bomb, Practice, Target, 100 lb., M75

CHARACTERISTICS

Length overall.........................2.66 ins.
Weight.............................0.54 lb.
Diameter.............................1.0 in.

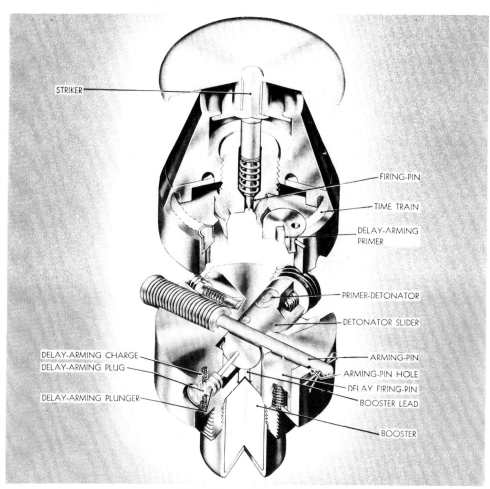

FUZE, BOMB, NOSE, AN-M104

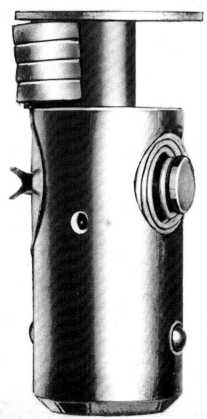

FUZE, BOMB, NOSE, M108

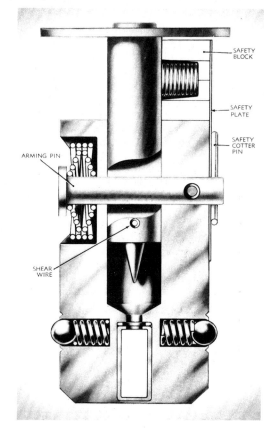

FUZE, BOMB, NOSE, M108

FUZE, BOMB, NOSE, M110

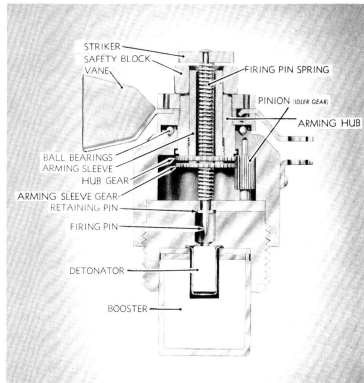

FUZE, BOMB, NOSE, AN-M110A1

FUZES, BOMB, NOSE,
AN-M110A1, STANDARD—M110, LIMITED STANDARD

These are nose fuzes of the arming vane type with mechanical delay arming and are designed to function on impact.

Striker and firing-pin form a unit held in the fuze by a pin passing through the firing-pin behind the end plate. Safety in the unarmed position is secured in the AN-M110A1 by a C-shaped safety block placed between the striker and the delay-arming mechanism. In the M110 fuze this block is made in three segments.

Operation of the delay-arming element can be understood more clearly by reference to the illustration of the AN-M110A1 fuze. The arming vanes are mounted upon a hub to the lower face of which is staked a gear with 33 teeth. The arming sleeve is threaded within the hub and turns with it on ball-bearings. A gear with 34 teeth is staked to the lower face of the sleeve and both gears mesh with an idler pinion in the fuze body.

When the bomb is released from the airplane the entire arming assembly, including the sleeve and its gear, begins spinning as a unit in the air stream under the impulse of the rotating vanes. Since the sleeve gear has one tooth more than the hub gear it necessarily lags behind for the distance of that one tooth, or

1/34 revolution, for each complete turn the sleeve and hub make together. This lag serves to withdraw the sleeve, threaded into the hub, a distance corresponding to that 1/34 revolution.

The result is that of a gear train with a reduction ratio of 34 to 1 between the revolutions of the arming hub and the withdrawal of the sleeve from its threads. After 260 revolutions of the arming vanes the sleeve is completely withdrawn from the C-shaped safety block which is then thrown clear of the fuze by centrifugal force. The fuze is now fully armed and the firing-pin is held from contact with the detonator only by its spring.

When the bomb strikes the target the resistance of this spring is overcome and the pin is driven into the detonator, firing the integral booster charge and the main explosive charge of the bomb.

The AN-M110A1 differs from the M110 in being constructed of stronger parts to insure functioning when released at high air-speeds. A single C-shaped safety block is employed instead of one consisting of three segments. The M110 has reduction gears with 57 and 56 teeth and is armed after approximately 455 revolutions of the arming vanes in the air stream.

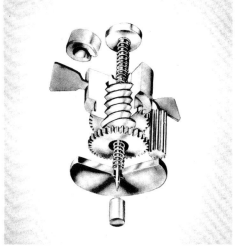

FUZE, BOMB, NOSE, AN-M110A1—MECHANISM

BOMBS
M110

Bomb, Practice, 20 lb., AN-M48
Bomb, Fragmentation, 20 lb., AN-M41
Bomb, Fragmentation, 20 lb., AN-M41A1

AN-M110A1

Bomb, Gas, Persistent (HS), 115 lb., AN-M70
Bomb, Fragmentation, 20 lb., AN-M41
Bomb, Fragmentation, 20 lb., AN-M41A1

CHARACTERISTICS

	M110	AN-M110A1
Length overall	3.58 ins.	3.7 ins.
Weight	0.62 lb. (aluminum) 1.1 lb. (steel)	1.02 lb.
Diameter	1.75 ins.	1.75 ins.

FUZES, FLARE, M.T., M111A2, STANDARD—M111, M111A1, LIMITED STANDARD

These are nose fuzes which may be set to function after a predetermined time or on impact. They represent a combination arming vane and arming pin type and are armed by a mechanical delay mechanism.

The three models are mechanically similar but vary in setting-time ranges. The M111 may be set from 15 seconds minimum to 93 seconds maximum; the M111A1 and M111A2 may be set from 5 seconds minimum to 92 seconds maximum. The safety block of the M111 and M111A1 fuzes is in three segments, the M111A2 has a single C-shaped block.

The mechanical delay-arming device of the M111 and M111A1 operates on the same principle as that employed in the M110, the M111A2 operates the same as the AN-M110A1 fuze. The arming sleeve of the M111A2 is withdrawn from the hub by the lag between a gear of 34 teeth on the sleeve and one of 33 teeth on the hub. Both gears mesh with an idler and a reduction ratio of 34 to 1 is obtained. The arming sleeve of the M111A2 fuze is withdrawn from the safety block after approximately 260 revolutions of the arming vanes; the M111 and M111A1 vanes make 455 revolutions before the fuze is armed. Centrifugal force throws the block clear of the bomb.

The fuze is now fully armed but the cocked firing-pin is restrained from striking the primer by a half-round pin under a shoulder of the firing-pin body. This half-round pin is controlled by the time mechanism.

As the flare or photoflash bomb falls away from the plane the arming wire is withdrawn from the vane stop and the arming-pin. The arming-pin is forced out by its compressed spring and withdraws the inner end of the pin from a slot in the timing disk. The disk is now released and revolves under the impulse of the clockwork mechanism. A timing-disk lever, which has been adjusted for the desired delay, bears on the edge of the timing disk. At the proper time this lever falls into the slot vacated by the arming-pin. The timing-disk lever is connected through the firing lever to the half-round pin and releases it to turn from beneath the shoulder on the firing-pin. The firing-pin spring now drives the pin into the primer. Flame from the primer passes on to the booster charge of black powder.

BOMBS
M111A2

Flare, Aircraft, Parachute, AN-M26
Bomb, Photoflash, M46

CHARACTERISTICS

	M111A2
Length overall	4.5 ins.
Weight	1.4 lb.
Diameter	1.75 ins.

FUZE, FLARE, M.T., M111

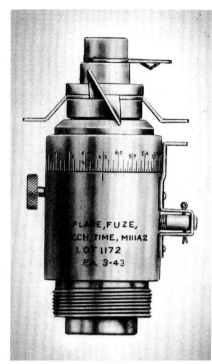

FUZE, FLARE, M.T., M111A2

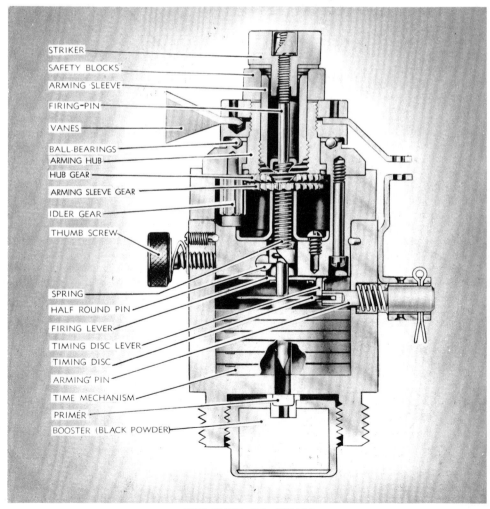

STRIKER
SAFETY BLOCKS
ARMING SLEEVE
FIRING-PIN
VANES
BALL-BEARINGS
ARMING HUB
HUB GEAR
ARMING SLEEVE GEAR
IDLER GEAR
THUMB SCREW
SPRING
HALF ROUND PIN
FIRING LEVER
TIMING DISC LEVER
TIMING DISC
ARMING PIN
TIME MECHANISM
PRIMER
BOOSTER (BLACK POWDER)

FUZE, FLARE, M.T., M111A2

FUZES, BOMB, NOSE, **AN-M120A1**, STANDARD—**AN-M120**, LIMITED STANDARD

The AN-M120 and AN-M120A1 are impact fuzes of the arming-pin type with mechanical delay arming. Delay arming is accomplished in the AN-M120A1 by clockwork within 1.90 ± .15 seconds after removal of the arming-pin.

When the arming wire is removed from the arming-pin a spring ejects it from the fuze. This frees the arbor on the time mechanism cylinder and the cylinder begins to rotate. After the cylinder has rotated for 1.90 ± .15 seconds the detonator slider-pin is cleared and the detonator slider is pushed by its spring until the slider lock engages a hole in the side of the slider. This locks the slider in the armed position and alines the detonator with the firing-pin and the booster lead-in.

The firing-pin, which has been held in the safe position by a restraining spring, is driven into the detonator upon impact and ignites the explosive train.

The AN-M120A1 model contains a lead azide lead-in in place of the tetryl lead-in in the AN-M120. The primary difference between the AN-M120 and the AN-M120A1 is that the arming time has been reduced from 2.5 seconds in the former to 1.90 ± .15 seconds in the latter fuze. In the AN-M120A1 the striker head and the arming elements have been strengthened.

BOMBS
AN-M120 AND AN-M120A1

Bomb, Fragmentation, 23 lb., AN-M40
Bomb, Fragmentation, 23 lb., AN-M40A1
Bomb, Fragmentation, 23 lb., M72
Bomb, Fragmentation, 23 lb., M72A1

CHARACTERISTICS
AN-M120 AND AN-M120A1

Length overall	4.6 ins.
Weight	1.1 lb.
Diameter	2.3 ins.

FUZE, BOMB, NOSE, AN-M120

FUZES, BOMB, NOSE, **AN-M126A1**, STANDARD—**AN-M126**, SUBSTITUTE STANDARD

The M126 fuze is identical in mechanism and functioning to the M110 but contains a detonator instead of an integral booster. The AN-M126 will arm in approximately 1,250 feet of air travel after release.

The AN-M126A1 fuze is mechanically identical with the AN-M110A1 except for a detonator which replaces the integral booster. It is fully armed after 750 feet of air travel.

BOMBS
AN-M126 AND AN-M126A1

Bomb, Gas, Persistent (HS), 100 lb., M47A2
Bomb, Incendiary Liquid, 100 lb., M47A2
Bomb, Smoke (WP), 100 lb., M47A2

CHARACTERISTICS

	AN-M126	AN-M126A1
Length overall	3.12 ins.	3.24 ins.
Weight	0.68 lb. (aluminum) 1.16 lb. (steel)	1.10 lb.
Diameter	1.75 ins.	1.75 ins.

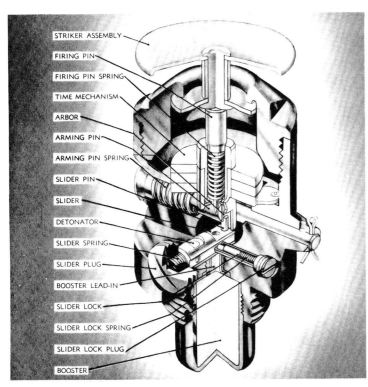

FUZE, BOMB, NOSE, AN-M120

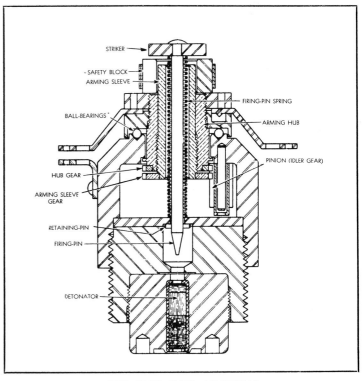

FUZE, BOMB, NOSE, AN-M126A1

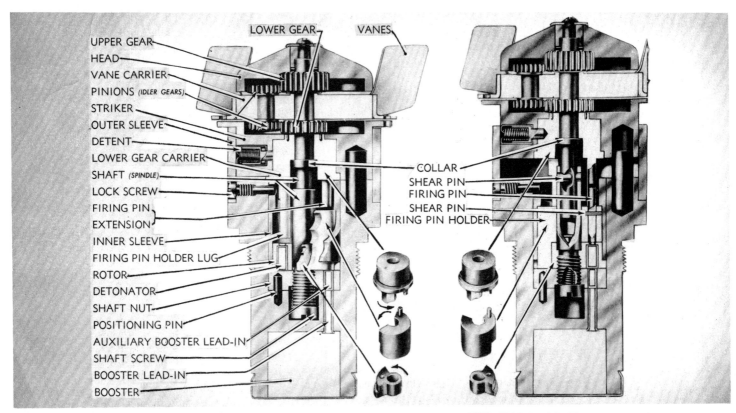

FUZE, BOMB, NOSE, AN-Mk. 219—UNARMED POSITION (LEFT), ARMED POSITION (RIGHT)

FUZE, BOMB, NOSE, AN-Mk. 219— LIMITED STANDARD

The AN-Mk. 219 is a nose fuze of the arming-vane type with mechanical delay arming.

When the arming wire is withdrawn the vanes rotate the vane carrier and drive a reduction gear train. The reduction gear train reduces the relative rotation to one turn of the shaft for 23 turns of the vane carrier. As the vane carrier revolves, the upper pinion turns the upper gear and advances the central shaft on its threads until stopped by the shoulder on the shaft screw. During this operation the lower gear carrier and striker are raised and the lug on the lower gear carrier is disengaged from a slot in the inner sleeve. The lower pinion then turns the lower gear and gear carrier through approximately 340°, bringing into alinement the firing-pin extension, firing-pin, detonator, auxiliary booster lead-in, booster lead-in, and booster. As this rotation is completed a locking detent engages the lower gear carrier to maintain proper alinement of the explosive train.

Upon impact the head, vane carrier, striker, and lower gear carrier as a unit shear the shear pin in the shaft and the

FUZE, BOMB, NOSE, AN-Mk. 219

firing-pin extension engages the firing-pin. The firing-pin cuts through its shear pin and strikes the detonator, igniting the explosive train.

BOMBS

Bomb, Fragmentation, 30 lb., Mk. 5 Mod. 3
Bomb, Demolition, 100 lb., Mk. 4
Bomb, Chemical, 100 lb., Mk. 42
Bomb, Depth, Aircraft, 325 lb., AN-Mk. 17 Mod. 1
Bomb, Depth, Aircraft, 325 lb., AN-Mk. 17 Mod. 2
Bomb, Depth, Aircraft, 325 lb., AN-Mk. 41
Bomb, Depth, Aircraft, 350 lb., AN-Mk. 44

Bomb, Depth, Aircraft, 350 lb., AN-Mk. 47
Bomb, Demolition, 500 lb., Mk. 12
Bomb, Demolition, Light Case, 500 lb., Mk. 9
Bomb, Depth, Aircraft, 650 lb., Mk. 29
Bomb, Depth, Aircraft, 650 lb., Mk. 37
Bomb, Depth, Aircraft, 650 lb., Mk. 38
Bomb, Demolition, 1,000 lb., Mk. 13
Bomb, Demolition, Light Case, 1,000 lb., Mk. 9

CHARACTERISTICS

Length overall.........................5.5 ins.
Weight.............................4.0 lb.
Diameter.........................2.3 ins.

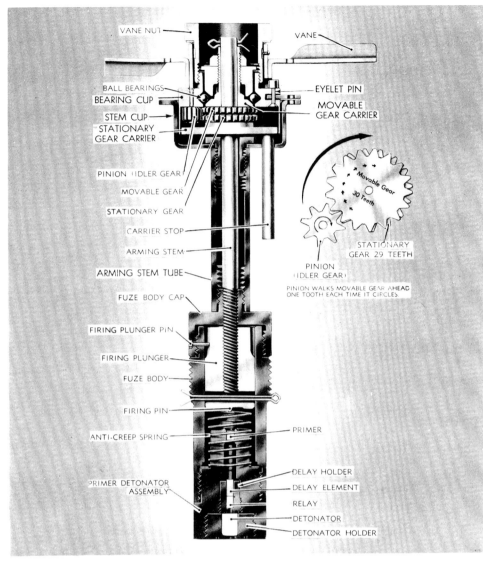

FUZES, BOMB, TAIL, AN-M100A2. AN-M101A2, AN-M102A2

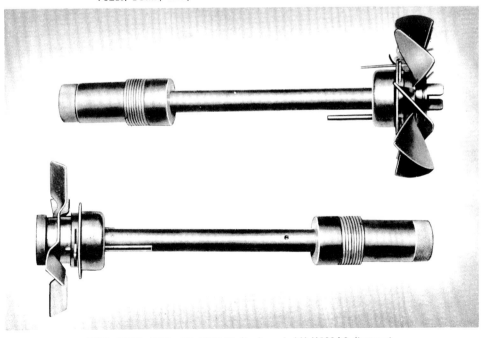

FUZE, BOMB, TAIL, AN-M101A1 (top), and AN-M101A2 (bottom)

FUZE, BOMB, TAIL, AN-M100A1— LIMITED STANDARD

FUZES, BOMB, TAIL, AN-M100A2, AN-M101A2, AN-M102A2—STANDARD

These are tail fuzes which are designed to function on impact and which may be equipped with M14 primer detonators to provide delays of 0.01 second, 0.025 second, or 0.1 second, or nondelay action.

These fuzes are of the arming-vane type and have mechanical delay arming. The arming vanes, delay-arming mechanisms, firing mechanisms, and explosive components of the three fuzes are alike. The lengths of the arming-stem tubes and arming stems, and the overall lengths differ on each model. These variations are necessary to locate the arming vane in the air stream so that these vane type tail fuzes may be used in bombs of various sizes.

Mechanical delay arming is accomplished by a reduction gear train between the arming vane and the arming stem. This reduces the rotation (unscrewing) of the arming stem to one turn for each 30 revolutions of the arming vane.

The arming vane is fitted to the bearing cup so that the eyelet pin fits into grooves in the arming vane and vane hub. The vane is then locked on by a nut. The bearing cup contains a pinion gear and rotates with the vane on fifteen ball-bearings about the movable gear carrier.

The movable gear carrier is fastened to the arming stem by a pin. On the extended surface the movable gear carrier contains a gear which meshes with the pinion gear. The pinion gear is rotated by its contact with a stationary gear held in the stationary gear carrier. The rotation of the pinion gear is communicated to the movable gear and as the movable gear carrier and arming stem unscrews, the whole bearing-cup assembly is moved rearward.

To prevent rotation but provide for axial movement a carrier stop through the stem cup is screwed fast to the stationary gear carrier.

As the vane rotates, the arming stem is unscrewed from the firing mechanism. When the stem is completely separated from the firing plunger the fuze is armed. This occurs after 175 revolutions of the arming vane.

The firing mechanism consists of a firing plunger held in the unarmed position by being screwed to the arming stem. As the arming vane rotates, the arming stem is unscrewed from the plunger. A firing-plunger pin riding in a slot in the plunger prevents the plunger from rotating but permits axial motion for firing.

When the arming stem has been completely unscrewed from the plunger the firing-pin is armed but restrained from striking the primer by an anti-creep spring.

Upon impact, the plunger firing-pin overcomes the resistance of the spring and the pin strikes the primer.

The explosive train is ignited and the flame passes successively through the primer, the black-powder delay element, the relay, the detonator, and on to the adapter-booster and bomb charge.

The A2 series require less air travel for the arming process than the A1 series. The A2 series require but 175 revolutions of the arming vane as compared to 675 revolutions in the A1 series. In addition, the arming vane in the A2 fuzes has been strengthened and the number of blades reduced from 8 to 4.

BOMBS
AN-M100A1

Bomb, General Purpose, 100 lb., AN-M30
Bomb, General Purpose, 100 lb., AN-M30A1

AN-M100A2
Bomb, General Purpose, 100 lb., AN-M30
Bomb, General Purpose, 100 lb., AN-M30A1
Bomb, General Purpose, 250 lb., AN-M57
Bomb, General Purpose, 250 lb., AN-M57A1
Bomb, Fragmentation, 260 lb., AN-M81

AN-M101A2
Bomb, General Purpose, 500 lb., AN-M43
Bomb, General Purpose, 500 lb., AN-M64
Bomb, General Purpose, 500 lb., AN-M64A1
Bomb, Chemical, 500 lb., M78
Bomb, Incendiary, 500 lb., AN-M76
Bomb, Semi-Armor-Piercing, 500 lb., AN-M58
Bomb, Semi-Armor-Piercing, 500 lb., AN-M58A1
Bomb, Semi-Armor-Piercing, 500 lb., AN-M58A2

AN-M102A2
Bomb, Chemical, 1,000 lb., AN-M79
Bomb, General Purpose, 1,000 lb., AN-M65
Bomb, General Purpose, 1,000 lb., AN-65A1
Bomb, Semi-Armor-Piercing, 1,000 lb., AN-M59
Bomb, Semi-Armor-Piercing, 1,000 lb., AN-M59A1
Bomb, General Purpose, 1,000 lb., AN-M44
Bomb, General Purpose, 2,000 lb., AN-M66
Bomb, General Purpose, 2,000 lb., AN-M66A1
Bomb, General Purpose, 2,000 lb., AN-M34
Bomb, Light Case, 4,000 lb., AN-M56
Bomb, Light Case, 4,000 lb., AN-M56A1

CHARACTERISTICS

	AN-M100A1	AN-M100A2	AN-M101A2	AN-M102A2
Length overall	9.2 ins.	9.2 ins.	12.2 ins.	16.2 ins.
Weight	2.7 lb.	2.7 lb.	2.9 lb.	3.2 lb.
Diameter	1.5 ins.	1.5 ins.	1.5 ins.	1.5 ins.

FUZES, BOMB, TAIL, M112A1, M113A1, M114A1—STANDARD

These three fuzes are identical in all respects except the lengths of their arming-stem tubes and arming stems, and the length overall. These variations permit use of these fuzes with bombs of various sizes and properly locate the arming vanes in the air stream.

These fuzes arm with approximately 80 to 100 feet of air travel and may be used in operations at extremely low levels. They have cocked firing-pins and are classed as supersensitive. However, a delay element is provided to permit the plane to leave the target area before the bomb explodes. Use of the appropriate M16A1 primer detonator permits a delay period of 4 to 5 seconds or of 8 to 15 seconds.

The fuze head includes the arming vane, vane holder, and vane nut which rotate as a unit. The arming vane is attached to the arming stem by a cotter pin which passes through the vane holder and the stem. The connection is direct and each complete turn of the arming vane rotates the arming stem a full revolution.

The arming stem provides delay arming since it is threaded to both the body cap and the plunger and must unscrew from the plunger before the plunger is ready to function. This requires approximately 18 to 21 revolutions. A pin through the fuze wall engages a groove in the plunger and prevents its rotation with the stem. When the fuze is fully armed the plunger and

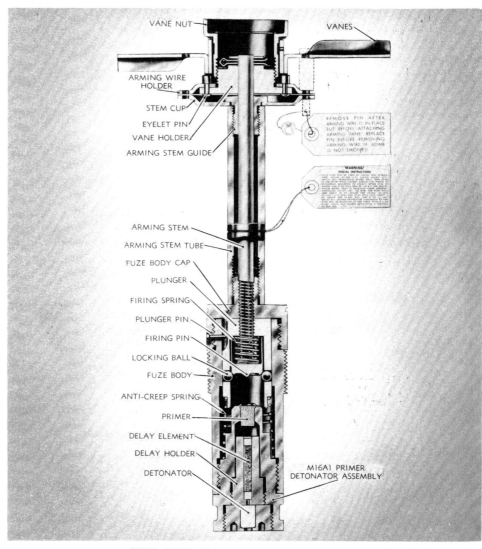

FUZES, BOMB, TAIL, M112A1, M113A1, M114A1

BOMB FUZES (Continued)

firing-pin are restrained from moving forward by an anti-creep spring.

The firing mechanism is made up of a plunger, firing-pin, cocked firing-pin spring, locking balls, anti-creep spring, and retainer. The locking balls neutralize the pressure of the spring on the firing-pin until the moment of impact when plunger and pin are carried forward by the force of inertia with sufficient energy to compress the anti-creep spring and force the locking balls into recesses in the fuze wall. The unlocked firing-pin is then driven against the primer by its compressed spring.

The explosive train includes primer, delay charge, relay charge, and detonator. The flash from this train ignites a charge in an adapter booster to function the bomb charge.

BOMBS
M112A1

Bomb, General Purpose, 100 lb., AN-M30
Bomb, General Purpose, 100 lb., AN-M30A1
Bomb, General Purpose, 250 lb., AN-M57
Bomb, General Purpose, 250 lb., AN-M57A1
Bomb, General Purpose, 300 lb., M31

M113A1

Bomb, General Purpose, 500 lb., AN-M43
Bomb, Semi-Armor-Piercing, 500 lb., AN-M58
Bomb, Semi-Armor-Piercing, 500 lb., AN-M58A1
Bomb, Semi-Armor-Piercing, 500 lb., AN-M58A2

Bomb, General Purpose, 500 lb., AN-M64
Bomb, General Purpose, 500 lb., AN-M64A1
Bomb, General Purpose, 600 lb., AN-M32

M114A1

Bomb, General Purpose, 1,000 lb., AN-M44
Bomb, Semi-Armor-Piercing, 1,000 lb., AN-M59
Bomb, Semi-Armor-Piercing, 1,000 lb., AN-M59A1
Bomb, General Purpose, 1,000 lb., AN-M65
Bomb, General Purpose, 1,000 lb., AN-M65A1
Bomb, General Purpose, 1,100 lb., M33
Bomb, General Purpose, 2,000 lb., AN-M34
Bomb, General Purpose, 2,000 lb., AN-M66
Bomb, General Purpose, 2,000 lb., AN-M66A1

CHARACTERISTICS

	M112A1	M113A1	M114A1
Length overall	9.6 ins.	12.6 ins.	16.6 ins.
Weight	2.3 lb.	2.5 lb.	2.8 lb.
Diameter	1.5 ins.	1.5 ins.	1.5 ins.

FUZES, BOMB, TAIL, M115, M116, M117—STANDARD

These are tail fuzes of the arming vane type with mechanical delay arming mechanism identical with that used in the AN-M100A2 fuze previously described. Use of the proper M16A1 primer detonator permits delay firing of 4 to 5 seconds or 8 to 15 seconds after impact.

The fuzes differ one from another only in the length of the arming stems and arming tubes and in overall length. This permits use in bombs of various sizes and properly locates the arming vanes in the air stream.

The arming vanes make from 150 to 170 revolutions before the stem is completely withdrawn from the plunger and the fuze is fully armed.

The firing mechanism is identical in every respect with that of the AN-M112A1 fuze.

BOMBS
M115

Bomb, General Purpose, 100 lb., AN-M30
Bomb, General Purpose, 100 lb., AN-M30A1
Bomb, General Purpose, 250 lb., AN-M57
Bomb, General Purpose, 250 lb., AN-M57A1
Bomb, General Purpose, 300 lb., M31

M116

Bomb, General Purpose, 500 lb., AN-M43
Bomb, Semi-Armor-Piercing, 500 lb., AN-M58
Bomb, Semi-Armor-Piercing, 500 lb., AN-M58A1
Bomb, Semi-Armor-Piercing, 500 lb., AN-M58A2

Bomb, General Purpose, 500 lb., AN-M64
Bomb, General Purpose, 500 lb., AN-M64A1
Bomb, General Purpose, 600 lb., M32

M117

Bomb, General Purpose, 1,000 lb., AN-M44
Bomb, Semi-Armor-Piercing, 1,000 lb., AN-M59
Bomb, Semi-Armor-Piercing, 1,000 lb., AN-M59A1
Bomb, General Purpose, 1,000 lb., AN-M65
Bomb, General Purpose, 1,000 lb., AN-M65A1
Bomb, General Purpose, 1,100 lb., AN-M33
Bomb, General Purpose, 2,000 lb., AN-M34
Bomb, General Purpose, 2,000 lb., AN-M66
Bomb, General Purpose, 2,000 lb., AN-M66A1

CHARACTERISTICS

	M115	M116	M117
Length overall	9.63 ins.	12.63 ins.	16.63 ins.
Weight	2.7 lb.	2.9 lb.	3.2 lb.
Diameter	1.5 ins.	1.5 ins.	1.5 ins.

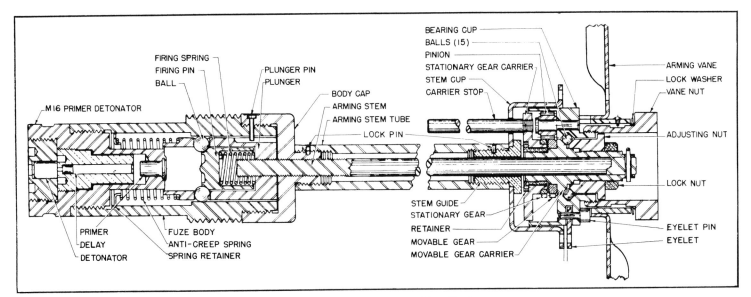

FUZES, BOMB, TAIL, M115, M116, M117

FUZES, BOMB, TAIL, M123, M124, M125—SUBSTITUTE STANDARD

These are special-purpose fuzes used with aircraft bombs when long delay periods are desired. They are made with fixed delays of 1, 2, 6, 12, 24, 36, 72, and 144 hours. The different delays are obtained by variation in strength of solvent contained in a glass ampoule and by variation in thickness of celluloid which has to be dissolved by solvent before functioning can occur. As supplied to the service each fuze is stamped with the delay period for which it has been manufactured.

The delays mentioned, however, are only approximate and vary greatly with the temperature, being much shorter at high temperatures and longer at low temperatures. The accompanying table shows the period at which detonation will occur at various temperatures.

The three models are identical in functioning and mechanism, differing one from another only in the length of the tubes, arming stems, and in overall length. The different lengths are necessary in order to locate the arming vanes properly in the air stream when the fuzes are assembled in bombs of different sizes. The fuzes of this series are of the arming vane type with delay arming accomplished by a reduction gear assembly similar to that used in fuzes of the AN-M100A2 series. The rotation of the arming stem of the M123, M124, and M125 fuzes, however, screws the stem into the fuze; in the AN-M100A2 fuzes the stem is withdrawn for arming. The space required for the deeper entry of the stem into the fuze is obtained by placing an arming block, serving as a spacer, between the stem cup and the vane stop eyelet.

When the bomb is dropped the arming wire is pulled from the fuze, releasing the arming block and permitting the vanes to rotate. After approximately 400 feet of air travel the arming stem advances suffi-

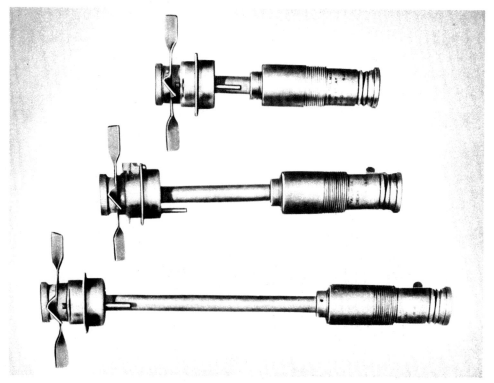

FUZES, BOMB, TAIL, M123, M124, M125

Nominal delay period	TEMPERATURE				
	115° F	90° F	75° F	55° F	25° F
1	0 hr. 15 mins.	0 hr. 20 mins.	0 hr. 30 mins.	0 hr. 45 mins.	2 hrs. 10 mins.
2	0 hr. 20 mins.	0 hr. 50 mins.	1 hr. 0 mins.	1 hr. 30 mins.	3 hrs. 15 mins.
6	1 hr. 0 mins.	1 hr. 30 mins.	2 hrs. 0 mins.	3 hrs. 0 mins.	11 hrs. 0 mins.
12	1 hr. 15 mins.	2 hrs. 30 mins.	3 hrs. 50 mins.	9 hrs. 0 mins.	30 hrs. 0 mins.

Nominal delay period	80° F	55° F
24	8 hrs. 0 mins.	24 hrs. 0 mins.
36	15 hrs. 0 mins.	37 hrs. 30 mins.
72	38 hrs. 0 mins.	96 hrs. 0 mins.
144	70 hrs. 0 mins.	135 hrs. 0 mins.

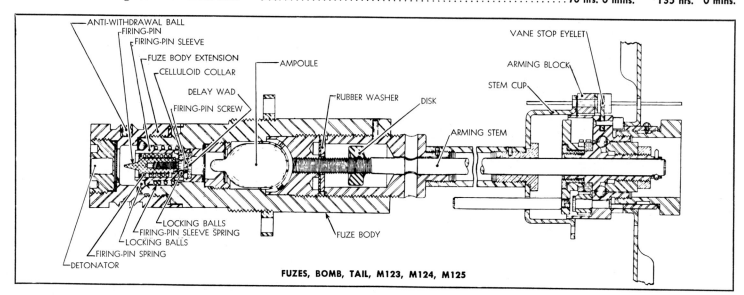

ANTI-WITHDRAWAL BALL — FIRING-PIN — FIRING-PIN SLEEVE — FUZE BODY EXTENSION — CELLULOID COLLAR — DELAY WAD — FIRING-PIN SCREW — AMPOULE — RUBBER WASHER — DISK — ARMING STEM — VANE STOP EYELET — ARMING BLOCK — STEM CUP — LOCKING BALLS — FIRING-PIN SLEEVE SPRING — LOCKING BALLS — FIRING-PIN SPRING — DETONATOR — FUZE BODY

FUZES, BOMB, TAIL, M123, M124, M125

BOMB FUZES (Continued)

ciently into the fuze to crush a glass ampoule containing a solvent. The released solvent filters through a delay wad and attacks a celluloid collar. After a total of approximately 1,000 feet of air travel the stem has advanced sufficiently to seat a disk against a rubber washer, thus sealing the vane end of the fuze against entrance of water and leakage of solvent.

The firing-pin and its spring are mounted within a sleeve and held in a cocked position by eight balls seated in a groove beneath the shoulder of the firing-pin screw and there retained by the celluloid collar mentioned above. The sleeve, too, is surrounded by a spring and is held in position by a second set of locking balls which are released only if an attempt is made to withdraw the fuze from the bomb.

Action of the solvent on the celluloid collar weakens it until it can no longer hold the balls in the groove. The compressed spring then exerts its force on the pin, pushes the balls aside, and drives the pin into the detonator, exploding the booster charge and the main explosive charge of the bomb.

ANTI-WITHDRAWAL DEVICE—All fuzes of this series incorporate an anti-withdrawal device which will detonate the bomb immediately upon any attempt to unscrew the fuze.

The fuze body is assembled to the body extension by a loose threaded joint, and the whole assembly is screwed into the fuze cavity of the adapter booster.

An eccentric groove, tapering from a maximum depth of approximately 1/4 inch to a minimum of approximately 3/32 inch is machined about the periphery of the fuze body extension. A steel ball 1/4 inch in diameter is held in the deeper section of the groove. Should any attempt be made to unscrew the fuze, the ball wedges tightly in the shallower portion of the groove and locks the body extension to the adapter booster. This permits the body to unscrew from the body extension. After the fuze body has moved through approximately two turns the balls which support the firing-pin sleeve are pushed into recesses in the body and the sleeve is freed in much the same manner as the firing-pin in the normal operation of the fuze. The sleeve spring then drives the entire sleeve and firing-pin assembly into the detonator to explode the booster and the high-explosive charges.

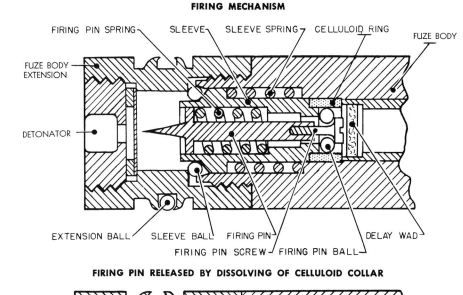

FIRING MECHANISM

FIRING PIN SPRING — SLEEVE — SLEEVE SPRING — CELLULOID RING — FUZE BODY — FUZE BODY EXTENSION — DETONATOR — EXTENSION BALL — SLEEVE BALL — FIRING PIN — FIRING PIN SCREW — FIRING PIN BALL — DELAY WAD

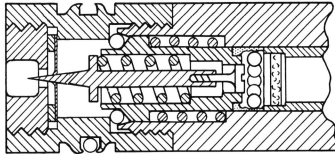

FIRING PIN RELEASED BY DISSOLVING OF CELLULOID COLLAR

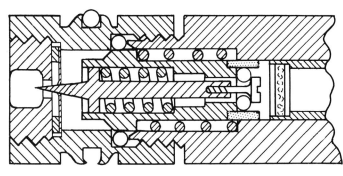

FIRING PIN RELEASED BY ANTI-WITHDRAWAL DEVICE

BOMBS

M123
Bomb, Demolition, 100 lb., M30
Bomb, General Purpose, 100 lb., AN-M30
Bomb, General Purpose, 100 lb., AN-M30A1
Bomb, General Purpose, 250 lb., AN-M57
Bomb, General Purpose, 250 lb., AN-M57A1
Bomb, Demolition, 300 lb., M31

M124
Bomb, Demolition, 500 lb., M43
Bomb, General Purpose, 500 lb., AN-M43
Bomb, General Purpose, 500 lb., AN-M64
Bomb, General Purpose, 500 lb., AN-M64A1
Bomb, Semi-Armor-Piercing, 500 lb., AN-M58
Bomb, Semi-Armor-Piercing, 500 lb., AN-M58A1
Bomb, Demolition, 600 lb., M32

M125
Bomb, Demolition, 1,000 lb., M44
Bomb, General Purpose, 1,000 lb., AN-M44
Bomb, General Purpose, 1,000 lb., AN-M65
Bomb, General Purpose, 1,000 lb., AN-M65A1
Bomb, Semi-Armor-Piercing, 1,000 lb., AN-M59
Bomb, Semi-Armor-Piercing, 1,000 lb., AN-M59A1
Bomb, Demolition, 1,000 lb., M33
Bomb, Demolition, 2,000 lb., M34
Bomb, General Purpose, 2,000 lb., AN-M34
Bomb, General Purpose, 2,000 lb., AN-M66
Bomb, General Purpose, 2,000 lb., AN-M66A1

CHARACTERISTICS

	M123	M124	M125
Length overall	9.63 ins.	12.63 ins.	16.63 ins.
Weight	2.9 lb.	3.1 lb.	3.4 lb.
Diameter	1.45 ins.	1.45 ins.	1.45 ins.

FUZE, BOMB, TAIL, AN-Mk. 228—STANDARD

This fuze is of the arming-vane type with mechanical delay arming. It is designed for delay action of 0.08 (±0.01) second after impact.

Arming is accomplished by rotation of the arming vane and its shaft which turns an upper gear meshing with a pinion. This gearing reduces the ratio of rotation to 1 turn of the shaft for 23 turns of the vanes. Rotation of the cap turns the upper gear and unscrews the shaft until it is stopped by a shoulder on the vane-shaft extension. During this operation the lower gear carrier is raised and a lug is released from its seat in the inner sleeve. This frees the lower gear and carrier to rotate under the impulse of the lower pinion. The lower gear carrier and the striker turn through approximately 175° to bring into alinement the firing-pin extensions, delay elements, detonators, and the leads of each explosive train. These units are locked in the armed position by pins.

To insure functioning of the main high-

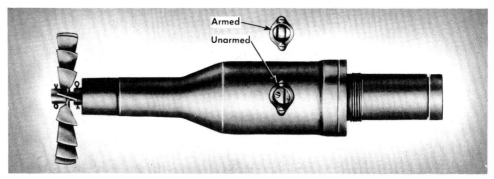

FUZE, BOMB, TAIL, AN-Mk. 228

explosive charge in the bomb, this fuze is equipped with two independent firing mechanisms, each with its own explosive train. Each mechanism consists of a firing-pin extension and a firing-pin. One pin is slightly longer than the other and ignites its primer and explosive train a fractional part of a second ahead of the shorter pin.

On impact of the bombs the striker and lower gear carrier cut the shear pin which passes through the supporting collar and central shaft, and drive the firing-pin ex-

tensions against the pins. These strike the primers and the flash is passed on to the explosive trains which consist, in each case, of a delay element, detonator, auxiliary booster lead-in, booster lead-in, and booster charge.

BOMBS

Bomb, Armor-Piercing, 1,000 lb., AN-Mk. 33
Bomb, Armor-Piercing, 1,600 lb., AN-Mk. 1

CHARACTERISTICS

Length overall.......................16.36 ins.
Weight..............................10.5 lb

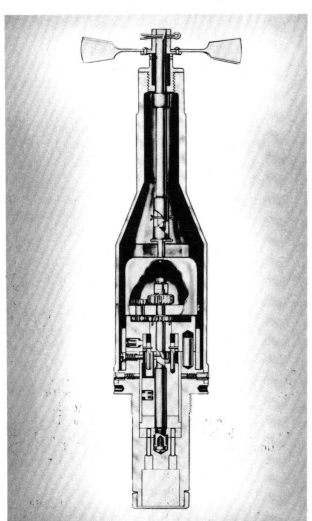

FUZE, BOMB, TAIL, AN-Mk. 228—UNARMED POSITION

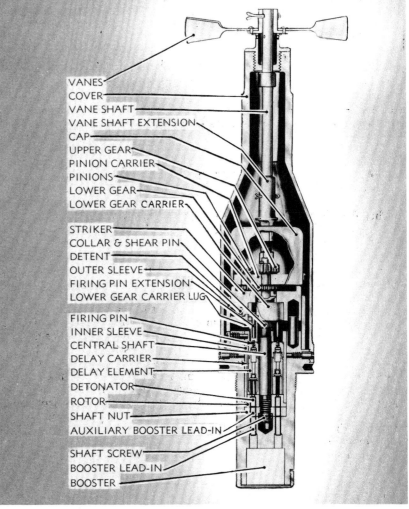

VANES
COVER
VANE SHAFT
VANE SHAFT EXTENSION
CAP
UPPER GEAR
PINION CARRIER
PINIONS
LOWER GEAR
LOWER GEAR CARRIER

STRIKER
COLLAR & SHEAR PIN
DETENT
OUTER SLEEVE
FIRING PIN EXTENSION
LOWER GEAR CARRIER LUG

FIRING PIN
INNER SLEEVE
CENTRAL SHAFT
DELAY CARRIER
DELAY ELEMENT
DETONATOR
ROTOR
SHAFT NUT
AUXILIARY BOOSTER LEAD-IN

SHAFT SCREW
BOOSTER LEAD-IN
BOOSTER

FUZE, BOMB, TAIL, AN-Mk. 228—ARMED POSITION

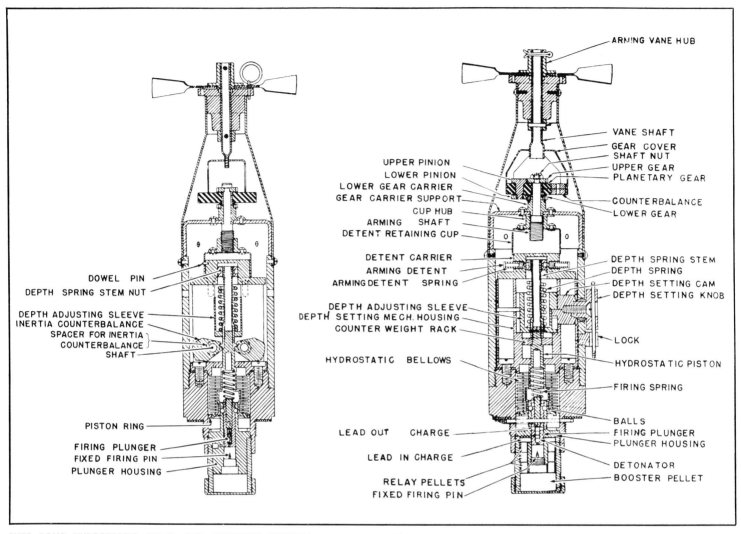

FUZE, BOMB, HYDROSTATIC, AN-Mk. 230—UNARMED POSITION

FUZE, BOMB, HYDROSTATIC, AN-Mk. 230—ARMED POSITION

FUZE, BOMB, HYDROSTATIC, TAIL, AN-Mk. 230—STANDARD

This fuze is used with depth bombs dropped from airplanes against such submerged targets as submarines. It is of the arming-vane type with mechanical delay arming and may be set to function by hydrostatic pressure at depths of 25, 50, 75, 100 or 125 feet. Depth settings are made by an external knob.

Hydrostatic fuzes of this type must be regarded as consisting of two distinct units: the vane-actuated delay arming unit which completes its cycle of operation while the bomb is in the air; and the firing unit which depends upon hydrostatic pressure for its operation and which does not begin to function until the bomb has entered the water. The fuze cannot be set to detonate on impact nor can the arming operation be completed unless the bomb is released from sufficient height to permit of at least 110 revolutions of the arming vane before it strikes the water. As a corollary thereto, the hydrostatic mechanism is inoperative at normal atmospheric pressures.

Mechanical delay arming is accomplished during the free fall of the bomb by rotation of the arming vane and vane shaft, connected by a gear train which reduces the ratio of rotation to 1 turn of the shaft for 23 turns of the vane. Rotation of the shaft screws it into the detent retaining cup, raising the cup until it clears the arming detents which are then expelled from engagement with the nut at the head of the depth spring stem. Impact with the water spins two inertia counterbalances from engagement with lugs on the stem and the fuze is fully armed and the depth mechanism freed for action. The counterbalances prevent downward travel of the freed arming stem and detonation of the fuze on impact.

As the bomb submerges, water is admitted to the hydrostatic bellows through openings in the body sleeve and in the housing of the depth mechanism. The bellows are free to expand in only one direction, downward, and as they expand under pressure of the admitted water they carry with them in that downward travel the hydrostatic piston, the piston ring, the counterweight rack, and the depth spring stem and nut—all moving as a unit. Both firing spring and depth spring are thereby compressed.

Functioning of the firing mechanism at various depths is governed by compression of the depth spring as positioned by the setting knob which extends through the fuze body. The knob may be set and locked in any of five positions, providing for explosion at depths of 25, 50, 75, 100, and 125 feet. The knob is a part of the depth-setting cam within the fuze body, and a lug or boss is machined off-center on the inner face of the cam to engage a slot in the depth-adjusting sleeve which surrounds the spring. When the fuze is set for detonation at a depth of 25 feet, this lug is in its lowest position and the spring is at maximum expansion. With each setting for increasingly greater depth the lug is raised toward the vanes of the fuze and the spring is compressed within the sleeve for a corresponding distance.

The further the depth spring is compressed the greater the pressure which must be exercised upon the hydrostatic piston by the bellows to move spring and sleeve downward and compress the firing

spring. Although the pressure is greater, the distance the piston moves is the same for all depth settings.

The firing plunger is locked within its housing by steel balls which are forced into recesses in the piston after it has moved downward approximately ⅜ inch. This frees the firing spring which drives plunger and primer against the fixed firing-pin. The flame passes from the primer-detonator to the lead-out and lead-in charges, which are brought into aline-

ment by the descent of the plunger, and from them to the relay pellets and the booster charge which ignites the main explosive charge of the bomb.

BOMBS

Bomb, General Purpose, 500 lb., AN-M64
Bomb, General Purpose, 500 lb., AN-M64A1
Bomb, General Purpose, 1,000 lb., AN-M65
Bomb, General Purpose, 1,000 lb., AN-M65A1
Bomb, General Purpose, 2,000 lb., AN-M66
Bomb, General Purpose, 1,000 lb., AN-M66A1

FUZES, BOMB, HYDROSTATIC, TRANSVERSE, AN-Mk. 234, STANDARD—AN-Mk. 224, LIMITED STANDARD

FUZE, BOMB, HYDROSTATIC, TRANSVERSE, AN-Mk. 234—The AN-Mk. 234 is an arming-pin type of fuze which is issued in three subassemblies: pistol, booster, and booster extender. It may be set to function at a predetermined depth of 25, 50, 75, 100, or 125 feet.

The assembled fuze fits into a transverse tube in the bomb. Arming-pins are located in either end of the fuze—one actuating the functioning of the pistol-firing mechanism, the other actuating the booster extender and booster to aline the explosive train.

On the exterior of the pistol head are the depth-setting knob and the lock screw with safety clip. The depth-setting knob also serves as a water port. When the fuze is unarmed the port is closed by a plug and a neoprene tube connector which are attached to the arming wire. Upon release

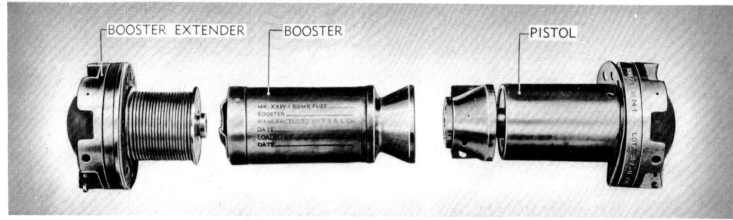

FUZE, BOMB, HYDROSTATIC, TRANSVERSE, AN-Mk. 224

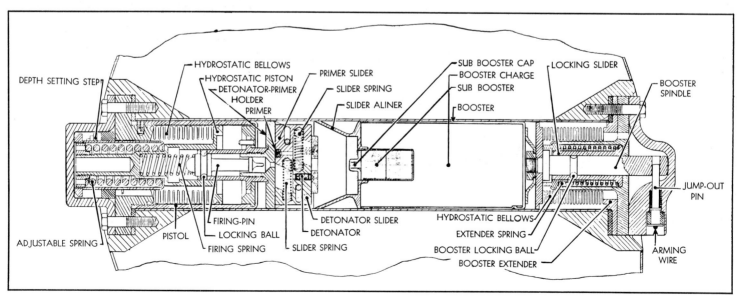

FUZE, BOMB, HYDROSTATIC, TRANSVERSE, AN-Mk. 234

BOMB FUZES (Continued)

of the arming wire the plug and tube are pulled from the pistol, uncovering the water port. A second arming wire is attached to the bomb jump-out pin in the booster extender. On release this arming wire is withdrawn and the jump-out pin is ejected. This admits water to the bellows and also unlocks the booster spindle.

As the bomb submerges, the water entering the booster extender arms the fuze. Water pressure expands the hydrostatic bellows and pushes the booster can toward the pistol. This movement is retarded by resistance of the extender spring until the balls which unite the booster spindle and

slide drop out of their position. The bellows now drive the booster forward with greater impetus and the slider aliner engages the detonator and primer sliders. These are moved inward against their springs until they are alined, at which time the subbooster cup enters the slot of the detonator-primer holder and comes into contact with the detonator charge. All the action in the booster extender is accomplished before the bomb reaches a depth of 20 feet.

During the process of arming in the booster extender and booster the hydrostatic bellows of the pistol are expanding.

As the bellows are extended they advance the hydrostatic piston and compress the firing spring and the adjustable spring. The adjustable spring controls the depth at which the firing mechanism will function by restraining the advance of the piston. The amount the adjustable spring must be compressed is predetermined by rotating the depth-setting step to the proper position under the lugs on the spring housing. The depth-setting step has four stepped surfaces, each expanding the adjustable spring so that an additional 25 feet of depth is required to provide the proper hydrostatic pressure for compressing the adjustable spring and actuating the firing mechanism.

The firing-pin is held in the safe position by locking balls. These drop into recesses when the piston has advanced sufficiently and free the firing-pin. The compressed firing spring then drives the pin into the primer, igniting the detonator, subbooster, and booster.

FUZE, BOMB, HYDROSTATIC, TRANSVERSE, AN-Mk. 224—The AN-Mk. 224 fuze is similar in mechanism and functioning to the Mk. 234 fuze. It consists of three subassemblies: pistol, booster, and booster extender.

The pistol of the Mk. 224 is set for depths of 25, 50, 75, 100, and 125 feet by disassembly and not externally as in the Mk. 234. Each depth-setting requires a different firing-pin spring or combination of firing-pin spring and auxiliary spring as follows:

Depth	Firing-pin Spring	Auxiliary Spring
25 ft	Yellow	
50 ft	Black	
75 ft	Black	Green
100 ft	Yellow	Red
125 ft	Black	Red

The different firing-pin springs and auxiliary springs are supplied separately and the desired spring or springs must be inserted before installing the pistol in the bomb.

The head of the Mk. 224 pistol contains a jump-out pin which closes the water port before withdrawal of the arming wire.

This fuze is armed and detonated in the same manner as the Mk. 234.

BOMBS

AN-Mk. 234 and 224

Bomb, Depth, Aircraft, 325 lb., AN-Mk. 17 Mod. 1
Bomb, Depth, Aircraft, 325 lb., AN-Mk. 17 Mod. 2
Bomb, Depth, Aircraft, 325 lb., AN-Mk. 41
Bomb, Depth, Aircraft, 350 lb., AN-Mk. 44
Bomb, Depth, Aircraft, 350 lb., AN-Mk. 47
Bomb, Depth, Aircraft, 650 lb., Mk. 29
Bomb, Depth, Aircraft, 650 lb., Mk. 37
Bomb, Depth, Aircraft, 650 lb., Mk. 38
Bomb, Depth, Aircraft, 700 lb., Mk. 49

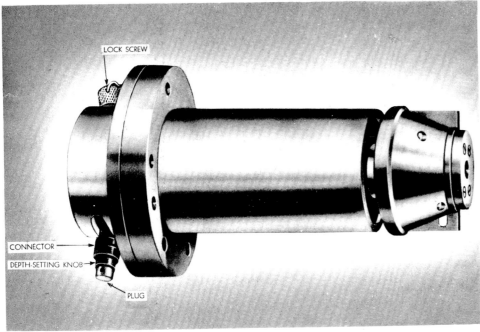

FUZE, BOMB, HYDROSTATIC, TRANSVERSE, AN-Mk. 234—PISTOL

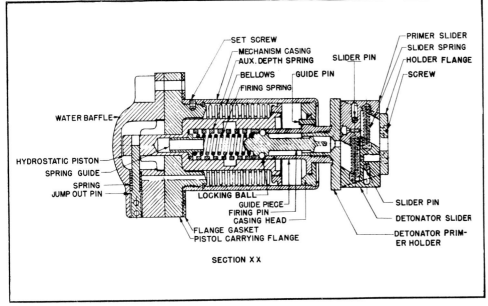

FUZE, BOMB, HYDROSTATIC, TRANSVERSE, AN-Mk. 224—PISTOL

369

2.36 INCH H.E.A.T. ROCKET M6A2—LIMITED STANDARD

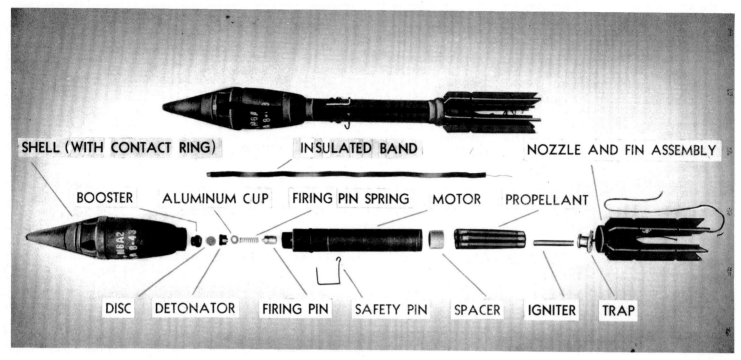

SHELL (WITH CONTACT RING) — INSULATED BAND — NOZZLE AND FIN ASSEMBLY

BOOSTER — ALUMINUM CUP — FIRING PIN SPRING — MOTOR — PROPELLANT

DISC — DETONATOR — FIRING PIN — SAFETY PIN — SPACER — IGNITER — TRAP

2.36 INCH H.E.A.T. ROCKET, M6A2

The 2.36 inch H.E.A.T. Rocket, M6A2, with shaped-charge loading is fired from a Bazooka-type launcher at ground targets. The rocket is effective against the armor plate of tanks and armored vehicles. After penetration it has the effect of throwing a white hot metal spray.

This round is a modification of the original M6 rocket, now obsolete. Except that the contact ring was not removed from the ogive, the changes are the same as for the M6A1. This modification was performed in a Theater of Operations, and the designation M6A2 was applied to distinguish it from the M6A1 modification performed at arsenals in the Zone of the Interior.

The practice round, inert loaded to conform to the live round, is the 2.36 inch Practice Rocket, M7A2.

CHARACTERISTICS

Range . . . . 600 yd.
Dispersion . . . . 8.5 mils
Velocity . . . . 265 f/s
Service temperature limits . . . . 0° to 120° F.

Burning time:
  At 0° F. . . . . 0.08 sec.
  At 120° F. . . . . 0.03 sec. (estimated)
Type of stabilization . . . . Fixed fins
Length, overall . . . . 21.6 in.
Weight of round, loaded . . . . 3.4 lb.
Fuze . . . . B.D.—simple impact type

Motor assembly:
  Diameter, outside . . . . 1.25 in.
  Length . . . . 8.32 in.
  Weight (less propellant) . 1.82 lb. w/fuze and fins
  Material . . . WD1025 or WD X1025 C.D. steel

Propellant . . . . . 0.136 lb. solvent extruded double base powder, 0.375 in. O.D. by 0.08 in. I.D. by 4.15 in. long
Type of loading . . . Five sticks held by pulpit trap and cardboard spacer

Shell assembly:
  Caliber . . . . 2.36 in.
  Length . . . . 8.8 in.
  Filler . . . . Pentolite
  Weight, filler . . . . 0.5 lb.
  Weight, total . . . . 1.57 lb.
Type of ignition . . . . . Electric squib in aluminum case, centered in motor
Launchers M1, M1A1, M9, M9A1
Packaging . . . . Packed fuzed, one per fiber container, 20 containers per wooden box

2.36 INCH H.E.A.T. ROCKET M6A3—STANDARD

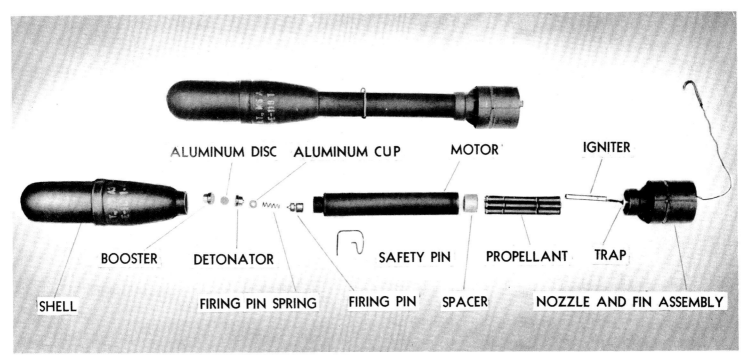

2.36 INCH H.E.A.T. ROCKET, M6A3

The 2.36 inch H.E.A.T. Rocket, M6A3, with shaped-charge is fired from a Bazooka-type launcher at ground targets. The rocket is effective against the armor plate of tanks and armored vehicles. After penetration it has the effect of throwing a white hot metal spray.

This round is the same as the M6A1 rocket except for a hemispherical ogive and cylindrical fins.

The practice round, inert loaded to conform to the live round, is the 2.36 inch Practice Rocket, M7A3.

CHARACTERISTICS

Range	600 yd.
Dispersion	6 mils
Velocity	265 f/s

Service temperature limits.........0° to 120° F.

Burning time:
At 0° F.	0.08 sec.
At 120° F.	0.03 sec. (estimated)

Type of stabilization......Fixed ring shroud fin

Length, overall........................19.4 in.

Weight of round, loaded..............3.4 lb.

Fuze.................B.D.—simple impact type

Motor assembly:
Diameter, outside	1.25 in.
Length	8.32 in.
Weight (less propellant)	1.74 lb. w/fuze and fins
Material	WD X4130 or WD 8630 steel tubing

Propellant....0.136 lb. solvent extruded double base powder, 0.375 in. O.D. by 0.08 in. I.D. by 4.15 in. long

Type of loading...Five sticks held by pulpit trap and cardboard spacer

Shell assembly:
Caliber	2.36 in.
Length	8.8 in.
Filler	Pentolite
Weight, filler	0.5 lb.
Weight, total	1.64 lb.

Type of ignition......Electric squib in aluminum case, centered in motor

Launchers................M1A1, M9, M9A1

Packaging....Packed fuzed, one per fiber container, 20 containers per wooden box or one per fiber container, 10 containers per wooden box

2.36-INCH WP SMOKE ROCKET **M10**—STANDARD

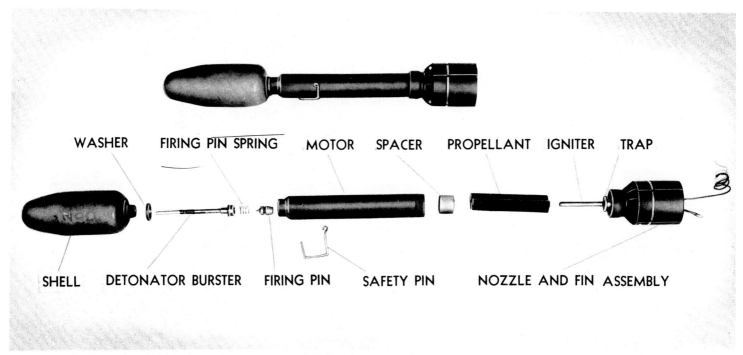

WASHER   FIRING PIN SPRING   MOTOR   SPACER   PROPELLANT   IGNITER   TRAP

SHELL   DETONATOR BURSTER   FIRING PIN   SAFETY PIN   NOZZLE AND FIN ASSEMBLY

2.36-INCH WP SMOKE ROCKET M10

The 2.36-Inch WP Smoke Rocket M10 (formerly the T26E2) is a WP filled shell with the M6A3 rocket motor. It embodies a special burster assembly not present in the T26 and T26E1 rockets and supersedes and cancels these two former developmental rockets. The rocket is used for laying down smoke screens and as an effective casualty producing weapon against enemy personnel in foxholes, trenches, pillboxes, etc.

CHARACTERISTICS

Range.............................600 yd.
Dispersion...........................6 mils
Velocity...........................265 f/s
Service temperature limits........0° to 120° F.
Burning time:
  At 0° F........................0.08 sec.
  At 120° F..............0.03 sec. (estimated)
Type of stabilization.......Fixed ring shroud fin
Length, overall..................17.1 in.
Weight of round, loaded...........3.4 lb.
Fuze.................B.D.—simple impact type
Motor assembly:
  Diameter, outside.................1.25 in.
  Length..........................8.32 in.
  Weight (less propellant)..1.74 lb. w/fuze and fins
  Material..WD X4130 or WD 8630 steel tubing

Propellant......0.136 lb. solvent extruded double base powder, 0.375 in. O.D. by 0.08 in. I.D. by 4.15 in. long
Type of loading...Five sticks held by pulpit trap and cardboard spacer
Shell assembly:
  Caliber...........................2.36 in.
  Length............................5.9 in.
  Filler..............................WP
  Weight, filler.....................0.9 lb.
  Weight, total.....................1.64 lb.
  Type of ignition....Electric squib in aluminum case, centered in motor
Launchers.................M1A1, M9, M9A1
Packaging.........Packed fuzed, one per fiber container, 12 containers per wooden box

3.25-INCH A.A. TARGET ROCKET M2—LIMITED STANDARD

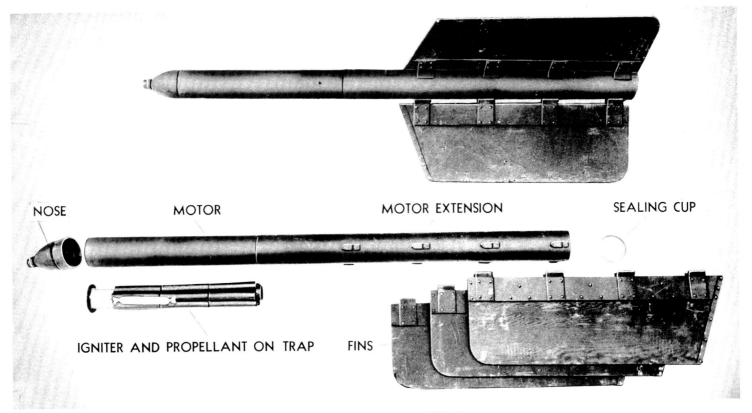

3.25-INCH A.A. TARGET ROCKET M2

The 3.25-Inch A.A. Target Rocket M2 is designed to simulate low flying aircraft in the training of antiaircraft gun crews. The large fins act as a target.

This rocket has not been fired for specific data on range and dispersion.

CHARACTERISTICS

Range..................1,700 yd. (estimated)
Dispersion..........................No data
Velocity..................530 f/s (estimated)
Service temperature limits.........30° to 120° F.

Burning time:
  At 30° F...............0.25 sec. (estimated)
  At 120° F..............0.10 sec. (estimated)
Type of stabilization.................Fixed fins
Length, overall.........................59.1 in.
Weight of round, loaded.............35.1 lb.
Fuze..............................No fuze
Motor assembly:
  Diameter, outside...................3.25 in.
  Length..............................25.25 in.
  Weight (less propellant)............8.44 lb.
  Material..WD 1010 to WD 1025 steel tubing
Propellant......3.2 lb. solvent extruded double base powder, 0.875 in. O.D. by 0.281 in. I.D. by 5 in. long

Type of loading..18 sticks strung on a 6-wire cage
Shell assembly:
  Caliber............................3.25 in.
  Length.............................4.1 in.
  Filler........Solid cast nose except for $1\frac{1}{8}$ in. axial hole
  Weight, filler......................None
  Weight, total.....................5.83 lb.
Type of ignition.....Electric squib contained in cardboard cartridge in nose. Ignition aided by auxiliary igniter bag tied to cage
Launchers.........Target Rocket Projector M1
Packaging.......Either two or three rounds per wooden box

3.25-INCH A.A. TARGET ROCKET **M2A1**—STANDARD

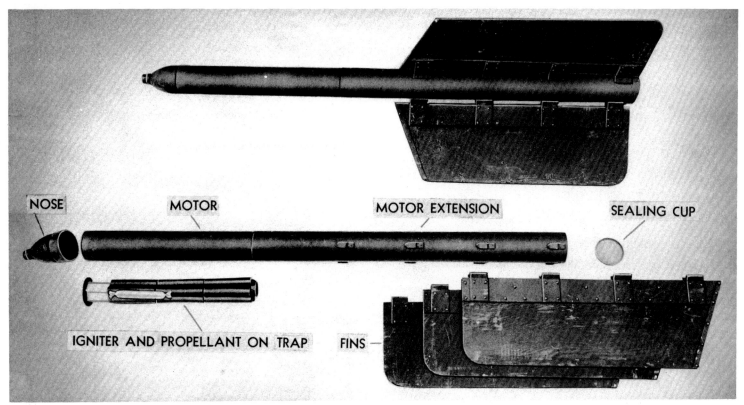

3.25-INCH A.A. TARGET ROCKET M2A1

The 3.25-Inch A.A. Target Rocket M2A1 is identical to the M2 Target Rocket except for a flare attachment which burns from 20 to 30 seconds. The flare is ignited by the ignition cartridge when the rocket is launched.

This rocket has not been fired for specific data on range and dispersion.

CHARACTERISTICS

Range.................1,700 yd. (estimated)
Dispersion.........................No data

Velocity...................530 f/s (estimated)
Service temperature limits........30° to 120° F.
Burning time:
   At 30° F...............0.25 sec. (estimated)
   At 120° F...............0.1 sec. (estimated)
Type of stabilization.................Fixed fins
Length, overall......................59.9 in.
Weight of round, loaded....36.3 lb. (estimated)
Fuze............................No fuze
Motor assembly:
   Diameter, outside.................3.25 in.
   Length.........................25.25 in.
   Weight (less propellant)...........8.44 lb.
   Material..WD 1010 to WD 1025 steel tubing
Propellant.......3.2 lb. solvent extruded double base powder 0.875 in. O.D. by 0.281 in. I.D. by 5 in. long

Type of loading.....Eighteen sticks strung on a 6-wire cage
Shell assembly:
   Caliber..........................3.25 in.
   Length.......................7.5 in. w/flare
   Filler.......Solid cast nose except for 1⅛ in. axial hole
   Weight, filler.......................None
   Weight, total........7 lb. w/flare (estimated)
Type of ignition.....Electric squib contained in cardboard cartridge in nose. Ignition aided by auxiliary igniter bag tied to cage
Launchers..........Target Rocket Projector M1
Packaging............Probably similar to M2

4.5 INCH H.E. ROCKET M8—LIMITED STANDARD

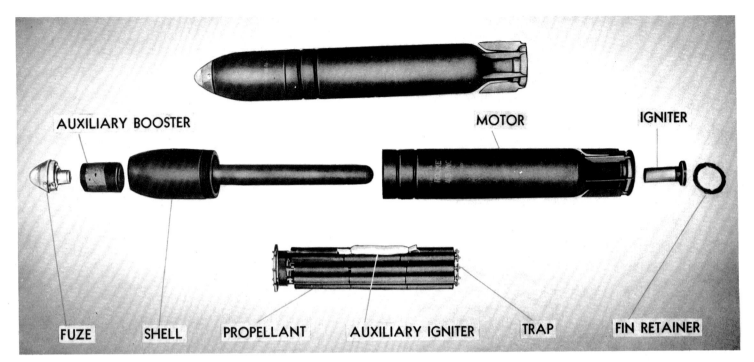

AUXILIARY BOOSTER MOTOR IGNITER

FUZE SHELL PROPELLANT AUXILIARY IGNITER TRAP FIN RETAINER

4.5 INCH H.E. ROCKET, M8

The 4.5 inch H.E. Rocket, M8, is used for attacking lightly fortified ground targets and against personnel from aircraft or ground launchers.

The practice round, inert loaded to conform to the live round, is the 4.5 inch Practice Rocket, M9.

CHARACTERISTICS

Range..........................4,000 yd.
Dispersion.......................15 mils
Velocity:
   Full charge.....................850 f/s
   Reduced charge.................760 f/s
Service temperature limits:
        20° to 90° F.—Full Charge
        50° to 130° F.—Reduced Charge
Burning time:
   At 20° F.............0.3 sec. (estimated)
   At 130° F.............0.12 sec. (estimated)

Type of stabilization.....Folding fins opened by acceleration
Length, overall...............31.1 in. w/o fuze
Weight of round, loaded.............38.1 lb.
Fuze....P.D. M4, M4A1, M4A2, selective SQ or delay, P.D. T4

Motor assembly:
   Diameter, outside..................4.5 in.
   Length............................23.29 in.
   Weight (less propellant)...........11.65 lb.
   Material......WD 1025 welded steel tubing

Propellant:
   Full charge...4.65 lb. solvent extruded double base powder $\frac{7}{8}$ in. O.D. by $\frac{9}{32}$ in. I.D. by 5 in. long
   Reduced charge......4.2 lb. solvent extruded double base powder $\frac{7}{8}$ in. O.D. by $\frac{9}{32}$ in. I.D. by 5 in. long

Type of loading:
   Full charge....30 sticks strung on 10-wire cage
   Reduced charge.27 sticks strung on 10-wire cage

Shell assembly:
   Caliber............................4.5 in.
   Length.............................7.5 in.
   Filler................................TNT
   Weight, filler......................4.3 lb.
   Weight, total...........14.5 lb. to 15.25 lb.

Type of ignition.....Cardboard igniter cartridge containing electric squib and backed by plastic cup pressed into motor venturi. Two auxiliary ignition bags tied to wire cage

Launchers...M10, M12, M14, T27, T27E1, T31, T33, T34, T36, T38, T46, T46E1, T47, T57, T58, T60, T61

Packaging........Packed unfuzed, one per fiber container, two containers per wooden box. One fuze and one auxiliary booster per fiber container or metal can, 15 containers or cans per metal box

4.5 INCH H.E. ROCKET M8A1—LIMITED STANDARD

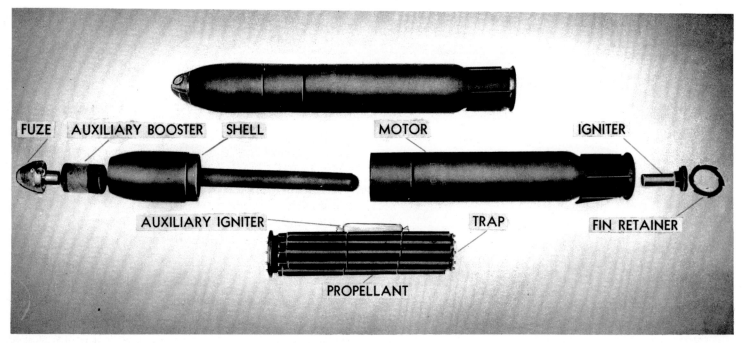

4.5 INCH H.E. ROCKET, M8A1

The 4.5 inch H.E. Rocket, M8A1, is used for attacking lightly fortified ground targets and against personnel from aircraft or ground launchers.

This rocket differs from the M8 by an increased thickness at the threaded end of the rocket motor, use of a rocket motor steel with greater yield point strength, and coarser threads remachined in the base of the rocket shell.

The practice round, inert loaded to conform to the live round, is the 4.5 inch Practice Rocket, M9A1.

CHARACTERISTICS

Range............................4,000 yd.
Dispersion ....15 mils
Velocity..........................840 f/s

Service temperature limits.....−10° to +105° F.
Burning time:
    At −10° F.........................0.3 sec.
    At +105° F.......................0.13 sec.
Type of stabilization.....Folding fins opened by acceleration
Length, overall...............31.5 in. w/o fuze
Weight of round, loaded.............38.8 lb.
Fuze....P.D. M4, M4A1, M4A2, selective SQ or delay; P.D. T4
Motor assembly:
    Diameter, outside....................4.5 in.
    Length..........................23.49 in.
    Weight (less propellant)............13.2 lb.
    Material......WD 1025 to WD 1030 welded steel tubing
Propellant.....4.65 lb. solvent extruded double base powder, $7/8$ in. O.D. by $\frac{9}{32}$ in. I.D. by 5 in. long
Type of loading..30 sticks strung on 10-wire cage

Shell assembly:
    Caliber............................4.5 in.
    Length.............................7.5 in.
    Filler..............................TNT
    Weight, filler.......................4.3 lb.
    Weight, total..............15.7 to 16.1 lb.
Type of ignition...Cartridge igniter containing electric squib backed by plastic cup is pressed into venturi. Ignition aided by two auxiliary bags tied to cage
Launchers....M10, M12, M14, T27, T27E1, T31, T33, T34, T36, T38, T46, T46E1, T47, T57, T58, T60, T61
Packaging...Packed unfuzed, one per fiber or metal container, two containers per wooden box. One fuze and one auxiliary booster per fiber container or metal can, 15 containers or cans per metal box

4.5 INCH H.E. ROCKET M8A2—LIMITED STANDARD

4.5 INCH H.E. ROCKET, M8A2

The 4.5 inch H.E. Rocket, M8A2, is used for attacking lightly fortified ground targets and against personnel from aircraft or ground launchers.

This rocket represents a change from the M8A1 as the strength of the rocket shell was increased at the base to prevent deflection of the metal under pressure of the burning propellent gases. The length of the rocket shell and rocket motor thread engagement is greater than in the M8A1 rocket.

The practice round, inert loaded to conform to the live round, is the 4.5 inch Practice Rocket, M9A2.

CHARACTERISTICS

Range .... 4,000 yd.
Dispersion .... 15 mils
Velocity .... 840 f/s

Service temperature limits ..... −10° to +105° F.
Burning time:
  At −10° F. .... 0.3 sec.
  At +105° F. .... 0.13 sec.
Type of stabilization .... Folding fins opened by acceleration
Length, overall .... 30.5 in. w/o fuze
Weight of round, loaded .... 38.2 lb.
Fuze ..... P.D. M4, M4A1, M4A2, selective SQ or delay; P.D. T4
Motor assembly:
  Diameter, outside .... 4.5 in.
  Length .... 23.49 in.
  Weight (less propellant) .... 13.2 lb.
  Material ..... WD 1025 to WD 1030 steel— both welded and seamless tubing used
Propellant .. 4.65 lb. solvent extruded double base powder, $\frac{7}{8}$ in. O.D. by $\frac{9}{32}$ in. I.D. by 5 in. long
Type of loading . 30 sticks strung on a 10-wire cage

Shell assembly:
  Caliber .... 4.5 in.
  Length .... 7.4 in.
  Filler .... TNT
  Weight, filler .... 4.3 lb.
  Weight, total .... 15.7 lb. to 16.1 lb.
Type of ignition ..... Cartridge igniter containing electric squib backed by plastic cup pressed into venturi. Ignition aided by two auxiliary bags tied to cage
Launchers ... M10, M12, M14, T27, T27E1, T31, T33, T34, T36, T38, T46, T46E1, T47, T57, T58, T60, T61
Packaging .... Packed unfuzed, one per fiber or metal container, two containers per wooden box. One fuze and one auxiliary booster per fiber container or metal can, 15 containers or cans per metal box.

FUZE AUXILIARY BOOSTER SHELL MOTOR IGNITER

AUXILIARY IGNITER TRAP FIN RETAINER

PROPELLANT

4.5 INCH H.E. ROCKET, M8A3

The 4.5 inch H.E. Rocket, M8A3, is used for attacking lightly fortified ground targets and against personnel from aircraft or ground launchers.

This rocket is a modification of the M8A2 rocket by the addition of a locking burr to each fin blade to assist in rigidly maintaining the fin in full open position during flight.

The practice round, inert loaded to conform to the live round, is the 4.5 inch Practice Rocket, M9A3.

CHARACTERISTICS

Range.................................4,000 yd.
Dispersion..........................15 mils
Velocity.............................840 f/s

Service temperature limits.....—10° to +105° F.
Burning time:
  At —10° F........................0.3 sec.
  At 105° F........................0.13 sec.
Type of stabilization.....Folding fins opened by acceleration
Length, overall...............30.5 in. w/o fuze
Weight of round, loaded...........38.2 lb.
Fuze.....P.D. M4, M4A1, M4A2, selective SQ or delay; P.D. T4
Motor assembly:
  Diameter, outside...................4.5 in.
  Length..........................23.49 in.
  Weight (less propellant)...........13.2 lb.
  Material.....WD 1025 to WD 1030 steel—Both welded and seamless tubing used
Propellant.....4.65 lb. solvent extruded double base powder, 7/8 in. O.D. by $\frac{9}{32}$ in. I.D. by 5 in. long
Type of loading...Thirty sticks strung on 10-wire cage

Shell assembly:
  Caliber............................4.5 in.
  Length.............................7.4 in.
  Filler...............................TNT
  Weight, filler.....................4.3 lb.
  Weight, total...........15.7 lb. to 16.1 lb.
Type of ignition.....Cartridge igniter containing electric squib backed by plastic cup. Assembly pressed into venturi. Ignition aided by two auxiliary bags tied to cage
Launchers.......M10, M12, M14, T27, T27E1, T27E2, T31, T33, T34, T36, T38, T46, T46E1, T47, T57, T58, T60, T61
Packaging......Packed unfuzed, one per fiber or metal container, two containers per wooden box. One fuze and one auxiliary booster per fiber container or metal can, 15 containers or cans per metal box

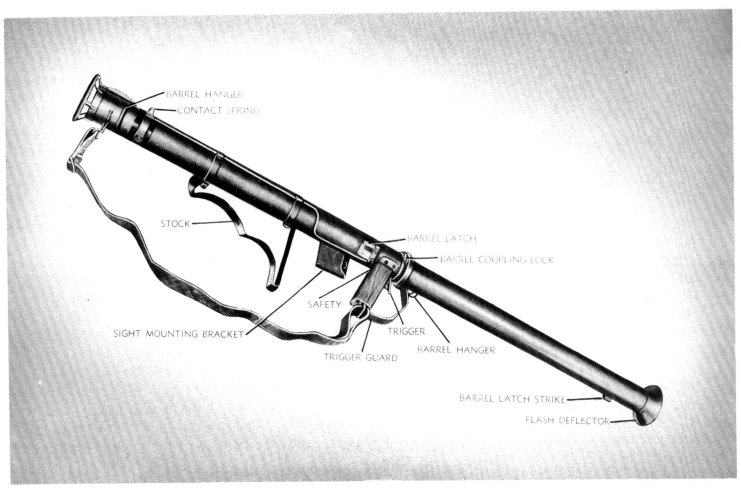

THE 2.36 INCH ROCKET LAUNCHER, M9, HAS A TUBE THAT MAY BE UNCOUPLED INTO TWO PIECES

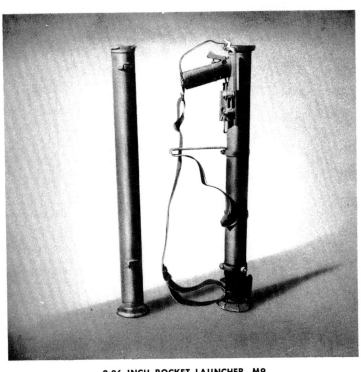

2.36 INCH ROCKET LAUNCHER, M9

The 2.36 inch Rocket Launcher, M9, is an electrically operated shoulder weapon. It is similar to the M1A1 launcher except for improved sighting, a tube that may be uncoupled into two pieces, and a magneto-operated instead of a battery-operated electric firing circuit.

CHARACTERISTICS

Weight, total . . . . .16 lb.

Rails or tubes:

    Length . . . . .60 in.

    Number and arrangement . . . . . . .Single tube may be uncoupled into two 31-inch lengths. Stock and trigger assembly attached to rear section

    Composition . . . . .Smooth bore steel tube

    Mounting . . . .Fired from shoulder in standing, kneeling, or prone position

Elevation . . . . .By operator

Traverse . . . . .By operator

Rate of fire . . . . .Not specified. Weapon must be sighted before firing each round

Firing mechanism . . . . . . .Pressing trigger generates current to fire the rocket

Fire control equipment . . . . .Horizontal bar sight with range adjustments from 0 to 700 yd.

ROCKET TARGET PROJECTOR **M1**—STANDARD

ROCKET TARGET PROJECTOR, M1, IN FIRING POSITION

ROCKET TARGET PROJECTOR, M1, IN TRAVELING POSITION

The Rocket Target Projector, M1, is used to launch the 3.25 inch rocket target. The rails are mounted on a two-wheel carriage and are lowered into traveling position for towing. The mobility of this launcher permits firing courses to be set up quickly.

CHARACTERISTICS

Weight, total............................750 lb.
Rail or tubes:
   Length...............................132 in.
   Number and arrangement....Two parallel rails guide single rocket in launching
   Composition....................Steel tubing
   Mounting........Rails mounted on two-wheel carriage with pneumatic tires
Elevation............................0° to 60°
Traverse..................By moving carriage
Rate of fire.......One to two rounds per minute (estimated). Rate of fire of secondary importance. After loading personnel take cover at maximum distance permitted by firing cable
Firing mechanism..Electric current supplied by dry cells in reel and battery box. Cable on reel permits remote firing
Fire control equipment.Direct and indirect laying; sighting and leveling devices provided

4.5 INCH 3-TUBE A.C. ROCKET LAUNCHER M10—STANDARD

4.5 INCH 3-TUBE A.C. ROCKET LAUNCHER, M10, MOUNTED UNDER WING OF FIGHTER PLANE

The 4.5 inch 3-Tube A.C. Rocket Launcher, M10, is a cluster of three plastic tubes used for firing rockets from aircraft. One cluster is mounted under each wing of fighter aircraft. The cluster may be jettisoned after the rockets are launched. The fin-stabilized 4.5 inch rockets M8, M8A1, M8A2, M8A3, T22 and T41 may be launched from this cluster.

CHARACTERISTICS

Weight, total...........................82 lb.
Rail or tubes:
    Length.................. ....120 in.
    Number and arrangement.......3-tube cluster
    Composition.........................Plastic
    Mounting........Clusters mounted on special
                    brackets installed on under-
                    side of aircraft wings
Elevation....4° adjustment possible. Clusters har-
            monized with aircraft machine guns

Traverse.........By changing direction of plane
Rate of fire....6 rounds released in 0.6 sec. when
                set for salvo
Firing mechanism..Selective single round or ripple
                fire electric firing mechanism
Fire control equipment....No special equipment.
                Clusters harmonized be-
                fore takeoff by use of
                boresight equipment
                and quadrant of plane

4.5 INCH ROCKET LAUNCHER M12—STANDARD

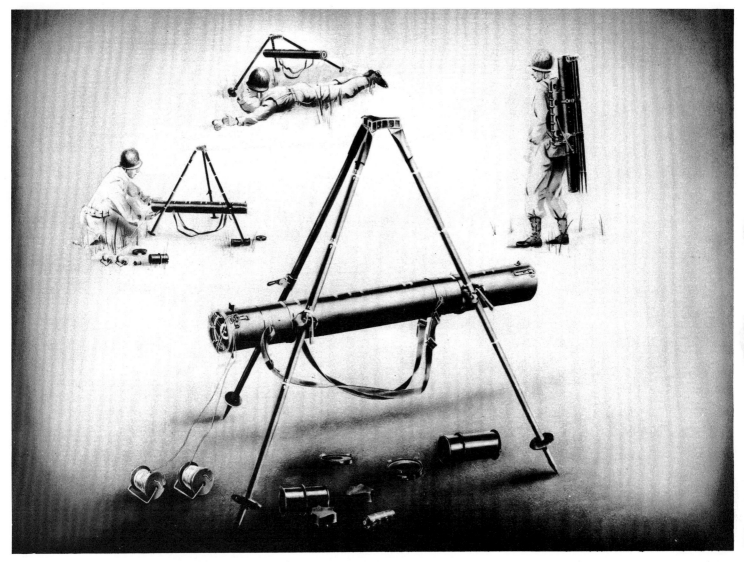

4.5 INCH ROCKET LAUNCHER, M12, IS AN EXPENDABLE PACKING CRATE TYPE FOR FIRING SINGLE ROUND

4.5 INCH ROCKET LAUNCHER, M12

The 4.5 inch Rocket Launcher, M12, is an expendable packing crate type of launcher that is loaded and shipped complete with one M8 or M8A1 Rocket with a special igniter. In firing position the launcher is slung under the tripod which accompanies the packed launcher crate.

CHARACTERISTICS

Weight, total . . . . 22 lb.

Rails or tubes:
    Length . . . . 48 in.
    Number and arrangement . . . . Single tube
    Composition . . . . Plastic
    Mounting . . . . Tripod

Elevation . . . . Fixed

Traverse . . . . By moving tripod

Rate of fire . . . . Discarded after firing one round

Firing mechanism . . . . Battery packed with launcher furnishes electric current. Ten-cap exploder may be used for salvo release of several rockets at the same time

Fire control equipment . . . . Folding peep sight and front stud sight

4.5 INCH 3-TUBE A.C. ROCKET LAUNCHER M14—STANDARD

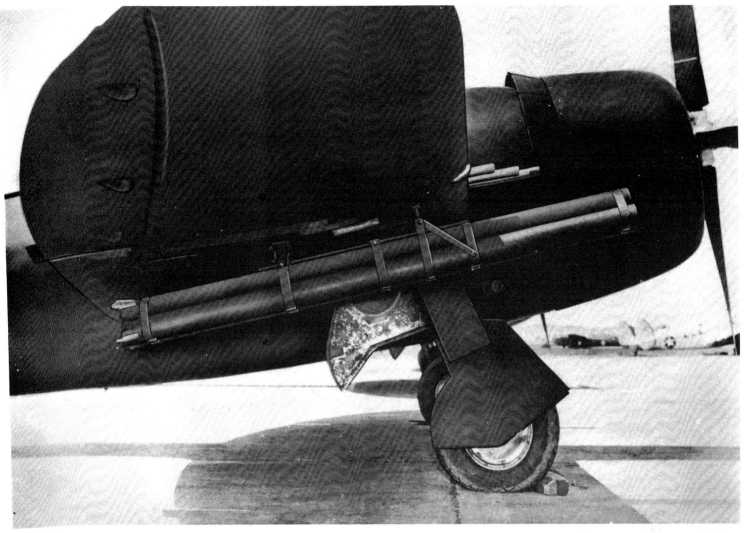

4.5 INCH 3-TUBE A.C. ROCKET LAUNCHER, M14

The 4.5 inch 3-Tube A.C. Rocket Launcher, M14, is a cluster of three steel tubes used for firing rockets from aircraft. One cluster is mounted under each wing of fighter aircraft. The cluster may be jettisoned after the rockets are launched.

This launcher is the same as the 4.5 inch M10 launcher except for steel instead of plastic tubes. This launcher may be used for fin-stabilized or spin-stabilized rockets (after slight modification).

CHARACTERISTICS

Weight, total..........................210 lb.
Rails or tubes:
    Length...........................120 in.
    Number and arrangement......3-tube cluster
    Composition...........................Steel
    Mounting..Clusters mounted on special brackets installed on underside of aircraft wing
Elevation....4° adjustment possible. Clusters harmonized with aircraft machine guns

Traverse.........By changing direction of plane
Rate of fire....6 rounds released in 0.6 sec. when set for salvo
Firing mechanism..Selective single round or ripple fire electric firing mechanism
Fire control equipment....No special equipment. Clusters harmonized before takeoff by use of boresight equipment and quadrant of plane

4.5 INCH 3-TUBE AIRCRAFT ROCKET LAUNCHER, M15, MOUNTED ON P-47 PURSUIT PLANE

4.5 INCH 3-TUBE AIRCRAFT ROCKET LAUNCHER, M15

The 4.5 inch 3-tube Aircraft Rocket Launcher, M15, is a cluster of three magnesium tubes used for firing rockets from aircraft. One cluster is mounted under each wing on an aircraft. The cluster may be jettisoned after the rockets are launched. This launcher is identical to the M10 Aircraft Launcher except that it is constructed with magnesium tubing instead of plastic tubing.

CHARACTERISTICS

Weight, total. . . . . .82 lb. (estimated)
Rails or tubes:
   Length. . . . . .120 in.
   Number and arrangement. . . .Three-tube cluster
   Composition. . . . . .Magnesium
   Mounting. .Clusters mounted on special brackets installed on the underside of aircraft wings
Elevation. .4° adjustment possible. Clusters harmonized with aircraft machine guns
Traverse. . . . . .By changing direction of plane
Rate of fire. . . .6 rounds released in 0.6 sec. when set for salvo
Firing mechanism. . . .Selective single round or ripple fire electric firing mechanism
Fire control equipment. .No special fire control equipment. Clusters harmonized before takeoff by use of boresight equipment and quadrant of plane